'Masterfully teases out the warring impulses wrestling in Davies' psyche. . .
Rogan is adept at relating the social history of the 1950s and 1960s to
Davies' brooding character and lyric obsessions. . . He uncovers psycho-
logical traumas everywhere and is fascinating on the bitchy rivalries between
1960s pop titans. . . Such tales make this oceanically researched biography
go with a swing'
Sunday Times

'In the traditi   akes
for a gripping read'
Evening Standard

'It's always a delight to encounter a biography which has been meticulously
researched, crafted with a near-obsessive passion and boasts abundant
original interviews. . . Davies' many fans have never been served this well;
Rogan interviews major players and delves deep into the archives to emerge
with the ultimate account of Davies' life, times and idiosyncrasies. . . Rogan
never loses sight of Davies' position as a quintessentially brilliant English
songwriter and pop-culture commentator, resulting in his own personal
masterpiece and another benchmark for music biographies'
Record Collector

'Rogan's strength is his dispassionate approach. He's not in awe of Davies,
nor does he have an axe to grind. . . He gives as definitive a view of the
man as anyone could hope for'
The Times

'Monumental. . . Shining through the violence, the personality clashes, the
litigation with former management, the volatile relationship with women,
even a mental breakdown, are the songs'
Daily Mail

'Gripping and hugely readable. . . teems with as much detail as a nineteenth-
century novel. . . Whatever's been previously written about the band is
rather overwhelmed by Rogan's book with its illuminating interviews with
Ray and Dave Davies and an abundance of supplementary testimony'
Uncut (9/10)

'Kinkophiles will enjoy the recreation of Sixties London and the accounts
of sibling mayhem'
Daily Telegraph ****

'Definitive. . . delineated by Rogan in impressive fashion. Nary a character or event of even minor importance in the Davies story is left undisturbed by the author's flair for asking the right questions of the right people (including Ray himself) and plundering archives that have remained under dustsheets for aeons. The wonder is that with so many facts and opinions to assemble, this tome remains so eminently readable'
Mojo * * * * *

'The most in-depth biography to date of the enduring pop genius'
Choice

'This doorstep biography portrays Davies as an ambitious man but a reluctant rock star, by turns outgoing and self-doubting, sporty and studious, cocksure and troubled. It's precisely these quirks that make him a worthy study, and Johnny Rogan is the man for the job, a writer renowned for going to extraordinary lengths to research his subjects. . . Rogan is rigorous and relentless, the kind of biographer who'll go as far as to invoke Freud and Laing in order to throw light on the notorious rivalry between Ray Davies and his tearaway brother. . . *A Complicated Life* serves as a social history as well as character study. Rogan illuminates the labyrinth of Swinging Sixties record labels, managers, bookers and pluggers, and spares no blushes in his depiction of the young Kinks'
Irish Times

'A terrific insight into one of Britain's greatest artists'
Shortlist

'Rogan chooses to delve deep into the period that will most interest potential readers of this book. . . Defiantly non-sensationalist. . . dogged, even-handed and punctilious in his research. . . scrupulously fair in his assessments of his subject's work and character, while also conceding that, in several ways, Davies remains an enigma. . . A valuable account of the working life of a complicated man'
Spectator

'This richly detailed and revelatory biography presents the most frank and intimate portrait yet of Ray Davies'
CGA Magazine

'One of the best rock biographers of his generation'
Irish Independent

JOHNNY ROGAN

Johnny Rogan is the author of over twenty books, including highly acclaimed biographies/musical studies of the Byrds, the Smiths, Van Morrison, Neil Young, Crosby, Stills, Nash & Young, John Lennon and Morrissey. His groundbreaking *Starmakers & Svengalis: The History Of British Pop Management* was adapted for a six-week BBC series. *Morrissey & Marr: The Severed Alliance* was one of the bestselling and most controversial rock biographies of its time, receiving various music biography of the year awards, and has been in print continuously for over twenty-five years. More recently, *Van Morrison: No Surrender* was chosen by the *Sunday Times* as one of its Top 10 Music Books of the Year. He is currently completing an epic two-volume study, *Byrds: Requiem For The Timeless*.

Timeless Flight: The Definitive Biography Of The Byrds

Neil Young: Here We Are In The Years

Roxy Music: Style With Substance

Van Morrison: A Portrait Of The Artist

The Kinks: The Sound And The Fury

Wham! (Confidential) The Death Of A Supergroup

*Starmakers & Svengalis: The History Of British Pop
Management*

The Football Managers

The Guinness Encyclopaedia Of Popular Music (co-ed.)

Morrissey & Marr: The Severed Alliance

The Smiths: The Visual Documentary

*The Complete Guide To The Music Of The Smiths &
Morrissey/Marr*

The Complete Guide To The Music Of Neil Young

Crosby, Stills, Nash & Young: The Visual Documentary

The Complete Guide To The Music Of John Lennon

The Byrds: Timeless Flight Revisited – The Sequel

The Complete Guide To The Music Of The Kinks

Neil Young: Zero To Sixty: A Critical Biography

Van Morrison: No Surrender

Morrissey: The Albums

Lennon: The Albums

Byrds: Requiem For The Timeless, Volume 1

Anthology Contributions

The Bowie Companion

The Encyclopedia Of Popular Music

The Mojo Collection

Oxford Dictionary Of National Biography

*Oxford Originals: An Anthology Of Writing From Lady
Margaret Hall, 1879–2001*

JOHNNY ROGAN

Ray Davies

A Complicated Life

VINTAGE

1 3 5 7 9 10 8 6 4 2

Vintage
20 Vauxhall Bridge Road,
London SW1V 2SA

Vintage is part of the Penguin Random House group of companies whose
addresses can be found at global.penguinrandomhouse.com.

Penguin
Random House
UK

First published in Vintage in 2016
First published in hardback by The Bodley Head in 2015

www.vintage-books.co.uk

A CIP catalogue record for this book is available from the British Library

ISBN 9780099554080

Printed and bound by Clays Ltd, St Ives plc
Typeset by Palimpsest Book Production Ltd, Falkirk, Stirlingshire

Penguin Random House is committed to a sustainable future for our
business, our readers and our planet. This book is made from Forest
Stewardship Council® certified paper.

MIX
Paper from
responsible sources
FSC
www.fsc.org FSC® C018179

"*Ray Davies – A Suitable Mind For Study*. If only Herr Freud was still alive, the results of his analytical survey of Ray's thinking mechanism would make fascinating material for a best-selling book. Few people can honestly claim to fully comprehend Ray's complex actions or to be able to penetrate his veneer of what appears to be self-inflicted paranoia.

It has become something of a joke between Ray and myself that every time we meet, either I ask him if he is still paranoid or he tells me that he is trying *not* to be paranoid. Quite a few other people – especially those involved in the pop business – see Ray in this way and he does nothing to alleviate their suspicion.

Question him on the subject and you are likely to get a long searching look that speaks volumes but, paradoxically, reveals nothing. What is going on inside his head, you wonder?"

Richard Green, *New Musical Express*, 13 February 1970

CONTENTS

ACKNOWLEDGEMENTS

I would like to thank everyone I interviewed since commencing this project, originally way back in late 1981. The research continued in earnest during the mid-Nineties and then into the new century. A number of key interviewees have never previously spoken about their involvement with Ray Davies or the Kinks, and never will again. It is salutary to consider how many contributors, major and minor, have since passed away. May the survivors continue to flourish.

Firstly, thanks to the original Kinks for their enlightening comments: Ray Davies, Dave Davies, Pete Quaife and Mick Avory. Pre-Kinks drummers: John Start and Mickey Willett. Later Kinks: John Dalton, John Gosling, Andy Pyle, Jim Rodford and Ian Gibbons. The 'golden era' managers: Larry Page, Robert Wace and Grenville Collins (the latter email only). The road managers: Peter 'Jonah' Jones, Sam Curtis and Ken Jones. Producer of their best work, Shel Talmy. Ray's first wife, Rasa Didzpetris, whose memories were particularly revealing. Backing singers Shirlie Roden and Debi Doss.

In addition to this core insider group, there were a wealth of other interviewees from Ray Davies' past, including college friends, fellow musicians, managers, actors, music business moguls, A&R heads, colleagues and associates. In alphabetical order: Brett Anderson, Don Arden, John Beecham, Danny Betesh, Chris Britton, Donnie Burke, Clem Cattini, Chris Dreja, Ursula Graham-White, Charlie Greene, Ian Hendry, Ken Howard, Colin Huggett, Terry

King, Billy J. Kramer, Barry Leith, Bunny Lewis, Steve Marriott, Mitch Mitchell, Jeanne Nathan, Paul O'Dell, Andrew Loog Oldham, Reg Presley, David Quaife, Dick Rowe, Ned Sherrin, Philip Solomon, Screaming Lord Sutch, Julien Temple, Robert C. Tannen, Clive Tickner, Lisa Tickner (née Warton), Nick Trevisick and John Turney.

Salutations to Yvonne Gunner and Patricia Crosbie for their exceedingly polite demurrals.

The dates and places of the interviews above, along with all secondary sources, are included in the end notes, which also feature additional interview material, biography, arguments, minor revelations and commentaries considered too arcane to be included in the main text.

Several other people have played a significant or historical part in assisting the completion of this book. Keith Rodger, from my secondary school days in the Sixties, usually bought Kinks albums during the week of release and educated me accordingly on his favourite group at a time when LP purchases were still a luxury. We both revered *The Village Green Preservation Society* from the day of its release.

During the early Eighties I began a lengthy correspondence with Kinks' collector extraordinaire, Doug Hinman. At the time, he was working on a voluminous world discography. This was followed by an ambitious chronology of the Kinks to which I contributed in what became a rewarding reciprocal research arrangement. Hinman kept me locked in Colindale Library for lengthy periods, attempting to track down some of the elusive gig dates still outstanding towards the end of his own years of research. I also recall visits to Companies House unearthing some of the limited companies formed by the Davies brothers and their managers, a task that benefited both of us. Doug was always there with follow-up information, questions and answers. Later, when I was researching my books on Crosby, Stills, Nash & Young and Van Morrison, he helped with lists of copyrighted song registrations, concert dates and other obscure information in what was a rewarding research exchange across the Atlantic. It seems so many years ago now, but we're still in contact to this day.

Peter Doggett, whom I also first met during the early Eighties, always had a keen interest in Ray Davies and the Kinks. There were so many discussions and shared reminiscences over the years that even we cannot recall them all. Doggett, through his work at *Record Collector* and as consultant on the many Kinks reissues, interviewed Davies on several occasions, most notably in the Nineties. After our preliminary meetings, he would often throw in several provocative questions to Ray on my behalf which frequently helped inform my continued appreciation of the Davies psyche. Peter was the only person to see a preliminary early draft of this book. Of course, we do now share the same publisher.

Neil Rosser, a documentary maker who interviewed me for programmes on the Kinks and the Byrds in 1995, kindly provided a wealth of unedited tapes from his research archive, which were fascinating and revealing.

Other Kinks fans from way back who helped me include Russell Smith, Carolyn Mitchell, Peter Seeger, Marianne Collins and Andy Neill. I thank them all.

During the past 30 years I have been involved in a number of television projects involving Ray Davies. Thanks to Cyriel Van den Hemel for bringing me in as consultant for the video documentary *The Story Of The Kinks* for which both Ray and Dave were interviewed. Plus the producers and film-makers who interviewed me on camera about the Davies brothers through the ages: Ken Howard (*Routes Of Rock*); Len Brown (*My Generation – The Kinks*); and the DVD company behind *The Kinks Performances*.

On a personal level, thanks to all my friends over the decades and, during the more recent years spent writing this book, to Jackie for all her love and support. Thanks also to everyone at Random House, notably Stuart Williams, Will Hammond and Richard Collins.

Since becoming a full-time author in 1981 I vowed to put writing books above everything else, including family, friends and loved ones. In that time I have disappeared for months or longer on writing retreat, strained relationships to breaking point and no doubt will continue to do so until I shuffle off this mortal coil. I don't know how many of these epic books are left in me now. Increasingly, you feel this could be the last time, but who knows? One of my biggest fears has always been that I might die midway through a book project, so it's a relief to deliver this in advance of the anticipated arrival and onslaught of the Grim Reaper.

PREFACE

The time and place of the interview had been arranged: a restaurant near the BBC. Then, Ray Davies' publicist contacted mine with an urgent caveat: "Are you OK with JR covering lunch costs? . . . I am booking a table for Ray and Johnny, so don't want to risk any awkward situations!" An innocent enough request, perhaps, but this priceless exchange was guaranteed to win a smile from those former Kinks associates who still regale the world with tales of Davies' thriftiness. An entire chapter of such comic scenarios could be constructed concluding with such punchlines as "No, it's too expensive", "Can you lend me a penny?" and "What *half* are you drinking?" The 'Low Budget' persona is now a well-trodden stereotype, but a role once assumed is not easily discarded. When I later point out that he is a multi millionaire, Ray grimaces, as if the very suggestion is an affront. In many ways, he is still a man of simple pleasures, far removed from the trappings and excesses of celebrity culture. He is also a wry and mischievous observer of the human condition. A contradictory figure, Davies has at times perplexed and infuriated ex-band members, managers, business associates and even some of his own family. Nevertheless, few, if any, deny his charm, humour and sensitivity. Resilient yet fragile, quietly spoken and impressively forthright, shy but audacious, sardonic and sincere, he seems acutely aware of his Janus personality. When the conversation gets too close to the bone, he is adept at neat aphorisms and evasive explanations for his eccentricities and more wayward

1

behaviour. Here is a man intrigued by the meaning of personal identity, so much so that he has even secretly changed his name by deed poll, losing his surname in the process.

There is a wistful quality about Davies that harks back to a troubled childhood and adolescence, memories of which are none-theless treasured. One of his most endearing traits is a capacity to remember characters from his past with wry affection and genuine curiosity. He asks about former manager Larry Page, now living in Australia. I tell him about Page's house on Avoca Beach and his current work with producer and former Easybeat Harry Vanda. "I wonder if Larry is still with that girl Jade?" Ray enquires. An affirmative answer about the marriage prompts a faraway look. "That's good!" he says, apparently satisfied.

A passing comment about ex-manager Robert Wace's father prompts another unexpected effusion. "A lovely man," he remem-bers, having never mentioned him in print before. Perhaps it's advancing years, but as he enters the autumn of his life, Davies sounds phlegmatic, positive and forgiving. He even waxes fondly on former road manager Sam Curtis, the most irreverent, outra-geous and acerbic commentator on the Kinks that I ever encoun-tered. Davies now acknowledges Curtis as one of the "great characters".

And so the roll call continues. A comment on his film work suddenly brings to mind Paul O'Dell, a close friend from college whose importance is discussed in the Hornsey chapter herein. They lost contact years ago. Recalling *Veronica*, their almost forgotten film project, Davies reminisces about its titular star, a mysterious figure whose surname neither of us can recall. "Veronica turned up to a Kinks gig in Leeds," Ray muses. "She went to Leeds University, settled in Leeds and had a family. She had a great face." And what of John Philby, the son of spy Kim Philby and a former drinking pal of Davies? "Did you meet him?" Davies enquires, eager to learn more. He then admits that he only recently heard of Philby's death, even though it happened several years ago. I mention how Philby had remained in north London and set up a joinery business, as if he was a minor character in one of Davies' affecting vignettes.

Talking about the lost and the dead seems fitting as Davies himself flirted with the Grim Reaper only a decade ago when he was shot in New Orleans. Now, as he celebrates his 70th birthday, full of fresh plans yet uncertain whether time will permit their completion, the list of obituaries in his circle inevitably multiplies.

The defining tragedy in his life was the sudden death of his sister Rene on a London dance floor in 1957. Arguably, it was this incident that intensified the enduring importance of family in Davies' life and work. Personal history runs through his entire oeuvre from 'Waterloo Sunset' to 'Come Dancing' via concept albums, notably *The Village Green Preservation Society*, *Arthur*, *Muswell Hillbillies* and *Schoolboys In Disgrace*. He lost another sister, Rose, when she emigrated to Australia with her husband, Arthur, accompanied by their son, Terry. Even though Davies was almost 20 years old, the departure of his nephew and sister produced an ineffable and disproportionate sense of loss. "It was the beginning and the end of everything," he now says. He also remembers, with great fondness, Rene's orphaned son Bobby, who ended up living with the Davies clan in north London. "His father was half North American Indian. One of the first gigs I went to see was Duane Eddy and the Rebels, and Bobby looked just like the drummer in that band. Who would that have been? He had glasses on like Bob."

Davies is full of such stories and reminiscences. It's rather like meeting Shakespeare and discussing Rosencrantz and Guildenstern instead of Hamlet and Ophelia. "I always write for the extras," he says, with a lopsided smile. That much is evident in his recent writings, but what is equally noticeable is the extent to which he connects with his 'composite characters' – part-fictionalized versions of real people fused with aspects of his inner self.

Oddly, there is an affection and empathy in his observations of such peripheral figures that seems absent when he reflects upon his only brother. His relationship with Dave was forged amid the white heat of Kinks conflicts, a process that has left both brothers baffled and suspicious about each other's motivations. "I don't really know my brother very well," Ray concludes, as if Dave has always been a stranger. Detachment has not tempered former frictions. If anything, their time apart since performing and recording as the Kinks in the mid-Nineties has exacerbated Dave's negative feelings. Sporadic broadsides have included colourful accusations that Ray is a 'narcissist', a 'vampire', an 'arsehole' –

and worse. Bizarrely, such insouciant tirades often end with Dave protesting how deeply he loves his brother. Ray's restrained responses convey a haughty magnanimity which, intentionally or not, perforate Dave's defences. "Ray does talk a lot of shit and the older he gets the worse he gets," he says. "Someone as experienced as you can read between those lines." It is this complex dynamic that has driven the career of the Kinks and continues to intrigue fans and foes alike.

The oft-described sibling rivalry somehow became normalized within the context of the Kinks. Ray's first wife, Rasa, observed the relationship from the home front. "It was obvious that there were going to be constant clashes and disagreements and I just accepted that as being normal between two brothers who were so very different. I'm not sure about bonding. Obviously they're brothers and there's a bond, but there are strong bonds and weak attachments . . . Dave is a personality who is much more receptive, emotionally. I think he would wish for a stronger bond and Ray is just shuttered off from it really and does what he wants to do and is the way he is. So it's never going to be the greatest love affair between two brothers. I accepted that that was the way it was going to be and, to me, it was pretty normal really. I was living in that environment."

Ray's relationship with Kinks alumni has seldom been straightforward. Some members have departed amid exasperation or acrimony, but are usually fondly remembered. Even when bass player Pete Quaife was undergoing dialysis treatment, Ray still spoke sentimentally of reuniting the original Kinks. Over the decades, he has grown closer to drummer Mick Avory, who remains the butt of a ribald humour that cannot disguise an irrepressible and special affection. Avory's involvement in tribute outfit the Kast Off Kinks has also kept Davies in sporadic contact with the group's subsidiary members. They now resemble grizzled war veterans, a veritable legion of substitute heroes, keeping the music alive, largely untroubled by the Davies brothers. Bassist John Dalton describes them as one great extended family. While Dave Davies seems ambivalent, if not hostile, towards their continued existence, Ray often dutifully appears when they perform in Tufnell Park at the annual 'Kinks Konvention'. Sometimes he joins them onstage for a short cameo, but more often complains that he has a head cold or sore throat and simply offers some encouraging words and thanks to the fans. At the November 2013 gathering, he hinted teasingly at some grand reunion. "I've got special plans for the boys. I can't tell them now because we've got to negotiate pay." When a wily audience member shouts, "They don't want any money," Davies turns towards Dalton and Avory and asks: "Can I have that as an affidavit?" A music hall Scrooge could not have phrased it better.

Davies' career in the music business now spans 50 years. It has been a remarkable odyssey. His reputation would probably have been assured solely as an innovative R&B-influenced pop composer. Of course, there was always so much more. Davies mined a strain of Englishness like no other songwriter from his generation. In common with several of his great contemporaries, he was an iconoclast at a time of immense social and cultural change. For all that, he was never comfortable as a clichéd symbol of the Swinging Sixties. He seemed fascinated and half in love with the world that he was leaving behind. Davies never forgot the Austerity years. For a full understanding of his life and work, it is not enough to appreciate the golden era of the mid-Sixties. An empathy with the moral, musical and social landscape of post-war London, particularly during the Fifties, adds a deeper understanding of the Davies psyche. It is no coincidence that so many of the key themes in his songwriting and biography – his sisters' lives, the prominence of the dance hall, the rivalry with his brother, his musical aspirations and the upheavals suffered by his extended family, his fascination with suburbia, class differences and changing sexual mores – all stem from that crucial era. Even in his prose and theatrical work, Davies returns obsessively to those times for inspiration or reflection.

Early press notices for the Kinks catalogued familiar influences – Chuck Berry, Big Bill Broonzy, the Beatles, the Rolling Stones – but by the late Sixties Davies was equally well known for his satirical portraits and subtle social commentaries. In discussing his work, it seemed valid to step beyond the influence of pop and blues legends to cite literary precedents as diverse as J. B. Priestley, George Orwell and Dylan Thomas.

For those of us who have followed the Davies brothers and the Kinks since 1964, it has been a roller-coaster ride, filled with excitement, hope, doubt and re-evaluation. A canon that once seemed in flux now looks settled. Late arrivals, younger listeners and latter-day music critics can appreciate the quality of Davies' work, albeit without the extremes of emotion, personal prejudices and uncertainties that came from witnessing the story as it slowly unfolded: the exhilaration of listening to 'You Really Got Me' and 'All Day And All Of The Night' on the wireless; the realization with 'Tired Of Waiting For You' that Davies could write plaintive, neurotic love songs; the stylistic setback presented by 'Ev'rybody's Gonna Be Happy'; the lyrical and musical mystery of 'See My Friend'; the failure of 'Waterloo Sunset' to reach number 1; the emergence of Dave Davies with 'Death Of A Clown'; the fear that 'Wonderboy' and a spell in cabaret might be the end; the sense of profound discovery upon first hearing *The Village Green Preservation Society* amid the sonic bustle of 1968; the non-television broadcast of *Arthur* and chart failure of 'Shangri-la'; pop chart redemption via 'Lola'; the initial tedium and puzzlement of the theatrical years; the evolution/devolution of the group into a hard rock 'American' act; the emergence of Ray Davies as a rock icon and national treasure; and lastly the realization that all these snapshot memories are now part of a generation's musical history. After every individual foible has been catalogued the music remains intact and, if anything, grows in stature. This is a point that both Ray and Dave Davies stress whenever they mull over their careers or confront their personal failings. "My work is better than I am," Davies admits. "I just don't live up to it. I'd love to be as good as 'Waterloo Sunset'." He is correct. That song, along with many others, will transcend the turbulence of the Kinks and the vicissitudes of his life.

Of course, the play is not yet over but we are currently watching the final act. Davies has long since become a grand elder statesman of British popular music. It is a fate he shares with several contemporaries including Pete Townshend, Paul McCartney, Mick Jagger et al. In what seems the ultimate revenge of the cult of youth, each of these stars has seen their Sixties selves elevated to retrospective godhead. An illustrious past eclipses present-day ventures, no matter how worthily executed. How must it be for Pete Townshend to be told that he really said it all with 'My Generation' or that his last great album was 1973's *Quadrophenia*? Davies too has been compromised by his own history. His post-millennium solo albums compete with a stream of higher profile Kinks deluxe reissues, archival collections and compilations, just as *The Village Green Preservation Society* and *Arthur* vied with budget Kinks packages back in the Sixties. Tellingly, he has contributed to that nostalgic trend by revisiting classic material via collaborations (the 'tribute' album, *See My Friends*), choral adaptations (*The Kinks Choral Collection*) and musicals (*Come Dancing* and *Sunny Afternoon*). This is both the curse and the triumph of the heritage act, forced by marketplace conditions and public expectation to confront their past at the expense of their present. Davies has accepted that challenge – just as he did in the 1960s and 1970s – by extending and expanding his work in related disciplines via television, film, theatre, musicals, experimental autobiography and short stories. The work is ongoing. The greater concern is the immemorial one – mortality. Ray Davies is currently planning an opera, teasing journalists about the likelihood or otherwise of a Kinks' reunion in 2014–15, planning a new solo album and wondering if *You Really Got Me*, the long-awaited major film on the Kinks, will be completed. "I've just got to work out how I want to spend the rest of my life," he concludes.

CHAPTER ONE

THE FAMILY

As their family name suggests, the Davies' lineage was part Welsh. Ray's grandfather Harry Davies was from the Rhondda Valley and worked as a slaughterman. He subsequently married a servant girl, Amy Kelly, of Irish descent. Their son, Frederick George Davies, settled in London and took up his father's occupation, eventually finding work at a cattle market in King's Cross. There, he met Annie Florence Willmore, born in 1905 to Albert Willmore and Catherine Emily Bowden. Frederick and Annie enjoyed a short courtship before marrying in the summer of 1924 in the borough of Islington. They rapidly produced a sizeable progeny, beginning with daughter Rosina (Rose) in 1924. Over the next decade and a half a veritable matriarchy was established comprising Irene Gladys (Rene) (1926), Dorothy (Dolly) (1928), Joyce (1930), Kathleen (Peggy) (1932) and Gwendoline (1938). All the girls were born and brought up in the King's Cross area, where Annie's mother Catherine (later known as Big Granny) still lived.

The Hungry Thirties was a time of deprivation when a full-time job was considered a prize to be treasured. Fred worked hard butchering cattle in an all-male environment. A convivial personality, he liked a drink and considered himself a ladies' man. He also attended Variety shows and was a capable tap-dancer, a pastime endearingly at odds with his day job. His wife enjoyed social outings but spent most of her time at home bringing up the children. As the product of a sprawling family herself, Annie Davies easily adapted to her domestic routine, rearing six girls –

but she was no shrinking violet. Known for her sharp tongue, she could be crude and forceful when riled. Years later, recalling a revealing piece of family folklore, Dave Davies told me of an incident when his mother challenged the conventions of the time in devastating fashion. Back then, public bars were predominantly male enclaves, where respectable women would never be seen. Older women congregated in cloistered 'snugs' accessible by separate entrances, while couples on a social outing drank in the saloon bar. Everybody had their place, as convention dictated. In what would have been regarded as a shocking breach of working-class etiquette, Annie stormed into the public bar like a crusading suffragette. "The girls were babies and she had two or three of them in the pram," Dave says. "She got so fed up with the old man being around the pub that she thought she'd surprise him. One day she walked into the pub and the old man was chatting up some floozie behind the bar. She went up to him and said, 'What are you fucking chatting up that old tart for?' Dad was playing the innocent, so she threw beer all over him, left the kids there and said, 'Sod this, you fucking look after them, I'm going out!' Then she stormed out of the pub leaving these screaming kids with my dad and this tart. He had beer all over his head."

The Davies children had a far from genteel upbringing and, in keeping with the times, there were health issues and near fatalities. Rene, the second eldest daughter, suffered a bout of rheumatic fever as a child that left her with a serious heart condition. For the remainder of her life she was a walking time bomb, cursed with the ever-present knowledge that death was merely a missing heartbeat away.

Rene's younger sister, Peggy, faced more immediate problems. In 1934, at the age of two, she was playing on the pavement outside the door of the family house when a large brewery lorry swerved across the street. The driver had been drinking and lost control of the vehicle which hurtled into metal railings, simultaneously impaling part of her arm. Peggy was rushed to hospital, then despatched to Wales for further treatment and a period of convalescence. A surgeon saved her damaged arm but the limb withered. The collision also left her partially deaf.

During the Second World War, at the height of the Blitz, family life was disrupted as many children were moved to the safer environs of the countryside. The Davies girls were set to depart but, at the eleventh hour, their mother had a change of heart. Instead, the entire family relocated from the inner city to East Finchley, eventually settling at 6 Denmark Terrace in Muswell Hill. It was a happy and necessary compromise that enabled Fred Davies to commute between north London and his workplace in Smithfield Market. His was a reserved occupation, which ensured that he did not have to serve in the armed forces. It also meant that the Davies family had a plentiful supply of meat.

Fred sported noticeably outsized clothes, with baggy trousers held up by braces. This sartorial eccentricity was a ruse that allowed him to smuggle meat from the cattle market or abattoir. Often he would return home laden with cuts. Like a music hall magician, he would produce a joint of meat from deep inside his trousers, followed by a sliver of liver or bloodied heart. Evidently, he was never rumbled. The routine continued during the early years of post-war rationing. Interestingly, both his sons would later become vegetarians.

Annie Davies was 39 when she became pregnant for what she assumed would be the last time. On 21 June 1944, there was great excitement in the matriarchal household when she gave birth to a son, who was christened Raymond Douglas Davies. It was an eventful evening in Denmark Terrace as a nearby air raid had blasted out several windows in the street, including their own.

The war years were also the dancing years for several of the older Davies girls. Ballrooms of romance – with evocative names like the Palais, Mecca and Locarno – proliferated and were made more glamorous by the presence of American servicemen with money and access to black-market goods. Adolescent girls seduced by nylons, chocolates and dreams of becoming a GI bride flocked to the halls as peacetime beckoned. The sisters were dance mad, especially Rene, who started dating a Canadian soldier, Russell Whitbread. Suddenly, there was a flurry of marriages. In June 1943, the eldest daughter Rosina (Rose) wed Gordon Arthur Anning, another serviceman. The ceremony was followed by a reception, with Fred providing a joint of meat and his wife acquiring some additional food from the American Services Club where she was working part-time. The married couple moved to nearby Highgate and, two years later, had a son, Terry. That same year, Rene announced that she was marrying her Canadian beau Russell in December, after which they would emigrate to North America.

Accommodating everybody in a three-bedroom house proved quite a challenge. Further complications arose when Annie Davies, now almost 42, discovered that she was pregnant again. Her fecundity was a marvel but also an embarrassment, and she kept the news from prying neighbours. Even her mother, Big Granny, was unaware of the event. On 3 February 1947, the peak year of the post-war baby boom, the second boy in the family was born: David Russell Gordon Davies. The effects of all this on Ray have provoked much debate among the brothers ever since. "When Dave was born, I felt like a little child of two whose parents suddenly go out and buy a dog. Of course a kid gets jealous." One teasingly symbolic moment, often recalled by Ray, became part of the family legend. While baby Dave was being paraded in front of his sisters, his brother became over-excited and ran out of the house, dodging outstretched hands as he tumbled forward, hitting the ground violently, fracturing his front teeth and bloodying his nose. The accident ultimately created that familiar gap-toothed smile. But what Ray remembered most keenly was the immediate effect upon his family. Suddenly, they turned away from the usurping infant and focused all their attention on his injury. He was the centre of attention once more. The event may even have kick-started his interest in music as his parents presented him with a ukulele soon after for braving his first visit to the dentist.

Dave Davies remembers another formative incident that occurred several years later when the brothers were playing in the front room. One of their uncles had left some boxing gloves around, so they decided to have a mock fight. Swinging wildly, Dave hit Ray with a lucky punch, knocking him off balance. As he stumbled to the floor he grazed his head against the family piano and lay still, seemingly unconscious. Hovering close to his face, Dave whispered, "Are you OK?" Ray bolted upright and punched his brother hard in the face. "It's symbolic of our whole relationship really," Dave maintains. "I felt the pleasure that I'd knocked him over, then concern that I'd hurt him. But all he really wanted was to get back at me." For Dave, the confrontation was a harbinger of worse to come. "I was quite a happy kid and Ray was a real miserable one. He was probably happy for three years until I was born and realized there was another boy in the family. 'What's that little bastard doing here?'"

Such a reaction is common enough among siblings of such a young age, as are their contrasting feelings towards each other. Psychoanalyst Peter B. Neubauer notes: "Differences in the evolvement of rivalry, jealousy, and envy may depend upon whether the child is an older or younger sibling . . . The younger child will, in the first years of life, take the circumstances of his environment as he finds them for granted . . . The older child, while feeling displaced, may later enjoy the younger's admiration, which the latter rarely experiences to the same degree." That Dave never felt a reciprocal admiration from Ray seems something of an understatement, despite occasional evidence to the contrary. It was part of a peculiar dynamic that they would continue to play out for the remainder of their lives.

Sigmund Freud concluded that all sibling relationships, irrespective of visible positive interaction, were based on "an unfathomably deep hostility" or "primal hatred", punctuated by the symbolic "intent to murder". In his view: "The elder child ill-treats the younger, maligns him and robs him of his toys; while the younger is consumed with impotent rage against his elder, envies and fears him." Ray Davies later translated Freud's theory into song, most notably in the lacerating duet 'Hatred', but it was also there in the feminized 'Two Sisters' and, most tellingly, 'I'm Not Like Everybody Else', a self-analytical howl of independence passed over to the younger brother to perform like some act of psychological transference. "I'm not a psychologist," Ray cautions, "but I think what annoys people about one another, and why I think children fall out with parents, and siblings fall out with each other, is because they see everything they hate about themselves in that other person. And it's familiarity that breeds contempt, not so much the things that are opposite. It's the embarrassment of seeing yourself in another person that makes you dislike them."

June 1949 was an occasion of treble celebration in the Davies family. Ray was five years old and two more of his sisters had just married in a joint ceremony: Dolly to Joseph Warwick and

Joyce to Kenneth Palmer. The newly-weds temporarily moved into the Davies' overcrowded home, now teeming with siblings and in-laws.

The multifarious Davies family tree provided more exotic fruit at the beginning of the Fifties. Peggy, independent of mind and irrepressible of spirit, had survived her childhood injuries and established herself as an unlikely star of the ballroom dance floor, along with her sisters. Tongues wagged when she started dating, of all people, an African. Before the influx of West Indians during the late Forties to mid-Fifties many people, even in London, had never seen a black person, let alone contemplated going out with one. Peggy's defiance of social convention evidently ran deep; she not only had sex with her boyfriend, but fell pregnant. This was a shocking development, likely to lead to ostracism, but Annie Davies proved remarkably supportive of her errant daughter. One solution to such a problem, of course, would have been a rushed wedding. Mixed marriages were rare then and any such couple was likely to meet social disapprobation, but even that was preferable to the shame of mothering a bastard child. Illegitimacy rates were as low as 5 per cent at this time and more than 50 per cent of children born out of wedlock were given up for adoption. Many argued that whatever the emotional deprivation felt by the mother or child, adoption at least removed the terrible stigma of illegitimacy, which was seen as infinitely worse. Peggy's options were limited, reduced further by the realization that her boyfriend had no legal status in Britain. Shortly afterwards, he returned to the Dark Continent, disappearing as mysteriously as he had arrived.

The child was named Jacqueline Michelle. She faced an uncertain future in an environment that veered between loving and hostile. Faced with the prospect of becoming a social pariah, Peggy nevertheless decided to keep the child. Mrs Davies allowed them to stay at the already overcrowded 6 Denmark Terrace, although it was hardly a matter of choice. Alternative accommodation was a near impossibility. Landlords did not welcome unmarried mothers – citing both financial and moral objections, if asked. It was difficult and often impossible to chase lost fathers for income support and no help was available from social services. Unmarried mothers were not allowed on housing register waiting lists, so there was no prospect of a much coveted council flat, or even short-term lodgings.

Jackie was accepted as part of the family, but was seen as an oddity in the local community. Inevitably, she was singled out at school and on the street, and suffered the familiar and expected prejudices of the time. Children teased her with the nickname 'Blackie Jackie', a rhyming monicker that Ray claims was even used by some of her younger cousins. Just as her mother had overcome a physical handicap and defied social convention, Jackie displayed considerable fortitude and was blessed with a sweet disposition. Dave Davies, only a few years older, always felt close and protective towards his niece, and Ray remembers cheering her up in sadder moments by singing a tune in her honour. Peggy, the perennial survivor, married an Irishman named Mike Picker a few years later, a union not entirely free from censure. They left Denmark Terrace to move into a new home, but Jackie was left behind to be raised by her grandmother. A potential victim of the times, she transcended her difficult upbringing, eventually moving to Los Angeles and marrying an established keyboard player.

The Davies household was always strapped for cash but money often seemed to appear unexpectedly from somewhere. At the beginning of the Fifties, Fred Davies acquired a car, a luxury beyond the budget of most working-class families of the era. He seemed unfazed by the recent 4d rise in petrol costs, which now stood at 3/6d per gallon. A period photo of the L-plated car reveals the proud father in his familiar braces, flanked by his wife and eldest daughter, Rose. In the foreground, a pensive looking Dave touches the vehicle's bonnet, as if it is capable of emanating magical powers, while the infant Jackie stares into the photographer's lens. Camera-shy Ray is conspicuous by his absence.

Even as a young boy, when he professed to be happy, Ray seemed unpredictable and difficult to please. "At a very early age I was forced to recite poetry on Sunday afternoons," he complains. In 1949, he was enrolled at the nearby St James Primary, a Church school where he sang in the choir until the age of ten. "Then I trained myself to sing out of tune so I could hang around with a gang called the Crooners instead. Our Scottish singing teacher Mrs Lewis said, 'Never mind, Davies – I hear crooners are making a lot of money these days.'" Ray found the regimented ethos of the school stifling at times, but that was the way of the world. Several of the teachers had served in the armed forces and were still readjusting to civilian life. "I picked up a sense of bitterness from some of them. There was one notable teacher who said, 'Yes, I'm wearing my demobilization suit – it's all I can afford on my wages.' I sensed from them that it was not a good world that I was coming into."

The sensitive child reacted uncertainly when faced with social occasions and entertainments – some of which left him cold. Discussing key experiences between 1950 and 1951, he reminisces about a promised trip to the circus, an opportunity to attend the panto *Dick Whittington* and even the chance to see some jugglers and comedians. None of these made much impression. "I think I saw Max Wall when I was a kid, but I'm not sure if it was the real music hall, or just a Variety night. They still had those at Stratford East when I was young. I wasn't sure about that kind of thing when I was a kid, though – I remember I walked out of the circus when I was six years old and the same thing happened with the pantomime at Golders Green Hippodrome. Now I wish I'd seen real music hall – I would have loved it, I'm sure."

One pastime that did meet with Ray's approval was the cinema. He was a fan of Burt Lancaster, fascinated by the actor's gleaming tombstone teeth which contrasted so markedly with his own. Fred Davies enjoyed taking his eldest son to the pictures, irrespective of what was on offer. "When I was five my dad took me to see *Bicycle Thieves* at the Odeon in Muswell Hill," Ray recalls. "A tragic little Italian film, all violin accompaniment. I didn't understand the subtitles but the pictures and the passion interested me." Filmed in 1948, *Ladri di Biciclette* is an existentialist tale of a man and his son's search for a stolen bicycle involving seemingly endless wanderings around the streets of Rome. The notion of Fred Davies sitting through a 90-minute black and white classic of Italian neo-realism may seem strange, but this family foray into foreign language cinema was not unique. The younger Dave Davies also remembers seeing a French film with Ray featuring a leonine misfit, so alienated from his world that he invents his own language. This briefly inspired the brothers to speak gibberish among themselves as an act of defiance against the adult world.

It was one of the few occasions when Dave felt some kinship with his sibling.

Another formative experience that marinated in Ray's memory banks was being taken by his father to the celebrated Festival of Britain at London's newly rebuilt South Bank in 1951. The Festival was promoted as a "tonic for the nation", a phantasmagorical vision of a more optimistic future in which the possibilities were supposedly endless. The event, which attracted more than eight and a half million visitors, served as a political and propagandist coup, an opiate for the masses, an emblem of gratitude to the survivors of the war, a promise of technological advancement – and much more.

The spectacle was meant to be educational rather than merely entertaining and those seeking simpler pleasures were directed to the suitably named Pleasure Gardens in Battersea Park which included a Fun Fair featuring modern American-styled mechanical rides. The major attractions on the South Bank were the rocket-like Skylon, an imposing 300-foot-high tower made of steel and aluminium, and the grandly named Dome of Discovery, the largest hemispherical edifice in the world, whose interior included a model of the solar system. Almost as thrilling, for youngsters and adults, was the presence of an escalator, whose stairs moved as if by magic. An exhibition titled 'Home Of The Future' and an opportunity to watch a film in three dimensions were among the other highlights. Considering that basic foodstuffs, not to mention luxuries such as tea and sweets, were still under ration, there was a certain perverse wonder in observing these technological miracles.

For Ray Davies, only a month away from his seventh birthday, the Festival of Britain was a puzzling spectacle. "I was just an infant and was a bit confused by it," he recalled, 60 years later. "They had this thing called a Skylon and I asked my dad what it was and he replied, 'I think it represents the future.'" Ray was uncertain what his father meant and later became wary of any utopian notions of progress. Symbolically, neither the Skylon nor the Dome survived their time. They were dismantled and consigned to history. It was enough to spark conflicting feelings about what the future might offer.

Three years later, he had similar feelings after glimpsing the opening of Nigel Kneale's television dramatization of George

Orwell's *Nineteen Eighty-Four*. Broadcast live on a Sunday evening
(and starring Peter Cushing as the doomed Winston Smith) the
unnerving drama attracted the highest viewer ratings since the
Coronation. It was preceded by warnings alerting viewers to its
disturbing content. Much to his indignation, Ray was ushered off
to bed after being told that he was too young to watch the drama.
In protest, he obtained a copy of the novel from the local library
and was profoundly affected by its contents. Its dystopian vision
seemed to chime with his pessimistic view that all was not well
in his world. Orwellian themes would come to dominate much
of his recorded work in the early Seventies. Somehow it all went
back to that first reading of *Nineteen Eighty-Four*, and the impressionable visit to the Festival of Britain where the 'future' was
played out before his eyes. The area around the South Bank
attained a psychogeographical significance in his life, partly
inspiring one of his most memorable compositions, 'Waterloo
Sunset', a subsequent teleplay *Return To Waterloo* and a collection of short stories. In 2011, a cavalcade of cultural events was
arranged to celebrate the spirit of the original Festival of Britain,
including a series of pop concerts curated by Ray Davies. "It's
poignant to me that sixty years on when we are celebrating its
anniversary I still feel that the future is upon us," he said. "At
the time we were in a period of terrible post-war austerity and
we are going through a similar phase now."

The Festival of Britain may have symbolized the arrival of a
new age in certain eyes, but there was a paternalistic concern
about the state of the proletariat. Class consciousness was pervasive and inescapable. It was ever present in newspaper articles,
nuanced in didactic columns of concern, and reinforced via church
sermons and BBC radio broadcasts. It was as if there was a need
to create and establish a revitalized, idealized notion of everyman
among working-class communities still recovering from the
brutality of a world war. Concepts such as duty, patriotism,
decency and right thinking were common virtues seen by many
as the very essence of Britishness. Benign condescension was
wielded by even the most restrained and seemingly reasonable
voices. Novelist/playwright J. B. Priestley captured the mood of
the period well in his delightfully innocent yet subtly subversive
reflections on the emergence of an aspiring, suburbanite culture

whose membership valued conformity and homeliness above all else. Addressing BBC listeners in the summer of 1951, he announced: "Let us – like the good Home Service types we are – be cosy together. For that I take to be the mark of our Home Programme, the cosiness of plain easy folk . . . Between the raucous low brows and the lisping high-brows is a fine gap, meant for the middle or broadbrows; and you and I, in our homely fashion, fill that gap nicely. We can be cosy together in it. We can talk about bilberry pie." That last sentence could so easily have been voiced by a character named 'Arthur' or housed within an invitation to join an imaginary Village Green Preservation Society.

The British government also seemed conflicted about the moral health of the nation. Germany's defeat in the war had vanquished an external threat, but there was still fear of the enemy within. That same year, Guy Burgess and Donald Maclean were exposed as spies and defected to the USSR. The news was kept from the public, as was the embarrassing revelation that the traitors were homosexual. With the old British Empire already in retreat, it was difficult to escape the impression from contemporary commentators that, beneath the victorious façade, something was rotting in the body politic. A reported increase in figures for gross indecency between men, buoyed by convictions for sodomy and bestiality, either testified to some sort of moral stagnation or indicated a concerted clampdown on such activities by the police and judiciary. Perhaps both points of view were true.

These anxieties were made manifest in 1952 when the popular *Sunday Pictorial* ran a three-issue special titled 'The Evil Men'. The investigation by Douglas Warth pulled no punches. "Homosexuality is an unpleasant subject, but it must be faced if ever it is to be controlled . . . a number of doctors believe that the problem would be best solved by making homosexuality legal between consenting adults. This solution would be intolerable and ineffective. Because the chief danger of the perverts is the corrupting influence they have on youth. Most people know that there are such things – 'pansies' – mincing, effeminate young men who call themselves 'queers'. But simple, decent folk regard them as freaks and rarities. They have become, regrettably, a Variety hall joke. There will be no joking about this subject when people realize the true situation." Warth was adamant that this "unnatural sex vice" was corrupting the country to such an extent that it represented an even greater threat than incipient Nazism. Indeed, in an extravagant flourish, he equated the two. "I have watched it growing," he wrote, "as it grew in Germany before the War, producing the horrors of Hitlerite corruption, and as it grew in classical Greece to the point where civilization was destroyed. I thought, at first, that this menace could best be fought by silence – a silence which Society has almost always maintained in the face of a problem which has been growing in our midst for years. But this vice can no longer be ignored. The silence . . . is a factor which has enabled the evil to spread." The reassuring panacea was eternal vigilance by parents, educators and the establishment.

The year 1952 brought Britain a new monarch, Queen Elizabeth II, the first pop chart courtesy of the *New Musical Express* and, not incidentally for the Davies' family, the end of tea rationing. For Dave, it all seemed to pass in an evanescent blur. "When you were the youngest in the family . . . it was like a Fellini film – faces everywhere." Ray was also caught up in the frenetic activity but the ceaseless movement seemed to have a disorientating effect. "I can't explain what my childhood was like. It was like a dream childhood . . . The family had a lot of people living in the house: eight siblings, *seven* sisters, one brother." This peculiar miscalculation was not some harried journalist's typing error, but Ray speaking directly to the camera in a sanctioned television documentary on his life broadcast in 2010. Had he really lost count of his siblings or was he creating an additional sister for his own amusement or to confuse viewers and commentators? Either way, it seemed to testify to an underlying dissatisfaction about his place in the world. "No disrespect to where I grew up," he cautions. "I love my family, but I was bored by being in the house. I did all the things like Christmas and birthdays and New Year's and waiting for the Saturday afternoon football reports. Most people call it lonely, but I was just isolated . . . It was a sense of loving where I was from but also a sense that I belonged somewhere else. When I was a kid, I heard the sound of the night train. I could hear it in my bedroom." The train not only symbolized adventure, but escape from surroundings that were simultaneously familiar, reassuring and suddenly confusing.

Later in the year, there was another temporary addition to the family house when Rene returned from Canada for an extended stay. Several years before, she had left war-ravaged London only to discover that life abroad was nothing like the idyllic alternative she had imagined. Transatlantic communication was conducted solely by Air Mail correspondence, which was reassuring, but no substitute for the human voice. Like many GI brides, she missed her family. Adjusting to Canadian customs was surmountable, but her resolve was undermined by her husband Russell, who was a heavy drinker and prone to violence. They had a young son, Bobby, who accompanied her on the trip to London and attended school while she sought a temporary job.

Rene was immediately struck by the personality differences between Ray and Dave. The younger brother was confident, cheeky, mischievous and happy-go-lucky, whereas Ray seemed preternaturally quiet. It was as if he had taken on the burdens of the world while internalizing his feelings. Restive and anxious, he found it difficult to get a good night's sleep. His insomnia had been present as long as he could remember and would remain with him for the rest of his life. "My sisters used to take turns walking me around when I was a baby, trying to get me to sleep. The only way they could get me to sleep was to play gramophone records. All night, as long as it took. It was a wind-up record player. When it wouldn't work, one of my sisters just moved it around with her fingers." Rene, already aware of his neuroses, offered reassuring words to soothe his troubled mind. If he was still awake in the early hours, she would cuddle up beside him in bed until he slept. Even then, he seemed restless and uneasy. At times, he was plagued by nightmares and alarmed the family with scary displays of sleepwalking that threatened his own safety. Dave remembers one such incident during which Ray woke the entire household, screaming in fear, convinced that he was being chased by a tiger. Running from the house, eyes wide yet still asleep, he ended up in the garden where he was shaken into consciousness by his mother. The significance of the tiger was never unlocked, but there was no doubting his genuine fear and confusion.

Rene remained the loyal sister and surrogate mother, but she had her own family and health problems to deal with and soon returned to Canada, hoping that her life might somehow improve.

Coincidentally, the gap between her departure and next return to England (1952–7) was the precise period that Dave felt most distanced from his elder brother. "During the time when Ray was eight to thirteen, he was very quiet, deep and lonely. He never shared anything – least of all his mind. And as a little boy I felt completely left out of his life."

In addition to Rene, Ray had another mother figure to fall back on. Rose, the eldest of the sisters, had always been there for him since his birth. She now lived in Highgate with her husband (Gordon) Arthur Anning. Their home was a sanctuary for both brothers in times of trouble.

In September 1952, Dave started school at St James Primary where his boisterous personality soon attracted the unwelcome attention of his first female teacher. He ran away, instinctively bypassing his own home in favour of his more understanding elder sister's. "I was five years old and I was crying and banging on Rose's kitchen door.

'I won't go back to school!' I said through sobs.

'But you have only been in school for three days, love!'

'Well, there's a mistress there who shouts. She scares me. I threw some plasticine at her. Then I ran home.'

'What did you tell Mum?'

'That we had the rest of the day off. She tried to take me back to school. I ran away to you.'

"Mum guessed where I had gone and left me there. Ray and I were always running away to Rose's. Rose never actually sent us home, now I come to recall; we always left of our own accord. I think she believed in making us face up to our punishment alone . . . When we were children, Ray and I depended a lot on Rose. She was married before we had grown up, and her house was a continual haven in the storms of childhood . . . . Rose was the one who really understood Ray. They had a sort of understanding between them that overcame everything, even silence. The only time there was any closeness between Ray and me was when we were in trouble. We would face the storm of Mum's anger together. Ray would smile at me, shrug and say, 'Don't worry, it'll blow over by tomorrow and if it doesn't there's always the next day.' He was quite a philosopher, really."

CHAPTER TWO

'THE NEGRO'S REVENGE'

Although family life for Ray Davies was unquestionably chaotic, he retained fond memories of his childhood years. Saturdays had been party time at 6 Denmark Terrace for as long as he could remember. His father's custom was to enjoy an evening at the local pub, after which he would invite his drinking friends and extended family back to the house for a sing-song. A crate of beer enhanced the mood. Everyone crowded into the front room and congregated around the family piano. All the girls could play, with varying degrees of proficiency. Several of them even created their own vocal ensemble, in imitation of the Andrews Sisters. The soundtrack for the evening was impressively eclectic, a trip through the musical century featuring bombastic show tunes, jazz standards, lachrymose country laments, modern pop ballads and even hymns. Highly charged emotional renditions of 'I'll Take You Home, Kathleen' or 'Danny Boy' were complemented by comedy numbers and cockney music hall staples – 'My Old Dutch', 'Bye Bye Blackbird', 'Roll Out The Barrel', 'Down At The Old Bull And Bush', 'Doing The Lambeth Walk' and 'Where Did You Get That Hat?' A religious song could be instantly undercut by a bawdy singalong of adulterous intent such as 'Who Were You With Last Night?', 'Hello! Hello! Who's Your Lady Friend' or 'Hold Your Hand Out, You Naughty Boy'. The spirit of the Blitz was recaptured on a round-the-table rendition of Vera Lynn's 'We'll Meet Again'.

Although expensive parlour songbooks were available in the

West End, most families favoured cheaper publications of lyrics without musical notation, bought from outlets like Woolworth's. Titles such as *The Hit Parade* and *The Magazine Of Song Hits – The Correct Lyrics Of Thirty Songs* were self-explanatory. The seasoned drinkers seldom had any inclination to consult these transcriptions for accuracy, preferring to rely on folk memory or improvisation. Fred Davies had a particular affection for Gus Elen, the Victorian music hall artiste known as the 'coster comedian' who was still performing in the 1930s. His vocal style was idiosyncratic but appealing, replete with inflexions adapted from the fruit sellers, meat tradesmen and market traders who inhabited Fred's world. Elen even dressed like a costermonger onstage while enacting his tribute to alcohol ('Half A Pint Of Ale') or lamenting an overbearing wife ('It's A Great Big Shame'). Dave Davies remembers his father singing the latter with particular passion.

Ray had his own party piece, the show tune 'Temptation', recorded by Bing Crosby (1933) and Perry Como (1945), and later featured in the 1952 musical *Singin' In The Rain*. The highlight of the night was invariably an hilarious closing routine from Fred who, after imbibing sufficiently, would explode into animation, cascading across the floor like a Gene Kelly or Fred Astaire. This would culminate in a slapstick rendition of Cab Calloway's 1931 popular jazz tune 'Minnie The Moocher', after which Fred would usually end up in a heap, laughing uproariously as his audience applauded his efforts.

Ray was delighted by these family extravaganzas. The more they drank and sang, the louder and more expressive they became, like fictional characters come to life. His sisters in their heavy petticoated flared skirts resembled marionettes as they performed the latest dance routine seen at the local Palais. Aunts and uncles were also present, none more intriguing than Annie Davies' brother – the dapper and stylish Uncle Frank Willmore. With his pencil moustache, greased-back hair, pinstripe suit and polished shoes, he resembled a well-to-do wartime spiv. Even more than Fred Davies, he was steeped in the street market subculture of King's Cross and spoke in that strangely baffling mixture of music hall English laced with cockney rhyming slang. The secret argot was in full flow whenever he was conducting business or parlaying with his pals in the local pubs or marketplace, safe in the knowledge that prying passers-by or off-duty policemen would be oblivious to his dealings. "Frank was an old school kind of cockney," says Dave Davies. "He wasn't a spiv exactly but he always had his wits about him. Like he'd say, 'Oh, blimey, don't mention that when the rozzers are about . . .' He lived down the Cally [Caledonian Road] and was embedded in that cockney culture. He and my mum were closer in age and grew up more matey than some of her other siblings. They were very close. Of course, my dad and Frank were always in the pub so they got on very well too."

Frank was a funny character, almost a caricature, whose comic ways provided endless entertainment, particularly after a few drinks. On one occasion, he commandeered a wheelbarrow to transport their inebriated Aunt 'Lil home from Archway after some ill-advised late-night party. He spent most of the journey swearing in exasperation. Streetwise, confident and provocative, Frank always spoke his mind, a trait he shared with his sister, Annie. When Ray went through one of his uncommunicative phases, it was Uncle Frank who provided the amusing rejoinder that everyone remembered. He called his nephew "a miserable little bleeder". Ray would later honour Frank's memory by assuming his image in the enchanting video production of 'Come Dancing'.

A more distant and meeker character in Ray's early life was 'Uncle Son', another of his mother's brothers, who would later be immortalized in song on the album *Muswell Hillbillies*. Sensitive and quiet in comparison to the irrepressible and uproarious Frank, Uncle Son had fought in the Second World War and endured tough times working for the soon to be nationalized British Railways. "I can't remember talking to him but he came to see me when I was very young, just before he died," Ray recalls. "He had TB from working on the railway and he died because of his job." Like others in the family, the caring Uncle Son was also struck by his nephew's shyness and introspection. "He drew me a picture of a train. He couldn't draw, but he thought he was giving me something by drawing a train for me." The picture elicited a rare smile from the withdrawn child.

Dave Davies also spoke in almost mythical terms about his compassionate uncle. "I would have known him when I was really young as one of Mum's brothers. I haven't got any clear memories but Uncle Son was often spoken about as being someone special. He was a kind, generous, warm man. My mum would say, 'Oh, Uncle Son would have liked you' or 'Uncle Son would have liked that.'" Often, it seemed as if she was preserving the memory of her brother through constant repetition of his good deeds and thoughtful ways. Despite the size of the extended family, it was considered important that close relatives were treasured and their lives remembered. That attitude was passed through the generations and survived in the lyrics and music of the Davies brothers, both of whom referenced family members in song like storytellers passing on folk memories. Resilience was ever important. "At the time things didn't always seem comfortable," Dave recalls, "but you had to be an optimist. Things did right themselves. My mum and dad and their families grew up through two world wars. They were enforced optimists. It was live for today – and we'll deal with tomorrow. During the Blitz they didn't know whether they were going to live for another day or another week. I can't imagine what that must have been like. But we were brought up in the tail end of that culture. It was a very supportive family. That's the good feeling I always get from the past."

Although more considered, Ray expressed similar feelings, acknowledging that the family's longevity and endurance meant that they remained close-knit yet open to new ideas and fresh musical influences. "These people had lived through World War II. Their culture had survived that, so it could survive anything. They weren't anti-youth at all – they [later] embraced rock 'n' roll and my dad liked some blues but, generally speaking, more traditional music was played . . . I always tried to get the approval of my parents because they owned the gramophone. It was a musical house, everyone played something – just not necessarily very well. We had enthusiasm and commitment. My mum and dad were happy we were expressing ourselves."

Another of Ray's happier memories was attending football matches at Highbury with his father, an avid Arsenal supporter. This ritual began when Ray was "five or six". He remembers the thrill of being taken on the 212 bus from Muswell Hill to Highbury, then walking to the ground by way of Blackstock Road, before turning into Avenell Road. "It was then that I saw the stadium for the first time, glittering and palatial between streets of terraced houses. As we got closer, I could hear the crowd cheering and singing. It turned out to be one of the most enduring moments of my life."

The boy was enchanted, not just by the football, but the sight and sound of the accompanying brass band, who played rousing marching songs during which their leader would throw a baton in the air that he retrieved with the expertise of a seasoned juggler. Fred Davies held his boy above his head so that he could witness the spectacle in all its glory. Even the smells of sweat and charcoal-cooked food were alluring and intoxicating. At half-time, Fred proudly presented his son with "a weak tea and soggy meat pie" as if it was a delicacy to be savoured. Tellingly, Fred spoke of Arsenal as if it was a church rather than a football club. "My father instilled in me the belief that Highbury was the most hallowed of places and the stadium itself epitomized the noblest spirit of Corinthian sporting endeavour. He had seen the great Arsenal side of the 1930s dominate English football . . . Having a club like Arsenal to support must have given Dad a sense of purpose and place particularly in the post-war austerity of 1950s London with the old British Empire crumbling around him."

Fred Davies was clearly a more complex character than some of his contemporaries assumed. Convivial to a fault, he also had a quiet side and liked to escape the chattering household throng by retiring to the sanctuary of his allotment where he could talk to his plants, safe in the knowledge that they would not answer back. Drink and football provided a similar escape.

Both his sons inherited a passion for football, with Ray emerging as an accomplished school soccer player. Unfortunately, the boy seemed prone to injuries, some of which he kept secret. He was plagued by a back problem which never entirely disappeared but, more alarmingly, there was evidence of self-harm. Later, Davies mentioned being discovered by his mother hitting his bruised shins with a hammer following a football match. "I had no way, as a child, of conveying how I felt to people. I guess to a confused kid you want to see less of the hurt. So I tried hitting my leg to see if a bruise would come up, and it did. It was just an experiment. Kids experiment with these things. It was nothing drastic like putting oranges in your mouth and hanging yourself up with garters. I just hit myself on the leg and a bruise came up. My mother saw it and she was shocked. She would be – quite rightly. It sent, I guess, the shudders of doubt in her mind about whether I was really here." Even before this disturbing incident, Ray was displaying a recklessness that bordered on the dangerous. He discovered a 'Carbolic' concoction in the kitchen ("the stuff you used to put down the sink to clean it out") and dared himself to taste it. "I drank a bottle of that for a laugh. Not good. It was worse than Epsom salts." His mother was concerned enough by his introversion and odd behaviour to arrange a visit to a child psychologist.

A revealing family photo of the period captures Ray Davies at his gloomiest. While his sister Gwen smiles like a Hollywood starlet, he stands in the background, arms tightly folded, his eyes staring at the floor, avoiding the camera. The remainder of the scene is strikingly normal by comparison. Dave sits on the ground, studiously playing with a mechanical toy, the acme of contentment. Jackie, no longer a baby, positively beams radiance, while carefully clutching a fair-haired doll. It seems like the perfect family portrait, spoiled only by the despondent aloofness of a boy who clearly wishes he was anywhere else. "Gwen inspired the song 'Come Dancing', so it was a good symbolic shot," Davies says. "It's me looking like an edgy thirteen-year-old. It also looks very American. I'm dressed like somebody from the television series *My Three Sons*."

Ray's edginess and retreat into quietude and the safety of his own imagination were not untypical of an adolescent searching for space amid the hubbub of an overcrowded household. In larger families there is often greater competition to be loved, a feature, according to some psychologists, more likely to exacerbate sibling rivalry. This, in turn, may create an over-stimulated inner world demanding a kind of psychic retreat. Psychoanalysts specializing in this field suggest that "the inner world of an only child is quieter, their dreams less populated by events with a lot of people". Conversely, Ray Davies' dreams were over-populated to such an extent that he was susceptible to vivid nightmares, sleepwalking and ultimately insomnia. It was akin to a sensory overload.

The psychological complexities multiply when we consider the confluence of mother figures in this saga. As Dave Davies acknowledges, his parents were old enough to be his grandparents. For Ray, Rene and Rose served as emotional buffers against internal and external hostilities. Yet, the maternal figure was also a shifting presence. Ray was later shocked to learn that he had once considered his eldest sister to be his mother. "I called Rosie 'Mum' until I was five years old . . . She said that, and I couldn't believe it. Maybe that had a lot to do with the way my relationship with Dave was formed because I've never really had a brother relationship with him. I always thought that my nephew, Terry, who is Rose's son, he's only a year younger than me – I felt like he was my brother."

In their study 'Oedipal Sibling Triangles', S. A. Sharpe and A. D. Rosenblatt posit the theory that in families with a large number of siblings some of the children may create triangular relationships among themselves independent of the mother/father/child model. Amid these constellations, they note that "a big brother transference will usually entail attitudes of mingled admiration and more openly intense competition". Commenting on the type of long-term fraternal conflict familiar to the Davies brothers, they conclude: "Siblings have easier access to acting out their wishes and desires, whether hostile or loving, and this results in a greater intensity of feeling, which in turn becomes less easy to relinquish . . . the narcissistic blow to the self-esteem that results from the loss of the battle means that there is far greater investment in continuing the battle rather than giving it up . . ."

While Ray was displaying disconcerting signs of introversion and withdrawal, his younger brother appeared to be heading in the opposite direction. Dave thrived on attention and loved noise – the everyday bustle of family life and the prattle and clatter of the school playground invigorated his imagination. "I often got chased by infuriated neighbours who claimed I'd wiped my hands on their clean washing. I made mud pies and threw them at smaller boys, and I let off stink bombs." This sounded like the world of Richmal Compton's *Just William*, but there was another more sensitive side to Dave Davies which was equally compelling. Even at a very young age, he had a keen interest in girls that separated him from his fellow pupils. In 1954, he became infatuated with a "new girl in the class", Gillian Richardson, who stood out from the rest, not least because she was wearing her previous school's green blazer, in striking contrast to the red uniform of St James Primary. "I really fancied Gillian, but I felt a bit sorry for her . . . she was from another school and seemed to be lost. I wrote her a love letter and the teacher found it and took it to the headmistress. I was called into her office." Dave was mortified to learn that the head intended to read out the note in front of the entire school at Monday morning assembly. Worse still, he was to be paraded before them like a criminal. What followed was the longest weekend of his pre-pubescent life. "I was absolutely terrified. On Monday morning, I went in early to see the headmistress to beg and plead. I caught her as she was coming into school and said, 'Please, Mrs Lewis, don't read that letter.' She said, 'What letter? Oh, that! I threw it away.'"

The incident did nothing to diminish his romantic interests or sexual precociousness. Within four years, he would be following girls home on his bike and, at a later date, would face expulsion from school following a public liaison with his then teenage love. His pre-pubescent behaviour marked him out as a buccaneering romantic figure in marked contrast to his elder brother. "I never had sex at the age of seven," Dave stresses, in jest. "I'm sure I would have tried. You must consider that I was surrounded by beautiful women. All my sisters were voluptuous and in the prime of their womanhood. I suppose I was eager . . . and felt comfortable in the presence of girls."

In 1955, Ray Davies sat the dreaded 11-plus examination. The elite minority considered academic were allowed access to a grammar school; the remainder could choose between a technical school or secondary modern. Gwen, the sister closest to Ray in age, had passed the exam back in 1949 and secured a place at nearby Tollington Grammar. Both her brothers would fail that all-important test and, in doing so, were left with little or no chance of entering a profession.

That autumn, Ray passed through the gates of the recently built William Grimshaw Secondary Modern, a large building which boasted its own playing fields and athletics track, with facilities designed for up to 600 pupils and a staff that would soon rise to 40 in number. Upon arrival, Davies' teachers laboriously recited the school rules, informing him that he had been allocated to Harvey house, named after the eminent sixteenth-century physician William Harvey. The house system was an affectation borrowed from the public school system. Pupils at William Grimshaw spoke about their particular house as if it was made of bricks and mortar, but no actual buildings ever existed. The 'houses' were nothing more than an abstraction in the collective imagination of their inhabitants. These invisible edifices only truly came to life as teams on sports days. That aside, they remained the fairy-tale equivalent of the emperor's new clothes, an organizational mirage by which a concept could be concretized.

Ray Davies may have thought he had a lively imagination, but seemingly he was no match for his own school. When recalling the more troubled part of his schooldays, especially his visits to a child therapist, he wrote of his sense of being an outsider or misfit. He imagined being discussed in the same tone reserved for the local eccentrics, the fallen women or the queers who loitered around public toilets like those "evil men" that the *Sunday Pictorial*'s Douglas Warth had warned Britain about back in 1952. Such fancies merely underlined the extent of his sensitivity. It was true enough that schools, particularly in the Fifties, were conformist and conservative by nature. Verbal bullying was frequently accepted as character building and taunts based on creed, complexion or skin colour were often tolerated, not least because most pupils shared the same religion and ethnic origin.

Despite his lurid imaginings, Davies was neither bullied nor ostracized. His athletic abilities, both on the football field and running track, ensured that he was admired. Even when he went into his shell, it was initially seen as nothing unusual. For the first two years at William Grimshaw, before his brother joined the school, Davies seemed reasonably settled and well-adjusted, but he was not at peace. There was a noticeable sadness about his demeanour which would not go away.

The ubiquitous presence of the extended Davies family provided Ray with therapeutic support. All his sisters lived nearby, including Joyce and her husband Ken Palmer, who had moved next door to 5 Denmark Terrace. In 1955, a new family arrived at number 4, having bought the street's newsagent/sweet-shop. The Joneses had three children: two daughters and a son, Peter, who soon acquired the nickname 'Jonah'. One of the first commandments issued by his overbearing father was to have nothing whatsoever to do with the Davies family, whom he considered as common as muck. The prohibition piqued Peter's interest, but his initial encounter with the brothers merely confirmed his father's prejudices. He had been innocently invited to participate in an 'apple fight' across the garden fence separating their respective houses. At first, it was fun, then it turned nasty. Jonah became agitated and angry when the brothers were joined by two of their cousins and proceeded to shower 'apple bombs' in his direction. The hapless human target felt humiliated and hurt. "All of a sudden it was four against one. The ground rules were that you only threw soft apples. So I picked up a hard one, aimed it at Dave, hit him on the forehead, and knocked him out. He was the first person that I consciously hurt in my life." There was no further comment about the incident, but a mysterious retribution awaited. "A couple of days later our garden shed went on fire. I don't know how it happened. I think they set fire to the shed." It would be a long time before Jonah tackled the brothers again.

*

The mid-Fifties was a time of acceleration. It could hardly have been otherwise in a country suddenly released from the shackles of post-war austerity. The coronation of a young monarch, followed by the end of rationing and the emergence of a thriving labour market, brought new opportunities particularly for those entering the workforce. Changing tastes in popular music were subtle, but significant, spearheaded commercially by Bill Haley & His Comets, whose 'Shake, Rattle & Roll' had enlivened the charts, serving notice of more to come. In January 1955, 'Rock Around The Clock' entered the UK Top 20, climbed to number 17, then dropped out. The disc gained a second lease of life when it was featured in the film *The Blackboard Jungle* and by November it was number 1. Its success was a personal triumph for a 35-year-old music publisher, whose effect on the life of Ray Davies, as both saviour and nemesis, would prove profound.

Edward Kassner, an Austrian-born Jew, had already experienced tragedy and good fortune in unequal measure. When Hitler annexed Austria in 1938, Kassner's family faced a future of ruination, concentration camp incarceration and death. Miraculously, the boy would be spared their fate. "He was tipped off by his friends that they were rounding up Jewish boys," says his eldest son, David. "He fled through Belgium and got caught trying to cross the border at Aachen twice. On the third occasion, a German soldier caught him but let him go saying that he hadn't signed up to shoot young boys." As Kassner walked – then ran – towards freedom, he was still convinced that the soldier would shoot him in the back. Silence meant salvation. Kassner subsequently traversed from Holland to Belgium, eventually reaching England. What he left behind was his family doomed to die amid the horrors of Auschwitz.

In common with other refugees, Kassner was interned, then deported to Australia, but subsequently joined the British Army, serving as an interpreter attached to the Canadian tank corps. He married in 1944 and, following his early interest in music, formed the Edward Kassner Music Co. Ltd on a shoestring budget. Success quickly followed when one of his own compositions, 'How Lucky You Are', was covered by Vera Lynn just after the war. Sheet music sales proved a lucrative business and over the succeeding years Kassner secured substantial publishing income on songs recorded by the leading popular vocalists, including Frank Sinatra, Perry Como and Nat 'King' Cole. A voracious expansionist, he extended his operation to New York in 1951, acquiring the Broadway Music Corporation whose catalogue included such evergreens as 'You Made Me Love You', 'I'll Be With You In Apple Blossom Time' and 'Take Me Out To The Ball Game'. It seemed ludicrous to think that any rock 'n' roll tune could compete with these standards, but Kassner, via a conjunction of instinct and luck, stumbled across the perfect song. He paid a modest $250 for the publishing rights to 'Rock Around The Clock' which made him millions of dollars and helped establish Edward Kassner Music as one of the most powerful music publishers in the world. Kassner's accession did not depend on rock 'n' roll, but the arrival of this new music, accompanied by rapid social change on both sides of the Atlantic, transformed everything.

The year 1956 was when the cult of the new threatened to overwhelm the old order by the sheer force of its assault. There

was no concerted movement, simply a series of seemingly superficial changes that would gain momentum in strange and unexpected ways. Those seeking the secret origins of the Swinging
Sixties need look no further than this remarkable year when life
in England suddenly lost much of its greyness. At first it was
simply a series of unremarkable fads that seemed to have captured
gullible young consumers, but their new spending power would
soon attract magazine proprietors, jukebox manufacturers,
B-movie film-makers, record companies, concert promoters and
merchandisers of every persuasion.

America loomed large in the public imagination. The year began
with the Davy Crockett craze which saw youngsters sporting
raccoon hats, singing along to the chart-topping 'The Ballad Of
Davy Crockett' and queuing to see the Disney film of the same
name. It was innocent enough, but indicative of the subtle persuasion that children could exercise on more permissive parents still
adjusting to post-war affluence in the new age of the enlightened
consumer. A feeling of ersatz glamour was in the air. It was there
in the neon signs of Soho where coffee bars, most famously the
2I's, sprang up seemingly from nowhere, with a contrasting clientele of well-scrubbed teenagers and studiously disgruntled beatnik
types. It was there onstage where a girl named Norma Sykes was
transformed, Cinderella-like, into the exotically named Sabrina,
an abstract creation whose finest asset was not her singing voice
but a curvaceous figure, highlighted by a stupendous 40-inch bust.
It was there at London's Royal Court Theatre where a young
playwright named John Osborne presented *Look Back In Anger*,
a new type of play which took drama out of the drawing rooms
of the upper classes and into the claustrophobic confines of an
impoverished bedsit, where a young married couple, Jimmy and
Alison Porter, offered a fresh take on modern life that was at
once funny, resentful and quietly revolutionary in its peculiar
mundanity. In popular literature, *The Outsider* became the
publishing phenomenon of the year. Its author, the self-proclaimed
'genius' Colin Wilson, was another of those brash young men
whose anti-establishment views and unguarded arrogance divided
critical opinion.

It was in popular music that these cultural changes were to
have the most profound and lasting effects. In February 1956,

Lonnie Donegan achieved chart success with an adaptation of Leadbelly's 'Rock Island Line'. This spearheaded another craze: skiffle. Based on the negro rent parties of Depression-era America, this working-class roots-based music transformed any young street kid of whatever age into a potential player. All you needed was a household implement like a washboard and thimble or a double-bass constructed from a broom handle and tea chest and a handful of folk and blues tunes. The effect was liberating.

Amidst these homegrown changes arrived the greatest pop phenomenon of the age: Elvis Presley. The single 'Heartbreak Hotel', which entered the UK charts in the spring of 1956, represented a clarion call to any sensitive listener, sated by the staid Tin Pan Alley balladeers of the moment. There was something indefinably evocative about the disc. Presley's voice, so youthful, yet so mournful, sang in almost elegiac recognition of a loneliness beyond redemption, accompanied by a stark piano accompaniment in curious contrast to a throbbing bass line which highlighted the song's central drama. Of course, Elvis was also a consummate rocker whose aura of brooding sexuality proved intoxicating.

The Davies family invited rock 'n' roll into their home with the same welcoming smile they offered to every other musical style. Back in Canada, Ray's beloved sister Rene had already fallen for Elvis' sultry charms and had even sent over some rock 'n' roll discs which were swiftly assimilated into the family repertoire. Before long those Saturday evening singalongs featured an Elvis impression, sandwiched between Fred Davies' 'Minnie The Moocher' and sister Dolly's moving renditions of Slim Whitman's 'Rose Marie' and 'Indian Love Call'. The old show tunes were still family favourites, but what Rene called 'the new music' was also accommodated. This dualism appealed to Ray who embraced modernity but never at the expense of a treasured past.

"My sisters bought be-bop and dance records from their generation and a lot of middle-of-the-road," he remembers. "When my sister emigrated to Canada after the war, it meant we had Elvis Presley records before anybody else did. I said, 'We've got an Elvis Presley here, he's called Lonnie Donegan.' Lonnie was quite cool at the time. So we had access to a lot of music, old and new."

That summer a new disc arrived, 'Blue Suede Shoes', a Top 10 hit for both Carl Perkins and Elvis Presley. Like the young skifflers on the street, Davies caught himself thinking, "I could do that. I could make a song like 'Blue Suede Shoes'." It was an exhilarating thought, at once presumptuous yet eminently possible in this new world of youthful rebellion. The same month that 'Blue Suede Shoes' entered the charts, the music paper *Melody Maker* paraded a provocative and enticingly rhetorical headline: 'Shall We Surrender To The Teenagers?'

The military metaphor was apt. Looming in the background was the Suez Crisis, which saw Britain threatening to invade Egypt in violation of a UN charter, a political act that severely divided public opinion in what was otherwise seen as an age of adult consensus. That unrest was played out in microcosm for the remainder of the year in a series of newspaper headlines focusing on the irresponsibility of youth. 'Rock 'n' Mayhem' and 'Youth On The Rampage' screamed the regional press as the film *Rock Around The Clock*, a fantastic money-spinner for publisher Eddie Kassner, provoked an orgy of razor-slashed seats, broken light bulbs, impromptu aisle-jiving, smashed milk bottles and police constable baiting from teens and Teddy boys. The rock 'n' roll craze resembled nothing less than an assault on British decency. More worryingly, its newest stars, the "crippled" leather-clad Gene Vincent and the disconcertingly effeminate Little Richard (memorably described by the music press as "an animated golliwog"), suggested that much worse was to follow. "It is nothing more than an exhibition of primitive tom-tom thumping," insisted the much respected BBC Orchestra conductor Sir Malcolm Sargent. "The amazing thing about rock 'n' roll is that youngsters who go into such ecstasies sincerely believe that there is something new and wonderful about the music. There is nothing new or wonderful about it: rock 'n' roll has been played in the jungle for centuries."

Sargent's view was echoed in the national press with the then broadsheet *Daily Mail* suggesting: "It has something of the African tom-tom and voodoo dance." The paper went on to provide a sociological perspective on the phenomenon which concluded with high-minded moral authority: "It is deplorable. It is tribal. And it is from America. It follows ragtime, blues, Dixie, jazz, hot cha-cha and the boogie-woogie, which surely originated in the jungle. We sometimes wonder whether this is the Negro's Revenge."

By the end of the year, rock 'n' roll had devolved from the jungle into the realms of prehistoric man as Tommy Steele, Britain's first major teenage star, charted with 'Rock With The Caveman'. Meanwhile, the Suez Crisis was living up to its name. Its endgame not only threatened the mental and physical health of Prime Minister Sir Anthony Eden, but persuaded Buckingham Palace to cancel that year's Royal Command Performance. The pneumatic phenomenon Sabrina, who was intending to perform Ray Davies' favourite song 'Temptation' in front of the Queen, was crestfallen by the news. Worse followed when the British government was forced into an humiliating climbdown. It was not military might that prevailed but the threat of economic sanctions, punctuated by a drain on gold reserves and the prospect of a devaluation in sterling. The Suez debacle made Britain look feeble and morally compromised in the eyes of the world. Any lingering delusions about the power of the British Empire all but ended here.

At least the parties continued at 6 Denmark Terrace. Annie Davies celebrated Christmas and the New Year by perfecting her new theme song, a melodramatic reading of Malcolm Vaughan's 'St Therese Of The Roses'. Letters from Canada testified to Rene's continual marital problems, which were now coming to an unhappy head. In January 1957, she watched Elvis Presley perform "from the waist up" on *The Ed Sullivan Show*, then prepared to leave for Britain with her young son, Bobby. This time she would not be returning.

Partly thanks to the iconography of Elvis and other rock 'n' rollers, sales of acoustic guitars shot up in early 1957. Ray Davies coveted a Spanish guitar, but could not persuade his parents to purchase one. Instead he was forced to find solace tinkering on the piano in the front room. For a time he even took lessons. In common with many youngsters of the period, Davies' keen interest in popular music pointed unerringly towards America. It was a trend that bothered many cultural commentators who tended to equate the New World with crass commercialism. *Melody Maker*, despite championing jazz and blues, could find no redeeming qualities in its bastard offspring, which they damned without apology. "Viewed as a social phenomenon, the current craze for rock 'n' roll material is one of the most terrifying things ever to have happened to popular music. And, of course, as in all modern forms of entertainment, we blithely follow the lead of the American industry. When father turns, we all turn."

The anti-American sentiment was the key issue here. Despite all that had been written about Teddy boys, jungle rhythms and rock 'n' roll delinquency, these criticisms were mere distractions from the central issue. It was the American influence that united detractors. It was not too difficult to locate the origins of such prejudice among the general public. While the inhabitants of the USA understandably regarded themselves as the liberators of Europe, their image in Britain was rather different. The mean-spirited saw them as late arrivals with big guns who secured glory with a minimum of sweat. They were 'Yanks', GI Joes, flash, brash and vainglorious, who stole the hearts of impressionable girls with a combination of nylons, chocolate, charm and well-nourished physiques. As the cliché went, they were "over paid, over sexed and over here". Even after the war, the stereotypes lingered for more than a decade. The Yanks had even played a part in the recent Suez Crisis, silencing the roar of the toothless British lion. For many that too was unforgivable.

One might reasonably have expected such reactionary views to remain the preserve of those who still clung to the nostalgia of Britain's Great Empire, but this was not the case. Anti-American sentiment brought together the most unlikely bedfellows. Fuddy-duddy colonialists and dyed-in-the-wool conservatives suddenly found themselves allied with young Marxists and radical thinkers in a united attack against a common enemy. They may have disagreed on just about everything else, but the curse of 'Americanization' transcended political and even class barriers. It was nothing less than a battle for the soul of a newly disenfranchised youth, supposedly perverted by the mindless vacuity of mass culture. One headline neatly summed up this modern malaise: 'Are We Turning Our Children Into Little Americans?'

The accusation was directed against politicians and parents, but the real targets were the teenagers themselves, who had sold their souls to the cult of Elvis, to rock 'n' roll music, to garish neon signs, to milk and coffee bars where girls took on the images of high school prom queens and boys imitated surly movie stars in the mould of James Dean. While hip teenagers championed modern trends at the expense of traditional values and outmoded

entertainment, others saw something more sinister – a philosophical, aesthetic and moral conflict between nature and artifice,
a veritable battle royal between the authentic and the ersatz.
Arguably, the rift was felt more keenly among left-wing enthusiasts and reformers than it was in the common rooms of right-wing
Tory diehards. Rock 'n' roll was not only about self-empowerment
and rebellion, but a passive surrender to the hidden persuaders
of advertising and the consumer driven profiteers who were
systemically stripping working-class culture of its roots. Cultural
commentators complained of the sad "glorification of youth" and
lamented all that was about to be lost. They saw the jukebox
supplanting the pub piano which, in turn, signalled the end of
the weekly singalongs so loved by Fred Davies and his generation.
All this would be replaced by a phantom culture, like the pre-
packaged pulp literature and mindless music consumed by the
proles in George Orwell's *Nineteen Eighty-Four*.

Folk song revivalist Ewan MacColl was in the front line of
dissenters. "I became concerned that we had a whole generation
who were becoming quasi-Americans, and I felt this was absolutely
monstrous. I was convinced that we had a music that was just
as vigorous as anything that America had produced, and we should
be pursuing some kind of national identity, not just becoming an
arm of American cultural imperialism."

Contemporaneous studies such as Raymond Williams' *Culture
And Society* and Richard Hoggart's *The Uses Of Literacy* also
lamented the Americanization of modern society with unabashedly
partisan zeal. Hoggart's description of a mundane coffee bar had
the tone of a religious pamphlet mixed with the portentous prose
of a science fiction novel: ". . . most of the customers are boys
aged between 15 and 20, with drape-suits, picture ties and an
American slouch . . . they put copper after copper into the mechanical record player. About a dozen records are available at any one
time; a numbered button is pressed for the one wanted, which is
selected from a key to titles . . . almost all are American; almost
all are 'vocals' and the styles of singing much advanced beyond
what is normally heard on the Light Programme of the BBC.
Some of the tunes are catchy; all have been doctored for presentation so that they have the kind of beat which is currently popular
. . . the 'nickelodeon' is allowed to blare out so that the noise

would be sufficient to fill a good-sized ballroom, rather than a converted shop in the main street . . . Compared even with the pub around the corner, this is a peculiarly thin and pallid form of dissipation, a sort of spiritual dry-rot amid the odour of boiled milk. Many of the customers . . . are living to a large extent in a myth-world compounded of a few simple elements which they take to be the American dream. They form a depressing group . . . they have no aim, no ambition, no protection, no belief."

Ray Davies was at once a part of this eerie congregation yet simultaneously detached from it. He empathized with American youth culture and the neon-bright barbarism of rock 'n' roll but also felt pangs of loss for much that would be left behind. He mourned the decline of the big band orchestras that had provided the soundtrack of his elder sisters' youth. At the start of the Fifties there had been 89 Variety theatres in London, but the majority had now either gone or faced imminent closure. The mass production of television sets was effectively killing off a generation of entertainers. Many music hall performers relied on routines that had remained unchanged for years, as they traversed the old theatres, the length and breadth of Britain. Television's immediacy meant that they could no longer rely on the public's amnesia to sustain their livelihoods. Predictable punchlines were now common currency, dance routines over-familiar and audience expectations impossible to match. Suddenly, once confident troupers were like nervous magicians, whose tricks were known to their audience in advance. They were suddenly anachronistic.

"That was the 'People's Music'," Davies recalls, "and it just died". He was not alone in lamenting that loss. Strangely enough, his words echoed those of that quintessentially Angry Young Man, John Osborne. Writing in 1957, the iconoclastic playwright struck an uncharacteristically nostalgic note when offering the following elegy: "The music hall is dying and with it, a significant part of England. Some of the heart of England is gone, something that once belonged to everyone, for this was truly folk art." Ray Davies could hardly have put it better and, for much of his life, would attempt to rediscover that lost folk art in song. Like a social historian turned lyricist, he would recreate that prelapsarian world of working-class labour, leisure and solidarity so beloved of Richard Hoggart in Kinks' vignettes like 'Dead End Street' and

'Autumn Almanac'. It was there too in the satirical and ambiva-
lently affectionate observations of suburbia in 'Shangri-la' and
the songs celebrating England's village greens. And when the
excesses of American stadium rock – that even Hoggart could
never have envisaged – became the norm in the early to mid-
Seventies, Davies would dress up and play the part of a music
hall comedian in a new context. He looked passé by then, but it
was as if he was reminding his loyal constituency of a time and
music that had sadly died out.

CHAPTER THREE

RENE AND ROSE

In 1957 family tragedy threatened to unravel Davies' already fragile psyche. There were celebrations when his still teenage sister Gwen married her boyfriend, Brian Longstaff. Rene was just back from Canada and more supportive than ever, encouraging her brother's musical interests with her Elvis eulogies and record purchases. Before long, she was living at 45 Stanley Road, Hendon, in an uneasy relationship with her visiting husband Russell, who was still a private in the Canadian Diplomatic Corps.

On 20 June, the day before Ray's 13th birthday, the boy was thrilled to receive the perfect present from Rene – the Spanish guitar that he had so desired and pestered his parents about since the beginning of the year. Guided by Rene, he practised on the instrument while she accompanied him on the family piano, playing show tunes, including selections from *Oklahoma!*. Although in good spirits, and only 30 years old, Rene was far from well. Her doctor had prescribed tablets to alleviate her heart problems and she was instructed to avoid excessive exercise. However, nothing could quell her love of dance halls and the prospect of an evening at the Lyceum Ballroom in the Strand proved irresistible. Ray watched her from the front room window as she sashayed down the road. "We'd played a few songs together. Then she got a bus down to the West End." He would never see her again.

There was no expectation that anything fatal might occur, even though she was defying her doctor's advice. "It was her decision," he adds. "It was her way of saying, 'I'm in control of my own destiny.'" Late that Thursday evening, tragedy unfolded. While on the dance floor she suffered left ventricular heart failure. She was rushed to Charing Cross Hospital but nothing could be done to save her life. "She died in the arms of a stranger on the dance floor," Ray remembers. "It was poignant that it was on [the eve of] my birthday when she bought me my first guitar. I took that as being a sign. It has to be a sign from somebody."

News of the death reached Denmark Terrace sometime after midnight. "I remember waking up hearing my mum screaming, wailing downstairs," Dave says. "It was terrible. I thought, 'Oh God, what is this?' I heard my dad coming upstairs and he was ashen-faced. He sat at the end of my bed and I knew what he was going to say before he even opened his mouth. He was crying and he said, 'Rene's dead!' It was a terrible shock for everybody."

What made the unbelievable news frighteningly real for Dave was the look on his father's face and the tears in his eyes. "He'd come from a time where men were men. He'd grown up in that culture of stiff upper lip where you don't show your feelings. But I think my dad was a very sensitive man. When Rene died that was the first time I'd ever seen a male member of our family cry."

The funeral passed in a blur of beer and sandwiches with Ray literally shocked into silence. He returned to school, seemingly broken by the tragedy. "Clearly, I couldn't cope," he acknowledges. "Death scares people, and when you're young you're not meant to be an unofficial mourner, so my brother Dave and I were kept from the funeral. Maybe it would have been better if we'd been there." What followed was "the great silence" – a lengthy period when the boy retreated into himself, resisting all attempts at communication. At first, his quietness provoked little comment. Many children went through phases of introversion. Educational institutions of the Fifties valued conformity and deference, so such behaviour was usually considered a virtue rather than a source of concern. The euphemism "very reserved" on school reports often disguised more serious problems. Years later, in a wonderful piece of self-diagnosis, Davies suggested that he might have been suffering from an excess of 'normality'. There is some evidence to suggest that even his contemporaries initially interpreted his diffidence as nothing out of the ordinary. Fellow pupil Rita Lack, who was there throughout 1957, spoke about Davies' shyness and withdrawn presence during those final four weeks of the summer term in a revealingly positive light. "Ray sat in front of me in the third year at senior school and I have fond memories of his quiet, selfless nature. He was a perfect gentleman and didn't go through that disruptive self-centred, arrogant phase so many teenagers do. He was a very private and much respected class-mate."

How long the great silence lasted is a matter of conjecture. Ray has variously described it as months, an entire year – or even longer. "I wasn't a rebel. I was very quiet. I went through a period when I was passive and didn't speak for a few years. I hardly spoke when I was in a quite difficult situation." Ray's passivity was akin to a sense of helplessness, a veritable surrender to fate in which he was no longer controlling events, they were control-ling him. The emotional trauma he suffered during this period was exacerbated by concomitant physical ailments and related injuries, most notably his on/off back pains which he often kept secret from family members and school sports masters.

The death of his sister at such an impressionable time in his adolescence thrust Davies deeper into his own imaginary kingdom, a place of detachment in which he was an observer, who no longer needed to participate. At times, he felt pervaded by a sense of unreality, as if everything on the outside was a carefully staged theatrical performance populated by animated marionettes. "Life was like a reproduction," he concluded, when recalling that trou-bled time, "it was not the real thing."

*

While Ray retreated inward, the outer world suddenly looked more enticing. British rock 'n' roll was gaining momentum. Skiffle was still strong, along with mainstream entertainment. Tommy Steele was dominating the charts and even had a movie made in his honour, chronicling his rise to fame. The same week that Rene died, EMI's Columbia label launched the career of another aspiring teenager, Larry Page. His career would later become entwined with that of Ray Davies, but there was already a link that nobody mentioned during their later times together. Page's real name was

Leonard *Davies*. The son of a Welsh-born father, he was raised in Hayes, Middlesex, home of EMI Records. Like many local lads, he joined the EMI factory after leaving school and was placed in the packing department. The local pub provided a welcome outlet on weekends and, fortified by beer, he would occasionally sing something over the microphone. One girl said he was pretty good, which was sufficient encouragement to persuade him to audition for EMI. Improbably enough, they offered him a recording contract. At the time his debut disc 'Start Movin'' was released, he was still standing at the factory's conveyor belt packing his own record. Within a month, he was topping the bill at the Palace Theatre, Reading. The *Sunday Pictorial*'s showbiz correspondent, Jack Bentley, soon provided him with a catchy nickname – 'Larry Page – the Teenage Rage'.

For one moment, it seemed as though Page might be the fortunate recipient of the rampant anti-Americanism that even stretched as far as the Director General of the BBC, who informed senior staff of the importance of promoting songs "capable of performance in a British way". His jingoism was echoed by the Orwellian-sounding 'Controller of Sound Entertainment' who suggested: "We should look at existing programmes with an eye to the ultimate possibility of removing the American element and replacing it with something un-American, if we can find it . . ."

British record companies were of the same mind. Page's producer Norman Newell regularly scoured the US trade magazine *Billboard* for cover material and unearthed 'That'll Be The Day' by an obscure Texan outfit the Crickets, whose lead singer was Buddy Holly. "It won't be released in this country because it's terrible," Newell reportedly told Page. The producer dutifully 'Anglicized' the recording which meant removing the distinctive guitar solos and emasculating its rock 'n' roll power. Page merely followed orders. "It was the biggest load of crap you ever heard, but I was the first person in Britain to cover a Buddy Holly song and I had the opportunity of meeting him."

Thereafter, there was an air of desperation about Page's singing career, but the dearth of home-grown teenage talent in Fifties Britain, compared with the USA, meant that the press was ever willing to offer free publicity. Page had learned this lesson well. He knew how obsessed the media was with the notion of teenage stars surrendering their adolescence and potential audience in order to get married. For better or worse, that had been the key narrative in the respective sagas of Tommy Steele, Marty Wilde and Terry Dene. So it was that Larry boldly announced his engagement to a young fan, Ann Ward, following a whirlwind eight-hour romance. Thereafter, the phone never stopped ringing. Their marriage at Caxton Hall was attended by a posse of journalists and made front-page news in the national press. Considering that Page had never enjoyed a pop hit, the exposure was incredible. Even his interfering mother Mrs May Davies contributed to the drama by threatening to boycott the wedding on the grounds that the couple were too young. Naturally, she relented at the last minute. When the marriage later hit troubled waters, Page was in the news again, addressing a full-scale press conference. It was evidence enough of the enduring power of a human interest story.

Alas, none of this was sufficient to save Page's recording career. By the end of the decade, the Teenage Rage was history. Nevertheless, he had served a remarkable apprenticeship in the music industry, witnessing the staid bureaucracy of record production, the power of publishing and the ease with which the media could be fed a story or cajoled by a gimmick. If he could only put that experience to use in some fashion, might there yet be a way to alter the downward trajectory of his adult life? It was a tantalizing consideration.

While the arc of Larry Page's recording career was being played out, Ray Davies was enduring growing pains that were distressing to behold. Following the summer break, he returned to school in the autumn of 1957, still haunted by the death of his sister. By now, the great silence could no longer be ignored either by his mother or his form teacher. He seemed suspiciously prone to injuries throughout this period, damaging his back during a football match when he fell heavily against a goal post. "It was a really bad injury. I bled internally. I was told I had a 'bad back', nothing more detailed than that. The doctor said I shouldn't worry, it would go away. I should rest and not play sport for a year. Of course, being thirteen, I ignored that." His physical pain was mirrored by his mental anguish. After another visit to a child psychologist it was decided that he should attend a special school for a couple of days a week at 43 Pembridge Villas in Notting

Hill so that his condition could be monitored. "It turned out I learned quite a bit there. I felt the world was a lie, though I couldn't put my finger on what I was worried about, but when they tried to prove otherwise, somehow I would put up a verbal argument." While at Pembridge, he was mentored by a female psychologist in one to one sessions which he vaguely remembers lasting "a year or two". Over time, the therapy proved productive. "This wonderful person explained to me that you probably will never get over your insecurities. And I was really young when I was told that. I got a slight advantage because I always remembered what she said. She was very convincing. She justified what she said. She was an extraordinarily incisive person. I think when I became an adult I still kept thinking, 'I'm not going to grow up'."

While acknowledging that the sessions were helpful, Davies later claimed that they initially made him feel like a misfit alongside his fellow pupils back at William Grimshaw. Certainly, his absences were unusual but there is no evidence of any serious teasing, let alone harassment. Perhaps he was just lucky. School bullying is an inexact science based on a combination of irrational prejudice, petty resentment and timing. In the Fifties, the overweight were the favoured target, largely because they stood out in the immediate aftermath of post-war rationing. Those unfortunate enough to wear spectacles, along with the enfeebled and part foreign, were also unlikely to escape playground taunts. Of course, charm, wry humour or simply good luck might prove enough to ward off the bully's barbs. Davies' deficiencies were inward rather than visible, so he was never an obvious target. For all their prejudices, Fifties' children existed primarily in a black and white universe devoid of moral complexities. There was still a strong sense of regimentation and deference inculcated by parents using such rejoinders as "mind your own business". It was considered impolite to pry so children avoided gossip while perfecting the mannered art of incuriosity. In short, Davies' two-day absences rapidly became routine. They submerged into the essence of his character, as if they were broken-rimmed spectacles, ill-fitting trousers or an unmended torn blazer.

A further disruption in the Davies' household occurred when, in consultation with Ray's psychologist, it was agreed that he should move to Yeatman Road, the Highgate home of his eldest sister and surrogate mother, Rose. Her husband Arthur was a stern, patriarchal figure, worn down by the austerity years and disillusioned by the failures of successive governments and the state of the British Empire. His brother, a daredevil fighter pilot, had been killed in action and posthumously awarded the Victoria Cross. Arthur, whose poor eyesight prevented him from becoming a flying ace, felt diminished by his brother's achievement and embittered about his death. "A lot of people in the family thought that he was a bitter man," Ray Davies adds, "but he was just frustrated. People gave up their lives and their youth for the war. They had been promised a new world, and what did they get? Motorways and concrete."

Arthur and Rose provided Ray with a stable upbringing that was far more conventional in its routine than the noisy chaos he had witnessed at his parents' home. By now, his nephew Terry had fully taken on the role of younger brother in place of Dave who, conversely, had found his own fraternal figure in Rene's son Bobby, who had stayed on at 6 Denmark Terrace after his mother's death. Although Ray had yet to be coaxed out of his inner world, there were gradual signs of improvement. The Anning household suited his temperament, allowing him to readjust to the daily exigencies of life. Arthur, who worked as a welder in a plastics factory, secretly dreamed of a new life abroad, but never allowed his fantasies to deflect him from the rigorous routine instilled by his own military minded father.

Although Ray's physical and psychological health appeared to be improving, there was another traumatic incident that impacted on both brothers. "Ray went into hospital for something," Dave recalls. "I can't even remember what it was. He had to stay overnight – he was there for a few days." In the middle of the night, Dave had a strange, almost paranormal feeling. "It was about three o'clock in the morning. I woke up and I couldn't breathe. I was dying. I rushed into my mum's room and I said, 'Mum, I can't breathe'. She said, 'What's the matter with you, you silly little sod? Here's a glass of water, drink that.' I was shaking and feeling really bad. Eventually, she managed to calm me down. The next day, my mum [went] to the hospital and when she came back she said, 'It's really strange. Last night, Ray said that he nearly died . . . He had to have a tracheotomy so that they could help him breathe.' That's so strange. There were many occasions like that where me and Ray had emotional or telepathic links." While Dave talks of such empathic connections, the enduring impression of this tale is the lack of either. While picturing Ray almost dying in hospital, Dave could neither remember the location nor the reason his brother was admitted in the first place. Even when researching his own book, the younger brother could only recall his own psychic reaction, while advancing no details whatsoever of Ray's medical condition or emotional response to the near-death experience.

The hospital episode was another memorable moment in time for Ray. It had actually taken place at St Thomas' Hospital on Westminster Bridge overlooking the Thames. Ray recalls he was 14 at the time, dating the incident as 1958. "It wasn't life-threatening at first. I'd fractured my jaw and broken my nose as a kid. The jaw needed to be reset, so they had to break the jaw. They gave me a tracheotomy and the balloon burst and I nearly died in the night. My lungs collapsed in hospital." The event passed in an almost hallucinatory haze, captured in memory via evanescent images of being wheeled out on to a balcony by nurses and left alone in meditative repose as the Thames (the "dirty old river") flowed beneath like blood pumping through veins. It was an intense visual image, later rechanneled into the narrative of 'Waterloo Sunset'.

Ray returned to Arthur and Rose's house with his neck supported by a brace. The medical procedure had worked and over the succeeding months his confidence returned. Like a reluctant explorer, Davies expanded his surroundings beyond the seemingly ineluctable environs of Highgate and Muswell Hill. "I needed to get out to find my space, find my world. I went on lots of long walks, went to the West End. I loved riding on buses." A pivotal moment occurred when he was 14, going on 15. He instinctively boarded a 134 bus in north London on the front of which were the enticing words: 'Dolphin Square, Pimlico'. Davies never reached that destination. Instead he alighted at Leicester Square, in touching distance of the theatres, dance halls and coffee bars of Soho. In doing so, he was re-enacting that final journey taken by his sister Rene a few years before.

The Lyceum Ballroom was nearby in the Strand, but Ray was distracted and entranced by the throbbing life force that was Soho. The notorious square mile provided a visual feast of exotic entertainment for any teenager experiencing its temptations for the first time. An electric urgency emanated from every street. Sights, smells and sounds merged into one another: garishly lit arcades pulsated with the throb of pop hits interspersed with the whirling reel of one-armed bandits and the electro-thud of pinball machines; striptease clubs advertised their erotic delights to passing punters with inviting black and white framed photos of models, their breasts and legs exposed as much as legal and moral decency allowed; foreign restaurants, predominantly Chinese, offered curious culinary fragrances; and so it went on. It was not merely the peculiarity of place but the oddness and preponderance of its characters that appealed to Davies. He had always, almost deliberately, assumed the role of observer and here was a cast list worthy of his imagination: the intimidating, barrel-chested man on guard at the strip club, the gang of unruly kids and sometimes strange men in the pinball arcades, the bohemians and coffee bar cowboys, the well-dressed office workers trying to look respectable, and the occasional down and out traipsing through the streets.

Soho joined Waterloo as another of Davies' touchstones. In addition to its other pleasures it offered plentiful music and encouraged him to spend even more time playing guitar. For his 15th birthday, he received a 30-watt Watkins Dominator amplifier and also acquired a Maton electric guitar. It was enough to revive the "I can do that" philosophy that he had previously felt after first hearing 'Blue Suede Shoes'. The new equipment inspired dreams of performing, albeit not beyond a radius of a handful of pubs. Songwriting would come much later, although there were a handful of rudimentary attempts, including his first composition 'Rocky Mountain', a Country & Western pastiche "about the rocky skies of Arizona". Another composition he likened to the style of Perry Como, adding that it was unrecordable. There were also two inchoate works in progress: a Chet Atkins-inspired melody that would later evolve into 'You Really Got Me' and an instrumental titled 'South' which would one day form part of 'Tired Of Waiting For You'. Dave also recalled an experimental piece ("a horrifying, discordant set of shrieks from the guitar") which he found intriguing. Alas, Ray regarded the instrumental as too disturbing and never played it again.

Even though the Davies brothers were living separate lives in different households, their mutual interest in music unexpectedly brought them together. Dave credits his brother-in-law Mike Picker (Peggy's Irish husband) as a crucial catalyst in uniting them. He taught Ray the rudiments of classical guitar and encouraged his interest in harmony by playing along with the pop hits of the day, notably the songbook of Buddy Holly which the elder brother revered. Picker was also keen on country music and introduced the brothers to Hank Williams. While tutoring Ray, he encouraged Dave's interest in guitar technology, a fascination that would later mould the music of the Kinks. "Mike was from an older genera-tion but he was quite an influence. He was also into electronics and built amplifiers and guitars. He knew all the jazz chord progressions, but at the same time he liked modern music. He introduced us to Big Bill Broonzy. Mike and Peg had a television and that's where we first saw him."

Big Bill Broonzy had already achieved legendary status among UK blues enthusiasts. An ancient from the late nineteenth century, his music, once the preserve of black audiences, had found new converts among post-war white jazz enthusiasts and folk song revivalists. His down home Arkansas blues later found favour in Europe. A year after learning to write, he visited Britain for the first time in 1951, returning twice the following year. In 1957, he even appeared on prime-time Saturday evening television amid the incongruous setting of Jack Good's pop programme, 6.5 *Special*. The following year, several of England's premier blues musicians arranged benefit concerts to help pay for Broonzy's throat operation in his home city of Chicago. That August, cancer of the mouth ended his life.

Broonzy's influence on the later blues explosion of the Sixties was significant. Long John Baldry, a near contemporary of the Davies brothers, was among the converts. "I consider myself to be lucky beyond description to have been able to see Broonzy at the 100 Club, singing and playing not more than a few feet away. He was such an idol to me."

Ray Davies experienced a similar epiphany, albeit via a television clip rather than a live performance. "It was an archive documentary made in Belgium of him playing in a club. What amazed me – and I was just starting to play the guitar – was his dexterity and power. He was a big man with powerful hands . . . Broonzy, to me, was different from all the other blues people. He was a singular artiste, apparently he toured the UK and Europe without a work permit – he just flew in and did the gigs and got paid." Looking back, Davies went as far as describing the Broonzy discovery as a moment that "changed my life". More remarkable was the realization that they shared something almost indefinable, a spirit that transcended all the obvious differences of age, class, colour and nationality. "It didn't matter that Big Bill Broonzy was black and came from Chicago. What mattered was that he sounded like me. He had rough edges to his music. There was nothing really contrived about him and he sounded working class. He didn't try to be anything other than he was." Broonzy achieved the not inconsiderable feat of forging a musical link between the brothers as well as providing some welcome rapport between father and son. Ray remembers Fred Davies disparaging young teenage pop stars with their "high voices" while embracing the muscular urban blues of classic Broonzy. "Now he sounds like a *real* man," the father concluded.

Dave's interest in popular music was encouraged by Ray, although his motives were not entirely altruistic. "I was quite shrewd when we started out. We got pocket money but my brother bought the records. I persuaded him." While Ray carefully saved his money, the spendthrift Dave splashed out on singles like Johnny And The Hurricanes' 'Red River Rock' and other favourites of the day. "This was a big step forward. It meant my elder brother was beginning to accept me and it mattered a lot." Ray's apparent magnanimity may have been sincere, but it was expressed in words that suggested cold calculation rather than fraternal affection. "I saw it best to be friends with him because we were going to be together for a long time. We made the peace and forged a relationship. There was a lot of rivalry, of course, but that's the same with all siblings."

A few weeks before Christmas 1959, Dave took the bus down to Selmer Musical Instruments in Charing Cross Road accompanied by his father, who signed a hire purchase agreement of

£1 9s 5d per week for a £29 Harmony Meteor guitar. Before long, the 12-year-old Dave was playing blues records and exchanging chord sequences with his wildcat schoolfriend George Harris, as well as spending additional weekends with his musical mentor, Mike Picker.

The ever-encouraging Picker also took the brothers to see their first gig, featuring Duane Eddy, supported by Frank Ifield and Kathy Kirby, at the Finsbury Park Empire in April 1960. Dave almost missed the show after becoming involved in a mock sword fight with his niece Jackie in the garden of 6 Denmark Terrace. They were fencing with bamboo sticks when she accidentally poked him in the eye. When Mike and Peg arrived to pick up the brothers it was clear that Dave required medical attention, but he refused to attend a hospital until after the show. The concert had a powerful effect on many budding pop musicians, including both Ray and Dave, who later added some of Eddy's tunes to their repertoire.

The precise moment when Ray and Dave first appeared onstage together remains conjectural. Dave, arguably the more reliable when it comes to specific dates and places, reckons it was at "the Clissold Arms, the old man's local across the road" some time in 1960. Whether they even had a name is uncertain, but he remembers them briefly calling themselves the Kelly Brothers (the maiden name of their paternal grandmother). Ray has a different story. "It was in the [Bald Face] Stag in East Finchley," he claims. "I was fourteen, and my brother was eleven, and I remember drinking beer before the show and thinking how wonderful it was to be grown up. We played Shadows and Cliff Richard hits and early R&B like 'Memphis Tennessee' and, for some reason, in north London 'Ghost Riders In The Sky' was always being requested."

Although the Davies' parents allowed and even encouraged their sons' interests, they had no expectations of either pursuing a musical career. Dave, in particular, was considered too undisciplined, even by his mother. "I always thought he'd become a mechanic or something. He always used to like motors. He's not like his brother. Raymond was always more studious than David."

Ray's progress at William Grimshaw was nevertheless erratic. He had ceased attending special school two days a week but found it difficult to adapt to the regimentation of his secondary modern. Morale among some staff seemed low and Davies detected something deeper and more disheartening. "Maybe it was an England that was lost . . . an England that suddenly stopped." Describing himself as "an early realist", he sounded cynical about the future. "I think that my problems were that I knew what was coming. School bored me . . . I was not fooled by the promise of the late Fifties."

Unsettled at school, Davies was seduced by an ad in the London *Evening Standard* offering the chance to apprentice in layout and design for a magazine based in Holborn, not far from his beloved Soho. He hoped to secure some job experience, but instead felt like an office boy. He had little rapport with his fellow workers, whom he regarded as trade union militants in constant combat with their employers. Much of the day they sat around playing card games. When he once worked through his tea break, the reaction was predictably hostile. His depiction of his time there was suspiciously reminiscent of scenes from the Boulting Brothers' film, *I'm All Right, Jack*. A box office smash that same year, this wonderfully satiric comedy exposes the shallowness of the new consumer society, while also taking to task morally bankrupt capitalist employers. However, its keenest target are the lazy workers, languishing on the shop room floor, ever ready to down tools at the slightest provocation. They too spend most of their time playing cards. One character sums up their attitude in a piercing precis: "The natural rhythm of the British worker is neither natural nor rhythmic, or much to do with work." The satire reaches its apogee in the person of Fred Kite, the head of the works committee, played by Peter Sellers, whose confused parody of Marxist/Leninist rhetoric provides the finest comic moments. Defending a worker from the threat of the sack, he offers the immortal line: "We do not and cannot accept the principle that incompetence justifies dismissal: that is *victimization*."

"One of my favourite characters is Fred Kite in *I'm All Right, Jack*," Davies acknowledges. "Because he takes himself so seriously, he's the funniest person in the film. My humour is a bit like that. I put myself down; I over-blow myself. I become a bit conceited." Davies' brief experience of working in the print industry inculcated a lingering contempt for what he saw as the corrupting aspects of trade unionism and its subjugation of the individual voice.

Conversely, he also came to fear the power of corporate institutions. His attitude is encapsulated in the innocent bafflement and disillusionment of the other key character Stanley Windrush, played by Ian Carmichael. By the end of the film, betrayed by all sides, he seeks salvation in the rural sanctuary of a nudist colony. All of these leitmotifs echoed down the years informing Davies' work from the classic *The Village Green Preservation Society* through to the class conflicts crudely dramatized in the *Preservation* series of albums.

Davies' work experience was mercifully brief, lasting a few months at worst. Improbably, he was permitted to return to William Grimshaw Secondary Modern, an almost unprecedented concession for an early school leaver. Presumably, his previous troubled time and necessary absences at Pembridge Villas played a part in persuading the headmaster, Mr Charles Loades, to make an exception and allow him back. The decision was to prove life-changing.

CHAPTER FOUR

THE RAY DAVIES QUARTET

It was a new Ray Davies who entered the sixth form in September 1960. Gone was the disturbingly quiet introvert who shied away from social interaction. In his place was a vibrant team captain who seemed determined to excel at football, cricket and running. "I decided, all of a sudden, that I had to win everything. I wanted to be a footballer and an athlete. I loved track and field. I became a kind of leader of things rather than someone that was passive. I had to be good at something." He later claimed that the Grimshaw girls, who had previously ignored his taciturn ways, now voted him "the best arse in the school". His sporting prowess even extended to running for Highgate Harriers and amateur boxing. "I did quite well in the School Championships until I came up against the Schools Champion of Great Britain. I hit him three times and hurt my hands. He knocked me out in the first round."

Sport also inspired a close friendship with neighbour Peter 'Jonah' Jones, who accompanied him to Arsenal's home matches and played alongside him in the William Grimshaw First XI football team. "Ray was really competitive. He wanted to be top dog. He was such a good athlete – that guy could *run*. He's been running ever since. He excelled at cricket and boxing too. When he was allowed to perform like that, he became extrovert, but when you took him out of that environment he went right back into his shell again. Walking to school in the morning we used to talk about so many things. Ray was open and shared things with me then. Later, that totally disappeared."

Despite his understated friendliness, Davies was still unpredictable and subject to mood swings, as Jones discovered after making a seemingly innocuous remark about his brother. One afternoon, they were discussing soccer tactics and Jonah suggested that Dave lacked the coordination to excel as a football player. Retribution was swift. "Ray pinned me down on the ground and started to punch the daylights out of me. He wanted to absolutely crucify me. He said, 'I'm the only one that can put Dave down!' I thought, 'This is unbelievable.' In those early days, Dave really looked up to Ray because he was so good at everything."

By now, Jonah was fraternizing with both Davies brothers in defiance of his father who still regarded them with disdain. "It took me a long time to actually walk through the front door of their house. There was this long passageway and at the end of it I could see this light under the door. Everybody was congregated in the parlour by the kitchen. I could hear all the laughing, and the carrying on. I just wanted to go in and be part of it."

What Jones witnessed as he entered the Davies' inner sanctum filled him with wonder. "Annie, the mother, was holding court in her chair in the parlour with a cup of tea in her hand and a fag in her mouth. Fred was the court jester. He'd come in the house from the pub pissed out of his head, dancing and singing. I'd stand in the corner, just taking it all in – and I never wanted to leave. I could have stayed in that corner for the rest of my life and I would have had everything I ever wanted. It was absolutely magical, a wonderful feeling. They were the roughest and the most happy family. There was warmth and happiness, arguments and fights. Total war or total pleasure. It was completely alive and coming from my house, two doors away, which was always miserable and lifeless, this was completely different. I saw how open they were and how much fun they had. The door was always open, the kettle was always on, and there were people coming in and out all the time. It was a hub of activity."

Before long, Jones became a regular guest at the Davies' weekend parties, much to the rancour of his father. Contrary to expectations, he discovered that they were an unusually spiritual family. "They used to have seances in the house." Dave regaled Jonah with stories of his sisters reading tea leaves or playing with a ouija board. There were even spooky tales of strange murals on the wall upstairs. Jones was intrigued by such apochcrypha, the more so when he was allowed upstairs, a rare privilege for visitors. "There was such a weird energy there. I can't explain it but there was something evil *and* beautiful in that house. If you went up to the bedroom and saw the drawings that Ray had done on the wall it would blow your mind. They were really weird . . . really scary stuff. I'm very sensitive and alive to spirituality which is why I got on so well with Dave. We could sit in a room, not say a word and have a stimulating conversation. We were cosmic brothers."

Ray was less open to spiritual matters and more interested in playing music. While continuing to appear in local pubs with his brother, he also hung out at the nearby Highgate Jazz Club which had become even more popular with the emergence of the trad boom. The retro Temperance Seven, resplendent in striped jackets and boater hats, looked back to the Thirties with the surprise chart topper 'You're Driving Me Crazy', followed by another megaphone-led hit, 'Pasadena'. Both Mr Acker Bilk and Kenny Ball & His Jazzmen also enjoyed their greatest commercial success at the peak of the revival and there was even a spin-off film directed by Richard Lester, *It's Trad, Dad!*. Although Davies preferred the Dixieland originals played at his family's weekend parties, he took pleasure in listening to band versions of 'When The Saints Go Marching In', an influence that would re-emerge later in his career.

During the summer term, Davies submitted a short story for publication in the *William Grimshaw School Magazine*. Titled *Race Against Odds*, the 700-word piece described a gentleman horse-racing enthusiast, Bert De Lord, who falls into debt at the hands of a local bookmaker and ends up accidentally betting his future on a rank outsider named Flash which unexpectedly romps to victory, thereby saving the day. It was of passing interest to see that, even at this stage, Davies was crossing the social and class divide, incorporating a spiv and an aristocrat into his fictional universe.

In September 1961, Davies returned to William Grimshaw to join the upper sixth, a privileged position for a secondary modern pupil. Although his school record was at best average, he had set his sights on going to art college. This could still be achieved without any academic qualifications, but an A-level in Art would assist his passage to the nearby Hornsey College of Art and Design. The notion of even sitting an A-level exam at William Grimshaw was an achievement, but concentrating on a single subject meant that Davies was not stretched unduly.

One influential mentor was his art teacher Mr Bond, who provided extra coaching after school. "He wanted me to explore my creativity, rather than just dab paint on paper, and to build up a body of work." Bond was sometimes impatient with his pupil for spending too much time on the running track, but Davies enjoyed extracurricular activities. During lunch breaks he regularly attended an informal music class among whose ranks was a convivial character with a cheeky sense of humour named Peter Quaife.

Born on 31 December 1943, Peter was the son of Joan Kilby, a fun-loving single mother who became pregnant during the war after a fling with an American serviceman. The Blitz baby was born Peter Alexander Greenlaw Kinnes in Tavistock, Devon, far away from her gossipy neighbours in north London. In 1947, Kilby married Stanley Quaife, who already had a daughter, Ann. Four years later, they produced a son: David Melville. Stanley ran a grocer's shop, but he was far from rich and they rented a council flat at 59 Steeds Road on the nearby Coldfall Housing Estate. According to David, the family were reasonably close then, although Ann never got on that well with her stepmother and left school at 14, moving into her grandmother's house. Peter had started playing guitar in his pre-teen years, initially as therapy for a gruesome hand injury sustained when he impaled himself on a spike while playing in a corporation rubbish dump. He also broke his foot after someone dropped a gravestone on him in another piece of horseplay. The accident-prone kid was well liked and enjoyed telling improbable stories about his imaginary adventures. His stepfather, an electronics buff, was supportive of his musical interests and helped him secure equipment, including a guitar. "I first heard Pete playing guitar in the front room," his brother David remembers. "It was 'Peggy Sue'. One Sunday afternoon, he played it at a neighbour's house for a girl he fancied, but he didn't go out with her."

Quaife arrived at William Grimshaw at the same time as Ray Davies, but was allocated to a lower form, so there was little contact between them. Pete was aware of Ray's exploits on the football field, but that was all. "Although we were the same age, we hadn't really been friends. Ray was the outsider then, a quiet thoughtful person. So we'd never spent time together. He wasn't always there – literally. He wasn't at school – and then he was again. I'm not sure if I really noticed."

It was during a class run by Mr Wainwright that the pair found a common interest. "The teacher wanted to know if any of us could play music. I already had a Czechoslovakian-imported Futurama guitar at home with a pick-up that my dad had helped me choose. So I put my hand up. At first, I thought I was the only one but then I noticed Ray do the same. It was suggested we bring in our guitars the following week, so we did. I played 'Apache' by the Shadows, which I thought would go down well. Ray was into Chet Atkins' finger-picking and he completely outclassed me on his Spanish guitar with a note perfect version of 'Malagueña'. I'd no idea he could play that well." Encouraged by their teacher, the idea of forming a school group was mooted. Quaife recommended a pupil in the lower sixth who not only played drums but actually owned a full kit.

John Start, born on Christmas Eve 1944, lived on Ringwood Avenue, only minutes away from the school gates. He had played drums since the age of eight, largely as musical therapy for a bad stutter. His tutor was George Pearson, a musician based in Friern Barnet, a cycle ride away from Muswell Hill. Pearson was a regular on the BBC Light Programme's *Workers' Playtime*, one of the most popular radio shows of the era. During the skiffle boom, Start teamed up with a couple of school friends to form a makeshift group whose signature song was Lonnie Donegan's 'Rock Island Line'. An occasional observer was Pete Quaife, whose mother Joan had known Start's parents since the war when they each attended the local British Legion. During their later years at William Grimshaw, the boys became closer, with Quaife spending much of his spare time at Ringwood Avenue. Evidently, he was going through an unsettled phase.

"Pete wasn't very happy at home really," Start says. "He didn't like his stepfather particularly well, so he'd call by on his way back to the council estate. He was always reluctant to go home. We'd watch wrestling on Saturday afternoons, eat baked beans on toast and do all sorts of fun things." Their shared love of pop music inspired a memorable outing to the Finsbury Park Empire on 4 April 1960 where they witnessed one of the greatest pop package tours of the period, featuring Eddie Cochran and Gene Vincent. The show made a lasting impression, not least because of the tragic events that followed 13 days later. While driving back to London, the car that was carrying Cochran and Vincent careered off the road, hitting a lamp post. Vincent smashed a collarbone and Cochran's songwriting companion Sharon Sheeley suffered a broken pelvis. Cochran was thrown through the front windscreen and never regained consciousness. His influence inspired countless figures among the British rock 'n' roll generation, including Quaife, Start and the Davies brothers, all of whom testified to his importance.

Start was introduced to Ray Davies by Quaife during a school lesson break and immediately recognized him as the recent star of the running track. Beyond that, his knowledge of his background and personality was virtually non-existent. "He was quiet and aloof in his way. He held himself very upright. You would never have guessed that he came from an amazingly poor house, as I would soon find out." It says much for Ray's introspection and love of privacy that Start had never heard anyone mention his history. He knew nothing about Ray's spell as a disturbed child, the death of his sister, his long period living with Rose in Highgate or the agonizing back problems which prompted his studiously, military-style bearing and posture. "I had no idea of any of this, but I always found Ray to be quite a difficult character. I felt a good deal of depression in him, that's all I can say."

According to Start, the musicians were already rehearsing as a trio when Ray suggested that his brother, then in the fourth form, might be a valuable addition. Quaife was invited to see the Davies brothers perform together at a local pub, probably the Clissold Arms, and was duly impressed. Oddly, but not untypically, Ray had kept his brother in the dark about the new group. As far as Dave was concerned, he and Ray were still working informally as a duo. Expanding the enterprise had never been discussed. It was finally revealed in a tentative exchange that Dave remembered as unfolding in a series of conspiratorial asides.

*

"Pete used to come to our performances sometimes and walk home with us. One night, after he'd been at our house, Ray came into our room.

'Dave, did you hear what Pete said tonight? Did you hear him hint that he might join us?'

'Yes, funny wasn't it?'

There was a brief silence.

'No, I think it's a good idea.' Ray looked at me.

'You mean muck up our duo? It would mean the end of everything we've worked towards. We'd have to start all over again.'

Ray didn't argue. 'Well, think about it, Dave. I know it would mean a big change but he is a very good guitarist. We could make ourselves a group, maybe take in that drummer friend of his. Think about it.'

I thought all night. Another person in our act? It didn't seem right. But if Ray wanted it, it would be selfish of me to refuse. 'I think Pete would be a big help,' I said at breakfast.

Ray looked relieved. 'I thought you were dead choked so I made up my mind to tell you I'd given up the idea. You sure, Dave?' I was sure. And thank goodness I was. We would never have got anywhere without Pete."

*

Whether Ray was quite as magnanimous as Dave described is debatable, but it was not long before the group began appearing as the Ray Davies Quartet. In an attempt at democracy, they were sometimes called the Pete Quaife Quartet or the Dave Davies Quartet, depending upon which member secured the booking. Their first show was an 'Autumn Dance' at William Grimshaw. John Start recalls that they were ill-prepared, having rehearsed briefly in the school's green room. "I can't even remember if Dave played. We only did one number, maybe two. There didn't seem to be anyone in charge. Nobody was singing."

The Shadows were the most popular group in the UK at this time, so it was hardly surprising that instrumentals were favoured at subsequent rehearsals. Another big influence was the Ventures, an American guitar group, who had 'crossed over' into the UK market two years earlier with the Top 10 hits 'Walk Don't Run' and 'Perfidia'. "I was a great fan of the Ventures," Dave Davies recalls. "They had a great track called 'No Trespassing' – the B-side of 'Perfidia' – which I loved. It was a raunchy little throw-away instrumental that I always felt was a strong influence on my playing style." Completing the Quartet's repertoire were some standard rock 'n' roll songs, including 'Johnny B. Goode', 'Move It', 'Money' and 'Do You Want To Dance'.

After their fleeting debut in the school assembly hall, it was agreed that Quaife should change instruments, so he traded in his Futurama guitar for a Framus bass. Although both Ray and Dave insist that the switch was decided by lots, Quaife suggests otherwise. "I was basically threatened . . . In the beginning I was lead guitarist playing 'Apache' by the Shadows. After the school dance we decided to get a bit more serious. I was given the shortest matchstick and they made it that I'd get the shortest and, if I didn't, Ray would break it and give it back to me. That's how I became the bass player."

The rhythm section was now complete, but inexperience and poor equipment sometimes caused problems. Towards the end of the year, they secured a booking at Muswell Hill's Athenaeum Ballroom and were booed off the stage. John Start remembers that they could hardly be heard due to the weak wattage of their amplifiers while the sloping stage resembled a cliff face that threatened to swallow his ungrounded drum kit. "I was terribly embarrassed about the whole thing. I was playing with my legs around the kit to try and stop it moving forward. The others had their own problems. At that stage Pete wasn't that much of a guitarist in all honesty. He was a reluctant bass player and Ray was always on at him for not knowing what he was doing. I used to pity him. Pete was elevated above his station as a musician, but I always held him in great respect. He was a lovely fellow. As a personality he was the nicest one. He deserved a lot better than Ray Davies, I can tell you."

Although Start avoided any conflict with Davies, he was wary of his darker moods. Like many others, he observed striking differences between the brothers. "Ray was a tetchy, difficult, almost bad-tempered person. There was something there I didn't like. He wasn't at ease with the world. Dave was the opposite. He was exhibiting all the emotions of somebody that had been able to free himself of the ties of being the second male born after so many girls. Ray must have worn the crown of the king figure heavily in contrast to Dave's very free outlook on life."

Ray's attitude towards home and family was curiously ambivalent. In one important sense, his memories of childhood would become the lifeblood of his songwriting, a secret portal back to a lost Eden where all things were seemingly in harmony. As much as Davies connected to that time, part of him was running away from those experiences. By his own admission, he felt a paradoxical love for his family that was manifested in a sense of displacement, of not quite belonging. As he entered his teenage years, Dave became more conscious of his brother's socially aspirational ways. It was evident from his less pronounced London accent and preference for living in Highgate with his sister Rose and her husband Arthur. They had a bathroom, a car and middle-class luxury goods that made Ray feel more comfortable. That, at least, was Dave's view.

Pete Quaife went much further, insisting that incipient class consciousness ultimately had a malignant effect on Ray's psyche. "I'm not sure he can ever be really happy. I think the root of his problem is that he was ashamed of his upbringing, his father, his mother, the house they lived in. Everything. Dave never had that problem and, in a way, the saddest thing was that it never mattered . . . It was always just Ray's problem."

The class consciousness described by Quaife was symptomatic of the times. Adjectives like 'respectable' or 'vulgar' were sometimes applied to families on the thinnest of pretexts. The open-house philosophy advocated by the Davies clan, not to mention their regular weekend parties, were seen by some as indicative of the lower orders at play. That was certainly how Mr Jones at number 4 regarded their behaviour. Neighbours often complained about the noise and late-night revelry, no doubt with justification. There was a confrontational, even brazen element to the parents' view of the world. Dave saw it as a *carpe diem* reaction to the uncertainties of living through the war, but others were not so sympathetic. The Fifties was an age of reserve and conformity, not exhibitionism. Many working-class families disguised their poverty behind closed curtains and opened front doors warily. It was a policy designed to discourage visitors. Some ensured that even their children's close friends were kept waiting on the door-step for fear that they might gossip to their parents about what went on inside a neighbour's family home or accidentally provide an inventory of its contents and shortcomings. Annie Davies, brash, outspoken and antagonistic when roused, seemed oblivious to such niceties and welcomed everybody without discrimination or restraint. Whether this was a virtue or a character flaw largely depended upon the observer's social status and sense of decorum.

When John Start first visited Denmark Terrace, he was impressed by the strong sense of family loyalty. "It was a very loving environment. They had these sing-songs on Saturday evenings. Often, my drums were left there and used, probably by Dave, at those get-togethers." It was also noticeable how family members came to the rescue when numbers were needed at important gigs. Gwen's husband, Brian Longstaff, helped them book some shows and even provided transport, while Joyce's spouse Ken Palmer secured a series of dates at Hendon Police College. Although Start was well liked, he detected a gulf between his lifestyle and that of his school fellows. "Dave and Ray always saw my parents as wealthy, certainly compared to their own. My father had done rather well after the war. He was a retail jeweller. When everybody was still eating bread and dripping and cooking rabbits, we lived in a modern, beautiful four-bedroomed house in a very good area."

The class divide appeared to bother Ray, at least from Start's perspective. He concurs with Quaife's theory that Davies felt embarrassed or ashamed about the state of the family home. "I don't think Ray liked me being there seeing it. He was all right with Pete because he knew he lived on a council estate. The actual fabric of the Davies house was very poor. Windows were broken. We often rehearsed there in this tiny, smelly room at the front of the house. The mother – overweight – came out in the most filthy apron a lot of the time. I didn't see much of the father. I don't think he was amazingly well. He spent most of his evenings at the Clissold Arms where we occasionally played." Unsurprisingly, Ray felt more at ease whenever they relocated to Start's upmarket abode on Ringwood Avenue.

The foursome continued working at youth clubs, church dances, coffee bars and local pubs, gradually honing a more varied reper-toire, albeit with a strong reliance on Fifties material from Buddy

Holly, Chuck Berry and Little Richard. Vocals were shared between Ray and Dave, with the younger brother belting out the more raucous material such as 'Good Golly Miss Molly'. "I did more singing then," he admits. "It was so haphazard though. If I brought a song to the band I'd sing it. If it was a Lightnin' Hopkins song or later a number like 'I'm A Lover Not A Fighter', I'd do it. Ray preferred the Buddy Holly type of song like 'Peggy Sue'."

With neither brother considered strong enough to fill the role of lead vocalist, they were in need of a front man. The ever-loyal 'Jonah' Jones was desperate to become more involved, having already played maracas, tambourine and sang along onstage at several early gigs. At this point, he was more interested in blues music than the others, and had been entranced after hearing the guttural sound of Elmore James' 1959 recording 'The Sky Is Crying'. Although an adequate singer, Jones' junior status distracted Ray from acknowledging his promise. "The biggest mistake I made was not playing an instrument. Ray was an un-believable guitarist in the early days, given the technology then. While they were practising, I was more into sports." Instead, Jones stuck around, looking after the equipment and later serving as assistant road manager for the Kinks.

An alternative candidate for lead singer emerged in the person of Rod Stewart, yet another William Grimshaw pupil, one year younger than Ray. A self-confessed spoilt child, whose Scottish father owned a newspaper shop on Archway Road, Stewart had more in common with Davies than might be supposed. Living several miles away, he felt a little isolated from the local commu-nity around the school. While other pupils could socialize or get up to mischief between four o'clock and teatime, or meet later in the evening, he was obliged to travel home. By his own admis-sion, he spent much of his time in his bedroom playing with his model train set and listening to Al Jolson records. Nevertheless, he was an imaginative child, whose distance, emotionally and geographically, inspired a certain vicarious glamour. In common with Ray, he was a fine footballer, careful with his money, and confident enough to challenge convention and enjoy music from a previous generation. Just as Davies had recently transformed himself from a gauche outsider to a football captain, Stewart found a similar salvation through sport. He had been placed in the 'C' stream in his year which, in a secondary modern school, was akin to academic abandonment. With little or no prospects, he seemed destined to drift into who knew where. In a revealing combination of apathy and disdain, he developed what was then known as "the American slouch". Every day, John Start would see him heading home, shoulders hunched forward in resigned defiance of the world. From a certain angle it looked as if he was cowering in fear of a vicious thrashing. "Rod looked like a beaten animal," Start says. It was all the more impressive when Stewart somehow assumed the position of prefect, house captain and a privileged place in the school football team alongside Ray and Jonah. In some respects, he resembled a tarnished parody of the idealized figure later captured in song by Davies in that *Boy's Own* tale 'David Watts'.

Stewart had already been playing with another local group, the Moontrekkers, when he first encountered the Ray Davies Quartet. Being in the same year as their drummer John Start, he was aware of their progress and was willing to try out as their singer. Stewart's fondness for Al Jolson had encouraged a distinctively gruff vocal inflexion that he would later put to use during the mid-Sixties blues boom. It was in evidence during rehearsals at Start's home in Ringwood Avenue where the band often convened. Mrs Start found Stewart's raspy voice so grating that she insisted the group leave the house and rehearse in the adjacent garage. Evidently, there were no protests from the others. "I don't think any of us thought he was a good singer," Start says. "We just didn't have anybody else. We didn't choose him. He auditioned with us. My mother didn't like his voice because it was so gravelly and awful." Nevertheless, with his love of football, fellow school background and capacity to be moulded into a promising blues singer, Stewart ostensibly looked the part, but something was missing. Reportedly, he played only once (possibly twice) with the Quartet, appearing at the nearby Coldfall Youth Club. "Rod was very aloof and independent," Start concludes. "He didn't want to be part of the group really. I think he just saw us as his backing band."

As for those subtle similarities between Davies and Stewart on a psychological level, Quaife was intrigued, but uncertain. "The comparisons you make between Ray and Rod are persuasive but, looking back, I'm not sure how aware we were of them at the time. More simply, I don't think those two liked each other, or maybe that was just Ray. He was very competitive, even then. I always felt Ray wanted to be Big Bill Broonzy while Rod saw himself as Eddie Cochran." Elsewhere, Quaife reiterated those tensions. "I could see Ray thinking, 'This guy's gonna take over if he stays' and I don't think he liked that at all." In one of his opaque asides, Davies facetiously referred to Stewart as "the Elvis Presley of Muswell Hill" and displayed an amnesia worthy of Stalin while discussing his involvement in the story. He had no recollection of ever performing onstage with Stewart and even denied attending rehearsals in his presence. "No," he insisted, when challenged. "He *may* have rehearsed *without* me. It could have been true. He was more interested in pop stuff than us."

On reflection, the most amazing aspect of this episode is that four future stars – the Davies brothers, Quaife and Stewart – should have been attending a London secondary modern school at the same time. It is tantalizing to consider a parallel world version of this story in which Rod Stewart's bluesy yowl combines with Dave's raunchy guitar sound and Ray's songwriting genius to produce a hybrid supergroup of possibly greater commercial appeal or impact than the Rolling Stones or the Kinks. But history turns on such moments. Considering Ray's controlling personality and creative leadership, it seems unlikely that he could have contained as powerful an ego as Stewart in the group, although the later Townshend/Daltrey combination in the Who provides pause for thought.

For his part, Stewart hints that personality differences might have caused friction. "I was real cocky, and that obviously comes from insecurity. I was real aggressive, taking the piss out of people all the time". Instead, Stewart returned to the Moontrekkers, playing the same circuit as the Davies brothers, before embarking on a longer road to superstardom.

There were a couple of half-hearted attempts to find another singer, but no suitable candidates emerged. Another local boy of Greek/Cypriot origin named Pete Georgiou attended a rehearsal, showcasing his act with a rendition of Cliff Richard's 'Living Doll', but he too was deemed unsuitable. "He was there *before* we auditioned Rod Stewart," Start believes. "Rod was definitely after. Pete G came and went and I don't think he did any gigs with us. It may have been that he just didn't mesh with Ray. I thought he was a lot more melodious than Rod Stewart." Quaife vaguely recalls two other candidates, a South African Elvis Presley fan, whom no one else remembers, and a "Jewish girl" from a rich family who lived in a palatial apartment block overlooking Highgate Hill. "That was Sue Redmond!" exclaims John Start, suddenly thrown back in time over 40 years. "She was a nice girl, reasonably tall, obviously Jewish. Pete fancied her but I don't think there was anything very romantic. She was really an eleva- tion of his social climbing skills. It's as high as he ever got, I would think. Sue was maybe a year older than Pete. She had been to a posh school and had recently left. Pete may have met her at a jazz club close by, which Ray also went to occasionally. Pete probably chatted her up and told her he was a guitarist. We liked going to her place. It was the most expensive apartment and her father had these wonderful sculptures. They had their own lift which went right up outside their front door. It must have been the premier block of flats in north London." During those visits, it was suggested that the Quartet might serve as her backing group, financially assisted by her wealthy father, but nothing concrete materialized.

Ray Davies fully appreciated the importance of money in advancing the Quartet's prospects, a view that was regularly conveyed to John Start. "It got to the point where I actually asked my father if he'd buy uniforms for us. Ray's parents had provided for him and Dave, bought instruments and gave as much moral and financial support as they could. Ray couldn't see why my parents couldn't fork out £5 a head on a pair of trousers and a shirt." Start's father proffered the money, somewhat reluctantly, and the group were kitted out by an outfitters in Wood Green in a silken uniform that included smartly "buttoned waistcoats". The imaging did not come without a price. "My father was a bit mean, and there was always a gripe," says Start. Ray suffered unspeakable torment whenever Mr Start uttered the words: "When are you going to pay back that money?"

As summer 1962 approached, more pressing problems concen- trated attention. Ray had his A-level art exam to consider and both Quaife and Start had other commitments. But it was the hellhound Dave Davies whose life was about to be turned upside down. For the past year, he had been dating Susan Sheehan, a Muswell Hill resident who attended Henrietta Barnett School in Golders Green. "Sue was introduced to me by a mutual friend. She seemed like a grown-up woman, but she was only a year older than me. I thought she was much more developed than the girls in my class. It was that old cliché – love at first sight. A special attraction." The pair consummated their relationship, a daring act considering their respective ages. Thereafter, they enjoyed regular sexual contact and were inseparable as friends and young lovers. Susan even appeared onstage with the Davies brothers singing along on the Harry Belafonte/Odetta comedy duet, 'Hole In The Bucket'.

Dave's recklessness proved his undoing when he was discovered by truancy officers in part congress with Susan in the sumptuous grounds of Kenwood House, near Hampstead Heath. They notified the school authorities and retribution was swift. Mrs Davies accompanied Dave to a meeting with the headmaster, Mr Loades, who administered corporal punishment, after which he informed the boy that he was expelled with immediate effect. While Dave remained defiant about the outcome, Susan and her parents were mortified. She too was forced to leave school and ended up working at Selfridges in Oxford Street as a sales assistant. The romance continued over the summer, but soon there was more drama when Susan revealed that she was pregnant. Dave was surprisingly stoic upon hearing the news. His immediate reaction was to buy her a cheap engagement ring and set a wedding date. "If I hadn't had such a big family it might have been more of a drastic experience. I was used to the family set-up. There were always kids around in our family. I felt more comfortable with the idea of a baby than someone from a smaller family."

Dave's mother did not share Dave's carefree attitude but reacted with "shock and horror" at the prospect of her youngest son becoming a married father at the age of 15. The Sheehan family were equally, if not more, aghast and a plot was hatched to keep the teenagers apart. In a well-intentioned but cruel act of deception, the parents not only segregated the couple but convinced each of them that the other no longer wished to be involved. Somehow the subterfuge worked. Susan was subsequently spirited away to an unmarried mothers' home from which Dave was barred access. He was even prevented from seeing his newborn daughter, Tracey. It would be 30 years before he would encounter either of them again.

At a time when Dave seemed on the brink of maturing into a more thoughtful, caring and sensitive being, the great deception, partly perpetrated by his mother, had lasting effects. Wrongly believing that he had been rejected by Susan, he felt hurt and dis-illusioned. The enforced separation unleashed a barely suppressed rage, later manifested via drunken revelries, constant partying and a mindless promiscuity that would follow him down the remainder of the decade. "I was totally emotionally devastated," he says. "I cannot recall a time in my life where I felt so absolutely dreadful as that time when we were separated. The first few months after our separation I felt terrible. It does haunt you. After that, maybe I was always looking for Sue in another woman."

Ray, despite his distance from his brother over the years, was also caught up in this emotional drama. He understood the symbolic significance of the incident with an acuity that never diminished. In privately produced film experiments, photos, record sleeves and even an album (*Schoolboys In Disgrace*) he would retrace the psychogeography of this traumatic event and replay the action as if it was a crucial part of his own autobiography.

CHAPTER FIVE

HORNSEY

While Dave Davies was bereft, lost in the voracious revel of his senses and wary of the uncharted topography of the future, his elder brother exuded a fresh confidence and relative certitude about his own prospects. The William Grimshaw years had ended in unexpected triumph, garlanded by the news that he had been accepted as a student at Hornsey College of Arts and Crafts. A formal interview with the influential principal Herbert 'Harold' Shelton confirmed his induction. The fiscally conscious student was even more pleased to learn that he would be receiving a full grant from the Middlesex County Council. For this, he had to thank his ailing father who was no longer able to work as a slaughterman but found employment as a gardener in the community. At the precise moment the council's means-tested calculations were taking place, he had been out of work for most of the year. According to Annie Davies, in a conversation with her son Dave, Ray hoarded the grant money with the frugality of Shylock, seldom spending a penny.

Ray Davies' arrival at art college resembled an over-familiar script from the pages of the life story of many a budding pop or rock luminary of the age. His recent nemesis Rod Stewart had enrolled at Hornsey the previous year (minus any qualifications) only to leave because he was supposedly colour blind. Across London and beyond into the suburbs and other cities, a veritable roll call of musicians attended art schools, among them John Lennon, Pete Townshend, Ronnie Wood, Keith Richards, Eric

Clapton, Freddie Mercury, Bryan Ferry, Brian Eno and numerous future members of the Pink Floyd and the Bonzo Dog Doo-Dah Band. For most of them, it was a stimulating interlude during which they could escape from the straight world of everyday work and indulge their imaginations, avant garde interests and bohemian pretensions under the aegis of a vaguely constructed course of work. As Ealing-based student Pete Townshend remembers: "It was a clearing house and music was something that was considered to be OK, and not something that you did after hours. It was part of your life. You could sit in a classroom with people painting *and* playing."

Art schools frequently attracted bright, imaginative students, who were not academic or exam-fixated. Elitist universities demanded sometimes impossibly high marks in GCE passes, way beyond the aptitude of working-class pupils, even those lucky enough to have won a place at grammar school. It was no coincidence that countless later rock and pop musicians were former art students while their university counterparts – Mick Jagger, Paul Jones and Jonathan King – were so rare that their alma maters were paraded in the press as if they were members of the House of Lords.

"That was the remarkable thing about art schools," says the academic Dr Lisa Tickner (née Warton), who started on the Intermediate course at Hornsey in 1961. "They were in their way higher education for people who didn't have academic qualifications. It's a key thing. There was a real mix-up of people and that was part of its enchantment. It was very old-fashioned, a mix of quite traditional skills. You had to do craft. I remember one of my first lessons was being taught how to sharpen a pencil, which was actually a bit crazy."

When Davies started at Hornsey in the autumn of 1962, revolutionary changes in teaching methods and courses were underway. Up until then, students usually entered the four-year National Diploma of Art and Design at the age of 16. They would then take the Intermediate examination after two years, followed by another two years of specialization. There was a high failure rate, even among promising students, and widespread dissatisfaction about the course, prompting complaints that it produced "neither good industrial designers nor satisfactory art teachers". A degree qualification, the Diploma in Art & Design, was planned to take its place and Hornsey was among the colleges selected to teach Fine Art and Graphic Design at the new level. The death of the Intermediate ensured a move away from a strictly vocational course to one that was more liberal and culturally centred.

"Most people were pleased when the new Dip AD was introduced," Dr Tickner remembers. "It was much more creative and less regimented. But some people missed the old Intermediate and actually lamented the loss of the craft-based system." Although art colleges operating under the new system maintained what was colloquially termed "the genius loophole", which allowed them to recruit students without GCEs, the more general requirement was now five passes at O-level, a challenging task for the average secondary modern pupil.

Davies was enrolled in the Foundation Course, along with Pete Quaife who barely lasted a month before being expelled for what he euphemistically termed "Teddy boy behaviour". The truth was that Quaife, unlike Davies, felt alienated by the class and cultural differences between himself and the other students. "I got thrown out because I didn't really fit into the pattern of what they wanted. I thought I was going there to be taught how to draw, but it turned out to be a place for organizing marches – ban the bomb . . . and so forth. That's all it was about. I didn't learn anything at all." Quaife wasted no time securing a job at *The Outfitter*, a men's fashion magazine situated in the West End. Coincidentally, Dave Davies was also starting work nearby in the stockroom at Selmer's music shop. The pair gravitated towards each other, united by a shared love of blues music and fashion. Quaife was already an aspiring Mod, while Dave simply liked to wear anything that might cause a reaction. Every available lunchtime they would visit the specialist record shop Dobell's in Charing Cross Road, which stocked imported LPs of obscure American jazz, blues and folk performers. They would next hit the local shops and boutiques in search of colourful clothing. Even at this early stage, Dave was unabashed about wearing women's hats or fancy shirts, despite their effeminacy.

When he wasn't meeting Dave for lunch, Quaife hung out at the Strand Lyceum with Patricia Thomas, another aspiring Mod who worked at *The Outfitter*. Occasionally, they would share sandwiches with a young secretary and fellow clothes horse, Cathy McGowan, who would later become an icon for young Mods as a presenter on the influential television music programme, *Ready, Steady, Go!*. "We were Mods in those days," Pat recalls. "Pete was an absolute clothes fanatic. He talked about nothing but the latest gear and this group he was in. It was called the Ray Davies Quartet then . . . He was a lot of fun. I remember how the door would burst open. Pete would dash in, very excited about the record he had just bought. It was usually by Chet Atkins." During half-term holidays or afternoon breaks, John Start would visit *The Outfitter* and accompany Quaife on one of his Carnaby Street expeditions.

By now, Ray was a more distant presence, ensconced in the heady environs of art school, amid a clique of students for whom self-reinvention seemed almost requisite. While no social gadfly, he attended college parties and dances, frequented local coffee bars and pubs, and spent many hours sauntering around museums and art galleries. He even attended theatre school at the weekend and still played football at least once a week. In his more introspective moments, he occasionally visited London Zoo in Regent's Park where he would stare reflectively at the primates, whose antics may partly have provided the inspiration for the song 'Apeman' years later.

Davies' busy calendar left less time for the 'group project' with Dave, Pete and John, which was suspended for long periods. Quaife and Start found that it was a lot easier to deal with the Davies brothers when they were separated. Although there were no physical outbursts between them, Start remembers a lot of shouting and verbal tensions at key moments. His most pleasant memories are the dates when he and Pete travelled together in his mother's car. "She lent us her Anglia and my drums and Pete's guitar were sticking out the back while we were eating fish and chips on our way to a gig. That's when we had the most fun." Occasionally, the Quartet played at the Railway Tavern in Crouch End, a favourite haunt for Ray's student friends, but those two worlds never came together.

At Hornsey, Davies was surrounded by surprisingly approachable middle-class girls, some richer than others. Dress sense disguised poorer origins and Ray self-consciously wore a suit and tie for a brief period. Among the hipper elements, class origins were seen as anachronistic but they had subtle significance, admitted or not. "Art school was still a place where you got some nice girls who were filling in time before marriage," says Lisa Warton, who befriended Ray during his first term. "My parents were scrambling across the bottom of the middle class in a sense . . . and I went to the local grammar. I left school at sixteen. I had fallen in love with art school. I didn't know the word 'bohemian' but I thought it was some kind of route out of the suburbs. I was an only child of elderly parents neither of whom had gone to university and they were bitterly disappointed because this was not the route that I was supposed to take." Warton nevertheless oozed sophistication compared to Davies, and her speech pattern – classic Received Pronunciation – indicated her parents' aspirational hopes. At lunchtime, the students congregated at Stan's Café on Crouch Hill, where the menu offered beans on toast for a shilling, or egg and chips for 1/6d. The more affluent clientele dined on steak and chips at a hefty 3/6d. "I remember one girl who *always* had steak at Stan's," Lisa says. "She got engaged during the course and had a diamond engagement ring." Among the clique was Clive Tickner, whose father was an assistant bank manager, and his affluent sculptor pal Mick Dunn, both of whom hailed from Middlesex. There were other more exotic creatures including "a strange guy called Colin who was older and had a glass eye". Lisa also remembers "a Maltese guy called Joe who I went out with for about twenty-four hours before he discovered I wouldn't sleep with him". Summing up, she adds, "There was a real social mix but everybody was equal in the face of talent, or the lack of it."

Decades later, Ray Davies would provide a satirical portrait of his time at Hornsey in the song 'Art School Babe'. The female protagonist, with her ruby red lips and ghostly white make-up, resembles actress/singer Juliette Greco, the poster icon of the bohemian set. She lives in a bedsit and smokes joints for ostentatious effect. Ray's narrator plays the pathetically unsuccessful seducer, pretentiously quoting Proust, Ferlinghetti and Sartre, while failing to impress. It's a humorous, evocative re-creation, but somewhat stereotypical, like a Sunday supplement or period piece drama made for mainstream viewing. While there were a number of posh grammar school girls among the Hornsey set, exotic fruit of the calibre of the 'art school babe' were atypical. As one of Davies' circle attests, by way of contradiction: "What Ray is talking about in that song sounds much more like the world of Antonioni's *Blow-Up* than the world of a rather minor north London art school. I don't remember any beatniks at Hornsey then. I think we were all fairly well-dressed and middle class. It was tweed jackets more than jeans. The girls I knew were fairly straightforward and not in any way eccentric." Perhaps the 'art school babe' was the great exception or a fanciful creation reconstructed from falsely nostalgic images of the period.

Davies, despite his innate shyness, found some kindred spirits at Hornsey and was no longer the sad, pensive personality so familiar from the early days at William Grimshaw. Fellow student Mordechai Beck remembers him as a slightly mysterious figure who regularly disappeared after the early morning lecture. Beck assumed he was spending his time in some pub or coffee bar but was impressed to discover that he had been taking time out to practise jazz guitar. Clearly, he still enjoyed playing the detached observer. "At art school my source material was cafeterias, train stations, motorways, isolated people, bag ladies, tramps. People like me have a tendency to become too introspective and that might be frightening . . . There's a bit of the vampire in me as well, sucking life out of the world." In the accepting atmosphere of Hornsey, Davies' eccentricities went unnoticed and may even have been encouraged. "The teachers were quite radical," one of Ray's contemporaries recalls. "I remember them saying 'Forget everything you've learned about perspective – don't look at the object, look at the spaces in between.' They were full of new ways of looking at things, at least to me."

Davies' abiding passion at Hornsey was not art, painting or sculpture, but cinema. It had been a budding interest ever since he had seen *Ladri di Biciclette* with his father as a child. He became intrigued by the documentary format after watching an episode of John Grierson's *This Wonderful Life* (broadcast on Scottish TV from 1957) which included footage from *Men Of Aran* (1934) by Robert J. Flaherty. The scenes of farming and fishing on the Aran Islands, against a powerful backdrop of rolling waves, left a lasting impression. While his friends were praising the classic, star-studded 1960 western *The Magnificent Seven*, Davies attended a screening of the original *Seven Samurai* (1954) by Japanese director Akira Kurosawa. What sounded like an academic excursion was, it transpired, a happy accident. Ray's brother-in-law Ken Palmer (Joyce's husband) had accompanied him to the Hendon Classic to view what they assumed was a naturist film. Ten minutes into Kurosawa's masterpiece, Ken turned to Ray and enquired: "Where's all the tits then?" It was all part of Davies' early film education. At art school, he first discovered Ingmar Bergman, the Swedish director whose oppressive, medieval moral allegory *The Seventh Seal* (1956) was already a cult cinema favourite.

Student politics was still lukewarm in the early Sixties, but attracted the attention of some of the more radically minded. Across at Ealing Art School, for example, Pete Townshend was a member of both CND and the Young Communist League. The closest Davies came to political engagement was an encounter with fellow student John Philby, a well-travelled, public school-educated member of the Young Socialists. His father, Kim, a senior officer in British Secret Service Intelligence (MI6), had worked with the CIA and FBI in Washington and was closely involved in the investigation of double agents Burgess and Maclean, during their defection to Moscow in 1951. For a time, Philby Senior came under suspicion as a collaborator but was cleared of spying and declared blameless by the Foreign Secretary in a House of Commons speech in 1955.

John Philby saw little of his father, who left his family the following year and moved to Beirut. The boy's mother Aileen, a self-harming alcoholic, rapidly declined in health thereafter and suffered a fatal cardiac arrest in 1957, the same year that Ray's sister Rene died of heart failure. Philby, like Davies, was devastated by the news. "I was only thirteen and her death was a terrible blow. She'd been a wonderful mother. But none of us children were invited to the funeral . . . to this day I don't know where she's buried." Philby was taken in by an aunt and uncle, placed in boarding school and arrived at Hornsey with hopes of becoming a painter, but it was politics and partying that dominated his thoughts.

"John Philby was a familiar sight, always around," says Lisa

Warton. "He wasn't particularly one of a group, though he had a good-looking girlfriend for a bit. He was a nifty dancer at parties, very cool." Although Philby and Davies came from completely different backgrounds, they had more in common than either realized, both outsiders with troubled histories. Independent and wary, they were a little too reserved to establish any deep connection, although they would continue to meet after college.

The apolitical Davies preferred to engage with politics on the big screen. Revealingly, he cited the work of Soviet director Sergei Eisenstein as his major interest at the time. Watching *Strike*, *Alexander Nevsky*, *Battleship Potemkin* and *Ivan The Terrible*, Davies was struck not just by the camerawork, strong images and mannered design, but the commentaries and observations on capitalism, nationalism and revolutionary fervour.

Davies' cinematic education was provided primarily by Paul O'Dell, a well-dressed fellow student from Hendon. O'Dell had an intellectual air, an independent spirit and an aficionado's love of film. What that engaging persona disguised was a troubled upbringing and a fascinatingly circuitous route to art college that few, if any, of his colleagues learned about. O'Dell's parents, Harvey and Gladys, had a tempestuous marriage, punctuated by fiery rows. Often, his mother would seek sanctuary at the local cinema or take a bus to the West End to see the latest releases. "I was quite often carted off to the cinema as a result of those arguments. Given the vividness of those outings, it was no wonder I became hooked, if I wasn't already, on cinema."

Although bright and imaginative O'Dell, in common with Ray Davies, failed the 11-plus. He was consigned to a secondary modern in Haringey. Just as Ray had been seriously affected by the death of Rene as an adolescent, so Paul had to deal with the sudden death of his mother in 1955 when he was only 12. His father "fell to pieces" and Paul was subsequently looked after by a series of guardians. It was an extremely dispersive experience. In common with the majority of secondary modern pupils in the Fifties, O'Dell left school at 15 for an uncertain future. Over the next three years, he would attempt to find his way working at a printers, a small advertising agency and as a designer of posters for the Moss Empires chain of theatres. His life was transformed on 26 January 1961 when a local authority childcare counsellor introduced, then placed him in the hands of, new guardians whose influence on his life was to prove incalculable.

Gilbert and Hilarie Beaven lived in Crooked Usage, an upmarket area of Hendon. He worked as a research chemist and she was a language teacher. For O'Dell, this was akin to bridging a class and cultural chasm far wider than that experienced by Ray when he'd moved from Denmark Terrace to Rose and Arthur's house in Highgate. By comparison, O'Dell was living among the privileged elite. Almost imperceptibly, he acquired middle-class trappings and aspirations. "My guardians felt I should realize my potential. They were intellectual people au fait with theatre, cinema and literature. I suddenly became imbued with all this culture, classical music and everything, which I hadn't really listened to before." O'Dell began frequenting the National Theatre and attending evening classes, where he befriended several influential tutors. "We used to go to various flats in Hampstead, listen to jazz and talk about cinema and art. It was heady stuff. By the time I got to Hornsey I was fired up to achieve something. A lot of that was to do with Hilarie and Gilbert, but I think the secondary modern school stigma was also a factor."

After enrolment, O'Dell re-established the college's ailing film society – the grandly titled, mock Latin Hornsoria Kinematographic Society (note the prophetic 'K'). Inspecting the resources, O'Dell was appalled by the facilities on offer. The projector had a cracked lens, so the first film shown in the new term was completely out of focus. "Apart from the cracked lens, they'd been showing widescreen films without an anamorphic lens, which was ridiculous." It was enough to provoke a series of requests to the principal for new equipment. O'Dell's two associates in the enterprise were Clive Tickner and Lisa Warton. "Paul was the leading light," Clive says. "He would suggest the films, write a review he would get from somewhere, find a cover image and Lisa (a trained touch typist) would type up and photocopy the programmes. There was always a stark black and white image from Eisenstein. We weren't allowed to charge entry for films hired from the BFI (British Film Institute) but you could charge *for entry by programme* which was a shilling. We had to ring the BFI, pay for the film in advance and collect it from the post office."

Fellow students Mick Dunn and Ray Davies helped out. "I'm

certain Ray would be happy to recognize that Paul O'Dell knew more about film than the other three of us," Warton says. O'Dell was keen to promote the Western genre, recognizing the depth and pathos in popular movies of the Fifties such as *High Noon*, *The Searchers* and *Rio Bravo*. He shared, if not promoted, Davies' interest in Eisenstein and, thanks to contacts at the BFI, he was able to acquire rare prints. "He was the *real* film buff," acknowledges Lisa Warton. "We wanted to show European nouvelle noir, and we also showed silent films. We later screened the whole of D. W. Griffith's *Intolerance* (1916), which is incredibly long. We got an old but experienced silent film accompanist to come in and play the piano. We had to have a break every time we changed the reels." In order to compensate for O'Dell's more esoteric excursions, the Film Society would occasionally show more recent films, notably François Truffaut's *Jules Et Jim* and Jean-Luc Godard's *A Bout De Souffle*.

"We were very keen to give the *idea* of a cinema," O'Dell stresses. "We played music before the film started and by the end of the Easter term had persuaded the college to buy a second projector so that films could be screened without a break between reels." Thereafter, the Film Society thrived. Undoubtedly, the key to its success was O'Dell's passion and eclecticism. There were yet more films from Griffith (years later O'Dell wrote the book *Griffith And The Rise Of Hollywood*), plus National Film Theatre-style seasons of Ingmar Bergman and Alfred Hitchcock, and oddities such as the entire cycle of episodes, back to back, of the American science fiction B-movie serial *Captain Video*.

Ray Davies dutifully attended the art house screenings, but cavilled about the modest entrance fee. "I was usually taking the money at the door," Lisa remembers. "Each week he would ask how much it was and I'd say, 'It's still a shilling, Ray!' But he was very keen on film and he came almost every week."

Art college also brought new musical opportunities. Occasionally, Ray played in a duo with Tottenham-born Geoff Prowse. Two years older than Davies, Prowse was an accomplished painter, budding composer and talented jazz pianist. Often, they were augmented by bass player, Stuart 'Maciejewski'. Back on Highgate Hill, Dave Davies could also be found experimenting with jazz alongside former school pal Lou Lewis in the coal cellar of the

Victoria Arms. "He was into clarinet playing because his dad played the instrument in Benny Goodman's band," Dave recalls. "There were lots of pictures on the wall of Artie Shaw and autographed photos of musicians from that era. I was into Django Reinhardt and Diz Disley." Although the brothers still had much in common musically, their get-togethers were sporadic at best and it was difficult to avoid the impression that they were gradually drifting apart.

There was great excitement at Hornsey when the entertainments officer successfully booked Alexis Korner's Blues Incorporated for the end of term 1962 Christmas dance. Korner, already 34, was a blues enthusiast extraordinaire. His band became a veritable clearing house for budding R&B stars featuring, at various times, future members of the Rolling Stones, Manfred Mann and Cream, among others. At the time of the Hornsey appearance, the drummer was the inimitable Charlie Watts who was virtually being stalked by several members of the recently formed Rollin' Stones (still minus the 'g') who were desperate to acquire his services. The Stones opened proceedings that evening and made a good impression according to both Lisa Warton and Ray Davies. "I seem to remember they got paid £50 and Mick Jagger had a cold," the penny-wise Ray recalls. His other enduring memory is befriending one of the girls involved in booking the bands. "I thought she'd be good to latch on to because she would give me free tickets." Others remember the unforgettable sight of Brian Jones playing slide guitar.

Korner's credibility attracted the blues lovers at the college, plus a large number of Christmas revellers, including Watts' girlfriend (and later wife) Shirley Ann Shepherd, a senior student who spent the evening dancing to every song. Lisa Warton was dressed uneasily in a redesigned frock from her mother's wardrobe. Although enchanted by the band's performance, it was the sense of a new liberating influence that lingered longest. While fretting about her appearance, she was taken aside by an older girl who proclaimed with absolute authority: "You're fine. It doesn't matter what you're wearing. We can wear *anything* at our age." It was a sentiment with which Dave Davies would have wholeheartedly concurred.

Ray Davies was impressed by both bands. "Alexis arrived

onstage dressed in a wonderful black leather jacket, the musical attire of the time, and he sang in this gravelly London voice. They were trying to copy American blues but there was something about it that made it sound Kensington. I think it was Alexis' voice – Kensington Blues!" After the show, Davies was bold enough to seek Alexis' advice. Korner suggested that he should visit the Piccadilly Jazz Club in Ham Yard, opposite the Windmill striptease club in Soho. There, he would find Giorgio Gomelsky, a jazz and blues evangelist, whose myriad interests included film-making and promotion. He had already run blues nights at the Marquee, then in Oxford Street, and would later find success managing and producing the Yardbirds.

At this point, Gomelsky was on the lookout for young, blues-loving musicians to add some spice to the repertoires of the senior jazz players who played at the Piccadilly. Among them were the remnants of the Dave Hunt Confederate Jazz Band, a trombone-heavy trad outfit who were now calling themselves the Dave Hunt Rhythm & Blues Band. Tom McGuinness (later to join Manfred Mann) had already auditioned for them, but was immediately put off by their trad trappings. "There was a collision of styles. Dave Hunt was basically a jazz musician. He was trying to make the transition to R&B but I knew he wasn't going to do it with me. So I turned down the job . . . I understand Ray Davies didn't."

Indeed, Davies was happy to be considered a competent enough guitarist to secure a stand-in spot with the ensemble. Despite their new title, Hunt's band paid only token tribute to R&B. They were essentially a jazz-influenced unit of professional players, adapting to changing times. Four days before Christmas, Davies joined them at the Piccadilly but, prior to their performance, he was distracted by the young support act. It was the Rollin' Stones, whom he had seen less than a week before at the Hornsey Christmas dance. Either Hunt or another band member casually dismissed them as a glorified skiffle group and instead invited Davies for a pre-gig free drink. Ray was terribly torn, but as the Stones began their short set, something willed him to stay. "I saw the energy. I saw Brian Jones – a total star. I saw Keith . . . I saw Jagger, not so prominent then. They stood in a line, the three of them, all in their round button collars and their little shirts. The sound was exciting . . . I think that was the best I've ever seen them play." Impressive as they were, the Stones could hardly compete with the promise of a free drink. By the time they were starting 'Roll Over Beethoven' Davies was heading anxiously for a pub in nearby Archer Street to collect his gratis pint which he held as reverently as if it were the Holy Grail.

Ray spent Christmas with his family and various relatives. On New Year's Eve, the Ray Davies Quartet reconvened for a surprise booking at the London Lyceum, opening for Cyril Stapleton and His All-Star Orchestra. "I don't know how we got the gig, but it was top-notch," says John Start. "It was the biggest thing we did, a West End theatre. We did four numbers, maybe five, including 'Walk Don't Run'. It didn't go down amazingly well. There were no screaming girls. I remember feeling quite insignificant. We certainly didn't come away thinking, 'We showed them!'" For reasons Start did not understand, the night held a particular importance for the Davies brothers. The Lyceum was the venue where their sister had collapsed and died five years before also while listening to a big band orchestra. It was a strangely reflective way to end the year, but it did not bring the brothers together or unify the group. Instead, Ray decided to stay with Dave Hunt in the hope of securing better gigs in the West End and gaining greater experience.

During the second term at Hornsey, Davies became even more closely entwined with Paul O'Dell, that aloof but culturally astute student who had been conspicuous by his absence at the recent Christmas school dance. "Sadly I didn't go when the Stones played second on the bill. I was working my way through the symphonies of Mahler." O'Dell and Davies bonded when Ray discovered that the well-dressed young man was not merely showing but actually *making* films. Nevertheless, communication between the pair was guarded. "Ray was quite reticent, if not difficult to talk to. You certainly had to draw him out. Outside our film interests, we didn't have a great deal in common. He always seemed to be a very private person, wrapped up in his own thoughts and world."

O'Dell unexpectedly entered that world after asking the appealing question: "Would you like to make a film?" They were joined in the project by another student whose forename provided the project's title: *Veronica*. "It was about a guy who had a crush on a girl," Ray recalls. "I think he killed her in the woods." Davies played the lead part and the atmosphere was heightened by accompanying music from O'Dell's current passion, Gustav Mahler. "It was made over six months," O'Dell reveals. "We didn't have a script, it was all improvised. There were often times when Veronica or Ray couldn't make it. We shot this rather passionate love scene in the park and when we cut it together there were scenes where the grass was quite short and other scenes where it was waving above their heads. The story was basically about two people coming together. The Ray character tries to make love to Veronica, she resists, he gets a bit violent and leaves her on the ground, to all intents and purposes – dead. It was just an idea and we improvised it."

The footage was shot in the grounds of Kenwood House, beside Hampstead Heath. O'Dell had no idea that the location and improvised storyline had any deeper significance, but for Ray the romp in the grass with Veronica held special meaning. For it was in that same spot in Kenwood that Dave Davies had been discovered in flagrante delicto with Sue Sheehan, an event that culminated in his expulsion from school and subsequent discovery that she was pregnant. Not for the last time, Ray was siphoning his younger brother's experiences as fertile subject matter for his own designs.

Veronica was completed, but the film was later lost and only a series of stills currently survive. O'Dell and Davies also collaborated on a second effort, *The Return*. "It was about somebody coming back from holiday and finding their girlfriend had left them," O'Dell remembers. Unfortunately, that project was unfinished; all that remains is a single still of the participants: O'Dell, Davies, Jenny Howard, Su Statlender, and cameraman, Michael Flaum.

A third short film by O'Dell titled *Bridge* commenced production later in 1963 after Davies had moved on. Whether Ray ever saw the *completed* version is uncertain, but the theme and locale were significant. Filming was undertaken on Hungerford footbridge and Charing Cross Station, pre-empting the subject matter of 'Waterloo Sunset' by three and a half years. If the older Davies had ever considered filming a promo for that song, this would have been a fitting inspiration. "We were so noble and so immature," Davies concludes, when recalling these art school experiments. However, there is little doubt that O'Dell's confidence, affluence, sophistication, smart sartorial style and genuine appreciation of film as a serious art form each played an important part in forming Davies' world view during his time at Hornsey.

CHAPTER SIX

THE BOLL-WEEVILS

Harbingers of the cult of youth realized that 1963 symbolized a sudden erosion of the old order as teenagers paraded their discontent, while spending freely on glossy magazines, clothes, pop records and entertainment. The effect was kaleidoscopic rather than linear: the cast list included young pop singers, musicians, clothes designers, dramatists, novelists, photographers, filmmakers, artists and models, each working at different speeds and stages of development but buffeting against one another, then coalescing in a single moment of history to create what became known in tabloid journalese as the birth of the Swinging Sixties.

Cultural and stylistic changes were incandescent. Designers like Mary Quant were busily brushing aside the conservatism of Fifties dress with new youth-orientated styles. Furniture became showy, geometric and unashamedly non-utilitarian, with Formica replacing natural wood. At the cinema, the latest box-office hero was James Bond, a peculiarly British Secret Agent whose lascivious amorality, suave cynicism and obsession with new technology and gimmicky gadgetry was an apt comment on the times. Groundbreaking books such as Michael Shanks' *The Stagnant Society* and John Robinson, the Bishop of Woolwich's *Honest To God* questioned prevailing attitudes towards community and religion, candidly and provocatively. The great British class conflict, so prevalent in the work of such working-class writers of the Fifties as John Braine, Keith Waterhouse, Alan Sillitoe, Shelagh Delaney and David Storey, had now made the transition to the big screen.

Among the acclaimed films of 1963 were *The Loneliness Of The Long Distance Runner*, *This Sporting Life* and *Billy Liar* – all of them glimpses of the proletariat from the inside, inspired by northern working-class writers.

All this creative activity was played out against a backdrop of political unrest and moral uncertainty among an older generation caught between two worlds. As one cultural commentator noted: "It is impossible to question that the events and character of the year 1963 stand out as more remarkable than those of any other year in Britain since the War – and that they represented the central hinge of one kind of Britain from another."

Even the elements conspired, as if some unknown force was dictating events. The year began with weather befitting an approaching apocalypse. It was the most severe winter on record since 1740. While London was shrouded in fog, a blanket of snow stretched across Britain, driven inexorably by blinding blizzards and numbing temperatures that had already succeeded in freezing rivers, immobilizing public transport, raising the unemployment rate to 3.9 per cent, marooning a family on a Dartmoor farm for 60 days, escalating the incidences of hypothermia among the poor, aged and infirm, and encouraging eccentric prophets to herald the arrival of another Ice Age.

An impressionable young audience, barricaded in their homes by the weather, tuned in to Saturday night television's *Thank Your Lucky Stars* and witnessed four young, mop-haired musicians whose chirpy effervescence and melodic infectiousness rendered the climate irrelevant. Thereafter, the Beatles would change everything in pop music and fashion, spearheading a year which was later celebrated as marking the apotheosis of the British teenager. At the end of February, the group topped the charts with 'Please Please Me', an achievement that signalled the imminent death of the trad bands, dance crazes and ephemeral fads that had dominated the pop world during the previous two years. An even bigger hit followed with 'From Me To You'. Within months the chart-conquering Beatles would be joined by a legion of fellow travellers including Gerry And The Pacemakers, the Searchers, Billy J. Kramer With The Dakotas, plus Manchester rivals the Hollies and Freddie And The Dreamers. The long apprenticeship served by the Beatles and several of their contemporaries in

Germany ensured that they were the undisputed kings of the beat boom. Davies, who had first heard the Beatles' debut disc 'Love Me Do' the previous October, welcomed the Liverpool explosion but was also heavily influenced by a similar revolution occurring in London clubs. While national radio was still more comfortable with solo singers and family entertainers, the city's hipper haunts were offering the R&B music championed by Cyril Davies, Alexis Korner, Graham Bond, John Mayall and newcomers the Rolling Stones, the Downliners Sect and the Yardbirds.

Ray Davies was on the cusp of this new movement having appeared regularly in Soho clubs with Dave Hunt's band since the first week of the year. In addition to a residency at the Piccadilly Jazz Club, they were playing sporadic dates at the Station Hotel, Richmond, the spiritual home of the Rolling Stones. Davies was intrigued by the older players in Hunt's ensemble. "The pianist played 'Honky Tonk Train Blues' better than Bob Crosby And The Bob Cats. He used to tell me off for making the wrong changes. It was a jazz band but they could get money by playing R&B."

In order to supplement his income, Davies still played occasional gigs with his younger brother. Dave Hunt's saxophonist, Lol Coxhill, was aware of Ray's non-jazz work and oozed wisdom and cool in equal measure when offering advice. "He's the one who told me I should join a group. He said, 'Make your own music, because you're no good at mine!'" Somehow, Davies continued to compartmentalize his activities with the aplomb of a secret agent.

Amid the winter gloom, the Ray Davies Quartet (carelessly billed on a poster as the 'Ray Davis Quartette') appeared at Hornsey Town Hall for a St Valentine's Day dance supporting the Harry Pitch Band, whose leader's main claim to fame was blowing the harmonica on Frank Ifield's massive number 1 hit, 'I Remember You'. Several of the Davies' clan attended, congregating beside the stage and shouting encouragement. Among them was 'Jonah' Jones, still sweating after lugging the group's equipment aboard a local bus. The Quartet returned to the Town Hall for an Easter Dance that was well received. "I felt a lot more comfortable up there than I did at the Lyceum or the Athenaeum," recalls John Start. "They had a submarine bar downstairs and we played upstairs too. We did rather well there." Full of confidence, the Quartet next made a rare foray into R. G. Jones Recording Studio in Morden, Surrey, where they cut an obscure Dave Davies composition, tentatively titled 'Morning Sunshine'.

Soon after, Ray Davies left Dave Hunt for a more raucous spin-off ensemble – Hamilton King's Blues Messengers. King, a drummer and harmonica player, had been an occasional singer in the Hunt band, but now assumed lead vocals. Davies was content to adopt a cameo role. "It was strange coming in that curve at the end of that era. I used to sit and play with that band. Singers stood. The musicians only stood if they had a solo. I wanted to play and I learned a lot from these jazz players . . ."

Although it sounded a little staid from Davies' description, others noted the show's excitement with relish. Pianist Peter Bardens recalls Ray coming out of his shell and playing the showman, urged on by the band leader. "Hamilton King was this West Indian, a big bear of a fellow. He used to play harmonica and sing in a very high-pitched voice. Ray was very good . . . playing [the guitar] behind his head, rolling on the ground and kicking his legs in the air. He only sang on one or two numbers."

While Ray was advancing professionally, his brother was in danger of being left behind. It probably helped Dave's prospects when he was fired from his job at Selmer's for falling asleep at work after one late night too many. With more time to rehearse with Pete Quaife and John Start, he moulded the band into a tighter unit, renaming them the Ramrods in honour of the Duane Eddy instrumental 'Ramrod'. No doubt he also remembered performing 'Riders In The Sky' with Ray, which was later a hit by American act the Ramrods. John Start dutifully stencilled the new name 'RAMRODS' on his drum kit as evidence of their latest reinvention. Despite Ray's continued absence, Dave has no recollection of working in the interim as a trio. "No, there weren't any gigs," he says. "Not really. We were just getting it together and trying to find an identity, a sound."

Evidently, they succeeded. By early summer, Ray had another of his epiphanies and, in the spirit of the age, decided to commit himself to his brother's enterprise. "I was amazed how Dave had improved because I was the guitarist, the serious deep-thinking musician. I'd gone away to college and played in clubs and I came back and there was this crazed kid with really big hair playing these amazing guitar licks and he was terrific. I thought, 'I must get in on this!'" The decision was partly expedient as Hamilton King's band was already breaking up, but Ray could easily have sought another experienced outfit. What he saw in the Ramrods was the triumph of youth over experience and an opportunity to enter a lower league that might eventually lead to achievement on a par with the Rolling Stones, or even the Beatles. "Dave and I weren't playing much music together at this time but he did come down the club and sensed that I was after something that I couldn't articulate musically. He played me a record that seemed to be a bridge from what I was playing to what I aspired to be doing. I wanted to play Big Bill Broonzy with drums."

The disc that provided this missing link was 'Country Line Special' by Cyril Davies & His Rhythm & Blues All Stars on Pye International Records' R&B series. It sounded like Chicago blues transposed to London with a fierce and frantic harmonica accompaniment from its leader who appeared to be channelling the work of his great idol Little Walter for a new generation. It was at once pure and invigorating, a call to arms for Ray Davies who saw a completely new direction in which he might play a major part.

In several later interviews, Ray spoke as if he had usurped Dave as 'leader' of his own band, a perspective coldly contested by others in the group. "Ray didn't take over," Dave retorts. "It wasn't like that at all. He'd been playing with more accomplished professional musicians, but it was music that was on the way out. I think he liked the idea of getting a band together with me and Pete. Although the stuff Ray was playing with Hamilton King was R&B, it wasn't really what he wanted to do, particularly when there were other groups like the Stones around doing similar things to what we were doing."

Both John Start and Pete Quaife were aware of Ray's growing interest in R&B. "We used to go to the Marquee on a Thursday night," the drummer recalls. "Ray was very into blues and R&B, Sonny Boy Williamson and Big Bill Broonzy. He also came with me and Pete to Studio 51, the Ken Colyer Club, where we saw the Rolling Stones." Despite such interaction, neither Quaife nor Start has any memories of Davies working with other bands. "We played in the West End with Ray, but I never heard of the Dave

Hunt Band," Start insists. "There was a lot about Ray I didn't know. He wasn't upfront talking about many things." It says much about the psychological dynamic in the Ramrods that Ray was able to disappear and pursue a parallel career without the rhythm section ever finding out.

Ray's new beginning was also a time of endings. That summer he abruptly left Hornsey College of Art after the principal Harold Shelton told him that there was no opportunity to pursue film studies as part of the syllabus. Uncertain about his future, Davies hoped to enrol at the Central School of Art & Design, but missed the application deadline. He already knew he lacked the discipline or talent to succeed as a painter. "This was 1963 and art was going in a different direction. There weren't any Impressionists any more, they were all doing copies of chocolate boxes." Ray felt that he was "good but not great", a realization that drained his commitment to painting. Instead, he applied successfully for a place at Croydon School of Art in the autumn to study theatre and design.

During the same period, drummer John Start ended his 18-month association with the group. There had never been any conflict, but no great intimacy either. After Easter, Start had little or no contact with the group, mainly because he was studying for six O-levels, a not inconsiderable task for a William Grimshaw pupil. "I had other things going on. At weekends I used to go dinghy sailing. Pete came down occasionally, but he wasn't a sailor. I was very keen. That, to me, was what life was all about, sitting in a boat, sailing across the water in the salty air. I didn't want to stay in London with funny geezers like Ray Davies. I think I left by June, but I can't remember the *exact* moment. There was nothing formal. I didn't say, 'I'm never going to play with this group again.' But it was almost a release not having to be with Ray. That's the feeling I got. I didn't feel I was part of something that was going to go anywhere. It didn't mean anything to me at all. I didn't feel that Ray was particularly talented or clever. Unconsciously, it was just a release to be away from some-body that was a bit *troubled*. That's how I would sum it up."

Up until our interview in 2012, Start remained blithely unaware of Ray's emotionally disturbed childhood and adolescence, the details of which proved retrospectively instructive. "I picked that up somehow, even though I didn't know anything about it then. One of the reasons I didn't want to continue with the group was because I felt ill at ease with Ray. Now that I know more, I'm very glad I didn't continue with them. I was a fragile, stammering, jittery, blushing, nervous teenager with a difficult father. I didn't get any fatherly support from Ray, him being the older male as it were. It was more like *he* needed support from somebody and I wasn't in a position to offer that." Start completed school that summer, consigned his drum kit to history, then trained as a quantity surveyor for three years in Portsmouth, after which he became a wholesale jeweller. He never spoke to Ray or Dave Davies again.

Reduced to a trio, the others briefly fell in with local agent Danny Haggerty, who promised them access to US air bases, which were popular with aspiring R&B acts of the time. The hope was that such bookings might lead to a tour of Germany. Instead, the boys faced the indignity of playing as a makeshift backing band to the black bodybuilder and occasional singer Rick Wayne, who entertained the Americans with his displays of muscular prowess while his inappropriately named accompanists, the Musclemen, played a selection of instrumentals, usually climaxing with Duane Eddy's 'Shazam!'. During the set, Ray Davies and company would be asked to pass Wayne one of his smaller weights. As they feigned a feeble collapse, the black Adonis came to the rescue, effortlessly lifting the dumbbells as if they were made of cardboard. The Wayne experience ended abruptly when Ray was unable to attend a booking due to illness. Quaife recalls a final gig where he and Dave were forced to appear alone and did not get beyond an uneasy rendition of Cliff Richard's 'Do You Want To Dance' before being ignominiously ushered from the stage.

This humiliating interlude encouraged them to seek a professional drummer via the Musicians' Union. The successful candidate was Mickey Willett, a former member of Tommy Bruce & The Bruisers. He was first approached by Pete Quaife, who was impressed by his credentials and assurance. Several years older than Ray, Willett was confident and competent enough to win his approval.

Another character free and eager to assist the group was their neighbourhood friend, Peter 'Jonah' Jones. Since leaving William Grimshaw, he had been working as a car mechanic at the firm Henley's Jaguars. His foreman, Albert Medland, an ex-army commando, took exception to his longer than average hair and decided to teach him a lesson. One afternoon, Jones was called into Medland's office and set upon by six charge hands who proceeded to hold him down and attack his hair with a pair of clippers. He was left on the workshop floor, bruised and humiliated, with clumps of hair missing. Medland, fearful that he had gone too far, arranged for the boy to be driven to a barber's in the hope that a proper haircut might limit the damage. That night, Jones reported the incident to his imperious father who offered little sympathy. "You should have done what your foreman told you," he chided. Jones promptly quit his job, sabotaging Medland's Jaguar in a last act of retribution. Thereafter, he was able to spend more time fraternizing with the Davies brothers, driving the group to local gigs, setting up the equipment and occasionally joining them onstage. It was an exciting time.

Ray Davies, meanwhile, continued to veer between the worlds of art and pop music and simultaneously encountered a fellow excursionist, Barry Fantoni. An artist of Italian/Jewish ancestry Fantoni was an alumnus of Camberwell College of Arts and Crafts, from where he was allegedly expelled for setting fire to a chair. Reinstated, he became a scenester about town, occasionally teaching a painting course at Croydon Art College, providing magazines with illustrations and cartoons, and playing tenor saxophone at night. He remembers first encountering Davies one Saturday afternoon, a few months before, at the West End club, the Kaleidoscope. They were each auditioning for a spot in Hamilton King's Blues Messengers. As well as playing tenor saxophone, Fantoni was required to sing along with Davies on the chorus of King's cover of 'Money'. Barry was impressed by Davies' enthusiasm and unsurprised when the burly King took him on. Fantoni's services were not required.

The cartoonist was equally struck by Davies' guitar playing and felt he had a fair chance of succeeding in the pop game. Fantoni himself was part of this new age of opportunity and achieved a certain notoriety that summer when one of his Pop Art 'paintings', *Nude Reclining*, was admitted to the Royal

Academy's Summer Exhibition credited to the pseudonymous 'Stuart Harris'. It was actually a collaboration with fellow *Private Eye* cartoonist William Rushton and depicted a judge, a cardinal and a general ogling a book of pin-up models. The so-called satire boom had reached its apogee in mid-1963 with *Private Eye* magazine hitting the mainstream and the recently launched BBC television show *That Was The Week That Was* (produced by Ned Sherrin) attracting 12 million viewers. Strangely enough, considering what was to follow, Sherrin's irreverent series rapidly lost its edge and much of its audience. It was almost as if news events – cultural and political – were speeding forward with such alacrity and improbability that they were *beyond* satire.

On 3 June, the reformist Pope John XXIII died at the age of 81. The most revered Pope of the century, his demise inspired tributes throughout the world and particularly in Ireland where his photograph would remain on display in Catholic households for a generation and more. Northern Ireland journalists noted incredulously that his death was privately mourned even in some liberal Protestant homes where acknowledging the papacy had previously been synonymous with apostasy. In the racially torn United States, Martin Luther King announced that he had a dream and inspired a new generation to demonstrate publicly against institutionalized injustices. At the Berlin Wall John Fitzgerald Kennedy made his famous freedom speech; within months he would be slain by an assassin's bullet.

Normally, such earth-shaking news would have rendered events at home irrelevant, but these were exceptional times. It was a strange accident of history that saw Britain consumed by a dramatic and rapid series of social, political and cultural changes that would transform the decade more completely than any turning of a calendar. The sudden death of Labour leader Hugh Gaitskill at the beginning of 1963 was a relatively small-scale event, but set in motion the rise of Harold Wilson, whose prominence grew with each passing month. Politics provided the greatest sensations of the year as stories of espionage and scandal enthralled the British nation.

On 1 July, Ray Davies' Hornsey colleague John Philby was returning by ferry from the Isle of Wight when he was floored by a newspaper headline revealing that his father had defected to the Soviet Union the previous January. For the 17-year-old Young Socialist it was a life-changing event. Kim Philby had finally been exposed as the 'Third Man' – the masterspy who had assisted KGB agents Donald Maclean and Guy Burgess in fleeing to Moscow back in 1951. The belated exposé was a terrible embarrassment to Conservative Prime Minister Harold Macmillan who, when serving as Foreign Secretary eight years before, insisted he had "no reason to conclude that Mr Philby had at any time betrayed the interests of this country".

If the endorsement of Philby now brought Macmillan's judgement and leadership into question, so too did the ongoing Profumo affair. The embarrassing spectacle of a Cabinet Minister's liaison with a teenage 'call girl' might normally have passed unnoticed were it not for her fleeting sexual involvement with Captain Evgeni Ivanov, a prominent naval attaché from the Russian Embassy. Profumo at first denied the charge but under scrutiny from the Secret Service confirmed his indiscretion and resigned. Wilson, without overstating the case, spoke of "disclosures which have shocked the moral conscience of the nation". The scandal proved sufficient to focus attention on the Tory party as a whole and the newspapers were full of wild and whirling stories concerning a network of organized prostitutes busily servicing various Members of Parliament, wealthy landowners and High Court judges. A report commissioned by Macmillan and produced by Lord Denning was remarkable for its detailed descriptions of homosexuality, kinky sex and perverted orgies. It was akin to reading the fulfilment of Douglas Warth's fall of the empire, anti-homosexual diatribes of 1952.

In keeping with the times, accomplished film track composer John Barry, already famous for his James Bond themes, issued a tellingly titled single, 'Kinky', as an oblique comment on the era. *Private Eye* even amended Macmillan's oft misunderstood catchphrase from the Fifties ('You've Never Had It So Good') into the ribald 'You've Never Had It So Often'. Such highly publicized outrage reinforced the view among British youth that their elders were not necessarily their equals or betters. The vestiges of Victorian respect for politicians and statesmen who hid vices behind cant denouncements of juvenile delinquency and adolescent promiscuity gradually gave way to an insidious cynicism. This was the age of the instant event when incidents and trends converged upon and replaced each other with giddy rapidity. Arctic winter, papal death, presidential assassination and even a preposterously executed Great Train Robbery flashed past in a blur of headlines.

None of this appeared to affect the Davies family's capacity for partying. Cine camera footage captures them in the year of scandal and Beatlemania, cavorting around the front room while music plays in the background. The sisters still look lithe and eager to dance. Peggy, peroxide blonde in imitation of Marilyn Monroe, appears stylish and assured. Dave Davies, fresh-faced with exceptionally long hair for the period, writhes frantically, arms waving, as his partner and young niece Jackie attempts to keep up. Ever the observer, Ray sidles into the room, looking stylish in a French-style Beatle haircut, unafraid to show that gap-toothed smile. He manages to look simultaneously engaged and distant but, most notably, *happy*. By far the strongest presence on camera are the nephews and cousins, milling in the foreground. Bobby Whitbread who, only a few years before, had lost his mother Rene, his father Robert and his home country of Canada, appears the most exuberant and celebratory of the entire bunch. It is as if adversity has amplified his appetite for life.

In September 1963, Ray Davies enrolled at Croydon Art College, but he seemed permanently distracted. Much of his time was spent in the college canteen playing guitar and mouth organ, while fellow students looked on. This was hardly surprising as, by now, Davies was committed to playing music semi-professionally. Dave, still a dominant figure in the group, had changed their name from the Ramrods to the Boll-Weevils, this time adapting a name from 'Boll Weevil Song', the B-side of Eddie Cochran's 1959 single, 'Something Else'. Arguably, pop music had never been as much in vogue in the UK as it was in late 1963, largely thanks to the Beatles whose popularity would soon reach unprecedented levels. After seven weeks at number 1 with 'From Me To You', they had released the strident, wailing 'She Loves You', an exuberant litany with a magical catchphrase ("Yeah, Yeah, Yeah") that was echoed in newspaper headlines whenever their name was mentioned.

The Beatles arrived at the perfect psychological moment, re-inforcing a working-class assault on fashion, music and cinema.

Their influence spread through every stratum of British society, even reaching the ears of a tall, plummy young man whose tastes had been refined in the august environs of one of the country's leading public schools, Marlborough College. Robert Wace, like many from his class and generation, was being prepared for a position in the family business. His father owned the process engravers Wace & Co. in London's Farringdon Road. They supplied printing blocks to advertising agencies and Robert was employed as a sales representative, a low rung on the ladder to success. Observing the onset of Beatlemania, Wace dreamed of breaking free from the tedium of everyday employment and seeking fame as a minor pop star. He found a welcome ally in his best friend, Grenville Collins, a share dealer who worked at the London Stock Exchange. He too was intrigued by the rise of the Beatles and particularly their suave manager Brian Epstein who, despite his inexperience, had already established himself as the most successful pop mogul since Larry Parnes back in the Fifties. Collins agreed to play 'manager' to Wace's putative 'pop star', but first they had to face likely disapprobation from their respective employers. Robert's father considered the entire idea preposterous but reluctantly allowed his son a year's grace to prove himself with this silly pop business. Thereafter, he expected him to return to the long term security of Wace & Co. or even use his public school connections to get a government post at the Ministry of Defence

It was while hanging around Denmark Street, Soho's Tin Pan Alley, that Collins and Wace met Terry Kennedy, a music entrepreneur, who would later manage the Ivy League, co-produce Donovan, enter publishing with Southern Music and establish the King's Agency with madcap manager Reg Calvert. Kennedy was not interested in signing Robert Wace but, knowing he was seeking a backing group, provided a phone number of an acquaintance: Mickey Willett. The drummer was happy to set up a meeting between Wace and Collins and the other Boll-Weevils on a Sunday afternoon rehearsal at the Athenaeum Ballroom in Muswell Hill.

Ray Davies was struck by the society duo, whose upper-class demeanour eclipsed anything he had ever seen, even at art school. They were only a couple of years older than him, but oozed a sophistication and confidence that was alluring. "I think they were looking to break out of a society they possibly felt they were trapped in. The privileged leisure classes trying to break into the common. It was quite groovy to be working class and I guess we were." Wace came up with an intriguing proposition. He promised to secure them lucrative engagements on the society circuit in return for a brief solo spot in the act.

The arrangement proved beneficial to both parties and, according to Willett, some try-out demos were recorded with engineer Bill Farley at Regent Sound Studios in Denmark Street. They proved uninspired. Fortunately, the promises of well-paid gigs, including debutante coming-out parties, turned out to be true. Dave Davies' diary documents a rehearsal showcase at the Duke of Edinburgh pub in Wood Green on 15 September, revealing "lots of Grenville and Robert's friends were there". Wace had some calling cards printed with the new group name, 'Robert Wace & The Boll-Weevils'. These were distributed like confetti among his affluent associates and a succession of private bookings followed.

As well as financing a clothes-buying spree at John Stephen's fashionable boutique in Carnaby Street, Collins and Wace somehow pulled off a major coup that at first seemed unbelievable. With a gumption that bordered on the presumptuous, Robert had phoned the NEMS agency office of the great Brian Epstein. Even more remarkably, he was put through by the receptionist, possibly on the strength of his voice alone. Wace's perfectly enunciated speech and persuasive public school demeanour immediately differentiated him from the usual barrow boy boasters and music biz hustlers that Epstein disdained. Wace sounded like a social equal, at the very least, and his message was simple: "I know this really good group. Why don't you come along and see them?" Epstein had a thousand reasons to decline the invitation. The Beatles were in constant demand and two other major acts, Gerry And The Pacemakers and Billy J. Kramer With The Dakotas, were topping the charts. He was also in the process of launching the career of his latest protégée, Cilla Black. Insanely busy as he must have been, Epstein agreed to attend a Boll-Weevils' rehearsal upstairs at the Camden Head pub in Islington. Perhaps, his decision wasn't as crazy as it seemed. Over the past year, he had not only supervised the Beatles' extraordinary ascension to pop fame, but expanded his interests. There were lesser but still promising signings, including the much respected Big Three and the Fourmost, who were rewarded with two Lennon/McCartney hits, 'Hello Little Girl' and 'I'm In Love'. It was almost as if Epstein believed that the Top 20 could accommodate every act that played at the Cavern. Although some groups – notably Kingsize Taylor And The Dominoes and the Swinging Blue Jeans – resisted his advances, the reflected glory of the Beatles and the possibility of acquiring one of their discarded compositions was almost irresistible. For all that, Epstein was well aware of his Achilles' heel. On two other occasions, when he had signed acts who were not channelled through EMI or placed in the fastidious hands of producer George Martin, the results were dismal. Both Tommy Quickly and the Remo Four had been passed over to the Pye label and languished in obscurity. Even when gifted with a Lennon/McCartney composition, 'Tip Of My Tongue', Quickly's career stalled. The curse of Pye would not easily be forgotten.

Dave Davies' diary exclusively reveals that the Epstein audition took place on Thursday 26 September, a remarkably early date considering that Collins and Wace had barely arrived themselves. It underlined that the society duo was already thinking beyond merely hiring a backing group for Robert. Indeed, Wace did not even sing at the audition, a clear enough indication that the focus was on the Boll-Weevils. "We were merely considering all possibilities," Collins claims. "We thought that the group was very very good indeed. Through luring Mr Epstein it was, in a way, a confirmation and a frame of reference for us. We were total beginners in what, in those days, was called 'the music business' . . . The group was rehearsing in London anyway and Mr Epstein was curious."

The timing turned out to be terrible and the audition anti-climactic. Drummer Mickey Willett had booked a holiday in Manchester that week and announced that he was unavailable. Even Jonah wasn't around to offer moral support, musical accompaniment or assistance with the equipment. Epstein arrived punctually and was "courteous and pleasant" according to Collins. He listened politely, even attentively, but said little. Then he disappeared into the night, frozen with indignation at having to help Robert Wace start his cold-stalled car.

"Fingers crossed," Dave wrote in his diary, evidently without too much conviction. If Epstein ever entertained the notion of extending his NEMS empire with a parallel series of beat groups in the capital, then it was soon forgotten. "He turned them down," Wace says, "although he was interested in Ray as a solo artiste. I don't think he was *terribly* interested though – he wasn't exactly bursting the door down as they say. Lots of people can express interest but it wasn't much more than that." Grenville Collins recalls Epstein advising them "to get rid of the group and promote Raymond Davies as a solo singer", a conceit that nobody entertained. What Epstein's visit did confirm was an underlying interest in the group which Collins considered a positive outcome. "It is always valuable to see what else is happening. It puts one's own endeavours into the context of the over-all."

On Saturday 28 September, the group ended an eventful week supping champagne at a wedding reception for which they received a £15 fee, part of which had to be shared with their deputy drummer for the evening, Johnny Bremner. Robert Wace, who supposedly had his front teeth capped for cosmetic assurance, enjoyed his solo spot, although he had a mere handful of cover songs in his repertoire – Trini Lopez's 'If I Had A Hammer', Freddie And The Dreamers' 'I'm Telling You Now' and the Buddy Holly songs 'Rave On' and 'Peggy Sue'. Possibly in unconscious deference to Epstein, he was already planning to add a couple of recent Merseybeat chart-topping hits, Gerry And The Pacemakers' 'I Like It' and Billy J. Kramer's 'Bad To Me'.

No live tapes exist of the Boll-Weevils, with or without Robert Wace, but their standard set list was revealing, not least because Ray had no featured vocal. Still uncertain about his abilities, he deferred to his younger brother on the more raucous offerings and preferred to sing in unison on other tunes. Wace remembers those times as a period when the group was a genuine democracy rather than a vehicle for Ray Davies' unfolding talent. Their repertoire included two showcase numbers – Howlin' Wolf's 'Smokestack Lightning' and the gutsy Berry Gordy composition 'Money', currently one of the highlights of the Beatles' live show and a prime candidate for their forthcoming album, *With The Beatles*. The rest was standard beat group fare with a noticeable Rolling Stones influence in the song selection. "Ray and Dave were singing R&B numbers like 'Little Queenie', 'Poison Ivy', 'Route 66' and several other Chuck Berry and Bo Diddley numbers," Wace recalls. "Dave was singing a lot more then. We were always a bit worried about Ray's vocal ability in those early days. He didn't have much of a voice compared with Lennon and McCartney or Gerry Marsden. But he did improve his technique a great deal. He realized the limitations of his voice and worked on the strengths. I was doing my four numbers at the end and they were having a good laugh. We were having a great time. I didn't have enough confidence to stay up there for half an hour. It was mainly for a particular social circle. One night, we went outside of the circle and I didn't enjoy it very much."

This was an understatement *in excelsis*. Wace was ignominiously booed offstage before even completing his short set. What had been politely tolerated, even applauded, by his society friends in Knightsbridge was considered laughable in the harsher surroundings of an East End club. His act had been exposed for what it was – an unintended camp comic fusion of Buddy Holly and Noël Coward. The humiliation instantly squashed Wace's dreams of pop stardom, but it was not all bad news. After the show, Ray suggested that the Boll-Weevils should consider turning professional, with assistance from their society svengalis. Wace agreed to work more closely with Collins in a dual management set-up that was closer to a gentleman's agreement. Employing stock-broker logic, Grenville initially offered to throw in half his earnings from the City in return for a 50 per cent share of the group's profits. All things considered, it was a generous offer, with no strings attached.

Faced with the prospect of securing a record deal, Wace and Collins returned to Regent Sound Studios on 19 October and financed the recording of two songs, the Dave Davies' Merseybeat pastiche 'I Believed You' and Leiber & Stoller's familiar Coasters' hit 'I'm A Hog For You, Baby'. 'Jonah' Jones, their ever-supportive assistant road manager, was invited to provide a Bo Diddley shuffle to embellish the rhythm. The session confirmed that the younger brother was still a powerful presence, even as a fledgling pop songsmith. "It was probably one of the first things I wrote," Dave says. "It was done in one afternoon and I just stuck some words on. At the same time I wrote another song, 'One Fine Day'. There were other half ideas that didn't get recorded. One I had that resurfaced years later as a demo was 'Do You Wish To Be A Man'. I was a big fan of Hank Williams and I later wrote a couple of songs like that, folky things that nobody particularly picked up on." The demotion of Dave's material would be partly down to his own indolence but mainly a result of his brother's later flowering as songwriter. At this point, however, Ray had no ambitions or even any intentions of succeeding as a composer. All that would change before the end of the year.

Three days after the Regent Sound visit, the brothers, plus Quaife, signed preliminary contracts, engaging Wace and Collins as managers. A separate document dated 29 October was produced for drummer Mickey Willett, appointing Collins as manager with Wace adding his name as a witness. The slight discrepancy in the dating may have been a matter of convenience or the first indication that Willett's standing was less secure than that of the others.

One unexpected outcome of the signing was the belated revelation that Pete Quaife was actually the son of an American serviceman. "I don't think Pete knew," says his younger half-brother, David. "That was the first time I knew, and Pete was sitting there. He probably had an idea about it but he didn't want to ask. [Collins and Wace] spoke in a different language. They said, 'Mrs Quaife, you've got to sign this', then Dad stood up and they said, 'but you're not his father'. It was a shock to the family."

In another of their perennial rethinks, it was decided that the name Boll-Weevils was too obscure for a pop group. Instead, they settled on the Ravens, a title borrowed indirectly from Edgar Allan Poe's poem *The Raven*, which had partly inspired the current box office hit comic horror movie of the same name, directed by Roger Corman and starring Vincent Price and Peter Lorre as rival magicians. The Ravens sounded dark and mysterious, but it was almost too good a group name. Several other minor UK bands of the period had also borrowed the moniker and an American outfit of the same title were about to release a single. Until their orbits collided, however, the various Ravens could happily co-exist.

Booking dates and communications with Ray and Dave were initially frustrating for the management as the Davies family had no telephone at Denmark Terrace. The ever-amenable Jonah came to the rescue by allowing them to place and answer calls from the newsagent's, much to the fury of his father. When the messages extended beyond dusk and late into the evening, Mr Jones became inconsolable. "It used to drive him crazy," his son attests. He still disapproved of Peter associating with the Davies' clan, the more so when he learned of their late-night partying and forays into the West End. Enforcing a new policy, he started bolting the front door at 10 p.m., forcing his son to seek refuge in the local police station. The duty sergeant became used to the sight of the bleary-eyed teenager turning up in the early hours and asking permission to sleep in one of the empty cells. A happy routine was established in which the sergeant acted like a benevolent hotelier, providing cups of tea and an early morning call. At 6 a.m., when the news-papers arrived, Mr Jones would unbolt his door and his son would stumble through, weary as an over-walked dog. Jonah knew better than to complain. It was part of the price of befriending the Davies brothers.

By now, Ray Davies was becoming used to the society soirées that Wace and Collins were providing, but there was competition. The champagne and caviar circuit was dominated by the more modish A Band Of Angels, featuring singer Mike D'Abo, who would later replace Paul Jones in Manfred Mann. Nevertheless, Robert and Grenville boasted some impressive high society contacts, several of whom now regarded pop groups as acceptable entertainment. The Beatles' recent appearance before the Queen Mother at the Prince of Wales Theatre melted many old prejudices. For the younger aristocrats, the presence of a pop group at a private party was de rigueur.

On 10 November, Lady Jacqueline Rufus-Isaacs, daughter of the third Marquess of Reading, celebrated her seventeenth birthday with a lively musical set provided by the newly named Ravens. With her model looks, Jackie was already a poster girl for the nobility and was later described as "one of the most vivacious party-goers of her generation". It is salutary to consider that she was actually nine months older than Dave Davies.

Suddenly, it seemed as though there was no limit to the social heights in which the group soared. Robert Wace regularly appeared with a female companion, who turned out to be no less than the Dowager Countess Cowley. Jane Elizabeth Mary Aiyar was the daughter of Ramiah Dorasawamy Aiyar, a fellow of the Royal College of Surgeons. In February 1961, she married Denis Wellesley, the fifth Earl of Cowley, a direct descendant of the Duke of Wellington. The following year, she assumed the title Countess Cowley, although Wace would have known that under Debrett's rules of etiquette she should be introduced in company as Lady Cowley. Evidently, she preferred the nickname 'Tiger', especially when roaming the pop jungle in her new guise. "Countess Cowley is some cookie," wrote one 'Smart Set' columnist. "Everybody calls her Tiger – with reason. She has black eyes and masses of black hair and a certain animal quality so dear to the hearts of male chauvinist pigs." Tiger's vivacity and outrageous confidence appealed to the Davies brothers who were amazed by her ability to cross class thresholds with such assurance. Not restricted to the society circuit, she was happy to turn up at a working-class club or youth hostel gig dressed as though she were attending a ball. It was another sign of liberation and shifting values among the junior aristocracy of which Collins and Wace were now honorary members.

CHAPTER SEVEN

THE POWER PLAYERS

Playing at debutante parties was a curious, but not unpleasing, digression. Class consciousness was still present and the north Londoners were often treated with the same benign condescension that their hosts would display towards a favourite tradesman. Certain boundaries were still in place that could not be breached. Performance fees were modest but there were plenty of perks, particularly at private parties where champagne flowed freely and finger food was available in the kitchen. The clientele – invited guests rather than paying customers – were relaxed and indiscriminate in their tastes. For them, the Ravens were merely an optional extra, an adjunct to the evening's entertainment. In this respect, it was an easy gig, as undemanding as a wedding date and a lot more fun.

Not that everyone was happy. Drummer Mickey Willett, older and more worldly wise, found himself placed in a difficult position as the business conduit between the Davies brothers and their management. His attitude towards Collins and Wace was like that of a fired-up shop steward addressing an aggrieved factory owner or corporation head. Class politics was always an underlying factor in any discussion, even if it was never stated. It was an inverse prejudice that the society entrepreneurs had already experienced when attempting to sell the Boll-Weevils or Ravens to the sharper club owners and small-time operators who worked on the fringes of show business. Often they were treated like dilettantes playing the game of pop for their own amusement. At such moments, their urbane demeanour may have worked against them. One experienced road manager, who later worked with the Davies brothers, betrayed exactly that bias from the very first time he encountered the high society pair. "How they became their personal managers, I haven't the slightest idea. Collins and Wace were just there to make money. All they knew was that people were making money out of it. They knew nothing about the business but they had the group play society dos. Wace booked them to play in a tent for the horsey crowd. I heard him on the phone saying, 'Oh yes, darling, you'll adore them. They say things like "fuck" – you'll love them. They're quite crude.' And he was right. They loved it!"

'Jonah' Jones recalls one such booking in "the south of England" where he spotted actress Lynn Redgrave among the revellers. "They had a circus fairground there, it was amazing, an absolutely crazy party. We were so rough it must have been comical for that high society crowd. They could let their hair down, dance and enjoy the music. We crossed boundaries."

One of the first public bookings for the Ravens was at Muswell Hill's Northbank on 23 November. It was an unforgettable experience for David Quaife, who had never seen his brother perform professionally before. "I was about thirteen. Peter 'Jonah' Jones was on the maracas, and they were playing 'Little Queenie'."

The atmosphere was understandably subdued as this was the evening after President Kennedy's assassination in Dallas. It was almost surprising that the performance was allowed to take place. The Saturday newspapers contained photos of Jackie Kennedy bending over her husband's body, alongside details of the prime suspect, Lee Harvey Oswald, whose first reported words were "it's all over now". In New York, UN delegates, upon hearing the grim news, had expressed hope that the assassin was neither a Negro nor a Jew. In London, Prime Minister Alec Douglas-Home appeared on television within hours of the tragedy announcing: "There are times in life when mind and heart stand still and one such time is now." He went on to pay tribute to "this young, gay and brave statesman, killed in the full vigour of his manhood, when he bore on his shoulders all the cares and the hopes of the world". The assassination left a feeling of helplessness and an encroaching sense that the events of tomorrow were nothing more than a scarily empty page.

Ray managed to see some of the news bulletins on television that terrible weekend and it profoundly affected his view of America. He felt a lot safer in north London. Notwithstanding the society outings, small gigs kept him grounded in his local community. "One afternoon the vicar invited us to play for the old folks in Crouch End Church Hall and afterwards this little old lady in a woolly hat waited for me by the door and said: 'Ray, this is wonderful music. It really got my feet tapping.'"

While Collins and Wace plotted their next move, there were rumblings of discontent among the Ravens, primarily instigated by Mickey Willett, who started asking some provocative questions. "The only sore point in the entire business came with the bookings and the money. Ray and Dave looked to me somewhat because I was older and had experience. I had to sort things out with Robert. There was a gig in Lewisham and we were getting about £5 each which, in those days, wasn't bad. We were told that the managers were getting their small cut. Maria (my girlfriend, later wife) happened to find a purse in the ladies' toilet that belonged to the girl who ran the place. When Maria opened the purse she found a bill made out to Robert and Grenville for something like £64. I told Ray and Dave about this and they were up in arms. That was the start of the rot."

When he approached Wace, Willett was told that the bill included a variety of other reimbursed expenses connected with the booking. It was a plausible explanation, and nothing more was said. Wace was understandably indignant about being challenged in such a manner, particularly as his partner had already invested a substantial sum of his earnings supporting and promoting the group. They were only just starting in the business themselves and already there was mistrust and suspicion. The carefree Dave Davies dismissed such concerns in his usual cavalier manner, but his brother was more likely to brood over such matters. Willett could not rid his mind of how much his managers might be making, even while conceding that the Ravens were making decent money on the society circuit thanks to their backers. Having unwittingly cast himself in the role of the group's treasurer, he greeted each booking with an accountant's cockatrice countenance. One evening, there was a double booking: a pub date, followed by a party thrown by a Greek tycoon. The Ravens left the pub at closing time, drove to a large house in Notting Hill and set up their equipment. They played before the salubrious gathering till long after midnight. Willett, who had to get up for work early the next morning, was keen to go home and Ray Davies had college commitments to consider. As they were leaving, Willett claims he was confronted by Wace who supposedly offered them £20 or more on behalf of the hosts to extend the set. "I had a word with the boys," says Willett, "but we were dead tired so we packed up and left. The next day when we saw Robert and Grenville again they said, 'You bloody fools! Why didn't you stop and play? You were going to get £100 each from Aristotle Onassis if you'd played a couple of hours longer.' I said, 'That's a bloody difference from what you said last night, Robert!' Robert felt I'd misunderstood and said it was definitely £100 each. But if that had been the case I'd have played until my arms dropped off!"

Wace was adamant that this was another example of Willett misreading events and conjuring a conspiracy theory where none existed. "It wasn't Aristotle Onassis' party, it was George Livanos'," he points out, puncturing one of the drummer's florid memories. "A friend of mine who was a society swell organized this party for [shipping magnate] George Livanos who was one of the richest people in the world. His money made the Onassis family look like paupers. They were all Greeks there and basically they got excited and kept saying, 'If you play for another fifteen minutes, we'll give you an additional £20', but it certainly wasn't £100. They did this two or three times actually until, as I recall, one of the waiters made a pass at Dave. The waiter was drunk, made a pass, and they wouldn't play any more. And that was it."

The personality clash between Willett and the management, made worse by the fact that it was based on misinterpreted motives and misunderstandings, was becoming irksome. Wace and Collins felt that they had treated the group fairly and generously and resented the negative influence of the drummer whose suspicions were causing unspoken friction. Although Willett believed he had the support of Ray Davies when questioning the financial arrangements, the chief Raven said nothing himself. Ironically, Willett's outspokenness was undermining his own standing. By his own admission he was always an outsider, a late addition to the group

who lived several miles away in Palmers Green. He seldom social-
ized with the others, outside of gigs and rehearsals, and missed
several meetings between the group and their management at the
Davies' home. More pertinently, he was several years older than
the brothers and slightly detached from their milieu. While they
adored blues musicians and Carnaby Street fashions, his musical
tastes were more mainstream and he preferred smart suits and
shorter hair.

When Wace and Collins politely suggested that his attitude
and image might be wrong for the group, nobody jumped to
his defence. He was not disliked by anybody, merely expendable.
Events came to a head after a press reception at the *Daily Mail*
when the drummer was informed that his services were no longer
required. Pete Quaife recalls that he was chosen to impart the
bad news, but Willett already knew who was responsible. There
was no question of long term notice or compensation as he
realized after re-reading the fourteenth paragraph of the management contract he had signed with Grenville Collins only weeks
before: "This agreement shall be determinable by the personal
manager at any time by giving seven days' notice in writing to
the performer . . ."

Hurt and indignant, Willett instinctively turned to Ray Davies
who responded with an emotional commitment worthy of Pontius
Pilate. "When I confronted Ray on this he got upset and said, 'To
be honest, Mike, I don't want you to go, but what can I do?' We
parted good friends, though I was annoyed at the time. I felt I
was being pushed out for being their spokesman . . . Ray and
Dave were very gullible in those days. Wace was the villain of
the piece as far as I was concerned. He was instrumental in getting
me out. He got at Dave first . . . I said to Robert and Grenville:
'I'll take the pair of you on outside now!' I was really fuming. I
was livid that they'd gone behind my back and persuaded Dave
to get at Ray to get me chucked out. We never had any problems
before this." In common with John Start, Willett never spoke to
the Davies brothers again. There was no full-time replacement
available. Instead, they hired an even older drummer than Willett
to deputize for the remainder of the year.

While the Ravens were still adjusting to line-up changes, newspapers were full of stories about the Beatles. When Epstein had

attended the Boll-Weevils' rehearsal back in September, 'She Loves You' was number 1, but since then events had escalated. 'She Loves You' did not merely repeat the chart-topping longevity of 'From Me To You' – it actually defied gravity. It hit number 1, went down, then returned to the top at the end of November. During the interim, the Beatles had appeared on *Sunday Night At The London Palladium* and, a month later, the Royal Variety Performance in front of the Queen Mother. The popular press proclaimed the birth of a new phenomenon: Beatlemania. And 'She Loves You' was *still* at number 1. Eventually, it was only the Beatles themselves who could remove this refluent disc, with another of their own songs. With advance orders of one million, 'I Want To Hold Your Hand' entered the charts at number 1, the first disc to achieve this distinction since Cliff Richard's 'The Young Ones' back in January 1962. For the next two and a half years, every Beatles single would do the same, establishing their godhead as the most consistent chart-toppers of all time.

Brian Epstein was still the envy of the pop world and the ultimate measure of entrepreneurial success. He was not an easy act to follow and the onset of Beatlemania did not necessarily mean that newer groups were guaranteed success, let alone signed. The competition was intense. As neophytes in the management business, Collins and Wace were struggling to find any record company or publisher seriously interested in the renamed Ravens. Wace dutifully hawked their hastily recorded demos around Tin Pan Alley only to be stone-walled. One exception was Tony Hiller, a 36-year-old former song and dance man, who worked as general manager at the London offices of the American song publishers Mills Music. He displayed old-fashioned courtesy and actually accepted the demos for consideration, but did not act quickly enough. Faced with prevarication, Collins and Wace continued their search. What they needed was a more powerful ally to negotiate the shark-infested waters of the business, an experienced, uncompromising figure who could manipulate the record company A&R men, agents, producers and other architects of fame. They found the perfect master of pop *realpolitik* in Larry Page.

Since his retirement from pop singing at the end of the Fifties, the former Teenage Rage had relocated to Wales where he attempted to find contentment as a pub landlord surrounded by memorabilia from his all too brief golden era. Living off past glories was a vacuous pastime. Page missed the cut and thrust of showbiz and determined to find a way back in. A meeting with the garrulous Eric Morley of Mecca Enterprises proved productive. In a reverse of recent trends, Mecca were converting failing regional theatres, cinemas and older ballrooms into dance halls in order to exploit the youth demographic. Morley needed a consultant manager and provided a simple remit: target a venue, refurbish and relaunch, then check the takings after three months. If there was a profit, Mecca would increase their investment accordingly. Page applied this business method to the Orchid Ballroom in Coventry with impressive results. Before long, he was besieged by young singers, groups and myriad entertainers in search of bookings. Revelling in the role of talent spotter, Page staged contests at the Orchid usually for a nominal prize. This created a local buzz and, in turn, enabled Larry to take on managerial responsibilities for several of the acts.

Page still retained several contacts in Tin Pan Alley from his Teenage Rage days and his exploits did not go unnoticed. He was invited to attend a summit in Birmingham hosted by several key players in the industry. Chief among them was the imperious Philip Solomon, one of the most powerful, ruthless and historically underrated entrepreneurs of the Sixties. Originally, Solomon had hoped to become a vet, but his father decreed: "It wouldn't be proper for a young Jew." Instead, Solomon became a prominent player in the record industry, beginning in Northern Ireland. During the Fifties, he promoted various middle-of-the-road acts, notably Ruby Murray, then moved to London, setting up offices in New Oxford Street, assisted by his astute and glamorous wife, Dorothy. Over the next few years he would infiltrate every area of the music business with interests in management, publishing, production, record label ownership and, ultimately, pirate radio. An expert exploiter of talent, Solomon felt he could use Page as part of the cast list in his ever-expanding entrepreneurial empire. But he was not alone.

Another important figure in attendance was the renowned music publisher Eddie Kassner. Since the success of 'Rock Around The Clock' he had not been idle and, having witnessed the rise of the Beatles and the commercial power of the Lennon/McCartney writing team, he was keener than ever to acquire young talent. His masterplan was to finance a management company that would allow him access to new groups and songwriters whose publishing he could then acquire almost automatically. Since Page had recently proven himself in Coventry as a collector of young talent, he was deemed the perfect recruit. Choosing between the suitors was no easy decision for the embattled Page. Flattered, uncertain, intrigued but cautious, Page needed time to weigh up his options. These were powerful players, not to be trifled with. Solomon, in particular, had a persuasive personality and browbeating dominance that many found irresistible. It was even present at the hotel restaurant where they dined. "This food isn't fit for a pig!" Solomon told the maître d', who scuttled back to the kitchen in search of an alternative dish. Not that Solomon was satisfied. "Then he refused to pay the bill," Page remembers. "It was unbelievable."

The fourth party at the dinner table was Dick Rowe, head of A&R at Decca Records. Another music business veteran who, like Solomon and Kassner, was born in the Twenties, Rowe had spanned the ages, signing and producing countless acts from crooner Jimmy Young to rock 'n' roller Billy Fury and the premier instrumental duo and Shadows' offshoots Jet Harris & Tony Meehan. Rowe was a pleasant, avuncular figure who nevertheless had an astute understanding of management technique, calculated brinksmanship and expertly timed diplomacy. He had already gravitated towards the most powerful entrepreneurs of the past decade – befriending and negotiating with every major player from Larry Parnes to Don Arden. One of the few figures with whom he failed to establish a relationship was Brian Epstein – an error of judgement that had cost him many Merseybeat signings, including the Beatles. He had already rectified that error by signing the Rolling Stones and winning the everlasting admiration of their ingenu svengali, Andrew Loog Oldham. Rowe reserved his greatest respect for Phil Solomon, whom he regarded as "the shrewdest of them all". He later signed a string of Solomon artistes almost, it seemed, on demand. Page was not alone in concluding that "Solomon had Dick Rowe in his pocket and he *owned* the BBC".

After deep consideration, Page decided to throw in his lot with Eddie Kassner rather than Solomon. He figured, quite rightly, that

Kassner would be away in New York much of the time and therefore less likely to inhibit his own manoeuvres. Their partnership was formalized later that year when, on 24 October, Denmark Productions was registered as a limited company. It ratified the arrangement whereby Page, acting as general manager, would sign and nurture new talent and, if desirable, pass over their publishing to Kassner.

Page could be forgiven for thinking he had signed some kind of Faustian pact. Suddenly, his fortunes transformed in scarcely believable fashion. Dick Rowe, the discriminating dean of Decca, descended on Coventry as if it were the new Liverpool. Over the next 12 months he would acquire a small battalion of Page-managed acts, all of whom emanated from the Orchid Ballroom talent shows. Page was still congratulating himself on his Midas touch when he discovered an unpalatable truth. Eddie Kassner was pulling strings in the background via additional financial incentives. "Kassner had Dick Rowe in his pocket too!"

Rowe respected the music industry's power players but he was also a minor visionary in his own right. He had briefly defected from Decca a few years before to run the Top Rank label. That experience, along with his previous production duties back in the Fifties, allowed him to observe the British music industry unblinkered. Overriding the fiscal caution of his Decca boss, Sir Edward Lewis, he was happy to license material from independent producers such as the mavericks Joe Meek and Bunny Lewis. Rowe was especially enamoured of American producers who seemed capable of magically creating their own sound and had an arsenal of tricks beyond the imaginations of their staid UK label counterparts, some of whom still seemed stuck in the Fifties. Rowe dreamed of enlisting Atlantic label songwriter/producer Bert Berns, the man responsible for overseeing such international hits as the Drifters' 'Under The Boardwalk' and 'Saturday Night At The Movies' and co-writer of the Isley Brothers' 'Twist And Shout', made newly famous by the Beatles. Within a year, Rowe's fantasy would be realized but, in the meantime, he commissioned a relatively unknown American in the hope of adding some glitz to Decca's production roster.

Chicago-born Shel Talmy had arrived in Britain during the summer of 1962 with limited experience. He had trained as a recording engineer in Los Angeles, but worked with nobody of note. A friendly producer – Nik Venet at Capitol Records – had given him acetates and even allowed him to present them as his own work if he urgently needed a job. Talmy was merely intending to finance an extended holiday when he turned up at Decca Records seeking work. Dick Rowe entertained his vanities and listened intently as he bluffed and blustered, while playing the Beach Boys' 'Surfin' Safari' and Lou Rawls' 'There's Music In The Air' which he insisted he had a hand in producing. Rowe was amused by the braggadocio and cared little about the authenticity of Talmy's grander claims. The fact that he was an American and knew his way around a recording studio was enough. He even agreed to allow him a small royalty on the discs he produced for Decca, in addition to a fee. Rowe placed Talmy with Doug Sheldon – a singing actor managed by Bunny Lewis. Talmy failed to improve Sheldon's meagre chart record, but Rowe felt his production was competent, so placed the American with his latest discovery: the Phil Solomon-managed the Bachelors. Originally a harmonica playing trio from Dublin, Rowe had provided them with a group name and carefully chose their material which was squarely aimed at an elder audience.

In January 1963, the Bachelors charted with their debut, 'Charmaine', a chestnut written back in 1926. It was the first hit to credit the production team Shel Talmy and Charles Stone. Unfortunately, the next two singles, 'Faraway Places' and 'Whispering', fell outside the Top 30. Talmy was keen to produce the then unsigned Manfred Mann, but Decca scuppered the idea, possibly due to management rather than musical concerns. Rowe nevertheless kept faith with Talmy whose roll call of credits for the label included discs by Jimmy Powell, Tony Victor, the Young Ones and Wayne Gibson & The Dynamic Sounds. Rowe then literally sent Talmy to Coventry to choose one of the acts from the Larry Page stable of unsigned teenage stars. The lucky candidate was 17-year-old Rob Woodward, whom Larry, in a typically flattering gesture towards the visiting producer, had renamed Shel Naylor. Decca also signed Johnny B. Great & The Goodmen whose Talmy/Stone-produced single 'School Is In' was issued that summer. A third act that Page passed over to Talmy and Decca was the oddest of the lot. The Orchids (named after the ballroom) were a trio of schoolgirls from the nearby Stoke Park Grammar. For a laugh they'd entered one of Page's talent contests and come away with a pocket money prize of £1. Larry moulded their image, dressing them in regulation school uniform and arranging photo sessions in which they innocently sucked ice lollies. Hopes were high for their second single 'Love Hit Me', written exclusively by Talmy, and accompanied by the tag line: "Britain's Answer To The Crystals".

All five of these interconnected music businessmen – Kassner, Page, Rowe, Solomon and Talmy – were to play their parts in events leading up to the strange and convoluted saga of the Ravens' recording, management and publishing deal.

It was during the aforementioned visit to Tony Hiller at Mills Music that Robert Wace first encountered Shel Talmy. The producer vividly recalls him "clutching an acetate of the Ravens under one of his long arms" and saying he was "looking for a producer and a deal". Wace seemed an unlikely persuader. "He was a public-school type," Talmy says. "He blustered a bit and appeared very confident about things which he knew absolutely nothing about. And rock 'n' roll management was one of those things." Talmy, who later co-wrote a song with Hiller for Page's Orchids, agreed to listen to the acetate and was impressed enough to consider adding the group to his production conveyor belt.

Unfortunately, there were now political problems between Talmy and Decca. In a characteristic display of high-handedness, Phil Solomon was refusing to pay royalties to Talmy for work done on the Bachelors' recordings. The American was threatening legal reprisals and Dick Rowe was caught in the crossfire. Although Rowe attempted to remain neutral in the dispute, there was no way that he would ever offend the great Solomon. The Bachelors were soon to hit number 1 with another ballad 'Diane' (minus Talmy) and Solomon was promising more signings in the New Year. "Philip Solomon is a winner," Rowe told me, emphatically. "He just can't lose. He wouldn't care what he said or did. I've heard him have a row with a priest on the phone. I roared with laughter. He stood no nonsense." Forced to reconsider his position, Talmy commenced legal proceedings against Solomon then formed Shel Talmy Productions Ltd on 2 September. Thereafter, he felt free to find another label for his independent productions.

He retained links with Decca but realized this was not the best time to try and sell Rowe a new group.

While Talmy was still shopping around, Collins and Wace approached Larry Page. It made perfect sense. Page was slightly taken aback when he first received a phone call from Grenville Collins who identified himself as a stockbroker who had found "an absolutely super group". Larry agreed to audition the Ravens at a pub in north London and instantly expressed interest. The sound was raw but much more exciting than the groups he had nurtured back in Coventry. "Larry was recruited because he worked for a music publishing company," Wace says. "I felt that he would enhance the group's chances of success. Larry is an opportunist. It must be said that he was *never* the manager of the group, although he may like to think of himself as one. Larry had this management company called Denmark Productions owned by himself and Eddie Kassner. They had a 10 per cent interest on live gigs and records, but they didn't have any management concerns. They had a piece of the Kinks and the right to place Ray Davies' music. It was a very dangerous thing to do. I only made one mistake and that was getting involved with Eddie Kassner. From Ray's point of view, and mine too, it was a very bad mistake. But all Page had was a subcontracted piece of the action. A lot of people in those days owned different parts of groups."

Wace's testimony, of course, is blessed by hindsight and cursed by litigation. From Page's perspective, the management/publishing axis was crucial in enabling Ray Davies to achieve success in the first place. "Kassner was very good news for them," he insists. "Wace would be bloody selling ties somewhere if it hadn't been for Kassner. Wace knew nothing whatsoever. He came to me, he *begged* me to see the group. Without that, they would be nothing . . . You can say a lot of things about Eddie Kassner but without that man the group would still be the Ravens playing in a little pub. He gave me the chance of going out and signing whoever I wanted to, and it was through that that they got their break. Ray had a good basic talent, but he needed a lot of coaching."

What Ray also needed was a record contract. With the assemblage of an extensive expert entrepreneurial team, that now seemed eminently likely. Davies recalls that once Page learned of Talmy's involvement as probable producer, a meeting was arranged between the various parties which proceeded smoothly. Coincidentally, the new Orchids single 'Love Hit Me' was about to be released in December by Decca and all the key players were involved – Rowe, Kassner, Page and Talmy. The record was played on television's *Ready, Steady, Go!* and *Juke Box Jury* (in an edition uniquely featuring all four Beatles). The promotion testified to the power and influence of Larry Page and his business cohorts.

In the circumstances, the Ravens seemed near certainties to join Decca Records which already housed the Orchids, Johnny B. Great and Shel Naylor. Suddenly, news came through that the label had declined the north Londoners. Why? It was a broken sequence in an otherwise straightforward trajectory. Rowe had already signed three of Page's Coventry acts via Talmy and, over the next three months, would add two more – the Pickwicks and Little Lenny Davis. Tellingly, perhaps, the last two did not feature Talmy as producer. Could it be that the real reason for Rowe's shock rejection of the Ravens was the "Phil Solomon business"?

It was certainly a puzzling development. Some assumed that Rowe may have regarded the Ravens as too close in style to his recent R&B signings, the Rolling Stones. But that hardly made sense. He hadn't seen the Ravens play live and their demo sounded more like a Beatles-influenced beat group. In any case, Rowe would soon sign other R&B acts, notably the Nashville Teens and the Moody Blues. By any yardstick, the Ravens sounded a better bet than the other Page acts whom Kassner and Talmy had railroaded through Decca with nonchalant ease. Rowe kept quiet about the Solomon/Talmy dispute but it gave him cause to adjust his critical spectacles to the Ravens' disadvantage.

The Decca rejection was not merely a setback, but a massive shock. It meant that the industry players would have to shop more vigorously for a deal. Kassner and Page had lesser clout with the EMI group of labels whose rosters were, in any case, oversubscribed with beat groups and R&B hopefuls. Columbia would soon sign the Animals and the Yardbirds, HMV already had Manfred Mann and Parlophone was dominated by Epstein acts. The best hope, it seemed, was the smaller Philips Records. Their senatorial A&R manager Jack Baverstock recorded a couple of songs with the Ravens, listened back to their two Beatles' pastiches, 'I Believed You' and 'I Took My Baby Home', then promptly rejected them. The material sounded too derivative and they lacked a vocalist of power and distinction. Within a few months Baverstock would sign the more raucous and authentic Pretty Things, whose rough-hewn R&B made the Ravens sound anaemic by comparison.

Page and Kassner were now running out of options. It appeared that the Davies brothers and their management had been cursed by a combination of bad timing and record company politics. Meanwhile, Talmy had found another label willing to take him on as an independent producer. Still reeling from the Solomon dispute, he had approached Pye Records, the fourth and smallest of the leading UK record companies. For years, the company had been living off past glories courtesy of its two major acts, Lonnie Donegan and Petula Clark. The recent beat group explosion promised a fresh start. At this point, Merseybeat still ruled the UK charts. The Rolling Stones had yet to achieve a Top 10 hit, while Gerry And The Pacemakers and Billy J. Kramer With The Dakotas flourished. Pye boasted the best Liverpool act outside the Epstein stable. The Searchers had hit number 1 with 'Sweets For My Sweet' in the summer, recently reached number 2 with 'Sugar And Spice' and were poised to return to the top in the New Year with 'Needles And Pins' and 'Don't Throw Your Love Away'.

Pye's chairman was the commanding Louis Benjamin, already a pillar of traditional showbusiness. Born in London's Stoke Newington in 1922, the son of a Jewish cobbler, he was educated at Highbury County Secondary School, which he left aged 14 to join Moss Empires as an office boy. By 1945, he had become assistant manager of the London Palladium. In 1959, when Moss Empires' parent company ATV acquired Pye Records, he was appointed sales controller and, within four years, became managing director. His tastes were unashamedly populist and it was Royal Variety Performances rather than beat groups that appealed to his aesthetic. However, the Searchers' success suggested that a new market was opening up and Benjamin was willing to take a risk on Talmy.

The American producer was accompanied by the powerful

lawyer Marty Machat, who was more used to making deals on behalf of championship boxer Sugar Ray Robinson, and was renowned as a skilled negotiator. However, Chairman Benjamin was canny and Talmy uncharacteristically careless. Shel was offered a 2 per cent royalty for the artistes he produced, but was liable for all studio costs and, of course, had no ownership of the product. Furthermore, any act he delivered was signed directly to Pye rather than through his own production company. It was a tough deal, allowing Benjamin to acquire fresh talent without overpaying for the privilege. A recording session was arranged for the beginning of the New Year, leaving Page, Wace and Collins to negotiate the finer points with Benjamin. Not that there was much to discuss. As he had shown with Talmy, the Pye man was unyielding. He offered the company's standard contract of the time: a three-single deal with five one-year options of renewal; royalty rates at 2 per cent of the disc's retail price in the UK and 1 per cent on foreign releases. It was hardly generous but, as Page, Kassner and, by now, Benjamin well knew, the Ravens had nowhere else to go. "Decca, Philips and EMI had turned them down," Page reminds us, "so what do you reckon I should have done? Not done a deal? If you got a deal on the table back then, you didn't turn it down."

With all the frantic activity surrounding the Ravens, it was difficult for Ray to concentrate on his art school studies. He was frequently late arriving at college in the morning, often with his guitar in hand. Students and tutors became used to the sight of the slightly detached character sitting in the refectory, strumming and playing harmonica. "He was obviously drawn towards the theatre, possibly even performance as well," tutor John Turney recalls. "I got on fine with him. I can remember him being a very animated person. There was almost *too* much going on. It didn't really impinge on theatre design as such. He had a lively mind. He seemed to get on well with the other students, but there was possibly a bit of friction because he was very independent. He was quite a strong person. He went his own way."

Davies' continuing interest in film, along with his studies in theatre design, were put to unexpected use during his spell at Croydon. By chance, he was introduced to society and fashion photographer John Cowan. Born in 1929, Cowan was already established at the time. He was known for his use of angular shots, particularly on sessions with his glamorous girlfriend, Jill Kennington. Oddly enough, he did not undertake a series of promotional photo sessions with the Ravens – which would have produced a fascinating archive – but was temporarily seduced by a far more ambitious project. Following up the work he had done with Paul O'Dell, Ray Davies decided to produce a short film featuring the Ravens. Cowan was intrigued. Robert Wace believes the idea was inspired by the Beatles, whose film *A Hard Day's Night* would commence shooting in the New Year. In common with Richard Lester's direction, Cowan employed jump shots along with his customary trick of having his subjects hanging from buildings and other objects. Davies remembers one comic sequence in which the group were filmed entering a car wash with the vehicle's bonnet left open for comic effect.

Cowan was a generous but imposing figure, and an avid gun collector who always seemed to be dressed in denim, set off by desert boots. Like Wace and Collins, he was well over six foot, which must have appeared transfixing when all three were together.

Filming continued over several weekends in December, but neither Wace nor Collins could afford to finance the project indefinitely. Sadly, the film was never completed and no archive footage is known to survive. Davies' enduring memory of those cold, wintry shoots is an incongruously erotic image of Jill Kennington offering them hot tea. Three years later, she would appear alongside David Hemmings in Michelangelo Antonioni's *Blow-Up*, which Davies always regarded as the high water mark and symbolic death of the Swinging Sixties.

Davies' parallel life at art college was set to end as Christmas approached. Music was no longer a mere pastime now that managers, publishers and record companies were involved. "By then he was already playing gigs so he missed quite a bit of time," recalls John Turney. "Basically, one could see that music was his main interest." The idea of pursuing pop music as a career was generally regarded as nonsensical to the majority of the adult population. Ray knew that most pop groups had a short lifespan and he already had a contingency plan for a very different future. "I didn't think it would last more than six months. I wanted to make enough money so that I could pay my college fees and go to Spain and study guitar under Segovia. That's what I wanted to do . . . I still wanted to go back to college and learn stuff."

Davies found a sympathetic ally in Freddie Crooke, the head of Theatre Design at Croydon, who listened patiently to his concerns and, contrary to expectations, advised him to take a sabbatical, recharge his batteries, find himself, then return to Croydon if his musical ambitions remained unrealized. "Freddie Crooke was the sort of man who would tell him that," adds John Turney. "He wouldn't say, 'You must stay on and do this'. He suggested he stick with the music rather than stay on in a half-hearted way."

Even the supportive Crooke did not envisage Davies succeeding as a pop musician. "I always thought he'd develop as an actor rather than in a group. His interests obviously led to performing in front of the public in one way or other. He wasn't a very practical sort of person really. But then few artistic people are. He fulfilled himself in a way better suited to his talents than building scenery."

The rest of December passed in a blur. On New Year's Eve, the group celebrated Pete Quaife's 20th birthday at a Carnival Ball at Hornsey Town Hall. After packing away their equipment, they rushed over to the Lotus House in Edgware Road to perform at a private party for several of the showbiz elite. Collins and Wace were entertaining the influential impresario Arthur Howes, booking agent for the Beatles, among others. Having been turned down by Brian Epstein, the pair still hoped to bathe in the reflected glory of the Fab Four. Howes, in ebullient mood, said he was impressed by the group's performance and agreed to add their name to his list of illustrious clients. Drunk on champagne, they could hardly believe their ears. "The Arthur Howes connection was the next major step for them," Wace stresses. For Davies, the chance to be associated with the man who promoted the Beatles was probably as important an accolade as securing a record contract. It was the perfect end to a remarkable year.

CHAPTER EIGHT

KINKY BOOTS

It would be no exaggeration to claim that 1964 began on a wave of intense optimism. After the political purgations of the previous year everyone was keen to look forward. Harold Wilson, the premier-in-waiting, spoke about "a new Britain" promising "1964 is the year in which we take our destiny into our own hands again". Evidently, the saviours of the age were to be found among the new teenagers whose creative talents, originality and determination promised to vanquish the corruption so brutally exposed among the political elite during 1963. "This is the time for a breakthrough to an exciting and wonderful period in our history," Wilson announced, "in which all can and must take part. Our young men and women, especially, have in their hands the power to change the world. We want the youth of Britain to storm the new frontiers of knowledge, to bring back to Britain that surging adventurous self-confidence and sturdy self-respect which the Tories have almost submerged with their apathy and cynicism."

The BBC also paid homage to youth by launching a new television programme devoted to popular music. On New Year's Day, *Top Of The Pops* was broadcast for the first time as a kind of visual equivalent to the Radio Light Programme's long-running *Pick Of The Pops*. Both were designed to reflect, rather than determine, the public's taste. *Top Of The Pops* was wonderfully democratic, embracing fashionable beat groups, showbiz familiars, modish singers and old-style sentimental balladeers, without any sense of incongruity. Although aimed primarily at the young record buyer, the show also served as family entertainment. Its rule of thumb was the weekly pop chart, the contents of which would provide the performers deemed suitable for inclusion. Pop charts in the UK had been around since 1952, but they had never seemed as important as on that memorable New Year's Day when the cream of British disc jockeys – Jimmy Savile and Alan Freeman, later abetted by David Jacobs and Pete Murray – combined to co-host the show. The Beatles' 'I Want To Hold Your Hand' was still number 1, 'She Loves You' at number 2 and the Liverpudlians' latest album *With The Beatles* had even infiltrated the *singles* charts at number 14. For pre-adolescents, teens and young-at-heart adults, the programme was unmissable. Its chart rundown was regarded as stock market share listings by the tycoons and denizens of Tin Pan Alley; it provided DJs with playlists for the weekend; and for pop stars and young viewers it came to be seen not merely as a barometer of success, but of status and achievement. For those caught up in its numerical mythology, it mattered intensely. That familiar line – "it's number 1 – it's *Top Of The Pops*" – bestowed instant immortality.

Although still ambivalent about his prospects, Ray Davies was now ready to enter this competitive pop game in earnest. In January, he returned to Croydon Art College, merely to ensure that he qualified for that term's grant. Once the money was safely banked, he was gone, never to be seen again. The canny timing coincided with further good news when, much to his relief, Robert Wace learned that Arthur Howes' New Year's Eve promises had not been fuelled by champagne and excess bonhomie. The Ravens were officially invited to join his lustrous agency – but not under that name. A metamorphosis had occurred.

Nobody is entirely certain of the *exact* moment when the Ravens became the Kinks but a decision appears to have been made just before the year-end meeting with Howes. The origins of the name – who coined it, when and why – have sparked conflicting anecdotes but, as everyone agrees, it was a title that was 'in the air'. It could hardly have been otherwise considering the political and sexual scandals of the previous year. Profumo's affair with the 22-year-old Christine Keeler had spiralled into a public debate about the morality of the nation. As early as March 1963, *Time* magazine reported: "On the island where the subject has long been taboo in polite society, sex has exploded into the national consciousness and national headlines. 'Are We Going Sex Crazy?' asks the *Daily Herald* . . . 'Are Virgins Obsolete?' is the question posed by the solemn *New Statesman*. The answers vary but one thing is clear: Britain is being bombarded with a barrage of frankness about sex."

There were even public warnings from the barons of Fleet Street. One month later, the *Sunday Mirror* confronted a familiar menace with the cautionary headline: 'How To Spot a Homo'. Lord Denning's report into the Profumo affair provided newspaper columnists, satirists and readers with a veritable smorgasbord offering sensational yet shocking details of sexual depravities. There were rumours of High Court judges engaged in orgies and a naked, masked Cabinet Minister serving dinner clad only in a lace apron offset by a card around his neck reading: "If my services don't please you, whip me". The indefatigable Lord Denning confirmed that no member of the Cabinet was involved but, in scotching the more lurid tales, he conceded that young call girls had attended "perverted sex orgies; that the man in the mask is a 'slave' who is whipped; that the guests undress and indulge in sexual intercourse one with the other; and indulge in other sexual activities of a vile and revolting nature." The buzzword for such behaviour was 'kinky', a term picked up by satirists on television's *That Was The Week That Was* and frequently used by the British public as shorthand for any perceived aberration. "I seem to remember Dusty Springfield being described as 'kinky'," Robert Wace recalls. "The word was around."

'Kinky', as previously noted, was the title of an instrumental single issued at that time by John Barry. The word also became associated with a revamped television series, screened that autumn of 1963. *The Avengers*, which first aired in January 1961, was a popular detective drama starring Old Etonian Patrick Macnee as John Steed and character actor Ian Hendry as his tough but compassionate associate, Dr David Steel. After 26 episodes Hendry, fearful of being typecast as the avenging doctor, declined to renew his contract. Director Sydney Newman, a Canadian who had trained under Davies' hero John Grierson, then made the bold decision to cast a woman in Hendry's place. Honor Blackman, previously famous for playing upper echelon, cut-glass-voiced

English roses in the Fifties, was transformed into the leather-clad heroine, Cathy Gale. "I'm a first for television," Blackman announced. "The first feminist to come into a television serial; the first woman to fight back. Cathy is all anthropologist, an academic, all brain and what she doesn't have in the way of brawn, she makes up for in motorbikes, black boots, leather combat suits and judo." Unsurprisingly, it was the 'kinky' leather and boots that grabbed the public's attention. "The leather thing was extraordinary," she says. "The fact that I happened to choose leather for my fighting outfit was a pure accident. Cathy led a very active life and I soon realized that skirts were out of the question. When your legs are flying over your head, the last thing you want to worry about is whether your stocking-tops are showing. It happened right at the beginning of the series; I split my trousers in close-up, with my rear in full view of the camera . . . The only things you can wear with leather trousers are boots, so they kitted me out with calf-length black boots, and the leather thing was born."

Coincidentally, the boutique-loving Dave Davies also had a penchant for such outlandish garb. At one point, he purchased thigh-high cavalier boots from a theatrical agency and also enjoyed wearing plastic macs, another sexual signifier of the time. The 16-year-old had also taken to parting his hair close to the centre, a daringly effete style, still associated with the Victorian aesthete Oscar Wilde. It seemed the word 'kinky' had been specially invented for Dave Davies' sartorial stylebook. On the other hand, one music press myth claimed that it was Ray's more sober style that had inspired the group name. Supposedly, a studio engineer spotted him wearing a grey pullover, tweed trousers and orange tie and declared him a 'kink'. In another reworking of the story, a passer-by in a pub was so taken aback by the sight of Dave and Pete that he blurted out, "You should be called the Kinks". Hovering in the background, Larry Page relished the moment and took the man's advice.

For his part, Robert Wace credits an Old Etonian and society swell. "It was thought up by a friend of mine, Ozzie Armandeus, who had come to see them a couple of times. To my recollection, he was the one who came up with the name." Each or all of these accounts may be true, particularly when you consider the date.

Honor Blackman was about to enter a recording studio at Decca to make a comedy single with Patrick Macnee titled 'Kinky Boots'. After that she would quit *The Avengers* to become the provocatively named Pussy Galore in the new James Bond film, *Goldfinger*. On 6 December, Christine Keeler, who could well claim credit for bringing kinkiness into mainstream argot, was sentenced to nine months' imprisonment. Finally, on Christmas Eve, a week before the Ravens played in front of Arthur Howes at the Lotus House, the *Daily Mail* entertained its readers with a cartoon of a young girl, kneeling at her bedside in prayer. The caption read: "All I want for Christmas is a Beatle, failing that, a pair of *kinky* boots, a fab leather jacket, black tights and £500,000 for Oxfam."

As the leading image maker in the group's orbit, it was inevitably Larry Page who insisted that the title 'Kinks' must be adopted immediately. He had already rechristened all of the performers in his Coventry stable of acts and the Ravens were forced to follow suit. Initially, every member of the group hated the name Kinks, but Page was adamant. He pointed out that a short name would stand out on billboards, an obvious asset for a group likely to be a bottom of the bill act over the next few months. They were even bamboozled by a plausible psychological ploy pointing out that the letter 'K' was so unusual that it would mesmerize anyone who happened to see the group's name while scanning a newspaper or music press article. Pye Records, of course, also went along with the management's decision.

As he had done with the Orchids, Shel Naylor and Johnny B. Great, Page could not resist playing the experienced tutor. Even before Christmas he had taken Ray Davies into Regent Sound Studios to co-write an instrumental, 'Revenge', which would later appear on the first Kinks' album. "I sat down with Ray and told him that the one thing that would sell records would be riffs. Just riffs all the way through. We concentrated on trying to write material with stock notes where you didn't need a good singer . . . We'd sit around the piano and work out ideas." At this stage Davies was still uncertain about his vocal abilities, but Page was quick to remind him that employing somebody else would cost money. "I thought it was a waste of time bringing in a singer which would mean yet another split. I encouraged him to sing and write because he was really doing neither."

Page was equally keen to nurture Davies' songwriting, not least because the entrepreneur received a healthy commission from Eddie Kassner for any composition that was passed over to the publisher. One of Larry's standard tips was to personalize a song by including the words 'You' or 'Me' in the title. It was an old Tin Pan Alley trick to provide a lyric with universal appeal. In later years, Page would carefully select songs with titles such as 'With A Girl Like *You*' and 'Anyway That *You* Want *Me*' and 'Give It To *Me*' in order to provide the Troggs with sizeable hits. Ray evidently proved an eager accomplice and quickly came up with three songs that fitted the formula: 'You Still Want Me', 'You Do Something To Me' and 'I Don't Need You Anymore'.

On 17 January, events took an unexpected turn when Page received an urgent phone call from Arthur Howes in Paris where the promoter had just watched the Beatles perform at the Olympia Theatre. His advice to Page was categorical: "You've got to get in there straightaway. They did a number last night and brought the house down." The song was a cover of Little Richard's 'Long Tall Sally', which the Beatles would not release until five months later. Seizing the opportunity, Page persuaded the Kinks to work up a cover version. Three days later, the group entered Pye Studios to record the aforementioned 'You' and 'Me' songs, plus Ray's earlier composition 'I Took My Baby Home' and 'Long Tall Sally'. "I thought it would be a good idea to do a standard for the first thing out of the box," producer Shel Talmy says. "We were doing it entirely differently from everybody else. I wasn't knocked out by it, but I thought it was OK."

It must have been both exciting and intimidating for Ray Davies to record his first session for a record label. He remembers that as they were leaving the studio, one of Pye's employees quipped: "Hey, fellows, you just made a flop!" It would prove an accurate prediction.

With 'Long Tall Sally' scheduled for release in early February, the Kinks urgently needed a new drummer. Since Mickey Willett's departure, they had been unable to recruit a permanent replacement. Talmy had employed famed session drummer Bobby Graham for the studio recordings but he was too busy for promotional work or touring. Dave Davies was keen to appoint the outrageous Viv Prince, a fellow raver whose fearless party exploits were much admired. Prince was not available and missed the opportunity, which may have been a blessing in disguise considering his raucous reputation. Instead, he would join the Pretty Things a few months later. The search for a drummer, like much else during this frantic period, was done in haphazard fashion. Both Davies brothers, and even Larry Page, recall placing an advert in *Melody Maker* supposedly reading: 'Drummer wanted for a smart go-ahead group'. But this ad never appeared. In fact, they themselves responded to a small ad in the paper: 'Drummer. Young, good kit, read, seeks pro-R&B group. MOL 4615'.

Based in East Molesey, across the Thames from Hampton Court, Mick Avory was a hard-working, down-to-earth character with a lugubrious demeanour and placid personality. He had originally started playing drums, aged 13, in a local skiffle scout troupe (The First Molesey Skiffling Scouts), replacing another lad who had switched to mandolin. He then learned to read music and joined an older jazz ensemble who had a residency at the Osterley Hotel. After leaving school, he was employed as a snow clearer, a painter, a fireplace maker, an excavator on a building site and, finally, a pink-paraffin delivery man. He still played part-time in various small groups, notably the Shadows-influenced Hilights, and briefly took lessons in the hope of becoming a jazz drummer. Most impressively, after frequenting the Crawdaddy Club, he began rehearsing with Mick Jagger, Keith Richards and Brian Jones in a prototype Rolling Stones. In one bill from the period, a certain 'Mike Avery' is listed as a member of the group for a forthcoming appearance at London's Marquee club on 12 July 1962. Some rock writers later described him as one of the founding members, but this was an exaggeration. Always modest, Avory admitted to me that he never actually played live with the Stones. "They were rehearsing for the Marquee gig in the top room of a pub, the Bricklayers Arms. Mick Jagger phoned me and I went along to the audition. I said I'd do the gig but, as it turned out, they wanted a full-time drummer. I wasn't really available for that as I was still working during the day so, after about two rehearsals, I dropped out. That was my big chance of being a Stone."

When the Rolling Stones signed to Decca and hit the charts with 'Come On', Avory knew that he had made a mistake, but he was not bitter. He concluded that there were plenty more R&B groups in London and awaited his second chance. It came via a phone call from Robert Wace which his mother had fielded while he was at work. "Some posh la-di-da gent rang about a vacancy in a group," she told him. Avory was invited to play for the Kinks at the Camden Head pub in Islington. Perhaps it was Wace's posh voice that inspired a shocking fashion *faux pas*. Convinced that the Kinks must be a smartly attired group, Avory had a severe haircut and headed for the audition dressed in a conventional shirt and tie. What he encountered was a flamboyant and arty bunch, who delighted in making fun of his appearance. "Ha, he's just got out of prison," Dave joked. Avory was bemused by the 16-year-old guitarist whose effete dress was almost intimidating. "I was wearing a plastic mac buttoned to the neck, moccasins, and I had shoulder-length hair. When Mick asked me what I was drinking I said 'pineapple juice' and he practically passed out."

The younger brother could not resist playing the homosexual for outrageous effect, much to Avory's consternation. Quaife, the friendliest of the bunch, joined in, while Ray looked on in detached amusement. "It was actually Pete's fault in the first place," Dave adds. "He introduced the camp thing from people he used to work with in *The Outfitter*. He started doing all the hand movements. We used to mimic homosexuals in a derogatory way, and it caught on. Because it shocked people we realized it was getting us attention . . . It was funny when Mick first appeared. He'd just come off a building site, virtually, and was thinking, 'I don't know about these geezers . . .' So me and Pete deliberately camped it up even more to test and shock him. After a few months he was worse than all of us. He had these great big builder's hands going [limp wristed] . . . It just goes to show that maybe there's a closet queen in all of us, dear. Sometimes the most macho people are trying to hide the female side of their nature."

The homosexual humour continued when they discovered that Avory was a former Boy Scout. Ray Davies quietly observed the commotion, seemingly more fascinated by Avory's quizzical reaction than his drumming ability. "Poor old Mick! It was an attitude with Mick rather than his playing . . . Always look at the person rather than how good they are at what they do. I had this theory – it's like the guy in the movie *The Hustler* who says, 'I know you *can* do it, but *will* you do it?' I look for performance and I look for energy and people who have an original take . . . I didn't think about his audition – I thought about his *presence*, and it was a good one." Although Avory was, in many ways, the antithesis of the art school-educated Ray Davies, his interest in jazz was a plus and he even had an oblique family connection to film work. His father had trained as a sculptor at St Martin's Art School and had designed models for the 1958 film *The Vikings*, starring Kirk Douglas and Tony Curtis.

Avory's amiability was almost enough to win him a place in the Kinks but he still faced the pressure of a second audition in front of all three managers and agent Arthur Howes. They recognized his competence and were clearly relieved to find a suitable candidate at such short notice. Larry Page was struck by Avory's pliability, which he hoped might diffuse any tensions between the Davies brothers. "Mick would do anything you told him because he's not the brightest person in the world. He'd just sit there thumping away like mad. But he was no problem. Mick was like a little puppet."

However, there was one dissenting voice who chose to keep his counsel. Dave Davies had been playful and outrageously funny during the audition, but he was not entirely convinced. Perhaps Ray's positive reaction caused him to cast Avory in a more critical light, but it was a worrying development. "I don't think Dave thought I was the right guy, to be honest," Avory acknowledges, "so I used to get a bit of stick from him. I thought that was just him but later I realized that it was Ray who thought I was more suited [to the group]. But they never agreed on anything anyway. I just happened to be in the middle of it."

In different circumstances Dave might have challenged Avory's appointment but, with a television commitment looming, time was running out. Once Ray and the management had accepted Avory, Dave felt obliged to concur. "He was the best drummer we'd seen but I didn't really have a gut feeling that he was the *right* guy. But the pressure was mounting to do stuff, and he looked good. He was a nice guy, played well, but I wasn't happy with it from the start."

On 1 February, the four-piece played their first gig billed as the Kinks at Oxford's Town Hall, supporting EMI Columbia's R&B

specialists, the Downliners Sect. There were no adverts in the local paper, ensuring a small turnout, slightly boosted by several members of the Davies family who loyally made the trip. Six days later, Pye Records rushed out the Kinks' cover of 'Long Tall Sally' and that same evening the group made their television debut on *Ready, Steady, Go!*. It was a prestige spot which Page had secured in the wake of the Orchids' brief appearance the previous month. A veritable tribe of Davies' sisters, cousins and assorted friends staged a 'fan invasion' outside the studio. Among the ringleaders was niece Jackie, clutching an autograph book and jointly leading the line.

Ready, Steady, Go! was also the scene of an explosive outburst from Dave Davies. Michael Aldred, a junior presenter on the show, clearly preferred to interview the younger Kink rather than his more celebrated brother. Aldred's motives were not entirely journalistic. A homosexual, he had taken a fancy to the teenager with the girlish looks. Dave was flustered by Aldred's unscripted but anodyne questions and angered by Pete Quaife's amused reaction. He even threw a punch at the bassist to relieve his humiliation. "Dave was very excited and pissed off," says Quaife's brother, who attended the show. "There was nearly a punch-up afterwards. Aldred didn't hide it, and it was illegal in those days."

In preparation for their television launch, the group had gone on a shopping spree at various London boutiques. They emerged with a uniform of sorts, highlighted by thigh-high boots, leather jackets, leather and cloth caps and a smattering of tweed. A photo session was arranged with Bruce Fleming, a regular at Ronnie Scott's, whose portfolio featured an impressive selection of jazz greats including Stan Getz, Chet Baker and Dexter Gordon. He had recently started photographing beat groups and the Kinks' assignment provided the opportunity to attempt something different. His most memorable portrait was an iconic shot of the quartet looking sinister and 'kinky', with Dave and Pete brandishing whips as if they were auditioning for a sadomasochistic blue movie. There was another aspect to the new image, unseen in the photos but strikingly noticeable on television. Against his better judgement Ray had agreed to have his front teeth capped to hide that distinctive diastema smile which had been part of his visual identity ever since his brother was a baby. After seeing himself on *Ready, Steady, Go!* wearing pre-operational crowns, Ray thought that he looked like Bugs Bunny. The effect was made worse by his admission that he was suffering terrible back problems and contorting in agony.

That same month, the group played a lunchtime set at Liverpool's Cavern where they were filmed performing their single 'Long Tall Sally' by Granada Television. It remains a fascinating document of the time. Ray, dressed in a smart shirt and cufflinks, plays electric guitar and blasts away on a harmonica, but the effect is slightly eerie. He resembles nothing less than a clone of himself. The facial image appears safe but strangely devoid of personality. Such concerns played on Davies' mind when he returned to the dentist to complete his procedure. The drill was already whirring when he abruptly jumped from the chair and left the room. "I said, 'If I'm going make it, I'm going to make it on my songwriting,' and I think it's worked. I'm less visual than other people." Looking back, Ray saw his refusal of cosmetic dental surgery as akin to an artistic statement of intent: "It's the most important decision I've ever made."

CHAPTER NINE

MARCH OF THE MODS

Despite a front-page ad and television promotion, 'Long Tall Sally' failed to reach the Top 30. It was listed at number 42 in *Melody Maker*'s Pop 50, the lower regions of which were often vulnerable to chart hypers with a 'promotional budget'. Perhaps the *Ready, Steady, Go!* cameo had been enough to propel the record this far, but it disappeared the following week and was seldom played on radio. Few could argue that it deserved a better fate. It was a fairly passionless cover, unsuited to Ray's vocal range. "Dave would have been better singing it," he agrees. "He was the Little Richard expert in the band." Revealingly, Dave was never even considered. Having shared lead vocals with his brother when they were first discovered, his role was now secondary. He would never be featured as main vocalist on any UK single issued under the Kinks' name.

February was also the month when the complex management arrangements between the various parties were finalized. Having formed a company, Boscobel Productions, Collins and Wace signed the contracts binding them to the Kinks and Larry Page. However, their solicitor chose a curious and unfortunate method of drawing up separate agreements for both the management parties that would subsequently prove contentious. On 12 February, each Kink signed a five-year agreement with Boscobel allowing them to retain 40 per cent of the group's earnings as well as granting them the rights to place their song publishing. Fourteen days later, a separate agreement, to which the performers were not parties, was concluded between Boscobel and Denmark Productions appointing Larry Page as manager of the group on a 10 per cent remuneration for the duration of the previous agreement. Ray Davies approved of this arrangement, fully realizing that he had simultaneously assigned Kassner all rights pertaining to the placement of his and Dave's musical compositions. In cold print, it was Page whose position was most threatened by these separate agreements since he was not signed directly to the Kinks, and Collins/Wace could legally appoint any person to carry out these obligations. It was understood, however, that Page should undertake such duties and the agreements did no more than put into legal form, albeit clumsily, what the Kinks had already accepted since late 1963.

Page evidently regarded the contracts as watertight, in spite of their unusual form, and proceeded with his managerial plans unperturbed. "There weren't three managers, there was only one manager and that was me," he argues. "The other two knew nothing about the music business, didn't interfere and at that stage of the game left everything to me. It was only when the money started appearing that the problems arose. They were going to bathe in the reflected glory. Their contract was with me and *my* contract ensured total control, otherwise I wouldn't have touched it. I wouldn't have got involved with a couple of Hooray Henrys, as they were, unless I controlled the situation."

Page's disparaging comments underline the extent to which class conflict played a part in this unfolding saga. He had recently met Robert Wace's father, who took umbrage at his London working-class accent. It was an insult not easily forgotten. For Ray Davies, too, it was a strange feeling to be connected with mentors whose personalities, backgrounds and experience were so different. "Our managers were conservative, upper class, whereas Larry was working class. That was critical. You could see the class system in action by the way they behaved with each other." The notion of Page and Collins/Wace as mirror opposites was even reflected in the titles of their respective companies. Denmark Productions took its title from Denmark Street, the slightly seedy area of Soho where Page and Kassner rented offices. Boscobel Productions was named after 45 Boscobel Place in Knightsbridge, where Robert Wace lived.

Collins and Wace could congratulate themselves for even reaching this far in the shark-infested music business. But they had already paid for the privilege. Their original 40 per cent management commission had been whittled down, and they were each now on 10 per cent. In addition to Page, agent Arthur Howes took his 10 per cent share. "And just for the record, Arthur wanted Larry Page out from day one," says Wace, who points out that he and Collins expended considerable effort actually defending their future nemesis. If true, Howes' objection was unexpected, not least because he had previously worked with Page and booked him as a performer during the Teenage Rage days. "I would say that is wrong," Page says of Wace's allegation, "but nothing surprises me in this business. If you've got a chance of dealing with two people, one of whom knows what he's talking about and one who *doesn't* then, quite possibly, it's beneficial to deal with the one who doesn't know what he's talking about . . . You think how much they know now and how much they knew then. It was very, very little. They were very empty people."

By March 1964, Page was actively promoting the songwriting of both Davies brothers via his deal with Eddie Kassner. With Shel Talmy still working with Page's Coventry acts, two singles appeared on Decca in rapid succession: Shel Naylor recorded Dave's composition 'One Fine Day' and the Orchids covered Ray's 'I've Got That Feeling'. Neither broke through but that was hardly surprising. The Davies brothers were far from competent, let alone established, writers. "'One Fine Day' is just a chorus really," Dave admits. "It has the same chords in the verse as it does in the chorus." As composers, there was little to choose between the brothers at this point but that would soon change. Dave appeared to regard songwriting with the same dread that he had previously reserved for school homework. Although Kassner and Page were eager for him to write more, and certainly had numerous artistes available to record his compositions, the younger brother preferred partying to penning songs. Ray was very much the opposite and, just as he had done with his singing, would eclipse Dave as the chief contributor to the Kinks. It was another crucial shift in the power structure that would never be adequately resolved.

That same month, Page was excited to hear that Ray had written some new songs, including one that both brothers felt might be a hit. The origins of 'You Really Got Me' went back to the end of the Fifties when Ray was living with his sister Rose and tinkering on the piano. Several years later, he adapted the melody in the jazz blues style of Mose Allison and added some rudimentary lyrics. Both Davies brothers had recently attended a rare screening of *Jazz On A Summer's Day*, a documentary of the 1958 Newport Jazz Festival starring Chuck Berry, Gerry Mulligan, Mahalia Jackson, Thelonius Monk, Anita O'Day and Dinah Washington among the cast list. Berry had already provided the template for the recent Merseybeat and R&B boom, influencing both the Beatles and the Rolling Stones, who made full use of his repertoire. Ray was equally entranced by Gerry Mulligan whose saxophone work was still in his mind while working on the piano-led prototype of 'You Really Got Me'. Although Dave Davies was not eligible for a co-writing credit, it was his sonic contribution that transformed the composition. Over the past year, he had been experimenting with sound, initially using a low-wattage Elpico amplifier that he had bought from Les Aldrich's electrical shop at 29 Fortis Green Road. In a moment of frustration, he started attacking the amplifier, firstly with a knitting needle (according to Ray) and then more thoroughly with a razor blade, slicing the speaker cone to create distortion. He then attached the Elpico to a Vox AC30 amp, turned the lower amp to maximum volume and revelled in the outrageous sound emanating from his guitar. It was quite unlike anything heard in British pop music of the period. The 'Marconi of Fuzz' had, partly by accident, created the power chord, influencing a future generation of hard rock and heavy metal guitarists in the process.

On 18 March, the song was demoed at Regent Sound Studios, along with two other compositions: the older Ray Davies' blues shouter 'It's Alright' and a never to be released obscurity, 'It's You'. Page was pleased and encouraged that Ray had expanded upon their previous collaboration 'Revenge' while still using the 'You' and 'Me' blueprint. Pye International had recently issued 'Louie Louie' by American group the Kingsmen, which employed a similar *C-F-G* chord progression whose simplicity appealed to Page. "I based the act on 'Louie Louie'," he claims, in overstated fashion. "I was a great fan of the Kingsmen. It was just a riff – that was the whole thing." Although 'You Really Got Me' was certainly insistent, its commercial appeal was uncertain. Pye prevaricated for the present, not least perhaps because the Kinks were scheduled to commence a 43-date tour at the end of the month.

Agent Arthur Howes had proven himself worthy of his 10 per cent commission by adding the Kinks to a package tour that he was co-promoting with Harold Davison, who represented the headliners, the Dave Clark Five. The north London quintet were undoubtedly the group of the moment, partly thanks to an accident of history. In January, their exuberant beat classic 'Glad All Over' had dislodged the Beatles at number 1, prompting the national press to wonder 'Has The Five Jive Crushed The Beatles' Beat?' It was conveniently forgotten that the Beatles' single had already been top since the beginning of December and its fall had more to do with gravity than rivalry. Nevertheless, the Five were ludicrously credited as purveyors of the 'Tottenham Sound', a genre owned exclusively by themselves which was predicated on an unrelenting thumping beat. It was captured with military precision on their succeeding hit 'Bits And Pieces', which was currently heading for second place in the Top 20. Also on the bill were the Hollies, an accomplished Manchester outfit with a breathtaking harmonic blend whose impressive run of hits for EMI's Parlophone label was currently gathering steam with their latest chart entry, 'Just One Look'. Completing the line-up was Pye recording artiste Mark Wynter, best known for his 1962 hits 'Venus In Blue Jeans' and 'Go Away Little Girl', plus Butlin's Holiday Camp regulars the Trebletones and Decca's Mojos. The Kinks were placed second from bottom and no doubt happy to be so.

Before setting out on the long tour, Davies was given the customary coaching of Larry Page who was keen to push the provocative 'kinky' image. "I taught Ray and Dave how to hold their guitars," he says. "Not play them, but hold them. You hold it as if you were holding your prick – you have it right in front of you and you play it. When the camera comes on you, you grip it so that they can see every little bit of nervous energy in your hand. When the camera comes on your face it's got to be that aggression all the time. And those were the things I went through. Same as their stage act where I put one of them on one side and one on the other and they'd skip into the middle. It was always aggression – the whole thing. It had to be."

The tour opened in Coventry, where Page had promoted his stable of acts, but this was no happy omen. *New Musical Express* reviewer Richard Green (whose acerbity had earned him the nickname "the Beast") was dismissive of the Kinks whose four-song set consisted of familiar R&B staples. He felt they "relied too much on entirely copying the Rolling Stones with long hair, tie-less shirts and even Jagger-type dances". Worse still, he suggested that the group should be demoted to bottom of the bill. One week later, the Mojos entered the chart with 'Everything's Al 'right' and Green's wish was granted. It was a ruthless but fair decision by Arthur Howes who was sufficiently concerned to despatch road manager Hal Carter in a concerted attempt to improve the Kinks' stage image.

Carter, who had worked with Larry Parnes' acts, including Marty Wilde and Billy Fury, had enough showbiz nous to add a professional veneer to the Kinks without diluting their natural raucousness. He was warned off any further gentrification by the Hollies' ever-supportive Graham Nash who barked: "Leave them alone . . . they're OK as they are." Ray remembers slightly modifying the set so that the stock R&B numbers were not so noticeable, but they still could not rid themselves of the Stones comparisons. Dave proved predictably untameable and, lost in manic abandon, almost sabotaged the set. "I made a right idiot of myself. We'd just got to the end of a number and I went jumping up and down like we always do, when it suddenly occurred to me that the floor was an awfully long way away. I'd jumped right off the stage and fell into the orchestra pit. The audience loved it. They all thought it was part of the act. There was blood dripping down my face and yet the audience never did realize that it wasn't supposed to happen."

The tour was beset by rivalry among the leading acts, much of it directed against the Dave Clark Five, who had their own PA system and a swagger that some considered undeserved. Tour manager Malcolm Cook, who took over from compere Frank Berry after the opening dates, remembers "a lot of trouble" almost culminating in a punch-up. There were even attempts to sabotage the Five's equipment in what sounded like a clear case of jealousy. "They actually cut their mains cable," says Cook. "It was very dangerous, unprofessional, stupid and unnecessary. But what do you do?" For Ray Davies it was a revealing insight into the politics of a package show.

Pye Records now felt the need to issue a second single to coincide with the tour. On 17 April, they released 'You Still Want Me' b/w 'You Do Something To Me'. Producer Shel Talmy was scathing about the disc, rightly seeing it as a retrograde step. "'You Still Want Me' was done at the same session as 'Long Tall Sally'," he reminds us. "I did not want that to come out but Pye decided to release *something*. It was Louis Benjamin's idea. It was just thrown out." Ray Davies was similarly deflated, and with good reason. Both songs betray the group's lingering debt to rudimentary Merseybeat and sound like pastiches. Ray deliberately disguises his London accent and sings like a Liverpudlian uncertainly undertaking elocution lessons. Despite a front-page ad in the *NME*, sales of the single were negligible and radio play virtually non-existent.

"'You Still Want Me' and 'Long Tall Sally' may have got a few plays but I was never happy about those records," says Dave. "The production was soft and I didn't like them. We had a rough sound but when we got in the studio it would be all smoothed out." Dave was also suspicious about the B-side 'You Do Something To Me', which reminded him of his previously rejected composition, 'I Believed You'. "It has a similar chord progression," he points out. "What's strange is that some time later Ray came up with a similar song that *he* wrote. It's based on the same chords." Teasingly, he adds: "So that was the first major rip-off – no! The first *influence*!" The failure of the second single was a serious setback which threatened the future of the Kinks as a recording entity.

In a further attempt to reinvigorate the group's image, a change of clothes was deemed necessary. The previous month, Larry Page had launched the Pickwicks, another Coventry group whose first Decca single was a big-beat treatment of the 1920s evergreen 'Apple Blossom Time'. Having named the group, Page decided to play up the Dickensian 'Mr Pickwick' image by decking them out in frock coats, top hats and fake whiskers. They looked as though they were auditioning for a television costume drama. Coincidentally, the Kinks also adopted a Dickensian persona while appearing on the Dave Clark tour: Ray was nicknamed

Filch (from Mrs Filch, the laundress in *A Christmas Carol*), Dave became the Artful Dodger and Mick emerged as the villainous Bill Sykes (both borrowed from *Oliver Twist*), while Pete took on the role of Pip from *Great Expectations*, but was soon re-christened Crutch Quelch. What sounded a cruel putdown was actually a malapropism provided by a fan from Liverpool who, for some reason, could never properly pronounce Quaife's name. The Kinks might well have ended up resembling extras from the musical *Oliver!* but Page was happy enough for them to choose something colourful to enliven their visual look. On a rare day off, they were taken to the London theatrical costumiers M. Berman Ltd and dressed in pink/red hunting jackets, frilly shirts, black pants and riding boots. As an image, it combined and reflected the very different personalities of their management team. Page, whose love of a distinctive uniform was evident in his promotion of the Orchids and the Pickwicks, was reminded of his Teenage Rage days when his standard look was a red blazer, set off by dark trousers. For Collins and Wace, the hunting garb was emblematic of the aristocratic country gentleman made more subversive via its adoption by a group of long-haired, working-class parvenus. It was an apt comment on the times.

Perhaps the only positive aspect of the tour was the emergence of 'You Really Got Me' as a stage favourite. The group played an extended version which ended suddenly after which Ray would announce playfully: "Well that's enough of that then" and move on to the next song. According to Dave, "It used to have a very abrupt ending. So abrupt, in fact, that when we'd finish playing it, the audience just sat there quietly. We had to yell at them, 'Come on, you lot, clap!'" It was not long before the clapping became tumultuous. "It used to blow away people at gigs," Dave adds. "It was like 'What the hell was that?' It was such an unusual song, even the chord changes weren't normal for the time."

The central two-chord riff drove the song in unrelenting fashion. Watching from the wings, Hal Carter noticed that the composition opened *in medias res* with the words, "Yeah, you really got me . . ." Taking Ray aside he suggested a more personal introduction, replacing 'Yeah' with the softer 'Girl' so that female fans could identify with the lyric upon first hearing. Ray was impressed, and agreed. The only remaining concern was Pye's continued reluctance to confirm a recording date. "The record company said it was too repetitive and didn't have a happy-go-lucky melody," Ray remembers. "It didn't sound like the Beatles, but we persevered, playing it [on tour] and the song itself got a cult following. I thought the Kinks were special and, one way or another, we'd make it."

By mid-May, the nationwide tour was complete and the Dave Clark Five were whisked across to America where 'Bits And Pieces' was heading for the Top 10. They were now transatlantic stars with a prestigious booking on *The Ed Sullivan Show*. Clark was emerging as a canny business brain whom the money-conscious Ray Davies had good reason to envy. By comparison, the Kinks were still at the starting blocks, hopeful but uncertain of a breakthrough hit. Soon, they were back on the bread and butter circuit of ballrooms and small halls, at least one of which summed up their appeal with the condescending observation: "If you like the 'Rolling Stones' – you will love The Kinks". At another date they were billed as 'the Kinks from Liverpool' and erroneously referred to as '*Decca* Recording Artistes: The Kinks'. Dick Rowe would have smiled wryly at that slip.

Pop star aspirations inevitably encouraged female attention for the still teenage group. Dave and Mick took voracious advantage of their bachelor status, but their colleagues were slightly more restrained. Peter 'Jonah' Jones remembers driving Ray to the flat of a tall, attractive girl, possibly a former art student, about whom Davies confided absolutely nothing. "Ray was just finding himself with women at that time," Jones suggests. "He was experimenting." Pete Quaife had a steadier relationship with a statuesque, long-necked upmarket conquest, Nicola Stark, whom Jonah affectionately nicknamed 'Giraffe'. The assistant road manager was also felled by Cupid's arrow. One afternoon, a beautiful beauty queen and aspiring model walked into the family newsagent's in Denmark Terrace and agreed to a date. Jones was smitten. Everyone was impressed, not least Ray, who mischievously referred to Jonah as "our star roadie".

On 15 May 1964, the Kinks appeared at the Goldhawk Social Club in Shepherd's Bush, a venue synonymous with the latest teenage subculture: the Mods. The original Mods – or Modernists as they were more accurately known – were closely related to the beatniks of the Fifties. Their favourite music was the cool jazz of Charlie Parker, Miles Davis or John Coltrane; their sartorial style was formed by French or Italian fashions; their favoured habitats were coffee bars and clubs. In certain ways they were not unlike the middle-class art school types with whom Ray Davies had recently associated. However, the denizens of the Goldhawk were second-generation Mods, a new, predominantly working-class species who loved various forms of black music and R&B rather than jazz. Among the distinguishable, if clichéd, characteristics of the 1964 Mods were smartly styled cropped hair, tailored suits with razor-creased trousers, Fred Perry sports shirts, Vespa or Lambretta scooters ornamented with multiple mirrors, disposable income and a devotion to purple hearts (amphetamines). They had already gained some media exposure two months before after invading the quiet seaside resort of Clacton but that was merely an aperitif for what was to follow. Two days after the Kinks' show at the Goldhawk, a mass of Mods descended upon the beaches of Margate and Brighton for the Whitsun weekend. They were accompanied by their leather-clad rivals, the Rockers, who resembled Teddy boys on motorcycles, with an image redolent of Hell's Angels and Fifties American rock 'n' rollers such as Gene Vincent & The Blue Caps. Clashes between the two groups ended in a trail of destruction, scores of arrests and some hysterical reporting in national newspapers. The most famous comment on this riotous feast was provided by Margate magistrate Dr George Simpson who spoke of "these long-haired, mentally unstable, petty little hoodlums, these sawdust Caesars who can only find courage like rats, hunting in packs".

The Kinks played at the Goldhawk Social Club several times in 1964, but their connection with Mod culture was largely incidental. Among their ranks only Pete Quaife, later to purchase a Vespa complete with an army-green Parka coat, ever adopted the image. The premier Mod group at the Goldhawk were the Who – a name they would not fully adopt until later in the year. In February, they had supported the Kinks at the club under their previous name the Detours, but the headliners had not made much of an impression. Guitarist Pete Townshend was aware that the Kinks had since made some progress on the package tour circuit but felt put off by their image. "We were still an amateur band when we'd supported them at the Goldhawk . . . We were very much caught up in the Mod ethos. The Goldhawk was a Mod club and we all thought they looked *ridiculous*. They came in with their long hair and their draped jackets and frilly shirts and we thought they looked like wankers . . . Dave's hair was very long and he really did look a bit old-fashioned to me already. I know that sounds incredibly snooty, but nonetheless."

What the Kinks could offer the Mods was a selection of R&B classics that always went down well with the dancers. Over time, Townshend concluded that there was something more to their appeal, possibly based on a subtly androgynous image. "Probably in the days of the Mods, people were much more open to that. In the Mod era, boys wore eye make-up and there was a lot of boys dancing for boys and trying to dress for boys – and not necessarily with anything sexual going on, but in order to enchant or seduce. Ray had that. Ray and the Kinks – even though they weren't Mods – somehow they managed to become a Mod band in spite of their funny, kinky outfits. I never could get what the outfits were about, really. I suppose it was just a gimmick of the time."

Ray Davies was in a quandary for most of that busy May month, veering erratically from one mood to the next like a weathercock in an emotional storm. The night after the Goldhawk gig, he felt euphoric after experiencing an intense reaction from an audience at the Savoy Ballroom in Southsea impressed by a spirited performance of 'You Really Got Me. "It was the only song where they all stood up and clapped at the end, but it was different from anything else in the set and I just knew we'd make it." That high was succeeded by near despair. Terry Anning, the nephew who served as his substitute brother, was emigrating to Australia, along with his parents, Rose and Arthur. The boy did not want to leave, but had no choice in the matter. "On the day they went to Australia, we went on tour," Davies recalls. "It was our first tour in the van. So it was the beginning and end of everything." The next evening, after an appearance at the Scene in Redcar, Yorkshire, Ray fell into a maudlin state, lamenting the departure of Terry and the loss of his beloved sister and surrogate mother, Rose. He recalled that she had taken the instrumental tapes that he had made while staying at her house. Several years later, he would channel all his misery into the song 'Rosy, Won't You Please Come Home'.

Two days later, a third version of Ray Davies was on display following a show at Sheffield's Esquire Club. This time he was back in control, but still vulnerable and romantically needy. That night he was introduced to a teenage girl who would change his life. She had hitched from Bradford with a friend named Sue, who was then going out with Mick Avory.

"What's your name?" Ray asked.

"Rasa," she replied.

"What does it mean?" he enquired.

"Dewdrop," she translated, explaining that she was of Lithuanian extraction.

"So, do you drop?" Ray quipped, in a crude attempt at humour.

Rasa had no idea what he was talking about, so merely smiled, leaving him intrigued. He soon discovered that the pretty blonde 18-year-old was still at school. She seemed mature and confident for her age and had an obvious interest in music. Her fine-boned, high-cheeked face was reposed but mobile, lit by piercing almond eyes that assimilated and absorbed everything he said. They made tentative plans to meet again, exchanging addresses and promising to write to each other. Geographical distance and band commitments seemed likely to thwart any blossoming relationship. Still, there was a definite spark and sense of fortuitous timing about the meeting with Rasa. After the hectic tour with Dave Clark, the manic euphoria of Southsea and the dark melancholia of Redcar, he now felt a reassuring equilibrium.

CHAPTER TEN

THE MYSTERY OF
'YOU REALLY GOT ME'

The story of 'You Really Got Me' is one of the most celebrated and mysterious fables in rock history, a saga steeped in myth, muddied by conflicting memories from all the parties involved in its creation and dissemination. Music critics later made portentous statements about the variant recordings, but factual certainties have turned out to be notoriously subjective, based on an audible authenticity unchecked for decades. The original tapes and record-ings, recalled with such passion, are like relics buried beneath sand.

Ray Davies still speaks about the origins of the song as a Chet Atkins'-styled instrumental captured on a Grundig tape recorder in the front room of his sister Rose's house in Highgate. Time dissolves in his many retellings of the story. Sometimes he is a schoolboy of 15, or 16, then he places himself at art college, two years later. It is one of his most enduring memories, yet it escapes straightforward chronology. According to its composer, the tape still exists somewhere in Rose's house in Adelaide and was once considered an archival candidate for the Kinks' box set. Ray promised to track it down but either thought better of the idea or simply abandoned the search. It has never surfaced.

The same fate has befallen the Regent Sound demo of the song first attempted in March 1964. This supposedly featured the "sudden ending" which was later used for dramatic effect in concert. It remains unheard by the public, as does any live version from the period, none of which are known to have been taped. Much more remarkable is the disappearance of the original studio version recorded at Pye's own studio with producer Shel Talmy. A crucial part of the Kinks' recorded legacy, this was a tape of immense historic importance, but it appears to have vanished. "There has to be an acetate around *somewhere*," Dave Davies says with an incredulous air but, if so, none has appeared at auction or even on bootleg tape. "There probably is a good version lying around," Ray adds, then corrects himself. "I don't know where the tape is. It's never been out." Even the multifarious labels that have acquired the rights to the Pye catalogue since the Seventies onwards have never located a single take from this particular session. All that remains is the familiar classic recording, untainted by comparison with its enigmatic blueprint.

It was mid-June when the Kinks entered Pye Studios to complete what was likely to be their final attempt at the recording. "I remember when we previously did it with Shel," says Dave Davies. "It had a Ronettes drum sound with lots of Phil Spector-style echo. The guitar was lost in the mesh of echo which totally defeated the whole point of it. Our idea was the funny guitar sound I had which everybody thought I was crazy doing. Shel was a big fan of Phil Spector and saw himself as an American entering into a new venture. He was very enthusiastic, but we all hated it. We heard it and it didn't sound anything like it did live."

It is something of a critical commonplace to claim that the original unreleased Pye version was over-produced and heavily influenced by Spector. In the music press of the time, Talmy had already been criticized for trying to make the Orchids sound like the Crystals and the Ronettes, but there is no aural evidence available to prove whether he ever employed the same trick with the Kinks. Whenever he was questioned about the Spector influence on his version of 'You Really Got Me' he seemed genuinely perplexed, pointing out that it was merely "slower and more R&B influenced".

"We did it about twenty-five per cent slower," Talmy estimates, "and, if you picture the riff, you'll see that it really works well with blues. It certainly wasn't a Phil Spector version. I don't know what that is. It was extremely good and a totally different concept from the one that eventually came out. We all liked it at the time."

That last sentence is contradicted by both Davies brothers and if Talmy was ever under any illusions that Ray liked the recording, then he soon learned otherwise. Over the next few weeks Davies fretted about the session and refused to accept mongrel apologies. He had a face as long as a late breakfast whenever the topic was discussed. "I became obsessive about it because I didn't know if I'd write other songs. I thought that this was the only record I'd ever make that I was really pleased with. I'd just come off a [tour] date and I had a sore throat – a really bad, gravelly sore throat. I sounded more like Georgie Fame impersonating Paul Robeson . . . And the guitars sounded untidy and it was just swamped in echo. No doubt you've interviewed Shel Talmy who says it was perfect, but I think you'd go with the [later] one I wanted."

Initially, Davies could get no support when petitioning to re-record the song, not even from the other Kinks, who felt he was over-reacting. Pete Quaife evidently had no great faith in the composition. "When I played the song first for Pete, he said he didn't care for it. It didn't sound commercial enough for him – not pop enough." The management also greeted Ray's request for a re-recording with caution. They were understandably wary of crossing swords with Pye, especially as this was the third and last single that the company was obligated to release under their contract. Ray persisted with an obduracy so intense and entrenched that Collins and Wace feared he might break up the group. Fortunately, Davies found an ally in Larry Page whose penchant for political intrigue proved decisive. "I'd already demoed those songs and I didn't like what Shel had done. I didn't think the magic was there. Therefore, I went along and had a meeting with Louis Benjamin and asked him if he could either use the demos or readjust the mixes so that the song would sound right. And Louis said it couldn't be done because they had a producer who would have to be given credit. I said that didn't interest me at all. All I wanted was for the record to be right when it came out. And Benjy refused. So I said, 'At the moment I'm talking to you as their manager. Now I'll talk to you as a publisher and tell you that either the song gets changed or the records don't come out.' And that's what happened because the power of a publisher is such that he can stop it."

Benjamin huffed and puffed about the unnecessary re-recording and the awkwardness of changing the release date but his objections were mere bluster. Contractually, Pye was not responsible for paying for the sessions so the record company had little to lose by submitting to Page's demands. The person most affected by the decision was Shel Talmy. After learning of Page's powerplay, he convinced himself that the former Teenage Rage was angling to produce the Kinks. Although the pair had worked successfully together on a number of Page's Coventry acts, their relationship deteriorated hereafter. Talmy's hostile reaction was understandable. It hardly seemed fair that he should be responsible for the costs of a second session when the first had seemed perfectly adequate. He still insists that the original slow version "would have been a number 1 hit", an opinion impossible to counter given its unavailability.

It was left to Robert Wace to resolve the Talmy issue with a combination of diplomacy and hard cash. "Ray was so sure that the recording of 'You Really Got Me' was terrible and wouldn't be successful that I personally paid for it to be re-recorded at IBC Studios. He was saying that if it went out he'd pack it in. The original was flooded in echo and they wanted a much drier recording that was less produced. Talmy thought the original was great as it stood, and Pye wouldn't pay for it to be re-recorded. I felt Ray had a lot of drive and should be given his head. To be honest, I didn't particularly like 'You Really Got Me', but he was totally convinced that it was a smash."

In mid-July, the group gathered at IBC in Portland Place, a studio that Talmy always preferred to Pye's own. Ray Davies had got his wish, but at what cost? His demands had offended the imperious Louis Benjamin, caused friction between Talmy and Page and left Collins and Wace puzzled by the entire affair. Ray felt a dark foreboding at the moment of his imminent triumph, reinforced by the belief that he had alienated Pye Records to such an extent that only a hit record could possibly save the Kinks from extinction.

Convinced that Talmy was only there under duress, he feared that the producer might terminate the session after the first unsuccessful take. His concerns ultimately proved unfounded but were real enough in his own mind, particularly at the start of the recording. It seemed that he was required to dance an intricate tarantella of self-deceit simply to complete the recording. Seeking reassurance, he focused on his younger brother, always an oasis of self-confidence whatever the circumstances. Dave was predictably unfazed and even betrayed an air of arrogance about his performance, as if it were of no more importance than a rehearsal. He had, after all, been playing the song live for months. "It could have been our last shot in the studio for Pye," he admits. "Ray always said it was a desperate moment, but I never thought of it like that. It was just exciting. When we went to IBC the song started to sound like it should with no echo, just a dry recording. Ray was in more of a panic about it than I was. I was having a great time. But there was a lot of tension around. I remember laying in the guitar solo. I said, 'All right, let's just do it.' It seemed everyone around me was panicking and I couldn't understand that. It always surprised me that people felt under pressure because I didn't at all. Maybe Robert and Grenville thought we were going to blow it with Pye; maybe the other version was all right and this might not sound so good. There were all these things, but they didn't bother me. I just wanted to get on with it."

The defining moment in 'You Really Got Me' occurs in the 74th second when Ray screams the ambiguously encouraging words, "Oh no!" Dave responds to this entreaty by unleashing a blistering guitar solo whose power is amplified by the brevity of its execution. It left Ray transfixed. "That moment before his solo, those few bars, I remember it in slow motion. I shouted to Dave, he glared back . . . and played himself into rock 'n' roll history." Looking back at that remarkable session, his words resemble those of an athletics coach reflecting on a winning race. "When that record starts it's like four people doing the four-minute mile, there's a lot of emotion. It was a great experience standing next to Dave when he played that because I was shouting at him, willing him to do it, saying it was the last chance we had. There's determination, fight and guts in that record. 'You Really Got Me' was, in a way, a computerized version of all that we were doing."

The historic importance of 'You Really Got Me' as a cultural artefact of the mid-Sixties beat and R&B boom is indisputable, but even the final version retains its mystery. Determining who actually played on the record (beyond the nucleus of the Davies brothers, Quaife and session drummer Bobby Graham) is no easy task. There are no surviving session logs at Pye or IBC to confirm the identities of the other participants. Individual testimonies and memories are clouded or confused by the different times and locations of the two recordings. It is not even entirely clear if the same session musicians appeared on both recordings. Over 30 years ago, Talmy told me: "Glyn Johns was the engineer . . . Jimmy Page played rhythm guitar, Jon Lord played organ and Perry Ford played piano." Even then, this seemed questionable. There is no detectable organ on the record, unless it was mixed out of existence. Other details are similarly vague or contentious. The Davies brothers cite Arthur Greenslade as the piano player rather than Perry Ford, and even Jimmy Page believes he played rhythm on subsequent LP tracks rather than this one. At least all the parties are in agreement about Bobby Graham's contribution. "Avory was not involved," confirms Talmy. "That was no slur against Avory though. He was a new member and didn't really know the stuff – that's why we used Bobby." Even these comments sound a little disingenuous. Considering Avory had been playing 'You Really Got Me' almost nightly for several weeks on the Dave Clark tour, he obviously knew the song far better than his substitute. Of course, Talmy always liked to have his own team of musicians on call and drummers were invariably seen as the weakest link.

Ray later claimed that the doleful Avory had been handed a tambourine to play as compensation for his usurpation by Bobby Graham. Even that morsel of mercy was denied him by Talmy who insists that he himself played the tambourine in a sonic, cameo equivalent of film director Alfred Hitchcock, who frequently appeared as an extra in his own films.

One canard that dogged the Kinks for years was the suggestion that Jimmy Page might have played lead guitar on the group's early hits. This unfounded rumour always irked Dave and Ray and survived far longer than it should have done, despite consistent denials from everybody connected with the group. Decades later, in a wonderfully condescending compliment to his sibling, Ray said: "My brother Dave hasn't got much going for him, but to try and take that stuff away from him is bullshit. He invented that guitar sound. I wrote the song, but it wouldn't have been anything without his work."

On 4 August, 'You Really Got Me' was released, a few days after a return appearance on *Ready, Steady, Go!*. Coverage of the single in the music papers was minimal but the television exposure, along with extensive promotion on pirate radio, ensured an instant chart entry. "It was amazing hearing it on the radio," Dave recalls. "It was like having sex for the first time. I remember coming out of Arthur Howes' office in Greek Street, turning on the transistor and it came on. I was mesmerized. It seemed like it was somebody else. I couldn't get it out of my head." Within a month, the disc dislodged the Honeycombs' 'Have I The Right?' at number 1. It was the first time that Pye Records had achieved *consecutive* chart toppers. Earlier that year the Searchers had reached number 1 with 'Needles And Pins' and 'Don't Throw Your Love Away' and Sandie Shaw would soon do the same with '(There's) Always Something There To Remind Me'. The once unfashionable Pye label was having a vintage year and Louis Benjamin was overjoyed. His response, not untypically, was to insist that the Kinks complete their debut album post haste. Amazingly, their deadline was the end of August.

The summer of 1964 was a golden era for British R&B groups. Suddenly, they were not mere chart contenders but dominant taste makers. The Animals, who had relocated from Newcastle upon Tyne to London, catapulted to the top of the charts with 'The House Of The Rising Sun', a daring folk/blues standard whose subject matter vividly detailed the moral ruination of a young man ultimately doomed to spend his life in sin and misery following a visit to a New Orleans brothel. Its risqué theme escaped censorship and DJs responded uncharacteristically kindly to its intimidating four-minute length, a possible record for a chart-topping single at that time. The song was replaced at number 1 by the Rolling Stones' cover 'It's All Over Now', their first climb to the summit. By mid-August, the top spot was secured by Manfred Mann's 'Do Wah Diddy Diddy', another group much loved by the producers of *Ready, Steady, Go!*. Although the Kinks were fourth in line among the R&B giants that summer, Ray Davies could rightly boast that his group was the only one among the quartet to reach number 1 with a self-penned single.

'You Really Got Me' has been praised frequently for its sonic innovation but little attention has been paid to its lyrics. On one level, they could be dismissed as scarcely more than a moronic chant, leavened by a strangely insistent, almost neurotic declaration of commitment. Maybe that was the point. The intensity and uncomplicated nature of the composition fits perfectly with its musical starkness of tone, both in the insistent riff and occasional distortion. Davies even includes a reference to ongoing insomnia: "I can't sleep at night". The sentiments are direct, earthy and anti-romantic, a reaction against the trappings of the early Sixties love-lorn ballad "without all that moon and June stuff."

The public image of the Kinks in the pop firmament of the time was less than positive. It was easy to knock their Neanderthal lyrics and unforgivable grammar – even the title 'You Really Got Me' would prompt the riposte: it *should* be '*You've* Really Got Me'. Although the Beatles had released 'You Really Got A Hold On Me' on *With The Beatles* at the end of 1963 that was not one of their compositions but a cover of an American act, the Miracles, featuring Smokey Robinson. Evidently, far better was expected of British state-educated musicians. The Rolling Stones would flout such conventions the following year with '(I Can't Get *No*) Satisfaction', but they were already considered beyond the pale. Ever since they had appeared on the pop scene, the Stones had stoked the fiery ire of an elder generation with an image that was variously seen as dissident or degenerate. Promoted as an antithesis of the Beatles, the Stones' anti-authoritarianism was invariably measured by the length of their hair. Unlike the Beatles' cut – at first ridiculed but grudgingly accepted as a teenage fad – the Stones' shoulder-length locks were regarded as an affront to common decency. Similar barbs would be levelled against Dave Davies. It was a key issue in the great generational divide.

Criticism of the Stones' image had been unrelenting throughout 1964. In January, the *New Musical Express* referred to them as a "caveman-like quartet". The *Daily Mirror* quoted the president of the National Federation of Hairdressers offering them free haircuts, adding "one of them looks as though he's got a feather duster on his head." The *Daily Express* concluded, "They look like boys that any self-respecting mum would lock in the bathroom." Such sarcasm might have been expected from middle-aged reporters and mums and dads, but it was also present among some of their contemporaries. Journalist Maureen Cleave, an avatar of pop chic, friend of the Beatles and a confidante of John Lennon, casually dismissed the Stones as "a horrible lot". Sharpening her pen, she added: "They've done terrible things to the music scene, set it back, I would say, about eight years. Just when we'd got our pop singers looking neat and tidy and, above all, cheerful, along come the Rolling Stones, looking almost like what we used to call beatniks." There may have been more than a sliver of irony in Cleave's admonishments but, if so, it was largely lost on the readership of London's *Evening Standard*. Nor was it a one-off. Within two months, Cleave returned to the theme, this time more earnestly. "Never have the middle-class virtues of neatness, obedience and punctuality been so conspicuously lacking . . . The Rolling Stones are not the people you build empires with; they are not the people who always remember to wash their hands before lunch." One month after this appeared, 11 schoolboys were reportedly suspended and threatened with expulsion for sporting Mick Jagger-inspired haircuts. In July, all five Stones appeared on *Juke Box Jury* and the BBC received the predictable "deluge of calls" commenting adversely on the group's long hair and surly demeanour. That same summer Granada Television reported a number of complaints after 19-year-old student Nicholas Austin had appeared on that mainstay of middle-class academic respectability *University Challenge* wearing shoulder-length hair, rakish side whiskers and dark glasses. As if to compound these sins, he even had the audacity to chew gum throughout the broadcast. "Gum, dark glasses and hair as long as Mick Jagger's can hardly be considered suitable for a television appearance," wrote one irate viewer.

Later that year, the great debate even reached the courts when counsel for Jagger, defending his client on a driving offence, pleaded: "The Duke of Marlborough had hair longer than my client and he won some famous battles. His hair was powdered I think, because of fleas. My client has no fleas. The Emperor Caesar Augustus also had rather long hair. He won many great victories. Barristers, too, wear long hair in the shape of wigs with curled-up ends . . . Put out of your minds the nonsense talked about these young men, the Rolling Stones. They are not long-haired idiots, but highly intelligent university men." That last sentence was a calculated overstatement: Jagger was a dropout from the London School of Economics and none of the others had ever attended university. Nevertheless, it was a witty and persuasive plea, the more notable coming from a member of the judiciary rather than the pop press or media.

The Kinks had been blighted with accusations of copying the Stones almost since their inception. It was not merely the London R&B connection, the stage act, the song repertoire and the sartorial style, but the crucial issue of long hair. In truth, Ray Davies more closely resembled a Beatle than a Stone, while both Quaife and Avory had modest hairdos for the time. Such nuances were ignored amid the grander spectacle of Dave Davies, whose girlishly long hair almost outdid those of the Stones. The androgyny was underlined by an amusing press snippet revealing that Dave's sister Gwen, wearing slacks and an identical hairstyle, had been chased by a group of female fans who mistook her for the younger brother.

In order to improve their profile, the group's management appointed publicist Brian Sommerville, a dapper former Royal Navy lieutenant commander, whose previous major client was the Beatles. He arranged a series of pop paper profiles and interviews for the autumn, including a lengthy encounter with *Melody Maker* in which Ray Davies addressed the thorny issue of imitating the Stones. In defining the Kinks' image, he both confirmed and denied the irksome comparisons: "OK, so we've got the hair and all that, and some people even say the same attitude, but – well, come to that, you could ask 'Aren't the Stones another Beatles group?' because of their hair, couldn't you? Mind you – OK, so it's true. There's a bit of the rebel in us. But we are not doing a Stones. And we don't play R&B. That's best left to people like Muddy Waters, who know what it's all about. I call our stuff *expression*. It's an outlet to us. I know it sounds corny to say it, but you feel, when you're standing up there, that you want to get something out of your system. Everyone's got it somewhere – the expression and the need for an outlet. The audience want to experience it. So we help them. Doesn't that sound right?" That last sentence suggested rhetorical evasion rather than conviction.

Amid the flurry of interviews, there were a couple of oblique predictions from Davies about the musical future of the Kinks. Anticipating the sound of 1965 when he would write the groundbreaking raga-influenced 'See My Friend', he noted: "I like going to Indian restaurants and listening to the records there. I like that drone they've got on them." Even more remarkably, he anticipated the group's eventual incorporation of a brass section, which would not occur until the stage shows of the early Seventies. "We are still trying hard to develop. In about four years' time, or before then – you can never follow public taste – we might be augmenting the group to form a band. That was our original plan, if we hadn't had any luck with the records." The inoffensive pop profiles toned down the group's darker traits, but the Stones' comparisons continued in live reviews and music press news bulletins.

While the momentum was building, the Kinks opened for the Beatles in Bournemouth where Ray bore the brunt of John Lennon's sarcasm. "Can I borrow your song list, lads?" he quipped. "We've lost ours." As Ray recalls: "He meant that as a criticism of our style. I feel I could have been a friend of John's, but we were two people who were destined not to talk . . . We did not get on. He was very cynical . . . John made a few cruel remarks to me." In truth, Lennon was merely pulling rank, a common enough occurrence. The Bournemouth show was one of the few times when the Liverpudlians faced even a minor challenge from their support act. "I think it was the best gig we ever did," says 'Jonah' Jones. "My memory of it is that the audience was still singing 'We want the Kinks!' after the Beatles had started playing."

Two weeks later, on 16 August, the Kinks again supported the Beatles on a unique bill that included a third act, the High Numbers, soon to be rechristened the Who. Pete Townshend, by now familiar with the single 'You Really Got Me', was guardedly impressed. Comparing their sound to the Beatles and Stones, he admitted: "It seemed to bring something new to the spectrum. I'd heard wilder guitar playing because I'd listened to John Lee Hooker and Link Wray and a lot of dirty blues guitar. But in the field of rock guitar that percussive playing that Dave did – the kind of thing that a drummer would do – was quite unique." At the end of August, the Kinks again played with the High Numbers, this time in Blackpool alongside Pye rivals, the Searchers. Townshend listened to Dave's playing with a critical ear. "He wasn't very loud. He had a great distorted, funky guitar sound but he just used a Vox twin amp and I was already using great stacks of Marshalls. So we were at least five or six times as loud as they were. They weren't a particularly loud band, but they were a very driving band."

Part of that drive came from the aggressive interaction between the players. Pete Quaife remembers the onstage rivalry and animosity as each brother would goad the other, as if they were saying, "I'm going to be better than you". Townshend observed that same dynamic when comparing the Kinks to his own group. "Mick and Pete were quite cool characters in the Bill Wyman/ Ringo Starr mould. They were cool, laid-back guys and very easy to meet and spend time with – no grandeur, no edge. Ray and Dave were complex. There was no sense of them working *together*. They were both working outwards, both competing for the audience. It was very similar to the way the Who worked but in the Who, we *all* did it. There were four of us working it outwards. But with them, you had a sense that you'd seen it before, perhaps with the Everly Brothers, this sense that they're together but there's some tension going on . . . With Ray and Dave there was that feeling that they weren't really mates. There was tension there but it was because they *were* so different. Dave was very testosterone driven, very aggressive, very mean, very strong, very indifferent, careless. He had a Keith Richards thing about him: 'I don't give a fuck, I just play' . . . but very earnest, solid . . . Ray had a real longing. I watched them several times from the audience [and saw] him concentrating, reaching out and wanting to engage you. But when you met him in the flesh you'd think, 'This can't be' because he's not that kind of guy. If you met Mick Jagger, for example, you'd know that the guy you see on the stage . . . would do that. Mick stands in front of you, moves his shoulders, looks you square in the eye and you think, 'Stop moving! People will talk!' With Ray, he pulls himself up, looks a bit imperious and you start to realize you're dealing with somebody that's actually quite shy."

There was nothing shy about the audience reaction to the Kinks that autumn. On 4 September, an estimated one thousand teenagers at the Mecca Ballroom in Basildon New Town, Essex, nearly caused a riot after some of their number dragged Dave from the stage. Two days later, the group played the Princess Theatre in Torquay, unaware that a ghost from their recent past was lurking in the front seats. Former drummer John Start had spent the summer sailing in Dartmouth and could not resist taking his girlfriend to see the group, just as they were climbing the charts, appearing on *Top Of The Pops* and making headlines in the pop press. Start made no attempt to get backstage and would never see the group perform again. "What did I feel? I didn't feel I was missing out on anything. There were no regrets or anger that I might have done the wrong thing. There's never been that. It was a lovely evening. I don't know why I didn't see them afterwards or contact Pete. I didn't feel the connection somehow."

The next night, at the Streatham Ice Rink, it was Ray's turn to be hauled into the crowd during the harmonica-led Slim Harpo tribute, 'Got Love If You Want It'. Beneath the audience the ice literally melted, but there was enough left to chill the champagne which awaited Davies after the show amid breaking news that 'You Really Got Me' was number 1 in the charts. The group were still on a high 48 hours later when they took the stage at the 100 Club in Oxford Street, briefly accompanied by 'Jonah' Jones, reprising his role as backing singer and Bo Diddley-inspired accompanist. One week later, in Newcastle, there was another Stones-styled public disturbance when a hundred fans were crushed against a stage barrier, many of them fainting from lack of oxygen.

The Kinks' roadshow ground to a temporary halt in the early hours of 19 September when the car in which they were travelling collided with a lorry. Although they played another gig later that evening in Bury, the next three dates were cancelled on the grounds of "delayed shock". At least this gave Davies some free time to write the group's next single. Among the songs in contention was 'Tired Of Waiting For You', which Shel Talmy had marked as a likely winner. After further consideration it was decided to retain that title for the New Year. Larry Page, back from a lightning visit to Eddie Kassner in New York, advised Davies to err on the side of caution and compose something similar to 'You Really Got Me'. Even as that was happening, the Kinks' first album was rushed out to cash in on their current high profile. Asked by a journalist whether it was too soon to release an album, especially one that had been recorded with such haste, Ray was brutally frank. "You're right," he retorted. "The record company have to make their money, I suppose." Dave Davies later looked back with amazement at the time frame in which the work was completed. "The first album – we had a week to do it. I don't know how we managed. There were only about six original songs on that LP because of the time, and the rest were things we knew and could do very quickly. As I remember, the last sessions for that album, there were actually people hammering on the door to get in because we were running a bit over time."

Shel Talmy always maintained that, in the early to mid-Sixties, it was the least accomplished that spent the most time in the studio. He liked to record speedily, for economic as much as artistic reasons, and there was no prevarication with the Kinks whose familiar live set made up the bulk of the album. "We certainly had time to finish what we had. It was all ready. Benjamin wanted the album out to capitalize on the single, so we finished it quickly. It sounds terrible – it only took a week! The way it sounds is that we rushed it. We didn't. We're only talking about three-track. How elaborate could you get? That 'knocking on the door' story is a slight exaggeration."

CHAPTER ELEVEN

LOVE AND MARRIAGE

The Kinks was a credible debut which equalled, if not bettered, most other first albums from beat merchants of the period. Over-reliant on familiar R&B material, its major deficit was the lack of a new composition that might eclipse or distract attention from the pervasive presence of 'You Really Got Me'. It was standard procedure at the time to follow the Beatles' model on *Please Please Me* and *With The Beatles* by mixing original and cover songs to produce a varied set. Earlier that summer, the Fab Four had shown the way forward by including a complete collection of original compositions on the accompanying album to the film *A Hard Day's Night*. Ray Davies was in no position to compete with Lennon and McCartney and, in any case, was not given the option. A week after completing the sessions for *The Kinks* two new Davies compositions were recorded at Pye – 'I Just Want To Walk With You' and 'Don't Ever Let Me Go' – but these were consigned to the tape vault. "For a first album I thought it would be a very good idea to do some non-original stuff," says Shel Talmy. "On one hit song, Ray Davies was hardly established as the great songwriter that he is. Besides this, in the early Sixties, the singer-songwriter was not something that the public had latched on to . . . Early on, Robert Wace felt that we should be doing somebody else's stuff and Ray saw sense in that. Nobody disagreed with this material – there were no great traumas – nothing like that."

Instead, the public received what they probably expected: a

long player featuring reassuring material from the group's recent live set. Among the 14 songs are spirited versions of Chuck Berry's 'Beautiful Delilah' and 'Too Much Monkey Business', Dave's raucous reading of Don Covay's 'Long Tall Shorty', the Stones-influenced 'I'm A Lover Not A Fighter' and the harmonica-led cover of Bo Diddley's 'Cadillac'. The blueprint riff-based instrumental 'Revenge', the only known collaboration between Ray and Larry Page, receives a belated release, partly vindicated by its later inclusion as the opening theme to television's *Ready, Steady, Go!* courtesy of the Ray McVay Sound. Shel Talmy cynically contributes the out of place 'Bald Headed Woman' and 'I've Been Driving On Bald Mountain', two blues-based folk arrangements introduced by the astute producer for the sole purpose of securing a share of the publishing money. The remaining Ray Davies' compositions are a varied bunch: 'So Mystifying' betrays strong American phrasing; 'Just Can't Go To Sleep' indicates the continuing influence of the Beatles and the Shirelles; and 'I Took My Baby Home' sounds like a Coasters' tribute. 'Stop Your Sobbing' is a welcome pop outing with an engagingly vulnerable vocal and oddly paternalistic tone: the impatient admonition "Stop it!" is sung as if the narrator is addressing a recalcitrant child or a disobedient dog rather than a distraught lover. The album closes with 'Got Love If You Want It', whose unrestrained exuberance had recently encouraged audiences to pull Ray bodily from the stage.

The Kinks performed as well as could be expected in the album charts, peaking at number 3. For the remainder of the year, momentum was sustained via the traditional route of the pop package tour. During October, Billy J. Kramer With The Dakotas headlined a strong line-up of acts including the Kinks, Cliff Bennett & The Rebel Rousers, the Yardbirds and the Nashville Teens. The tour was promoted jointly by Arthur Howes and Brian Epstein with the intention of re-establishing Billy J. as a major chart force. Although Kramer's plaintive cover of Lennon/McCartney's 'From A Window' had recently reached the Top 10, he was discovering to his cost that the Olympian flame of Merseybeat had been momentarily passed over to a rival breed of R&B exponents, several of whom were lurking on his bill. The Yardbirds, although still several months away from breaking through as a chart act, already boasted a devoted cult following among the London blues and R&B set. In common with Pete Townshend, their attitude towards the Kinks was a mixture of restrained admiration and condescension. "I didn't see them as a blues band," says Yardbirds' guitarist Chris Dreja. Echoing the High Numbers' laughter at the Kinks' hunting jackets, he remembers "we used to call them the Cricketers" with Ray caricatured as their aloof eccentric captain. Nevertheless, there was no doubting the power and originality of 'You Really Got Me' which Dreja had at first assumed to be an American recording. Its provenance shocked everybody. "It blew me away to be honest," Dreja admits. For the R&B elite that had looked down on the Kinks as a well-meaning pop group, the single set an unexpected benchmark. As the first original composer of a UK R&B chart topper, Ray Davies felt as though he had won a race. "'You Really Got Me' was a different record for the time, there was nothing around like it. I remember I used to go down the Marquee and everyone was close to making a record like that. The Yardbirds thought they'd do it, but we did it first."

If Davies is to be believed, his contemporaries at first dismissed the Kinks' success as an accident of history or a lucky aberration that more rightly should have been achieved by a more authentic R&B group. "I don't think we were taken very seriously from the start. We were rushed in and out of the studio because they thought we wouldn't last and, as a result, some of our early records sound horrible. And when we had our first hit, I think other musicians were stunned. How could we make this blues-rock song and get a number 1? I don't think they've ever forgiven us." Even the Rolling Stones were supposedly taken aback. "I remember Mick Jagger's jaw dropping the first time he saw us. He couldn't believe that four such uncool people could have a bigger hit than he did. The Kinks were genuinely rebellious and threatening because we knew no shame."

Pete Quaife concurred, portraying the group's public image as "rather nasty little boys who loved to go around making lots of trouble and lots of noise and getting as many girls pregnant as we could. It was great from our point of view but a lot of people out there weren't too happy. We made the Stones look like sissies then. They were very conscious of their status and you could easily see the Stones were trying to climb up the ladder while we weren't. We were always sitting on the first rung of the ladder, fighting all the time and yelling at each other . . . Ray and Dave were very volatile. They could start a fight over absolutely nothing. I thought discretion was the better part of valour."

The *NME* reported more screaming for the Kinks, seemingly inspired by Dave's "crippled jockey" dance. Poor Billy J. Kramer must have felt a musical outsider among the coterie of R&B acts on the bill. In a rare moment of empathy, Davies sympathized with the Liverpool star whose act suddenly looked old-fashioned and unchallenging. "I really admired Billy J. Kramer. He just wanted to make good pop records. The Kinks, on the other hand, were under the misapprehension that they wanted to change the world. We did our bit."

The Kinks sometimes appeared aloof and, despite the presence of other R&B acts on the scene, from the Rolling Stones to the Yardbirds, Ray remained distant and detached. "I didn't feel a sense of solidarity with those other British bands as much as I felt a sense of rivalry. It was reassuring, in a way, to know that there were all these other people around, who were trying to express themselves in a similar way. But I never felt part of a movement."

Barely a week into the tour, there was an historic General Election in which Harold Wilson led Labour back into office for the first time in 13 years. Although Ray Davies could have voted that day, he made no effort to do so. Political apathy would remain an enduring trait for the rest of his life. The election result was seen by many as symbolizing a fresh beginning for the country, another sign that the Sixties was in full swing. As ever, Davies was sceptical.

On 23 October, the Kinks released their new single: 'All Day And All Of The Night'. It was the classic paradoxical follow-up inasmuch as it sounded uncannily like its predecessor, yet also radically different. Dave's guitar work, rawer than ever and chaotic in execution, is highlighted by abrupt key changes, a striking solo and a stronger melody line. Vocally the sound is cleaner, with Larry Page's protégé Johnny B. Great (John Goodison) hovering in the background. Talmy once again demotes Mick Avory in favour of the steadfast Bobby Graham. During the recording, Ray had the front to suggest a different drum pattern, prompting the amazed session man to exclaim: "Who do you think you are?" Davies' confidence back then should not be mistaken for arrogance. His aim was to create a record that had the intensity of a live performance and in this he succeeded.

The music's urgency is reflected in the lyrical construction. The previous single, 'You Really Got Me', had spoken of disorientation, emotional confusion and insomnia. 'All Day And All Of The Night' goes further, conjuring a 24-hour addiction to a girl whose physical appearance in the song is virtually non-existent. There is no characterization, no description, simply an all-consuming hunger for what is almost an abstraction. Even the opening three words – "I'm not content" – attest not so much to his need for the girl but, rather, to an existential exasperation at the state of the world. What emerges is a dark love song of immense frustration, detailing a frightening dependency and irrational possessiveness caught somewhere between John Fowles' *The Collector* and Alfred Hitchcock's *Psycho*.

Ray Davies was not fully aware of the emotional intensity he was conveying until he heard the words of a master composer. "Burt Bacharach wrote a review in one of the trades. A great writer, I really admire him very much. He said a strange thing. He said it sounded 'very neurotic'. I *was* writing about someone who was very neurotic and very concerned with getting laid, finding a girlfriend or maybe looking for his girlfriend who's run off with somebody else. To a seventeen-year-old, this is very important stuff." Bacharach's comments made a lasting impression. "I thought I was being put down at first, but then I realized he was complimenting it. It's youthful, obsessive and sexually possessive."

Coincidentally, at the very moment Davies' neurotic hymn was released, Sandie Shaw was at number 1 with '(There's) Always Something There To Remind Me', a Burt Bacharach/Hal David composition chronicling a nostalgic walk through city streets in which every physical object serves as a painful reminder of all that has been lost in a relationship. Its neuroticism and abstract sense of place were more pronounced than anything Davies could yet produce in a pop song.

Reviewing 'All Day And All Of The Night', the *New Musical Express* concluded: "They could get very close to number 1 with this one." In the end it was kept from the top by the Supremes' 'Baby Love' and the Rolling Stones' 'Little Red Rooster'. Although the sales figures were worthy of a number 1 hit, the competition was unprecedented. Late 1964 saw the biggest volume of singles sales in pop history. It was the apotheosis of the British beat boom and the Kinks were now prominent members of a cast headed by the Beatles and the Rolling Stones.

Louis Benjamin was well aware of the sales surge and managed to squeeze more product out of Ray Davies. In late November, the EP *Kinksize Session* appeared, just in time for the Christmas market. Its opening track was a less than exciting cover of the Kingsmen's 'Louie Louie', the garage group staple that Davies once described as "the best rock 'n' roll song ever written". Already familiar from their early live performances, it is often cited as an important influence on 'You Really Got Me' and even 'All Day And All Of The Night'. Of course, the Kinks were not alone in creating new riffs from old. The Kingsmen themselves had covered 'Louie Louie' – an obscure R&B number recorded by its composer Richard Berry in early 1956. Moreover, variations of the arche-typal riff would appear at least three times the following year in such hits as the Who's 'I Can't Explain', the McCoys' 'Hang On Sloopy' and Sam The Sham & The Pharaohs' 'Wooly Bully'. Whenever rock went back to basics, some adaptation of the 'Louie Louie' riff would never be far away. Completing the EP were three nondescript Davies' compositions, 'I Gotta Go Now', 'Things Are Getting Better' and the song once given away to the Orchids, 'I've Got That Feeling'.

At the time of the EP's release, the Kinks were still on the road, part of an even larger package tour headed by Gerry And The Pacemakers, along with Gene Pitney, Marianne Faithfull, the Mike Cotton Sound, Bobby Shafto, Kim Weston and the Earl Van Dyke Band. Bassist Jim Rodford, a recent recruit to the Mike Cotton Sound, was thrilled by the visceral power of the Kinks, who closed the first half of the show. "I watched them from the side of the stage and I couldn't believe it. The power and the energy. What they did to the crowd was unique. I haven't seen anything like it since. The reaction was unbelievable. It was animal. The wildest thing you've ever seen. Dave was down on his knees, hair dangling on the stage, playing to the skies. The crowd were going berserk

– rioting. Later, I worked [on bills] with the Beatles and the Who, and they didn't have the same effect on me. Not *that* power. The Kinks were just something else."

While Dave Davies went wild at every opportunity, Ray was still canny enough to conduct some publishing business. In a tactical pitch worthy of Eddie Kassner, he offered the angelic Marianne Faithfull a song he had recently completed: 'There's A New World Just Opening For Me'. It was not so much rejected as completely forgotten about. Despite her bohemian sensibility, enhanced by association with the Rolling Stones, Faithfull felt uncomfortable in the presence of the Davies brothers. "The Kinks were very gothic," she wrote, years later. "Creepy and silent. They never spoke. They were uptight and fearful of everyone. Terrified. Underneath which there was all this weird dysfunctional family stuff going on."

Faithfull's recollections did not tally with those of others on the tour. John Beecham, the trombonist in the Mike Cotton Sound, recalls the camaraderie on the bus where Pete Quaife was the joker and Dave Davies the girl magnet. "We were in awe of the Kinks because everybody then was out for a hit record. Dave was a great guitar player. A lot of rock guitarists have their set licks but he was like a jazz musician with his solos. He would be different every night. Their live version of 'Louie Louie' was exciting." Ray was animated onstage, but quieter in company. "He was the one you'd least notice probably because he was shy. Pete would read a music paper and shout, 'Ray, see what they're writing about us now?' And Ray would cringe. That's not what he wanted."

Ray had good reason to feel a little strange during the tour. His personal life had been unsettled since encountering the exotic-ally named Rasa Pupyte Emilija Halina Didzpetryte on that date in Sheffield back in May. Since then, they had exchanged letters and promised to meet again. Over the summer, the Kinks appeared on the regional television show *Discs A Go-Go*, alongside Bradford soul singer Kiki Dee, who was then signed to Fontana Records. Dee had been contacted by Rasa via a friend who knew the singer's sister, Betty Matthews. Asked to pass on a message to Ray, Kiki gave him a paper with Rasa's name and a London telephone number. It says much for his state of mind that he phoned her that very night.

Davies had dated several girls during this period, as well as enjoying groupies on the road, but his first encounter with Rasa made a profound impression. They arranged to meet at Tottenham Court Road Tube station, an assignation that Ray had already romanticized in his mind's eye as though he was directing a film. When he saw her halfway down the stairs, idly perusing the Tube map, back turned but instantly identifiable due to her long blonde hair, he paused momentarily to savour the scene. For a brief second, he pondered the perverse possibility of abandoning the tryst in order to preserve its cinematic perfection in his imagination. At that point she turned around. After a Chinese meal in Soho, they walked to the Thames and talked at length.

Rasa has only fleeting memories of that memorable London date. "He's romanticizing, I think. The Ice Princess – that's what he called me. I don't know why. Maybe it's because my hair was long and blonde and I was wearing this rabbit fur coat. I might have looked like somebody from Norway among the ice fields." They certainly had much to discuss.

Rasa's life story reads like a touching fable. Her father had been a college professor of literature in Lithuania when the family had fled the country in 1948. She was born in Blomberg, Germany, on 5 April 1946, the youngest of four children. As refugees, they had settled in England, living in Bradford since 1951 among the Polish/Lithuanian community. Rasa received a strict Catholic upbringing and was discouraged from associating with boys or the more precocious English girls in her locale. Her parents secretly hoped that she might become a nun or a teacher but, even before she was a teenager, the girl harboured fantasies of something more glamorous. She dreamed of becoming a ballet dancer under the tutelage of Ostap Buriak, director and master of the newly founded 'Krylati' (The Winged Ones). Regrettably, her parents could not afford to pay for this. Often, Rasa would stand outside the dance studio, peering through a window, enviously watching the other Lithuanian girls in their tutus. Her father found some work as a translator but poor health, exacerbated by kidney and bladder problems, meant that he earned considerably less than other Lithuanians employed in the local factories. His wife, a seasoned multi-tasker, had been a talented tailoress in Moscow, specializing in corsetry and dresses. In Bradford, she worked briefly for Levi's tailors and supplemented her income by taking in two lodgers, while also cooking and cleaning for Mr Yablon, a Jewish solicitor, prominent in the community. Every day after school, Rasa would meet her mother at his palatial home, pretending to school friends that she lived in a flat surrounded by luxurious white carpets, silver cutlery and a fancy television set.

The early Sixties British beat boom intoxicated Rasa's imagination and she somehow persuaded her parents to allow her to attend a Beatles' Christmas show. In a similar act of rebellion, she applied for a part-time job at a local coffee bar, surreptitiously working after school several times a week. It was there that she first learned of the Kinks' existence from her friend Sue, who had met the group when they played the Bradford Gaumont on 5 April. Thereafter, Sue began dating drummer Mick Avory, who provided access to concerts whenever the Kinks played in the vicinity. Sue spoke seductively about the group's sexy looks and long hair and inspired that aforementioned fateful, life-changing expedition to Sheffield which had left Ray smitten. Evidently, it had been quite an adventure. Rasa was still in her school uniform, complete with blazer, beret and satchel, when she made her way to a secret rendezvous with Sue in the ladies' toilet at Chester Street bus station. There, she changed into a miniskirt, set off by stockings, held in place by a threepenny bit attached to her suspender belt. It was a remarkable transformation. The girls hitched a ride to Sheffield from a lorry driver but were stopped by police on the motorway and taken into custody for questioning. Sue concocted a story, claiming that they were art students who were intending to interview Ray Davies in Sheffield for the Bradford College of Art magazine. Having received no reports of any missing girls, the police officers accepted their tale and magnanimously drove the 'students' to the Sheffield Empire, treating them to tea and biscuits along the way. Sue ensured they gained access to the dressing room after the performance where the Kinks were in various states of undress. For Rasa the convent girl, the scene was impossibly exotic and she felt captivated by the lead singer. "I basically fell in love with him," she admits. When Ray belatedly heard the full details of this unlikely odyssey he was amused and fascinated. It was like a chapter from a romantic novel.

And now there was more. Rasa had an elder sister, Dalia, who had recently moved to London. This meant that Rasa could also visit the capital and perhaps relocate there after leaving school. She was hoping to audition for a place at RADA (Royal Academy of Dramatic Arts) having played the fairy Oberon in an all-female school production of *A Midsummer Night's Dream* the previous year. It seemed a good idea, but she and Ray were rapidly over-taken by events. Any dreams of becoming a Shakespearian actress ended that summer when the romance with Ray deepened and the relationship was consummated at her sister's home in Willesden. Back in Bradford, she faced the task of fending off a former boyfriend, who still appeared forlornly at her front door desperate to rekindle their relationship.

There was also a dreaded visit to 6 Denmark Terrace where Rasa was introduced to Ray's family. Annie Davies was far from welcoming. "She wasn't very happy that Ray was with a girl that wasn't English, let's put it that way. There was something that was said, but I can't remember exactly what it was." Although all the Davies daughters were now married and living away from home, the house was still a hive of activity. "That was my first experience of being with cockney people," Rasa says. "Mrs D was a real cockney from the Cally, a big lady, and she had a grandchild living with her [Jackie], and the dog, Susie. Gwen lived around the corner down the bottom of an alley with her husband, Brian, and their three daughters. Fred, the dad, was wonderful. He played the spoons and they'd play the piano on Saturday and Sunday nights. It was a tiny terraced house, but the actual strength of the family bond was unbelievable. They had a good, solid, cockney London upbringing. It was amazing. I'd never experienced anything like it in my life."

On a reciprocal visit to Rasa's home on Bradford's Howard Street, Davies experienced a similar cultural jolt. "Behind the front door of the house, it was Lithuania," Rasa explains. "The food, the speech, the church, the school, everything was Lithuanian. What did they think of Ray? My mother thought he was abso-lutely wonderful; she called him her golden boy. For my father, it was all very strange. It must have been quite a shock."

In September, Rasa returned to St Joseph's Convent School at the precise moment when 'You Really Got Me' reached number

1 in the charts. That same week, the Kinks appeared on *Top Of The Pops*, much to the amazement of her school friends and teachers. The nuns at St Joseph's took a dim view of her pop star association, which was already proving disruptive. When Ray himself turned up in Bradford some weeks later to meet Rasa for a lunchtime date in Lister Park, minor mayhem ensued. Word spread and they ended up being pursued by a gaggle of schoolgirls in full uniform. "It was like a scene from St Trinian's," Rasa recalls. Subsequently, the harried twosome were approached by local journalists in search of a human interest story. Embarrassed by the publicity, the convent suggested Rasa should leave St Joseph's. This was a bitter blow to her parents, but the girl already harboured a far greater revelation: she was pregnant with Ray's child.

For the sake of decorum, the news was hidden, even from members of Rasa's family. "I knew I was going to be in so much trouble. A Catholic girl, convent-educated, Lithuanian. I wish I'd spoken to my mum, but I think there was a feeling of shame because I was pregnant. I knew I had to get married, it had to be a Catholic church, and it had to happen quickly." Any hope of keeping the engagement secret ended on 9 November when Judith Simons, the pop specialist at the *Daily Express*, revealed that the wedding was to take place the next month. Evidently, she had been tipped off by a colleague after a list of forthcoming marriages had been published in the *Bradford Argus*. Rasa's father sheepishly noted, with marked understatement: "Ray has been hoping to keep the event quiet as he thinks it might harm the group."

Davies was less concerned with the reputation of the group than he was with protecting his own privacy. He was never a lovable or sexy pop star in the traditional mode and concluded, quite rightly, that marriage would not affect the Kinks' popularity. Since the revelation about John Lennon's marital status, even over-cautious pop managers had become less paranoid about the implications of matrimony on their young charges. A greater test for Davies was fulfilling the terms of the Catholic Church's *Ne Temere* which decreed that all non-Catholics in a mixed marriage had to submit to religious education by a local priest with a view to conversion. Any children from such a union had to be baptized and brought up in the Catholic faith. The ruling also had serious implications for the bride. If she was later to divorce, she would remain married under canon law and could not remarry in a Catholic church.

A far greater worry than theological conundrums arrived 11 days later when Robert Wace appeared after a show at Shrewsbury's Granada Cinema clutching a telegram with a grim message. Rasa had been hospitalized.

While visiting her sister Dalia in London, she'd rushed to catch a Tube train and stumbled and fell on the platform. By the time she returned home, abdominal pains told her something was terribly wrong and she was taken to Bradford Infirmary. Robert drove Ray to the hospital that same night where they learned that Rasa had suffered internal bleeding. Mercifully, her foetus was unharmed. The local press reported that Ray was comforting his betrothed after she had been admitted following a bout of influenza. The pregnancy would remain a secret, at least for the present.

Adjusting to the notion of marriage and impending fatherhood proved quite a challenge. Even in hospital Ray and Rasa had not been spared the disruption of relatives, friends and well-wishers, with their ceaseless chatter and curiosity. It seemed to bring them closer together. Almost imperceptibly, they were experiencing a mutual dependency. Ray was surprised, even shocked, to discover that Rasa's presence was challenging everything that was once comprehensible and contained in that intensely private world of his imagination. "He really needed somebody he could confide in emotionally," was Peter Quaife's impression. "Ray is very introverted as a personality, very enclosed. He doesn't like to come out of his shell."

Differentiating between love, desire and need was neither desirable nor necessary at this point. It was only later that Davies would ponder such matters. "I don't think I should have got married when I was so young . . . I needed a crutch more than a marriage . . . it was all too much for me to handle."

Rasa was unimpressed. "Well, no one forced him to marry me!" she counters. At least Davies acquitted himself adequately with the local Lithuanian priest, completing his instruction in the faith.

The wedding took place on 12 December at St Joseph's Church,

Packingham, Bradford. Davies defied convention by arriving a considerable time after his bride-to-be had entered the church. Playing on the groom's jitters, PR man Brian Sommerville cheekily quipped: "I've got tickets to South America in my pocket, if you want them!" By this point a crowd, estimated at 150, had already congregated outside, flanked by 13 policemen. When Ray stepped out of the hired cream and red Riley, a group of fans surged forward, prompting Annie Davies to drag her son inside the vestibule. Dave, taking the honours as best man, was already there, talking to Eileen Fernley, Rasa's chief bridesmaid, whom he had been dating on and off over recent months. Thereafter, the ceremony was conducted with civilized restraint. It was a pleasing spectacle for the guests, among whom were all three Kinks' managers. Pete Quaife and Mick Avory were conspicuous by their absence for reasons unexplained. There may have been a fear that the presence of all four Kinks might turn the wedding into a media circus.

Rasa, uncharitably referred to as Ray's "stateless refugee bride" in the local paper, was dressed exquisitely in a white satin dress and shoulder-length veil, held in place by a decorative coronet. She was flanked by three bridesmaids in Lithuanian national dress, each carrying a single chrysanthemum. By the time the family priest, Father Dunleavy, announced, "I now pronounce you man and wife", the crowd outside the church door had swelled to over 300. There was almost a scuffle as the married couple struggled to reach their getaway car, which was chased through the adjoining streets. Eventually, the vehicle found its way to the family home at 31 Howard Street where a small reception awaited them.

Decades on, Larry Page still remembers what followed with a wry, vivid humour. "I'd driven Ray overnight from Oxford to Bradford. There was this little terraced house [the Didzpetris home]. We were sitting on the arms of the couch having the breakfast luncheon. The press were there. We had Ray's family in one room and her family in the other. It was like a United Nations summit. Finally, the priest stood up and said how wrong he'd been, he'd misjudged groups totally, and what wonderful boys he'd found Raymond and David to be, and now he'd like David to say a few words. And Dave stood up and said, 'Well, I'm too pissed to say anything really!' Magic."

The irrepressible younger brother disgraced himself with aplomb that morning. At one point he was discovered in an upstairs bedroom by his sister Peggy having sex with the leading bridesmaid. By the end of the luncheon, he had succeeded in offending Father Dunleavy, not merely by his drunkenness, but the sarcastic tone in which he referred to him as 'Holy Joe' and 'Vic' (an abbreviation of vicar). Dave was obliviously unaware that calling a Catholic priest a vicar was the height of ecumenical ignorance.

Oddly, there was no wedding album to commemorate the day. The sole photo opportunity back at the house featured a couple of hastily taken shots of Ray pretending to bite into his mother-in-law's Dundee cake while Rasa giggled nervously in the background.

Later that day, the couple flew to London, accompanied by the Kinks' management, then boarded a train for their honeymoon at a hotel in Exeter. "It was all very dramatic," Rasa recalls. "I got dressed and left my parents. I was the last daughter, the last child of the house and I just left. Now, I think, 'How did *they* feel?' After this massive fuss and wedding and all those people, suddenly they were left alone in that big house and I'd gone. I was the baby of the family. It must have been difficult for my parents, but I didn't give them a thought. What does that tell you about youth?"

Ray was only allowed a three-day break, after which he was required to return to the capital for television and recording commitments. That same week, the *NME* had published its influential annual poll, a must read for pop stars and pop fans alike. With 'All Day And All Of The Night' still in the charts at the time the poll was conducted, the Kinks seemed guaranteed a healthy showing. Instead, the results underlined how competitive 1964 had been, even for a group that had come close to achieving two consecutive number 1 hits. It was probably no great surprise that the 'Best New Disc Of The Year' was won by the Animals' groundbreaking 'The House Of The Rising Sun', but the votes of the discerning *NME* readership could not lift 'You Really Got Me' higher than seventh place, outflanked by the Beatles' 'A Hard Day's Night', the Rolling Stones' 'It's All Over Now' and 'Little Red Rooster', Manfred Mann's 'Do Wah Diddy Diddy' and even Dusty Springfield's 'I Just Don't Know What To Do With Myself'.

This trend continued in the 'Best R&B Group' section where they finished fourth beneath the Rolling Stones (who polled almost as many votes as everyone else combined), the Animals and Manfred Mann. As for 'British Vocal Group', they were lucky to get sixth spot behind the Beatles, the Rolling Stones, the Bachelors, the Searchers and Manfred Mann. Their best showing was runners-up spot in 'Best New Group', albeit way below the Stones. What the poll revealed most clearly was the need for constant vigilance in a swiftly changing marketplace. Despite the swing away from Merseybeat, the Kinks still faced intense competition – even in their specialist R&B field – from the Animals and Manfred Mann. Clearly, the Beatles and the Stones were on another planet in terms of popularity.

The Kinks' management fully understood the implications of this poll. It was telling them that the group needed to work even harder, touring and recording. For Ray Davies, destined to become a father in 1965, it was not a welcome prospect.

At least there was time for an end-of-year party. On 31 December, the Kinks saw in the New Year on the two national channels, appearing on BBC 2's *The Beat Room* and ATV's *The New Year Starts Here*. A pensive looking Pete Quaife celebrated his 21st birthday backstage, posing with a bottle of champagne, a cigar and a floorful of greetings cards. There was still time to return to 6 Denmark Terrace where the Davies family was awake and in festive mood. Upon entering the front room, Ray noticed that 'You Really Got Me' had been added to the list of favourite party pieces. It was an accolade as important as any poll result.

CHAPTER TWELVE

AUSTRALIA

While Ray settled down with his wife in a rented attic flat in Muswell Hill's Midhurst Gardens, his 17-year-old brother was lost in a social whirl of clubbing, shopping expeditions, bleary-eyed revelries and one-night stands, seemingly fuelled by an endless supply of purple hearts washed down by Scotch and Coke. Even among the promiscuous pop elite, his rampant sexuality was regarded as exceptional and insatiable. At times, it read like a tawdry tale. On one terrible occasion, he awoke next to a tearful girlfriend whose bruised face betrayed an act of violence of which he had no memory. The scene was one great imponderable puzzle. He felt himself detached, a mere vessel of forces and emotions over which he had no control. Everything had the transparency of shattered glass. Those were the worst moments. At other times it was playful high jinks, a sexual experiment in which debauchery was a moral abstraction that Dave Davies had single-handedly consigned to the Victorian age. His mother – unusually tolerant of illegitimacy, black babies, divorce and drunkenness – found her moral compass stretched to breaking point upon discovering her son in bed with five girls. Clearly, he required new premises to satiate his love of orgiastic excess. Before long, he found a home in Connaught Gardens where he was joined by Mick Avory, fresh from leaving his mother's house in East Molesey. The three-bedroom shag pad was elaborately furnished with an elephant's foot as a table, a goat's head on the wall and a display featuring the guitarist's buccaneer sword.

As if to compound the contrast with his newly-wed brother, Dave became even more unconventional in his entertainment of sexual aberration by accentuating his effeminate image. On the recent tour with Gerry And The Pacemakers, he had been introduced to compere Bryan Burdon and expressed amazement at his stage make-up. "It's slap," Burdon informed him. "Don't you wear any?" Walking away, Dave retorted, "No, I think it looks a bit poofy!" Days later, both he and Quaife were applying foundation with abandon. Soon, they were taking fashion and cosmetic tips from the showgirls in their circle.

Dave's feminine looks attracted attention, especially from homosexuals. On one occasion, he invited the finely tailored singer Long John Baldry back to a hotel. He remembers them kissing and holding hands, but draws a veil over anything else that might have happened. A more profound encounter involved Michael Aldred, the young presenter on *Ready, Steady, Go!* who had interviewed Dave the previous year. Their friendship developed into a sexual relationship which was consummated when Aldred moved into the spare room in Connaught Gardens. It was a remarkably reckless decision which could have destroyed Davies' career had it ever been made public. Aldred was emotionally volatile and not universally loved. "He was one of those poofy, in-people of the Sixties," Quaife recalls, "a horrible guy."

Aldred was far too possessive for a free spirit like Dave Davies and the relationship ultimately foundered. What is more incredible is the casual attitude of Dave, who seems to have been immune to the stigma attached to homosexuality which was illegal and seen by many as both a perversion and a blackmailer's charter. "It didn't seem strange to me because it's *me*, I suppose. It was the times. The pop world was showbusiness. There's always been a homosexual element there. I was always surprised, when we first had success, how many homosexual people there were in showbusiness. But it didn't faze me. I didn't feel any qualms about it. It just seemed very experimental and fun. A bit of a laugh, a bit of a tease. I almost did it as an act of rebellion and provocation. I never considered that it was illegal. In the circle of people I knew, it was quite common and I'd obviously never experienced it before. I always considered myself a woman's man anyway. It's very difficult to answer this because it didn't seem a terrible problem to me at the time. I never considered myself a homosexual, although I had relationships with men. One of the more meaningful I treated more out of friendship than a sexually driven relationship which, probably from his point of view, that's how he wanted it to be . . . This was Michael Aldred – and that's why the friendship broke down. That's what all the tension was about."

Dave's greater interest in girls no doubt saved him from further scrutiny and, for all his irresponsibility, he was discreet enough to keep his bi-sexuality hidden from his managers, producers and publishers. Larry Page spent the next 30 years innocently unaware of any instance of homosexual behaviour. "My biggest problem with him was the girls, not the fellows . . . He was always crumpet mad so the Long John Baldry story I just do not understand. My God, the thought of Long John Baldry is quite unreal."

The promiscuity and sexual experimentation may well have been worsened by the loss of Dave's original girlfriend, Susan Sheehan. While Ray was allowed to marry and bring up his child, the younger sibling was expelled from school, robbed of his lover and prevented from seeing his daughter, Tracey. Did both brothers suffer a form of arrested development? Ray suggests as much, indicating that the brothers' success at such an early age may have left them partly frozen in time. "I don't think we were allowed to finish growing up because when we had our first hit Dave was 16 and I was 19 and he never finished school and I never finished college. I dropped out. So I didn't go through that completion. There's a certain amount of us that's incomplete. I think of me as an incomplete person."

The Kinks opened 1965 with a full calendar of dates, including plans for a world tour. In mid-January their new single, 'Tired Of Waiting For You' – held over since the first album sessions – was released. Its gestation had been as long as that of 'You Really Got Me', having been first conceived as the instrumental 'So Tired' several years before. It was indicative of Davies' struggle as a lyricist that he could not find suitable words for the tune. He was reduced to completing the composition while on the Tube to the studio and, even then, could not get beyond the chorus. The remainder sprang forth after the backing track had been done. Just before Christmas, Dave returned to the studio to overdub a guitar part to boost its appeal. It was certainly a brave departure after the recent heavy riff-based hits. Part of the song's appeal lay in Davies' now familiar neuroticism. Years before, he had been inspired by the simplicity of 'Blue Suede Shoes' with its reductive admonition: "You can do *anything*, just stay off of my blue suede shoes". There is something of the same in 'Tired Of Waiting For You' when the narrator allows his beloved to "do what you like" as long as she avoids the sin of unpunctuality. The 'waiting' could be a euphemism for sexual gratification but in the acutely anxious mind of its narrator it is the brief passing of time that seems overwhelming. It is sung with a strange mixture of tenderness and petulance and what emerges is not a song of lusty innuendo or high romance but something closer to a domestic quibble. The repetition of the song's title in the chorus emphasizes the narrator's neurotic fixation recalling the same frustrated cries of 'All Day And All Of The Night'. Although uncredited, Rasa adds a harmony part to the lyric she surely inspired, and also appears on the B-side, 'Come On Now', a showcase for Dave Davies.

The management expressed faith in Ray's new work, but could not afford to take any chances. Knowing that the group would be abroad while the song was climbing the charts, they arranged for them to pre-record some key television performances. "We were supposed to do *Top Of The Pops* in Manchester," Dave recalls. "We went to the airport and there was no room on the plane, but because it was us they actually took people off the plane and flew us up to Manchester. That had never happened [before]. You felt that you could do anything you liked. There was a lot of bravado, a sense of how much can I get away with? It was like taking drugs." That same month, there was another appearance on *Ready, Steady, Go!* where the familiar red hunting jackets were replaced by a new uniform of bottle green.

By then, the group were already abroad. First there was a trip to Paris and Marseilles where a filmed performance was entered for the Montreux Television Festival. Included in the footage was an appearance aboard the battleship USS *Saratoga*. Upon returning to London they barely had time to pack their cases before boarding a 34-hour flight to Australia, accompanied by chart rivals Manfred Mann and fellow Pye act the Honeycombs, whose ranks included a female drummer, Honey Lantree. Even before they reached their destination there was trouble. During refuelling in Moscow, they were forced back on the plane at gunpoint after Quaife had dared make an innocent joke about the recently deposed Russian president, Nikita Khrushchev. Next, there was a stopover in Bombay, where the musicians were allowed several hours' sleep at the Sun 'n' Sands Hotel. The heat was stifling and Ray Davies' mind was racing with half-formed tunes that would later be translated into song. "I couldn't sleep. That's my curse. I've never been able to sleep. I got up early and went to the beach and saw these fishermen going to work at sunrise and they were chanting. It stayed inside my head."

On 19 January, the entourage at last arrived in Perth looking, as one local journalist wrote, "all pale and tired". The following evening they played their first show on Australian soil at the city's Capitol Theatre, with Manfred Mann headlining. Dave Davies was uncharacteristically sentimental at first, as if he was still adjusting to the culture shock. "The audience were marvellous to us on our opening night. They yelled just like they do in England . . . When we got back to the dressing room we were very quiet, each scared to say how we felt in case we sounded soft."

There was genuine emotion at the next date which took place in Adelaide, where Rose Davies had settled with her husband Arthur and son, Terry. After an emotional reunion, the brothers were invited back to her suburban home in Little Elizabeth. Ray was quite taken with the semi-detached house, complete with modern conveniences. It testified to how far the family had come from the poverty of post-war London. For all that, there was something soulless about the place, its homogeneous architecture betraying an artifice that could not be ignored, least of all by Ray who filed away the experience in his songwriting brain. For Dave, the encounter caused a sudden reversion to childlike helplessness and dependency. After settling in an armchair, he bleated: "Rose, I don't want to go to the show tonight!" Suddenly, he was talking irrationally about staying for a spell in Australia so that they could all be a family again. "Don't be crazy, Dave," Rose responded. It was enough to shock him out of his reverie. "Her voice was a bit sad, although she was smiling. She was right, of course. You can't go back in life. Though you can remember."

The atmosphere among the touring acts was a combination of camaraderie and competition. It could hardly have been otherwise considering the presence of Manfred Lubowitz Mann, a Jewish South African émigré, whose cynicism was already legendary in the pop business. He enjoyed a combative rapport with Ray Davies and was happy to play on his weaknesses. "I was terrified of flying, still am," Ray acknowledges. "It didn't help travelling with Manfred who was dispassionate about everything and taking the piss. It was like the prefects' room. Manfred was the head boy and we were the bad prefects." Manfred's mordant wit was also executed on hapless journalists. At one breakfast reception, a reporter excitedly enquired if he was a member of the Honeycombs. "Yes, I'm *Honey Lantree*!" Manfred shot back.

The competitive Mann felt immense satisfaction at his group's bill-topping status. He even challenged Ray about record sales, wagering that Manfred Mann's latest single, 'Come Tomorrow', would outchart 'Tired Of Waiting For You', a bet that the Kink would ultimately win. Although it was largely banter, Manfred's guitarist Tom McGuinness maintains there was a definite edge. "We were vying with each other to be the third biggest group in the UK." Coincidentally, they were about to encounter the band that occupied second position in that league. "It was Stones, Stones, Stones every time you picked up a paper," Dave Davies complains, "and all they said about us was 'The Kinks Are Coming'."

On 26 January, Brisbane played host to a Stones concert at the City Hall while the Manfred/Kinks package appeared at the nearby Festival Hall. "We were in the same hotel as the Rolling Stones," says Tom McGuinness, who vividly recalls a joint after-show party, spread across the corridors of an entire floor. "It was just drink and drugs and women. At two a.m. the manager turned up and locked all the doors and the lift. It was like a scorched-earth policy. He figured he couldn't save the floor so he just abandoned it. We weren't allowed to trash anywhere else. All I remember is staggering back to my room and finding every nook and cranny, including my bed, occupied by couples. I went to sleep in the bath. That was life on the road with the Kinks. I remember getting on very well with Ray. I seem to recall him thanking me because I'd warned him about the pitfalls of business and the importance of getting accountants and lawyers whom he could trust."

The morning after the party, tour manager Johnny Clapson,

who had the physique of a dancer and the ferocity of a drill sergeant, corralled everybody into a bus then on to a plane bound for New South Wales. While in Sydney, they were photographed on Bondi Beach, perversely dressed in winter clothing, which somehow managed to annoy the macho locals who threw sand and stones at them.

On 1 February, it was the turn of New Zealand to experience the phenomenon with reports of wild scenes in Auckland, Wellington and Christchurch. A few days later there was a show at the Hong Kong Football Stadium where Manfred Mann won the plaudits and the fan pandemonium. Exhaustion was setting in by the time they appeared at Singapore's Badminton Stadium. "We spent thirty-six hours in Singapore, but it was too hot and humid," Dave remembered. "We spent every moment we could in the swimming pool, but we felt pretty rough. I had been advised not to swim because of an infected ear, but due to the heat and my even greater obstinacy, I did. As I stood on the top board, I had an idea for a song . . . 'Got My Feet On The Ground'. I should have, too. It was a rotten dive and made my ear worse."

Brother Ray was also suffering, from a mosquito bite on his foot which became infected. He rested by the poolside of the palatial Goodwood Hotel, his spirits buoyed by a phone call from the London *Daily Mirror* confirming that 'Tired Of Waiting For You' was number 1. "I got a bottle of champagne and I got the waiter who brought it in, who couldn't speak English, to have a drink with me. That was one of the happiest times. Just that moment." When he consulted the *NME* chart later that week, Ray noticed that the single they had displaced at the top was the Righteous Brothers' 'You've Lost That Lovin' Feelin''. After hearing the Phil Spector-produced disc, he knew that there was no possibility of laurel resting. The pop marketplace was thriving with innovation on an almost weekly basis. "We all came to a halt after the Righteous Brothers recorded 'You've Lost That Lovin' Feelin','" he admitted later in the year. "That was the end. It was the perfect pop disc – as far as anyone could go."

Back in London, Rasa was still living in the rented top flat of a house in Muswell Hill that was already attracting pushy fans who would knock on the door at all times of the day hoping to meet the Kinks' frontman. His absence abroad appeared to make little difference. For his heavily pregnant wife, the world tour felt like an abandonment. "I suffered when he went to Australia. The woman downstairs was really lovely but I was quite pregnant by then. I remember sitting upstairs in that flat with a sloping ceiling. It was awful because I was lonely and pregnant. I had a pet name for Ray, 'my baby kangaroo'. He had a funny little belly because of the spinal problem, and a strange posture. Now, my baby kangaroo was in Australia, and I looked like a kangaroo too because my belly was out here! I remember crying and feeling really sad because he was away for quite a long time. Mrs Davies and the family were nice to me, but I did feel very alienated and alone. It was a very difficult time."

The Kinks still had new worlds to conquer and towards the end of their tour conducted a four-day reconnaissance mission in America. They had already achieved two US Top 10 hits with 'You Really Got Me' and 'All Day And All Of The Night' and recently appeared in a pre-filmed slot on the television show *Shindig!*. A prestigious spot on the high-rating *Hullabaloo*, miming their two hits, guaranteed them mass coverage and augured well for a forthcoming tour. Unfortunately, it was not an entirely happy experience. Ray was grumpy and spent most of his time in a hotel room still nursing his troubled foot. Dave was besieged by 50 girls but felt constrained by petty rules and reactionary comments. Soon after, he damned New York with the faintest of praise. "It's got a great night life. But you get people shouting corny things like 'Are you a Beatle or a girl?' as if you couldn't be anything else. We couldn't see any coloured groups. They were all in Harlem and it was too dangerous to go there at night."

Even the *Hullabaloo* appearance did not pass without incident. The producers suggested that the group perform a dance routine, as if they were Freddie And The Dreamers. "Ray didn't want to do it," Mick Avory recalls, "and neither did any of us. So we did our own dance in the corner. Ray and I did a waltz which was a much better idea. The Americans didn't understand . . . . it wasn't smooching, but that's the way they thought of it. They were shocked. The Kinks never conformed to anything." The innocuous dance was only shown fleetingly on screen, but the episode underlined the group's lack of cooperation, a cardinal sin on American television.

On St Valentine's Day, they arrived back in England. Ray Davies barely had time to get through customs before being told that he had to complete a new album within the next week. Press activity was also frantic. *Melody Maker* presented another challenge, asking, "Have the Kinks taken over from the Rolling Stones as Britain's top beat group?" A jet-lagged Dave Davies responded: "We would like to very much, but I don't think we could at the moment. But I think we might take over in a few months . . . Ask me the same question when our next song gets to number 1."

Such words were hubristic, not least because the Rolling Stones were poised to release 'The Last Time', a Jagger/Richards composition which would soon become their third consecutive UK number 1. Ray Davies seemed more distracted by a doppelgänger disc which was steadily climbing the charts, much to his disapprobation. "We came back from a world tour and heard this record. Dave thought it was us! It was produced by Shel Talmy, like we were. They used the same session singers as us, and Perry Ford played piano, like he did on 'All Day And All Of The Night'. I felt a bit appalled by that. I think that was worse than stealing a song – they were actually stealing our whole style!"

The record was 'I Can't Explain', a lowly Top 10 hit for the Who, the west London group formerly known as the High Numbers. "When they supported us, their music was nothing like 'I Can't Explain'," Davies complained. He had a point. The Who had already incorporated 'You Really Got Me' into their live set and Pete Townshend admits that they consciously copied the Kinks in order to secure a producer and record deal with 'I Can't Explain'. "I broke up the rhythm of it so that it had a chopped rhythm which aped 'You Really Got Me'. I made a demo of it specifically so it sounded like the Kinks. Perhaps that was a bit unnecessary, but I thought Shel Talmy would get it if we sounded like the Kinks. To make it different from what Dave Davies was doing I used a twelve-string guitar, a jangly sound. Using the guitar as a percussive tool [like Dave] fitted very much into the way I was playing at the time."

As it turned out, the Who were fellow travellers rather than copyists and swiftly went on to forge their own unique Pop Art style. Townshend maintains that he and Ray Davies had much in common due to their art school education and shared musical influences. Of course that was not enough to explain the uncanny parallels between their two groups. Again and again, Townshend and Davies, the Who and the Kinks, would find themselves sharing experiences as if they were in constant competition. The fraternal friction between the Davies brothers was echoed in the intense interaction between Townshend and singer Roger Daltrey. After the Kinks made their debut on *Ready, Steady, Go!* with a staged fan invasion outside the studio, the Who responded on their first appearance by cramming a hundred of their Mod supporters *inside* on to the dance floor. Both groups would become involved in High Court actions in the peak years of the Sixties and Townshend and Davies would be forever linked thanks to their later pioneering 'rock operas'. Even their respective management set-ups seemed strangely symmetrical. While the Kinks balanced the working-class Larry Page alongside the aristocratic Collins and Wace, the Who combined the Oxford-educated Kit Lambert (son of composer Constant Lambert) with the cockney, streetwise Chris Stamp, the younger brother of actor Terence Stamp. Lambert turned Townshend and Keith Moon into wine connoisseurs; Wace introduced the Davies brothers to fancy restaurants. At times their histories seem magically entwined.

On 5 March, the Kinks released their second, hastily recorded album. *Kinda Kinks* was an unappetizing dog's dinner. Built around the recent single 'Tired Of Waiting For You' b/w 'Come On Now', it displayed a tiredness and abject carelessness that was almost shocking. Clocking in at a paltry 27 minutes, the album was released only in mono in an attempt to save money. The material on offer included rudimentary R&B ('Look For Me Baby', 'Got My Feet On The Ground'), a Phil Spector pastiche ('You Shouldn't Be Sad') and an anaemic Tamla Motown cover of Martha & The Vandellas' current hit, 'Dancing In The Street'. Ray Davies' songwriting was generally uninspired but there were fleeting moments of promise. 'So Long' and 'Nothing In This World Can Stop Me Worryin' 'Bout That Girl' had a folk rock feel, 'Wonder Where My Baby Is Tonight' was a decent pop tune, and 'Don't Ever Change' and 'Something Better Beginning' (a single by fellow Pye artistes the Honeycombs) had a melodic grace, albeit clearly inspired by the Drifters' 'Save The Last Dance For Me'.

The familiar ruse of rushing out an album to cash in on a hit single still worked in early 1965, but it would not succeed for much longer. More sophisticated releases, notably by the Beatles and Bob Dylan, would soon expose records like *Kinda Kinks* as exploitative and anachronistic. Not that Louis Benjamin was concerned. He looked on proudly as the album climbed to second place in the *NME* charts, held off the top for a fortnight by *The Rolling Stones No. 2*. With Sandie Shaw's *Sandie* climbing to number 4, Pye's questionable policy was clearly paying dividends.

Ray Davies was well able to teach his Pye master some lessons in frugality. Since returning from Australia, he tried to spend more time with his wife, but still visited his mother's house for the odd meal. "All right, boy, what would you like?" became a regular refrain. Rasa, who was more familiar with Lithuanian cuisine, had to adapt to traditional British dishes. "I had no idea about English cooking, so the butcher down the road told me how to make steak and kidney pie and shepherd's pie. Ray would always ask, 'what's for dinner?' and I would tell him what I was cooking." Visits to expensive restaurants were considered luxuries by the newly feted pop star. Even Ray's mother was not beyond teasing him about his penny-pinching ways. "It was difficult," says Rasa. "She used to call him 'boy', as in 'come on, boy'. She'd say, 'Boy, Rasa can't go walking around in a smock and Wellington boots all the time. When are you going to get some clothes for this baby?' We had nothing for the baby. Nothing was bought. There was no cot, no clothes, nothing at all. I was totally unprepared for any of this. Mrs Davies nurtured me a little bit. It must have been hard for her because she adored Ray. It was a struggle. There was never enough money. We never rowed about it, but it was always a problem. I always felt guilty about asking for money because I didn't have my own."

Having been surrounded by solicitous sisters and a protective mother for so much of his life, Davies found sharing difficult. Selfishness was an easier option. "I was married and trying to have a family life which was very difficult. I continually used to watch my wife sleep and wonder why she was there." That sense of detachment was a disconcerting feeling that he kept to himself.

"Well, he was young," Rasa sympathizes. "He never said anything like that to me. It probably was hard for him being so young with his music career and me being pregnant. It must have been difficult for him. Ray is a very deep man and I never really knew what he was thinking or what he'd be like the next day or whether he was really happy. It wasn't easy. I think he was confused. When you hear him say, 'I was looking at my wife and thinking should she be here?', it sounds quite unkind. Apart from looking at it very personally, there's the other side of it which is *that's what he's like*. He could have said that about anybody he was with. It just happens to be Ray. I don't think he knew what he wanted, to be honest."

CHAPTER THIRTEEN

RAY'S CONSPIRACY THEORY

Ray Davies was unhappy and, after returning from Australia, voiced concern about fees, expenses, recording schedules, publicity commitments, business arrangements and security at live shows. Amid the chaos, his management attempted to address each of these issues with varying success. For most of their British concert dates, the group had been accompanied by their loyal road manager – the Davies' brother-in-law, Brian Longstaff. He ferried them around in an ambulance and enjoyed the vicarious excitement of fainting fans, car chases and constant media attention. The prospect of larger venues, longer concert tours and greater responsibility persuaded everybody that he needed help. Neighbourhood pal 'Jonah' Jones was unable to accompany the brothers on extensive tours due to family issues which required him to spend long hours assisting his father at the newsagent's in Denmark Terrace. Larry Page and Arthur Howes instead contacted the experienced Sam Curtis, who had worked with many acts, including the Shadows. He had already been approached the previous year to assist the Kinks on their first package tour with Dave Clark, but was busy elsewhere, so that job went to Hal Carter. With promises of a major excursion in the spring, Curtis agreed to assist on a handful of local dates. The first of these was an eye-opener in more ways than one.

"We did a show in London where Dave deliberately went onstage with his bollocks hanging out under his guitar. He was holding his guitar in front of him pretending he didn't know. But before he went onstage he pulled his trouser zip down and pulled his bollocks out to hang over his trousers." Asked whether any members of the audience were aware of this unusual action, Curtis answered incredulously: "Were the audience aware of his bollocks hanging out? If you were two feet away from a guy with his bollocks hanging out, could you see them? And it was all girls! The stage was only small – it was about eight foot from the back to the front of the stage." Dave was mauled by fans – a common enough occurrence – and the rest of the week's shows, including several dates in the north, were cancelled.

Dave's mischievous ploy was no doubt inspired by the example of singer P. J. Proby who, a couple of months before, had split his trousers onstage in Croydon and was banned by the ABC theatre chain, excoriated in the national press and replaced on tour by Tom Jones. The tightness and threadbare quality of Carnaby Street boutique clothes meant that accidental exposure was always a possibility as Ray Davies almost discovered the following month in Newcastle when his trousers were torn by over-excited fans.

For all their risqué and rebellious ways, the Kinks never courted bad publicity in the reckless fashion of the Rolling Stones and their fearless manager, Andrew Loog Oldham. Three days after Ray's minor pants episode, a trio of Stones (Jagger, Jones and Wyman) were arrested for publicly urinating against a garage wall. Subsequently, they were each fined £5 for insulting behaviour, confirming their reputation as British pop's premier anti-heroes.

Following what may have been a cancellation of convenience, Ray was able to complete some important outstanding business agreements. On 11 March, Kinks Productions was formed with the assistance of accountant Robert Ransom, effectively making the group a partnership. Twelve days later, Ray Davies (Entertainments) Ltd became the receptacle for his songwriting income. He had already complained to Collins and Wace about the amount of money he was paying out and they agreed to forego their management commission from his publishing royalties. It was a concession won without threats and appeared very generous in the circumstances.

In the background was the increasingly fragile relationship between Page and Collins/Wace. As the former recalls: "The

Hooray Henrys were starting to say 'We're paying Larry Page this ten per cent, it's a lot of money. Do we really need him?' You could feel the friction. Now, if I'd wanted to, I could have rowed them out. I could have taken them out, but I'm not like that. To me fair is fair. If we have an agreement, then we stick to it. But I could have taken them out with no trouble at all."

Page believes that such an opportunity came and went during a meeting with Ray Davies at the Kassner office when the money-conscious pop star reiterated his concern about commissions and deductions. Apart from seeking sympathy, it is difficult to avoid the conclusion that Davies was playing one manager off against the other two as a cost-cutting exercise. Page's magnanimity towards Collins/Wace also strains credulity considering his view of them as 'Hooray Henrys'. Perhaps Page realized that a *coup d'état* could not be achieved without the complete cooperation of the Davies brothers, who vacillated between their mentors depending on mood and circumstance. Page, in common with Collins and Wace, was probably biding his time in the belief that industry and commitment would be rewarded.

Even as he was establishing his new limited companies, Ray found himself denying rumours that he was leaving the Kinks. The story had reportedly been circulated by a rival group, at least according to Davies, who appears to have been the sole source. Tellingly, it was he who had phoned the music press refuting an account that may have existed only in his imagination. That same day, he was busy stirring further trouble by refusing to travel to Southampton for an appearance on the television programme *Three Go Round*. "I can't do it!" he informed his management. "I won't stand for this shit any more. I don't want to do it. I've had enough of this publicity." Considering he had just rung the music press himself, it was an unexpected outburst, but he was adamant. He declined to conduct any more interviews for the foreseeable future. His robust publicist Brian Sommerville was unimpressed. Turning to Davies, he said, "Don't be stupid. You're doing this job. You're either in the business or you're out of it."

Ray's sudden desire to retreat was symptomatic of a troubled mind. He was protective of his private life and concerned about impending fatherhood. "I feel very sorry for Rasa," he revealed to the press. "It's very hard at the moment because she is expecting her first child. I hope we'll have a little girl – I think I'd be jealous of a little boy." He did not mention his extreme thriftiness but confessed to practical failings that made him a comic liability at home. "I'm hopeless around the house too, I'm afraid. I put a plug in an amplifier once, and it blew up. My hand was all black. I put a bulb in a socket at home the other night. Same thing – black hand." Having just denied the breakup of the Kinks, he suddenly contradicted himself by projecting a completely different career in another medium. "I'm a collection of loose ends. I don't want to be a pop star. I think that this is just a part of my life which will come to an end. I feel like there are other developments in my life. For example, I should very much like to produce a film. Something artistic that would convey emotion and reaction."

The notion of Ray Davies the film-maker was a reminder of his lost art school ambitions. In other respects, he remained socially aspirational. He was now living a more middle-class life far removed from his humble upbringing in Denmark Terrace. The brothers still rehearsed there occasionally, working out ideas in the front room, whose ramshackle appearance and mustiness had been noticed by John Start several years before. Both Start and Pete Quaife had testified to Ray's mixed feelings about his former home, suggesting that he was sometimes embarrassed by its condition. Even Dave admitted that his brother had felt more settled in the loftier environs of Highgate, when he lived with Rose and Arthur. Ray had experienced his personal cultural revolution at Hornsey and Croydon and, since then, both brothers had been introduced to high society via their refined managers. Although the early Sixties was a time of upheaval and dilution of social class within the popular arts, that did not necessarily translate to the wider population. Social stratification was as entrenched as ever in most occupations, and disparities in class were still marked. Attempts by Collins and Wace to introduce the Kinks to polite society retained an air of Henry Higgins educating Liza Doolittle in Shaw's *Pygmalion*. "He was great, Robert, really funny," says Dave. "He'd go to these posh restaurants in Chelsea, order all this food, cut off a little bit of steak, take a chip, then push the plate away and continue, 'As I was saying . . .' Whereas we'd sit there and stuff away, going 'Hey, give us a bit' to each other."

Wace jokingly claims that one of his lasting achievements was teaching the Davies brothers how to use a knife and fork properly. He, of course, was the acme of good manners.

Even by the mid-Sixties, old values still ruled, despite all the talk of egalitarianism. Larry Page remembers being introduced to Wace's father only to suffer instant humiliation with the rejoinder: "What's that? What are you saying, boy? You sound like you've got marbles in your mouth." It did nothing to assist management relations. Robert Wace felt more comfortable in the age of the upstart and tolerated what Shaw's Professor Higgins would have called "kerb-stone English". He feigned an aristocratic snobbishness at times, which the Davies brothers responded to with teasing hilarity. It might have been assumed that Wace would have reacted to the Davies' family home in the same disparaging fashion as other sophisticated visitors. Instead, he paid no attention to dust marks, old furniture, a cracked window or Annie Davies' coarse apron. He seemed above such concerns. Dave remembers Robert happily chatting with his mother and eating beef dripping sandwiches, cuisine unheard of in the Wace household. Sometimes, he would take along his female friend Tiger (Countess Cowley). It may have been noblesse oblige or simply sociological curiosity, but his polite-ness was appreciated. Others were not so understanding or tolerant. Road manager Hal Carter was taken aback by the tiny front room from which he collected their equipment. His successor, Sam Curtis, who came from an upwardly mobile Jewish family, always looked down on the Davies brothers. He vividly recalls his first visit to Denmark Terrace during which a procession of visitors was passing through. Curtis was bemused by the chaotic scene and puzzled by the mother's vulgar open-door attitude. One detail that caught his discriminating eye was the supposed ethnic mix ("and it was all creeds and colours"), an unsubtle racial allusion to the presence of 'Blackie Jackie', the illegitimate niece who always seemed to be singled out solely because of the colour of her skin.

Annie Davies was now solely in control of running the house and keeping it clean, a difficult task for which Curtis felt no sympathy. He was unforgiving in his impressions. "They [Ray and Dave] came from a very bad home in my opinion. I felt uncom-fortable sitting down in it. Their home was dirty. It was a modern-day slum." Ask Curtis whether he regards the Davies brothers as the products of a working-class family, and the response is sarcastic and caustic. "It was a pig-sty family," he splutters, only partly in jest. "The area was very nice, there just happened to be a few slums in it, and they were one of them. You can't hold anything against the parents for being poor, but the place was always filthy when I visited. I never had a cup of tea there. I was offered one, but I couldn't possibly drink it."

Such snootiness was typical of the time. Curtis, a decade older than the Kinks, betrayed a class consciousness unaltered by recent events. It speaks volumes when a worldly road manager, immersed in the bacchanalian, backstage adventures of a long-haired pop group, could voice values that harked back to the upstairs/downstairs mentality of the Victorian era. "Sam was one of the great characters," Ray now notes, sympathetically, "but he was from another generation. He did the most obscene things with girls. I couldn't describe them – it's not lunchtime material at all. But he had a lovely wife, a red-haired girl, lived in Hendon."

While Curtis was obliged to visit the Davies home, others retained a respectful distance. Larry Page evidently never got beyond the front door, preferring to conduct any business back in Denmark Street. His most memorable encounter with Annie Davies occurred at a workingman's café near her home. Ray had arranged a meeting there but neglected to tell his mother who was expecting her son to come over for dinner. Somehow, she tracked him down, burst into the caff and, according to Larry, emptied a plate of meat, veg and gravy over his head. His response is not recorded.

On 19 March, the Kinks released their sixth single, 'Ev'rybody's Gonna Be Happy'. Inspired by their recent interaction with the Earl Van Dyke Band on the Gerry And The Pacemakers' package tour, the song was an attempt to capture the "punching rhythms" of the Tamla sound. "That's where 'Ev'rybody's Gonna Be Happy' came from," Ray Davies explains. "It wasn't necessarily written as a single, but more as an experiment. There weren't really any home studios in those days, so we had to come up with the master in a three-hour session. In effect the single was the demo of the song." It proved a baptism of fire for Mick Avory, who finally had the chance to appear on a Kinks' A-side for the first time. Of all their singles, he found it the most difficult to play due to the "complex rhythm" which contrasted strikingly with their earlier work. "It didn't help having all the wives and girlfriends clapping out of time," he grumbles.

At least it was fun for the participants. "Oh, I loved the song," Rasa says. "I remember putting the headphones on and the smell of the studio. Shel was there and they were all talking about acetates. I was learning stuff, and it was one of the best memories I had. We were all at that session. Everybody had to be there because everybody had to be happy!"

The slight but exuberant melody was superficially infectious yet oddly out of place in the Kinks' canon. It would have made a fine album track or notable B-side but lacked the immediacy, power and depth of 'Tired Of Waiting For You' or 'All Day And All Of The Night'. At the time of its release, Britain was hosting the Tamla Motown Revue featuring the Supremes, Martha & The Vandellas, Stevie Wonder, Smokey Robinson & The Miracles and the Earl Van Dyke Six – with special guests Georgie Fame & The Blue Flames. Tamla evangelist and *Ready, Steady, Go!* editor Vicki Wickham was swiftly on the scene to record the one-hour special *The Sound Of Motown* featuring the touring acts, plus the Temptations. Mod aficionados, pop's hip elite, black music commentators and later rock historians all acknowledged the tour's significance but the general public was less convinced. Ticket sales were sluggish. Unlike America, where Motown acts regularly reached number 1, Britain exercised a veritable colour bar at the top of the charts. The Supremes had overcome that innate prejudice with the catchy 'Baby Love' in 1964 but for the remainder of the so-called 'egalitarian' Sixties, long considered the golden years of Tamla Motown, only two other singles ever climbed to number 1: the Four Tops' 'Reach Out I'll Be There' (1966) and Marvin Gaye's 'I Heard It Through The Grapevine' (1969). Commercially, it was never a good idea to copy the Motown sound, even with the subtlety displayed by Ray Davies.

At the time of the Revue, Dave Davies admitted a sense of anti-climax. "We were disappointed with the Tamla Motown show as a whole, just because of the big build up." The Kinks attended an after-show party, but felt snubbed by the partisan retinue of fans. Pete Quaife was especially aggrieved. "I wandered into the dressing room and some of the Tamla fans recognized me. Well, they were really nasty. They started carrying on as though I wasn't good enough to be in the same room as the Tamla artistes. That was the end in prejudice."

The tribalism was a disappointment, not least because the Kinks had risked much in promoting the Tamla sound on their current single, even against the better judgement of their producer. Shel Talmy had been unconvinced by the song from the moment he heard the playback. "'Ev'rybody's Gonna Be Happy' was a single I did not want to put out. Ray did – I believe. He was in love with the song. I didn't like it, and I didn't think it was a single. It was the lowest chart record we ever had." As a follow-up to a number 1, the single was a relative disaster, peaking at a lowly 19 in the *NME*. Having fallen farther behind the Rolling Stones, the Kinks faced a fresh assault from the Yardbirds, whose experimental, harpsichord-flavoured 'For Your Love' was heading towards number 1 in the *NME* that same week.

The chart statistics were disconcerting and duly noted in America where 'Ev'rybody's Gonna Be Happy' was subsequently denied A-side status in favour of its flip side, 'Who'll Be The Next In Line'. It probably made sense at the time but the latter's world-weary vocal and vindictive lyric proved even less attractive and fell outside the US Top 40.

Even historical reassessment has failed to rescue 'Ev'rybody's Gonna Be Happy' from cultural obscurity. Its spontaneity can now be seen as a brave, if misguided, attempt to capture the impulsiveness of a live take within a studio session. In this, it shared the spirit of 'You Really Got Me' and 'All Day And All Of The Night' but it was too light in tone to be taken seriously. Psychologically, Pete Townshend was treading similar ground at the time, albeit in his distinctively iconoclastic way. The Who's latest Pop Art single, 'Anyway Anyhow Anywhere' featured feedback, echoing the opening of the Beatles' 'I Feel Fine'. In common with Davies, Townshend was picturing and capturing the Who's live atmosphere, but in a much more aggressive and adventurous fashion than the slapdash ''Ev'rybody's Gonna Be Happy'.

The Kinks urgently needed to regain momentum with a successful UK tour but they seemed plagued by a series of illnesses and mysterious mishaps. Scotland proved their undoing. In Stirling, Ray collapsed, supposedly from exhaustion and developing pneumonia. Dave complained of bronchitis, possibly in sympathy. By the time they returned from the north, Pete Quaife completed the triumvirate of breakdowns in typically dramatic fashion. A visit to the Odeon Muswell Hill to see the spy film *The Ipcress File* ended on a gory note. After going to the toilet, Quaife fainted, smashing his head on the stone floor. "I don't know what caused it," he said at the time. "Probably that bit of the film where Michael Caine grips a nail in his clenched fist so he won't break down during the brainwashing. There was a lot of blood – and that may have turned my stomach over. I wandered out into the cinema foyer and asked if I could have a glass of water because I'd just fainted when a woman behind me started having hysterics. Apparently, I had blood pouring from the cut on my nut." Conveniently, Mick Avory happened to be in the cinema and assisted Quaife as he was rushed by ambulance to Archway's Whittington Hospital and given stitches.

Such colourful copy elicited sympathy from the pop press despite Quaife's known penchant for exaggeration. The Davies brothers nicknamed him 'Pete Liar' on the grounds that his embellishments were as unconvincing as those of Keith Waterhouse's fictional character Billy Liar. Even decades later, Quaife was capable of transforming the group's on the road travails into grotesque scenes of Hogarthian decay. "I'd see a drop of blood and I'd faint and I had God knows how many diseases due to malnutrition. There was one point where all the skin on my hands started peeling off in great big chunks and that was because I wasn't eating the right foods and getting the right vitamins. We were drinking, and eating chips and baked beans. Just fast food really, nothing nutritional. All it did was just fill the hole . . . Consequently we were all dying."

What really happened at the Odeon Muswell Hill remains a minor mystery. "He said he fainted but nobody in the family believed it," says David Quaife. "Maybe it was a fight with some- body. He kept it quiet. He did bottle stuff up a lot."

Despite Quaife's concussion, it was only a matter of days before the Kinks were back on the road and heading for further trouble, this time in peaceful Denmark. On 8 April they played a show in Falster and the next night were scheduled to appear at the concert hall in Copenhagen's splendid Tivoli Gardens in front of approximately 2,000 fans. Nothing untoward was expected that evening. Only eight days before, the Rolling Stones had appeared at the same venue and the show had passed peacefully, a clear enough indication that, by comparison, the Kinks posed no security threat. It was to prove a severe miscalculation.

The set had barely begun when a wave of over-excited fans swamped the stage prompting the arrival of 40 police officers armed with batons. While the Kinks were ushered into a subterranean dressing room, police and concert-goers engaged in open warfare. "It was total chaos," Ray says. "The only thing that didn't get smashed was a big picture of Jim Reeves!" Amid the bloody scenes, the Kinks were taken back to their hotel where Dave, already hyped up to manic proportions, downed a bottle of brandy which he then threw in anger towards the bar, smashing a large ornate mirror to smithereens. Hotel security informed the police and, after a cat and mouse chase, Dave was bundled into a car and deposited in a prison cell. He was still hung over several hours later when he heard a familiar voice that sounded simultaneously soothing and authoritative. It was the imperious and unflappable Grenville Collins.

"Come along, David, we're leaving," he said.

Later that day, the group conducted a press conference before an unexpectedly forgiving Danish media. Some reporters took the police to task for what was considered a severe over-reaction, a view with which Dave Davies wholeheartedly concurred. His brother was not so self-justifying. "We wrecked a lot of places," he mused, enigmatically. Later, he described the 'Tivoli incident' as an act of political rebellion. "That night I saw a youth revolution against the establishment and it became big news in Scandinavia. Somebody said to us afterwards, 'Why can't you be nice and polite like the Rolling Stones?' We were doing our best to entertain and make people feel happy, but we knew how to finish a riot . . . Actually, I was terrified. We were locked in a room hearing the carnage around us. It's quite scary that, particularly when you know you've caused it. But the crowd just wanted to rebel."

On Sunday 11 April, the group arrived back in London and were whisked across to the Empire Pool Wembley for the celebrated annual *NME* Poll Winners' Concert. For as little as 7/6d, the audience were treated to a spectacular line-up featuring the Beatles, the Rolling Stones, the Animals, the Moody Blues, the Searchers, Freddie And The Dreamers, Herman's Hermits, Wayne Fontana & The Mindbenders, the Rockin' Berries, the Seekers, the Ivy League, Them, the Bachelors, Georgie Fame & The Blue Flames and Sounds Incorporated. Among the female solo performers were two of British pop's finest – Cilla Black and Dusty Springfield – plus the ingénue Twinkle. Recent chart entrants Tom Jones and Donovan completed the line-up.

On paper, the Kinks might have been expected to precede either the Rolling Stones, who closed the first half, or bill toppers the Beatles. Instead, the north Londoners' late arrival ensured they faced the ultimate poisoned chalice – following the Fab Four, who had triumphed as undisputed British and World Top Group in the *NME* Poll and were currently at number 1 with 'Ticket To Ride'. The Denmark debacle, possibly accentuated by nerves, a lack of rehearsal and an unfamiliar sound system, combined to produce one of the least memorable performances of the Kinks' career. They sped through desultory renditions of their number 1 hits 'You Really Got Me' and 'Tired Of Waiting For You' while Davies apologized for their lateness. Dave has no coherent memories of the event ("I was drunk") but Ray was burning with indignation and anger. Quaife was puzzled. "Ray flipped. He was screaming and yelling and going absolutely nuts blaming everybody."

Decades later, Ray began peddling an extraordinary conspiracy theory which he repeated in interviews, memoirs and even onstage during concerts. He claimed that the Kinks had attended the Poll Winners' Concert in anticipation of collecting an award for 'Best New Group'. He was shocked to be given a trophy for 'Runners-Up In the Best New Group' category. The winners were the Rolling Stones who, according to Davies, had won the 'Best New Group' award the previous year too.

Davies' conviction about this 'injustice' sounded genuine and won sympathy in some quarters, but it was totally misplaced. Firstly, the Rolling Stones did not win 'Best New Group' for *two* consecutive years as that category did not even exist the previous year. Secondly, his shock about being acclaimed as 'Runner-Up' was at best disingenuous. As previously mentioned, the *NME* had printed the poll results several months earlier, just before Christmas. The Stones had won a landslide victory as 'Best New Group' with 2,094 votes, ahead of the Kinks who registered a modest 685. In truth, the Kinks were extremely lucky to receive any award at all. Manfred Mann and the Animals were close behind with 675 and 668 votes, respectively. The paltry margin of ten votes was smaller than the sum of the Davies' household on a Saturday night. Ray's attempt to rewrite history was not merely eccentric but downright peculiar.

CHAPTER FOURTEEN

THE CARDIFF INCIDENT

In April 1965, the media creation known as 'Swinging London' was first trumpeted in all its garish glory in the *Weekend Telegraph*, one of the new 'super' Sunday supplements. American writer John Crosby expounded extravagantly about a so-called 'English Renaissance' to be found in many of the city's recently opened nightclubs. Like an animal entering the lair of Dave Davies, he unearthed a scene full of precious young things, wallowing in their exclusivity. The prose was excitable, almost to the point of intoxication: "In Soho, at the Ad Lib, the hottest and swingingest spot in town, the noise is deafening; the beat group is pounding out 'I Just Don't Know What To Do With Myself'; on the floor under the red and green and blue lights, a frenzy of the prettiest legs in the whole world belonging to models, au pair girls or just ordinary English girls, a gleam of pure joy on their pretty faces, dancing with the young blonde, the scruffy very hotshot photographers like David Bailey or Terence Donovan, or a new pop singer – all vibrating with youth." Like celebrants worshipping at the altar of adolescence, the *Weekend Telegraph* proudly proclaimed London 'The Most Exciting City In The World'. They were not alone. Within a month, the influential American publication *Newsweek* offered readers a cover story on 'The Switched-On World Of Jean Shrimpton'. By June, France's *Le Figaro* had rechristened London 'The European Las Vegas' while Spain's *Epoca* concluded it was "the happiest and most electric city in Europe".

The international appeal was not without some justification, certainly in reports from America where the British Invasion was in full swing. On 20 April, the *Billboard* chart, already bombarded by Liverpool groups over the previous year, now revealed a new phenomenon that made for extraordinary reading. The Top 3 American singles were acts from, of all places, Manchester: 1. 'Game Of Love' by Wayne Fontana & The Mindbenders; 2. 'Mrs Brown You've Got A Lovely Daughter' by Herman's Hermits; 3. 'I'm Telling You Now' by Freddie And The Dreamers. The Kinks – like guests at the Mancunian party – were at number 10 with 'Tired Of Waiting For You'.

The blessed investors in this unlikely Manchester invasion were the Altrincham-based agency/management company Kennedy Street Enterprises, which represented all three artistes. What they discovered in the days ahead was quite shocking. While the Americans had embraced the Beatles as if they were ambassadors of pop, there was an underlying resentment against several of the second wave of British invaders. The cheery Herman's Hermits and Freddie And The Dreamers were later accepted by more conservative listeners as Variety acts, but others were not so fortunate. Wayne Fontana & The Mindbenders, although top of the US charts, were allowed only an H-2 visa, entitling them to play a *single* public performance in America. This was based on the supposition that the act was not well known enough – absolutely nonsense considering they were number 1 in *Billboard*. Wayne Fontana, risking censure, spoke out on the matter. "It's jealousy. And plain childishness. At first they were not going to grant me a visa at all. We had to get letters of confirmation from *Billboard* and *Cash Box* about my being number 1 before they would admit my being 'well known' in America. With so many American artistes in this country – Screaming Jay Hawkins, the Walker Brothers and P. J. Proby to name three – all being granted extended work permits, I cannot understand the American attitude." The words of Wayne Fontana served as a warning that few, if any, heeded. For managers, performers, publishers and record companies, the American market was still seen as the promised land.

Larry Page was already plotting a US Invasion of his own. With the three Mancunian groups dominating the American listings, it seemed more imperative than ever that the Kinks should exploit their singles success there with a major tour. "At that time they were one of the very first English groups and I think what you had to do was to make an impact there and then. If we'd left any country a bit later, someone else would have been in there and they'd have been the new Beatles or the new Rolling Stones. They *wanted* it. They wanted to work."

One week after the 'Mancunian chart treble', the Kinks were despatched to France for concert and television appearances. By now, Ray was thinking in terms of presenting a complete one-act show rather than the usual 20-minute slot. He even approached his agent Arthur Howes about the concept but was rebuffed. Amid the familiar world of package tours and short sets, an elongated performance was considered impractical. After their show in Paris, Davies employed Pete Quaife as a mouthpiece to explain his latest idea. "We thought it would be great if we could tie the whole thing together and do sketches in between numbers and then have a finale with everyone coming on at the end and singing and jumping around. The only trouble was that it would need a tremendous amount of rehearsing to put a show like that together . . . but this is a definite 'thing' we've got into our systems so we're hoping very much that our next tour will take this form." It would be another decade before Davies translated this vague concept into a successful theatrical presentation.

Paris was an eye-opener, even for Dave Davies. Accustomed to swanning around nightclubs in Swinging London, he was shocked to discover that the Parisians had far more debauched forms of entertainment. He and Ray were invited to one club where, late into the night, a veritable farmyard of animals was let loose on the dance floor for the entertainment of the patrons. A surreal spectacle followed in which pigs and sheep were partnered by humans in a bizarre *danse macabre*. Years later, in an unintentionally provocative aside, Dave referred to the venue as "the best club of its kind". This provoked a wry riposte from one journalist, agog at the casual depravity of a lost age: "It's hard to imagine, in these more judgemental times, a decade in which a man could not only spend an evening in the intoxicating company of the lower mammals, but had a choice of venue."

Here Ray Davies also discovered transvestitism. Caught up in the strange netherworld of French nightlife, he noticed his manager in congress with an Amazonian goddess whose allure was strangely disconcerting. "Robert Wace was dancing with this beautiful black woman, who was wearing a tight dress. Incredible. And I stole her. It was back to my place and there was the stubble. I'm not mad about stubble. It makes your face very red." In other interviews, Davies reversed the roles, claiming it was his manager who left the club with the 'girl' only to discover the truth when the daylight outside betrayed a spiky growth on 'her' face. In the alternate telling she also changes skin colour to become a blonde Marilyn Monroe lookalike.

Davies' flippancy disguised concerns about the limits of experimentation in an age of sexual licence. "You didn't think of it as sleeping with men. I cannot sleep with men because it's a gay situation. I think I'm more a voyeur. I like watching people. I observe people, I take it in. I've got a great recall system. It's just being part of the experience. And this could be said about my whole attitude to the Sixties. Yes I was there, but I was watching it happen. I won't knowingly *make* it happen. The same applies to sexual activities. I was there but I was not part of the action . . . I was trying desperately to have a semblance of normality. But there's part of me that goes into the night and becomes not Mr Hyde but Mr Mysterious." The Parisian episode would partly inspire one of his memorable compositions, the decade-closing 'Lola'.

On the same day the Kinks travelled back from France, Bob Dylan arrived in London for a series of concerts, culminating in a memorable performance at the Royal Albert Hall. His presence transformed the British music scene that spring, not least because he had successfully crossed over into the teenage market. His singles 'The Times They Are A-Changin'' and 'Subterranean Homesick Blues' both hit the Top 5 in quick succession. In the wonderfully democratic pop press of the time this meant that he was featured in the *New Musical Express* and *Melody Maker*, alongside Val Doonican, Tom Jones, Twinkle, the Seekers, the Beatles, the Rolling Stones and the many other established stars and chart debutants of 1965. He was also a candidate for lavish colour photo spreads in girls' magazines like *Jackie* and *Boyfriend*. There were even decorative centre-page cut-outs intended for pre-teen bedroom walls, where Dylan's face could be placed alongside the other pop stars of the day. At the same time, his albums *The Freewheelin' Bob Dylan*, *The Times They Are A-Changin'* and *Bringing It All Back Home* were in the Top 10, two of them hitting number 1. Journalists were intrigued by his gnomic pronouncements and the articulacy of his work. British Tin Pan Alley songwriters, adept at copying any new style, initially felt ill-equipped to offer anything similar. The only candidate for the title of Britain's Dylan was Scottish folk singer Donovan, who wrote his own material and appeared regularly on *Ready, Steady, Go!*. At the moment of Dylan's chart breakthrough Donovan enjoyed two Top 10 hits: 'Catch The Wind' and 'Colours', much to the pleasure of Louis Benjamin's Pye label.

Dylan not only altered the very notion of what constituted a pop star but inspired a new generation of songwriters, many from the beat boom era. Lennon and McCartney acknowledged their debt immediately. Everyone else of significance was influenced on some level, including Ray Davies, who would subsequently be freed to write about whatever he chose. The final restraint on his songwriting came in the immediate aftermath of 'Ev'rybody's Gonna Be Happy'. Its failure brought great pressure from the management and record company to revert to the old formula. Ray maintains that everyone's confidence was dented, except his own. "Their heads went down after that. I thought it was still great because I knew what I had on the backburn. The other guys didn't know that. Mick Avory thought he'd be living back in Thames Ditton. You can imagine them being disillusioned because they didn't have my awareness of what was coming." But did Davies have any real knowledge of what lay ahead?

While Dylan was receiving a president's welcome in England, the music press reported further complaints from the second wave of British invaders seeking work in the USA. The Animals had attempted to record a live album at Harlem's Apollo Theater but, just as they were preparing to go onstage, the US Immigration Department intervened, blocking the show. Other touring groups felt bamboozled by the arcane regulations and various radio and television unions they were obliged to join in advance of performing. While the Musicians' Union back in Britain could be equally draconian, there was a growing sense that, to quote the

Animals' drummer John Steel, the Americans "have got it in for the invasion by our groups".

The situation even drew the ire of the senatorial and sober Derek Johnson, the most experienced and rational voice at the *New Musical Express*. Expanding his role as news editor and singles reviewer, he provided a rare, cerebral reflection on the problems facing touring musicians in the USA. In an indignant flourish, he wrote like a political commentator addressing an issue of international importance. "At this moment, America is striving desperately to seek peaceful solutions to the problems in Vietnam and her own Deep South. Why then is she, at the same time, unashamedly creating another international incident, by being deliberately hostile to the British pop business? For, make no mistake, America's attitude to our artistes is far more important than a mere squabble within the entertainment industry. It nibbles at the very roots of Anglo-American relations. For many decades, during which America had been undisputed top dog in the music business, the steady flow of artistes from the States into this country has continued unabated – and we have always welcomed them warmly . . . Suddenly, in the course of a year, the entire picture has changed. For the first time ever, thanks initially to the Beatles boom, Britain has assumed the role of champions of pop . . . Quite dramatically, our own boys and girls find themselves dominating the American hit parade.

"What happens? Sandie Shaw and Twinkle are banned outright . . . The Hollies and Wayne Fontana & The Mindbenders are kept hanging about for days before reluctantly being issued with H-2 visas . . . Reason given by the American Embassy in Britain for these restrictions are either that 'the artistes are insufficiently well-known in America to warrant working there'. . . or that they have nothing original to add to the American show business scene. The reason for the Americans' dictatorial attitude is simply – sour grapes. They bitterly resent the success of our artistes after themselves being on top for so long. And in true American tradition, they cannot bear to be the underdogs."

On 30 April, the same day that Derek Johnson's warning was published, the Kinks embarked on a nationwide UK tour supported by the Yardbirds, the Riot Squad and Goldie & The Gingerbreads. It was their first package tour as headliners and their most arduous to date. Relations within the group were already strained and would soon worsen. "We hated the sight of each other," Dave says. "We were dashing around the country doing one-nighters. We were tired out so much after a long drive. We lived off sandwiches and snatched meals." Ray Davies presented an equally bleak snapshot of the mid-Sixties' touring circuit. "In those days you arrived at the ballroom, the promoter and his bouncers grabbed you and locked you away in the dressing room, which was usually no more than a big cupboard, and then they'd come back and unlock you when it was time to go on. It was terrible, but you had to put up with it, and it led to a few strange scenes."

The euphemism "strange scenes" encompassed a wide range of aggressive and insulting behaviour. Road manager Sam Curtis recalls a litany of simmering conflicts almost from the outset of the tour. "Whatever you wanted to do for them, they worked against it. When it came to presentation, they weren't concerned. They had their own ideas about what they wanted the kids to see. When I picked them up they would deliberately make us late and ensure I had to drive faster, no matter where they were going. We'd all be ready and Ray would be off somewhere. You couldn't say, 'Come on, we've got to go now!' He'd say, 'Fuck ya, we go when *I'm* ready!'"

On one occasion, Ray uncharacteristically vented his frustrations with a display of mindless vandalism more typical of a Seventies rock star. "We did a show and the Yardbirds went on and they were going down bloody well. And what did Ray Davies do? He went into this lovely dressing room with beautiful tiled showers, tore the metalwork off the wall and threw it onstage during the Yardbirds' act." Arguably, this was less a comment on pop star rivalry than simply letting off steam. A year before, the Kinks had been a more united outfit aspiring towards pop fame. Now there were different pressures, both from within and without.

Sam Curtis detected an increasing schism in the line-up as the tour progressed. "Ray and Dave had nothing in common with Mick and Pete. The attitude I saw was that they had them along simply because they needed a bass player and a drummer. They were just a couple of geezers . . . The Kinks could be together for a hundred years, but the drummer and the bass player would never have a chance . . . They could never be shareholders, not even in the bus fare." This was a suspect assessment considering that Quaife had been there since the William Grimshaw days and Avory, on paper at least, was part of the business set-up. However, Avory had been the butt of their jokes since his recruitment and they took perverse delight in antagonizing the mild-mannered Kink for easy laughs. Curtis remembers one recording session during which Mick was allowed to set up his drum kit only to be laughed out of the studio when a session musician took his place. The group dynamics became more complex and brutal on the road. "It was the brothers against Mick," Curtis remembers. "Peter Quaife I don't include – he was just *there*. He wasn't the type of guy to get involved in aggravation . . . Peter was of a different background, a different class. He had no experience, he was just a nice guy trying to find his way. You'll notice that in none of these controversies will you find Peter Quaife. The only whipping boy was Mick Avory . . . I think he had a lower IQ and he was naive. There was nowhere else for him to go in the world other than where he was . . . You could insult him and treat him like dirt and it still didn't matter. He would just tolerate it."

The good-natured Avory was frequently pushed to the precipice of fury by the heartless goading of the brothers, whose taunting was unrelenting in its viciousness. "These guys could provoke the Pope!" says Curtis. "They didn't need anything. They would come down in the morning to go off on tour and when they'd see him they'd say, 'Morning, cunt!' How would you feel? If somebody says that to you in the morning you just feel like going out with them, don't you? But then, if he didn't he'd starve because he couldn't do anything else. What was he going to do, become a star on his own with a drum kit?! He's got the personality of a cucumber sandwich . . ."

The relationship between the parties was further complicated by the fact that Dave and Mick shared a house. Instead of bringing them closer together the arrangement exacerbated tensions. The two subsidiary Kinks, meanwhile, valiantly attempted to avoid the psychological conflict between the brothers and kept their own counsel. Pete Quaife became involved in a relationship with Genya 'Goldie' Zelkowitz (from support act Goldie & The Gingerbreads). This limited his interaction with the group during the potentially troublesome after-show festivities. Avory had no such outlet, relying instead on his kind-heartedness, self-deprecating humour and non-confrontational personality to maintain the peace. Unfortunately, these positive traits merely served to infuriate Dave at a time when he felt in creative conflict with his brother.

"For the first two years, it was just touring, partying and travelling," Dave says. "Mick and I were sick of seeing each other every day. The Mick thing came about because of something that happened between me and Ray. We were undecided about something. I think it was as silly as what we were going to do in the set. I wanted to do some different songs. Ray said, 'I don't want to do that.' I was getting frustrated that we were banging heads so I approached Mick, who seemed totally uninterested. That freaked me out and really irritated me. That's where things started to go wrong for me and Mick. I felt we were buddies but, in the end, he wasn't making any decisions at all. On reflection, I was asking the wrong guy. I should have spoken to Pete as we were good mates. Perhaps there was something subconscious going on between me and Mick. Maybe we were just fed up with each other and I just didn't want him around any more. Mick was getting a bit overshadowed by my antics. He'd be quietly sitting in the background and I was always out there being outrageous, getting stoned, and talking all night. That maybe created a bit of tension, whereas Pete and I were very outgoing and used to get off on each other, messing around. Pete didn't want to get involved between me and Ray. Mick stood away from it. Probably he didn't want to upset Ray, but it ended up in a fight. A big punch-up. It was the following night at Cardiff that it almost became fatal when I smashed Mick's drums and I was hit with the cymbal."

The lead-up to that momentous moment in the Kinks' career was almost equally violent. "It actually started the night before in Taunton," Quaife points out. "Dave got invited to a party which meant that he would do as many drugs and as much booze as he could possibly shove down his throat. We decided we'd better get him back before any damage was done . . . In the car he started fighting with Ray, and at the hotel he went after the road manager [Sam Curtis]. Then he attacked the night porter. Mick and myself decided to get away from it all because the guy was going nuts." Quaife and Avory reached the hotel staircase when they were confronted by the frightening spectacle of Dave Davies consumed by an overwhelming fury. "The mood was dangerous and we didn't know what would happen. He came flying after us at speed, clutching this suitcase which he let go. We were still moving when it came soaring through the air, then it smashed into Mick's back. Hard."

The drummer was momentarily shaken, but stayed on his feet. Quaife was astonished at the sudden change in Avory's countenance. His eyes widened and his fists clenched. It seemed as though he was seized by an insensate anger that nobody had ever witnessed before. "That's it!" he repeated to himself as he turned towards his adversary. What followed was a snarling conflagration of scratches and blows as the two battled like mad dogs in a back alley. Quaife recalls Avory pounding his large fists into Dave's head and body causing enough damage to knock him out several times. Ray adds that Mick had his brother in a wrestler's headlock as the blows rained down. Amazingly, Dave kept coming back for more, seemingly numbed by a combination of pills and booze that made him feel super-strong and invulnerable. In the end both parties suffered cuts and bruises but Dave came off worst with two black eyes. Sam Curtis was transfixed by a trail of blood stretching across the staircase. Momentarily, he found himself wondering what Ray Davies might say or do if anyone from the hotel dared suggest he should contribute some small payment for the damage. It was a funny yet typical consideration. Who knew what tomorrow would bring?

The night of reckoning occurred at Cardiff's Capitol Cinema and Theatre on 19 May. As a precautionary measure, Curtis had ensured that the brothers and the rhythm section travel from Taunton in different cars. When they arrived in Cardiff the parties were placed in separate dressing rooms and kept apart until they were due onstage. Even then, Ray and Dave and the rhythm section made their entrances independently from different sides of the theatre, like competing animals in a circus. "The stage hands thought we were crackers," Curtis says. What followed was nothing less than the most controversial, violent and disturbing incident in the Kinks' entire career. The eyewitness accounts and press reports are surprisingly consistent considering all the high drama. "I remember that night vividly," says Ray. "It was one of the first times we had separate dressing rooms. They pushed us onstage, and Dave had been beaten up by Mick the night before, so he had sunglasses on. Both his eyes were black. He did the first number, then he turned to Mick and spat at him. Then, crack!"

More pertinently, as press reports confirm, Dave wandered over to Avory, exchanged a few choice words, then kicked his prize drum kit across the stage. "He was getting on my tits," Dave explains, "so I said to him he should play the snare drum with his cock, it would sound better. Then I knocked his drums over. His drums were hallowed ground for him at the time. Now, he'd probably do it himself."

Sam Curtis vividly recalls the moment when Dave casually stepped back from the microphone and demolished the drum kit with a perfectly executed kick. The 2,500 teenagers packed inside the auditorium at first howled with delight at what they assumed was a well-rehearsed stunt. Avory was furious and humiliated. While the audience continued laughing, he was on his knees, scrambling around in the debris of his drum kit like a wounded animal. Curtis watched helplessly as the much abused drummer finally lost control and lashed out in retaliation. "Mick picked up his high-hat cymbal, came over and whack! Fortunately, Dave managed to step out of the way slightly because if he had not moved that thing would have gone through his head down to his neck. Those cymbals are *sharp*."

The instrument grazed his head, knocking him to the floor. Among the select observers was the Yardbirds' guitarist Chris Dreja who, after witnessing the assault, almost needed treatment himself. "I was standing in the wings watching. He delivered what to me was like an execution – a beheading. Seriously. It was such a violent act. He hit him over the back of the head. I was absolutely stunned. I remember *shaking*, then thinking, 'He's killed him.' The drummer just ran off stage and out of the theatre. Poor guy."

Pete Quaife confirms "Mick picked up a cymbal and whacked Dave across the head as hard as he could." Most agree it happened in the break between the set opener 'You Really Got Me' and the start of 'Beautiful Delilah'. Quaife's other memory is of Ray shrieking in horror: "My brother! My brother! He's killed my little brother!" The singer's own account is more detached, with no sign of any emotion or active involvement. "Dave was lying on the floor after Mick had just hit him with a cymbal. Blood was everywhere. Everybody rushed over to Dave to see if they could help him. I stood there. I was looking at my guitar and wondering what would have happened if the chords of 'Beautiful Delilah' had been different. The place was in chaos."

After surveying the scene and concluding that Dave was not dead, Sam Curtis rushed off in pursuit of the hapless drummer. "Mick thought he'd killed him and ran out of the theatre. Can you imagine the scene? This guy wearing the hunting jacket and frilly yellow shirt running through the streets of Cardiff with hundreds of girls chasing after him because he's one of the Kinks. And he's *running for his life* because he thinks he's killed someone."

While Dave was taken to the Cardiff Royal Infirmary for treatment, the MC announced the cancellation of the Kinks' second show. Curtis, meanwhile, was still scouring the streets of the city in his car, pulling up alongside groups of girl fans asking if they'd spotted the missing Kink. "Finally, I found him sitting in a café where a woman was nursing him like a mother. The boy didn't seem to know what was happening. I told him, 'There's only one thing to do. Take that jacket off, undo your shirt, get down to Cardiff Station and hide in the waiting room. The first train that comes along, I don't care where it's going, get on it. I want you out of town!' By now, I knew the police were back at the theatre and had started to search the hotel for him."

"They wanted to do Mick for GBH [grievous bodily harm]," Ray adds. "We were at the police station, Dave was in the hospital, and this guy was saying to me, 'Look, I want your brother to press charges.' Mick had nearly killed him. And Dave wouldn't, to his credit. It left me terrified, though."

Soon, the national press learned of the assault. With no comment from the Kinks, they pestered Curtis for an official statement. All he could give them was a grim perspective on the sad affair: "This looks like the end of the road for them. I think the group must break up now. I've seen this coming on for a long time. They've all been tensed up and something had to break."

Curtis' comments were engagingly frank and, years later, Larry

Page also acknowledged: "There was no way that they were ever going to play together again. The police were putting out bulletins for Mick Avory, who ended up with me, still in his stage suit. They were looking for him, and it was very serious. It was the *end* of the Kinks."

Confusion reigned over the next few days as the participants scattered. Dave Davies convalesced at the home of his sister Joyce and brother-in-law Ken Palmer. Avory stayed very briefly at the house of Page's music journalist friend Keith Altham, then quietly moved to his mother's place in East Molesey. He would never return to the rave pad in Connaught Gardens, which Dave subsequently took over. Pete Quaife spent several days in limbo, uncertain about his future, but already assuming the worst. "Everything was a bit upside down. Nobody really knew what was happening. Had we split up? Had we decided to go our own different ways? For about a week it was total confusion. I personally had no contact with anyone. I just stayed at home and counted my losses!"

Ray Davies, for once, had sound reasons to fear for the future. He not only faced the prospect of losing a drummer and possibly dissolving the Kinks, but had to contend with domestic dramas. Four days after the 'Cardiff Incident', Rasa gave birth to a daughter, Louisa Claire Rasa, at Alexandra Maternity Hospital in Muswell Hill. The baby's arrival in the midst of the biggest crisis ever to embroil the Kinks merely added to the emotional turmoil. This was no time for celebrations. Even as he was awaiting news of the birth, Davies sat hunched over a piano at his parents' home in Denmark Terrace, busily completing a new composition, 'I Go To Sleep', that Eddie Kassner required as a matter of urgency. "That song was commissioned by Peggy Lee," Davies says. "She was one of my older sister's favourite singers and I got to write a song for her. It was such an honour . . . There's something in casting songs for people – it's a real art form. I did have her voice in mind when I wrote it. If you listen to the bridge ("I was wrong . . ."), the lyrics evoke to me her voice, her style. I wrote that bridge for her." That same week, the group's all-important new single was released and a major US tour was tentatively scheduled for the following month. It seemed as if everything was happening at once – and yet no one knew what was happening.

Issued at the height of the rumours about Dave Davies' near decapitation, 'Set Me Free' was a demulcent, reflective ballad which Ray sang in a higher register than usual. It was one of his most moving vocal performances of the period, but the circumstances of its recording and release were never fondly remembered by its composer. After the relative failure of 'Ev'rybody's Gonna Be Happy' he had bowed to pressure from his record company, publishers and management to come up with something resembling "the old Kinks' sound". This implied another 'You Really Got Me' or 'All Day And All Of The Night' but, by now, there was a trend to alternate slow-paced ballads with fast rock-based numbers. In a calculated attempt to please all parties, Ray completed a mid-tempo, yearning lament in the vein of 'Tired Of Waiting For You' while borrowing a title that had already featured in the lyrics of 'You Really Got Me' ("please don't ever *set me free*"). "To say the least, I was pressured into doing it. That song was about freedom, in the sense that someone's been a slave or locked up in prison. It's a song about escaping something. I didn't know it was about my state of mind." In contrast, the flip side, 'I Need You', was a clingy, intense burst of garage rock, complete with a feedback opening from Dave Davies at the beginning of the track.

'Set Me Free' was shipped the same weekend as Louisa's birth. Incredibly, the very next day Ray could be found in London's Regent Sound Studios demo-ing the completed 'I Go To Sleep' and six other new compositions with minimum accompaniment. At short notice, Larry Page had brought in drummer Mitch Mitchell from fellow Pye act the Riot Squad, whom he also managed. For a few days, at least, it seemed that Mitchell (later the drummer in the Jimi Hendrix Experience) was in line to replace Avory, but Page still hoped for a reconciliation. Having heard that Dave was not intending to press charges, he phoned each of the Kinks individually requesting their presence at a Friday afternoon meeting. Each member turned up expecting to see Page alone. "As you can imagine when they all sat down in the room, it was dynamite. I didn't mess around. I just said, 'OK – there's an American tour starting soon' – and I didn't give them time to ask anything. At the end of it, I just said, 'Any questions?' And Mick Avory said he needed new cymbals because he'd smashed them over Dave's head."

In the aftermath of the Cardiff debacle, Page attempted to school Avory in the art of public relations. They concocted a story intended to cajole journalists into retrospectively reporting the onstage violence as an unfortunate accident. Given Curtis' public admission and other printed reports, it seemed a hopeless undertaking. Avory's explanation was ridiculously unconvincing but the press voiced no scepticism. "It was part of a new routine we had worked on for our song 'You Really Got Me'," he said. "The idea was that Dave should wave his guitar at my drums and I should pretend to hit him with the cymbals, but I really did hit him. When he fell over and everyone rushed onstage I felt such a fool, especially when I realized I had injured him." A photo session was arranged with the four Kinks huddled together holding the 18-inch cymbal that had felled the guitarist. Many years later, Avory amended the received account, pointing out that it wasn't the large cymbal pictured, but a smaller one that did the damage. "There was nothing left of the kit – there was only the high-hat, which is the pedal cymbal. So I turned that upside down and whacked him over the head with it." Every other eyewitness to the event agrees that it was indeed the high-hat cymbal, but none support his very belated claim about turning the 'weapon' upside down.

The positive press campaign was not entirely successful despite some diplomatic comments from Ray, who bleated: "I'm sorry about my brother and also that Mick's been upset." When sections of the music press suggested that the group should have continued the tour, Dave was wheeled out for an explanation. "I would have been hurt and annoyed if the boys had carried on without me," he said, while two girls backcombed his hair, carefully avoiding his damaged scalp. "A substitute would not have produced the same sound and that would have meant that the kids were not getting what they had come to hear – the Kinks."

What nobody mentioned was an unofficial ban from many city hoteliers, wary of the group's reputation after hearing about the violence in Cardiff. "There wasn't a single hotel in the country that would let them in," claims Sam Curtis. "That's why they couldn't tour. You couldn't come home to London every night. Word went out. The minute I went in to book them – 'No way'. Who wants blood all over their carpets or equipment torn off the wall?" Like the press, the hoteliers would soon be mollified, but a brief cooling-off period was deemed necessary.

On 26 May, 'Set Me Free' entered the *NME* charts at number 22, peaking at number 9 three weeks later. By previous high standards, this was relatively disappointing. Only a few months before, the group had been challenging the Rolling Stones but had now fallen far behind their major rivals. In different circumstances, Louis Benjamin might have expressed concern but the Pye chairman was happily distracted. That same week, Jackie Trent had climbed to number 1 with 'Where Are You Now?' soon to be followed by Sandie Shaw's 'Long Live Love'. Pye's double chart-topping achievement confirmed that they were still a force in the marketplace. Louis was content.

By contrast, Ray was angry and bitterly disappointed by what he felt was an artistic compromise on his part. "I'm ashamed of that song," he announced, a few months later. "I can stand to hear and even sing most of the songs I've written, but not that one. It's built around pure idiot harmonies that have been used in a thousand songs." Davies had this same downbeat mood as final preparations were underway for their much anticipated American tour. It did not bode well.

CHAPTER FIFTEEN

THE GREAT AMERICAN DISASTER

On 5 June, the Kinks played at the Astoria cinema in Rawtenstall, Lancashire, their first date since the cymbal incident in Cardiff, 17 days before. This low-key gig provided a chance to gauge the temperatures of the key combatants, away from the glare of the city press. Dave and Mick responded well to the entreaties of their management and maintained the peace simply by staying out of each other's way. Although their personal and working relationship never fully recovered, they learned the virtues of mutual tolerance. Once Dave ceased to use Mick as a buffer between himself and his brother, a semblance of civility re-emerged, but it would remain fragile. "I think that during the first year of our success I really abused myself," Dave admitted, one year on. "I was willing to do absolutely anything that was excessive, drinking and things like that. Then I started to realize what I was doing wrong when Mick and myself had a big punch-up onstage . . . At that particular time I wasn't writing . . . and I was thinking even less . . . From then on, I could still do a lot of things I'd done before, but with reservations."

While Dave was reassessing his priorities, Ray became increasingly entrenched in family, financial and career quandaries. He secretly dreaded the forthcoming tour of America and fretted over the cold war that was hotting up between his respective managers. "He was being hit from all sides," says Larry Page. "People were trying to influence him wrongly. He saw the Hooray Henrys as money, as stability, but I was the only person in there with any musical knowledge who could have guided them at all."

"I'm sure Ray saw us as money, stability and background," counters Robert Wace. "He had met my father. He knew that the Wace group was a very big public company. They knew who they were getting involved with. We had the relationship with the band. They understood what we'd done for them. Basically, Larry's an opportunist and he wanted to go to America. I wasn't very happy about that but he pointed out that Eddie Kassner had an office over there. Arthur Howes said, 'Let him go – it should be interesting to see what happens.' We wanted to see how Page would measure up. We felt that he was bad news for the group, being divisive and playing one off against the other. He was trying to row out Shel Talmy as producer. Everybody was rather bored with Larry Page. We'd probably have jacked it in ourselves because we were tired of having him around. You've got to remember that Grenville and I weren't exactly paupers."

Wace's disdain was palpable but, in allowing Page to get closer to the group, he was playing a perilous game. The weary resignation in his comment "we'd probably have jacked it in" indicates frustration at his rival's growing influence. Not that Page was immune from hubris himself. In his estimation, any power that Wace and Collins exerted was nothing more than illusory. "If we ever discussed it with the Kinks at that stage, they were a bit of a joke." This was another misreading which failed to take account of the complex relationship between the Davies brothers and their wealthy mentors. "They were extraordinary," says Dave, "and we'd never met people like that before. They were both so tall that people sometimes thought of them as twins. Robert looked down his nose, but Grenville really had the voice. He came from a posh part of Liverpool and had acquired his accent at public school. They had a lot of connections, and social circles were much smaller then. This was before the celebrity era. There was a friend of Robert's called Xavier who said to me, 'I can get you a date with Princess Margaret for £500.' That was loads of money in those days. It was amazing. These society people didn't give a shit about anything. I took girls into closets and cupboards. They didn't need much encouragement. High-society people could do anything they liked, so I just thought that was how you were supposed to behave." At different times, Dave befriended Wace and Collins individually, but also enjoyed Page's presence.

Ray's attitude was similarly ambiguous, depending upon his needs. While Wace claims "we had the relationship with the Kinks", it was Page who was more proactive on the creative side. "I was very, very close to Ray," he insists. "I had a good relationship with the group. Come on! I used to be in the [dressing] room when they were screwing around and everything else. We were all from a working-class background and that was the one thing that Wace and Collins weren't. They would just show up and say, 'Hello, hello – what! what!' There was no way that they could *communicate* with the boys. When there was trouble at Cardiff with the fight onstage, I was the one who sorted it out. I was the one who *could* sort it out. There would be no Kinks if I hadn't sorted them out. Now, if Wace had such a relationship with the boys, how come he didn't? He couldn't talk to Ray because he would just tell him to 'Get knotted'."

Sam Curtis had already seen enough to conclude that Ray Davies was a self-sabotaging creature who took perverse pleasure in making life difficult for everybody. "It might have been a bit different if Dave had been the oldest and not Ray, because Ray was very embittered. No matter what you did he would make sure there were problems. He wanted to be contrary. And the reason he was contrary was because he knew that anybody who spoke to him was only speaking to him for one reason – to make money. Nobody ever spoke to Ray Davies because they liked him! Nobody spoke to Ray or Dave Davies because they got pleasure from talking to them. People dealt with them to make money. In that position, why shouldn't he say, 'You want money – work for it – I'll be as awkward as I can.'"

Larry Page received a hint of what was to come while preparing for the US tour. "We got the contracts sent from America. These were standard contracts. Bear in mind that groups were a new thing. I went around to see Ray, sat there, showed him the contracts and said, 'Fine, you've got to countersign them with me.' I gave him a fountain pen and I watched him empty it on the floor. As he was talking to me, I saw the ink dripping out and he said, 'Oh, the pen's got no ink in it!' I said, 'I should bloody well think not. I've just watched you empty it.' So we got another pen. Then he said, 'I can't sign this because it says "Orchestra Leader" and they'll expect me to take an orchestra with me.' I said, 'No they won't, Ray. Groups are a new thing – just cross it out.' There was no way he wanted to put pen to paper to do the American tour. I don't know whether he was scared of committing himself. Ray just enjoyed being awkward. He really did. You had to coax Ray. You had to treat Ray like a little boy, humour him, be nice to him and pat him on the head."

Davies' passive-aggressive, oddly childlike behaviour was almost comical but it disguised genuine concerns that he preferred to keep private. Chief among them was a reluctance to be separated from his wife and baby daughter. He was also cynical about America, later referring to the Kennedy assassination of 17 months before as symptomatic of a country in crisis. His apprehension was heightened by fears about what might occur with promoters or American police if there was any repetition of the Cardiff affair. It continued to play on his mind. "The incident with Dave and Mick horrified me. I was scared it was going to happen again. Seeing people reduced to that level and talking to the police afterwards . . . it was a pretty horrible time."

While Ray ruminated, his brother made light of such concerns. "One thing worries me though," he joked with the press. "If I start running along a street, I don't want a copper shooting at me. I'm not used to bullets." For the other Kinks, the trip was nothing more than an exciting adventure. "I think I'd like to meet President Johnson and Presley, go to a cattle round-up and play the part of a Pony Express rider in a movie," was Quaife's innocent fantasy.

A couple of weeks before the US tour, Ray decided to invest in property for the first time. He was keen to retain his London roots rather than relocate to the stockbroker belts of Weybridge or Esher, the traditional route of the newly affluent pop star. To his amazement, a large house that he had envied as a child, was available at 87 Fortis Green. Built in 1805, it boasted up to nine rooms – according to press reports – including spotlighting, sash windows and a fashionable spiral staircase. At a hefty £9,000, it was three times the price of an average house, a formidable undertaking for someone yet to celebrate his 21st birthday. Fortunately, record sales and touring meant that the Kinks' gross income had risen to an incredible £90,000 per annum, although a vast chunk of that was swallowed by expenses, administration and sky-high tax rates. Even Ray was uncertain of his net income. However, he later wrote that he was able to arrange an *advance* of £9,000 from Kassner, an incredible sum in the circumstances. If true, this was a substantial commitment from the music publisher as Ray Davies still had no major cover hits to his name and the Kinks' last two singles had been modest successes, at best. The advance, approximately six times or more the average annual wage in 1965, also meant that Davies was able to buy the house outright without having to get a mortgage. It was an astute move.

The fancy house was a rare extravagance, out of keeping with his everyday spending. Even on the road, Ray was parsimonious. On entering a pub, he might politely hold the door open for his colleagues, ensuring that he would be last to reach the bar and it would likely be time to leave before he was asked to pay for a round. Another trick was to avoid carrying money altogether. During the Yardbirds/Riot Squad package tour, the musicians stopped off at a motorway café, where a familiar song wafted from the jukebox. "I was paying for my cheese on toast, while 'You Really Got Me' played," Ray remembers. "By this time we were headlining ourselves, and a muso from one of the support bands stood next to me. He assumed I was 'flush' because my record was playing on the jukebox, so he ordered a mega fry-up, thinking I would pick up the bill. I reached in my pocket and discovered that I didn't have any money on me. He ended up paying for me as well as himself."

"It took Ray five years to come to terms with success," Robert Wace attests. "By then, he had made a great deal of money as a songwriter. You know artistes that aren't able to handle wealth and he's not one of them. But he didn't have a very sophisticated attitude towards money. He's always been paranoid about it. He has this vision of himself as a tramp. He used to be the tightest guy with money I'd ever met."

Wace's view was corroborated by producer Shel Talmy, who reckoned Ray "made Rod Stewart look like a philanthropist". Even their faithful roadie Jonah conceded that "Ray was so tight it was unbelievable." Money was seldom far from Davies' mind, then or since. Five years later, he would damn all three of his managers and his publisher in the lacerating assault 'The Moneygoround'. For Larry Page, the song remains one of the most jawdroppingly hypocritical pronouncements ever featured on disc. "When I hear 'The Moneygoround', I can't believe it! That should give you a good insight into the way Ray thinks. Ray is the tightest bastard that ever lived. I've been in a car with him with Rasa. I've sat in the front and heard her say, 'Ray, what about that coat?' and he's said, 'No, you can't have it!' . . . 'Oh, Ray, please, it's very cold outside.' I'm sitting there listening to all this – 'No, it's a lot of money!' And it goes on and on and on. At the end of the day, he says, 'Oh, all right then . . . driver, will you go to Sketchley's?' It's a coat coming out of the dry cleaners! Now that gives you *some* idea. The boy was worth a lot of money, but he used to say to me: 'Larry, I want some chewing gum but I've only got a penny. Can you lend me a penny?' And that was Ray. Ray would *never* spend. He was a very careful person with his money. You never saw him put his hands in his pocket. Ray's pockets were sealed. Ray Davies never got screwed by anybody. *Never.*"

Interestingly, an unprompted Sam Curtis repeated the story of Rasa and the coat verbatim. Even Dave felt that Ray never surrendered his frugality. "He was miserly with his money and, in later years, he would be equally miserly with his emotions and affections."

The tendency to worry about absurdly small amounts of money was endearingly eccentric, but also indicated an almost childlike self-centredness. It was another fascinating insight into Ray's peculiar psychology but not one that Curtis entertained with any patience. "You can't rationalize the actions of somebody like that. Wealth is something that they were never able to assimilate. Personally, I don't think they ever will. Even if you told me that the Davies brothers had become like the nouveau riche, I wouldn't believe you. He may be a multi-millionaire now but, to me, Ray Davies will still question the price of an ice cream. If there's two pairs of trousers and one's £6 and one's £4, he'll see if he can wear the £4 ones."

Rasa learned to be both uncomplaining and resigned when confronted by her husband's Dickensian thriftiness. "The money?

Unbelievable. I used to buy my stuff from catalogues because that was the only way I could get anything for the house and so on. It was really hard not having any money."

Ray had good reason to feel a little disgruntled at the beginning of June. The Kinks' latest rivals, the Yardbirds, had just released their follow-up to the chart-topping 'For Your Love'. 'Heart Full Of Soul' was another thrilling record, this time pre-empting Davies' innovative use of Indian music. Only a month before, he had recorded a new composition, 'See My Friend', which had an unusual raga effect, but the Yardbirds had got there first. Indeed, they initially went further than the Kinks by experimenting with a genuine sitar. Producer/manager Giorgio Gomelsky masterminded the legendary session. "Some years earlier an Indian friend of mine had turned me on to ragas. Here was an opportunity to branch off into as yet unchartered musical territory. With my Indian friend's help we found a sitar and tabla player, not exactly in plentiful supply at the time, even in London . . . The sound was incredible, and we looked at each other awestruck. After a while, however, we came upon what finally proved to be an insurmountable obstacle: timing. Indian musicians have a different way of counting time and bars and we just couldn't communicate to them that they were supposed to stop after four bars." Gomelsky was about to berate himself for wasting money on "an outlandish experiment" when Yardbirds lead guitarist Jeff Beck brilliantly duplicated the sitar sound and saved the session. "It didn't turn out too bad for the Indian musicians either," Gomelsky adds, "because, aside from their session money, Jimmy Page, who had dropped in to see us, got so fascinated by the sitar that, on the spot, he convinced them to sell it to him, cloth included, for £25, quite a lot of money then." 'Heart Full Of Soul' would eventually climb to number 2, stopped only by the Byrds' majestic 'Mr Tambourine Man'. Having delayed the release of 'See My Friend' till after the American tour, Davies was again in danger of falling behind his rivals.

It was probably no coincidence that Ray was in a tetchy mood when interviewed that same week. This time his target was the record buying public whom he blamed for the current state of the charts, where Elvis Presley was number 1 with a five-year-old recording: 'Crying In The Chapel'. The Everly Brothers had also recently topped the *NME* chart with 'The Price Of Love'. For one strange moment, it seemed that some sort of Fifties revival might be underway, but it was really a testament to the remarkable eclecticism of the time. Unfortunately, Ray could only focus on the negative. "It makes you sick," he stormed. "They're all waiting for something different, so they buy Elvis Presley and Connie Francis and all that crap. No records are selling well but what do they want to buy that crap for?" He concluded his rant by laughing at the presence of Tom Jones' 'It's Not Unusual' in the US 'R&B' charts.

By the time the interview was published, Davies was safely abroad and missed the backlash, which was ferocious. *Record Mirror* was bombarded with indignant replies, many of them deemed unprintable. The more sober attacked Ray Davies for his presumption, damned the Kinks' live sound, complained about their "ponderous boring guitar work" and lampooned their "run of the mill records". A certain R. Phillips from Rotherham led the charge with a catch-all diatribe: "These pop music veterans with a career of at least 18 months' duration, with the most off key vocalist and the worst disc ('Ev'rybody's Gonna Be Happy'), are now connoisseurs of the industry. So the world's leading male singer and the greatest female singer are crap? The Kinks can dislike anything they like but they can't tell others what they should like."

On 17 June, the Kinks, accompanied by Larry Page and Sam Curtis, boarded a Continental Airlines flight bound for New York. Cine camera footage of the departure captures them in the moment: resplendent, puppy-playful and optimistic. The Davies brothers sit alongside Page and Curtis, all four pushing their noses back like children showing off. Ray even unzips his trousers to reveal blue underpants, specially bought for the trip. He is smiling and animated. Despite Ray's secret fears about the fate of the group after Cardiff, resentment of being taken away from his family, concerns about management, wariness of American police and general disgruntlement, he displays the tireless exuberance of a schoolboy enjoying an adventure into the unknown.

After arriving in New York, the Kinks were immediately taken to Manhattan to promote 'Set Me Free' on television's *The Clay*

Cole Show. Ray Davies still seemed in exuberant mood, encouraging the others to adopt public school speech, just like Collins and Wace, while claiming that they were former art school students who had met at university. Imitating the Beatles, Ray informed his host that they were all to be awarded MBEs (Most Excellent Order Of the British Empire) by the Queen on their return to England. "We feel only pop stars should get MBEs," he concluded. These mild spoofs may have been intended to display a similar humour to that of the much loved Beatles but, if so, they backfired. The Beatles' wit was based on clever wordplay, easily understood puns and affectionate retorts, but Davies' responses were edgier and seemingly intended to make the interviewer feel uncomfortable and foolish. Page remembers one run-through where a researcher politely enquired about Ray's hobbies outside music, only to be told, 'plating'. "What's plating, Ray?" he asked. Ray smiled enigmatically. The question was never asked on air.

It was already evident that the group had no intention of pandering to American expectations. As Ray attests: "We were very conservative and unyielding north Londoners who were waiting to see the football results. 'Why don't you have the football results in the *New York Times?*' We were on our own planet, we really were. Planet Kink. And if they weren't on our planet it was difficult for them to get along with us. So it was a collision of cultures."

While the Beatles had provided the model for sympathetic media attention via press conferences, quick-witted interviews, accommodating photo shoots and an amiable accessibility way beyond the call of duty, the Kinks were more remote and uncaring. "We didn't have the savvy of the Beatles or the Stones," Ray reflects. "They had a great publicity machine behind them. They were very personable people. Even the Stones had a great way of dealing with press. The Kinks were complete novices and rednecks. We didn't understand why we had to do all these interviews and things, so we didn't hit it off too well with the Americans. But the records were big hits. We just didn't understand the publicity part and how to deal with promoters from Las Vegas."

On 18 June, the Kinks appeared at New York's Academy of Music. Sam Curtis was aggrieved to discover a dusty auditorium, lacking the excellent facilities he had imagined. Some of the old stage hands felt contemptuous towards shaggy-haired rock 'n' rollers, particularly of the British variety. When Page arrived early at the venue, he was horrified by a billboard proclaiming the arrival of 'THE KINGS'. Convinced that Ray would refuse to perform if he ever saw such a title, Page persuaded the management to rectify the error immediately. In advance of showtime, there were further problems about who was supposed to top the bill. The Dave Clark Five naturally assumed they were the headliners but an inspection of the respective contracts indicated that both groups had been promised this accolade. Having argued among themselves, both acts were now ready to lynch promoter Sid Bernstein until it was learned that one of his close relatives had just died. The dispute was eventually settled by the toss of a coin.

When the Kinks took the stage, Page retreated to the rear of the Academy like a proud parent. "It was very emotional for me. I remember the old tears running down my eye. For this little band I'd found to be opening in America was sensational." Afterwards, at the Grantham Hotel, Dave was in his element, simultaneously fending off and inviting teenage girls into his room. "There were birds in the cupboards, under the bed," Curtis recalls. "They crawled all over the hotel." Ray preferred to get a good night's sleep, but was still troubled by insomnia.

The next night, the group played at Philadelphia's Convention Hall, this time with additional support from the Supremes, specially recruited to replace the Moody Blues who, despite a recent UK number 1 with 'Go Now', had been declined a US visa. Page remembers Ray entertaining Mary Wells after the show. The talented former Motown singer – a hit songwriter in her own right – had heard Davies' demo of 'I Go To Sleep' and insisted, "I want that song!" Ray blurted, "You can't have it!" before explaining that it had already been promised to Capitol Records' star, Peggy Lee. Wells evidently accepted the disappointment with grace.

There was no time to rest as the tour brought them to Peoria, Illinois, a tedious trek involving a plane flight and a long bus ride. The booking was a severe disappointment, the turnout poor and the reaction tepid. It was at this point that unrest and irritability started to affect group morale and old grievances threatened to re-emerge. "The whole tour was problematical because of Cardiff," says Page. "During this stage everybody wanted to punch the life out of everybody else. It was my job to act as referee. I had to keep them to one side all of the time. We had a large bus and I had two of them at the front and two at the back, and I had to sit in the middle and keep them apart. Ray, of course, was enjoying it and provoking it all. Imagine me on the bus with the two of them at each end. I'd hear a little movement and I'd look round and Ray would say, 'I'm just stretching my legs!' Then, he'd run down the bus and go, 'you cunt, you cunt', and then he'd go back again. This is schoolkids' stuff . . . There were a lot of problems. Pete Quaife was a fairly cooling influence, but he had to be careful too. If he sided with Mick, he'd have the brothers against him and if he sided with the brothers, Mick would be on his own. Ray felt that anything to create a bit of excitement was the thing to do – and he certainly did."

The curse of Cardiff had far greater consequences than even Page admits. As a result of Dave Davies' injury there, the US visit had been delayed by a week. This meant that the itinerary had to be revised. Prestige locations were sacrificed along the way. In the Midwest and beyond, this created an embarrassing fiasco of low attendances at unsuitable venues, made worse by poor advertising and promotional confusion. It was more than enough to sap confidence, unravel fragile psyches and foster an atmosphere of cynicism and resentment.

On 21 June, Ray Davies 'celebrated' his 21st birthday in Chicago. Several attendees at the Arie Crown Theater presented him with cakes before the show. Shortly after the opening song, an electrical failure plunged the theatre into darkness. Page bolted backstage, fearful of the consequences. Such a caesura might easily spook the group, provoke a fight or prompt a walk-out. Their set had been deliberately paced to maximize the impact of 'You Really Got Me'. Page had advised Davies to open the show with a teasing few bars of the song, then play a full version mid-set and finally close the performance with a truncated coda emphasizing its familiar riff. "That way they'll get it three times," he had told the singer. The power cut put paid to that idea. Backstage, the boys looked deflated and drained of adrenalin, like boxers whose championship fight had suddenly been suspended in the middle of a round. "I had to gee them up to that bloody climax to start them going again." After a five-minute delay, power was restored and the Kinks completed the performance, but they were not happy.

Increasingly, Ray focused his thoughts on his family in London. He missed Rasa. Back at the hotel he sought solace via the trans-atlantic telephone, but hearing her disembodied voice, stilted by echo and time delay, merely darkened his mood. Her absence on his supposed 'big day' played on his mind, later prompting a bitter harvest. Sam Curtis recalls the entourage visiting a club afterwards where Ray was greeted by a standing ovation while the house orchestra struck up the chorus of one of their hits. Even the hardened road manager was moved by the affectionate spectacle, but the mood rapidly turned sour. Ray stopped, reached into his pocket, pulled out some loose change and threw it around the room, shouting: "Is this what you want? Is it my money you're after?" Later, Davies confessed to Curtis that the phone call to Rasa had proved upsetting, but Sam had little sympathy for his excuses. "Well, don't phone her then," he advised.

As they traversed the Midwest, things worsened. A date in Springfield, Illinois, proved upsetting for Curtis. "It was a school armoury! They were moving the school desks around when we arrived. It was only a small building, so they could only pay me so much. This went on all over the country. The promoters knew they'd made mistakes and bad bookings and they didn't want to pay." After another poorly attended show in Denver, the troupe endured a turbulent flight to Reno, prompting chilling memories of the 1959 plane crash in Clear Lake, Iowa, that took the lives of Buddy Holly, Ritchie Valens and the Big Bopper.

The show in Reno, Nevada, at the Centennial Coliseum was arguably the most disappointing yet. "This woman booked a stadium on the same night the rodeo came into town," Curtis says. "The place was empty. So the Kinks went on and did eighteen minutes instead of forty. I was given $1,000 instead of $2,000 and promised the rest at another booking in Sacramento. When we got there Sonny & Cher were on the bill."

By now, Ray Davies had lost patience with the promoters, the dwindling audiences and his management. "The Kinks didn't play the game," he admitted, 45 years later. "That's what worked against us. And I don't know why we didn't – possibly because we were slightly unpolished and got our own way, and we were young. Dave was seventeen and had to get a special work visa. So it was a tricky time." Unlike the Beatles, the Kinks were volatile, directionless and subject to temper tantrums when things went wrong. "The Beatles were refined," Ray adds, "and how brilliantly they were prepared for every situation. They had a wonderful press agent, Brian Sommerville, when they first toured America. Brian Epstein was totally behind them, pulling the strings, but in a good, positive way. I admire the way they dealt with America and in their careers generally. The Kinks were barely potty trained by comparison. It was just the nature of the way we worked . . . If we got angry, we played solos longer, things weren't organized."

Larry Page faced the twin problem of rapacious agents and appeasing his increasingly aggrieved singer. "We were getting situations where promoters were refusing to pay us because we'd only done forty-four minutes instead of forty-five. The following night it would be for the same promoter, and I'd say to Ray: 'They're refusing to pay us, don't worry we're going to fight it.' The next night Ray would do forty-six minutes, but all he would play would be 'You Really Got Me'. Now that's OK – you're telling the promoter what you think – but it's not fair on the fans." Curtis confirms that an extended version of the song was played in Sacramento although, obviously, it did not constitute the entire set. In retaliation, one annoyed promoter would later report the Kinks' "unprofessional behaviour" to a music union representative. More complaints would follow before the end of this fractious tour.

It was blessed relief when the Kinks reached Los Angeles where they were booked to appear on several television shows, culminating in an all-star gathering at the prestigious Hollywood Bowl. At last, the musicians were able to relax and enjoy their celebrity status. Tinsel Town provided positive snapshot memories of America that they would remember for the rest of their lives. Pete Quaife was mobbed at Disneyland; Mick Avory visited the Manne-Hole Club and was introduced to the great jazz drummer Shelly Manne; Dave Davies acquired his famous Gibson Flying V guitar and played alongside the Shindogs, featuring one of his and Ray's adolescent heroes, lead guitarist James Burton.

The indefatigable Eddie Kassner was also in Hollywood, busily flogging sheet music, organizing deals, arranging covers and feverishly networking on behalf of his clients. He introduced Ray to Dean Martin at a party and the following day the American turned up at Warner Brothers on a motorcycle, dressed like a rocker, accompanied by singer Buddy Greco. Martin expressed interest in covering one of Davies' songs, but later thought better of the idea. Not that Kassner was too concerned; remarkably, he had already licensed a series of new Davies' compositions to such performers as Peggy Lee, Cher, the Cascades and Bobby Rydell, with the prospect of more to follow.

Larry Page was also busy in Hollywood. Among his new contacts were Charlie Greene and Brian Stone, managers of Sonny & Cher, then heading to the top of the American charts with 'I Got You Babe'. Even by the cut-throat standards of Tin Pan Alley, the tale of Greene and Stone was worthy of a docudrama. As teenage press agents in Fifties New York, they had lived way beyond their means, renting a palatial penthouse apartment, sporting expensive suits, hanging out at the Copacabana and representing some star clients, including Sammy Davis Jr and Peggy Lee. In the summer of 1960, they moved to Hollywood and, in a daredevil prank, scaled the walls of the film lot Revue Studios, set up business in a vacant office and acted as if they owned the place. They enjoyed free phone facilities and even canteen meals courtesy of the studio, an arrangement that lasted several months until they were rumbled. Branching out, they opened a club, then entered the music business, representing and recording Billy Daniels. At Gold Star Studios, they met producer Phil Spector, whose arranger, Jack Nitzsche, introduced them to Sonny Bono and Cher La Pierre, then recording under the name Caesar & Cleo. In a supreme example of brinksmanship, they resold Caesar & Cleo as Sonny & Cher and later acquired solo deals for each performer on different labels, as if they were shares on the stock market.

Page was impressed, the more so when Cher agreed, or was instructed, to record Ray Davies' 'I Go To Sleep' for her forthcoming solo album, *All I Really Want To Do*. He even persuaded Greene and Stone to nominate him as Sonny & Cher's representative on a forthcoming UK promotional visit. What intrigued

Page most of all was the prospect of recording the Kinks at the aforementioned Gold Star Studios. Ray was thrilled by the idea and a session was completed featuring a new composition, 'Ring The Bells'. It was a decision guaranteed to irk Kinks' producer Shel Talmy, who had already crossed swords with Page over the re-recording of 'You Really Got Me'. Larry was unrepentant. "I thought some of the songs Shel was doing, the demos were better. To me, producing is a lot more than being in the studio – it's getting the thing right before you get there, which we always made sure was done." If Page was harbouring secret ambitions of displacing Talmy as producer, then this was a provocative powerplay, the outcome of which was likely to be gory.

Gauging the mood of Ray Davies, even at the best of times, was no easy task. By his own admission, he felt "in a mixed-up state" during that fateful week in LA. Both Page and Curtis were exasperated by his behaviour and received little support from the rest of the group, who knew better than to intervene. "Sam could have been due for a nervous breakdown I don't know how many times," Larry says. "He did a good job, a tough job, but he was treated like a bloody slave by them." Ray's actions were more mischievous than malevolent. His humour was quirky, frequently sardonic and seemingly intended to drive his manager to distraction. "I used to stand there watching them go on the screen and die wondering what Ray was going to say. It was totally unpredictable. You never knew what was going to happen. It's very tough. In LA, he refused to do a TV show because there was a coloured drummer. Now I know Ray's got nothing against coloured drummers, but everyday there was a little trauma. Everyday he would want to bring to everyone's attention that he was the man in control. We had this throughout the tour."

Sometimes, Page found himself unwittingly playing straight man in what sounded like a Ray Davies comedy routine. On one occasion, Larry mislaid a pair of custom-made prescription spectacles. Later that evening, he was astonished to discover Davies wearing them. Upon demanding their return, he was rebuffed by Ray who insisted he had bought them for his own use. A long argument followed before they were given back. While this seems like an obvious, if childish, practical joke, Page was almost convinced that Davies actually believed his own story. Nor was it the only example of the singer's eccentric behaviour. "I used to have to count my underpants and count my socks," Page complains. "But then again, as they say, possibly a true talent is very very close to the border of insanity. I don't know whether Ray was before his time, after his time, or where he was."

On reflection, all this sounds like displacement activity to release tension. Later in life, Davies liked to create characters and inhabit them, like a method actor. Page's bamboozlement indicates how successful Davies was in manipulating his creations for comic effect. There was a darker side to Ray's unpredictability, though. It was during a location shoot for the Dick Clark-hosted *Where The Action Is* that Davies lost his temper and became involved in a quarrel which ended in an exchange of blows. "We were doing a Dick Clark show [*Where The Action Is*] . . . Peter and Gordon were there. They had a changing room that was as big as a shoebox and somebody said, 'You wait until the Communists take over Great Britain.' Well, that was too much to take. I just lashed out at him. I wasn't drunk. You shouldn't say 'Wait till the Communists take over Great Britain.' It infuriated me."

Davies' reaction was astonishingly violent considering the innocuous remark. Sam Curtis, by now inured to tempestuous outbursts from both brothers, was unfazed. "One of the guys working there just said *something*. You must realize that if these people spoke to the Davies brothers thinking they were talking to ordinary people, they were wrong. You could turn round and say something innocent and finish up with the most unholy row. They weren't the type of people you could talk to in an ordinary way if you didn't know them, and the guys in America *didn't* know them. Like, I could turn round to you and say, 'Oh, don't be silly, don't do that' and you would say, 'Well, what do you mean?' But if you said that to the Davies brothers there was a punch-up or they'd smash a few bottles or knock a table over. 'What do you mean – you're calling *me* silly. I'm the great Davies!'"

The scuffle might have proven inconsequential but for the fact that the 'victim' turned out to be a representative of the American Federation of Television and Radio Artists. He had already exchanged words with Dave, who was stubbornly resistant to signing a union contract, and Ray's eruption only made matters worse. The Kinks' future in America was now on a knife edge.

Still upset, Ray returned to the Ambassador Hotel, locked himself in his room and refused to see anybody. It was the eve of the Hollywood Bowl concert, a star-studded spectacular featuring the Beach Boys, the Righteous Brothers, the Byrds, Sonny & Cher, Sam The Sham & The Pharaohs, the Sir Douglas Quintet, Donna Loren, Dino Desi & Billy and Ian Whitcomb. This was the show that Page rightly regarded as the pinnacle of the Kinks' achievement in the USA, the instant where all the tribulations of slogging across the Midwest playing school armouries and near empty auditoriums could be forgotten. In Page's imagination the Bowl was inextricably linked with his vision of the Kinks as a possible second Beatles.

On 3 July, Larry was fantasizing about that evening's Bowl concert and congratulating himself on having survived a rigorous 17 days on the road. All things considered, the visit had not gone as badly as he'd feared at the midway point. Ray Davies had been infuriating and there were problems with some promoters, but it could have been worse. Kassner had done good business in Hollywood, Page had met Greene & Stone and ingratiated himself with Sonny & Cher, and the Kinks had appeared on several important music television shows including *Shivaree*, *Shindig!*, *The Lloyd Thaxton Show* and *Where The Action Is*.

Page's reveries were abruptly interrupted by a phone call from Patrick Doncaster, pop columnist of the *Daily Mirror* in London. He started questioning Page about gossip that the Kinks, specifically Ray Davies, would not be appearing that night. Larry laughed off the rumour as nonsense, but was urged to check, just in case. When he reached Ray's hotel room, he was greeted by the threat, "I'm not going on." What Page considered the ultimate prima donna display may have been sparked by the previous day's fight, but Ray's mood had festered overnight. He had been on the transatlantic phone again in recent days speaking with Rasa, and had already insisted she should be flown over for the concert, along with Quaife's girlfriend, Nicola. Page had contacted Grenville Collins back in London who arranged a flight, but it was no easy task. "At that stage, it was very tough because Rasa was of Russian or Eastern bloc parentage. The Americans weren't too keen on getting them in, even given time, let alone short notice."

"I didn't have a passport," Rasa recalls. "I had what they called an alien's card. The only place I'd ever flown to before was Jersey, where my eldest brother was living. Robert and Grenville got me a passport. I don't know how they did it, but they got me one, just like that. They told me to go to their boutique and buy some dresses." With Ray thousands of miles away and unable to object, Rasa went on a shopping spree. "I must have had some money by then," she says, although Collins and Wace were always able to offer credit. "I bought this coat, not the fur one, but a shabby brown like a bear. I loaded my suitcase with clothes from the shop. I loved it. I thought, 'What am I going to do with my baby?' So I left Louisa with my mother. My poor mother!"

While Rasa was gleefully heading for the airport, events in America took a bleaker turn. Page continued the tired routine of coaxing Davies out of his negative state but, on this occasion, the manager's patience finally snapped. "I spent all day pleading, grovelling – and this was after a very heavy tour. It was totally degrading for me. I sat there and thought, 'What's it all about? I've taken these boys, I've given them every bloody thing. Here we are at the Hollywood Bowl, and Ray's refusing to go onstage!' And that was it for me. What am I going to do after that? Where am I going to put them where Ray won't refuse to appear onstage? And since then any act I've been associated with, the minute I see problems, I'm out. I don't work my arse off twenty-four hours a day with people who refuse to honour contracts."

The power game between Page and Davies had now reached a bitter climax in which both parties lost. Angry and humiliated, the manager waited till Rasa arrived and the Kinks were onstage at the Bowl, then abruptly departed. His destination was London, where outstanding business awaited in the happier environs of Tin Pan Alley. Although he informed the other Kinks of his plans that afternoon, he did not speak with Ray, who was infuriated when he heard the news. "Nobody abandons the Kinks," he muttered. It was a refrain that would rattle down the years, re-iterated in court rooms where counsel would allege that Page had left his charges "in the lurch". He always denied the imputation. "I'd had enough. If I hadn't left I'd have had a nervous break-down. Of course I didn't leave them in the lurch. I left Sam Curtis there. I left the publisher [Eddie Kassner] there. I left the agent

[Don Zacharlini] there. They were very well looked after. Sam was a very efficient roadie."

Curtis sided with Page, insisting that the controversial abandonment was of minimal importance. Indeed, he even went as far as questioning the relevance of Page's presence at all, implying that Larry may as well have stayed at home with Collins and Wace. "I could see no reason that he had to be there other than that they wanted him at their beck and call. Page leaving made no difference at all. They wanted Larry there as a whipping boy, somebody to have a go at, or make problems for. He must have realized they were doing this. Ray's attitude was 'You're making money out of me – have trouble.'"

Page missed the final week of the tour, including an unhappy Independence Day in San Francisco, where the Kinks were booked to appear at the Cow Palace on a streamlined version of the previous night's spectacular, headed by the Beach Boys. It was the same promoter who had booked the ill-fated Reno performance. Fearing non-payment because of lower than expected gate receipts, Ray allegedly demanded an advance in cash, which was not forthcoming. In the end, the Kinks did not play, but politely wandered onstage and waved to the crowd. The following day, they flew to Hawaii for a couple of shows, entertaining US troops at Schofield Barracks and appearing at Honolulu's International Center Arena. Davies was momentarily seduced by Hawaii's charms. "I thought it would be spoilt and commercialized, but I was wrong. There were still many beautiful, peaceful beaches where we could relax. Still, as soon as you got inland there were troops and bases. The atmosphere was tense – as if the H-bomb was going to fall any moment. It was an interesting place, and with lots of sunshine too." The visit even inspired a whimsical composition, released 15 months later: 'Holiday In Waikiki'.

For Rasa, the trip was the ultimate treat. "Waikiki was like a second honeymoon. I really enjoyed Hawaii and loved being in America. There was a picture of me in this posh Los Angeles hotel, lounging on this huge bed which could have accommodated eight people. Breakfast was brought in on a silver tray. I felt like a princess. In Hawaii, I was wide-eyed looking at everything. I remember seeing something behind me and then I walked straight into a telegraph pole. I had a big lump on my head. We visited

Diamond Head, a volcano [tuff cone] on O'ahu and there were all these lovely Hawaiian girls. It was a brilliant time."

Ray Davies appeared temporarily rejuvenated by the Hawaiian sojourn. The remaining handful of dates on the US tour passed without incident, proof enough that Page's absence was not disastrous. Far from opening the doors to anarchy, his departure seemed to quieten Ray's penchant for mischief, at least for the present. Sam Curtis performed the administrative tasks with his customary firmness. Unlike Page, his responsibilities were limited to specific functions, which ensured that he was largely immune to Davies' personal problems, capricious decisions or baffling mind games. "Larry could not make them perform better. He didn't have to arrange their transport, or put them to bed at night or get them up in the mornings, or get their meals. I did. If there was no Ray causing problems, then Larry wouldn't have to sort them out. And if Larry wasn't there, Ray couldn't make problems because there was nobody there to make them to. He couldn't make problems for me because I just ignored them. For example, in Hawaii, the shirts got stolen. Ray said, 'No way am I going onstage without my shirt.' So I turned around and said to him, '*Great*, don't go on!' Of course, they went on."

On 11 July, the Davies brothers boarded a flight to London, leaving Quaife and Avory to enjoy an extended holiday in Hollywood. Robert Wace was eagerly awaiting the brothers' arrival, knowing that the struggle for power over the Kinks' management had shifted firmly in his direction. Without having to lift a finger, he and Collins suddenly found themselves in an unassailable position thanks to Page's dramatic exit.

"The point is that management is about relationships," Wace reflects, in hindsight. "With due respect, you don't leave an artiste during their first American tour! While he was in America as our representative Larry Page was, to all intents and purposes, the manager. That group were capable of anything – you couldn't leave them. They were capable of getting involved in a fight or getting knifed. Grenville or I were on subsequent US tours. If even on one morning we decided to leave and not tell Ray, I would not expect to manage them on my return. Larry Page blew his stack. He ran into Sonny & Cher and at the first sign of the grass being greener he fucks off . . . We wanted Page out and we gave him enough rope to hang himself, and that's exactly what he did. When they came off the plane, Ray and Dave said, 'Get rid of Larry Page. We don't ever want to see him again. We want out of any involvement with Page, Kassner Music, Denmark Productions . . . thank you, goodnight. End of story.'"

CHAPTER SIXTEEN

A LEGAL MATTER

In spite of all the drama on the American tour, everything was preternaturally quiet for Ray Davies upon his return to the UK. He and Rasa spent some time at the Imperial Hotel in Torquay, Devon, after which they moved into and began furnishing their new home in Fortis Green. It seemed that Ray's most pressing concern was to enjoy a well-deserved rest from the group. The consequences of the recent stateside conflicts were still unknown. Indeed, there was even talk from some optimists of a return trip in the near future. Nobody yet realized that the complaints logged by the Reno promoter, the television union official and others unknown would prevent the Kinks from touring America for the best part of four years. Contrary to later reports, there was no official 'ban' as such, but something closer to a universal black-listing. Given the sensitivity of the Musicians' Unions on both sides of the Atlantic, the withholding of permits was not entirely surprising, but the lack of explanation and duration of the sanction seemed almost Kafkaesque. It meant that the group had little chance to compete, even with lesser rivals. All that was left was bitterness and an exile that, by the late Sixties, would diminish the Kinks' reputation in America to that of an obscure cult outfit.

Larry Page still knew nothing about his ineluctable fate. Ray had phoned him several times upon his return to the UK and, apart from a sarcastic reference to his abrupt departure, appeared both friendly and cooperative. Wace had visited his office to discuss various matters but also gave no hint that he had broken any obligations in coming home a week early. There was every reason to believe that things would continue as before.

Page's major adversary at this time was neither Wace and Collins nor the Kinks, but producer Shel Talmy. The music press reported a simmering dispute over the next Kinks' single. Page was determined to release 'Ring The Bells', the song he had produced at Hollywood's Gold Star Studios, while Talmy insisted that 'See My Friend' was still the favoured choice. "As their publisher I have the final say on any recordings by them," Page claimed, but Talmy stood firm, citing his production deal with Pye as paramount. Having previously taken on the imposing Phil Solomon in court, the producer was never likely to back down. "We had no power to release it whatsoever," Page now acknowledges. "Shel had a contract."

Talmy had enjoyed a reasonably productive relationship with Page prior to the Kinks' formation, but ended their association in anger. His contempt was still evident decades later. "Page!" he exploded. "The word that comes instantly to mind is guttersnipe. He was trying to wind up with the band without Collins and Wace, and without me. He wanted to be head honcho. Page was trying to ace out everybody else. He'd got Ray to record a couple of things in the States, then he tried to get them released. A charming fellow. I infinitely preferred Collins and Wace."

Page faced further criticism from within following the release of *Kinky Music*, an instrumental, orchestral album of Ray Davies' compositions. At the time, Ray was mildly sarcastic about the project but, in later years, railed against its creation. "That was appalling! Horrible! It's wonderful to have your work appreciated but that was just jumping on the back of a craze. Total and utter exploitation." Page was incredulous at the criticism, arguing that his project was an excellent marketing exercise in introducing Davies' work to a completely new audience. "I was out to boost him as a writer. That was the whole idea of *Kinky Music*. It was to boost his melodies. I spent a bloody lot of money doing the album to show people that, apart from 'You Really Got Me', he could write beautiful melodies. He got every penny that was due to him."

At the end of July, the new single, 'See My Friend', was released. An enchanting and intriguing composition, it was arguably Davies' most original work to date. Everything about the song – the poignant vocal, the ambiguous lyrics and the distinctive musical arrangement – seemed consciously constructed to provide an air of mystery. Even its title was a subject of confusion. On the record, it *clearly* stated 'See My Friend' and initially appeared in its first week on the charts under that name. However, in contemporary trade ads, later chart placings and subsequent compilations, it metamorphosed into the plural 'See My Friends'. Was this a pusillanimous act to distract attention from the song's homosexual undertones? The singular 'friend' was terribly suggestive at the time, particularly when placed alongside intimately sung words such as "she is gone" and the attendant revelation "now there's *no one* left – except my friend". It certainly implied more than mere friendship. Larry Page was concerned about the sentiments, rightly fearing a radio ban or limited play if the word 'friend' was analysed. Although Davies would later consistently use the 'plural' version, which merely implied a retreat into the security of male company, he was much more ambiguous about the composition in 1965. On the original single, he appears to sing both 'friend' and 'friends', as if intent on covering himself and dodging any censorship. He was considerably more explicit in a contemporaneous interview with the London *Evening Standard*'s scenester Maureen Cleave, admitting: "The song is about homosexuality. I know a person in this business who is quite normal and good-looking, but girls give him such a rotten deal that he becomes a sort of queer. He has always got his friends. It's like a football team and the way they're always kissing each other."

There were no similar comments in the music press, which would undoubtedly have regarded such subject matter as highly distasteful at best. Later, Davies became more circumspect about the theme. "It's patently obvious that the friends I'm singing about are not girls," he said in 1994. "They're across the river, it's a gulf! . . . I was thinking I have the choice to go there if I want . . . A lot of audiences think because I'm singing in the first person, it's me. People don't realize I'm like a novelist. I write characters. It worries me when people think that I am one of those characters." By 2011, his evasion had reached new levels of sophistry. "It isn't about sex," he insisted. "It's about a girlfriend. Maybe it's about lost opportunities. Playing across the river, maybe 'the river' is playing across the big pond. It's about loss, definitely. The loss of a person but also loss of career because we never thought we'd ever get back to America." This was taking the symbolism to an implausible level. As Davies well knew, the composition had been written and recorded well in advance of the American tour.

Musically, 'See My Friend' was equally fascinating, its raga drone echoing the experimental work recently conducted on the Yardbirds' 'Heart Full Of Soul'. Over the next year, pop's most adventurous innovators would continue to incorporate Indian elements in their work, a trend exemplified by the Beatles' 'Norwegian Wood', the Byrds' 'Why', the Yardbirds' 'Shapes Of Things' and the Rolling Stones' 'Paint It, Black'. Each of these owed a debt of sorts to Ravi Shankar's 1956 album *Three Ragas*, and several later recordings released by the Indian on Hollywood's World Pacific Records. Shel Talmy cites another likely source for Davies' inspiration when recalling a session he produced with John Mark of the Mark Almond Band. "He was a great guitarist and had just started listening to Indian stuff. He wrote a song based on a drum, raga-influenced. It was very melodic and I played it for Ray. The next day he came back with 'See My Friend'. That's how we did it. It was ahead of its time . . . very much a departure."

Davies insists the melodic inspiration came from that earlier trip with the Kinks to Bombay where he'd wandered out of his hotel at five in the morning and listened to fishermen chanting, after which he was chased by a large, angry dog. He sensed a spirituality in the voices of the workers that seemed perfect for the song. "I wanted a droning sound like the chanting people on the beach but I didn't have the Tibetan monks handy so I did it on the feedback on the guitar." Davies described the process of composing in similar terms to Wordsworth's recollection of emotion in tranquillity. "I'm of fairly average intelligence as a person, but there's a programme inside me that's programmed to remember significant events and that's what I'm good at. I can recount the emotion . . . I remembered the sound . . . I think it was quite a beautiful inclusion . . . Again, completely by accident – but the emotion felt right."

The happy accident occurred in the studio when Ray was playing "a very cheap Framus 12-string guitar" with a "quite bad" sound. "It had a great quality, but when I played it, I got too close to the microphone, and it started to feed back. And that provided the drone that ran through the record. I remember Shel Talmy saying, 'We'll never get all this sound on there, so I'll compress it.' It was a mixture of my stupidity, Shel's opportunism and engineer Bob Auger's technical ability."

*

On 2 August, Robert Wace took Ray to see solicitor Michael Simkins to discuss the arrangement with Kassner Music and Denmark Productions and devise a strategy to end that relationship. It must have been especially stressful for Davies who had just learned that Sonny & Cher were in London working closely with Larry Page. Although Page was perfectly within his rights to publicize or record another act, Ray was still bitter about the recent 'abandonment' and protective, if not possessive, when faced with tests of loyalty. "Artistes are very jealous people," Wace agrees, "and you could say, 'Hell hath no fury . . .' They do not like to think that one of their managers is having a romance with another act. If they're paying somebody, they want attention. They don't want it thrown in their faces."

The following day, Davies turned up at Pye Studios to confront Page. It was a bizarre turn of events in which the Kink found himself arguing against another act covering one of his songs. "Even as their publisher I tried to make him an important writer," Page points out. "I wanted another Lennon and McCartney in one man. But when I did 'I Go To Sleep' with Sonny & Cher at Pye he broke into the studio and said, 'Larry, you're stealing my song!' That was the man's mind." That strange episode was later recounted in court with Davies confirming: "I said, 'Get out of the studio, I don't want anything to do with you – get out of my life', and I just told him I did not want him to steal my ideas any more. I did not say 'songs', I said 'ideas'."

After the emotional exchange of 3 August, there was no going back for Davies who left the Page problem in the capable hands of Michael Simkins. The balance of power had now shifted inexorably towards the society duo, much to Page's chagrin. He always believed that they had systematically poisoned his relationship with Davies, thereby setting in motion one of the most famous legal battles in pop history. "The package worked but Collins and Wace did what I could have done earlier on. It's as simple as that. I think if we'd been able to continue without interference from the Hooray Henrys we would still have been in a very good situation. Ray is a fantastic talent. I liked Ray and if I'd had him on my own, I could have straightened him out. That I know."

The summer of 1965 was one of the greatest ever in pop. What was usually considered a quiet season in the music industry was dominated by several of the greatest singles ever released. Among the number 1 hits that flowed in rapid succession were the Byrds' 'Mr Tambourine Man', the Beatles' 'Help!' and the Rolling Stones' '(I Can't Get No) Satisfaction'. Even Dylan's six-minute wonder disc 'Like A Rolling Stone' was challenging for the top spot. The quality had seldom, if ever, been better. Davies was hoping that 'See My Friend' might be rewarded with a similarly high placing, but it only reached number 15 in the *NME*, dropping out from the listings after four weeks. To compound his misery, Sonny & Cher were all over the press and top of the charts on both sides of the Atlantic with the infectious 'I Got You Babe'.

Davies cut a miserable figure for most of that summer. His negativity poured forth like bile during interviews in which he seemed to complain about everything. The recent *Kinky Music* (credited to the Larry Page Orchestra) still preoccupied his mind and he virtually repeated the words used when he burst into the recording session with Larry Page and Sonny & Cher. "They copied all the thoughts that go into my songs from my records," he said. "They only elaborated on my ideas. So I must take some credit for the arrangements . . . If you play this LP and you play the records we made of the numbers you can see they had gone out of their way to make it sound like the way we sound. They've got a trumpet to sound like my voice. Whose idea was it in the first place? It must have been my idea." Davies sounded as though he was trying to convince himself as much as his puzzled interviewer from *Melody Maker*. Apropos of nothing in particular, he exaggerated his vocal abilities ("I could outsing Tony Bennett and Andy Williams put together"), reiterated his hatred of 'Set Me Free' and lashed out at Rolling Stones manager Andrew Loog Oldham, who had dared to dismiss a cover version of Davies'

'This Strange Effect' by Dave Berry as "boring". Like a hurt child, Ray retorted: "It's Andrew Oldham who is boring."

The greatest pain appeared to be reserved for the lack of critical or commercial recognition shown towards the doomed 'See My Friend'. It was as though the press and public had sided with Larry Page's negative view of the single. "[It's] the only one I've really liked, and they're not even buying it," he lamented. "You know, I put everything I've got into it . . . I can't even remember what the last one was called – nothing. Look, I'm not a great singer, nor a great writer, nor a great musician. But I *do* give everything I have . . . and I did it for this disc."

'See My Friend' was never a likely candidate for number 1, but it was a fleeting Top 20 success, heard by millions. It must have been a consolation of sorts when several of Ray's contemporaries later applauded its innovation, most notably Pete Townshend, who testified to its influence on the Who. Dave Davies recalls a similar accolade from the normally tight-lipped Mick Jagger. Barry Fantoni tells of "being in Marianne Faithfull's flat and Paul McCartney was eating a Dover sole that she'd cooked. They were looking at this little record player and it had Ray's 'See My Friend' on it and they just played it over and over."

Even if Davies had heard these compliments at the time, it is doubtful they would have lifted his glum mood. Solicitors were already preparing to do battle on his behalf. "I was a bit shattered by all that litigation," he later admitted. "It really went deep. I thought it was a team and the team was broken up and . . . I couldn't cope with it." This sense of betrayal was summed up in a handful of sentences in the music press that August. "You talk to someone and the next minute they're criticizing you. You think you've got friends and you haven't. You become wary of people. You become sick of people easily."

Davies sounded in need of another holiday. Instead, he was despatched to Berlin, where the Kinks were due to appear before 20,000 frenzied fans at the Waldbühne. Somehow, they managed to create almost as much pandemonium as they had done at Denmark's Tivoli Gardens earlier in the year. As the seats were unnumbered, volatile fans jostled for the best possible view in advance of the show. There were no alcohol restrictions so large sections of the crowd arrived with crates of beer which were

Ray Davies as a child.

Ray, the football star.

Ray, aged 8.

The winning athlete.

Paul O'Dell during the
Hornsey period. (Courtesy
of Paul O'Dell)

Frame enlargement from the film, *Veronica*.
(Courtesy of Paul O'Dell)

At Hornsey Art School. (*Left to right*): Paul O'Dell, Ray Davies, Jenny Howard, Su Statlender and Michael Flaum. (Courtesy of Paul O'Dell)

A surviving frame from Ray Davies and Paul O'Dell's lost film, *Veronica*. (Courtesy of Paul O'Dell)

Rasa Emilija Didzpetryte (*fourth from left*) at the Baltic Festival, Shipley, Bradford, 12 July 1964. (Courtesy of Rasa Didzpetris)

Ray and Rasa's wedding reception at 31 Howard Street on 12 December 1964. Rasa's mother admonishes Ray as he attacks her Dundee cake with a knife. (Courtesy of Rasa Didzpetris)

Grenville Collins (*left*) and Robert Wace (*right*), managers of the Kinks.
(© Rex)

Larry Page, who managed the Kinks in the Sixties and the Eighties.
(Courtesy of Larry Page)

Ray and Rasa celebrate the birth of their first child, Louisa Claire Rasa, at Alexandra Maternity Hospital, London: 23 May 1965. (© Mirrorpix)

Irrepressible road manager Sam Curtis, poses with police officers in America, while Dave and Ray look on.
(© Paul Gurvitz)

Posing with a cymbal after the 'Cardiff Incident'.
(© Pictorial Press Ltd/Alamy)

Mick Grace (*third from left*), temporarily replaces
Ray Davies in the Kinks: March 1966.

Ray in enigmatic pose. (© Rex)

liberally consumed. Tempting fate, the Kinks were supported by the self-styled lunatic of pop Screaming Lord Sutch, whose onstage shock horror theatricalism, 18-inch-long hair and quixotic attempts to stand for parliament had frequently secured press coverage in the UK. He began his performance by chopping up part of the stage with an axe. During his infamous set piece 'Jack The Ripper' he demolished a life-size dummy, which he then set alight, much to the consternation of watching stage hands. Finally, in parodic imitation of the Kinks' recent stage violence, he stabbed his saxophonist. "He was protected by a rubber mat around his chest. We'd break capsules and have pig's blood all over the place. There'd be animals' hearts and lungs which I'd pretend to pull from the saxophone player's body and throw into the crowd. That got everyone excited."

It was certainly a spectacular opening which left much of the audience in riotous mood. The Kinks barely made their way from the dressing room before being besieged by around 50 people while security guards looked on. A number of drunken fans invaded the stage, while others threw bottles indiscriminately, causing several injuries. Ambulance staff assisted the wounded. Still more attendees caused damage to public transport on their way home. After the debacle, the Kinks were met by a police escort and driven to a large concrete bunker and placed behind iron gates. This, it transpired, was their refuge and dressing room in preparation for the following night's show in Bremen. The Davies brothers complained about the various security breaches, but to no avail. Newspapers predictably condemned long-haired, rabble-rousing English groups while making little comment about the poor organization that precipitated the riot. Still reeling from recent events, Davies was even more despondent on the way home and hinted that the group might break up.

Far from curtailing foreign trips, the German visit was merely the prelude to a continental incursion, taking in Sweden, Finland, Denmark, Iceland, Germany, Switzerland and France. There was a further riot in Gothenburg, an overturned car in Stockholm, fighting between police and fans in Gelsenkirchen, smashed windows in Basel, and flying furniture in Kiel, the impact of which was serious enough to hospitalize Sam Curtis. The violent ritual had become so familiar that it was almost routine. Treadmill touring, home and abroad, could be debilitating, but the energy of youth conquered exhaustion. Were the Kinks overworked? "Cobblers," cries Curtis. "There were lots of groups that worked much harder than they did." Ray Davies made no public complaints about the itinerary, reserving his wrath for management, business matters, pressured studio schedules and the tastes of the record-buying public. The relatively short breaks abroad may even have provided a happy distraction from the legal disputes which were by now gathering pace.

On 2 September, Kassner and Page's Denmark Productions received a letter from solicitor Michael Simkins on behalf of the three senior Kinks stating that their original agreement with Collins and Wace's Boscobel Productions was unenforceable due to their then 'infancy'. Simkins added that Collins/Wace had committed a fundamental breach of their contract by engaging Kassner/Page on 26 February 1964 without the Kinks' consent. The letter went on to claim that the group had been unaware that Boscobel had assigned management and publishing rights to Denmark Productions, even though these provisions had now been in operation for more than 18 months. As a result, the Kinks had now drawn up new agreements with Boscobel, stipulating that managerial duties be conducted exclusively by Collins and Wace.

Kassner and Page immediately instructed their own solicitors to threaten legal reprisals if the terms of Simkins' letter were executed. On 14 September, Collins and Wace dutifully responded:

> We received your letter of September 8 and we would like to point out that there is no quarrel between our company and your clients, Denmark Productions Ltd, and as far as we are concerned there has been no breach by us of the above agreement. We have had a letter from Mr Michael Simkins, solicitor, representing the Kinks, stating that our agreement with them is determined, which, in view of the facts that the Kinks have offered to renegotiate a contract with us on much the same lines as the last, with a special clause saying that we must not farm off any of the management responsibilities, we have decided to accept that fact.

Although couched in very friendly terms, this correspondence clearly gave notice that Collins and Wace no longer considered themselves bound by their agreement with Denmark Productions. The gauntlet had been thrown down but the cost of disentangling the Kinks from Kassner and Page would prove greater than anyone could have imagined.

While the letters exchanged hands, the Kinks were busy promoting their latest EP, *Kwyet Kinks*. Its lead track, 'Wait Till The Summer Comes Along', was a folky, countrified tune, sung and written by Dave Davies, but erroneously credited to his brother. Its placing on the EP was odd since it was clear to everybody, apart from perhaps Pye Records, that the most scintillating song was on side two. 'A Well Respected Man', a brilliant send-up of the British middle classes, was like nothing else Ray Davies had composed up until this point. Its satiric thrust introduced a new strain to his songwriting that would continue on songs such as 'Dedicated Follower Of Fashion', 'Sunny Afternoon', 'Mister Pleasant', 'Shangri-la' and the various concept albums. The source material for 'A Well Respected Man' came partly from an incident that occurred at the Imperial Hotel in Torquay, where Ray and Rasa had stayed after the American tour. Davies detected old world snobbery and condescension among the guests and was inflamed when someone invited him to play a round of golf. "I said, 'I'm not going to play fucking golf with you. I'm not going to be your caddie so you can say you played with a pop singer.'" Davies spoke as if he had stumbled into a class war but 'A Well Respected Man' showed no such anger. Its tone was sardonic rather than bitter, poking fun at the hypocrisy of upper-middle-class manners. A secondary source for the composition was obviously Collins and Wace, whose world was not dissimilar to the subject of the song with its references to attending regattas and dealing in stocks and shares. Several Kinks insiders, including Shel Talmy, insist that the 'well respected man' was Robert Wace, whom the group would later nickname 'Bob the snob', much to his annoyance.

Dave Davies goes even further, arguing, "Robert was a big influence on Ray's writing because he was a big fan of Noël Coward and always fancied himself as a bit of a Noël Coward figure." In a television interview of the time, Ray acknowledged, "I can write a song about my manager" while a photo of Wace appeared on the screen. Of course, the song transcended any biographical origins, real or imagined, to emerge as one of the most piercing and hilarious pop satires of the era. Looking back, Davies rightly proclaims his subject "a composite character", adding, "I always create characters in songs and stories. I see hundreds of different people, and I create a single person out of their different characteristics. There was no *one* person I had in mind."

One of the biggest mistakes in the Kinks' career was Pye Records' decision to demote 'A Well Respected Man' to an EP rather than issue the song as a single. The label may have felt that it was too quirky or out of character with the group's previous work, although 'See My Friend' and even 'Tired Of Waiting For You' certainly departed from the familiar beat formula. There is little doubt that 'A Well Respected Man' would have challenged for number 1 in its own right. Disc jockeys loved the song which was played frequently at the time, ensuring substantial sales for *Kwyet Kinks*. The remainder of the EP was surprisingly impressive, easily surpassing many of the lesser tracks on their contemporaneous LPs. 'Such A Shame', a song of guilt and regret, lamenting "all the good times", is almost folk rock in its execution, while 'Don't You Fret' features Ray in his distinctive London voice, dreaming of coming home to his beloved for affection, favourite food and the obligatory pot of tea.

There was no EP outlet in America, so Reprise Records elected to release 'A Well Respected Man' as a single. It soon gained minor notoriety for the lyrical reference to liking 'fags', a word most Americans wrongly assumed meant homosexuals rather than cigarettes or public school underlings. Issuing such a determinedly British song may have seemed courageous on the part of Reprise, but it was a calculated gamble. That same year Herman's Hermits had enjoyed massive number 1 hits with two English music hall chestnuts, 'Mrs Brown You've Got A Lovely Daughter' and 'I'm Henry VIII, I Am', neither of which was issued in the UK singles market. Although 'A Well Respected Man' was a contemporary satire, there was an element of music hall whimsy in its lyrical and musical structure which appealed to an American public besotted with the concept of Swinging London. Although the Kinks were in no position to promote the record due to their US 'ban', it went on to climb to number 13 in *Billboard*, an impressive statistic in the circumstances.

Even after *Kwyet Kinks*, Davies was obliged to write a new single and, once again, complete a new album within the space of a week. Improbably, he complained of writer's block when all he needed was more time to put song to paper. Robert Wace arranged a visit from Mort Shuman, the famed American songwriter who, in collaboration with Doc Pomus, had composed some of the more enduring hits of the early Sixties, including the Drifters' 'Save The Last Dance For Me' and a series of Elvis Presley familiars, 'A Mess Of Blues', 'Little Sister', '(Marie's The Name) His Latest Flame', 'Kiss Me Quick' and 'Viva Las Vegas'. Shuman spent an evening with Davies during which he offered the standard songwriter's advice to write what you know. Privately, he wondered about Davies' living arrangements, voicing a variant of Cyril Connolly's memorable aphorism: "There is no more sombre enemy of good art than the pram in the hall."

Davies promptly composed and completed the new single, 'Till The End Of The Day', with the same self-conscious intent with which he had approached 'Set Me Free'. Arguing that 'See My Friend' had put the group "on a journey that went nowhere" he decided "it was time to get back to our rock roots". Given his revulsion for 'Set Me Free', it was odd that he should have compromised the group's sense of adventure by reverting to the old sound once again. However, he never voiced any misgivings about 'Till The End Of The Day', then or since, partly no doubt because it was a striking single with a strong riff in the tradition of 'You Really Got Me' and 'All Day And All Of The Night'. Judged in the context of 1965 – a year of great change and innovation in popular music – the single sounded disconcertingly regressive. It gave the impression that the Kinks were still stuck in late 1964 and no longer had the stomach for experimental efforts like 'See My Friend'. Even Mick Avory was thrust back into the shadows, humiliatingly replaced by a substitute session drummer, Clem Cattini, who would also appear on the forthcoming album. The Kinks were now playing it safe, at least for the present.

Ray Davies must have known that any hint of complacency would be dangerous in this age of creative invention. As recently as the Hollywood Bowl appearance he had witnessed the Righteous Brothers and the Byrds, whose singles, in their very different ways, testified to an American renaissance in pop. Even Sonny & Cher, for all their ersatz hipdom, benefited from the production skills of Sonny Bono and Harold Baptiste's sumptuous arrangement of 'I Got You Babe'. The recent folk rock explosion had altered the pop landscape in America, while back home Davies' leading contemporaries reacted to the protest boom with dissenting anthems of their own. In the weeks before 'Till The End Of The Day' entered the UK charts, the Top 10 offered the Animals' 'It's My Life', the Rolling Stones' 'Get Off Of My Cloud' and the Who's 'My Generation'. These were defiant cries of societal displacement and, in the case of the Stones and the Who, overt attacks on the conservatism of the establishment. Aloof, disgruntled, insolent and contemptuous, their lyrics championed the cult of youth in a mutinous glorification of the moment. In stark contrast, 'Till The End Of The Day' was a deceptively simple statement of the joys of commitment. In its almost manic evocation of personal fulfilment ("we do as we please") it displayed the familiar Davies neuroticism with power and passion, but in other respects it was a throwback to the birth of the Kinks. Momentarily, it made them sound slightly old-fashioned, still chained to the beat boom in a time of Pop Art. Unlike Townshend, Davies was never a songwriter with an eye for the big statement. He could not reach out to his audience and proclaim them 'my generation'. Nor was he attuned to the idealism and revolutionary fervour of the time. "The Sixties was a lie, a total lie," he subsequently said. As many of his later songs demonstrated, Davies was as much a traditionalist as an innovator, ever willing to mine the distant past for lyrical or musical ideas. His attitude was encapsulated on the B-side of their latest single: 'Where Have All The Good Times Gone'. Even Sam Curtis, no great fan of the Davies brothers, was impressed by the self-questioning title, pointing out that it sounded like the work of an old head on young shoulders.

Davies' timing was apposite. At the moment the B-side appeared, dark clouds were gathering: the economy was in trouble; sanctions were imposed on Rhodesia by the British government; and the BBC had just screened Ken Loach's *Up The Junction*, a searing adaptation of Nell Dunn's novel of slum life in Battersea with explicit scenes of abortion and working-class strife. It was a world away from the popular image of Swinging London, as Davies realized. "Everyone I knew seemed to be having a good time. But as a realist, I knew that the good times had to have a payback." Prime Minister Harold Wilson would no doubt have concurred. In November, he decreed: "the world has taken a step backwards."

'Where Have All The Good Times Gone' asks the question "will this depression last for long?" in startling contrast to the manic enthusiasm of 'Till The End Of The Day'. Both songs are extreme statements, but Davies does not present a simple dichotomy between optimism and pessimism or idealism and realism. The flip side is more than a critique of contemporary escapism for it indulges its own fantasies. "Let it be like yesterday," Davies sings, retreating into nostalgia. The composition captures the pressures he faced at this tumultuous time. Songwriting demands were now threatening to drain his pen dry. Lines like "get your feet back on the ground" and "worry bout a thing" echoed song titles on *Kinda Kinks* like a recycled wash. More pertinently, "yesterday was such an easy game for you to play" was not merely indebted to Paul McCartney's 'Yesterday' but repeated part of its lyric, almost verbatim.

In an attempt to break free from Kassner Music, Davies decided to sign with a new publisher, Belinda Music, a British subsidiary of Hill & Range, publishers of the Elvis Presley music catalogue. Belinda was run by the dapper Freddy Bienstock, a Viennese Jew who, like Eddie Kassner, had fled to America and found his niche in music publishing, assisted by his cousins, Jean and Julian Aberbach. Bienstock was preparing to buy Belinda, which was subsequently renamed Carlin, in honour of his daughter, Caroline. Like Kassner, Bienstock recognized the commercial potential of Davies' songwriting and used his considerable charm to secure the composer's signature on a five-year contract. Kassner was furious and reacted swiftly and devastatingly. Writs were served on Davies, Boscobel Productions, Pye Records and Belinda Music claiming damages for breach of contract and conspiracy. In a tactical powerplay, Kassner also announced that he was seeking an injunction to prevent the release of 'Till The End Of The Day', claiming publishing rights to the single and its B-side.

Although Pye Records went ahead and released the disc, it did not have an easy passage. The BBC was sufficiently intimidated by the dispute to prevent the broadcast of a live performance of the song on the Light Programme's high-rating *Joe Loss Pop Show*. Television exposure was also threatened when *Ready, Steady, Go!* cancelled a Kinks appearance and *Thank Your Lucky Stars* declined to promote the single until the issue was resolved. The drama lasted another couple of weeks, by which time a judge had ruled that the publishing monies should be placed in escrow pending the outcome of a High Court action that was still a long way off.

This probably explains the erratic chart progress of 'Till The End Of The Day', which went up and down, before finally climbing to number 8 in the New Year, a full two months after its original entry. The chart placing disguised its overall sales which were impressively high and worthy of a better showing had they been concentrated in a shorter time frame.

At the end of November, the new album, *The Kinks Kontroversy*, was rushed out with the same unseemly haste suffered by its predecessors. Even the cover artwork betrayed a scandalous lack of care, contradicting the vinyl label credits with the singular title *The Kink Kontroversy*. It was the 'See My Friend(s)' confusion all over again. Although arguably an improvement on the previous two Kinks albums, it was no great progression. Tellingly, the best two tracks are both sides of the recent single. Dave Davies shines on the live favourite, 'Milk Cow Blues', an R&B staple composed by Sleepy John Estes, while his own composition 'I Am Free' also impresses. Ray's songwriting seems laboured in places, ranging from the derivative R&B of 'Gotta Get The First Plane Home' to the beat-styled 'When I See That Girl Of Mine', the fatalistic 'The World Keeps Going Round' and the formulaic 'What's In Store For Me'. A new recording of 'Ring The Bells' emerges as one of his most affecting and perplexing compositions. The lyrics are celebratory to an almost excessive degree and, in the hands of a different producer or performer, might have been embellished by the toll of wedding bells or the loud ringing heard at the end of the later 'Big Black Smoke'. Instead, Davies offers a largely acoustic backing and a vocal so dolorous that it undermines the lyrical content. It is akin to rendering a victory speech in the tone of an elegy. The result is a more complex emotional statement. Two other songs anticipate future musical excursions: the calypso-style 'I'm On An Island' would be more fully explored on 'Holiday In

Waikiki', while the honky-tonk 'It's Too Late' pre-empts the country feel of *Muswell Hillbillies*. The closing 'You Can't Win' sounds like a bridge between the old R&B sound and his more lyrically conscious social commentaries. Nicky Hopkins' piano is mixed alongside a freak-out guitar break, reputedly the work of Shel Talmy, set off by a battling vocal harmony between the brothers. The song underlines how effective the album might have been if more time had been allocated to the project.

The Kinks Kontroversy entered the charts at number 10 on 8 December, then promptly disappeared. That same week, the Beatles' *Rubber Soul* entered at number 1 and stayed there until the end of February. The statistics expressed a truth that Ray Davies could not ignore. What the Beatles had achieved on *Rubber Soul* was nothing less than a reinvention of the album format. Hereafter, no British group of any distinction could afford to treat an LP as a rushed afterthought. It was now an art form in itself, something that Davies had been slow in discovering or acknowledging. From here on, Davies' songwriting would be more carefully considered and tailored for *both* the singles and albums market. Over a period of 13 months, the Kinks had released three albums but it would be another year before they issued another. It was time to slow down, reflect and consider.

A day after the release of *Kontroversy*, the Kinks returned to Cardiff for the first time since the cymbal incident with Avory. It brought back bad memories, which affected Davies' demeanour onstage. There was even a chilling moment when further violence might have occurred. One astute reviewer observed: "As they began their third number 'You Really Got Me', leader Ray Davies stormed off the stage after one of the microphones went dead. He wound down the curtain on the rest of the group who were still playing. He flung down his guitar and paced up and down in the wings as many of the dancers began booing and jeering. Then the group's road manager, Sam Curtis, wound back the curtain and pleaded with Davies to go on with the act as the other Kinks stood there bewildered. 'Not until whoever pulled out that mike lead puts it back' yelled Davies . . . the Kinks finally reappeared to a mixture of cheers and jeers to continue their act." Backstage, Davies thundered, "Every time we come to South Wales there is a fiasco."

A couple of weeks later, Davies made a surprise appearance on *Five O'Clock Club*, the children's television show, co-hosted by a puppet owl named Ollie Beak and his canine sidekick, Fred Barker. It was hardly the place for a serious interview, but Davies poured his heart out, railing against the iniquities of the music business and even threatening to retire. Asked about his career in showbiz, he responded: "I get sick of it sometimes. Like last week, I wanted to give it up completely. If it hadn't been for the other three I'd have packed it in . . . I dislike the pop business, but I enjoy playing. It annoys me intensely sometimes not to be able to do what I want to do . . . I'd like to stop playing for three months and just write songs."

Davies' disenchantment was understandable. That same day, the *NME*'s annual readers' poll was published and the results were disturbing to read. At the beginning of 1965, the Kinks had been touted as Britain's third biggest group, behind the Beatles and the Stones. All that promise had unravelled amid the personal and legal dramas of the succeeding months. In the 'British Group' category, they were rated 14th best in the country. The 'World Group' section was even more alarming as they were not even listed in the Top 20. Rivals, old and new, including the Animals, the Yardbirds, the Hollies, the Searchers and the Dave Clark Five, all made the final count, as did the Seekers, the Bachelors and even Peter, Paul & Mary, but the Kinks were nowhere to be seen. Ray had never been rated highly as a vocalist but an additional failure to appear in the Top 25 'Male Singers' section must have cut deep. Suddenly, in their classic mid-Sixties period, the Kinks were losing ground.

That same month, the Italian film director Michelangelo Antonioni arrived in the UK to commence preliminary work on *Blow-Up*, his tribute to Swinging London, starring David Hemmings. A principal setting for the shoot was photographer John Cowan's studio at 39 Princes Place in Notting Hill, where his girlfriend and muse Jill Kennington was filmed, along with the German model Veruschka. "The David Hemmings–and–Veruschka scene for *Blow-Up* was pure Cowan," says Kennington. "Antonioni must have seen him working – I never saw anyone else take pictures quite that way. The shooting on the floor downwards, completely fluid, unhindered by tripods, was typical

Cowan. Veruschka was the only person who could have done that scene like that." Kennington remembers the "excited whispers" among London's scenesters as Antonioni scouted the capital, turning up at restaurants, clubs and discotheques in search of visual inspiration. He even found his way to the Goldhawk Club in west London with a view to offering the guitar-smashing Who a part in the movie. This was a terrible slight to Ray Davies, who had worked with Cowan and Kennington on a film with the Kinks over a year before. The idea of using the Who never worked out and the role would later be handed over to another of Davies' rivals, the Yardbirds. Evidently, it had never even occurred to Antonioni to consider the Kinks, despite their penchant for onstage violence. Their standing among London's hip elite had clearly waned.

At least the festive season allowed fans to recall better times. On Christmas Day (with a repeat showing on 26 December), the BBC broadcast a *Top Of The Pops* special featuring the number 1 hits of 1965. It was a rare chance to see and hear 'Tired Of Waiting For You' on national television. The song had been number 1 only ten months before but suddenly that seemed an age ago.

As tradition dictated, the Kinks ended the year with an appearance on *Ready, Steady, Go!*. Ray had intended to write a satirical song about the show, but instead settled for a comic rendition of 'All I Want For Christmas Is My Two Front Teeth'. *New Musical Express*' Christmas edition also reassured Kinks followers about the future. "I've been halfway to giving up the Kinks on a number of occasions," Ray admitted. "Then I do a gig with the boys and we see all those kids have a raving time and are enjoying what we are doing so I change my mind, but one day I may get three-quarters to giving up and that will be the end for me." The words were ambiguous but sounded more positive than might have been expected. So concluded what would prove the most momentous and troubled year in the history of the Kinks.

CHAPTER SEVENTEEN

ENGLAND SWINGS

On 1 January 1966, American singer Roger Miller entered the UK charts with a topical tune: 'England Swings', a quaint, if slightly ludicrous snapshot of picture-postcard London where, alongside landmarks such as Westminster Abbey and the Tower of Big Ben, 'bobbies' (policemen) ride in regimented two by two on bicycles, flanked by children whose rosy red cheeks testify to the health of the nation. The anachronistic stereotypes conjured an American image of England timelocked around 1945. Cultural clichés have a resonance of their own and, despite laughing at Miller's well-meaning tourist brochure of London, its inhabitants appeared to rather enjoy living up to the image imposed on them from abroad. The only difference was that, instead of bobbies and rosy-cheeked children, the cast list consisted of pop groups, fashion designers, actors and photographers.

The year 1966 has frequently been regarded as the high water mark of the Swinging Sixties and with good reason. It was the year England won the World Cup, when London model Twiggy was acclaimed as the Face of '66, when the boutique boom reached new heights and the Union Jack became fashion's favourite flag on items such as bags, T-shirts and even knickers. Shifting moral values were evident in many of the London-centric films of the time: *Blow-Up, Modesty Blaise, Georgy Girl, Alfie, The Knack ... And How To Get It* and *Morgan: A Suitable Case For Treatment*. It was also a year of endings with the final episode of *Ready, Steady, Go!*, the gradual capitulation of pirate radio in the face of official disapprobation, the eclipse of the 45 rpm single in favour of increasing album sales and a last hurrah for old-fashioned beat groups, who either adapted to changing musical trends or fell from chart favour into obscurity.

For many cultural historians, the key date was 15 April when no less an authority than America's *Time* magazine officially declared 'London – The Swinging City'. Overflowing with intoxicating prose, their feature writer described a heady metropolis "alive with birds and Beatles, buzzing with minicars and telly stars, pulsing with half a dozen separate veins of entertainment". These sentiments were reiterated in other glossy magazines such as *Life*, whose caption writer spoke excitedly of the 'Spread Of The Swinging Revolution', and *Esquire* which rather presumptuously called London "the only truly modern city". The news spread abroad to France's *L'Express* which reiterated the belief that the UK was the place where "the wind of today blows most strongly". These words must have gladdened the countenance of Prime Minister Harold Wilson, the self-proclaimed architect of the country's white hot technological revolution who, only a month before, had led the Labour Party to re-election with a considerable majority.

In another sense, the Swinging Sixties was merely a marketing myth, a media creation and a distracting chimera, no less real than the scenic panorama presented in Roger Miller's 'England Swings'. Strictly speaking, it was not even *new*. Precisely one year before, John Crosby had 'invented' the same phenomenon in his celebrated piece for the *Weekend Telegraph* supplement, prompting other publications throughout Europe to proclaim the same.

The sense of déjà vu should have been noticeable but, if so, it was ignored by commentators and public alike. Evidently, the *idea* of the Swinging Sixties was such a welcome one that it was worth restating, even after less than a year. London was now entering the age of the repeat, recycling and feeding upon its own mythology.

Ray Davies responded to the times with his usual ambivalence. He was a part of Swinging London's extended cast list yet resolutely detached from its centre. He would produce two of the catchiest and most memorable anthems of 'Swinging' 1966 before releasing a third single that year, reminding the revellers that it was not all cakes and ale. His first broadcast to the nation was 'Dedicated Follower Of Fashion', a satiric thrust at Carnaby Street couture. Like 'A Well Respected Man', it was originally conceived as an EP track but, this time around, Pye realized its commercial potential as a single. The song was a triumph of camp comedy that brought a new dimension to the Kinks' image.

Despite its lightness of touch, the composition was born of violence in the Davies household. Although he never considered himself "a very sociable person", Ray felt obliged to throw the odd soirée at his house largely, one suspects, for Rasa's benefit. "The song came about after I'd had a violent punch-up at a party. All these awful Sixties trendsetters would come around and wear the latest fashions and I would have on a pullover . . . Anyway, it was an appalling party and these people were making snide remarks about me."

The main offender was a fashion designer who made the fatal mistake of suggesting that Davies was wearing flared trousers. "I had a slight flare, not amazingly so," Ray protests. Somehow, this innocuous exchange ended in bloodshed, with both parties rolling on the floor like schoolkids in a playground. "We had a punch-up and his girlfriend beat me up as well with her handbag – or was it his handbag? Anyway, I threw them out of my semi . . . And I got angry and started writing this song." Pounding on his manual typewriter, Davies completed the lyric in a single draft but what emerged displayed none of the rage that had inspired the composition. At worst, it was gently mocking, pinpricking the narcissistic foppery of the boutique fashion follower. There was a strong element of music hall humour in the recording that some likened to George Formby. When questioned, Ray was quick to point out that Formby had made a lot of money, which seemed justification enough for the song.

Not everyone was happy with the recording. Dave Davies considered it rather lightweight and novel for his tastes, while Pete Quaife lamented the hours spent in the studio perfecting the opening guitar strum which, in Ray's head, was meant to sound like a ukulele. Unfortunately, he failed to communicate his ideas to the others, resulting in countless takes and wasted studio time. Quaife felt exasperated. "He's always been a control freak. It has to be done his way or no way. We did that so many times, changing guitars, trying it on piano. When he realized he couldn't get the sound he wanted, he took the tape, rolled it across the floor and set fire to it. That's the kind of rage Ray could get himself into. And, of course, that fury affected everybody."

Davies felt haunted by the song after it climbed into the Top 5 and became an instant national anthem. Its pantomime qualities appealed to all ages but its composer was disconcerted when passers-by walked up to him in the street and shouted, "Oh yes he is!", as if expecting the riposte, "Oh no he isn't". At least Mick Avory made some belated capital from the disc. He subsequently metamorphosed into the 'dedicated follower' of Davies' imagination when he was hired as a male model at John Stephen's boutique in Carnaby Street and photographed in striped jackets alongside model Debbie Delacey for a spread in *Vanity Fair* and the soft porn magazine *Men Only*.

The Kinks' renewed high profile should have invigorated Ray Davies, but he seemed trapped in a downward spiral. Since the beginning of the year, the group had avoided arduous package tours in favour of sporadic excursions that allowed their temperamental leader more time to compose and record. Evidently, this was not enough. The fallouts from the publishing and management disputes of 1965 were ongoing and Davies still found it difficult to juggle domestic and career commitments. When he failed to come home after a late-night business meeting, a maudlin Rasa confided in her diary: "My love just does not exist. I am fed up, miserable and hurt. I haven't a home neither has Ray . . . he hasn't any time for home life or love."

At the beginning of March, a lightning one-week tour of Switzerland and Austria was undertaken. It began inauspiciously with a riot in St Gallen and ended in crisis when Ray was diagnosed with influenza, compounded by physical and nervous exhaustion. After returning to London, he retired to bed, leaving his harried managers and publicist to produce a press release apologizing for cancelled concert dates and television appearances. A forthcoming tour of Belgium was considered too costly to postpone. Since it was abroad, and therefore unscrutinized by the pop press, the management suggested the radical, if slightly preposterous, idea of hiring a substitute in the form of Mick Grace of the Cockneys. It was agreed that Dave should sing lead, with Grace filling in on rhythm guitar and making up the numbers onstage. There were no objections from Ray, who was clearly in no condition to rationalize the matter, let alone offer advice. Dave, still uncertain about the Mick Grace idea, sought his approval, but the meeting proved pointless. "Ray went bananas. Crazy. You couldn't talk to him. We were committed to do this tour so I took it on my own shoulders to do it. I would sing *all* the songs."

By now, Ray's problems at work and at home had reached crisis point. "We weren't getting on," Rasa admits. "He was being very difficult. I think he was ill. He was quite threatening and I said to him that I was going to call the police or I was going to leave him. I said something like: 'You need to see a psychiatrist, you'll have to go somewhere and get sorted, I'm going to call your doctor because you're behaving crazy. I've had enough, I'm going to leave you. I can't stand it.' Boom! We had a big black phone. He picked it up and hit me in the face, so I had a black eye. Then I *had* to call our doctor." Ray had never been physically abusive towards Rasa – either before or after this incident – but this time he had snapped. "A psychiatrist came and assessed him. Mrs Davies was against this, but I said that he should maybe go somewhere for treatment because he was behaving very bizarrely. Of course, he didn't go anywhere. That was a bad time."

According to Ray, there was a family intervention and a further contretemps with his sister Gwen, though Rasa has no memory of the latter. "Maybe I was downstairs when it happened. I don't know what that was about. I know that Mrs Davies wasn't happy for him to have psychiatric input. As well as being a loving family, they were also exceptionally volatile. They didn't always agree with Ray or me, and they were very interfering. Having said that, Mrs Davies was also helpful. But we lived too close to them. It was too incestuous, too close. They were quite powerful and controlling in their way. I just felt out on a limb because there was just me and all of the Davies's. If things were happening that they weren't happy with, it would make me feel bad and then there would be a problem. Ray was so difficult to live with anyway that I had to be very careful about what I said or did because it would always be *my* fault. So it was a difficult situation."

Looking back, Ray recognized his collapse as a culmination of the creative, recording, personal and business pressures that had almost ended the Kinks' career during 1965. "My art was the world that was also destroying me. Legal cases and publishing disputes. I don't think it was a nervous breakdown. I was extremely tired. I'm mentally too strong to have a nervous breakdown. I can pull myself through it. But when you're so exhausted the pressures get to you and you say, 'Oh, let me go to sleep.' Also, the crisis I had was a cultural crisis. I felt betrayed by the industry I was in. People expected me to be a performing animal at the circus, like one of those dancing bears – that's what I felt like. And I didn't want to be 'me' any more . . . I should have taken a holiday, I think." Further analysing his condition, he says: "I'm not a weak person. I don't crumble that easily. In fact if I have conflict with the outside world it makes me stronger, I just crumble later. I think everybody crumbles sooner or later. You're not human if you don't . . . You have to be vulnerable to write. But I'm also very strong. Very strong will."

While Davies convalesced, his fellow Kinks commenced their European tour, almost incognito. Hopes of passing off Mick Grace as Ray Davies were jeopardized when they were asked to appear on a French television show. Mick Avory remembers an amusing squabble between Grenville Collins and the TV director during which the former stockbroker announced in his poshest voice: "I understand every bloody word you're saying but I won't speak your filthy language. De Gaulle won't speak English, why should I speak French?" A compromise was reached when they agreed to focus on Dave as vocalist, filming only Grace's hands on the guitar. One magazine was allowed a photo shoot of this unique line-up posing beside a globe as if they were plotting world domi- nation. Grace looks uneasy, his eyes studiously avoid the camera, like an impostor caught in the spotlight. In Belgium, the masquerade was exposed one evening during an otherwise unremarkable set. Dave, pilled up to the eyeballs and fortified by alcohol in order to get through the nine-day nightmare, was suddenly distracted by an anxious looking spectator beckoning him to the apron of the stage. As Dave knelt there, preparing for a guitar solo, the concerned onlooker leant forward and whispered a warning in his ear. Pointing towards the rhythm guitarist, he said: "Dave – *he's* not Ray!" It was like a scene from *Invasion Of The*

Bodysnatchers, with the Belgium cast in the role as exposer of rock's greatest conspiracy – the removal and replacement of Ray Davies. Dave was so amused by the notion of his brother being displaced by a doppelgänger, unknown to everyone including himself, that he would collapse into sporadic fits of laughter for the remainder of the evening.

By the time the Kinks returned to the UK they learned that Ray had suffered a relapse. He had been acting strangely for several days, sometimes railing against Rasa and visiting members of his family, then settling into a calmer state. When a previously taped performance of 'Dedicated Follower Of Fashion' was aired on *Top Of The Pops*, he became agitated and tried to place the television in his gas oven. Whether he intended to roast the contents, symbolically re-enacting the witch's role in *Hansel And Gretel*, is not known, but the psychology was revealing enough. "To say the least, I was acting irrationally," he says.

Worse followed on St Patrick's Day when Davies unexpectedly rose from his bed in a state of agitation. In a cartoon reprise of his entire life, he became the athlete of his youth, running six miles to Tin Pan Alley, where he confronted and attempted to punch his publicist Brian Sommerville. His next encounter, after he was chased from the premises, was with his great nemesis, Kassner Music. Larry Page, as phlegmatic as ever, reacted to Davies' alarming appearance with a jaundiced shrug. "There was nothing unusual about that. It was like having afternoon tea with Ray. I can remember the incident with Brian Sommerville because his office was next door to us. I can remember the chaos." When Page informed road manager Sam Curtis of Ray's 'breakdown', he offered the withering response: "For all I know he was in a constant state of nervous breakdown. How would anyone know the difference?"

It was the best part of a week before Davies could piece together what had actually happened. "I was a zombie. I'd been on the go all the time from when we first made it till then, and I was completely out of my mind. I went to sleep and I woke up a week later with a beard. I don't know what happened to me. I'd run into the West End with my money stuffed in my socks, I'd tried to punch my press agent, I was chased down Denmark Street by the police, hustled into a taxi by a psychiatrist and driven off somewhere. And I didn't know. I woke up and I said, 'What's happening? When do we leave for Belgium?' And they said, 'Ray it's all right. You had a collapse. Don't worry. You'll get better.'"

Davies' physician prescribed plenty of rest, supplemented by a salad diet and the suggestion, never taken up, that he should join a golf club. Even Ray's turntable choices seemed tailored towards a mellower, less frantic sound. Frank Sinatra, Johann Sebastian Bach and Glenn Miller were among the eclectic list of names mentioned. Bob Dylan's *Bringing It All Back Home* and 'Maggie's Farm' were the only concessions towards modernity. "I couldn't listen to anything to do with rock 'n' roll, it made me go funny," he says. A spell listening to classical guitar music also helped. "It sort of cleaned my mind out and started fresh ideas."

Although concerts were cancelled and other professional commitments restricted, Davies roused himself sufficiently to conduct a handful of interviews, either from his sick bed or in a private area of the Soho club the Capricorn. The results were delightfully entertaining and eccentric, offering revealing glimpses into his troubled psyche. "I walked across the street on my first day out in a week and someone honked his horn at me from his car. I said, 'Sorry'. I thought about it later and realized that most people would have sworn at him but I wasn't acclimatized to modern living . . . I think I give people the impression that I'm a tough nut. I heard the other day the reason my music publishers hadn't phoned me was because they were too scared."

Davies later said that his fractured state in the spring of 1966 reminded him of the central character in the film *Morgan: A Suitable Case For Treatment*, based on David Mercer's television play. Morgan, overwhelmed by his own fantasies, perceives himself as an 'Apeman' and dresses up as 'King Kong'. Davies would later use a gorilla suit for a promotional film and write songs using both those titles. More pertinently, like Morgan, who retreats into an inner world of fantasy in preference to engaging with the concrete concerns of everyday life, Davies sought salvation in his own eccentricity. In the past, this type of behaviour would have been kept behind closed doors and hidden from the press, but the new psychiatry popularized by innovators such as R. D. Laing was reversing many of those old stigmas. Laing had already produced case histories suggesting that "communication within the family could become so disrupted that an individual member might seek refuge in madness". If Davies' 'breakdown' was in any way an escape from 'reality' then it was arguably a necessary one. As Laing noted provocatively: "There is little conjunction of truth and social 'reality'. Around us are pseudo-events, to which we adjust with a false consciousness adapted to see these events as true and real, and even as beautiful. In the society of men the truth resides now less in what things are than in what they are not. Our social realities are so ugly if seen in the light of exiled truth, and beauty is almost no longer possible if it is not a lie. What is to be done? . . ." Faced with 'pseudo-events', Ray Davies saw no reason not to play them out in the full glare of the industry media.

One journalist, Bob Farmer, was allowed into Davies' lair and provided a curious report on "that dark and sinister Kink whose long hair, lean face, and limp moustache makes him look like Rasputin and Attila The Hun rolled into one, but who is really of rather mild nature . . ." Davies' self-diagnosis was suitably direct. "I really need to have my days organized for me, otherwise I'm going to go out of my mind." His routine began the second he awoke, seemingly in a slightly nervous state. "If I lie down and relax for five minutes everything will be all right." A full hour could be spent dressing, washing and shaving, after which he would practise some distracting techniques. "I'd Hoover the whole house and go for long walks – anything to take my mind away from the songs." Asked for an additional interview, he suggested the China Garden in Soho's Brewer Street: "I've always liked Chinese food." Visiting the West End allowed him to see one or two of the latest films, including *Modesty Blaise* and *Alfie*.

There was something reassuring about Soho. It was evident in the self-reflective movies he watched and visible in the Carnaby Street boutiques which seemed to be inhabited by clones of the character he had created in 'Dedicated Follower Of Fashion'. There were even echoes of 'See My Friend' in the sitar sounds emanating from shop doorways. It was as if his creations and song lyrics had taken on a new, independent life. Even the music press fused two of his lyrical interests in an intriguing feature headline: 'Carnaby Street Goes Indian!'

Stanley Adams, whose boutique Adam West One was situated on the corner of Kingly Street, trumpeted the arrival of a new fashion based on "the Indian look" inspired by "all these recent records". A shipment of fawn and black jackets retailing at £10 were already on their way. "We'll call it the sitar jacket!" Adams declared in all seriousness. This was the surreal cityscape that Davies encountered on his sporadic constitutionals. Later, in the evening, he would take another long walk, consider some ideas, return home, drink some coffee, place his thoughts on paper and indulge himself with some peanut butter and banana sandwiches. Never an easy sleeper, he would retire to bed at 2 a.m., evidently satisfied, if a little confused.

Davies' neuroticism was also captured in a series of oddball revelations. "I worry about everything," he told *Disc.* "One night I went around to Barry Fantoni's flat and then remembered that I'd left the tap dripping at home. It was on my mind all the time – in the end Barry had to run me back to Muswell Hill so I could turn it off. If it's cold I put an electric fire near my pipes to stop them freezing. I get worried about those pipes. I slept next to them once." Clearly, nobody dared point out that the best way of avoiding freezing pipes was to heat the house gradually and regularly. That, of course, would have meant incurring a larger utility bill, an unwelcome prospect for the frugal Kink. "I keep thinking of getting insured but I haven't done anything about it yet," he added, when confronted with various premiums.

A steady but select stream of visitors were allowed into Ray's house during this troubled time. His chief supporter was the aforementioned Barry Fantoni, who was then hosting the pop/arts television programme *A Whole Scene Going* and had recently recorded a specially commissioned Ray Davies composition, 'Little Man In A Little Box', as a one-off single for Fontana. At a time when Davies was thinking of abandoning the Kinks and retreating from pop music, Fantoni's support was flattering. "When you look at Ray Davies' history, his interest in British musicals, he's extremely well-read, highly intelligent and not at all conceited. He's introverted but he's not conceited – always prepared to listen, always prepared to take the best and use it. What you have in Ray Davies is a songwriter of the excellence of Noël Coward or Ivor Novello. Just look at the lyrics and listen to the music."

Such commendation would have been less convincing if Fantoni was normally prodigal with his compliments, but this was not the case. Irreverent, iconoclastic and the possessor of a cynical sense of humour, typical of *Private Eye*, he was not merely waspish, but caustic. In common with Davies, he was instinctively suspicious of the Swinging Sixties scene and regarded its major players with an aesthetic disdain which corroded into contempt down the decades. "I just thought the Rolling Stones [were] stupid and foolish and sounded like it. The Beatles up to *Sgt Pepper* – none of them had seemingly done anything that would have offended anybody's granny and the songs . . . almost all of them owed something to somebody else . . . I can't get over some of the laziness in the Beatles . . . Pete Townshend was a very close friend. We met through *A Whole Scene Going* – he was the first interview we did . . . Pete can't write pop songs. He's got no talent for writing pop songs and his music's just drivel. It's just that he wore T-shirts with Union Jacks on them and that looked like and felt like it was something important . . . I couldn't see the point of the Who – couldn't see the point of the Stones either. The words and lyrics were just rubbish. If Chuck Berry had been born white in Dagenham that's what he would have sounded like."

For a songwriter as competitive as Davies, such opinions, no matter how philistine, prejudiced or unconvincing, were guaranteed to bring a smile back to his face. "If you flatter Ray, you'll be his friend for life," Rasa jokes.

By late April, Davies resumed promotional and touring activities, albeit tentatively. Evidence of his 'breakdown' was visible in a short-lived new look – a Zapata moustache that pre-empted the fashions of a year later. His re-emergence coincided with news that Mick Avory had been felled by tonsillitis and could not perform at a date in Nottingham. Ominously, he was replaced by Clem Cattini, the talented drummer who had played on most of *The Kinks Kontroversy*. If Avory's position was ever under threat, he was unaware of any machinations, but he seemed clearly distant from the central action. "I didn't really understand what a nervous breakdown was then. Did we talk about it? Not really. The managers would gather around, see how Ray was and get medical reports and then just take it from there."

A concerted attempt was made to improve travelling facilities with the appointment of Alex King, an experienced road manager who, like Sam Curtis, had worked with the Shadows years before.

King's wife, Shandy, agreed to run the Kinks' fan club, which also helped the organization. Against his better judgement, 'Jonah' Jones returned to the fold as Alex's assistant, even though he still had commitments at the newsagent's in Denmark Terrace. Before long, he moved into Alex and Shandy's house and, for a time, all went well.

Jonah was aware of Ray's much publicized health problems and the toll that stardom had taken on his personality. "He'd changed dramatically. I think he suffered with all the pressure, but he put it on himself. He didn't want to share it with the other guys in the band. Ray wanted to have control over everything. He was a control freak – and when he got control that's when he started to go crazy. Dave could be whizzed out of his brain, play guitar and still function. Ray couldn't do that. He couldn't find an escape; he couldn't go to clubs, hang out and socialize with people like Dave could. So there was a lot of animosity there. I chaperoned Dave to places like the Scotch of St James (when he was under age) because I felt he deserved to be there. We drank with John Lennon and Brian Jones – and Dave wanted to be with these people. Ray was so insecure about who he was. He didn't know who he was for a long time. I think he pushed a lot on to Rasa. Maybe he should never have got married. Ray had problems – he's always had them. But you have to love Ray for who he is."

Davies described his condition at this time as an "inner revolt" against the music industry itself. Freed from endless touring, he would often sit in a room in total darkness while ideas and semi-formed songs floated into his consciousness. Soon, they came in a torrent. Only six months before, he had felt drained of inspiration. Now, every passing observation, no matter how superficial or unlikely, provided inspiration for possible subject matter.

"I was learning how to write songs and enjoying the process. I never really listened to what anybody else wanted me to do. Probably some of the people around the band would have been encouraging me to keep to the original Kinks style . . . But I have never understood what this *idea* of the Kinks' original style was, apart from being very raw and energized, with minimal lyrics. I felt that I needed to develop."

This process might have happened earlier if Davies had not

been locked into the stamina-sapping routine of producing two to three albums per year. Now he had the time and energy to indulge his imagination. Even that insatiable taskmaster Louis Benjamin was no longer demanding the completion of an album within a week. The Rolling Stones had recently issued *Aftermath*, their most accomplished album to date. Like the Beatles' *Rubber Soul*, it was a firm indication that the conveyor-belt system of producing LPs to order had changed, irrevocably. *Aftermath* explored myriad lyrical themes, from triumphalist misogyny in 'Stupid Girl' and 'Under My Thumb', to time-travelling Tudor-style courtly love deference ('Lady Jane') and a satirical rejoinder directed against amphetamine addicted suburban housewives ('Mother's Little Helper'). On recent singles, '19th Nervous Breakdown' and 'Paint It, Black', Jagger had also used neuroticism and manic depression, tinged with a sprinkling of nihilism, to create a genuinely frightening lyrical landscape. It was almost as if he had reached into the darker areas of Davies' mind to show him a new way forward.

Ray's response was not to compose similarly bleak material, but create storylines based on imaginary characters, some snatched from aspects of his own personality. Throughout this period, journalists and fans were regaled with accounts of ongoing projects. There was much discussion of an EP based on people's professions or occupations, a musical revue whose contents were never coherently revealed and a seemingly endless list of songs: 'The Reporter (aka 'Mr Reporter'), 'Everybody Wants To Be A Personality', 'Party Line', 'Fallen Idol' and 'A Girl Who Goes To Discotheques'. A new album, tentatively scheduled for summer release, promised to be their most ambitious to date. An early plan was to link each track with sound effects. Thunderstorms, bongos, a metronome and a shepherd's pipe were some of the surprises suggested by Davies. In a mischievous moment, he even promised a lead vocal from Mick Avory on a new composition: 'Lilacs And Daffodils'.

What was most noticeable about Davies' latest plan was its parochial flavour. Taking his lead from 'A Well Respected Man' and 'Dedicated Follower Of Fashion', he was intent on displaying a distinctly English sensibility, far removed from the traditionally America-fixated rock market. "I hope England doesn't change," he said, fresh from his sick bed. "I'm writing a song now called 'You Ain't What You Used To Be' which expresses what I feel. I hope we don't get swallowed up by America and Europe. I'm really proud of being British . . . I don't care if a bloke votes Labour or Conservative as long as he appreciates what we've got here. We have so much that is great, compared with other countries, and people just don't realize it. I want to keep writing very English songs."

CHAPTER EIGHTEEN

SUNNY AFTERNOON

By late spring, Davies had completed the perfect English song – 'Sunny Afternoon' – a composition that he initially claimed completed a trilogy of satirical statements following 'A Well Respected Man' and 'Dedicated Follower Of Fashion'. In jocular mood, he said that its theme had first infiltrated his imagination following a financially painful meeting with his city accountant, Robert Ransom. According to the singer, the song was an exercise in therapy, a pleasing panorama in which he could contain all his secret fears about money, career and the future. It was also a testament to his indomitable and enduring competitive streak. Recently, he had been vacillating between leaving the Kinks and staying. "The first song I wrote out of that dip was 'Sunny Afternoon'." In an ingenious act of self-deception to spur creativity, he convinced himself of the need to conjure another number 1 hit. Only then, could he end the Kinks' career without disappointment or remorse. "If that had been my last record it was perfect . . . I could walk away and maybe get a proper job and be a regular person."

Producer Shel Talmy, a connoisseur of great pop singles, immediately recognized the potency of 'Sunny Afternoon' and was convinced that it could provide the Kinks with their first number 1 hit since 'Tired Of Waiting For You'. The recording session on 13 May was, says Davies, "one of our most atmospheric". Listening to the playback, he knew that they had completed something special. "I still like to keep tapes of the few minutes before the final take, things that happen before the session. Maybe it's superstitious, but I believe if I had done things differently – if I had walked around the studio or gone out – it wouldn't have turned out that way. The bass player [Pete Quaife] went off and started playing funny little classical things on the bass, more like a lead guitar, and Nicky Hopkins was playing 'Liza' – little things like that helped us get into the feeling of the song . . . I once made a drawing of my voice on 'Sunny Afternoon'. It was a leaf with a very thick outline – a big blob in the background – the leaf just cutting through it."

During the recording, Davies unveiled the composition like a conjuror reluctantly explaining a magic trick. "I played the intro on a mini-upright piano and went chromatic, playing down the lower register. Then I tried it on the acoustic guitar. It must have been frustrating for Nicky Hopkins, who played the piano on the record, because Shel Talmy made him watch me play it, and then copy my style." Hopkins never complained, but Quaife felt increasingly alienated by Davies' tyrannical tirades in the studio. Most of the bass parts were dictated from the piano and, more often than not, Quaife had no idea about the theme of the song and dared not make any creative suggestions. Davies was furtive and secretive, almost as if he suspected that his ideas might be plundered by studio spies. "That was the most annoying thing about playing with the Kinks," says Quaife.

The bass player remained subdued and tight-lipped in front of Davies, but some of his reservations and frustrations leaked out via the media. "What is happening?" he asked rhetorically. "Are we in the entertainment profession becoming a circle of senile old men and women gossiping about each other for the sake of it? . . . For God's sake, let us stop, and grow up. If not, let's get out and leave this business to the real professionals." In another aside, he revealed: "I have been offered a place at a college in California where they run a two-year course in scriptwriting. I can't go yet because of my work with the Kinks, but I shall go when that work is over."

While much of this sounded like the workings of a famously vigorous imagination, there was no doubt that Quaife was unhappy. Having experienced the conflicts between the brothers and suffered the role of middleman, he had retreated into stasis. "There was a lot of jealousy between Pete and Ray," Dave acknowledges. "While Ray and I had outward explosions of anger towards each other, Pete's jealousies were much more subtle and quieter. Pete was talented in his own right but he couldn't get a writing credit on a Kinks record, although he was obviously articulate and talented enough to do that. So there was considerable frustration."

The dynamic was further complicated by the presence of Ray's wife Rasa, who regularly attended sessions to add some beautiful high harmony to their most enduring songs. Dave always regarded her as a benign and ameliorating influence amid the macho posturing, a view with which Quaife at first concurred. Gradually, her attendance began to grate with Quaife, partly because it coincided with his own loss of power. Eventually, admiration turned into petty spite. "There was a lot of resentment there," he admits of himself. "The silly little bint from Bradford virtually running the damn studio. There was nothing you could say about it because if you said, 'Get her out of here', Ray would have taken a fit. The whole time was trying to keep the peace and that eventually entered into the music; you wanted to make a suggestion but you decided it would be best to keep your mouth shut because of the trouble it might make."

Quaife's jealousy and annoyance were not without foundation. Davies seldom listened to his suggestions, yet trusted his wife's commercial instincts. While writing on the piano at home, he could hear her humming one of his new tunes, always a good sign. Rasa could be relied upon to enthuse about a hit melody or suggest a possible B-side from the array of likely candidates sprouting from Ray's imagination. Stuck at home, she spent more time listening to current singles on pirate radio than any of the musicians ever did. With 'Sunny Afternoon', she provided her most significant contribution to date, not merely enhancing the high harmony, but providing the three words that closed the song. When Ray asked, "What do you think?", she gushed, "It's great, but why don't you add the words 'in the summertime'?" That small addition became an integral part of the chorus, much to everyone's satisfaction. Not that it was ever mentioned in the press or later interviews. "That was the only one where I wrote some words," Rasa admits. "Well, three words! To this day, my gripe is that he didn't ever give me credit for 'in the summertime'."

Oblivious to any underlying tensions, Davies petitioned for the immediate release of 'Sunny Afternoon'. He would later have good cause to berate his record company for its parsimonious percentages and short-sightedness in the new age of the album, but their singles policy proved appealing. "Pye Records was a great company for us at the time," he later admitted, with unexpected grace. "They broke us and I don't think anybody else could have done it because then it was a really young company and people were very go ahead and they'd take chances. I made 'Sunny Afternoon' at ten in the morning, finished cutting it at one o clock in the cutting room, took it up to the Managing Director [Louis Benjamin] played it to him and he said, 'What do you want?' I said, 'Get it out in two weeks . . .' I don't think I could have done that at any other company but Pye at the time."

Benjamin was almost as good as his word. The record was released on 3 June, missing Davies' deadline by a mere handful of days. Within a month, it would climb to number 1, displacing the Beatles' 'Paperback Writer', much to its composer's satisfaction. The single became forever associated with that memorable summer of 1966 when all things seemed possible and England was still in its dream stage.

'Sunny Afternoon' was a deceptively simple song whose jaunty tune and good-time chorus of drinking beer and lazing in the sun disguised the more serious concerns, expressed in the verses. More than any other chart composition of the time, it captured a national mood of delusional frivolity. Even in his weakened state, Davies knew that there was something ineffably alluring about 'Sunny Afternoon'. One reason he wanted to rush release the single was that it encapsulated not just the mood but the *temperature* of the times. On the day they completed the song at Pye's studio number 2 in central London, thermometers were registering an unseasonal high of over 80 degrees Fahrenheit. The city was experiencing that rarest of occurrences – an elongated heatwave. It continued for weeks, creating an almost Mediterranean climate. City gents loosened their ties and paraded the streets in shirtsleeves; parks were full of teenage girls and middle-aged women, sporting swimsuits and even bikinis, whose straps were lowered to the maximum level that decency allowed, much to the amazement of priapic schoolboys who had never witnessed such ample displays of cleavage and hidden flesh. Miniskirts were in the ascendant, as might be expected amid such heat. Boutiques continued to flourish, despite gloomy predictions of a recession. In Clifford Street, Mr Fish was selling shirts for six guineas and ties for two guineas, exorbitant prices which, for the moment, held firm.

London clubland, still the home of the pop and fashion elite, was opening its doors to an expanding clientele of affluent teenagers and young adults. The same month that 'Sunny Afternoon' was released, Sibyllas was unveiled at 9 Swallow Street and quickly became the hippest watering hole in town. It was not only frequented by pop stars but partly owned by George Harrison, as if confirming the spread of Beatlemania into high street business. Membership was seven guineas, meals (including wine) 30s. and miniatures a hefty 12/6d. With live groups and a 3 a.m. drinks licence, it provided the perfect end to a day in the sun. More sedate, but almost equally expensive, was Dolly's in Jermyn Street – five guineas' membership and a bottle of wine for 36s. Less affluent club habitués had the pick of the rest. The Ad Lib was perennially popular, along with the Cromwellian on Cromwell Road where, for three guineas' membership and an additional entrance fee of 7/6d, you could listen to records or live groups, sup beer at three shillings a glass, and even enjoy a steak garni for 12/6d. Lastly, for seasoned music watchers, there was Blaises in Queen's Gate, where famous visiting US groups played, and the entry fee was a bargain ten shillings with membership priced at only two guineas. At several of these clubs, and others like the Kilt on Greek Street, girls were allowed in cheaper, as chauvinism and tradition dictated.

The image of London as a centre of glamour was symbolized in the grand opening of the Playboy Club in Park Lane later that summer. Advertisements for bunny girls promised exotic opportunities and a lifestyle associated in the public imagination with James Bond movies. *Playboy* founder Hugh Hefner despatched one of his prized 'pets' to train the new recruits who were drilled in regimented fashion with a list of rules about the consequences of laddered tights, scruffy ears and tails, weight gain and incorrect posture. The organization considered itself an equal opportunities employer and even welcomed dark-skinned girls who were called 'chocolate bunnies', as if they were some tasty Easter treat.

Park Lane may have seemed a bit upmarket for the Kinks, but

several of their former deb associates from the early days visited the club and casino. 'Jonah' Jones' girlfriend even secured a prestigious spot as front-door receptionist, ensuring that the road manager was a regular attendee. Pete Quaife's younger brother Dave, who regarded Jonah as his laddish mentor, loved being driven around by the roadie in his flash Austin-Healey. He was even more entranced by his girlfriend, "a wonderful person" whose statuesque beauty proved invigorating. "I still remember her," David reminisces, "and she was *glorious*. She'd got that job at the bunny club just before it opened. She walked in with her new bunny costume and it altered my life completely."

Booming Britain had now reached its peak. Export sales were up, London night life was swinging faster than ever and the weather encouraged a mood of languorous contentment. Ominous signs of an economic caesura went largely unheeded. Newspapers fretted about the balance of payments but only those immersed in the media's business pages seemed remotely concerned. A freeze on wages and a squeeze on credit were about to be enacted by the government, but even these could not yet kill the party mood. It was as if a sizeable part of the population, and not just the bright young things, had bought in to America's image of 'Swinging London' and were living out that fantasy in an end-of-era display of collective narcissism. It took an outsider, ironically an American reporter then resident in London, to play the party pooper. Writing in the *New York Times*, Anthony Lewis warned of economic perdition, while marvelling at the complacency of a population, seduced by sun, cultural superiority and lazy disregard. "The atmosphere in London can be almost eerie in its quality of relentless frivolity. There can rarely have been a greater contrast between a country's objective situation and the mood of its people." A sudden reversal of fortune was only weeks away.

'Sunny Afternoon' encapsulated the summer mood in prescient fashion. On one level the song could be appreciated as a wry yet sympathetic comment on the plight of the fallen aristocrat who, taxed into oblivion by the Labour government, fantasizes about sailing away into tax exile, while contenting himself with the one luxury that cannot be taken away, a sunny afternoon in the summertime. The composition's darker aspects are pervasive, yet invisible to all but the most discerning listener. Those descending opening chords sound funereal, but rapidly break into a snappier rhythm that brightens the mood. There is a reference to the economic 'squeeze' and repeated pleas to "save me" and "help me", but even these add to the comedy. A sunny ambience is amplified by the presence of a 'big fat momma' whose pursuit of the narrator conjures images of a saucy seaside postcard rather than the symbolic government matriarch intended by Davies. Overall, the satire is less acerbic than the preceding 'A Well Respected Man' or 'Dedicated Follower Of Fashion', partly because Davies is singing in the first person, instead of pointing a finger at an imagined 'you'. Although the reference to a 'stately home' indicates the presence of landed gentry, the performance is so convincing that, for many, the singer and his narrator become one. "It was a bit like me at that time," Davies says of the narrative. With higher taxes in the 90 per cent region, nouveau riche pop stars were facing the same vicissitudes as lords of the realm.

Such nuances aside, the song's universal appeal lay in its wilful indifference. It was a perfect musical accompaniment to the extended heatwave and a national pick-me-up amid fears of economic meltdown. In many ways, 'Sunny Afternoon' echoed the sentiments of the Lovin' Spoonful's 'Daydream', a massive international hit earlier in the year that advocated escapism rather than political action. Even the Beatles had succumbed to the same resignation. While George Harrison was bemoaning their financial lot in 'Taxman', John Lennon, head in the clouds, hid away in his suburban eyrie and vegetated with apathetic affront. Exactly one week before the Kinks recorded 'Sunny Afternoon', the Beatles cut 'I'm Only Sleeping', the ultimate paean to indolence. Both songs revelled in the vacuous delight of doing nothing whatsoever.

For purchasers of 'Sunny Afternoon', there was an unexpected bonus in what was arguably the greatest B-side of the Kinks' entire career. 'I'm Not Like Everybody Else' was Ray Davies' great cry of independence against conformity. Originally, it was offered to the Animals with the intention that singer Eric Burdon would establish the song alongside the group's other hits of fiery protest: 'We've Got To Get Out Of This Place' and 'It's My Life'. Instead, it was left to Dave Davies to scream out the lyrics against a suitably dramatic guitar backing, leading to an intense crescendo.

Largely unheralded at the time, it remains a perfect summation of the lives and world view of both brothers.

'Sunny Afternoon' was part of Davies' self-therapy. "By then, I had a one-year-old daughter and I was trying to become normal as a human being. I wanted to write something that we could sing in the pub." The single's success radiated a fresh confidence which was evident in his interviews. That summer, he accepted an invitation from *Disc & Music Echo* to review the new Beatles album *Revolver*, knowing that he had earned the privilege after knocking 'Paperback Writer' from number 1. Far from being threatened by the groundbreaking work of the Fab Four, he sounded haughty and patronizing. He claimed that he had never listened to any Beatles album in its entirety, as if they were some obscure group barely worthy of his full attention. Nevertheless, he felt sufficiently qualified to point out that *Rubber Soul* was superior to *Revolver*. He was scornful about their forthcoming double A-side, dismissing 'Yellow Submarine' as "a load of rubbish" and suggesting that 'Eleanor Rigby' "sounds like they're out to please music teachers in primary schools". As for the rest of the album, now routinely paraded as among 'the greatest of all time' in numerous polls, he could hardly have been more withering. His comments – which caused no discernible backlash at the time – now appear refreshingly hilarious and iconoclastic in their lacerating disregard. What price 'Taxman' ("a cross between the Who and Batman"), 'And Your Bird Can Sing' ("too predictable"), 'I Want To Tell You' ("not up to the Beatles' standard"), 'Dr Robert' ("not my sort of thing") and, best of all, the epochal 'Tomorrow Never Knows' ("it'll be popular in discotheques"). "I don't want to be harsh," he added, throwing the Beatles a bone of consolation. "The balance and recording technique are as good as ever." While sparing some praise for 'Good Day Sunshine' and 'Here There And Everywhere', the only track he genuinely enthused about was, revealingly enough, 'I'm Only Sleeping', which recalled his week-long sleep at the peak of his spring collapse.

Within hours of the release of 'Sunny Afternoon', the Kinks faced another crisis as shocking in its implications as Ray's recent breakdown or the multiple dramas of spring 1965. Despite sterling attempts to stabilize the group, there were manifold fractures in the entire organization involving internecine disputes, under-lying tensions and hidden agendas. The conflict between the brothers had long since become an over-familiar pattern, doomed to endless repetition. 'Jonah' Jones, in common with Quaife and Avory, attempted to remain neutral when tempers flared, but his closeness to both brothers strained his loyalties. "I could never choose between them," he admits. "You couldn't do it or it would be all over." Nightclubbing with Dave understandably increased the bond between them. "Dave wore his heart on his sleeve. He was a total tearaway, and a lot of fun. I found it a shame that Dave was such an easy-going person that he let Ray walk all over him. But that's who Dave is."

Of course, it was not as simple as that, as Jones well under-stood. As open and giving as Dave was, he had an aggressive, confrontational side that could explode with little provocation. Avory and Quaife could testify to such violent episodes and Jones was not immune from similar outbursts. "He kicked me in the head a few times onstage when things went wrong," he recalls, as if such shocking behaviour was perfectly acceptable. "But that was on the spur of the moment. He came up later and apologized for it. Ray never apologized for anything. Dave knew when he'd stepped out of line and thought 'I shouldn't have done it.' I accepted that. When you're onstage there's a tremendous amount of energy projected from the band and the crowd. It's so moving and the adrenalin is flying and Dave thrived on that, so did Ray. Dave was speeding his brains out. That's what made him such a violent character. I think he used that as an escape from all the crap that he felt Ray was giving him. Dave used to go off in his own world and go crazy. Ray got his frustrations out by being the frontman. Ray kept too much inside. That was his downfall. He wouldn't express his feelings – he expressed them through his music."

When tensions were at their heaviest, Jones turned to Quaife for light relief. "Pete was a happy-go-lucky person, flamboyant, sociable and full of these amazing stories. He was seldom down. I liked him and he was good to have around. He was the weakest link (musically), but he was the statesman and the dandy of the band." By this point, of course, Quaife's contented veneer had been eroded by the toxic atmosphere. He too was under strain.

As was Ray Davies who had taken on so many responsibilities and still felt obliged to write constantly, while trying to keep the Kinks together.

By now, there were additional problems that extended to the road crew. Alex King was overwhelmed by marital difficulties and poured his heart out to 'Jonah' Jones, who was desperately trying to keep everyone sane, including himself. Jones' father had suffered a heart attack and Peter felt obliged to keep the newsagent business running smoothly. "I was working with the Kinks in the evening, coming back from a gig and opening the shop at six in the morning. I'd do a whole day, then go off and do another gig with the guys at night. It was unbelievable and I was really on the edge."

Jones was endangering his health and urgently required a break from the road; King also needed a sabbatical or a marriage counsellor; and Quaife should have been considering another career. Davies suspected that a conspiracy was afoot and vital information was being kept from him. "Ray was going absolutely crazy," Jones remembers. "He wanted to know what was going on. I was under so much pressure that I said to Ray that Alex had problems." Jonah even expressed fears that King might do something drastic to himself. If Jones was hoping for an expression of empathy, then Davies' response must have been devastating. "Ray said, 'That fucking bastard. If he wants to kill himself, I'll give him the gun.' I thought 'fucking hell!' That hurt so much because I knew if that's what Ray thought of Alex, then that's what he thought of me as well. For me, the real Ray reared his head. I knew how bad he could be. He'd fucked me up on many occasions . . . I tried to suppress it, but it really hurt me."

On the evening of 3 June, after a show at the Central Pier Marine Ballroom in Morecambe, Lancashire, the group journeyed back to London in separate vehicles. Eager to avoid stage door hangers-on, Quaife chose to accompany Jonah in the van. It was always easier on the nerves to travel long distances without having to contend with the Davies brothers, particularly when their adrenalin levels were still dangerously high following a performance. As their vehicle headed south, Quaife was chatting amicably to Jones, then dozed off. He was abruptly awoken by a sudden jolt, then a sharp pain, accompanied by the sound of smashing glass and a metallic ringing in his ear. The van had careered off the M6 motorway and crashed into a stationary lorry and tractor trailer. Reaching for the passenger door, Quaife was disorientated as it fell from his hand. Turning towards Jonah he was horrified to see that "most of the windscreen was hanging out of his mouth". According to Ray Davies: "Pete was so frightened he got out and ran across the road into the middle of the motorway with a broken ankle. And then his world caught up with him."

Peter 'Jonah' Jones' memories of that terrible evening are even more evocative and chilling in their detail. "I hadn't slept for about four days because of all the turmoil that was going on with Alex and Shandy, all the domestic side at home and all the problems with the band. So I drove back. Pete put a cushion down and within ten minutes he was asleep. I took off my seat belt because I was uncomfortable. I always used to wear my seat belt. The next thing I knew I'm waking up saying, 'Pete we've had an accident.' All of a sudden I could feel the blood on my teeth and the windscreen coming out of my mouth. Then, I was alone. Pete had gotten out of the vehicle. He'd banged his head and had concussion. He'd spun around and I think he broke his foot getting out while I was pinned inside. The engine that was in front of us was sitting beside me and the steering column had gone into my stomach and I was hanging out the front of the windscreen. I heard sirens. I could just move my right hand a little bit. The rest of me couldn't move at all. Then there was contact. A nurse crawled into the wreckage and was holding my hand and saying, 'Don't try to talk. Just squeeze my hand – once for "yes" and twice for "no".' She talked to me and kept me awake. They put an asbestos blanket over me as they cut me out with an oxyacetylene torch. I went through all sorts of pain as the adrenalin was starting to wear off then. Every time they moved a bit of metal, the pain was unbelievable. But that nurse kept talking and keeping me awake. I think if I'd closed my eyes, it would have been all over. My head was blown up, swollen as large as a football. All my face was smashed in, it was pretty horrific."

The casualties were rushed to Warrington Hospital. Quaife had a broken foot and cracked skull, while Jones suffered a fractured pelvis and head wounds. "He was in a terrible state," Quaife remembers. "I can still hear him screaming as they were pulling shards of glass from his tongue and mouth. We had serious injuries and needed time to recover. It made me think about my future." During his stay in hospital, Quaife was visited by his family, girlfriend Nicola and the other Kinks, albeit with one notable absentee. "Ray didn't come and I thought, 'You bastard.'"

Peter Jones has no recollection of either Davies brother visiting the hospital, nor of any messages of sympathy from the management. Indeed, it is difficult to avoid the conclusion that he was callously abandoned. He never worked with the Kinks again and does not recall seeing them after the accident. During his convalescence, he dreamed of a quieter life, possibly taking over the Denmark Terrace newsagent. A further shock awaited when he approached his father only to learn that he had given the business away to another local tradesman, George the Butcher.

The Kinks carried on, regardless. Television commitments were fulfilled, even though they were forced to lip-synch 'Sunny Afternoon' as a trio on both *Thank Your Lucky Stars* and *A Whole Scene Going*. Doctors estimated that the convalescing Pete Quaife would be unavailable for at least six weeks so a temporary replacement was required immediately.

CHAPTER NINETEEN

THE SEDUCTION

John Dalton was a reluctant Kink. A journeyman player, his main claim to fame, apart from attending the same school as Cliff Richard, was a stint in the Mark Four, a promising outfit that later evolved into the Creation. Dalton was endearingly down to earth with a convivial personality and ready wit. It was no coincidence that his closest associate in the Kinks would be the similarly even-tempered Mick Avory. Dalton had been working as a lorry driver, labouring on a building site, playing guitar occasionally and enjoying himself. He had no great ambitions. When Bill Fowler, a former road manager of the Mark Four, put his name forward as a putative Kink, Dalton was resigned about the outcome. His first meeting with Davies occurred at the Savile Row office of Belinda Music where Ray was conducting a guest review spot for one of the music papers. Evidently in imperious and dismissive mood, he was judging the week's new releases and firing offending discs from an open window when Dalton entered his sanctum. Davies seemed remarkably unconcerned about the audition, merely asking the puzzled candidate to "play a scale in D-Minor", which was enough to secure the job. Although he had only heard 'Sunny Afternoon' twice on the radio, Dalton was nonplussed to learn that he would be miming the song on *Top Of The Pops* that very evening. There was not even time to return home to change his clothes. Instead, he was reduced to borrowing a pair of trousers from substitute roadie Stan Whitley and squeezing into one of Quaife's stage jackets. "It was the first time

I'd stood in front of the cameras and I must have looked petrified," he says.

Days later, the group flew to Spain for a three-night stint at Madrid's Yulia Club. It did not go well. Dalton, a solid Fender Precision player, had inherited a Danelectro bass purchased for Quaife who had learned that the Who's John Entwistle played one on 'My Generation'. "It sounded like a honky-tonk piano on the bottom keys and I liked it." Dalton found it too flimsy to play, claiming that it had a twangy tone, like a banjo. In his hands, it seemed to drain the Kinks' live sound of any excitement. Taking advantage of their tepid performance, the promoter demanded a reduction in their fee, citing Quaife's absence as a breach of contract. Ray Davies stood firm, refusing to allow the group to reappear while insisting that the club owner had been informed of Pete's injury prior to their departure. The dispute intensified when police confiscated the Kinks' working permits and even threatened to arrest Dalton for impersonating Quaife. The new bass player was forced to wear sunglasses, a long coat and a different hairstyle while evading further attention from the authorities. Fearing that they might miss their next engagement in Oslo, Robert Wace despatched no-nonsense road manager Sam Curtis who, having survived the Kinks' Cardiff debacle, could be relied upon to pacify police officers and escort the group through Scandinavia.

Faced with a seemingly impossible deadline, Curtis plotted an extraordinary route taking them from Madrid to Paris, back to London Gatwick, then onward to Copenhagen where they were transferred to a private plane bound for Oslo. The plane blew a tyre along the way, but they arrived in time. "We eventually got to Oslo at 1.30–2 a.m.," Curtis recalls, "and the audience were still waiting. We did the show and we'd been going a good twenty-four hours from Madrid. We finished at 3.00 a.m., just as the sun was rising. While I went to bed shattered, out like a light, they went down to the beach to go swimming. No matter how tough it was, they were young people and they had the energy to do it." The group's managers subsequently informed the music press that they were suing the Yulia Club for £10,000, but nothing more was heard of the matter.

Settling back into live performance proved difficult for much of this period. Even before Quaife had left, the group had been involved with a row over top billing with the Small Faces, leading to the cancellation of a performance at the Edgware Town football ground. Upon their return from Oslo, they faced further barbs after declining to play their two recent hits, 'Dedicated Follower Of Fashion' and 'Sunny Afternoon', at disc jockey Jimmy Savile's Top Ten Club in Manchester. Davies countered that it was difficult to incorporate their slower paced satirical songs into a short, solid rock set and suggested that they might abandon clubs and ballrooms for summer season cabaret. In one interview he insisted, without a detectable trace of irony, that they were planning to add a comedy routine to their stage performance and wondered if their future lay in pantomime.

By the time the Kinks returned from Scandinavia, summer indolence had been replaced by the realization that England was in trouble. Prime Minister Harold Wilson unveiled a series of austerity measures in July, including cuts of £100 million from the overseas budget, 10 per cent increases in petrol duties, excise and surtax, and a limited allowance of £50 in foreign exchange for holidays abroad. There were severe restrictions on hire purchase and, toughest of all, a freeze on all wages and prices for six months. This was the squeeze predicted in the lyrics of 'Sunny Afternoon', but far worse than anybody had expected. The *Observer* summed up everyone's shock with the science fiction-like headline: 'The Day It All Stopped'. Over the succeeding months, the image of Swinging London with its dolly birds, bistros and boutiques would be replaced by reports of club closures and entrepreneurs unable to survive the bruising pinch of hard economics. Ray Davies appeared unsympathetic when discussing British society during that eventful month. A professed socialist, he sounded more like some High Tory blaming poverty on the poor. "I have very little time for those people who are considered to be downtrodden. It's their own fault and I hold them in contempt."

Denizens of Swinging London were further awakened by news of injustices abroad, the spectre of Vietnam, and whether Britain would become involved in the war. Equally disconcerting were reports from Northern Ireland in a year during which the Catholic population was celebrating the 50th anniversary of the Easter Rising, Protestants were solemnly remembering the Battle of the

Somme, and the Queen and the Duke of Edinburgh were preparing for a summer state visit. Tensions were at their highest for years and, for once, extensively reported in the mainstream British press. The realization that sectarianism was on a neighbouring doorstep in all its anachronistic splendour was a spectacle almost too terrible to consider for Swinging London habitués still immersed in the gospel of fab and the epistle of optimism. Liberal journalists, confronted by Orangeism at its most virulent, recoiled in horror. The *Observer* even resorted to a narrative more suited to an anthropological study of an alien race: "They are a touchy people . . . Bigotry is a casual, unchallenged reflex here: it is difficult to find any institutions, even individuals, it has not tainted. This is a sick, sick country."

This was the end of the fantasy, the bust following the boom, the full realization that sectarianism and war were part of the British experience as much as miniskirted dolly birds, picturesque bobbies on bicycles and Union Jack knickers. But there was occasion for one last escape into celebration. With 'Sunny Afternoon' still in the Top 10, England overcame West Germany in the World Cup Final at Wembley Stadium. Ray Davies' composition became an anthem of the victory parade and instantly one of the most memorable songs of 1966. Even Harold Wilson sang along, knowing that the fates had conspired to suppress speculation about the worst peacetime freeze in British history in favour of a jingoistic celebration of sporting achievement. As one newspaper concluded: "Pay may be frozen but elation is boundless."

Ray Davies' reaction to the economic chill was an appointment in New York with Allen Klein, the self-styled 'Robin Hood of Pop'. An accountant with a peculiar penchant for auditing record companies to within an inch of their ledger books, he had first come to prominence extracting monies on behalf of Buddy Knox, the young singer who had secured a million seller with 'Party Doll'. Word spread swiftly of Klein's financial feats and he soon represented a cavalcade of clients, including Bobby Darin, Bobby Vinton and Sam Cooke. Ever the expansionist, Klein next turned his attention to the UK and, at the height of the British Invasion of the US charts, added the Dave Clark Five and, most profitably, producer Mickie Most, via whom he was able to bag the Animals, Herman's Hermits and Donovan. In what was arguably his finest coup, he won over the young svengali Andrew Loog Oldham, manager and producer of the Rolling Stones. When the Stones' contract expired in July 1965, Klein had confronted Decca's chairman Sir Edward Lewis and renegotiated their deal, as reported in the US press, for $1.25 million. It was a remarkable achievement but, as with many of Klein's negotiations, there was a sting in the tale. Unbeknown to the Stones, the money was not paid into the publishing company they had formed (Nanker Phelge Music), but an American subsidiary (the deceptively titled Nanker Phelge USA) controlled by Klein himself. This fact would not emerge until several years afterwards, by which time Klein was in litigation with the Stones and about to embark on a similar course of attrition with the Beatles.

It was the Animals' road manager Peter Grant (then a junior associate of the notorious entrepreneur Don Arden and later manager of Led Zeppelin) who first alerted Robert Wace to Klein's alleged acumen. Ray, never averse to the prospect of making more money, was keen to meet Klein and propose a deal. Soon after, the music press revealed that the American had been approached to be the group's business manager and was to renegotiate their contract with Pye, just as he had done for the Stones with Decca. It was also hoped that he might break the impasse with Kassner Music which was still bound for the High Court in London. Klein was represented by the paper-sharp lawyer Marty Machat who had established an impressive client list including Dinah Washington, Sam Cooke, James Brown and the Four Seasons. Machat had also been instrumental in setting up the notorious Nanker Phelge USA for which Klein was eternally grateful. More pertinently, the attorney had completed the original production deal with Pye, which Davies was also keen to address in the near future. This, in turn, alerted Shel Talmy who was still represented by the ubiquitous Machat. In the midst of the action, the imposing Pye chairman Louis Benjamin flew to New York, determined to defend his interests in his inimitable style.

These extended negotiations meant that the Kinks' projected summer album was delayed by several months. Benjamin was unfazed and already had a contingency plan in place. He was currently preparing a very different album, culled from previously available material and set for release in September. Late 1966 saw

Britain's two premier groups, the Beatles and the Rolling Stones, issue greatest hits collections in the home market for the first time in their careers. *A Collection Of Beatles Oldies . . . But Goldies* and *Big Hits (High Tide And Green Grass)* represented a coming of age, reminding listeners and the artistes themselves that they were already the equivalent of heritage acts, whose remarkable run of hits qualified them for a rare privilege, unlikely to be repeated for many years, if ever.

The Kinks were not in the same league but that did not stop Benjamin, who not only recycled the group's work, but dared to release the commemorative album at a discount price. *Well Respected Kinks* appeared on Pye's Marble Arch subsidiary at a bargain 14/6d, easily less than half the price of a regular album, thereby ensuring substantial sales. It charted at number 5 that autumn, a few months ahead of the more prestigious Stones/ Beatles collections which, of course, were only available at full price. Benjamin's coup was daring and innovative. Although the Kinks would ultimately be cursed by similar compilations in the future, whose unwelcome presence would distract attention from their regular releases, Davies was initially impressed by Benjamin's clever marketing. "We were very pleased about that," he said the following year. "It made the LP charts . . . something rare for a budget release. Sales apart, it was certainly interesting from our point of view since it covered about two years of our disc history from 'You Really Got Me' onwards."

Shel Talmy was less impressed. Ever aware that his production deal with Pye should have been better, he now faced the additional danger of losing the Kinks amid the negotiations over the group's future. The combination of Davies' caprice and expediency, Benjamin's realpolitik, Klein's ruthlessness and Machat's conflicting interests, offered minimal security. Impassioned when roused, Talmy had already voiced his wrath against Larry Page in the heat of battle and felt even more upset by Benjamin's machinations. The Pye chairman would remain his greatest adversary.

"Louis Benjamin is a shit," he declares in a tone that does not invite contradiction. "He's one of the most obnoxious people you're ever likely to meet. He's a bum, he's garbage. He's like a little East End ton-up boy who got a couple of breaks. The people around Pye lived in fear of him. He was a petty tyrant. The Kinks never really got exploited like they should because Pye wasn't the label it should have been, because Louis Benjamin was running it . . . He was too interested in intimidating everybody else around him. Their promotion was suspect, not necessarily because of the promotion but because Benjamin would sit in his ivory tower issuing edicts all the time about various things that had nothing to do with the records. He had everybody running scared."

Talmy's comments were highly prejudicial and spiteful but indicated the resentment felt towards Pye Records by several of its seasoned acts and their business representatives. Ray Davies both praised and damned the company, but never verbally attacked its chairman. His manager Robert Wace was of similar mind. "On a personal level, I liked Louis Benjamin. My comments on Pye are unprintable. As a record company they didn't handle the Kinks badly. But their whole attitude to artistes explains why they haven't got a record company today. You can't take all the cream and not pay the artiste well. And that's what they did. Consequently, while they had a thriving record company with Petula Clark, the Searchers and Sandie Shaw, their cheapskate attitude meant that all their signings were trying to get away from them."

Benjamin was determined to retain the Kinks and hammered out a new five-year deal, which was accepted by Davies. Among the terms was a clause allowing Pye to repackage the group's work in any way they chose, without restriction. It made economic sense for Benjamin and Davies, but would ultimately cheapen the Kinks' recordings in the marketplace. Robert Wace concedes that they were renegotiating from a weak position, despite the recent chart-topping success of 'Sunny Afternoon'. "Our deal got extended in order to get a higher royalty rate, which was probably a mistake, in hindsight. The Kinks were not earning a phenomenal amount of money. The original deal was two per cent and the improved deal was eight per cent. They were not a really big band saleswise. We never had as much clout as we would have liked."

One result of their lack of clout was a very detached relationship with the rapacious Allen Klein. Having acquired the Stones, and with serious designs on the Beatles, he never had the commitment or inclination to invest time and money into the Kinks' convoluted affairs. "We neither made nor lost in the Klein situation," Wace confirms. "He didn't really have that much to do with

Kassner [publishing]. His real job was to get a hell of a lot of money from Warner Brothers in the States, and he never really brought it off. Allen never did anything harmful to the Kinks whereas he may have been a bit more dangerous where the Beatles and Stones were concerned. I think he was rather put off by my and Grenville's background."

Klein did have time to complete one piece of sharp practice. According to Davies, he passed a demo of the recently composed 'Dandy' over to another of his clients, producer Mickie Most, who then recorded the song with Herman's Hermits for US release. Ray had written 'Dandy' (originally titled 'Randy Dandy') after seeing the film *Alfie*, starring Michael Caine as the eponymous amoral womanizer, whose cynicism and lothario attraction are ultimately upended by encroaching middle age. Davies' treatment is sympathetic and ribald, with any underlying censure buried by the closing words, "Dandy, you're all right!" Steeped in music hall tradition, the song was a perfect vehicle for Herman's Hermits, whose US reputation had been made by reviving vaudevillian vignettes of far older vintage. By the end of the year, their version would climb into the American Top 10 – the best selling Davies cover song of all time. It was sufficient to win the composer the unexpected epithet: 'Britain's £100,000 a year songwriter'. "I don't look on myself as the star songwriter of the moment," he demurred at the time. "It's just that people used to visualize my songs as impossible for anyone else. But now, because I'm having hits, they realize my songs might be worthwhile for them too. You can say the same about Paul Simon who, as far as I'm concerned, is much more in demand than me at the moment. A year ago, when he didn't have hits but was still writing good stuff, nobody was interested. Now they all fall over themselves to record Paul Simon songs. Dylan's another example."

Davies' modesty was well placed. He well knew that Simon had recently enjoyed vicarious chart success with the Bachelors' 'The Sound Of Silence', the Seekers' 'Someday One Day' and the Cyrkle's 'Red Rubber Ball'. Dylan, of course, had been a constant presence and touchstone, the more so since the Byrds' transatlantic number 1 with 'Mr Tambourine Man' in 1965. In terms of productivity, Davies could boast an impressive array of covers in his own right, a list that included: 'Revenge' (Ray McVay); 'Just Can't

Go To Sleep' (Formula One); 'Something Better Beginning' (Honeycombs); 'Emptiness' (Honeycombs); 'I Go To Sleep' (Peggy Lee; Cher; Applejacks; Truth; Marion; Adrian Pride; Fingers; Lesley Duncan); 'When I See That Girl Of Mine' (Bobby Rydell); 'I Bet You Won't Stay' (Cascades); 'This Strange Effect' (Dave Berry); 'A Little Bit Of Sunlight' (Majority); 'Little Man In A Little Box' (Barry Fantoni); 'All Night Stand' (Thoughts); 'Oh What A Day It's Gonna Be' (Mo & Steve) and two recent compositions earmarked for the next Kinks album, 'House In The Country' (Pretty Things) and 'End Of The Season' (Uglys). "I had no idea that anyone else would ever connect emotionally with anything I wrote," Davies says. "I was doing it solely as self-expression. I thought my lyrics were my own secret world, with an agenda of their own."

Ray's 'secret world' did not translate easily into the marketplace. Apart from 'Dandy' and 'This Strange Effect', none of these covers, along with many others that followed in the late Sixties, made any commercial impact whatsoever. Whereas Lennon/McCartney songs almost guaranteed success, including several number 1 hits, Ray Davies could not even compete with the formulaic tunesmiths of London's Tin Pan Alley. His reputation as a great songwriter was established solely by his work with the Kinks at this point, despite all the efforts of publisher Eddie Kassner.

Although there is little evidence to suggest it could have been otherwise, Shel Talmy maintains that a breakaway into solo work might have enhanced his reputation. "Ray is one of the most prolific writers I've ever run into. He might go home and come back the next day with forty songs. With the amount of stuff he wrote, there was no way we could record everything. Had Ray wanted to he could have been the biggest singer-songwriter from this country as a solo. He obviously never wanted that and needed the security of a band. I think he's one of the great songwriters of our time. He should have been right up there with Lennon and McCartney, and is not. He never had the publicity that the Beatles had. In the public's eye he was never as revered as Lennon and McCartney. Kassner worked as a collection agency. Davies is still basically an undiscovered asset. There are lots of things there that could be done successfully now."

Davies found songwriting inspiration in the most unlikely places.

Sometimes, the germ of an idea or even a song title might emerge from a chance encounter. So it was in the late summer of '66 when the Kinks, still without the convalescing Pete Quaife, found themselves playing a 'Big Beat Festival' charity event at Rutland's County Agricultural Showground. The promoter, a former army major named David Watts, hired the Kinks as bill toppers for £450. Inexperienced in pop matters, Watts over-estimated the likely attendance figures for a show in Rutland and suffered the embarrassment of watching 60 police officers and assorted Alsatian dogs patrolling the site in expectation of a disturbance. On this occasion, there was no Kinks'-related riot to report. The passive and largely undemonstrative audience merely cheered and clapped politely after watching the 30-minute set.

Counting his losses, the stoical promoter invited the Kinks to his nearby Georgian mansion for an after-show party. When they arrived, Dave Davies noticed that Watts was wearing pink socks which the guitarist regarded as a coded indication of homosexuality. That feeling was reinforced later in the evening when an all-male party of guests arrived, some of whom were, according to Ray, accompanied by young boys. In keeping with his sock colour, Watts provided copious bottles of pink champagne, a type that even the debutante-loving Dave had never previously tasted. With inhibitions loosened, several of the male guests danced together and reportedly kissed each other in degenerate abandon. Mick Avory, whose appreciation of homosexual humour had grown ever more keen since his first audition for the Kinks back in 1964, joined in the camp spirit and performed a mock strip-tease. At one point, he accidentally dropped his trousers, much to the amusement of Ray, who always enjoyed seeing the drummer make a fool of himself. Seizing the moment, the mischievous singer turned to David Watts and pointedly asked him if he fancied Avory. Ray became more intrigued when the promoter professed a preference for his younger brother. Emboldened by champagne, Ray came up with an extraordinary proposition, encouraging Watts with the idea of wooing his brother and settling down with him as a gay couple in Georgian splendour. "I felt that would be the right thing for him to do," he later claimed. "I genuinely thought that this was the perfect match. I felt I could trust David Watts with my brother."

Dave, meanwhile, was touring the house and ended up in an upstairs room, pedalling furiously on an exercise bike which provided a brief surge of sobriety. Oblivious to his brother's machinations, he was taken aback when Watts appeared in the doorway in lustful appreciation. "Everyone was acting in a camp way," Dave explains. "I thought they were just getting it from us, taking the piss – but it was a gay party . . . Unbeknown to me, Ray had been talking to David . . . He tried to marry me off to David Watts really because he had a nice house and he thought I'd be really secure living with David. Poor David Watts! . . . He'd really taken it on board seriously that we were going to be a couple living in his home. And I didn't know anything about it."

Eventually, the two Davids retired to the back garden to resolve the embarrassing affair. Ray watched the proceedings with a voyeur's delight, keenly observing that they were holding hands on a double swing under a willow tree overlooking a lake while Dave attempted to break the news gently that he was uninterested. He may even have mentioned that he currently had a regular girlfriend whom he would marry a year later. "There was an awful row," he concludes. "David Watts was crying and it was terrible – and all because of Ray's meddling."

Over the years, Ray perpetuated the idea that the incident was not some cruel jape but an example of his true concern for his brother's future. Playing the honest broker, he even pointed out, with plausible glee, that he had negotiated on Dave's behalf, securing him a half share of the palatial home in the event of a breakup. Dave was unsurprisingly cynical about this display of magnanimity and argued the opposite, claiming that Ray had acted like a white slave trader and attempted to betroth him to Watts in exchange for the lease to his Georgian house. "What stuck in my mind the most," he wrote, "was the fact that my older brother, whose guidance and defence I had counted on, was ready to trade me for a piece of architecture. This time he had been thwarted." It spoke volumes about the brothers' relationship that Dave never considered all this to be some elaborate joke at his expense and a supreme example of Ray's quirky humour. The incident later provided Davies with a song title ('David Watts'), a coded tribute to his brother's putative seducer.

CHAPTER TWENTY

FACE TO FACE

By the autumn of 1966, Pete Quaife had still not returned to the group. He was living in Copenhagen with Danish fiancée Annette Paustian, whose cousin Lisbet Thorkil-Petersen was dating Dave Davies. Rumours persisted that the bassist was intending to abandon pop music and join British European Airways as a designer. "When Pete came home from hospital, he changed completely," his brother David remembers. "He just didn't want to go to work. He said, 'No, I'm not feeling up to it.' My theory is that while he was lying there in hospital, he was thinking about what to do. You've got time to think. So he decided to be his own person without the harassment."

This period of uncertainty seemingly ended on 11 September when Quaife confirmed that he was leaving the group. By the end of the month, he had resigned his partnership in Kinks Productions and Dalton was confirmed as his replacement. Coincidentally, the group were in Denmark at the time, and tensions were high. "We'd been friends for a long time," Davies says, "so of course I was sorry that he left. But I think the time had come, for him and for us." Back in London, Quaife's old friend John Start learned of the news but was far from surprised. "That's the trouble with a pop group. You're in a car for hours and hours. You can imagine what a trial it must have been for Pete. He was the sweetest guy terrorized by that blinking Ray Davies." The word 'terrorized' may be too strong, but Quaife himself admits that the tensions were almost overwhelming.

The Scandinavian tour was blighted by all too familiar scenes of rioting fans threatening to break up the stage and, on one occasion, attacking a police station. While Quaife was signing his exit papers, Ray became embroiled in a dispute with a Copenhagen promoter who was incandescent about the group's refusal to play at a venue they insisted was unsuitable. In retaliation, he confiscated their equipment which interrupted their schedule, resulting in a late arrival in Malmö, Sweden, where they could only perform a 15-minute set. The knock-on effects of these petty disputes drained morale and motivation. Unsurprisingly, the Scandinavian Musicians' Union took a dim view of such behaviour and promptly banned the Kinks from returning in the foreseeable future. Although these temporary setbacks proved minor, the reputation of the group undoubtedly suffered. Even before Ray's illness, the Kinks had been unreliable and disruptive; now they seemed constantly plagued by postponed concerts and rearranged itineraries. Agent Arthur Howes announced that he would not be accepting any further bookings for the remainder of the year, a clear enough admission of his lack of confidence. The Kinks' management also felt the strain, caught as they were in the conflict between Ray Davies' caprice and health issues and further burdened by the constant need to placate promoters whose support was required in order to keep the group solvent. "The cancellations were very tedious," says Robert Wace. "It was down to Ray growing up. I got very bored and fed up with it. Very often I was angry with them because I don't like letting people down. A couple of promoters were hit very hard. It affected the Kinks' credibility as a live act. There was a period when they were very difficult to book. When their agency agreement with Arthur Howes ran out, I had to convince Harold Davison to take them on. He was very reluctant."

In later years, Davies sometimes wondered whether he should have taken the plunge and launched a solo career at this point. The strain of live performances and lengthy business negotiations had clearly taken their toll and all his energies now focused on songwriting and recording. Ideally, he would have followed the Beatles' recent lead and transformed the Kinks into a studio entity, but economically that was never viable. Touring income was still a necessity and his only other solution was to dissolve the group, a risky venture in 1966. Instead, he elected to inhabit both worlds, performing and recording as the Kinks but simultaneously isolating himself. Increasingly, he retreated into a domestic routine. "That's what parents do when they've got children," he says. "I saw the fright of being thrust into the world of popular music and being on *Top Of The Pops*. I felt a little intimidated by it and wanted to be grounded by something. I thought it would be safer for me emotionally with all the temptations that lie out there . . . I thought it would be good for me to get some stability in my life, and it worked for a long time. I didn't really see the Swinging Sixties. I stayed at home writing the songs. I had to continually deliver. I had to be disciplined."

His brother was aware of the increasing schism in their world views and personalities, but felt that it worked to the group's advantage. "We were inventing rock 'n' roll. People used to say I lived the life and Ray wrote about living it. Ray's technique for survival was observing the scene. He's never been any good about showing his feelings. If I got upset, I'd cry and shout. Ray's always been withdrawn."

The extra time that Davies allowed for songwriting was revealed on the next album. On 28 October, the delayed *Face To Face* appeared, boasting 14 original compositions. Its scope and depth remain remarkable. Although the original idea of connecting each track with musical effects and sound montages was regrettably compromised, thereby depriving Davies of pre-empting the Beatles' *Sgt Pepper's Lonely Hearts Club Band* by a year, several motifs are retained, notably the thunderstorms and splashing water on 'Rainy Day In June' and 'Holiday In Waikiki', respectively. The opening track, 'Party Line', is preceded by a loud, ringing phone, answered by Grenville Collins ("Who's that speaking, please?") whose clipped received pronunciation anticipates the class consciousness displayed on several of the succeeding tracks. There is even a sly hint of sexual ambiguity, years before 'Lola', in the arch consideration, "Is she a she at all?"

'Party Line' and 'You're Looking Fine' (another Dave Davies cameo) are inspired rock workouts, reminiscent of the R&B-styled Kinks, but provide only glimpses of the eclecticism on offer. Overall, the album encompasses every aspect of Ray Davies' songwriting and arranging skills. Lyrically, there are psychoanalytical confessionals, philosophical meditations, music-hall romps and light-hearted satires lampooning bourgeois values and dramatizing class conflicts. "You could tap into all cultures and styles and not be ashamed of music hall, Eastern music, West Indian music," Davies says. "I didn't want to pretend I was a Jack Daniel's drinking bluesman from the American South. I enjoyed the Englishness of what I was doing, writing songs about suburbia and having fun with words. I was relating to a world that I was familiar with." Although two songs were inspired by the 1965 US tour – the wry comment on commercial exploitation in 'Holiday In Waikiki' and the poignant, retro sounding 'I'll Remember', written on harmonica during a stay in Seattle – the remainder are far removed from the American landscape. "When we realized we couldn't go back, I withdrew into complete Englishness and quaintness. Everyone was making albums to define the drug culture, but we withdrew into this world that was alien to what other bands were doing."

The musical palette on *Face To Face* is no less intriguing, not solely due to the clever sound effects, but the ingenious employment of Nicky Hopkins who provides harpsichord, piano and melodica to embellish the work. He even "partly inspired" 'Session Man', an incisive satirical stab at a working musician bound by union rules and pay scales, who flits from orchestras to pop groups, without discrimination. It was typical of Davies, who always admired Hopkins' attitude and ability, to couch his tribute in the form of a tongue-in-cheek attack. Hopkins was encouraged to offer "something *classy*" and promptly provided a classical harpsichord flourish which producer Shel Talmy used as a lavish opening.

The satirical songs on *Face To Face* are akin to an album within an album. There's 'Dandy', a rake's progress comment on Swinging London values, and 'Little Miss Queen Of Darkness', which capture the frantic amorality of London clubland. The nouveau riche with their fancy cars and rural hideaways are taken to task in 'House In The Country' and its sister song 'Most Exclusive Residence For Sale', a cautionary tale documenting the financial fall of an aristocrat who squanders his fortune on girls and jewellery. The presence of 'Sunny Afternoon' in this new context is a revelation, transforming a classic single into a complementary album track that comments even more sardonically on the new aristocracy.

What lingers long after the demise of Swinging London are the album's more nakedly introspective and peculiar moments. 'Too Much On My Mind' invites the listener into Davies' troubled psyche, invoking an image of an insomniac obsessive, plagued by tortured thoughts that shake the very life from his brain, slowly fracturing his "poor demented mind". Hopkins' stately harpsichord accompaniment brings an almost regal dignity to this drama of mental decay.

The instrument is used to equally impressive effect on the yearning 'Rosy, Won't You Please Come Home', a desperate plea for the return of Ray's lost sister. Tellingly, Davies does not even bother to disguise the biographical inspiration by changing the character's name. Both Ray and Dave have testified to their traumatized reaction to the emigration of Rose, along with nephew Terry, to start a new life in Australia. In the brothers' personal mythology, it ranks alongside the tragic death of Rene as a symbol of ineffable loss. Rose, simultaneously a sister and mother figure, was not only missed but morbidly mourned. Ray captures the full poignancy of this loss in one of his plainest yet most affecting lines, "Rosy, how I miss you, you are all the world to me". It is not merely the words but the frightening vulnerability in the vocal that captures the full extent of his desolation. He sounds uncannily like a child whose mother has been taken away, without explanation. That disorientation is echoed in the description of the broken, morose matriarch, seemingly unable to adjust to her daughter's departure, while keeping her old room intact and unaltered, like a shrine. Always at his best as a songwriter of the heart, Davies would often siphon material from his own life, seldom changing the names to protect the innocent, yet forging creative work of even greater emotional impact as a result. In this song, he does not merely tell the story of Rose Anning (née Davies), but conjures a fictional recreation, a 'meta Rose' capable, it seems, of reversing history. In his narrative, she still lives abroad but even though years have passed, he still calls for her return. The fantasy element lies in her tantalizing availability. There is no mention of her husband Arthur, who is conveniently written out of the story. Indeed, the 'home' that he wishes her to return to is not even her marital abode in Highgate, but the imaginary empty bedroom in Denmark Terrace. This is not just a story of loss through geographical distance but more pertinently of time itself. 'Home' lies not in the present but in a lost past that can only be reclaimed in fantasy. The 'meta Rose' is still the mother figure that he knew as a child, but also a vehicle for his speculations on class conflict. Although located somewhere across the sea, she does not appear to be living modestly in a middle-class suburb of Australia like his elder sister but has joined the upper classes. Significantly, it is her social mobility that causes the emotional rift by which they do not know her any more.

Davies' inner world is also the subject of the elliptical 'Fancy', a composition completed in the immediate aftermath of his spring 'breakdown'. "It was at a time when people really wanted to find out what was wrong with me. All my life I've been able to keep them out." Here, he returns to the psychiatrist's chair during childhood and adolescence when reserve and opacity were his best weapons against a hostile universe. "No one can penetrate me" he sings, seemingly addressing both his past and present. The song has that same mysterious quality as 'See My Friend' and employs his trusty 12-string Framus guitar to emulate its sitar sound, this time in the form of a single droning note.

The journey into fantasy is completed in the strangest song on the album: 'Rainy Day In June'. Ostensibly a meteorological metaphor of Davies' breakdown state, it goes way beyond that straightforward sunshine and storm dichotomy into a realm of misty shadows and disappearing light. Portentous and fore-boding, the song moves from the naturalistic to the fantastic like the plot of a Dennis Wheatley novel. The back garden is transformed into a Tolkien landscape in which a crinkle-headed demon snares a butterfly and even gnomes are too terrified to scream, while treasured items perish or are entombed forever. The familiar and the phantasmagorical oscillate in the troubled mind of the observer who sees the altered terrain as a place of "no hope, no reasoning". It has an hallucinatory quality, made more disturbing by the intensity of description and cinematic sense of movement. There is nothing else quite like this in the entire Davies canon.

Face To Face sold reasonably well, climbing into the Top 10 of the album charts, while never achieving the critical credibility of an *Aftermath* or *Revolver*. Even at this juncture, the Kinks were still considered a singles group, a perception that they would never quite shake off despite the quality and sophistication of Davies' songwriting. Ray knew this, but he valued the dysfunctional companionship of the other Kinks in preference to pursuing his interests alone. Selfish and sentimental, he realized that he missed the presence of Pete Quaife, despite the recent frostiness between them. When he discovered the bass player had returned to his family's council house in Steeds Road, he conducted a charm offensive, tinged with a certain ruthlessness according to Quaife's brother David, and persuaded Pete to reverse his decision. Quaife returned as speedily and mysteriously as he had departed, leaving the unfortunate Dalton to find work as a coalman.

Four days later, on 18 November, the new Kinks' single 'Dead End Street' was released. The group had been tardy following up the summery 'Sunny Afternoon', but Davies and Pye resisted the temptation to pluck a track from *Face To Face* as a stopgap. Singles were still the lifeblood of pop and treasured artefacts in their own right. 'Dead End Street' was a daring record whose musical construction testified to Davies' authorial vision. Shel Talmy produced what might easily have been the finished track, employing two bass guitars, an electric and acoustic 12-string guitar, piano, drums and French horn. Later that night, Davies began tinkering with the arrangement, convinced that it needed to be stripped down. In his mind, a dour trombone part was required in place of the French horn with the intention of providing a more downbeat feel, like some colliery band providing an accompaniment to the 1926 General Strike. Grenville Collins was despatched to a local pub and returned with a competent player who added the new brass part, complete with an improvised ending. "That was the beginning of the end for Shel [Talmy]," Ray says, "because I didn't like the version he did." What finally emerged was quite a surprise.

Although Davies seemed inimitable as a songwriter, the denizens of Tin Pan Alley vainly attempted to master his style. The same October week that 'Dead End Street' was recorded, a single appeared whose novel theme attracted instant attention. Former rivals Manfred Mann were the fortunate recipients of 'Semi-Detached Suburban Mr James', written by professional tunesmiths Geoff Stephens and John Carter, and produced by Shel Talmy. The song satirized middle-class suburban values and aspirational marriage with a caustic wit, straight out of the Davies school of songwriting. Eminently commercial, it rapidly climbed the charts, narrowly missing number 1. It was anticipated that the Kinks might attempt something similarly light and wry with their new single, possibly in the vein of 'Dandy' or 'Sunny Afternoon', but Davies had already moved on.

'Dead End Street' is the distorted mirror image of 'Sunny Afternoon', a bleak portrayal of urban working-class poverty far removed from the languid landscape presented in Davies' memorable summer chart topper. The song's origins were multiple rather than singular, percolating over several months as Davies reflected on the state of the nation and recalled the severities he had witnessed growing up. Oddly, for a song so closely associated with English proletarian life, 'Dead End Street' owed its original inspiration to Depression-era America. Davies remembers reading "a book about the life and times of Al Capone, the American gangster" and being struck by images that seemed strangely contemporary, with scenes set against a backdrop of unemployment and poor housing conditions "very similar to those we are experiencing today". His meditation was reinforced by conversations with his Lithuanian in-laws, whose lives as refugees had been marked by acute deprivation. The large Davies family were no strangers to hard times themselves, having struggled through the war years and beyond. Ray's own cultural interests as an adolescent – reading the work of George Orwell or perusing the paintings of Hogarth – meant that images of the working-class poor had been with him since at least the Fifties. Although he had embraced some of the hedonism of the Sixties, Davies was never seduced by the fantasy pop world and was always cynical enough to see through its artifice. "I wanted to write about the cold reality, the lies and the deceits. The Sixties were just beginning to be shown to be a lie."

Social injustices and scary anachronisms were ever present. As 'Dead End Street' was being pressed, the nation was still recovering from news of the Aberfan disaster. A Welsh village primary school at the bottom of a hill had been buried beneath an ocean of slurry from a slag heap. The death toll was 144, including 116 children. It was an image that many people found difficult to comprehend, like some dark fable from the Victorian age. The National Coal Board was accused of gross negligence. How could this have happened in a supposedly modern, technological society?

With 'Dead End Street' Davies was asking similar questions about the city of his birth. The 'squeeze' he had predicted in 'Sunny Afternoon' was now biting hard, industries were in decline and even record sales were down. Five days before the Kinks' new single appeared, the *Sunday Times* declared "Beatlemania is at an end", a self-fulfilling prophecy that most music press readers would have understood as meaning something deeper – an acknowledgement that pop was growing up. 'Dead End Street' remains a testament to that maturity in its social realism. The figures Davies describes are destitute, with no hope of employment or even the dream of emigration. Their working-class fatalism ironically echoes the stoicism of the aristocratic wastrel in 'Sunny Afternoon' who has lost almost everything, but at least retains the delusion of escaping abroad, albeit with no visible means of achieving his aim.

If 'Dead End Street' has a weakness, it lies in Davies' failure to create a sufficiently rounded central character to convey the message emotionally. It could be accused of chocolate box bleakness, like a Christmas edition of *Oliver Twist* or *Bleak House*, minus the happy ending. With its rapacious rent collectors, leaking sink, freezing room and peeling ceiling, 'Dead End Street' offers details and description but its narrator sounds little more than a helpless voice. Therein, perhaps, lurks a subtler comment on proletarian fatalism. Additionally, there is something timeless about 'Dead End Street', as if it was commenting on the city's poor over the ages. It conjures images of Hogarth, Dickens, Orwell, the Hungry Thirties and, most tellingly, post-war rationing (a bread and honey sandwich replaces the traditional Sunday roast dinner).

What seems a song about the past was, in fact, nothing of the sort. Living conditions in certain inner-city areas were far worse in the Sixties than they had been in pre-war times. Slum housing, unscrupulous landlords and an overstretched social welfare system meant that some families were still trapped in the age of austerity rather than enjoying the brave new world promised by successive Conservative and Labour governments. Hazardous coal tips and overgrown bomb sites were visible reminders not only of the past, but of all that still needed to be changed. A contemporary investigative report in *The Times* offered a harrowing description of a London dwelling that made Davies' dead end street sound more like an exclusive residence by comparison: "There was no water, except for a cold tap in the backyard down three flights of dark rickety stairs. The one lavatory for the eleven people in the building was too filthy to use. Cooking facilities had to be shared. The house was rat infested and the walls . . . ridden with bugs and beetles."

'Dead End Street', the most unlikely of modern anthems, reflects its time more accurately than some of its Swinging Sixties purchasers appreciated. Synchronicity decreed that it was released less than 48 hours after BBC 1 had screened *Cathy Come Home*, the groundbreaking *Wednesday Play* written by Jeremy Sandford and directed by Ken Loach. One of the most moving and celebrated television moments of the Sixties, *Cathy Come Home* tells the story of a young, London-based family who, through ill fortune, suffer a downward spiral into homelessness and separation. Filmed like a docudrama, including the use of hand-held cameras, its verisimilitude had a powerful effect, most notably in the images of squalor depicted in tenement houses and overcrowded hostels and the heartlessness encountered along the way. The play attracted six million viewers and considerable coverage in the press. Whether it assisted sales of 'Dead End Street' is debatable, but it certainly made the song topical. When the BBC's current affairs programme *Panorama* subsequently featured a piece about slums in the capital, 'Dead End Street' was chosen as the accompanying music. This thrilled Ray Davies even more than news that the single had infiltrated the UK Top 5, an impressive statistic for such a courageous composition.

'Dead End Street' might have fared even better if the BBC had been more amenable about broadcasting a black and white film that Davies had made to promote the song on *Top Of The Pops*. "It showed slums and poverty and they wouldn't run it, I guess they prefer films about running around in parks, jumping over chairs." The BBC ban was not due to the film's social commentary, as Davies implied, but its depiction of a funeral procession which was deemed to be in poor taste. "I don't think it's sick," Dave Davies countered. "It's too funny to be sick. We're tired of doing the same old thing. We thought this would be different." Indeed it was. Ray's dark comedy featured the group dressed as undertakers and pall-bearers, with Dave appearing as a grieving widow. It ended with a Keystone Kops-style chase, sped up for humorous effect. "Our roadie, Stan [Whitley], played the corpse," Dave points out. "You could sing about poverty and inequality, but you couldn't show a funeral on TV!" Its ban was doubly upsetting for Ray, who had always wanted to experiment with film as a complementary medium to his musical endeavours. "I now look upon making a song as a production – rather like making a film," he explained. "I know it's the wrong way to do it, but it makes it more exciting for me. You know how actors live their parts? Well, I try to do that. I try to get into the character I am writing about. Producing a successful song is just a question of getting the most important ideas – the basic story of the song."

Purchasers of 'Dead End Street' received a welcome surprise with another non-album B-side that ranked alongside the Kinks' best work. 'Big Black Smoke' appears to shift through time and space in similar fashion to its A-side. The moral saga of a pure country girl seduced by the city is a familiar trope that could have come from a Thomas Hardy or Henry Fielding novel, by way of the later Edna O'Brien. Yet, the scene is firmly set in Swinging London with its bowling alleys, cafés and coffee bars and references to cigarettes and purple hearts (amphetamines). The effect is unsettling and stimulating, as if we are watching scenes from two different centuries – the bad Victorian girl and the Sixties runaway united in one song – with Davies using both to comment on the timeless theme of corrupted innocence. The descending bass line, by now a signifier of bad news in a Davies narrative, is predictably employed, but the song ends with a bravura performance from Dave Davies as a town crier repeatedly shouting an impassioned "oh yea". It is akin to a sudden jolt, joyous and arresting, as our senses are bombarded and the narrative terrain dissolves, shifting time once more from Sixties London to the previous century, or even earlier, when town criers declaimed news in stentorian tones armed with a warning bell. Here, the single instrument is replaced by the pealing of church bells, amplifying the message into an epic production.

The inclusion of a high-quality B-side was a stamp of honour among the elite exponents of mid-Sixties pop in the UK. If done frequently, it established a brand loyalty and faith in the performer that transcended the occasional dud single. "We were trying to put out two good songs," notes Shel Talmy. "If Pye had done their job properly, they would have promoted them as double A-sides and both of them would have got up there. Whatever lack of success the Kinks had is strictly to do with Pye. It was a terrible label to be associated with." Talmy's prejudices against Pye obscure a valuable argument. As he should have known, or cynically chose to forget, double A-sides at this point were predominantly the preserve of the Beatles who were blessed with such quality material that choosing between A- and B-sides was often impossible. Few others faced the same dilemma and larger labels than Pye hardly followed the trend. The Yardbirds had – only once – faced a similar dilemma in 1965 and issued 'Evil Hearted You'/'Still I'm Sad'. Neither the Rolling Stones nor the Who, to pluck two convenient examples, had yet to issue a double A-side, despite their prominent positions as purveyors of exceptional work. Indeed, it was noticeable how uninspiring their B-sides were in comparison to the best of the Kinks in 1966. In retrospect, Talmy is probably correct in suggesting that Davies' reputation as a songwriter and the Kinks' historical importance among the contemporary pop elite would have been enhanced by a double A-side. As it was, minor classics such as 'Big Black Smoke' and 'I'm Not Like Everybody Else' were left to the cognoscenti and permanently treasured.

As 1966 ended, Davies sounded as weary and detached as ever. "Once you've had a number 1 record you can only repeat yourself. You go on *Top Of The Pops* and stand there and sing the song." The Kinks did not even appear on the final edition of *Ready, Steady, Go!* that Christmas. In an uncharacteristic display of fraternal concern, Ray left music press readers with a charitable festive thought, laced with drama: "I'm worried about Dave. I might leave the group but I want Dave to be emotionally and financially secure first." The plea sounded sincere and heartfelt at the time, but was it genuine? When reminded by this author of the quote – which he had either forgotten or never read – Dave smiled, shook his head and, searching for a suitable response, enquired: "Can you use the word 'cunt'?"

CHAPTER TWENTY-ONE

LIVERPOOL SUNSET

"I'd like to own the group. I'd like to run them by myself." That was Ray Davies' message at the start of 1967 as the Kinks departed for Germany, supported by opera trained David Garrick, a Collins/Wace signing who had come tantalizingly close to chart success for Pye Records with a cover of the Rolling Stones' 'Lady Jane' and the catchy American obscurity 'Dear Mrs Applebee'. His repertoire would be enhanced by covers, notably Davies' 'Dedicated Follower Of Fashion' and 'Dandy'. By now, the management were keen to extend their entrepreneurial empire, having learned the lesson that concentrating on one major act can severely limit your power in the industry. Of course, this policy had to be balanced against Ray Davies' insecurities, fears, suspicion and possessiveness. The ousted Larry Page could have provided such a warning from the managerial graveyard. Among his sins, from Davies' prejudiced perspective, had been an over-keenness on Sonny & Cher. Collins and Wace proceeded cautiously, adding singer Leapy Lee to their books. He was given a rare Davies' composition, 'King Of The Whole Wide World' which the songwriter produced and arranged. Collins/Wace also established a working relationship with Andrew Loog Oldham, the flamboyant Rolling Stones manager, whose independent label Immediate was the acme of hipness. In a delightfully subversive move, Oldham encouraged Robert Wace to co-write and record a novelty record for the label with producer Mike Leander – 'Changing Of The Guard' b/w 'Reverse Thrust' – under the pseudonym The Marquis of Kensington.

Although unsuccessful, it probably provided psychological closure for Wace, who had been booed off the stage three years before when fronting the prototype Kinks' antecedent, the Boll-Weevils.

Surprisingly, Oldham was also willing to allow Wace to represent one of Immediate's hottest acts, the Small Faces. The young Mods had already enjoyed several hits with Decca under the proprietorship of the intimidating Don Arden, who zealously guarded his investment with a combination of foul-mouthed bluster and bulging muscle. When Arden heard that impresario Robert Stigwood had approached the group, he turned up at his offices with a couple of hired thugs and hung the unfortunate Australian from a fourth-floor window, while providing a lecture on managerial etiquette. According to Oldham, Wace had actually witnessed this incident from the street below. Soon, Robert would take over their management, which Arden had already sold on to agent Harold Davison. Taking on such a high-profile group risked incurring Ray's wrath, not least because the Small Faces were undergoing that same subtle shift from R&B merchants to witty experimentalists that the Kinks had previously undertaken.

By the end of the year, the new signings would scale fresh peaks with 'Itchycoo Park', a distinctive London song, celebrating drug-induced indolence. A similar mood was detectable on the following year's 'Lazy Sunday' (which echoed 'Sunny Afternoon' thematically) and the 'concept' album *Ogdens' Nut Gone Flake*. Wace was long gone by then, having passed the group back to Oldham after a brief but unhappy interlude during which the group failed to appear at a May ball. It taught him a valuable lesson about pop management as well as throwing a more positive light on his relationship with Davies. Ray's frugality had long been a source of hilarity and exasperation, but it was infinitely preferable to the reckless largesse of Steve Marriott and his fellow Faces whose career was already tottering on the precipice of perdition. "The Small Faces cost us money!" Wace laments. "To be perfectly frank, we were glad to be shot of them. If you gave the Small Faces £10,000, they'd find a way of spending £15,000. They'd go down to shops like Granny Takes A Trip on the King's Road, spend £500 on clothes and send the bill to the manager. Those sort of things used to happen in the Sixties. They were always running around in limousines, running up bills at tailors and hairdressers.

Whatever money they had, it went. You're either careful with money – or you're not. Ray Davies and the Kinks were the total reverse of the Small Faces. There was never a time in my management of the Kinks when they didn't have £100,000 on deposit." And even then, Ray still felt he didn't have enough money.

For all his foibles, Davies found a measure of contentment at this time. One year on from his breakdown, he had detached himself sufficiently from the pop treadmill to enjoy a domestic routine that was predictable but pleasurable. "[It] was one of the happiest times of my life," he recalls. "I had my friends; I used to play football on a Sunday; life was music and writing and touring with the band." His marriage also seemed more stable. Rasa was relieved to discover that there was no repetition of the psychodramas of 1966. Although Ray retained many of his eccentricities, life at 87 Fortis Green had never been better. Coaxed by Rasa, he had even agreed to pay for a kitchen extension, which increased the value of the property. While digging, the builders unearthed an ancient well. Further research revealed that it had originally been used to supply water to the local community.

With her new kitchen and now driving a fashionable Lancia, Rasa at last acquired a modicum of independence and some much-needed spending money. "I didn't see a lot of Swinging London," she says, "but I did enjoy the era and the clothes. My stamping ground was Miss Selfridge in Oxford Street. I used to drive down from Fortis Green and go to the King's Road and Carnaby Street, but not anywhere else. I liked the Sixties' buzz, the swinging clothes and the boutique that Grenville and Robert owned. I had a small group of girlfriends in Muswell Hill who all had kids. We were quite bohemian. We'd meet up in the local café up the road so I did have a life outside of home by then, but Swinging London probably passed me by a bit."

It was not only marital relations that had improved. There was also evidence that Ray's often antagonistic relationship with his brother had cooled – at least for the present. Both Dave and Pete Quaife had married their respective Danish sweethearts in low-key, almost secret, ceremonies. Suddenly, Ray was not the only domesticated Kink.

In contrast to their family lives, the group were happy to discuss work projects, albeit in highfalutin fashion. The usual compendium of semi-realized ideas, abandoned EPs, vague solo plans and imaginary schemes was mentioned in interviews or news snippets, and just as quickly forgotten. Apparently taking Ray's cue, his fellow members added their own obfuscating exaggerations. The normally reliable Avory spoke about rehearsing Dylan's 'Absolutely Sweet Marie' and 'Most Likely You Go Your Way And I Go Mine' which fooled many readers, this author included. Quaife, a more transparent raconteur, nurtured ambitions of writing a novel and spoke portentously of a three-volume work, *The Priest And The Physician*, in which he intended to present a philosophical argument for and against religion. It seemed designed to make Ray Davies look a dullard by comparison.

A new single, 'Mister Pleasant', was seriously considered for UK release, but instead came out in Holland. With Nicky Hopkins on barrelhouse piano and the Mike Cotton Sound's John Beecham allegedly on trombone, the song has an upbeat, music hall feel but there is no disguising the cruel sarcasm directed at the genial suburban man who is ultimately cuckolded. The continental B-side, 'This Is Where I Belong', a stark paean to domesticity with a treasured sense of place and enduring faith in simple verities, is punctuated by Ray's promise not to seek "that house upon the hill". Surprisingly, the single climbed to number 2 in the Dutch charts. Later, there was a memorable mimed rendition of 'Mister Pleasant' broadcast on the German TV show *Beat Club* featuring Grenville Collins on piano and hirsute English disc jockey Dave Lee Travis on trombone.

Ray Davies had already part written a composition that was to have a far greater impact than the sour and satiric 'Mister Pleasant'. It emerged in the spring of 1967, when pop was in flux. There had always been a generation gap of sorts in the modern history of popular music but it was now widening and turning in on itself in the oddest fashion. In recent years, the cult of youth had been promoted by several of its leading practitioners. Mick Jagger had declared that "old people are a drag" and sung as much on 'Mother's Little Helper', while pop's other great spokesman Pete Townshend was forever stuck with the words "Hope I die before I get old" from 'My Generation'. Even Ray Davies had displayed some of these same prejudices back in 1965 when he slated record purchasers for supporting older artistes such as Elvis Presley and Connie Francis. Since then, though, derailed by his breakdown, he had sought solace in Frank Sinatra, a singer whom many of his fans might well have called 'square'.

Now, a family man, keen to keep his marriage intact, Ray fashioned a song that not only connected various events in his life, from childhood to maturity, but also challenged the aesthetic divide in contemporaneous pop. "I wanted to write something that was like a little standard that other people could play and you could hear on muzak." The song was titled 'Waterloo Sunset'.

At a time when the forward-looking iconoclasts – Lennon, Jagger, Townshend et al. – were, in common parlance, becoming more 'far out', Davies was looking back and attempting to reconnect with an older generation. "That's where I differed from my contemporaries, and why I didn't always feel in tune with them. I wrote 'Sunny Afternoon' when I was twenty-one years old, and I wrote it so my granddad could sing it. I didn't write it to make my parents angry. It was the same with 'Waterloo Sunset'. I wanted everyone to like it. I didn't exclude adults from my audience. I basically wrote for my family because I came from an environment where everybody sang and was musically inclined. I never had this hatred of adults that everyone said they had. I don't believe that Pete Townshend hated old people and wanted to die before he got old, because he got along really well with his dad. I think the generation gap was blown up by the press more than by the individuals involved."

The so-called 'generation gap' was actually more complex than either Davies or the contemporaneous music press acknowledged. For many popular music historians and commentators, 1967 was supposedly the year when 'rock' emerged as the new dominant form. It was the year of Jimi Hendrix, Cream and Pink Floyd – harbingers of progressive, 'underground' music. Even the lexicon of popular music was subject to significant change. It would not be long before LPs became 'albums', artistes were renamed artists, groups started calling themselves 'bands' and 'serious' pop musicians renamed their 'art' form 'rock'. The Monkees, a 'manufactured' American group, were featured heavily in the music press and later patronized by snooty music writers who should have known better. It was difficult to avoid the growing schism between pop and rock.

The story of 1967 passed down by the rock press and related media has become received wisdom for countless recyclings of that era. Even more than the Swinging London myth, it has a reassuring familiarity, full of tales of rock revolution – the Human Be-In in San Francisco, the Technicolor Dream in London, the arrests and brief imprisonment of Mick Jagger and Keith Richards, the attempt to raise the Pentagon by the 'Armies of the Night', Haight-Ashbury, the International Monterey Pop Festival, *Sgt Pepper's*, the Maharishi Mahesh Yogi and transcendental meditation, the Summer of Love, freak-outs, love-ins and the invention of the hippie. This was counter-culture history at its epoch, yet it was far removed from the everyday experiences of pop fans, music press readers and radio listeners – particularly in Britain.

The UK singles charts – which over the previous three years had not only provided stylistic diversity but rewarded experimentation – suddenly looked rather staid. Dylan, supposedly incapacitated, but indisputably absent, was much missed. There would never be a 'Like A Rolling Stone' in the Top 10 again. Producer Phil Spector was also in psychic retreat which meant mini-masterpieces such as 'You've Lost That Lovin' Feelin'' and 'River Deep Mountain High' were now history. Even Ray Davies' old rivals the Yardbirds had mislaid the hit formula that had once brought innovation to the chart listings. Sadly, they were not alone.

The standard-bearers – the Beatles and the Rolling Stones – still Britain's top two groups – followed tradition by treating the singles charts as the high church of cultural achievement. In February, the Stones released a thrilling double A-side combining the lustful energy of 'Let's Spend The Night Together' with the madrigal melancholy of 'Ruby Tuesday'. It seemed a certain number 1 but was ultimately blocked from the top by MOR vocalist Petula Clark, whose reading of Charlie Chaplin's 'This Is My Song' sold a million. A couple of weeks later, the Beatles entered the fray with their most adventurous single to date: 'Penny Lane'/'Strawberry Fields Forever'. Amazingly, it too failed to reach the top, losing out to Engelbert Humperdinck's lachrymose 'Release Me'. A glimpse at the year's best-selling records makes salutary reading, with such artistes as Engelbert Humperdinck, Petula Clark, Vince Hill, Harry Secombe, Val Doonican and Frank and Nancy Sinatra dominating the listings. Indeed, the true chart champion of 1967 was undoubtedly Humperdinck, who returned to the top at the end of the 'summer of love' with 'The Last Waltz', whose phenomenal sales eclipsed all comers. It was nothing less than the triumph of the 'mums and dads', a target market that had never truly disappeared.

That year signalled the shift from singles to LP sales and was seen by many as a great migration whereby serious practitioners conquered a new form, commercially and aesthetically. This was at best a half-truth. The Beatles' *Sgt Pepper's Lonely Hearts Club Band* was a landmark release, a massive seller and a cultural phenomenon but so, in a very different way, was the record it supplanted at the top. *The Sound Of Music* had already celebrated its 100th week in the Top 10, most of them at number 1. It had been displaced periodically by four celebrated albums – *Help!*, *Rubber Soul*, *Aftermath* and *Revolver* – but on each occasion it had returned to the summit like a long-distance runner outlasting a sprinter. Amazingly, it did the same to *Sgt Pepper's* – thereby usurping four classic Beatles albums in a row. Like some great monolith, the soundtrack album was ever present but seldom, if ever, commented upon. It was considered irredeemably uncool, a cultural phenomenon that required no explanation or understanding. What it represented was a parallel triumph for the mums and dads in the albums listing. Nor was it an isolated success. In the same chart there were two albums by Herb Alpert & The Tijuana Brass, and best-sellers from the Seekers, Jim Reeves, Tom Jones and Mantovani. If rock revolution was in the air, then the British public was lagging behind the zeitgeist and seeking contentment in easy-listening music. It was difficult to resist the impression that a phony war was underway between two generations of pop listeners in 1967, and the early victors were those middle-aged consumers supposedly vanquished by the beat boom four years before.

This was the perplexing pop landscape into which 'Waterloo Sunset' was released in May 1967. When Ray Davies spoke about the song in terms of 'muzak' he was, consciously or not, partly responding to a demand that most of his great contemporaries would never have acknowledged. The composition had a lengthy gestation and, in common with 'You Really Got Me' and 'Dead End Street', required revisional studio work before Davies was satisfied. An early version featuring Nicky Hopkins on piano was deemed "awful" by Ray, although Shel Talmy disagreed. "There were two recorded," the producer claims. "They were the same except for the piano, and one was a bit slower than the other."

Davies insists he had supplanted Talmy as producer, working earnestly on the arrangement over several sessions. "I knew it was going to be a special record. I had the sound in my head of what it would be like. It was very easy. We recorded it over a three-week period. We went in and did the back track first, just strumming twelve-string guitar, drums and bass. [Dave] didn't play on the first back track. Then, I worked out a part with my brother all the nice little counterpoint, all the little riffs. [A] week later we went in and did the vocals. The last thing I did was the lead vocal. I had an ear infection, so we did the vocal through a speaker rather than headphones. It gives the vocal a special quality . . . You can hear a bit of the sound coming back through the speaker. That's why I sing it in a gentle way." There was a strong element of possessiveness about the recording, which puzzled its composer. "It started as a real personal song. When I finished it, I knew I'd done my best work . . . I wanted to keep it inside me, keep it for me. It's a very selfish thing and also a very stupid lack of business sense. That's why I took my time making it and I gradually let it out in small bursts because everybody had to like it in the band. Avory had to like it, Quaife, Dave . . . in the end everybody thought it was great."

The other participants acknowledge that it was a unified effort that transcended any lingering resentments about Davies' autocracy in the studio. Dave remembers discussions with Ray back at Fortis Green about the song's structure. The younger brother suggested a "slap back echo effect" similar to the guitar sound produced by Fifties players. Both Pete Quaife and Rasa were heavily involved in the construction of the 'sha la la' chorus and angelic coda. The signature use of the descending bass line introduction set the mood, allowing the song to flower in similar fashion to 'Sunny Afternoon'. However, on this occasion, there was no satirical intent, but something deeper which Ray found difficult to discuss, let alone analyse. The other Kinks did not hear the complete song until well after they had finished their parts when Davies sang them the lyrics for the first time. He invited no comment. After the single was pressed, it was premiered back in Muswell Hill in front of his discerning niece Jackie and his favourite sister Rosina (Rose) who had evidently heard his plea on 'Rosy, Won't You Please Come Home' and returned from Australia for a short holiday. Days later, Pete Quaife, visiting his local pub, noticed that several people, in response to radio play, were singing a line or two and looked happy. It augured well.

'Waterloo Sunset' remains one of the most evocative songs in the Davies canon. It is also one of his most personal statements, albeit couched in an air of mystery. The opening description of the "dirty old river" recalls Kern and Hammerstein's 'Ol' Man River' from *Show Boat* in which the river is also personified as some strangely knowing elemental force. Davies' lyric has a telescopic quality focusing from distance on to a scene seemingly beyond his reach. Like a spectator watching a staged performance, he cannot enter proceedings, only observe, reflect, appreciate and learn. At other times he resembles an omniscient but oddly vulnerable deity, disorientated by dazzling taxi lights and dizzied by the busy crowds congregating near Waterloo Station. He empathizes with his characters Terry and Julie but they too are beyond his reach. The narrator is alternately too lazy or fearful to become part of the madding crowd, but retains a voyeuristic fascination with proceedings. "I was almost making a little documentary rather than singing to the girl. I was singing from [the perspective of] the observer looking down."

The tone of Davies' narrator is gentle, loving, but disturbingly unreachable. In 'See My Friend', the speaker was left abandoned and alone with nothing but his 'friend' (or 'friends') across the river. Here, even that physical consolation has gone, replaced by a seemingly wilful separation from humanity. "I don't need no friends" he sings poignantly, rather than defiantly. It is a song of isolation and acceptance. Paradisiacal contentment is to be found in observing the sunset over Waterloo which itself becomes an almost religious meditation. In the final verse, Terry and Julie cross over the river, safe and secure in their own company and so attached that, like the narrator, they require no friends or seemingly anything else beyond the satisfaction of observing the sun setting over Waterloo.

Ray Davies was at his obfuscating best when discussing the

composition with the music press of the period. At first, he claimed it had been tentatively titled 'Liverpool Sunset' and was originally conceived as a song about the twilight of the beat boom, which had rendered redundant most of the Merseybeat acts who'd played the circuit when the Kinks first rose to fame. Even while he was putting those lyrics together, the Beatles had announced the release of their own odes to Liverpool with the double A-side 'Penny Lane'/'Strawberry Fields Forever'. "It happens a lot with my numbers," he said. "I work on a theme only to find as it nears completion someone else has come up with exactly the same melodic or lyrical idea." This incident alone evidently persuaded Davies to switch the geographical location and theme of the work. Next, he decided to write a London song. "I wanted a place that sounded good without sounding corny (like Bethnal Green)". Recalling connections with Waterloo from his student days, he enshrined its bridge as an unlikely haven of romance.

The above was the accepted story until a decade later when Davies backtracked. Weary of talking about the song, he put a new spin on the tale for a couple of American journalists. "I knew it was going to be 'Waterloo Sunset'," he claimed. "I said that thing about Liverpool Sunset because I was pissed off with certain things that were going on at the time and I just said it. It was right at the time, but when I look back on it, it's difficult to relate to now." These comments were so vague and riddled with ambiguity that it was uncertain what he was actually saying. How could the words be "right at the time" if they were indeed wrong and there never had been a 'Liverpool Sunset'?

Thirty years later, in 2006, he recanted once more, admitting that his original explanation was indeed true. "It *was* going to be called Liverpool Sunset," he confirmed. "At that stage it was about the death of Merseybeat, though subconsciously, it was probably inspired by my admiration for the Beatles . . . I sensed that the Beatles weren't going to be around long. When they moved to London, and ended up in Knightsbridge or wherever, I was still in Muswell Hill. I was loyal to my origins. Maybe I felt when they left [Liverpool] it was all over for Merseybeat."

The second circular mystery for source hunters is the origin of the song's two central characters. At different times, Davies claimed that he had tinkered with the names Mabel and George and

Bernard and Dorothy before settling on the more modern Terry and Julie. "If you look at the song as a kind of film, I suppose 'Terry' would be Terence Stamp and 'Julie' would be Julie Christie," he said. At the time, Stamp and Christie were starring in John Schlesinger's popular film adaptation of Thomas Hardy's *Far From The Madding Crowd*, so the connection was extremely topical. Unfortunately, some later journalists mistook Davies' words to mean that 'Waterloo Sunset' was *about* Terence Stamp and Julie Christie, as if they had taken time off from the film set to visit the bridge. Ray later said that if the fictional 'Terry' had to refer to somebody, it was probably his nephew Terry, the boy who had been taken to Australia by Rose and Arthur against his adolescent wishes. Not that it mattered. Within the song, the characters of Terry and Julie are undeveloped and remain phantom figures, symbolically crossing the bridge, like a thousand other people. Dave Davies reckoned that they could just as easily have represented Ray and Rasa. "Ray's never been very good at emotional things. He projects them on to characters in songs." Indeed, he was also thinking of his elder siblings. "Terry and Julie are to do with the aspirations of my sisters' generation, who grew up during World War Two and missed out on the Sixties. Sometimes when you're writing and you're on good form, you get into the frame of mind where you think, 'I can relate to *any* of these things'. It's something I learned through art school – let the ideas flow."

"I imagined it," Ray finally said of the characters and the song. "But when I imagine things I imagine the truth. It's so much better when it comes from how you imagine it than how you report it." In the end, Davies became suspicious of his own narration. "It doesn't mean anything. But when you hear the record, it means a lot. All the colours are there. I had to go into the studio and produce that record because that made up for me not being a painter. When I did the mix, I came down to Waterloo Bridge, to see if it worked. It was my substitute for not being able to paint it."

If the song was impressionistic rather than naturalistic, it was still possible to connect its parts with key events in the composer's life. Later, in self-analytical mode, he opened up about the personal aspects of the lyric which he had kept carefully hidden from the music press since the Sixties. "'Waterloo Sunset' is an accumulation of several memories . . . It's a remembrance of the time I went with my first girlfriend, who became my wife, to the Embankment and thought about our future and just absorbed the atmosphere. The other time was when I was in hospital at St Thomas' after quite a serious injury when I was a child and the view of the river and the romantic attachment I have to it. And then, as a student, I did a few months at Croydon Art School while I was waiting to go to another school and I used to get the Tube down to Charing Cross and change there. I saw a lot of the station. So it's a culmination of all my desires and hopes – it's a song about people going to a better world, but somehow I stayed where I was and became the observer in the song rather than the person who is proactive . . . I did not cross the river. They did and had a good life apparently. It's the totality of it. It's the ideas and sounds mixed together. It's a bit like an audio picture rather than a 'sonic sound' that triggers you. It allows people to interpret their own dreams within the song. And most people like to daydream. Sometimes, people's lives are so complex and difficult, they're so busy dealing with the realities of the world, they like being taken off for a week somewhere, an emotional trip with music . . . lots of people make those records."

Even while acknowledging the greatness of 'Waterloo Sunset', Davies has sometimes downplayed its importance, insisting that it "wasn't a great advance on what I'd done before". At the time of its release he was slightly offended when journalists pointed out that it was similar to the New Vaudeville Band's novelty hits, 'Winchester Cathedral' and 'Finchley Central'. "I can't see it, although *everyone* seems to mention it," he conceded. "Maybe it's because they are both place names." Even then, the comparison sounded heretical, even ludicrous, but it probably helped ground Davies. He was no doubt relieved when *Disc*'s Penny Valentine phoned to tell his managers it was the best song he would ever write, although even that could be construed as a backhanded compliment and denial of future greatness.

In his heart he knew 'Waterloo Sunset' was not perfect. Later, Davies picked at the composition, finding faults. Why had he written "I don't need *no* friends"? It sounded like Marlon Brando in *On The Waterfront*, rather than a Londoner, he complained. He was embarrassed to discover that he had repeated a rhyme

in successive lines (". . . Friday night . . . home at night") which
a more disciplined lyricist would have altered. Although the ambience worked, some of the imagery sounded forced. In describing
the hive of human habitation around Waterloo Station, he could
have made an analogy with buzzing bees or worker ants but
instead chose the ugly simile "swarming like flies" conjuring images
of excreta and rotting flesh. It was a jarring and ugly image in
the middle of an otherwise uplifting song. But few, if any, noticed
such nuances. It was akin to pointing out a smudge on *The Mona
Lisa*.

'Waterloo Sunset' climbed to number 2 in the charts, stalled
by the Tremeloes' revival of the Four Seasons' 'Silence Is Golden'.
Aesthetically, this seemed a terrible injustice, but was actually no
worse than what had happened to the Stones and the Beatles
earlier in the year. And unlike their discs, 'Waterloo Sunset' was
let down by 'Act Nice And Gentle', which broke the recent tradition of high-quality Kinks' B-sides. In America, the single did not
even reach the *Billboard* Hot 100. Its failure to reach number 1
in the UK was also underlined in the *NME*'s influential end-of-
year readers' poll where it was conspicuously absent from the
'Best British Disc This Year', where even Engelbert and the Dave
Clark Five were represented. Tellingly, there was no producer's
credit on either side of the record, evidence enough of the separation between the parties. Talmy was stoical about the loss of the
Kinks, which he described as an amicable split. "After four years
we decided it was probably a good time to do other things and
try other ways. That's basically what happened. We needed a
break from each other. It would have been nice to take a year
off and resume, but that's not the way it happened. There was
some talk [in the Seventies] of us going back and doing some
more singles but that never got resolved."

Ray remembers turning to his brother in the studio and saying:
"This producer doesn't know what he's doing." It was never a
question of technical competence, but, rather, a decline in empathy
and communication. "No disrespect, but when songs get so
personal and you can't convey those ideas . . . if you can't reach
out to that person, there's no point in having a relationship. When
I realized I could take over myself, that was a shining moment."

The break with Talmy testified to Davies' controlling nature, independent spirit and money-consciousness. Manager Robert Wace was unsurprised by it all. "The Kinks had their sound and the contribution of Shel was simply to take down the performance," he declares. "On two occasions he wanted to put out recordings by the Kinks that the act wanted to dissociate themselves from. That was part of the reason why Shel Talmy was never respected by the Kinks. If you don't have confidence in the producer you're working with, then ultimately the guy's got to go . . . There comes a time when the act resents paying the producer a percentage . . . they get fed up and want to do it themselves."

Wace's use of the plural obscures a decision that was solely the prerogative of Ray Davies. It was not without negative consequences. Even Wace admits that Talmy's departure meant there were far fewer commercial songs in the future and may have precipitated the Kinks' decline as a singles act. Under Talmy's tutelage they recorded 11 Top 10 hits in under three years – only three more would follow in his absence. If not the end of an era, it certainly represented the closure of another phase of Davies' career.

What followed was even more extraordinary. Suddenly, Davies was in retreat mode once again. "I went out with Grenville and Robert, my managers, and said, 'Look I've done 'Waterloo Sunset', what more do you want? I've done all these records, singles and I want to do something else.' They said, 'Well, old boy, just keep giving us singles, and we'll see if anything comes along.' I was kind of bored with what I was doing and, looking back now, it would have been a good time to call a halt to the band for a bit because Dave was doing quite well and I should have gone off and done other things. I'm not sure what happened to prevent that."

In fact, Davies had made a bid for freedom within a fortnight of the release of 'Waterloo Sunset'. While promoting the record, he expressed a wish to curtail performances with the Kinks and possibly employ a stand-in, as they had done the previous year with Mick Grace. This would leave him free to concentrate his energies on songwriting and production in a similar way to Brian Wilson, who was no longer touring with the Beach Boys. "I still intend to sing on the Kinks' records," Davies added, "because my work is written around the group. There is no question of my severing *all* connections with them. It's possible I may also undertake work of an individual nature as long as it does not conflict with my interests in the Kinks." This sounded suspiciously like a resignation note and it was no surprise when the *New Musical Express* offered the headline: 'Ray Davies Quitting The Kinks?' An exasperated Robert Wace was forced to issue a denial and, days later, Ray telephoned the music paper with a terse message: "It is difficult to find a substitute for a lead singer. So I will appear on Kinks shows." As a commitment of faith, it sounded hollow at best.

CHAPTER TWENTY-TWO

HIGH COURT DRAMA

While Ray Davies was considering his future in the Kinks, his nemesis Larry Page was readying himself for their battle royal in the High Courts of Justice. Since his split from Davies, Page had guided the career of the Troggs, who had already enjoyed three massive hits in 1966 with 'Wild Thing', 'With A Girl Like You' and 'I Can't Control Myself'. The last had appeared on Larry's own label Page One Records, confirming his entrepreneurial expansionism at this crucial juncture. This time around, Page ensured that he produced the act, co-wrote their B-sides and was even more heavily involved in their image and publicity. For Davies, it must have been a daunting proposition to confront an adversary at the height of his powers, the more so given Kassner's involvement as the aggrieved publisher. Davies' determination to extract himself and the Kinks from Page's Denmark Productions and thereby break the publishing arrangement with Eddie Kassner would prove one of the most important and stressful decisions of his professional life.

The court case commenced on 23 May 1967 and featured a procession of witnesses including the management, publisher, accountant, road manager and, of course, all four Kinks. It was a tense time. "I had to spend three to four hours in the bath every night trying to get my facts and dates together," Page remembers. On the steps of the High Court, the Kinks were their usual knockabout selves, but betrayed a more mannered appearance in front of the presiding Judge Widgery (who later became Lord

Chief Justice). "The Kinks on the witness stand were not the same as the Kinks on tour," Page wryly notes. "The Kinks in the court room were suddenly nice boys, with nice suits and haircuts, perfect gentlemen."

There were several light moments during the hearing, as is often the case when pop music is placed under the judicial microscope. Page recalls feeling puzzled during his cross-examination when opposing counsel alleged that he had referred to Grenville Collins as "a burn". "I said, 'Do you by any chance mean a 'burke' – as in *Burke's Peerage?*'"

For Ray Davies, the most amusing aspect of the case was the prospect of witnessing Mick Avory take the stand. That, at least, promised to provide some humiliating comedy, the equivalent of a taciturn schoolboy being interrogated by a stern headmaster. As it turned out, Avory's saturnine countenance and plain honesty made him an unlikely star witness. He was the only member of the group questioned specifically about Larry Page's alleged abandonment of the Kinks in America. In what could easily have been damaging evidence for Davies' side, Avory confirmed that he had not been bothered nor objected to Page's departure and had assumed the manager had pressing business to attend to back in London.

When Page took the stand he was calm and restrained, always a wise move according to seasoned litigants and learned counsel. "I could have been vindictive," he says, perhaps feeling he missed a chance to launch some brickbats at the opposition. The Davies brothers, more easily goaded than Page or Avory, found it more difficult to remain emotionally calm. Dave recalls lapsing into histrionics at one moment, pointing theatrically in the direction of Kassner and Page, like a person in a televised courtroom drama. His brother was impressed by his confidence. Ray's evidence included details of the moment he burst into the session when Page was recording 'I Go To Sleep' with Sonny & Cher in London after returning from America. In a devastating comment against his former manager, he testified: "I hated him . . . because he made a promise to me, he had broken it, and left the group high and dry and it seems he rushed back making deals everywhere with our songs with other people, and I was disgusted with him."

Robert Wace, who also appeared in the witness box, remembers

Judge Widgery unravelling the complex subtexts involving management and publishing. "The crux of the case was that Page broke the fiduciary trust between the parties. The relationship had broken down. There was no goodwill or trust between the parties. Kassner started the lawsuit because he wished to hang on to the publishing rights. That's what the lawsuit was all about. It had nothing to do with management. Kassner would have set aside the claims of commission for live gigs and records. That was peanuts. Music publishing – that's what it was all about. The judge turned around and said precisely that. It took him four days to find out. The penny dropped."

Indeed, the learned Widgery pointed out that Denmark Productions did not appear to be particularly interested in the 10 per cent management clause or even in claiming any damages. Although as a company they did not obtain commission from placing Davies' songs with any particular publisher, Kassner's role as chief shareholder ensured that he stood to make a substantial profit from such material if he controlled the placing rights. Page himself admitted in evidence that, without the publishing clause, the 10 per cent would not have been adequate. Indeed, he had received a substantially increased remuneration for handing Davies' songs to Kassner after the chart success of 'You Really Got Me'. Davies, of course, was aware that Kassner was handling his songs and had assigned them over one by one himself, making a lot of money as a result. While Page claimed he was motivated by the loss of the 10 per cent management commission, the judge accepted that the publishing clause was the real bone of contention.

His Honour Judge Widgery conceded that Page was largely responsible for transforming the Kinks' earnings into the £90,000-a-year bracket and decreed that several comments casting aspersions on his conduct were "unfounded and not justified at all". Nevertheless, he responded positively to Davies' aggrieved words on the stand, which he alluded to in his summing-up. "It was not until I saw the four members of the group in the witness box that I began to realize the seriousness of what Mr Page had done. Mr Page knew the group intimately, and could have foreseen their reaction. By his action, he destroyed the trust that was vital for the continuance of a relationship between them."

Nevertheless, several objections put forward by Boscobel's counsel left the judge unimpressed. The argument that the original contract was invalid because of the Kinks' "infancy" was dismissed as Widgery concluded that they were mature enough to sign such an agreement. Similarly, the suggestion that the group had been unaware of or did not approve of the assignment of publishing rights to Denmark Productions was considered "absurd". However, after reviewing all the evidence, Judge Widgery concluded that Denmark Productions' contract with Boscobel Productions was 'frustrated' and no longer tenable. Page's £6,000 court bid, as the press noted, had failed.

If the Kinks left court in victorious mood, any celebrations were short-lived. Page and Kassner were unwilling to accept defeat, even at the hands of a High Court judge, and an appeal was immediately lodged. Page vowed that he would return stronger than ever and take the case all the way to the House of Lords, if necessary. Nor was this mere bluster. Judge Widgery's ruling on 'frustration', a defence that Boscobel had only included in an amendment less than 24 hours before the action, was clearly open to question. The doctrine of 'frustration' was generally applied to contracts which become impossible to perform due to some supervening event, such as war, flood or famine, for which neither party is responsible. Was that applicable in this instance? It was one of several issues that Denmark Productions' counsel felt could be overruled. It would be another year before the case would wind its way to the Appeal Court.

Larry Page was haunted by Ray Davies' comments in court. Even a decade and a half later, he still felt embittered about the way his relationship with the group had ended. In private moments, he recalled conversations he'd had with Eddie Kassner and Phil Solomon, older and harder men, whose cynicism and love of realpolitik had made them successful in a cut-throat business. "I was always told in the music business that the artiste is always the enemy, they're animals. I was told this with the Kinks as well and I used to say, 'No, not these boys – they're different.' At the end of the day, it proved to be right. It did. They were the enemy, and they did turn out to be animals. The sad thing was that I still admired Ray like mad as a writer and performer. And the group too – I loved the boys; I really did. They were just pricks as human beings. That was the terrible thing. When it came to treating people with respect, they just didn't like it. People were treated like dirt."

Sam Curtis, the vivacious road manager who had testified on behalf of Page and Denmark Productions, concurred. "They always spoke to people like dirt, including me. These people, the Davies brothers, are exceptional. *Very* exceptional. They are exceptional for their talent and they are exceptional for their *grossness*. They think that their talent entitles them to live in a world of unconventional disorder."

While Judge Widgery had been preparing his summing-up, the Kinks flew over to Northern Ireland for a show at Belfast's Starlite Ballroom. There, they were greeted by Ursula Graham-White, an attractive, statuesque scenester and art student, who invited them to stay at her parents' palatial home. The daughter of a Second World War spy, psychiatrist and university lecturer, Ursula was the type of upmarket girl who would have appealed to Dave Davies, while her arty background meant she had much in common with Ray. That summer, she was renting a house with several other girls in Belfast's Fitzroy Avenue, a haven and 'crash pad' for several of the city's hipper musicians. A frequent visitor was Van Morrison, who spent time there with Ursula's musician boyfriend and later husband, Mick Cox. Almost every weekend there was a party and the Davies brothers were invited to drop by before they returned to England for a show in Bristol. The party turned out to be a premiere of sorts for *Sgt Pepper's Lonely Hearts Club Band* which had been released that very day. They all sat around listening to the album, amazed by its innovation and caught up in the zeitgeist, knowing that, across the water in London clubland and in the homes of the hip, everyone was doing precisely the same.

Ray Davies also listened to *Sgt Pepper's* at Fitzroy Avenue but remained obstinately unmoved. The previous year he had been lukewarm about *Revolver* and betrayed a similar disdain for this new work that the world was praising. Although he admired the Beatles, his competitive instincts meant he could never love them. Indeed, he seemed to avoid consciously listening to their latest songs, as if fearful that they might contaminate or influence his own ideas. Rasa remembers him composing on the piano, while she was doing the washing-up in the kitchen and listening to the radio. "Whenever the Beatles came on, he'd say, 'Can you turn that off, please?' He didn't like me listening to the Beatles. I think there was a rivalry there. He wouldn't be complimentary. No way."

Sgt Pepper's was an instant cultural phenomenon and its closing track, 'A Day In The Life', attracted lavish praise as the most ambitious and probably greatest achievement ever realized by a popular music group. Ray Davies said nothing, merely giving the impression that he regarded the work as overrated. In a subsequent interview, he even lampooned the Beatles by suggesting that the Kinks were busily working on a song titled 'A Hole In The Sock Of'. In keeping with those serious times, some people assumed that he was not joking and waited in vain for a mock epic that never appeared.

June 1967 was also the month of Monterey, the celebrated Californian pop festival that many saw as the ultimate flowering of youth culture and proof positive of pop's evolution into rock. Ray Davies claims that the Kinks were approached via their management, but could not appear due to their visa problems. No one else has confirmed this, but considering the festival was a non-profit venture and performers were expected to appear without a fee, it seems unlikely that Davies would have been interested. Among its other achievements, Monterey made Jimi Hendrix a star in his homeland and also transformed the career of the Who, paving the way for their conquest of America. Once again, Pete Townshend – without any conscious intention of doing so – had stolen Davies' thunder. Suddenly, the Kinks seemed more distant than ever from America – a near forgotten group who could not even secure airplay for a song of the quality of 'Waterloo Sunset'. Their world had diminished.

Summer solace was provided courtesy of Dave Davies who surprised his home nation with a solo single that climbed to number 3. 'Death Of A Clown' represented the younger brother's coming of age. He had recently secretly married his pregnant Danish girlfriend Lisbet Thorkil-Petersen and bought a house in Cockfosters for £9,000, but still acted like a young buck on a stag night, draining the last dregs of celebrity fame. 'Death Of A Clown' could be traced back to a saturnalian night of London clubbing after which the revellers were left strewn across the floor. When Dave awoke, bleary-eyed and stomach sick, he could hear 'See My Friend' playing in the background. Still disorientated, he interpreted the song as a mocking rebuke. Perusing the hung-over slumberers, he concluded that they were predominantly syco-phants, an adjunct to the rave scene of which he was the central cog. Life had become a circus in which he was cast as the perpetual clown. That notion was still in his head when he visited his mother in Denmark Terrace soon after. While tinkering on the front-room piano, a melody emerged along with the chorus: "let's all drink to the death of a clown". Encouraged by his brother, he persevered with the composition, expanding the circus imagery with images of a dead fortune-teller, a cowardly lion and a muted tiger. It sounded special. Ray added a bridge, then momentarily misplaced the lyrics, which were later found among his collection of old income tax forms. A session was immediately booked and the results were impressive. Rasa, uncredited as ever, provided a beautiful 'la la la la' soprano chorus which added an emotional depth to the song. At one point, she wandered alarmingly off-key, but somehow it added to the vulnerability of the composition. Ray was responsible for the ambient opening, plucking the strings from inside his Steinway piano with a guitar pick. The other highlight was Dave's drawled, slightly cracked, vocal which several critics decided was distinctly Dylanesque.

By now, the song was an obvious candidate for the group's forthcoming album, but nothing more. The younger brother had never sung lead on a Kinks' A-side and that was unlikely to change. Ray then recalled an odd incident from the past that caused a major rethink. At one ballroom date, Dave had sung 'Come On Now' (the B-side of 'Tired Of Waiting For You') and after the show a female fan happened to say: "He's a really good singer." Ray politely concurred, prompting the retort: "Well, why don't you let him sing all the time then?" Perhaps Dave deserved such a chance, albeit not under the group name. Soon afterwards, he was surprised to receive a call from Robert Wace enthusing about the possibility of issuing 'Death Of A Clown' as a single credited to 'Dave Davies'. "Robert would sometimes tell me things that Ray had said to him, but not to me. I think that was such an instance."

When 'Death Of A Clown' rapidly climbed the charts, the normally brash Dave became uncharacteristically nervous. Booked to mime on BBC's *Top Of The Pops*, he fretted unnecessarily and had to be reassured by his wife Lisbet that he would be fine. His appearance was one of the most memorable cameos of that summer. Dressed in a gold-braided three-quarter length coat, he resembled nothing less than a modern-day cavalier. Even when disc jockey Alan Freeman inadvertently introduced him as '*Ray Davies*' on a repeat performance, it did not spoil his victory. When the single threatened number 1, he sounded more relieved than triumphant. "I think if it had been a miss, a lot of people in the business would have been pleased. I've had the feeling for a long time that I was regarded by some people as just coasting along without offering very much. People used to think that all I wanted to do was rely on Ray and the group all the time. This record will change that, I hope."

When asked about the single's success, Ray sounded like a proud parent rather than an elder brother. "I do feel responsible for Dave because he's nervous and completely irresponsible himself. But this record has given him a lot of confidence." Years later, in darker times, Dave suspected that his competitive brother may have been resentful or jealous of the single's impressive chart position. "When it was mentioned or people patted me on the back, he always pointed out that 'Waterloo Sunset' had been a hit *before* 'Death Of A Clown'. One half of him wanted me to do it and the other half was worried in case it *did* work." Whether this was true or not, Ray's public comments at the time were invariably upbeat and supportive.

In September, *Something Else By The Kinks* was released. Its apparently throwaway title is a subtle tribute to Eddie Cochran whose 1959 single 'Something Else' had been a favourite of both brothers. In common with *Face To Face*, the work represents Ray Davies' flowering as a songwriter capable of sustaining an array of lyrical themes across an entire album. The bewildering but fascinating subject matter features mini-stories of schoolday nostalgia, homoeroticism, homeownership, nicotine addiction, cricket and sun worship. Musically, the eclecticism is equally breathtaking with flashes of psychedelia, hard rock, music hall, flamenco, folk and vaudeville. Arguably, *Something Else* is the most varied album in the entire Kinks' oeuvre, not least because Dave Davies is allowed an unprecedented number of songwriting contributions at a time when his muse is alight with ideas. In addition to the great 'Death Of A Clown', he offers a return to the group's rhythmic roots with 'Love Me Till The Sun Shines' and the hard-rocking 'Funny Face' ("a weird song about a guy who falls in love with a girl who is a lunatic."). One of the reasons these songs work so well is the undisclosed subtext. Both are disguised narratives about his frustration and pain over the loss of Sue Sheehan and the daughter he had never seen. The subject matter, obliquely expressed, contains a passion peculiar to that youthful voice and conspicuously absent from his later mid-period work. Within the context of *Something Else* these songs serve the dual purpose of enlivening the album with a harder edge and complementing Ray's more subtle and wide-ranging meditations.

Ray recognized his brother's contributions more charitably than he had in the past or would in the future. He was even inspired to write an allegory of their relationship in 'Two Sisters'. "I was twenty [something] and married . . . but Dave had a wilder life-style. I had my moments but, obviously, I can't talk about them . . . I looked at that situation I was in, particularly when we had a child, and I wrote 'Two Sisters' and the relationship with him having freedom and me having a house and responsibility. I made that work in a song." With a classical backing of harpsichord, cello and viola, Davies' domestic drama tells a simple tale of sibling rivalry, reconciled only when the sensible one (Priscilla) recognizes her own value as a parent with loving children. In a deft piece of characterization, Davies names the wayward, hedonistic sister Sibylla, conjuring images of the fabulously hip London club of the same title.

'David Watts', the album's startling opening song, also alludes vaguely to recent events, cheekily namechecking the homosexual major who had attempted to 'purchase' the younger brother after a show in Rutland. Beyond the teasing title, there is little to connect the actual David Watts with the narrative which owes much of its inspiration to memories of a talented schoolfriend from the William Grimshaw era. Davies ably captures the wonder of adolescent hero-worship in the hagiographical portrait of the protagonist – a sportsman, scholar, school captain and sex symbol, so noble and purely bred that he even avoids the advances of female admirers. It is also a song of envy, with the ever-frugal songwriter fantasizing: "I wish all his money belonged to me".

Musical diversity is evident on the contrasting 'No Return', a reflection on first love with a delightfully understated bossa nova rhythm, recalling Antonio Carlos Jobim. The rumbustious 'Harry Rag' (cockney rhyming slang for a cigarette – 'fag') follows, an arrangement that appears to be based on a sea shanty, complete with hearty cries and a rousing singalong, simultaneously warning and celebrating the effects of nicotine dependency from the point of view of the stoical smoker.

Satirical songs are also present, as expected. 'Situation Vacant' recalls the house-hunting narratives on *Face To Face*. In this alternate scenario, the beleaguered husband Johnny, browbeaten by an overbearing mother-in-law, seeks a better job but ends up losing his home and wife. Even the 'big fat momma' allusion from 'Sunny Afternoon' is diminished into a 'little momma' here. A warning against the dangers of social mobility, the song also keys into fears about the responsibility of homeownership. The composition is preceded by the more puzzling 'Tin Soldier Man', a brass-laden marching tune with the same condescending ambivalence as 'Mister Pleasant'. Davies' vocal follows the tuba's distinctive 'oompah' in what superficially resembles a modern reworking of 'The Grand Old Duke Of York' in miniature. With military fashions suddenly in vogue among the pop elite – including, of course, Dave Davies' cavalier regalia – Ray's polite satire on tin soldier conformity pinpricks the pomposity of his hipper contemporaries.

Those misguided commentators who had dared compare 'Waterloo Sunset' with the New Vaudeville Band's 'Winchester Cathedral' would probably claim prescient justification after listening to 'End Of The Season', the most vaudevillian of all Davies' compositions. Originally written in the weeks after his 1966 breakdown, it seeks idyllic distraction in the comfort of the pavilion. "It's about a cricket player," Davies says. "The cricket season's over, his girlfriend's gone to Greece and he's going to take up rugby . . . I really must have gone crazy!" Its allusive sound effects of birds chirping clearly date the song as an outtake from *Face To Face*. The Noël Coward persona that Davies uses to voice his satires on songs of quintessentially upper-class manners continues on 'Afternoon Tea', a nostalgic tale of platonic love among the tea rooms.

'Lazy Old Sun', the oddest and most experimental song on *Something Else*, owes its ambience to the use of the mellotron – a keyboard-operated cabinet including tape loops of brass, string and wind instruments, which the Hollies' Graham Nash had first introduced to Davies earlier that year. The singer's voice fades in and out of the track and the raga drone is complemented by a brass accompaniment more suited to a spaghetti western. "The song just didn't come off really," Davies says. "I didn't like a lot of the lines." Inconclusive musings on the meaning of the sun complete a rare example of Davies fully embracing contemporary psychedelia.

Something Else ends on a high note with 'Waterloo Sunset', but, despite the presence of two hit singles, sales were much lower than expected. It was disconcerting evidence that the Kinks were in danger of being shunted from the Sixties' high table in the new age of the album. Despite Davies' standing as a songwriter of distinction, the Kinks were still regarded by critics and audiences as a singles outfit whose natural habitat was the local dance hall or Granada cinema circuit. While the progressive bands that were emerging in 1967 played smaller, intimate venues or paraded their hip credibility on festival bills, the Kinks remained essentially a pop group. Pye Records realized as much and probably exacerbated that image by rushing out another budget album, *Sunny Afternoon*, on their cheap as chips imprint, Marble Arch. That November the pound was devalued by 14.3 per cent and it might be said that the Kinks' reputation as an albums band was devalued by a similar amount. It is doubtful that Ray Davies fully understood this at the time. If Louis Benjamin could be accused of being cheapskate with the Kinks' catalogue, Ray was of similar mind. When questioned about the budget release, his familiar frugality blinded him to any deeper implications. "I must say I'm pleased at all the low price albums coming on to the market – and that goes for the other Kinks, too. Hope the trend goes on and I think it will. It means lots of good 'buys' for the fans."

Sunny Afternoon went on to reach the Albums Top 10 in the run-up to Christmas, a substantial seller that eclipsed memories of the more important *Something Else*. It was a worrying development.

CHAPTER TWENTY-THREE

THE CABARET SEASON

The pressure to provide a follow-up to the formidable 'Waterloo Sunset' had been alleviated by the unexpected success of 'Death Of A Clown', but five months had now passed since the public had warmed to a new Kinks single. That long silence was broken in October 1967 with the release of 'Autumn Almanac', a deceptively understated composition that was nevertheless commercial enough to climb as high as number 5 (*NME*), ultimately outselling the more famous 'Waterloo Sunset'. It confirmed that the Kinks were still a major singles act with an inventive edge.

Disc jockeys and reviewers appreciated 'Autumn Almanac' as a pleasant sing-along with a quirky lyric, but it was far more than this. The song is debatably Davies' most carefully constructed composition, a veritable triptych in which each symbol and stanza combines to create an intensely visual experience. Like a director filming a nature documentary, rather than a pop songwriter producing a hit record, Davies daringly sets the scene with a close-focus image of a caterpillar crawling from a dew-soaked hedge at the break of dawn. It is an audacious opening for a supposedly commercial single, eschewing character or action in favour of a slow, almost static portrayal that is most remarkable for its ordinariness. Who else would dream of beginning a song with something as unsexy as a caterpillar? The composer describes the changing colour of autumn leaves, accelerating the alliteration and offering a precision of detail that is both thought-provoking and picturesque. He does not seek or imply profundity when presenting these images or suggest any deep symbolism or subtle subtext. Instead, summer's surrender to autumn is conveyed via the literally heart-warming application of hot tea accompanied by toasted currant buns. The lack of self-consciousness is refreshing. "That was the real step forward as far as I was concerned," Davies says. "I was writing about things I liked, rather than what I thought I ought to be writing about. It was inspired by the guy who did my garden. He'd say things like, 'Better get the leaves up', which was so wonderfully ordinary that I thought I should just start writing about normal everyday life in my songs."

The second verse features an endearingly evocative description of the leisure rituals of the working classes: Saturday football, Sunday roast dinner and holidays in Blackpool. It sounds like a reassuringly unchanged world, a setting equally applicable to his father's generation. Using the mellotron to create a brass backing, redolent of a Salvation Army band, Davies sings along in onomatopoeic fashion, like a child modulating his voice in imitation of a happy tune.

In the chorus, he playfully assumes the persona of the gardener, a hunchbacked figure from his childhood whom he later employed after purchasing the house in Fortis Green. "As I got to know him and learned about his love of gardens and plants I got to admire him. It's a song about seasons and people living with the world around them and being in touch with everything." His character's spine problems naturally recall his own tribulations during childhood. In a knowing message to family and friends, he includes a line about his "poor rheumatic back", provoking sympathy and smiles while staying in character. In subsequent interviews, he voiced valid satisfaction at the idea of incorporating the word 'rheumatic' in a pop single. This was, if anything, an understatement. Caterpillars, currant buns and roast beef were equally odd fare at the time. Even the song's title was unique. How many pop songs before 1967 had ever included the word 'almanac', in relation to autumn or anything else?

Davies' appreciation of 'native culture' was key to his development as a songwriter. With 'Autumn Almanac' he was not merely retreating into the parochial domesticity of Fortis Green, but expressing an essential Englishness that would heavily influence his work for the remainder of the decade. It was simultaneously a journey back to his childhood, to those memories of post-war austerity, the 1951 Festival of Britain, and trying to watch *Nineteen Eighty-Four* on television. In fact, George Orwell had pre-empted Davies in 'England Your England', an essay published in 1941 that described this native sensibility in terms that were echoed in 'Autumn Almanac'. Pondering the essential *privateness* of English life, Orwell wrote: "We are a nation of flower-lovers, but also a nation of stamp-collectors, pigeon-fanciers, amateur carpenters, coupon-snippers, darts-players, crossword-puzzle fans. All the culture that is truly native centres round things which even when they are communal are not official – the pub, the football match, the back garden, the fireside and the 'nice cup of tea'. The liberty of the individual is still believed in, almost as in the nineteenth century . . . It is the liberty to have a home of your own, to do what you like in your spare time, to choose your own amusements instead of having them chosen for you from above."

It would be easy to accuse Davies of finding comfort in old-world nostalgia or attempting to recreate the England that Orwell was observing from the perspective of 1941. However, 'Autumn Almanac', for all its garden cosiness, was also a timely reminder and an accurate reflection of the everyday lives of countless 'ordinary' people, many of whom had been untouched by the youth revolution. Sixties stylists, caught up in the insular glamour of their own milieu, were hardly likely to have noticed that a hobby as seemingly mundane as gardening had actually reached unprecedented levels of popularity in England. As suburbia expanded, garden centres sprouted exponentially; allotments were still carefully cultivated by the retired or newly married; and the BBC prepared the launch of the hugely popular programme, *Gardeners' World*.

Ray Davies, as best he could, continued to live between these different worlds: a dreamy husband rhapsodizing about home and garden; a celebrated pop star and regular on *Top Of The Pops*; and a frustrated film-maker with ambitions above his station. The class divide, so marked in his youth, had become blurred by wealth and homeownership. He still saw himself as a socialist, albeit one without much political conviction or engagement. He didn't vote, but connected with the people in his own way through his songwriting. On the terraces of Highbury, football supporters and pop fans chanted "Everton are going to crack, it's all part of the Arsenal attack" to the tune of 'Autumn Almanac'. As a regular attendee, Davies must have taken immense satisfaction in hearing his song transformed in such fashion. He connected with the man described so eloquently in 'Autumn Almanac' – but with certain reservations. Holidays in Blackpool (or indeed Torquay) no longer appealed and roast beef on Sundays was now off the menu. "I'm going off meat," he told an interviewer of the time. "Look at the people in this restaurant. You can always tell the people who eat rare meat all their lives. As they get older they begin to look like pigs – fleshy jowls, large ringed eyes like in the Hogarth paintings and little piggy eyes." Several years later, he would become a vegetarian, although his interrogator noted that he was eating scampi during this meditation on meat eaters.

In November, Dave Davies reappeared with a startling follow-up to 'Death Of A Clown'. 'Suzanah's Still Alive' (aka 'Susannah's Still Alive'), written entirely by the younger brother, is a treasured adjunct to the Kinks' discography that daringly displays the group's versatility during this incredibly productive phase. The rollicking piano drives the song, accented by Quaife's pulsating bass and Ray's wild harmonica playing. Dave provides one of his most exuberant vocals in a frantic performance and powerhouse production, complete with acerbic, flagellating lyrics. Asked about the song he claimed it was based on a book he had read "about a bird who never had any luck with the blokes". This was obfuscation worthy of his brother. Decades later, he admitted that it was another coded message to his muse Susan Sheehan, made more explicit by the adaptation of her name in the song's title. In a remarkable example of psychological transference, 'Suzanah' seems to merge into Dave Davies himself. The sexual allusions and references to the ameliorating effects of whisky and gin tell us more about his pop star life than the character he imagines trapped between bed covers, pining for a companion. He sings this song of suppressed pain with a combination of anger and exuberance – as if railing against the gods. The single proved a modest success, peaking at number 20.

As Ray Davies has frequently acknowledged, this was Dave Davies' time. A separate solo career was not only possible, but palpable. After two hit singles, Pye were keen for an album and a series of concerts were booked for the New Year. Then, everything unravelled. The shows were cancelled without explanation and the much-touted solo album was never fully completed. A third single, 'Lincoln County', a spirited, high-quality performance with a clever western theme, was delayed and postponed in order not to conflict with the Kinks' release schedule. By the time it came out the following summer, Dave sounded not only insecure but desperate. "I want people to know what's in me," he told the *NME*'s Richard Green. "I want to be taken seriously, but people never will. It's hard to say that to anyone . . . This record is all I've got in me, if people don't like it . . . do you think people might not like it? They must like it because I'm a normal person and it's a normal song. I will give up if people don't like it. If it gets into the Top 20 that'd be OK. Even if a few people I like play it, I won't mind. This is the first record I've done on my own that I've really believed in." Confirming his worst fears, the single received little or no airplay and failed to register on the charts. A fourth single, 'Hold My Hand', suffered a similar fate and nothing further would be heard of Dave Davies solo star for the next 11 years.

What had happened? Nobody knew for sure, not even Dave. He had always appeared confident, almost reckless, but when presented with the challenge of establishing a solo career he retreated into himself. "I didn't really want the responsibility," he now says. But it was more than that. In spite of past conflicts, the two brothers found it difficult to operate without the other in a professional setting. They had become an interdependent unit. Distance and friction could not destroy that fraternal bond – and the brothers each perceived the Kinks as an extension of their family, even at its most dysfunctional. Perhaps if the brothers had been at extreme loggerheads during this stage, either might have found the courage to pull away. Ironically, this was one of their calmer phases together and that most unlikely of adjectives 'supportive' was used on more than one occasion to describe their interaction. So it was that Dave squandered his best opportunity to establish a separate identity, a decision that he would have cause to regret by the mid-Seventies. For many fans, his abandoned solo album became one of the great lost artefacts of the era. That joyous sense of discovery in his songwriting would never be fully rekindled. When he finally got his chance to complete a solo album in 1980, he was a different person, responding to changing circumstances. Having played the frustrated sideman to so many of his brother's quirkier theatrical concepts, he no longer had much patience for musical subtlety, preferring to sacrifice himself on the altar of heavy metal and hard-rock bombast.

Ray Davies was also gripped by indecision throughout this period. Over the past year there had been desultory talk of a solo project, but little more. At least Dave had released singles and appeared on *Top Of The Pops*; Ray's breakaway effort stayed firmly inside his imagination. He found an alternate outlet for his songwriting when BBC 1 commissioned him to provide a series of topical songs for *At The Eleventh Hour*, an 'experimental programme' combining satire, comedy, poetry and pop. Davies' songs would be performed by resident singer Jeannie Lamb, backed by an orchestra. The discipline required to compose a song a week based around a specific news item was a challenge to be relished. It was rather like being transposed to New York's Brill Building, home of Tin Pan Alley where pop's great songwriters toiled in office booths, tirelessly producing material like factory workers on an assembly line. Davies' first effort, broadcast on 30 December, was the charity questioning 'You Can't Give More Than What You Have' followed by the post-festive 'If Christmas Day Could Last Forever'.

On New Year's Day, Ray Davies awoke to a news story that might have sprung fully formed from his own imagination. Five predominantly teenage typists at a ventilation and heating company in suburban Surbiton were reacting to the country's current economic malaise by giving up their tea break and working that half-hour for no pay. Hundreds of workers at the factory were ready to follow their lead in a campaign called 'I'm Backing Britain'. Thousands of Union Jack badges advertising that message were printed and, before long, everyone seemed caught up in the craze. A movement of sorts was born as workers throughout Britain offered support. Newspapers and politicians praised the young workers for rekindling the spirit of the Blitz. Prime Minister Harold Wilson and opposition leader Edward Heath both sent messages of support. Economists were consulted about whether the extra working time would affect productivity or the balance of payments. Trade union heads, fearful of their members being financially exploited, naturally voiced caution. An impressionable public, still full of New Year cheer and well-intentioned resolutions, decried the union leaders as either unpatriotic or humourless spoilsports. Their objections made little difference. In the end, recalcitrant shop stewards were brought into line and a clampdown by the more powerful unions meant that 'I'm Backing Britain' was history.

However, for a few weeks at least it seemed that the country had been acting out a scene from *I'm All Right, Jack*. The naive optimism of 'I'm Backing Britain' summed up a time when even a handful of young, working-class typists in suburbia could challenge the nation and get a reaction. All this greatly appealed to Ray Davies as it linked several of his hobby horses in one package. His disillusionment with trade unions (evident since his school-leaving days and later voiced in the song 'Get Back In Line'), his ever-present fascination with suburbia and the lives of everyday people, and speculations on the state of modern Britain were all subjects perfectly suited to his songwriting. Inspired, he rushed off his own 'I'm Backing Britain' for the 13 January edition of *At The Eleventh Hour*. His satire was parodied in the pop marketplace by fellow Pye artiste Jackie Trent who, along with songwriter husband Tony Hatch, composed 'We're Backing Britain' for the evergreen showbiz entertainer Bruce Forsyth.

That same weekend, a 'new' Kinks album appeared: *Live At Kelvin Hall*. Recorded at the Glasgow venue on April Fool's Day the previous year, it was already an anachronistic artefact, totally out of place in the heavier rock environment of 1968. Almost wilfully amateurish in its execution it captures, in brutal *audio-vérité*, the sound of a typical pop concert of the time, complete with fluffed notes, strained vocals and the constant, undulating bombardment of teenage screams. Responding to the baying cries, the Kinks occasionally rouse themselves on the upbeat numbers like 'You're Looking Fine' before surrendering 'Sunny Afternoon' as a sacrificial sing-along. Oddly, less attention is paid to the music than the swirling shrieks, which rise and fall as if trapped in a tape loop. Further lack of care is evident from the shoddy sleeve which erroneously credits 'All Day And All Of The Night' instead of 'Till The End Of The Day'. It could almost pass as rock's first bootleg in terms of quality, but remains a fascinating curio, whose redeeming feature is the frantic closing medley of 'Milk Cow Blues', 'Tired Of Waiting For You' and the 'Batman Theme'. "I'm still trying to justify that album now," Davies joked, over a decade later. "I think it was a good example of what it was like at a rock concert then. It may have 'historic' value. You've got to understand that for two or three years I never heard myself playing. No monitors . . . and with the audience, it was just a wall of sound . . . The pressure was enormous."

Davies diligently delivered his weekly quota of songs for *At The Eleventh Hour*, a list that included 'Poor Old Intellectual Sadie', 'Just A Poor Country Girl', 'The Man Who Conned Dinner From The Ritz' and 'This Is What The World Is All About'. A report on a suicide, 'Did You See His Name', was later attempted by the Kinks and there was a gentle satire of 64-year-old Malcolm Muggeridge, the intellectual broadcaster, journalist and Christian convert who had resigned as rector of Edinburgh University in protest against the Student Representative Council's unedifying interest in contraceptive pills and pot. Muggeridge, a brave, complex and sometimes contrary figure with a slightly quizzical demeanour, had been a comrade of George Orwell before the war and shared his interest and later disillusionment with Communism after visiting Russia as a correspondent. "I read up quite a bit about him," Davies claimed, "but I couldn't write anything against him for some reason. I just felt he was getting on. So I wrote 'Could Be You're Getting Old'. Never named him, but Muggeridge was who it was about." If Davies truly had 'read up' on Muggeridge, he would also have learned that he had been a good friend of Kim Philby, the double agent whose son John he knew from Hornsey College of Arts and Crafts.

Ray Davies' extracurricular interests meant that the Kinks were out of action during the early months of 1968. The previous spring, a prophetic Pete Quaife had announced: "We don't want to push ourselves as a popular group any more. To push yourself is death. The group has terrific contrasts in personalities and it's part of our success. It's probably one of the most physically violent groups. It doesn't take much to get us going. One wrong word and you walk away with a black eye. We haven't got many friends in showbusiness." Since Quaife's comment, the reduction in the number of live concerts and the sudden rise of Dave Davies as a solo star brought a new stability to the group. Ray and Dave, always a volatile combination, had been communicating well and supporting each other. Unfortunately, this meant that they required another outlet to release the suppressed aggression that could never be contained for long.

When the group reconvened for a one-off show in Coventry, Quaife was wearing a plaster cast on his arm. He informed the music press that he had suffered a fall at his north London home but the truth was he had broken his wrist after a contretemps with Dave. Neither party ever spoke publicly about the scuffle and Dave apparently excised it from his memory banks for ever more. It was a timely reminder of the dangers of coming between the brothers, even when they were seemingly at peace. "To be honest I was too damn scared at the end," Quaife later admitted. "The stress of being with those two was too much. They were a very dangerous group to be with. With Dave, all you had to do was blink your eyes in a certain way and – bang! You didn't know where it came from or why."

The incident made Quaife even more shaky and insecure, a psychological state that had been increasingly noticeable since the car smash back in 1966. At times, he resembled a nervous wreck. "He became very withdrawn," Dave Davies remembers. "Pete was always very chatty, liked making jokes, telling lies and exaggerating and being the centre of attention, but after seeing Jonah in such a terrible state that freaked him out. He wasn't the same. It made him a much more insecure and fragile person. He didn't seem himself at all. He became quite docile."

"It was like a creeping malaise," adds Quaife's brother, David. Even the age-old fraternal Davies bickering that he had once been able to ignore or transcend was now affecting him directly. "I couldn't take the way Ray and Dave would react to certain situations. You couldn't see it coming so you were constantly on guard. I remember there was a time when they were arguing about milk. Ray went on about pasteurized milk saying 'it isn't milk' and someone said, 'Don't be stupid – of course it's milk.' That's when they wrecked that café. So you really didn't know where it was coming from. The stress of living with people like that on a twenty-four-hour-a-day basis really got to me." There was scope for further tension ahead as the dreaded Denmark v. Boscobel action loomed in the distance, fraying nerves and leaving Ray Davies constantly on edge.

Back home, there were some amusing moments as Davies' eccentricity reasserted itself. He tried to fit in with standard pop star life but could not resist displaying his individuality at inopportune moments. "I had a party at my house and there were lots of hippies there. I didn't invite them. I think my then wife did. They were smoking pot and stuff and I put on a Max Miller album . . . vaudeville songs. All these stoned people were saying 'What's this all about?' And then I put on *We're Only In It For The Money* by Frank Zappa [The Mothers Of Invention]. I'm not a very sociable person. From Max Miller to Frank Zappa!" The wit of Miller and the cynicism of Zappa were suitable soundtracks for a return to the Royal Courts of Justice in the Strand.

The Court of Appeal sat from 25 March to 1 April, returning for further sessions from 1 to 3 May, concluding on 28 June. Their Lordships, Justices Winn, Harman and Salmon, differed in their interpretation of certain issues but would ultimately reach the same verdict. All agreed that the basis of Judge Widgery's findings the previous year regarding the doctrine of 'frustration' were "somewhat obscure". It was clear that Collins and Wace had actively sought to determine the contract and rid themselves of Page after contacting their solicitor, Michael Simkins, in the summer of 1965. Given this scenario, the ruling on 'frustration' was unanimously overruled. The matter of Page's leaving the group and returning to England on 4 July 1965 divided legal opinion. Lord Justice Winn supported Judge Widgery's ruling that this was a breach of contract, arguing that if Page had been in a *direct* contractual relationship with the Kinks (rather than simply via his company's agreement with Boscobel Productions) the group would have been entitled to dismiss him because of his conduct. Winn suggested that Page should have anticipated a reaction from Ray Davies extreme enough to have destroyed their relationship. It was a view with which Robert Wace fully concurred. "Where Larry Page made his mistake was in not telling Ray he was going back. That was the fundamental mistake. I think if Larry had stuck it out in the States it might have been a different case. But he wasn't capable of handling the group. I'm not saying it's easy.

The kind of problems that Ray posed for somebody were consid-erable and Larry had never been confronted with them on a day-to-day basis. It got to him. It reached him. And he cracked. He couldn't wait to get away. Maybe he did do a lot for the Kinks but, at the end, he couldn't get them to do what he wanted."

This was not the view of Lord Justice Salmon. He noted that all the complaints against Page had been repudiated by Judge Widgery, bar one: the controversial departure from the States. Widgery had concluded that this was such a serious breach by the plaintiff company (Denmark Productions) that it constituted a repudiation of the whole contract. But what did Page's conduct amount to? He was, as Widgery had found, under no obligation to stay to "the bitter end of the tour". He had told everyone, bar Ray Davies, that he was leaving, failing to confront the singer because he felt "that would only produce an outburst of temper-ament by that young man". Salmon was not convinced that such an action could justify repudiating a contract. "I find it very strange," he ruled in his lengthy summation, "that this can in reality constitute a fundamental breach of contract in any event, and, in particular against the background of all that Mr Page had done for the group . . . I am not satisfied that there was any real breach unless one puts the obligation upon the plaintiffs as high as an absolute duty to ensure that Mr Page should retain the goodwill and confidence of the Kinks – and this I am not prepared to do." As for Ray Davies' emotionally charged admission of "hatred" for his manager, Lord Justice Salmon was unimpressed. In a wonderful flourish, he offered an adage that could be applied, not only to Davies, but to any number of his contemporaries: "I think that almost anything a manager might do, however harm-less or trivial, could induce hatred and distrust in a group of highly temperamental, jealous and spoilt adolescents."

The vindication of Page, however, was not enough to save the publishing. Their Lordships agreed that Boscobel Productions had, with the full approval of the Kinks, repudiated the agreement in their letter of 14 September (see page 244). In Lord Justice Salmon's opinion this repudiation was completely unjustified and Denmark Productions should have claimed substantial damages for "wrongful dismissal". Instead they had chosen to fight for the publishing and 10 per cent of the Kinks' earnings since September

1965. Citing previous instances, it was stressed that it had long been settled that if a person employed under a contract of personal services was wrongly dismissed he had no claim for remuneration *after* the repudiation. In other words, if Page had been earning substantial sums under a long contract which was abruptly terminated, he could not simply "bask in the sun" and expect to draw a salary on the basis that he was *willing* to serve as manager. His sole claim would be for damages, which were not pursued in this case. Their Lordships concluded that the Appeal was misconceived and ordered that Denmark Productions be paid 10 per cent of the group's earnings from 30 June 1965 to 14 September 1965. That was the extent of their 'victory'.

The action made case law and thereafter the 'personal services' ruling became the bane of any manager who assumed he had total control over his charges. Page still maintains that he was right to leave the Kinks in America. As a manager he felt that his role demanded – if not obedience – a degree of respect. If Ray Davies chose to sabotage his manager's plans by playing the prima donna, then Page believed he was within his rights to retaliate by refusing to play the 'gofer' and should instead attend to more important matters. Wace was more circumspect. "You don't talk about respect! It's either there or it isn't. Either you can stand the drama that goes along with being the manager of a band or you haven't got the stomach for it and you cave in. You can't come back to Denmark Street and play the wheeler-dealer. They're not just a commodity . . . they're artistes and they're temperamental. Being a manager can be a remunerative business and you have to put up with being the whipping boy."

Wace's view would no doubt have provoked guffaws from many of the svengali-style managers who dominated mid-Sixties pop. Clearly, Page's philosophy of management did not include being treated as a "whipping boy" by anybody, least of all Ray Davies. "No fucking way!" Page concurs. "And that, no doubt, answers your question as to why Wace stayed for another four years. If that is his theory of what a manager is, then that is it. Why did he stay? . . . Don't ask me! You're talking about Ray Davies, so you're talking about something that is completely beyond logic."

While the High Court was busy determining Davies' future, the Kinks issued their new single, 'Wonderboy'. This was not some vibrant song about a powerful superhero, as might have been assumed from the title, but a lullaby to an unborn child. Rasa was pregnant and Ray in sentimental mode. "I thought it would be a boy, that's why I wrote the song." Pete Quaife, still bristling from his recent bust-up with Dave Davies and increasingly angry with Ray's creative direction and dominance, smelt blood during the recording which he saw as an embarrassing nadir. "'Wonderboy' was horrible. It sounded like Herman's Hermits wanking. Jesus, it was bad. I hated it. I remember recording it and doing the la-la-las and just thinking, 'What kind of bloody prissy, sissy nonsense are we doing? We're the guys that made 'You Really Got Me' for Christ's sake.' . . . I felt quite stupid doing it, to be honest."

Reviewers noted the song's philosophic lyrics, complete with simple aphorisms and a final warning that life is lonely. Had it been held over as an album track 'Wonderboy' would no doubt have been regarded as a hidden gem and a moving insight into Davies' sensitive side. Unfortunately, in commercial terms, it was a woeful choice for a single, as Quaife well knew. Although its lullaby charm had a lingering appeal, it was almost a private statement of parental joy let loose in an unsympathetic market-place. It scraped into the *NME* Top 30 for a single week, then disappeared forever, a statistic made worse by the fact that the group were energetically promoting the song on tour. Sales returns of 26,000 (a tenth of those for 'Autumn Almanac' and less than half of Dave Davies' 'Suzanah's Still Alive') were so dispiriting that they threatened the Kinks' very existence.

"It should never have been released," Davies said, suspiciously wise after the event. "I didn't want it released. We did it as a favour to someone." Whoever requested that favour – an unlikely tale in any event – was courting disaster. Davies found a consolation of sorts when he was told of a rumour that John Lennon had been playing the single consistently on a jukebox in some club or eaterie. The details were vague and apocryphal and never once mentioned by Lennon himself in *any* interview, but they provided crumbs of comfort. "I like to think that story's true," Davies says. "I would have liked to have heard him sing ['Wonderboy']."

An accompanying tour of the ABC/Granada cinema circuit was

promoted jointly by Altrincham accountant Danny Betesh of Kennedy Street Enterprises (agent for Herman's Hermits, Freddie And The Dreamers and Wayne Fontana) and Peter Walsh (manager of the Tremeloes and Marmalade). A predominantly pop line-up included the Herd, the Tremeloes, Gary Walker & The Rain and Ola And The Janglers. "The Kinks seemed sadly out of place," *Disc's* reviewer David Hughes observed. "They're not a teenage group by any standards, and Ray's beautiful songs do not suit a cinema stage. 'Waterloo Sunset' and 'Sunny Afternoon' are fantastic to sit back in the sun and listen to, but for crowds of fans who really want to scream loudly at lots of noise, they fall a bit flat. Still, Dave was very chuffed to be working again, and Pete Quaife was zany as ever, but Ray seemed a bit bored by the whole business – his 'sad clown' face forcing the occasional toothy grin to convince us he was really having a ball. The group also played it safe, sticking exclusively to a selection of its many hits, which were vocally good and instrumentally rather dire. And then, it was all over – ending as something of an anti-climax to the audience and I would imagine considerable relief to the artistes!"

The mismatched line-up was typical of the period. A year before, the Jimi Hendrix Experience had found themselves on a bill alongside Cat Stevens, the Walker Brothers and Engelbert Humperdinck. Such incongruous groupings, once the very definition of Variety, now looked hopelessly outdated. After witnessing the Kinks/Herd/Tremeloes combination play to quarter-full houses, one reviewer wondered whether this represented the death of the package tour. The urbane Danny Betesh, acutely aware of the fate of 'Wonderboy', offered Ray the conciliatory message – "Well, you've had a good run". Davies assumed he was referring to the end of their careers. The single and tour certainly provided a glimpse of pop star mortality for the Davies brothers, who both felt suddenly old. Dave had recently celebrated his 21st birthday and, like his brother, was a married father. He was young for a pop idol but no longer the sole kid on the circuit. The Herd's Peter Frampton, still a callow 17 at the start of the package tour, was British pop's newest pin-up dubbed the 'Face of '68' by *Rave* magazine. Dave was aware of the changing fashions. "They were the 'new faces of '68' and people didn't know if we were the old faces of '66 or what. I don't think that we were that big at the time . . . We were at the stage where we didn't want to work much. Ray was really into writing and when we did do live appearances they weren't really that rehearsed."

Ray was not only distracted by his songwriting commitments, but by troubles at home. For the past few months, he had been seeking solace in the company of a slightly older film-school teacher of East European extraction who patiently listened to his problems like an unpaid counsellor. He was drinking vodka heavily at the time which exacerbated his maudlin musings. "She just liked me," he says. "We used to go out and get pissed together . . . She was very kind." Occasionally, they would be joined by a couple of heavy drinking pals, including a face from the past: John Philby. Ray was intrigued to learn more about the adventures of the young man whose first year at Hornsey Art College had ended with news that his father had defected to Russia. Like Davies, Philby had abandoned any ambitions to become a painter after realizing that he "wasn't talented enough". He had also married young – courting a fellow art student, Katie, who subsequently moved to Canada and, according to Philby, killed herself. He was now working as a photographer for the *Sunday Times* and planning to set up a joinery business in north London. Recently, he had visited his father in Moscow for the first time, a trip most notable for its lack of revelations. "He offered no explanation for his career as a spy and I never asked for any." The master spy did confess that he missed two things from the old country: Worcester Sauce and mustard. He regularly listened to *Sing Something Simple* on the BBC's Light Programme. These were details that no doubt appealed to Davies who was also intrigued to learn that, since visiting Russia, John Philby had been tailed by members of the Secret Service. There was every possibility that they were observing the Kink and the spy's son at this very moment.

Ray's pregnant wife was largely oblivious to these furtive pub meetings and inebriated late-night phone calls. Sometimes, she suspected that he might be having an affair, but quickly put it out of her mind. There was never any confrontation resulting from the issue. "I was a pacifist person and didn't really have arguments – not then. Ray can be very dismissive or say something that means you can't actually reply to it. As in, 'That's the end of what I'm saying – and that's it.' So, yes, he was very hard to talk to at times."

The supposedly chaste encounter with the mystery woman ("I didn't want to be her lover") ended almost as casually as it had begun with Ray calling his 'counsellor' from a telephone box in the street. Her final words were "Well, thanks for all the good times and drinks and things", which he translated as meaning "thank you for the days". That last phrase inspired a lyric whose bittersweet nostalgia soon took on a more profound significance.

'Days' was recorded at Pye's basement studio and completed during late May, amid mounting tensions in the group. Ray's secrecy – by now a familiar trait in his professional and personal life – was evident in his reluctance to discuss his songs or provide any feedback about the vocal arrangements, which were usually added after everyone had provided their part. Pete Quaife was increasingly disillusioned by Ray's attitude and felt the Kinks were in danger of devolving into a backing band for his solo record-ings. At home, Quaife would voice conspiracy theories, insisting that the music had been artificially altered. David Quaife remem-bers listening to a Kinks' single only to be interrupted by his brother, who retorted: "That's got nothing to do with what we recorded. Ray's changed it." The bassist believed that "little bits had been cut out". "That was a shock because Pete always felt he was part of a gang. Dave Davies didn't know what was going on either. There was a lot of talk that the music on record wasn't the same as what they recorded."

In later years, Davies consistently recounted the memorable story of watching Quaife scribble the word 'Daze' on the tape box of 'Days' as a bitter complaint about the soporific nature of the song and its tortuous recording. Having already shown scant regard for 'Wonderboy', which he deplored, Quaife was now stepping on Davies' dreams once more. A furious exchange followed, culminating in Quaife leaving the studio, angry and disenchanted.

That, at least, was Ray's memory of events. Quaife was scathing in response. "That is so not true. Ray always insisted that we be in the studio whether we were involved or not. I think he looked upon us as his courtiers who had to sit around watching the master working. He loved that. So we had to sit there with nothing much to do but listen to this music. It would have been interesting if we knew what the goal was, but we didn't. I'd spend my time casually sketching little figures, having always been a cartoonist. I drew this little man with a raincoat and a hat. It was just on the side of one of the boxes of tape. Ray, who often did this, found something to make a huge fuss about and assert his authority. He started yelling and screaming that he was doing all the work and all I was doing was sitting around drawing stupid little pictures. Years later he came out with the story that I wrote 'Daze' on the box. I never did."

Quaife claims that Rasa was still laughing at his doodling when the atmosphere turned ugly. "I went, 'Fuck it, Ray, I'm out of here' and I just walked out. Rasa came running after me: 'Don't go, don't be like that.' I said, 'To hell with it, I'm not going to be spoken to like that.' . . . I just walked out of the studio and, as it happened, they didn't need me anyway, so it didn't hurt anybody."

Ray regarded Quaife's sudden exit as another bad omen. Everything was in flux. He was currently planning to move from East Finchley to Borehamwood, having been goaded by his sisters into purchasing a plush property more suited to his station. Rasa was also keen for a fresh start. "The reason I wanted to move was because I felt overwhelmed by his family. I thought it would be nice to move further away so that I'd have a little more control over my life. So we bought a lovely house in Borehamwood, where the actress Anna Neagle used to live. We still kept the house in Fortis Green though."

Joining them in their new home was Alfie, a springy Fox Terrier that they'd purchased as a pup. Ray and Rasa never settled properly in the Borehamwood Tudor house, and neither did Alfie. "I was upset about the dog," Rasa remembers. "He kept running away. So I chained him to three apple trees when I was out. He broke away from the chain and ran off. He was found and put into Battersea Dogs Home – and that was the end of that."

Just before moving to Elstree/Borehamwood, Davies conducted what sounded like a wake for his long history as a north London resident. After picking up a master of 'Days', he invited his parents, his sister Gwen and her family to a private premiere of the new single at Fortis Green. It was a special moment. The composition had a hymnal quality with its references to "*sacred* days" and "*bless* the night", the closest Davies had ever come to a religious meditation at this time. "I finished the song and there was silence in the room. It was obvious I was saying goodbye, not just to a house but to a way of life, a time, an inspiration. The song had an air of finality about it that I liked. Pop musicians are not supposed to go on forever and around this time I thought, 'Maybe it's the last record I'll ever make.' That's why it has that strange emotion to it. The band knew it too."

On 1 June, four days after Davies' falling out with Quaife, the Kinks were due to fly from London to Dublin for a ballroom date in nearby Bray. After boarding the plane, the bass player inexplicably sneaked off again prior to take-off. "We landed," Ray remembers, "we got in the car – and somebody was missing. Pete hadn't got on the plane. He had stood at the bottom of the runway and couldn't do it." Co-manager Grenville Collins was annoyed but calm enough to contact Rasa in London, who was despatched to pick up Quaife and place him on the next flight. She was not the ideal emissary. As Quaife's relationship with Davies deteriorated, his resentment towards Rasa built up, spilling over into envy and petty jealousy. "Rasa is a very sore point with me. I'll make no bones about it, I didn't like her and felt that she had no right to be there. But it was Ray's girlfriend [*she* was his wife] and we had to respect that . . . As always happens, when a girl enters the group, the group always suffers. With Rasa tagging along with us all the time, tempers began to sizzle and eventually the group began to splinter. Not that she cared!"

Blaming Rasa, of all people, for the Kinks' internal problems was neither logical nor convincing but testified to Quaife's festering disillusionment. He failed to board the flight to Ireland for a second time, resulting in the cancellation of the performance in Bray. The no-show was perceived as firm evidence of his petulance towards Ray and disregard for the group. But there was something deeper in his actions than simple spite. "By then I was suffering from claustrophobia, but I didn't tell them. It wasn't clever to admit weaknesses or offer excuses. I was very nervous. We'd been recording at Pye in Marble Arch, several levels under the street and that was an ordeal. No space. No windows. Before this, I'd always loved flying, but not any longer. It felt like being locked inside some metal cylinder. There was talk of returning to America the following year which meant long-haul flights and that was scary. I didn't want to do it."

Quaife nevertheless conquered his fears sufficiently to embark on a short tour of Sweden one week later. The venues were public parks, frequented by family audiences, most of whom regarded the Kinks as too loud and uncouth. Several reviewers preferred the wonderfully named support act Rainy Day Women and noted that the Kinks suffered "sound problems" at several of the dates. At least the shows were free from rioting.

The group returned to the UK in time for the release of 'Days' at the end of June. Reviews were respectful, even effusive, but the curse of 'Wonderboy' was not easily forgotten. *Melody Maker* reckoned 'Days' was "great" but in their accompanying guest review column, Who drummer Keith Moon was allowed some withering comments. "Memoirs of Ray Davies," he scoffed. "This sounds very much like a demo with Ray on acoustic guitar. I just heard a bass drum so Mick Avory must be on it as well. So it's the Kinks. Sounds pretty dated, like one of these songs Pete [Townshend] keeps under his sink. I dig what the Kinks do, but I've never thought of them as a group."

Keith Moon appeared to be voicing Pete Quaife's general frustration that the Kinks had become an almost silent vehicle for the singer. What would later be acknowledged as one of Ray Davies' greatest compositions was not considered so at the time, least of all by Quaife. The reason was largely a matter of continuity and context. 'Days' was fourth in a succession of singles ('Waterloo Sunset', 'Autumn Almanac' and 'Wonderboy') that were all reflective in tone. If Shel Talmy had still been producer, he would no doubt have advised Davies to employ the old trick of alternating heavier and lighter singles in the fashion exemplified so well by the combination of 'All Day And All Of The Night' and 'Tired Of Waiting For You'. As it was, fans craving what the music press would have called the "familiar Kinks sound" had now been starved of a high-energy single since 'Till The End Of The Day' back in 1965. Their only consolation was the B-side, 'She's Got Everything', tellingly a recording that was over two years old. 'Days' was respected rather than revered – that would come later.

The single peaked at number 14 (*NME*), a respectable position in the wake of 'Wonderboy'. Davies was nevertheless forced on the defensive. "I still have a lot of faith in our single, 'Days'," he said, almost apologetically. "If we like a record and like making it, it becomes a successful venture. After it's finished we're proud of it – but we never pretended to know anything about the sales or promotional side of music . . . Some releases are slow, and perhaps this is one of them. I don't think our image or position is altered by its moderate progress in the charts."

Davies was over-optimistic. The Kinks' reputation was further dented in October when they played a series of cabaret dates in Durham, appearing at such venues as the Top Hat Club and the Stockton Fiesta. When those dates were announced, Dave deflected embarrassing questions with some self-deprecating humour. "We've been doing cabaret for the past year but people haven't realized it. When we go onstage, it's like an act we do anyway. I think cabaret is the best thing for us. Why shouldn't we do panto-mime? We're doing *Jack And The Beanstalk*." Inside, Dave – the self-styled king of the ravers – was mortified.

While the Rolling Stones and the Who were still securing head-lines as iconoclastic and innovative rock acts, the Kinks were reduced to playing the scampi-in-a-basket circuit. Even Ray Davies could not sell this to the press, so Mick Avory was wheeled out as their most plausible spokesman. "You have to get into a new field," he announced, less than convincingly. "Mostly, on the performing side, we work abroad and now we've broken into the cabaret field up north. It pays well and it's given us a new chal-lenge . . ." Clearly, the Kinks were in need of reinvention on a massive scale.

CHAPTER TWENTY-FOUR

THE VILLAGE GREEN PRESERVATION SOCIETY

'The Year Of Revolution'. That is the phrase usually ascribed to 1968 – and with good reason. With the conflict escalating in Vietnam, peaceful demonstrations had given way to street fighting. In London, there were pitched battles between police and protestors outside the American Embassy in Grosvenor Square; Paris was the scene of rioting with workers joining students in revolt; in Belfast and Derry, civil rights marchers were attacked by police; across the Atlantic, Martin Luther King and Bobby Kennedy were assassinated, further traumatizing an America already at war with itself. Britain's rock aristocracy felt obliged to comment in song: the Rolling Stones recorded 'Street Fighting Man' and the Beatles completed 'Revolution'. While those titles sounded like a call to arms, the lyrics were self-questioning and ambivalent; they displayed a marked reluctance to bring down the establishment. Nevertheless, the idea of revolution was paramount to rock's premier spokesmen, as Mick Jagger's interview comments and John Lennon's pained confrontations with the Marxist press underlined. The *New Left Review* dismissed 'Revolution' as "a lamentable petty bourgeois cry of fear", while another radical paper, *Black Dwarf*, saw the song as evidence that the Beatles were "safeguarding their capitalist investment". In an open letter to Lennon, they scoffed: "That record was no more revolutionary than [the popular radio serial] *Mrs Dale's Diary*. In order to change the world we've got to understand what's wrong with the world. And then – destroy it. Ruthlessly . . . There is no such thing as a polite revolution." Lennon accused his Marxist detractors of being "on a destruction kick" and retorted: "I don't worry about what you – the left – the middle – the right or any fucking boys' club think. I'm not that bourgeois."

While Lennon was at least engaging in political debate, Ray Davies remained detached. Even when the 'revolution' extended as far as his alma mater, Hornsey College of Arts and Crafts, he made no comment on the student sit-in. The local press, by contrast, took up cudgels against the young upstarts, declaring: "A bunch of crackpots here in Haringey, or in Grosvenor Square, or Paris, or Berlin, or Mexico, can never overthrow an established system . . . We the ordinary people, the nine-to-five, Monday-to-Friday, semi-detached, suburban wage-owners, we are the system. We are not victims of it. We are not slaves to it. We are it, and we like it. Does any bunch of twopenny-halfpenny kids think they can turn us upside down? They'll learn."

Davies' political silence was hardly surprising considering the work that he was about to launch on the British public. For a year or more, he had been mulling over the contents of an album that would prove to be the most important and definitive of his entire career. The songs that he had stockpiled were distinctive, but far removed from any notions of revolution or radical chic. "I just immersed myself in being English and wrote about things that I cared about . . . I was writing old people's songs for a world I thought was vanishing." He knew that the material might be seen as uncool or reactionary but, in another sense, he had nothing to lose. "I didn't think I'd ever come back to America again. In many ways, my career was over. We were having hit singles in Europe and the rest of the world, but the sales were going down. I thought, 'Well why not write something about things you really care about.'"

Unlike the Beatles and Stones – let alone the three-piece blues-inspired outfits like Cream and the Jimi Hendrix Experience or psychedelic warriors such as Pink Floyd – the Kinks had little in common with the emerging British counter-culture. They did not play at their free festivals, frequent venues like the UFO or take to the streets. As Davies reminisces: "There were student riots in Paris, Mayor Daley had troops on the streets of Chicago because of the anti-war protests during the Democratic Convention – and there I was in England, writing 'Last Of The Steam-Powered Trains' and 'People Take Pictures Of Each Other'. The world was in turmoil, and that was my way of reacting. I felt that I needed to look inward, and to return to the way that England had been when I was growing up."

The origins of the new album could be traced as far back as late 1966 when he was tinkering with the idea of a solo album and a work loosely based on Dylan Thomas' *Under Milk Wood – A Play For Voices*. The first song completed was 'Village Green', the only truly detailed narrative that Davies would include on the album. It contains the essence of the project, with themes embracing time and loss, the city versus country conundrum, the erosion of old values and the inherent value in preservation. In the song, the narrator revisits his village having left years before to seek his fortune in the city – an idea vaguely recalling the moral fable 'Big Black Smoke'. What he discovers upon his return is corruption and change; the houses have been transformed into antiquities, crassly lauded by American tourists snapping photographs and uttering banalities. His first love, Daisy, has married the grocer's boy Tom, who now owns the village's fruit and vegetable shop. Nothing is the same. In the final lines, the speaker fantasizes about meeting Daisy again – laughing and talking about the village green. But this is a transparently fatuous dream in a world removed from time. Within the song, the village green itself has become nothing more than a museum piece.

Davies' storyline owed little to Dylan Thomas but recalled the work of an earlier influence: George Orwell. In Orwell's 1939 novel *Coming Up For Air*, the central character George Bowling returns to the country town of his youth only to experience sadness and disillusionment. His former sweetheart Elsie has married the tobacconist, a scenario not dissimilar to that of Tom and Daisy above. Unlike H. G. Wells' earlier *The History Of Mr Polly*, Orwell offers no happy ending or reinvention through escape. There is no second Eden.

Davies clung to his 'Village Green' for the best part of two years, knowing that he had something, yet uncertain whether it was appropriate for release, either as a solo effort or by the Kinks.

The arrangement and recording were completed amid an atmosphere of subterfuge and uncertainty. Pete Quaife found the process terribly frustrating. "Rehearsals took place at Ray's house, but they were often quite odd. He would keep us waiting for ages, then appear, play a song on a piano and we'd try it. Then he'd announce, 'You've got it!' and disappear again. I didn't know what to think."

Davies' vagueness had less to do with eccentricity than insecurity. 'Village Green' was delicate and had to be guarded from inappropriate influences, including those existing within his own group. "The only way I could record that was to tell Mick Avory that we were doing a soul track. I asked him to play like Al Jackson, the Otis Redding drummer, and to put some of those snappy fills in. Mick sat back, played it and thought, 'It's going to be good, a good soul track.' Then we brought in the orchestra. It wasn't until I put the vocal on that Mick realized he'd been totally conned. That's how dysfunctional we'd become."

By July 1968, under pressure from US outlet Reprise Records, Davies submitted a hotchpotch of songs for a collection tentatively titled *Four More Respected Gentlemen*. Labels were subsequently printed with a track listing comprising: 'She's Got Everything', 'Monica', 'Mr Songbird', 'Johnny Thunder', 'Polly', 'Days', 'Animal Farm', 'Berkeley Mews', 'Picture Book', 'Phenomenal Cat' and 'Misty Water'. Davies, in facetious mood, hinted that the work was a satire on English etiquette, featuring songs about table manners and outmoded customs. Much to the confusion of fans, *Four More Respected Gentlemen* never got beyond its arbitrary track listing as Reprise awaited the forthcoming Pye release in the UK.

In the third week of September, the elaborately titled *The Kinks Are The Village Green Preservation Society* was reviewed in the *New Musical Express* by Keith Altham. The 12-track album appeared in France, Sweden, Norway, Italy and New Zealand, but was mysteriously withdrawn in the UK with immediate effect as news filtered through that Ray Davies had changed his mind and elected to revise the work. A few weeks later, the plot thickened when a press release appeared announcing that the project was to be expanded into an 18-song two-LP set. Soon after, Mick Avory revealed in an interview that his colleague was working on a 20-*track* double intended for mid-price release. Ray Davies never mentioned this, then or later, but Avory's story made sense. Ever since Bob Dylan's 1966 groundbreaking twin-LP set *Blonde On Blonde*, the commercial and artistic possibilities of the double album had been self-evident. Pye Records, the least likely label to pioneer aesthetic innovation, had already sanctioned Donovan's two-LP set *A Gift From A Flower To A Garden* which charted in the spring of 1968. Its surprise success was not lost on Louis Benjamin. News that both the Beatles and the Jimi Hendrix Experience were readying double albums for the Christmas market also made the idea viable.

Instead, Davies elected to reconfigure the 12-track continental release, removing 'Days' and 'Mr Songbird', while adding 'Animal Farm', 'Big Sky', 'All Of My Friends Were There', 'Last Of The Steam-Powered Trains' and 'Sitting By The Riverside'. He now had a 15-song *single* album, a notable bargain for the time. New cover artwork was commissioned featuring the Kinks enclosed in hazy, psychedelic circles. On the rear, they were pictured wandering through the high grass at Kenwood House, the inspirational setting that Ray had already used for the film *Veronica*. This was another reminder to Dave of his liaison with Sue Sheehan, expulsion from school and the subsequent loss of his daughter, Tracey. It could hardly have been more symbolic.

On 22 November, the fifth anniversary of President Kennedy's assassination, *The Village Green Preservation Society* was finally released. It was a subtle conceit that did not trumpet its existence or attempt to bludgeon the listener with dogma. An elegiac feel permeated the work with expressions of longing and regret manifesting themselves amid light sketches and fractured tales of tarnished innocence, childhood memory, passing time and fading traditions. As Davies says: "The Village Green is where I set my imaginary world which almost existed before I came along. The album was a series of dreamscapes about an imaginary England. It's to do with innocence and lost youth and the permanence that life will continue to go on regardless."

The title track, described by Davies as the album's "national anthem", was intended as the equivalent of a rousing theme tune, if the work had ever been performed as a stage musical. Speaking about his conception of the preservation society, Davies said: "It's a shame that the Americans are more interested in our traditional values than we are. I'm not particularly patriotic – perhaps I'm just selfish – but I like these traditional British things to be there. I never go to watch a cricket match, but I like to know it's there. It's like not being able to read the *Eagle* any more. It's bad for people to grow up and not know what a china cup is – or a village green . . . I wouldn't die for the cause, but I think that it's frightfully important." His words sounded sincere, but Davies surely knew that his quaint, comic checklist of institutions to be preserved had a reactionary ring. As early as the second line, the patriotic ideal has already been compromised by the inclusion of the American cartoon character Donald Duck alongside British music-hall star Old Mother Riley, Mrs Mopp (from BBC radio's wartime comedy *ITMA*) and Sherlock Holmes. The parodic elements are ever-present, not least in the simple-minded chant that frames the song. Two years before, the Conservation Society had been founded in England with a policy promising to fight "against the menace of decreasing standards". The song discovers such 'menace' in the most unlikely and preposterous of places. Davies' narrator satirizes the very notion of preservation in a series of light-hearted lines. He playfully suggests we should preserve strawberry jam (which is itself a preservative, of course) and even the state of virginity. The retention of the George Cross and respect for those awarded medals (both seemingly serious considerations) are undermined by its ludicrously titled support group – the 'Custard Pie Appreciation Consortium'. Finally, there is self-parody. During the summer, Davies had completed the purchase of a Tudor manor house in Borehamwood, Hertfordshire, which he was busily refurbishing with small luxuries including, as he told reporters, a bar billiards table. In the song, which was recorded that same month, he suggests God saves Tudor houses, antique tables and billiards, a wry comment on his own climb up the social ladder. While the aforementioned 'Village Green' had described an idealized past, the recently composed title track strips away that poignancy to laugh with affection at our quixotic attempts to hold on to the artefacts of our youth. "The band played on the record," Davies says, "but I knew they were unhappy. If Hollywood had directed Muswell Hill and written it as a film script it would have looked like the Village Green. I was confusing

Hollywood with Borehamwood . . . Even though I felt out of place living in Hertfordshire, in the Village Green I felt I belonged."

'Do You Remember Walter' articulates the album's central themes of nostalgia and loss. Davies had created idealized figures before, most notably in 'David Watts', but in that song he was writing in the present tense while hero-worshipping the sporting scholar of his youth. Walter is a very different creature, an adult version of the boy hero, demythologized by age and passing time. "Walter was a friend of mine," Davies reveals. "We used to play football together every Saturday afternoon. Then I met him again after about five years and we found out we didn't have anything in common." Elsewhere, he added: "I wrote this song about friendship. It's about a real friend that exists. To me that was all important." However, the character in the song no longer exists in the present but lingers only in memory, an echo of a world that has long gone. Unlike Davies, the song's narrator never gets to meet the adult Walter. He merely imagines what he *might* be like – fat, married and averse to late nights. If they did meet, the speaker surmises, Walter would be bored, uninterested and unable to recall his name, which tells us as much about the narrator's state of mind as it does about the likely outcome. Once again, the ghost of Orwell's George Bowling is present; the imagined meeting with Walter echoes Bowling's bathetic reunion with his former sweetheart: "I was just a customer, a stranger, an uninteresting fat man . . . she'd simply forgotten my existence." Like Daisy in 'Village Green', Walter has become a phantom, whose personality and exploits can be preserved only in memory. In singing his story, Davies' gentle vocal captures the poignancy of lost time, but there is also a suppressed bitterness, even anger, driven by the sudden machine-gun drum rolls of Mick Avory.

'Johnny Thunder' takes Davies' mythologizing to levels far beyond the idealized characterizations of David Watts or the younger versions of Daisy and Walter. Like Walter and Watts, Thunder is a composite character roughly based, as Davies said, "on two people I knew". One was "someone I didn't want to fall out with. He was a bit older than I was at school, a complete hero, he was an outsider as well, the rebel. There's still part of that character that drives me. Johnny Thunder is somebody I still look up to, I changed his real name, but Johnny Thunder seemed to be a great idea."

A secondary inspiration was Marlon Brando's motorcycle rebel Johnny Strabler from the film *The Wild One*, which had been released in the UK earlier that year following a 15-year ban. In the movie, the misunderstood biker is asked "What are you rebelling against, Johnny?" and famously responds with the surly one-liner, "What have you got?" There are some similar rebellious traits in Davies' pasteboard creation, who vows never to end up like everybody else, a familiar enough comment among the songwriter's cast of misfit figures. But Johnny Thunder is also the name of a comic book hero – a member of the Justice Society of America – who, three summers before, had been resurrected from the archives for the story 'The Earth Without A Justice League'. Davies' Johnny Thunder is also a relic from the past, and a static figure amid the village green cast. Davies' characterization is so sketchy that Thunder resembles an unconvincing abstraction rather than a flesh and blood figure. Like some hunger-striking human dynamo, he lives on water and feeds on lightning – a superhero without a cause. Even his girlfriend – or devoted fan – Helena, seems detached from the barely existent narrative, and can only offer a reassuring prayer, "God bless, Johnny", echoing the title track's closing chant, "God bless the village green". "I can't for the life of me imagine now how I got my head around writing those songs," Ray wonders. "It was a totally strange mindset to be in."

Abstractions also dominate Davies' thoughts in the twin compositions 'Picture Book' and 'People Take Pictures Of Each Other'. Both are deceptively light-hearted romps, the former lazily executed with scat vocals as the narrator browses through a photo album recalling happy memories from childhood. In the latter song, he satirizes this very process while pondering the absurdity and pathos of photography as a means of proving one's existence or capturing the emotional experiences that truly characterize people's lives. Jaunty as these songs sound, they gouge deep into the heart of Davies' neuroses about family, loss, passing time and what, if anything, remains. "I'd rather have the actual things here, not just pictures of things we used to have," Ray adds, while acknowledging the futility of that wish.

'Sitting By The Riverside', a reminiscence inspired by Ray's fishing expeditions with his father during childhood, ostensibly sounds like an idyllic refrain, whose mood of lazy resignation recalls 'Sunny Afternoon'. Beneath the picture-postcard imagery, not everything is tranquil. The vaudevillian tune and light piano arrangement are interrupted by a menacing mellotron backing, like storm clouds gathering over a pastoral scene. "There's an element of lost youth in these things," Davies points out. "The person that one may become and the people we leave behind . . . Maybe it was an England that was lost, but could have been there. An England that suddenly stopped."

The title 'Animal Farm' takes us back to George Orwell but, contrary to expectations, it is not a song of farmyard revolution nor an allegory of the failure of Communism, but a celebration of simple country living set against the insanity of the metropolis. "That was just me thinking everybody else is mad and we're all animals anyway." Tellingly, the lyric does not focus on the present but conjures a longing for a time and place that the narrator has left behind. He imagines returning to Animal Farm with his girl, a triumphant homecoming that is not realized in the song's narrative and remains a fantasy. Arguably, the best produced recording on the album, the track became Pete Quaife's favourite. "The reason why it worked was because Ray relaxed for a while and allowed everybody to have some input. The only argument we had was on 'Animal Farm'. I wanted to do the intro on bass but Ray and Dave didn't agree. So I said 'fine' and that was it."

'Big Sky' momentarily takes us away from the village green concept. Inspired by a visit to the Midem Festival in Cannes, it was written after Davies observed music publishers scurrying around hustling for deals while he watched imperiously from his hotel balcony. He emerged with a complex, reflective lyric on the vanities of human behaviour when considered alongside the vastness of nature. Many listeners interpret the Big Sky as symbolic of God. "No, it's not about God," Davies said in 1969. "It's just a big sky." His comment sounded reductive and obtuse. Later, he confided that watching the businessmen at work had inspired his notion of "a being somewhat bigger than all the hustlers around me". If this is so, then Davies' God is a peculiarly impersonal deity, closer to the Victorian notion of the Supreme Being who is inactive in the universe, as opposed to the theist model of mainstream Christianity. His diffidence in admitting the theological theme was partly due to fears of misinterpretation. "I'm always wary about talking about God because I was told that I'm not religious because I don't go to church. I was told that at a very early age. But I think I'm quite religious, I just don't talk about it. If God's an influence on something, I don't want to tell everyone about it. If the influence is there it'll come out without mentioning it."

In common with 'Big Sky', 'All Of My Friends Were There' documents a recent event in the performer's life. On 1 July 1967, the Kinks appeared at the South East R&B Festival in Blackheath, London, on an impressive bill featuring the Small Faces, Georgie Fame and John Mayall. Davies was in a poor state before and after the show. "It was an R&B concert and I had a temperature of 104 but they asked me to do it because there was a contract. I had lots to drink and I thought, 'It doesn't matter'. The curtains opened and all my friends were sitting in the front row."

Davies' decision to turn his embarrassment into a song of high comedy and bathos proved inspired. His tale of shame and rehabilitation is related in the voice of a cockney music hall costermonger, recalling his father's favourite, Gus Elen. Midway through, Ray switches to his Noël Coward/Grenville Collins posh intonation ("oh the embarrassment . . .") while the arrangement speeds along like a Gilbert & Sullivan operetta. The final verse again shifts from rock 'n' roll to waltz time, amid reminiscences about returning to the old café, a refuge from happier days. A dominant 7th chord ends proceedings *in medias res*, leaving the listener with a shaggy dog story, unresolved. Looking back at the eccentric composition in 2003, Davies acknowledged: "If I'd done that song today, it would have been A&R'd off the album. But sometimes you need minor gems like that to set up the other songs, rather than just sticking to the ones that get played on the radio."

Two other distinctly un-*Village Green* compositions are 'Starstruck' and 'Monica'. Set against an Acapulco rhythm, the former gently chastises a starstruck groupie whose mind is "just not right". Seduced by urban artifice and intoxicants (wine and champagne) she can no longer distinguish between reality and stardom. In 'Monica', the narrator serenades a lady of the night who, despite selling her body, can never be fully bought. Davies' love of calypso, previously displayed on 'Holiday In Waikiki' and

'I'm On An Island', unexpectedly re-emerges in incongruous fashion. The subtle 'whore with a heart of gold' theme is delicately written, although Davies was frank enough about the subject matter at the time of its release. "It's about a prostitute – and the BBC has played it," he admitted. A few years later, he was back-tracking and contradicting himself. "I think I explained it enough for me and to various other people . . . I didn't actually say she was a prostitute, so it can apply to other people. If you say some-body is a prostitute or a hooker, you're restricted."

Expanding his lyrical palette, Davies daringly introduces a couple of songs that are pure fantasy. 'Phenomenal Cat' (regret-tably mistitled 'Pheonomical Cat' on the original album) resembles a Victorian fairy tale or children's story, reminiscent of Lewis Carroll or Edward Lear. The decorative flute opening (synthesized through a mellotron) sounds like some village hall amateur dramatic society production. There follows the tale of the obese cat, who chooses to live in a tree and eat endlessly. We learn of his history in thinner days when he travelled extensively and discovered the secret of life itself. That revelation inspires a serenity of sorts, manifested in a determined retreat from the world into wilful indolence and comfort eating. What great secret the cat unearthed we are never told.

Considering Davies' satirical bent, it is tempting to interpret the fable as an oblique comment on the search for spiritual enlightenment, not least among his leading contemporaries. An interest in Eastern philosophy, Buddhism, meditation, gurus and Holy Men accompanied the more publicized hedonism of the age. Pete Townshend followed the teachings of Meher Baba, the "compassionate father" who had taken a vow of silence in 1925 that remained unbroken for the rest of his life. "Meher Baba is the Avatar of the Age – the Messiah," Townshend said. "He can't do anything but good. He has completely and utterly changed my whole life and, through me, the group as a whole." Another well-known spiritual teacher had, for a time, entranced the Beatles.

Maharishi Mahesh Yogi was mocked by cynical journalists as the "giggling guru" and had a Cheshire Cat smile but, for John Lennon at least, offered the possibility of instant enlightenment. Lennon initially saw the Maharishi as the human equivalent of Davies' Phenomenal Cat, a contented figure who had acquired the secret of life. "John thought there was some sort of secret the Maharishi had to give you, and then you could go home," recalled Beatles' associate Neil Aspinall. "He started to think the Maharishi was holding out on him." Disillusioned, Lennon composed the barely disguised rebuke 'Sexy Sadie' which, coincidentally enough, was released as an album track on the same day as 'Phenomenal Cat'. Whether Davies had Lennon or Townshend in mind at any stage during the writing and editing of his song is conjectural at best, but, as a comment on the age's interest in spiritual regeneration, 'Phenomenal Cat' struck a topical chord. "I don't like to think there's a moral to it," Davies later said. "He ate himself to eternity. That's what he wanted to do." Elsewhere, he was equally as unforthcoming as his feline. "Phenomenal Cat went to Singapore and Hong Kong and decided it was just as well to get fat. I didn't, he did. It was completely his own decision."

The accompanying 'Wicked Annabella', a dark, gothic fairy tale, is given over to Dave Davies who takes on the role of narrator, ominously outlining the evils of Annabella, as if he is addressing a scared group of kids before bedtime. The cautionary tale recalls Hans Christian Andersen's *Hansel And Gretel*, a symbolic warning to children about the perils of entering the woods where demons enslaved by the witch Annabella lurk under stones. Dave relishes the horror, which is unsurprising given his love of Dennis Wheatley novels and later immersion in magic. Musically, the song is equally playful. Its bass and drums opening recalls the intro to the Rolling Stones' 'Get Off Of My Cloud', then morphs into a rhythm reminiscent of the Doors' 'Light My Fire', the ultimate irony in view of the Americans' use of 'All Day And All Of The Night' as a template for their recent international hit, 'Hello I Love You'.

Playful plagiarism is also the subtext of the most atypical song on the album, 'Last Of The Steam-Powered Trains'. Inspired by the familiar blues riff on Howlin' Wolf's 'Smokestack Lightnin'', which the Kinks themselves had performed live, the song is an onomatopoeic exercise, with the harmonica and guitar interlocking to imitate the rolling of a train, speeding towards a dramatic conclusion and coda relief. Davies casts himself as the last bastion of authenticity in contrast to his grey, middle-class friends. He proclaims to live in a museum, as if he is the curator of Britain's vanishing cultural heritage. As the assumed last song recorded for the album (session listings proving not entirely reliable), it is possible that Davies was attempting to unify the group by allowing them to play something in the old R&B Kinks' style. In one sense, 'Last Of The Steam-Powered Trains' is a farewell to the past but, paradoxically, it is also very topical: 1968 was also the year of the blues revival, not just in the UK but also in America where Canned Heat and Big Brother And The Holding Company (featuring Janis Joplin) were celebrating the influences of their great R&B predecessors. In the end, 'Last Of The Steam-Powered Trains' became a self-fulfilling act of preservation, establishing itself in the Kinks' live set for years afterwards.

The Village Green Preservation Society was a modest seller and – up until its critical and commercial rehabilitation in the Nineties – one of the most underrated albums of the Sixties. The most enduring myths about the album concern its reception and sales. Sources as well-written and reliable as the 2008 Kinks box set erroneously suggest that it did not receive a single review in the UK music press and was effectively disowned by Pye Records. But at a time when albums were not automatically reviewed in the British pop press, *The Village Green Preservation Society* certainly received a fair shout. Both Ray and Dave Davies trumpeted its arrival in pre-release interviews and, as previously mentioned, the 12-track version secured a lavish appraisal from the *New Musical Express*' leading light, Keith Altham. The revised work was acclaimed in *Melody Maker* by Bob Dawbarn ("easily their best LP") and accompanied by a revealing track by track commentary from Ray Davies, evidence enough of its cultural significance. *Disc & Music Echo* also applauded the songwriter's "words of wisdom", adding, "The Kinks may not be on the crest of a pop wave these days, but Ray Davies will remain one of our finest composers for many years." The album even attracted a rare mention in the broadsheets, where the *Daily Express*' sympathetic, chain-smoking columnist Judith Simons suggested: "Ray Davies has written a song picture of the gentler aspects of British life which could make an idyllic stage musical."

Simons may well have been primed by Davies or the group's management as the issue of the stage musical had already caused a rift with Pye Records. "Pye wouldn't give us any money to do our cabaret version of the album," Ray complained, referring not to the recent appearances at the Top Hat or Fiesta Club in Durham, but an intended tour of theatres or village halls that was never finalized. "They said we *could* have the money if we gave them a single, which we didn't."

Davies' intransigence was self-defeating as a new single would have provided television opportunities and additional publicity, both of which would have assisted the album's entry into the marketplace. Grenville Collins was so disenchanted by the impasse that he retreated in protest for a couple of months, but Davies declined to compromise. Still angry or petulant about Pye's limited budget, he felt the Kinks had been sidelined by their record company. "It was strange; they hardly spent a penny promoting those albums. We enjoyed tremendous success with hit singles and it was hard for Pye to think of us as a group who actually made albums as opposed to albums made up from a bunch of singles, shoved together for Christmas. On *Village Green* there was no obvious hit track that they could take and exploit – and I would've been offended if they had taken a single off, because it was an *album*."

Davies' intentions sound noble and there was no doubt that the Kinks were perceived primarily as a singles group, but it was unfair to suggest that Pye had done little or nothing to promote his work. Advertisements for *The Village Green Preservation Society* were duly placed in the major music publications, review copies were despatched and the response overall was positive. It is unlikely that Decca, EMI or Philips would have spent any more money at the time – and they too would probably have requested a single for the Christmas market.

In the wake of the album's original release, Davies admitted a slight disappointment that more people had not heard the record. Over the years, that initial regret hardened into acerbity and sarcasm. "It's the most talked-about record nobody's ever heard," he said in 2010. At other times, he has hinted, somewhat disingenuously, that the work was an act of self-sabotage and was never intended to achieve commercial success in the first place. "I wanted a record that would not necessarily get airplay but would be played for friends and at parties – just play the record like playing a demo. [laughing] And I achieved that and it didn't get any airplay at all. It became a cult record as a result."

The mystique surrounding *The Village Green Preservation Society* has been amplified by questionable assumptions about its sales receipts. Numerous commentators have highlighted its commercial failure, partly in misguided support of Davies' initial complaints about the album's reception. After reading his own words, reinforced by abrasive music press rhetoric, Davies has responded in kind, creating an ever-spiralling sense of injustice that continues to be echoed in commentaries on the record. This self-fulfilling prophecy has produced an unquestioned critical commonplace that warrants scrutiny. Championing the album for a 21st-century audience, writer Andy Miller reiterated Davies' sentiments, stressing that the sales figures were "an embarrassment", adding: "The humiliation was compounded by an awareness among the handful of people that got to hear it that in *The Kinks Are The Village Green Preservation Society*, Ray Davies had produced his best work to date." This conveys the false impression that the work was not merely a modest seller but an unprecedented commercial disaster, more befitting a limited edition or controversial record suddenly withdrawn from the marketplace. But in one of his periodic complaints about the album's performance, Davies calculated: "If we're talking about *The Village Green Preservation Society*, worldwide we'd be lucky if it did 100,000. I mean, even the people who talk about it haven't heard it." What Davies intended as a putdown actually makes a case for the album's popularity. One hundred thousand, although modest, is far from a disaster and certainly represents a lot more than "a handful of people".

Others have responded with horror at the album's non-appearance in the LP charts of the period, ignoring the group's downward trajectory since 1965. Even with the presence of two Top 3 singles, *Something Else* had failed to reach most of the charts of the time and, barring hits compilations, *not one* Kinks LP/CD released after *The Village Green Preservation Society* – totalling 21 albums on Pye, RCA, Arista, London, Columbia and Konk – could muster a single chart entry.

Nobody has ever studied or analysed the correlation between record sales and specific chart positions in UK albums listings of the Sixties. During the mid-Sixties, the *New Musical Express* merely featured a Top 10 which, by 1968, had been extended to a Top 15. Evidently anything lower was not deemed worthy of research, which says much about the continued dominance of the single format in the eyes of the pop press. Many mid-ranking releases that sold reasonably failed to register in the albums chart for a variety of reasons. Seasonal sales were a significant factor and any November release – like *The Village Green Preservation Society* – faced stiff competition and required significant numbers to achieve chart success. Who knew how close it came to that all-important Top 15? A record could easily chart for a single week at number 15 and yet sell fewer copies than another that did not chart at all. Staggered sales of albums, in contrast to the immediacy of singles, makes any judgements about chart positions even more hazardous. In addition, unlike singles, precise details of LP sales in the UK at this time are not generally available so any commercial conclusions about *The Village Green Preservation Society* are based largely on Davies' offhand remarks, unsupported by any documentation. Given the publicity, positive reviews and loyal fan base of the Kinks, there is every likelihood that the album was a *modest* seller. Contemporaneous plaudits, even for an unknown band, let alone an established group, would have guaranteed some limited success in the UK. Short of extant, detailed royalty statements or rediscovered Pye sales figures, we will never know for sure.

The response of the subsidiary Kinks to *The Village Green Preservation Society* was also a source of contention. "The decision to do the album wasn't unanimous," Davies insists. "Dave's reaction was *very* adverse." If Dave was hostile, the public never heard about it. Even before the release date he was telling both *Disc* and *NME* that "it's the best thing we've ever done". Twenty-eight years later, he was still saying, "it's a beautiful record". Ray also felt that Mick Avory was frustrated. "I should have left the band to do that record; that could have been the start of my solo career. I was thinking about some of the things that poor Mick Avory had to play. All he wanted was to be a jazz and blues drummer, and I brought in all these weird songs."

If Davies felt he was orchestrating a solo record, then it went unnoticed by the drummer. "It was more of a band effort," Avory says. "It was collaborative, rather than him writing a song and [us] going in like session men and just doing it." Ray also detected discontent from Pete Quaife, who had already stormed out at the end of the session for 'Days' and seemed in open revolt. Dave Davies remembers the bassist appearing onstage and playing a completely different set of songs from the other musicians, just to be awkward or register his disapproval. Yet, Quaife had nothing but retrospective praise for *The Village Green Preservation Society*. "Making that album was the high point of my career. It is something of which I am very proud. For me, it represents the only real album made by the Kinks. It is probably the only album made by us in which we all contributed something." Ray did not learn of Quaife's tribute until after the bassist's death and was astonished by his admission. As with everything else connected with the album, its historical standing appears to have conflicted its creators to such an extent that even their undiluted praise has been questioned.

It is tempting to cite the critical commonplace – frequently reiterated by Ray Davies – that *The Village Green Preservation Society* was an album uniquely out of time. Its conservatism, nostalgia and lack of psychedelic experimentation must have seemed deeply unfashionable in a year associated in popular memory with public unrest. Ray Davies' pastoral reflections had no place on the hectoring soundtrack of the Year Of Revolution. Or did they? As with all revolutions, the notion of counter-revolution is never far away. In tandem with the images of street-fighting men espousing Marxist philosophy, 1968 was also associated with an outbreak of nostalgia and escapism. Two of the most popular television programmes that year were *Dad's Army* and *The Forsyte Saga*, both of which looked back to a simpler England during the Second World War and the Edwardian era, respectively. Among the most popular books of the time were fantasies – from J. R. R. Tolkien's *The Lord Of The Rings* to Mervyn Peake's *Gormenghast* trilogy. Ray Davies' quaint songs about a wicked witch or phenomenal ballooning cat were hardly out of place here. His denunciation of city life and championing of the countryside also tallied with the new ecology movement.

The belief that the Kinks' album was fatally unfashionable is undermined by its form and content. 'Concept' albums, however ill formed or unrealized, excited the pop press of 1967–8. Apart from the obvious example of *Sgt Pepper's*, considerable coverage had been given to Keith West, whose single 'Excerpt From A Teenage Opera' had hit the Top 5. The song's central character was the deceased 'Grocer Jack', an elder version of Davies' Grocer Tom in 'Village Green'. There were wild and whirling reports of a full-scale teenage opera, all of which came to nothing. West was effectively a one-hit wonder, but the publicity he generated for the unrealized pop opera was completely out of proportion to his standing. All this emphasized the extent to which the pop press was impressed by ambition and novelty.

The *New Musical Express* was not the *New Statesman*. Pop journalists did not engage with politics and whether Ray Davies was reactionary or revolutionary was irrelevant and never discussed. He was the man who had written 'Waterloo Sunset', 'Autumn Almanac' and 'Days' – reflective and nostalgic odes that seemed to ask the pertinent question: is there any progression without retrogression? *The Village Green Preservation Society* was greeted in that same spirit and received the track-by-track analysis reserved for only the major artistes of that time.

Musically and conceptually, the album resonated with other strands in British pop. In the summer of 1968, the number 1 album in the UK LP charts was the Small Faces' *Ogdens' Nut Gone Flake*, a whimsical 'concept' album of sorts whose second side featured an extended song suite narrated by actor/writer Stanley Unwin. It was partly inspired by a lazy boat trip on the Thames and appeared even more fanciful than Davies' village green idea, which was almost radical by comparison. Moreover, the Small Faces' last hit, 'Lazy Sunday', had sounded like a thematic cross between 'Sunny Afternoon' and 'Sitting By The Riverside'. Clearly, Davies was in tune with the times in certain respects.

Beyond the populist heavy blues of 1968, there was also a 'back to roots' movement which was gaining momentum. Traffic were famously "getting it together in the country", the Rolling Stones had disavowed psychedelia after the career disaster *Their Satanic Majesties Request* and the Beatles had confined *Sgt Pepper's* to the Summer of Love. As early as March 1968, they were topping the charts with 'Lady Madonna', a wish-fulfilling attempt to record a genuine rock 'n' roll record, pre-empting the self-explanatory 'Get Back'. In America, Bob Dylan had started the year with *John*

Wesley Harding, a stark declaration, infused with biblical imagery, outlaw allegory and a landscape variously populated by the socially disadvantaged – the hobo, the drifter and the immigrant. After the electric maelstrom of 1966's *Blonde On Blonde*, its austere, acoustic setting was both challenging and prescriptive. It seemed that Dylan too was seeking salvation in old wisdom as a panacea to the political hectoring of the time.

The commercial shortcomings of *The Village Green Preservation Society* had little to do with the subject matter or the marketing. The album itself was not the problem – but, rather, the Kinks themselves. In a year of reinvention they were fatally branded as a pop group who had lost their way. Playing on a package tour with the Herd and the Tremeloes and appearing up north in cabaret were steps too far for a group that hoped to be taken seriously as albums artistes. Ray Davies, who had been sceptical about the Kinks' future since writing and recording 'Days', was left wondering whether *The Village Green Preservation Society* might become his unheralded epitaph.

CHAPTER TWENTY-FIVE

END OF THE SIXTIES

Ray Davies had good reason to feel concerned about the Kinks' career towards the end of 1968. Their reputation abroad – notably in the all-important American market – had shrunk to the level of a fondly remembered oldies act, unseen and unheard in years. The elongated 'ban' had taken its commercial toll and urgently needed to be resolved. In November, the same month that *The Village Green Preservation Society* was issued in the UK, the US trade magazine *Billboard* ran a news piece indicating that British acts were as viable as ever. Decca (US) mentioned three that they were eager to push stateside. The Who were obvious choices given their recent breakthrough but it was the other two performers that drew exasperated sighs. Leapy Lee, who had previously recorded a Davies composition and enjoyed the patronage of Collins/Wace, was a surprise name, having thus far achieved no hit success even in his homeland. Even more amazing was the 'latest UK discovery' whom Decca were presently promoting with a four-week tour of major American cities: Jonah P. Jones. The former Kinks' roadie, last heard of languishing in a Warrington hospital with Pete Quaife, had miraculously reinvented himself as a Decca recording artiste. His debut single, 'My Father', composed by hit songwriter Graham Gouldman, was garnering radio play and additional support in New York clubland. It seemed scarcely believable. While the Kinks were still prevented from touring America, their former roadie, William Grimshaw school-mate, tambourine man and failed candidate as lead singer, had won the support of Decca, the label that had turned down the Ravens and later signed the Who. In more colourful times, this would have smacked of a conspiracy.

Davies was distracted from such musings by major events at home. In November 1968, Rasa's father Aleksandras died. "A terrible moment," she remembers. One month later, on Christmas Day, Ray and Rasa celebrated the birth of their second daughter. Christened Victoria Jane in the birth registry, she was referred to in family documents and in person as Viktoria Jayne. Her first name, an alternate foreign spelling of Victoria, was oddly reminiscent of those old Kinks' liner notes where every 'C' was replaced by a 'K'. Jayne was inspired by Jayne Mansfield, the sexy starlet who had appeared in the rock 'n' roll cinematic classic, *The Girl Can't Help It*. Ray's prediction of a 'wonder boy' had proven wrong, but he was quick to write a song using her name, albeit without the 'K', which would emerge later in the year. Family commitments might have soothed his troubled mind but, since moving to his mansion in Borehamwood the previous summer, he had been unsettled. Geographically detached from the other Kinks and his casual friends in north London, he felt entombed in splendour. "It's so enormous and rambling and I'm so cut off from everyone, that I can't manage to get as much done as I'd like to," he told a visiting journalist. "So now I'm going to move back to a flat in London. I miss things like having people bang on the walls when I play music too loudly. I just want to be surrounded by people again." Fortunately, he had not yet sold his former abode in Fortis Green, so was able to return at his leisure. In the meantime, he kept himself busy by taking on multiple projects. "I find that when you sit down and try to write, you just *can't* – but if you're busy doing things all the time, then you can."

Ray found a welcome taskmaster in the person of Ned Sherrin, the avuncular television and film producer responsible for the celebrated satirical programmes *That Was The Week That Was* and *Not So Much A Programme, More A Way Of Life*. They had first met a few months earlier when Ray was invited to Sherrin's home in Bywater Street. "I think he wanted to meet my brother Dave really and got the wrong one, but was too polite to mention it. Ned had a nice Mrs Somebody who prepared scones and jam and then disappeared . . . At the time, I tended just to mix with pop music people – the pop and comedy worlds hadn't really started to spill over into each other much." Sherrin had been working with Columbia Pictures, which had recently acquired the film rights to Leslie Thomas' *The Virgin Soldiers*, a comic novel about National Service in Malaya. He was looking for a suitable candidate to compose the opening music when his co-writer Caryl Brahms, a sprightly near 70-year-old, suggested, "Why don't you use Ray Davies?" It was not an entirely eccentric choice as Davies had recently written the theme song for the film spin-off, *Till Death Us Do Part*.

"My knowledge of Sixties' pop radio and record charts was poor to non-existent," Sherrin modestly acknowledges. "The Ray/ Kinks connection was entirely down to Caryl who reeled off a list of hits – 'You Really Got Me', 'Dedicated Follower . . .' and 'Summer [sic] Afternoon'. I'd never heard of any of them at the time." Sherrin's ignorance of the Kinks' greatest hits, including their two chart toppers, was somewhat surprising given his involvement in commercial ventures such as the pilot episode of television's *Up Pompeii!* and various stage shows including *No Bed For Bacon* and *The Spoils*. Then again, as a former barrister he moved in social circles that tended to regard pop music as ephemera. Once introduced to Ray's more recent compositions he recognized the composer's potential beyond straightforward pop. In common with Barry Fantoni, Sherrin had the habit of praising Davies' work at the expense of his more illustrious rock contemporaries. "Ray's music really interested me – it seemed to catch the spirit of the moment. I thought the Beatles' music was charming pap and there seemed to be no relevance to the period in the Rolling Stones' lyrics – I just couldn't understand them."

Auditions soon began for *The Virgin Soldiers*, with the young actor Hywel Bennett securing the lead part. David Bowie, still a relative unknown, offered "a rather wooden screen test", according to Sherrin, "but we did use him in one dance scene as an extra." Davies was also offered an audition, but demurred. "Acting didn't really interest me. I was doing quite enough of it onstage with the Kinks. Ned said to me, 'You can do the audition and be a star, or you can work very hard for very little money and do the music', so I decided to do the music." At first, Davies wrote some "noble lyrics" to accompany the film's theme tune, but they were swiftly rejected. "Ned was very good at giving advice tactfully and kindly . . . I realized they didn't work when Ned very gently and humorously managed to get me to see it and we dropped them." The film was released later that year to mixed reviews.

The ever-accommodating Sherrin also offered Davies a song-writing commission for the BBC series *Where Was Spring?*, starring Eleanor Bron and John Fortune, both of whom had worked with the producer on his earlier satire shows. As with *At The Eleventh Hour*, Ray was required to compose a topical song every seven days for the Monday night programme. Among those that survive are 'Where Did My Spring Go?' a dark, yet amusing reflection on age, ill health and decay, with Davies echoing Shakespeare's Jacques in his gloomy but philosophical vision of approaching death: *sans* hair, *sans* skin, *sans* bones, *sans* everything. The song also has strong echoes of Nina Simone's contemporaneous hit, 'Ain't Got No . . . I Got Life'. Another extant recording, 'When I Turn Off The Living Room Light', opens with the daring and provocative question "Who cares if you're Jewish?" before moving into a lyrical equivalent of the proverb 'All cats are grey in the dark' with comic reflections on how physical imperfections magically disappear when the lights are switched off.

Sherrin was impressed by Davies' contributions and overall efficiency throughout the six-week series. The producer also gained some passing insights into the conflicting dynamic within the Kinks. "I witnessed the tension between them, especially Ray and Dave, but it wasn't discussed and didn't affect us." What struck Sherrin most forcibly was Davies' attention to detail. "Ray may have had a reputation for being quite a prickly person at the time, but as far as I was concerned he was never a moment's trouble: polite, attentive to what was needed, and then he went away, composed the music and delivered it on time."

Although there would be long periods when they did not meet, Davies and Sherrin became unlikely friends over the decades. The producer proved a valuable sounding board for the songwriter's more ambitious projects but it was his *joie de vivre* and epicurean tastes that were most attractive. Sometimes, they would consume epic amounts of wine as Sherrin, a fabulous raconteur, entertained his host with stories of the great and good. "After one meal in 1969," Sherrin remembers, "we'd had so many bottles that we went to the Jermyn Street Turkish Baths to sweat it out and simply carried on talking until morning."

Increasingly distant from his fellow Kinks, Davies maintained only intermittent communication, insisting that they attend meetings and rehearsals at his Borehamwood home. Pete Quaife, already disgruntled about his role in the group and ready to quit if things did not improve, was enraged by what he termed "Ray's ego". Davies' fraternization with television producers had made him insufferable to Quaife, who felt that his own contributions to the group had been marginalized over the past two years. The bassist boasted of writing songs inspired by the soft rock of Simon & Garfunkel and the Association but, if so, they were never recorded. "I'd heard songs he'd written," Dave says, "but he was never very forthright about playing them." That was probably just as well.

"I made attempts at writing," Quaife claims, a little vaguely. "Any ideas coming from anybody else were trodden down straight away. Nobody, by this time, could encroach upon Ray's area and expertise. If you came up with something – smack – it was gone. Whether it was good or bad didn't matter." On visits to Borehamwood, Quaife felt like a hired hand who would be kept waiting until his host entered the room and played something on piano without bothering to explain the tune or lyrics. Davies would just as abruptly conclude matters and disappear. Nobody was entirely certain if the session had ended or not. Sometimes, Quaife and Avory simply went home.

Ray Davies was astute enough to offer an olive branch, inviting Quaife to contribute to *The Virgin Soldiers*, an orchestral session which the bassist regarded as one of the highlights of his career. More importantly, Davies found a new vehicle for the Kinks via the television connections that Quaife privately loathed. Producer Jo Durden-Smith had recently contacted Collins and Wace about the possibility of Ray and the Kinks recording the equivalent of a 'pop opera' for Granada Television, roughly based on the rise and fall of the British Empire. Over dinner in Soho, Davies met the producer, a 27-year-old classics graduate from Merton College, Oxford, with an impressive CV. He had already worked on the current affairs programme *World In Action*, notably on their controversial investigation into Scientology. Durden-Smith had a keen interest in radical politics and pop culture, having recently produced documentaries on American group the Doors (*The Doors Are Open*) and the making of the hippie-styled hit musical *Hair*. His credentials, enhanced by youth and innovation, could hardly have been better.

Davies learned that he would be given carte blanche over the project and agreed that a musical drama based on the British Empire from the age of Queen Victoria to the present might be viable. The producer was keen, but they still needed an experienced co-writer. Having recently seen the play *Forty Years On*, Ray nominated Alan Bennett, a canny choice given his background in satire with the groundbreaking *Beyond The Fringe*. Bennett was ruled out when they found he was busy working on the stage play *Sing A Rude Song*. An even more promising candidate was John Betjeman, the future Poet Laureate, whose work chimed with Davies' in many respects. A founder of the Victorian Society in 1958, Betjeman was a celebrated critic of architectural brutalism and an active campaigner against the march of modernism. His light, comic verse had a sharp satiric edge with a sense of time and place that Davies should have envied. The poet could easily have been among the cast list of the songwriter's 'Village Green Preservation Society'. In common with Robert Wace, he was an alumnus of Marlborough College with a similarly mediocre academic record, having failed to complete his English degree at Oxford. What seemed a mouth-watering pairing was never realized. They were aiming too high. The third candidate was 32-year-old Julian Mitchell, an Essex-born playwright, screenwriter and occasional novelist. Like Bennett, he was homosexual, but Davies had been in showbusiness long enough not to raise an objection on that point.

Writing a pop/rock opera based around Queen Victoria and the erosion of the British Empire was hardly the sexiest of projects but it was not as unfashionable as it seemed. Like the 'Village Green' idea it was retro at a time of revolution, and had the scope to comment on contemporary events and mores by the very act of looking back. Victoriana was as vibrant and visible at this time as the Union Jack had been back in 1966. Along with Edwardian artefacts, it permeated the prevailing cultural landscape: Queen Victoria's eldest grandson Wilhelm II, the last German Emperor (Kaiser) and King of Prussia, had become an improbable style icon and had even inspired a hit single, 1967's 'I Was Kaiser Bill's Batman'. Field Marshal Lord Kitchener was now better known by young people as the inherited name adopted by the Portobello Road boutique I Was Lord Kitchener's Valet, which had recently moved premises to the equally trendy Carnaby Street. Military uniforms and regalia were more popular than ever, especially when used by pop icons such as Mick Jagger (who wore a colourful tunic on *Ready, Steady, Go!*), the Beatles (the *Sgt Pepper's* look) and, more recently, Jimi Hendrix. Aubrey Beardsley prints could be found decorating the walls of bohemian homes and long dresses straight out of Victorian costume melodramas had supplanted the miniskirt. Even the BBC Drama department had responded to the trend with an adaptation of John Galsworthy's *The Forsyte Saga*, which was about to transfer from BBC 2 to the main channel. For younger viewers, there was *Adam Adamant Lives!*, the story of a suave Victorian adventurer who, frozen in a block of ice, had been resurrected in 1966 Swinging London to face, not only contemporary villains, but a new, permissive morality.

As Ray Davies was commencing work on his pop opera, John Fowles' novel *The French Lieutenant's Woman*, set in the Victorian age, was published to international acclaim. On a more controversial note, Edward Bond's play *Early Morning* was performed legally for the first time, having previously been banned after a single staging at the Royal Court Theatre in 1968. A surrealist alternate history, it imagines Queen Victoria in a lesbian relationship with Florence Nightingale (whom she rapes), the royal sons as Siamese twins, and a heaven in which the participants devolve into cannibalism. The play's hero/anti-hero is Arthur who loses his mind before cajoling the cast into throwing themselves off the cliffs of Beachy Head. In Heaven, where a painless form of cannibalism is the norm, Arthur leads a working-class revolution and hunger strike in protest at the eating of human flesh, at which point Victoria nails him into a coffin. One commentator likened Arthur to the "flawed liberal would-be popular leaders of the earlier 1960s", while noting how much the first half of the play conjured images redolent of 'Swinging London'. "Bond's ghastly cannibal heaven, where no one feels the pain of being eaten any more, is clearly a parody of this triumphalist affluent society, where the dog-eat-dog ethics of Victorian capitalism are apparently to be run forever as a kind of whited, emotionally empty, sepulchre over which Victoria herself is still in undiminished charge."

Raymond Douglas Davies was no Edward Bond. He was unlikely to come up with anything as grotesque, absurdist or experimental as the playwright but, coincidentally, in personalizing the project, he creates his own Arthur. Inspired by memories of his brother-in-law Gordon Arthur Anning and beloved sister Rose, he uses their lives and emigration to Australia as key themes in his production. In common with his approach on 'Rosy, Won't You Please Come Home', Davies invents a meta-Arthur, stubbornly retaining the name and spirit of his brother-in-law, but altering many of the biographical details for dramatic convenience. As described by Julian Mitchell, the central character of Davies' work is Arthur Morgan who lives with his wife Rose in suburbia. They have a married son, Derek, who has two children: Terry and Marilyn. In this new scenario, it is Arthur's offspring who plan to emigrate to Australia. The action takes place on their final day in England. "Nothing happens very much," Mitchell notes, "everyone has Sunday dinner together." Arthur then takes the family on a boat trip and picnic during which he reflects on his own uneventful life. "It's a sad day for Arthur, seeing them off," Mitchell concludes. "People haven't been nearly as nice to Arthur as he's been to them and . . . What's it all about then? Is this what he's lived for? He's got the house, hasn't he? And the car? It's been a good life, hasn't it? Well, hasn't it?"

Granada's Jo Durden-Smith was happy to go along with an amended treatment, now titled *Arthur Or The Decline And Fall Of The British Empire*. "I thought it would be a nice idea to do it," Davies announced at the time, "but I didn't want to be restricted, so I built it round the life of Arthur . . . He's just like so many guys who are pushed through life within the confines of the establishment."

While Davies was composing material for *Arthur*, the Kinks released a new single in March 1969. It had been nine months since 'Days', an eternity in pop terms, but few found any great merit in 'Plastic Man'. Its heavy-handed humour lacked either the wit of 'A Well Respected Man' or the satiric bite of 'Dedicated Follower Of Fashion'. Touted as the first Kinks' song to feature all four members on vocals, it had little else to recommend it beyond a jaunty tune and an over-obvious novelty lyric. It was akin to a cartoon version of the Kinks. Few heard the admittedly odd B-side 'King Kong', which featured a warbling vocal reminiscent of Tyrannosaurus Rex's Marc Bolan.

Rather than play down 'Plastic Man' in the press, Davies foolishly trumpeted its importance. "This record has outgrown what a pop record can be," he announced, presumably through gritted teeth. "This record has more love for people. Sometimes you love a person so much. But he's got himself in a hole, and the only thing you can do is to kick him to get him out of it. People have had a go at me for using the word 'plastic', but it's the only word you could possibly use. You couldn't call a person a pathetic man . . . Certain people dislike it because they get certain truths about themselves. Nobody likes truth. But I admit truth." When in full flow, Davies sounded as though he was talking about himself as much as his imaginary 'Plastic Man'. Curbing the rhetoric, he concluded, more soberly: "It's probably not the greatest song I'll ever write, but it's the only song I could have written at this time. Even though I hated it when I first heard the acetate. But I think it could be a hit."

'Plastic Man' received reasonable radio airplay but a promotional film intended for BBC's *Top Of The Pops* was never shown, supposedly because the song contained the risqué word 'bum'. "It's ridiculous, but you're in the hands of a BBC monopoly," Davies complained. The lack of television promotion arrested the disc's progress, but it was never an obvious smash hit. Like 'Wonderboy' it peaked at number 28 in *NME*, selling a paltry 27,000 copies.

The chart statistics were less important than the shock news that accompanied the record's release. Pete Quaife had quit the Kinks. At first the management denied the rumour, but Quaife retorted: "I don't know why everyone's playing it down. I'm leaving. And that's it." Pressed for an explanation, he announced: "I'm sick of standing onstage and just playing two notes per bar. I want to do something more productive. There's no enmity. It's just that the other Kinks and I are going in different directions. I told them I was sorry but I couldn't take any more. I was fed up playing pretty bubblegum music . . . our tastes are not the same. I couldn't stick playing 'Sunny Afternoon' for ever. I want to do something more than just produce sounds. I can play that commercial stuff standing on my head . . . I'm leaving the Kinks on good terms. But I'd rather go to prison than play with them any more."

Perhaps the most surprising aspect of Quaife's exit was the nonchalance with which it was conducted. There were no intense discussions, stormy confrontations, arguments over compensation, or reservations about the wisdom of such a reckless career move. "That was his personality," says Dave Davies. "That's the way he would do it. He was very confident that what he was doing was right, so credit to him. There was a lot of quiet frustration and resentment going on with Pete. Ray and I were getting all the attention and he probably thought, 'I've had enough.' Creatively, he wasn't fulfilling himself. I remember one of the last gigs he did with us, we were onstage and he had his foot on the amp, playing all this weird shit over what we were playing. It was as if he really wasn't interested. Perhaps he thought that we were uncool and he wanted to do something else. That's the feeling I had . . . It was just as well he went because it wouldn't have got any better."

What the other Kinks did not know was that Quaife was on the edge of another breakdown. "Pete had a big flip out and trashed his flat in Lynton Grange," his brother David says. "When we got there, he was just sobbing. He'd lost it completely. Gone. He was married to Beden [Annette] and this was just before he went over to Denmark, permanently. Now, you look back on it and you think, 'nervous breakdown'. It was all too much for him."

Ultimately, the reasons for Quaife's departure were numerous: musical dissatisfaction, disillusionment with Ray's creative domination, wariness of the violent tendencies that were still likely to erupt at any moment, frustration at being treated like a session musician, the lack of financial remuneration, fear of flying and, more generally, that claustrophobia and nervousness he had experienced since the car crash with Jonah. Ray Davies was upset by Quaife's decision at the time but admitted that there had been a growing rift between them that was never likely to be resolved. "Pete Quaife was the true amateur. He enjoyed life, and he was my friend. The saddest thing was that we were very successful, and we toured, and we didn't talk to one another and [then] we weren't friends. The day we stopped communicating offstage was a good time to stop." There was no happy ending for Quaife. He had already formed a new group, Mapleoak, who later released a single on Decca, 'Son Of A Gun', which flopped. He would never record for a major label again.

Ray Davies immediately instructed Mick Avory to contact John Dalton and invite him to re-enlist as a Kink. Since leaving the group, Dalton had been employed as a coalman, lorry driver and foreman of his own yard in Wood Green, north London. Happily married with a baby boy and playing regularly with former Roulette John Rogan in Pastime, he was far from overwhelmed by Avory's entreaties. Ray was taken aback to learn that Dalton was prevaricating so improved his offer. Dalton was informed that sometime in the future, if things went well, he might secure a partnership in the Kinks, just like Pete Quaife had done back in 1964. What really won over Dalton, though, was news that the Kinks were planning to return to the USA before the end of the year. Visiting America sounded impossibly glamorous at a time when even a plane trip to the country was prohibitively expensive. Unfortunately, no contract was offered by Davies and any dreams of securing a partnership dwindled over the years to such an extent that even the original suggestion was forgotten. "It never happened," Dalton laments.

While the line-up was changing, Davies had been visiting Los Angeles, negotiating a deal to produce the Turtles' album *Turtle Soup* and attending meetings about a forthcoming national tour. The previous impasse was resolved when he signed a document of apology to the American Federation of Television and Radio Artists. After returning to England, he was amused to discover that the Kinks were heading for Beirut. Their recently appointed road manager Ken Jones – a Northern Ireland émigré who had served in the RAF – was keen to visit exotic places and persuaded the senior management to sanction the trip.

For new boy John Dalton, it was strangely reminiscent of his previous debut performance abroad when he was almost arrested by police in Spain. On this occasion, he accidentally walked through a plate-glass door in the hotel where they were booked to play above a boarded-over swimming pool. The sound of marching soldiers and tanks outside offered an unappetizing backdrop. A dispute with the promoter over money soon threatened to spiral into an international incident. The group were advised to leave the country at the earliest opportunity. Their passports were held until just before their plane departed.

Foreign quarrels also arose in Germany later that summer when the Kinks appeared at Hamburg's Star Club, a venue that had hosted the Beatles in the days before chart fame. Faulty equipment meant that Dalton's bass was mute so, midway through their opening song, the group walked off stage, carefully negotiating their way through the hostile crowd. Dalton ended up on the street, unaware of the ensuing drama back at the club. "I was so pissed off with it, I just wanted to get out of there. I couldn't believe what was going on. We'd played half a number. In the meantime, one of these bands had made a remark and so Ray landed him one. Then there was a full fistfight in the dressing room." Davies' latest altercation was merely another chapter in the history of the 'brawling Kinks' and a warning of what lay ahead.

On 21 June, an interim single appeared from the forthcoming album. 'Drivin'' was a pleasantly modest effort which, in common with 'Sitting By The Riverside', had been inspired by childhood memories of family outings in the countryside. Given Ray's aversion to driving, it was amusing for friends and familiars to hear him write a paean to the road. It would only be decades later that he finally passed his driving test, an achievement he greatly regretted. "Learning to drive was the biggest mistake of my life," he says. "It turned me into an arsehole." Rasa, the family chauffeur and occasional instructor, was one of his unwilling victims. "He was a nightmare. I was trying to teach him, but he was awful, dreadful. He nearly killed a woman on a zebra crossing. I said, 'I can't do this any more!'"

Following the disappointment of 'Plastic Man', something far stronger than 'Drivin'' was required to replenish Davies' chart fortunes. Alarmingly, the single failed to reach the *NME* Top 30, their first 'miss' since 'You Still Want Me' in that barren time before 'You Really Got Me'. Disillusioned, Davies began to wonder if the Kinks still had a future. The departure of Quaife, concomitant with the failure of recent singles, was ominous. "I believe that once the original members go, that's finished. It's all over then. It's only a cloning process and it's a one-way ticket to Vegas after that. Pete might not have been the most important member of the band but when you take one person out of a set-up, something in the chemistry changes and everybody changes as a result. When someone else comes in, he brings out different elements in most people. So, really, the band should have broken up then."

The Kinks seemed cast adrift in that summer of 1969. Their so-called 'pop opera' *Arthur*, now complete, was delayed in order to coincide with the television production scheduled for later in the year. In the interim, the Who had released *Tommy*, their lavish and bombastic double album, which was widely hailed as rock's 'first' pop/rock opera. In July, the Rolling Stones played a memorial concert for Brian Jones at London's Hyde Park attended by 250,000 people. The event was filmed by Granada TV as *The Stones In The Park,* produced by Jo Durden-Smith, who might otherwise have been commencing work on Davies' project. The following month, the most momentous gathering yet in rock history occurred in upstate New York at the Woodstock Festival. Among the star-studded cast was the Who, representing Britain, just as they had done at Monterey two years before. By now, *Tommy* was on its way to the US Top 5, having climbed to number 2 in the UK. It was difficult to escape the feeling that the Kinks had been usurped again.

In September, the group released their most important single in years. 'Shangri-la', the undisputed centrepiece of their forthcoming album, was among Davies' most accomplished compositions, a perfect distillation of the suburban dystopias that would dominate his work thereafter. "It embodied all my thoughts, fears, hopes and aspirations of a class that was moving from the tenement houses into aspiring to have their own owned houses . . . a shift in class. The Shangri-la becomes a curse because everyone has names on their houses, but they all look the same. There's fear in that as well, so it was double-edged." The idea had begun with a casual request from screenwriter Julian Mitchell who asked for a song about "Arthur's pebble dash nirvana". As with 'Animal

Farm' and 'Do You Remember Walter', there were echoes of George Orwell's *Coming Up For Air* in which the character George Bowling had described his street in West Bletchley as an endless row of identical semi-detached houses with interchangeable names like 'the Laurels' and 'the Hawthorns'. Davies developed these images of conformity to produce the most moving, subtly satirical and ambitious exposition of his songwriting life, a study in ambivalence that both derided and celebrated the fate of his anti-hero. At first he imagined the composition visually and drew a sketch of chimney pots stretching into an infinite suburbia. His disparaging vision of 'subtopia' was in keeping with those architectural critics who bemoaned the arrival of New Towns in 1946, but Davies also appreciated and articulated their popularity among the aspiring working classes in search of a more sedate existence away from the city centres.

The process of embourgeoisment was devilishly alluring, as Davies well knew when recalling his own troubled journey from Fortis Green to Borehamwood. "I tried living in a big house and I can't. I'm going back to a little house. I don't like to say what I've got and be happy with it. I'd wear hobnail boots by my fire rather than slippers. I can't stand slippers because they symbolize giving up to me. At the same time, I love the people who are like that. But I hate what's handed down when people get into the state where that's *all* they want."

'Shangri-la' captures exquisitely the duality described by Davies, both in its musical structure and ambivalent lyrics. The delicate acoustic guitar opening wrings out every ounce of pathos in the tale of the 'little man', seeking and finding contentment by acknowledging his station in life, submissive but happy in his comfy rocking chair. The narrator's mental anguish is evident as the arrangement speeds up and the comments become more caustic and condescending. A mock epic grandeur is achieved as the colliery brass collides with a stately harpsichord and church chorale while Davies calculates, in deadly detail, the price of satisfaction – summed up in the description of the radio/television set, rented for seven shillings a week. It is, in many respects, a devastating critique, albeit one told without anger. "I'm not laughing at those people in the song at all," Davies insisted, when challenged on the role of his condescending narrator. "They're brainwashed into that, they brainwash themselves. Their minds are like that: they're happy, really. It becomes a religion to them. The glory of being boring . . . It's a sense of greatness he's got around him that you can't penetrate because you feel you might upset him . . . The chorus of 'Shangri-La' is a bit of a chant – like 'See My Friend'. You accept it as your religion because you can't have anything else, whatever you've got is what you accept . . ."

Over five minutes long, the single 'Shangri-la' (retitled 'Shangrila') was a risky venture and, even before its release, Davies concluded that its running time might limit radio play or television exposure. "But there's nothing that can be cut," he said. If 'Shangrila' had reached number 1, Davies' reputation as one of the greatest song-writers of his generation would have been established beyond argument. There were precedents which offered hope. Far longer singles had achieved international success, notably Bob Dylan's 'Like A Rolling Stone', the Beatles' 'Hey Jude' and Richard Harris' 'MacArthur Park' – but they were the exceptions. Earlier that summer an equally audacious single – Procol Harum's 'A Salty Dog' – threatened to follow suit, but failed to reach the Top 30, despite selected radio play. The Kinks, already weakened by the successive failures of 'Plastic Man' and 'Drivin'', suffered the same fate in what was surely one of the great chart injustices of the era.

While fans were still awaiting the screening of *Arthur Or The Decline And Fall Of The British Empire*, complete with a prom-ised souvenir book to be published by Granada TV, Pye Records lost patience. Wary of losing the valuable Christmas market, they issued the album on 10 October to coincide with its American release. Critical response in the UK pop press was coolly favour-able, without fanfare. There was no sense of event accompanying *Arthur*'s arrival. Inevitably, there were references to the Who's *Tommy*, which did the Kinks no favours. Davies' subject matter seemed prosaic in comparison. Instead of a deaf, dumb and blind pinball-playing kid who turns his multiple handicaps to messianic advantage over the space of a double album, Davies' protagonist emerges as an arch-conformist whose crowning achievement is emigrating to Australia. Really, Davies had said it all in the great 'Shangri-la', which left the rest of the album sounding somewhat anti-climactic by comparison.

The work begins promisingly with the sprightly 'Victoria', a nostalgic and sardonic commentary on English society. Belatedly issued as a single, it registered in the *NME* chart for a single week at number 30, then dropped out. The remainder of the album was a well-produced but frustrating hotchpotch of average to good material, alleviated by fleeting moments of excellence.

Arthur had a greater unity of design than *The Village Green Preservation Society*, but that meant Davies was obliged to write to order, a process that seemed to drain some songs of empathy and emotion. The allegory between the character Arthur and the British Empire's decline and fall sometimes appears forced and awkward. The political songs on the album – 'Mr Churchill Says', 'Yes Sir, No Sir' and 'Brainwashed' – sound rather laboured, repeating the theme of military oppression to no great advantage. At least 'Some Mother's Son' (a title borrowed from the lyrics of 'Wonderboy') has conviction but even this seems compromised by Davies' affected voice. 'She Bought A Hat Like Princess Marina', ostensibly a playful commentary on the proletariat aping the royals, emerges as a music hall pastiche with Ray employing his upper-class accent, set against a grand harpsichord accompaniment. 'Australia', another song unlikely to survive outside the limiting context of the album, has a lightness of tone and knowing humour which would have suited his theatrical production. Its sardonic lyrics and fustian array of musical styles – everything from Caribbean and Beach Boys' surf to an extended progressive rock/blues workout, complete with a didgeridoo – is a great romp and wonderfully parodic. 'Young And Innocent Days' allows him to escape the straitjacket imposed by the concept to compose a more generalized reflection on the past in the vein of 'Days' or 'Do You Remember Walter', but the result falls short of their classic status. Similarly, the closing 'Arthur', effectively the title track, might have inspired something approaching 'Shangri-la' status but serves more as a lyrical/musical reprise. For all its strengths and ambition, the album ultimately sounds less impressive than either *The Village Green Preservation Society* or *Something Else*.

Whatever lingering hopes Ray Davies had for *Arthur* were blighted when Granada abruptly decided to cancel the television production, arguing that the project was too extravagant.

Scriptwriter Julian Mitchell was furious and placed the blame on producer Jo Durden-Smith for attending a meeting without preparing a proper budget. Manager Grenville Collins was equally indignant and threatened Granada with legal reprisals which were never executed. Davies was understandably shattered by the affair. "We got the director and the sets. It was only at the last minute that there were production arguments – and it got shafted. But our career hinged on that. I spent a year on [*Arthur*] – and it fell through. It was really hard." Years later, he spoke more fancifully, arguing: "*Arthur* was designed as a TV musical. If it had been done it would have pushed the boundaries of TV and art."

In America, the album failed to reach the *Billboard* Top 100, but it was not all bad news. Improbably enough, the Kinks had secured a following on the 'underground' music scene and suddenly became the darlings of *Rolling Stone* magazine. *The Village Green Preservation Society* had already been applauded, but *Arthur* achieved even greater cult status with critic Greil Marcus gushing: "*Arthur* is by all odds the best British album of 1969. It shows that Pete Townshend still has worlds to conquer and that the Beatles have a lot of catching up to do." The flame had been lit by Reprise Records, whose anticipation of the Kinks' imminent arrival, after the lifting of their elongated ban, had inspired a major promotional campaign. An elaborate package titled 'God Save The Kinks' was produced, including memorabilia and a compilation of edited songs, *Then, Now And Inbetween*.

Reprise's hype went into overdrive once the touring dates were confirmed. Bizarre promotional ideas were deliberately exposed to the press, including plans to recruit a battalion of teenagers to descend on Kennedy Airport on the day of the Kinks' arrival, in imitation of the Beatles' invasion of 1964. Further stunts included fake arrests for loitering, impersonating a police officer and income tax evasion. It was even hinted that the New York venue Fillmore East would be closed during their set in order to protect the hearing of the nation's youth. One internal memo at Reprise suggested the company should commission a ten-second spot on Top 40 radio "with a very seductive English chick, perhaps one of the lovelies in our own employ, intoning 'The Kinks are *coming*' over a very rocking passage from the album". Rather more reckless was the tasteless afterthought: "Arrange for the group to be arrested for possession or gang rape" and "for a number of paternity suits to be filed against Dave Davies". In the end, these sensationalist proposals were vetoed, but the Kinks were ever capable of producing their own PR disasters.

The US tour opened on 17 October at the Fillmore East where they supported the highly accomplished LA band Spirit. Nervous, under-rehearsed and seemingly ill-equipped, the Kinks received poor notices, with *Billboard* complaining: "Davies' lyrics were obliterated by the roar of the volume and further plundered by the group's musicianship, which suffered from the sameness of each song." They fared little better in Boston or Chicago where they opened for the Who, a reversal of the old order which did not go unnoticed by the Davies brothers. Already fractious and drinking heavily, Dave trashed a hotel room, then badly damaged his hand in a self-destructive display, resulting in the cancellation of several shows. The tour resumed in Detroit and Cincinnati, then traversed to the West Coast where the reviews improved markedly. A four-night stint at the Whisky A Go Go, attended by a combination of stars and hard-core fans, inspired lavish praise, although one critic was surprised to discover that Dave sang most of the songs while Ray "seemed content to play rhythm guitar and contribute occasional verses".

Behind the scenes, Dave was unravelling in lurid fashion. At the Hollywood Hawaiian Hotel, a groupie had offered him some LSD. Remarkably, he had never taken acid before despite its availability among London's hip elite. The Heaven and Hell drug had a profound effect on Dave's psyche – both positively and negatively. Unwisely mixing alcohol with high-potency LSD, he suffered a 'bad trip', broken intermittently by godlike flashes into eternity, the secrets of the universe and the meaning of life. His visions made the Kinks' career seem trivial by comparison. Confused and compromised by an excess of booze and sleeping pills – the antithesis of LSD – he threatened to abandon the tour and return to England. He sought his brother's counsel, pouring out his troubles, while hoping for sympathy and reassurance. Unsurprisingly, Ray remained emotionally detached throughout the fraught encounter, but sensibly suggested that they complete the tour after which Dave could do as he wished. Later, co-manager Grenville Collins played the wise owl, introducing Dave to yoga exercises which relaxed his troubled mind. After a further month on the road, the crisis subsided. Reprise expressed immense satisfaction, never realizing how close the group had come to wrecking their American comeback. Further dates were lined up in the New Year, presumably with Dave's approval.

By mid-December, Ray Davies was back in Fortis Green, reunited with his family. Over the Christmas break, he shared drinks with his father, who provided some inebriated advice. "My dad put his pint down and said, 'If you're going to tour so much you need one thing – a world hit, son. Write another world hit.'"

CHAPTER TWENTY-SIX

LOLA

Ray Davies faced fresh challenges at the dawn of the Seventies. It was a time when the Kinks needed to rebrand themselves as a contemporary band and conquer America, a territory that had remained tantalizingly out of reach since their mid-Sixties heyday. Following their recent return there, Reprise Records, a forward-looking label with hip credentials, was keen to promote the Kinks via frequent touring. Back in the UK, Pye – by no means unsupportive of their recent 'concept' albums – were ever eager to exploit their back catalogue. A sumptuous double album *The Kinks*, compiled by Ray Davies, who also promised to contribute an accompanying book that failed to appear, proved their most memorable vinyl archive collection, but the sales were disappointing. Davies was unforgiving and, in later years, conjured another of his conspiracy theories, maintaining that the emphasis on *The Kinks* had contributed to the commercial failure of *Arthur*. Although there was a four-month gap between the respective releases, he contracted the time frame in his imagination, while plotting a fantasy revenge. "I thought maybe I could wait until everyone left the building and blow up Pye Records and blame it on the IRA, but they don't have too many Irish acts. I don't know, it's just that they had this huge catalogue and they made use of it, coinciding packaging with something new we'd put out. They even did it to the detriment of *Arthur* and they brought a package out *that week* and that killed it off. It's a lack of imagination really. That's the thing I can't tolerate."

In a determined attempt to re-establish their standing in America, the group embarked on an extensive tour, which petered out by St Valentine's Day when the normally robust Mick Avory succumbed to illness. After returning to London, Davies had the luxury of a surprise break during which he was able to compose material for a new album, appear in a television drama and complete that potential 'world hit' that his father had demanded a few months before. For a song that would finish up as a risqué sexual mini-drama, 'Lola' had the most innocent of beginnings. Anticipating a lengthy absence abroad, Davies decided to leave his two young children with a baby lullaby, intoning the word 'lo-la' like a chant. Later, the chorus was enhanced by a novelty lyric in which an innocent young man encounters a transvestite. The narrative was based on several incidents, one involving Robert Wace in a Paris club and another featuring Ray at a date in Bridlington. The composite creation of 'Lola' was completed by additional real-life experiences involving Mick Avory whose late-night clubbing took him into a netherworld of extreme showbiz types, several of whom turned out to be of indeterminate sexuality. "I used to take Ray down transvestite clubs and have an entertaining evening and introduce him to different people. Whereas I just thought they were amusing characters, he could write about them."

The recording of 'Lola' required much tinkering. Wace coaxed Davies into conjuring a distinctive opening in order to attract radio play. That problem was solved when Ray purchased a Dobro guitar in Shaftesbury Avenue. A keyboard part was also suggested, which inadvertently coincided with discussions about hiring an additional player for their next American tour. It was agreed that they needed to embellish the sound in order to compete with more accomplished US groups, so Grenville Collins was assigned the task of finding somebody. It was Pete Frame, founder of the underground rock journal *Zigzag*, who recommended the next Kink.

John Gosling had attended Luton Grammar School with Frame, albeit in a lower form. A serious pianist/organist with teacher training aspirations, Gosling also sang and performed in folk clubs. A few years before, he'd played bass in a local group, the Challengers, whose repertoire included 'Long Tall Sally' and

'Ev'rybody's Gonna Be Happy'. Having passed the entrance exam at the Royal Academy of Music, he was heading towards his finals when Grenville Collins came calling. A comedy of communication ensued when Gosling thought the manager was offering him a job playing in 'the Kings'. "Who are they?" he spluttered. Collins reeled off the titles of several of their hits, reiterating the name: 'Kinks'. "The Kinks! Are they still going?" the pianist retorted. This faux pas was forgiven and Gosling was invited to attend a session at Morgan Studios, where Ray was now recording in 16-track. As part of the audition, Gosling contributed to a handful of songs, including 'Lola'. "That was the one they used for the single," he maintains, "even though the chords I played clashed with the vocal line in some places." The Davies brothers were impressed and did not even bother to audition anybody else. Risking his career, Gosling left the Royal Academy before his finals and agreed to accompany the group on their rearranged US tour and contribute to the forthcoming album.

On 22 May 1970, the tour reopened at the Depot in Minneapolis, a venue run by Danny Rapp of Danny And The Juniors fame. Midway through the set, Gosling's keyboards malfunctioned, leaving him 'panicked' until the sound crew intervened. The other Kinks remained oblivious to his plight. Within a week, Ray was called back to London on an urgent mission. With 'Lola' due for release on 12 June, the BBC were complaining that they could not promote the disc on radio or television due to his use of the brand name 'Coca-Cola' which transgressed the Corporation's rules on advertising. It was necessary to change a single word – 'cherry' replacing 'Coca' – an irksome and expensive substitution that required two plane flights. At least it provided an amusing news story which their recently appointed publicist Marion Rainford dutifully leaked to the music press. Journalists marvelled at Ray's '6,000-mile trip', supposedly completed in a 24-hour period. Evidently, there was further drama when the master tape of 'Lola', insured for £10,000, mysteriously disappeared somewhere between London and New York, only to be miraculously rediscovered. Ray returned to New York, missing the opening night of their double booking at Ungano's, but was otherwise unfazed.

The response to the new Kinks' line-up was generally favourable, even when they supported the heavy rock power trio Grand

Funk Railroad. The Englanders learned to play louder which went down well in large, popular rock venues but alienated more sensitive ears. After crossing the Canadian border, they received a devastating review – which they probably never saw – in a Winnipeg underground paper. It read like some pre-rock 'n' roll notice from 1956. "The Kinks from England are a no-talent group of very poorly groomed, not-so-young men whose success seems to lie in their ability to grow lots of long hair and scream unintelligible lyrics into a microphone. The noise was endless and piled layer upon layer until it seemed one's eardrums would break. There are no individual talents in this group. They merely make a pretence of playing music. If this was a sample of the new music coming out of England, perhaps it should stay there."

Back in the USA, John Gosling was adapting surprisingly quickly to the Kinks' customary wayward behaviour, joining in the drinking sessions and swaggering around hotels with bored abandon. Although Ray remained aloof at times, the others acted like adolescents let loose on their first holiday abroad. By now, the members even had nicknames, like characters in a children's comic. While playing a Saturday afternoon football match with John Dalton for Holbrook United, Ray learned that his bass player had been called 'Nobby' since his primary school days. Thereafter, that became his pet name in the Kinks. Gosling, whose long hair and beard made him resemble an Old Testament prophet was rechristened 'Baptist' (after John The Baptist). Dave, whose intense, unpredictable mood swings were becoming more prevalent, was referred to as 'Hyde', though not within his hearing. Avory assumed the alias 'One Step' because "he was always one step behind everybody else".

Ray, far from immune to mischief, provided one of the scarier moments on the tour. After dining at Martha's restaurant in Sausalito, several of the group were sauntering nearby when Gosling stopped to sit on a railing overlooking San Francisco Bay. John Dalton and road manager Ken Jones, observing the scene from the restaurant above, were joking about his buffoonery. "That fool will fall in, if he's not careful," Jones remarked. Dalton laughed, but then looked on astonished as the new recruit tottered and fell. "Ray had walked up, pretending to push him, and he lost his balance." Davies managed to grab his colleague's long tasselled coat but the seams came apart in his hands. Gosling, a non-swimmer, floundered helplessly in the water, clutching at the bay wall and lacerating his fingers on the attached barnacles. Dalton, fully realizing his pal's plight, sprinted out of the restaurant like the Flash, dived over the railing and swam Gosling back to shore. The spluttering keyboardist was whisked away, still cursing Ray who pleaded innocence. There was no hero's medal for Dalton, who suddenly realized everyone had left. Soaked to the skin, he trudged back to the hotel restaurant leaving little puddles in his wake.

Despite a delay in the American release of 'Lola', Davies was pleased when the Kinks were asked to promote the disc on the high-rating *David Frost Show*. The progenitor of the Sixties satire boom had become an internationally acclaimed broadcaster whose interest in British politics had never been blunted. He went out of his way to mention *Arthur And The Decline And Fall Of The British Empire* which was hardly surprising. Three years before, Frost and co-writer Anthony Jay had published *To England With Love*, a tongue-in-cheek commentary on the state of the country, which pre-empted Davies' own disillusioned musings. "Ruin and misery the pundit sees as he gazes upon his England," Frost wrote. "Huge debts, inefficient industries, antiquated unions, uncompetitive management, inadequate exports, depleted reserves, severely restrained wages, congested roads, decaying cities, irresponsible adolescents, irreligious clerics, escaped convicts, television addicts, short-sighted bureaucrats and myopic politicians. All trying to support the crumbling ruins of a derelict empire with an inadequate army, a doubtful currency and a Royal Mint with a hole in the middle."

By the time the Kinks returned from America, 'Lola' had entered the charts, jumping into the Top 10 after a mimed appearance on *Top Of The Pops*. "I had the cameraman blowing kisses at me from the floor," Davies joked. The BBC had banned the 'Coca-Cola' reference but offered no comment about the song's subject matter. Later critics would highlight 'Lola' as a work of subversion, breaking many boundaries and presaging the glam-rock years when words like 'androgyny' and 'bisexual' became music press clichés. At the time, however, 'Lola' caused little offence, except in Australia where a radio ban was imposed. The relaxed attitude elsewhere was a testament to the public's love of a good story. Sexual disguise had been a staple of English drama since at least the sixteenth century and the notion of men dressing as women was familiar to anyone who had read Shakespeare's *Twelfth Night* or *As You Like It* or enjoyed later Restoration comedy. It was there, too, in the musical productions of the armed forces during the war when soldiers dressed as women without attracting negative comments about their sexuality. Variety stars such as Old Mother Riley (played by Arthur Lucan and Roy Rolland) had also been popular from the Thirties onwards. By the Sixties, those old showbiz staples remained intact, notably with the success of entertainer Danny La Rue whose West End shows were box-office hits. On television, stars such as Benny Hill, Stanley Baxter and Dick Emery regularly played women in much-loved sketches and series. Considering this tradition, it was hardly surprising that 'Lola' escaped the censors' discerning pen. Four years before, the perennially shocking Rolling Stones had worn drag for a picture sleeve photo shoot that was used on the front page of the *New Musical Express* to promote their single 'Have You Seen Your Mother, Baby, Standing In The Shadow?' No outraged comments were forthcoming. 'Lola' was declared similarly safe, the vinyl equivalent of a saucy seaside postcard.

Davies enjoyed promoting 'Lola', while teasing journalists about the origin and 'meaning' of the song. "Lola is a real person and a very good friend of mine, a dancer actually," he said, rather too invitingly. "I'm not going to tell you what sex the person is though. It's a joke song, but it's very real." The scene setting was particularly important to Davies. "I like writing songs with stories about people. I live in a strange world to some, but I think the world is a lot stranger. Everything is really a great comedy with a stage manager somewhere watching the whole thing going along. I'm the one who treads dangerously, but if you read into the lyric, you'll see the song is only about friendship."

After completing his interview schedule, Davies departed on the annual family holiday to Mullion, Cornwall. This was not some intimate retreat but a gathering of the Davies siblings and their children in the countryside. It was not exactly the ideal vacation for Rasa who, since relocating from Borehamwood to Fortis Green, was regularly surrounded by various members of the Davies clan. The expedition to Mullion was undertaken by car and seemed to take an age. Trapped inside, Louisa and Viktoria would become cranky after a few hours, so stops and feeds were required along the route, while Ray snoozed contentedly in the front seat. He invariably complained about the number of super-fluous household goods packed into the boot, but Rasa knew that few luxuries awaited them on arrival. They would be spending the summer nights either camping or staying in bed and breakfast accommodation, an arrangement that Davies found reassuringly inexpensive. After settling in Mullion, Ray promptly disappeared, his head full of ideas for a new single about a man who wishes to escape city life and live like an ape. "I continued to deal with everything," Rasa recalls, with a stoic shrug. "I used to think that perhaps I did not need a husband!" Three days into the holiday, Ray received news that 'Lola' had climbed to number 1 in the *NME* charts, dislodging Free's 'All Right Now'. The Kinks were back in the big time.

During the summer, Davies was busily completing a new album and accompanying the group on weekend promotional forays to Belgium and the Netherlands. Renewed success encouraged exces-sive drinking and boorish behaviour, made worse by boredom on the road. After a performance in Reykjavik, Iceland, the musicians were eager to go home, but their plane was delayed for a few hours. Frustrated, they started boozing heavily, then attacked their duty-free allowances which were soon exhausted. On the plane, they even hassled passengers, offering to buy any extra bottles they could spare. Dave, resplendent in a sheepskin coat, turned feral, prowling the aisle on his hands and knees while growling like a dog and pretending to bite passengers' ankles. John Dalton was at his uproarious best until intoxication inspired a moment of madness. Frustrated by the realization that he would miss a football match because of the plane's late arrival time, he rose from his seat and shouted: "This is a hijack, take me to Cheshunt!" Flight staff were not amused and the group was fortunate not to be arrested or permanently banned by the airline. Instead, they were rushed through customs on arrival in London while security officers looked on sternly. Dalton was still recovering from a hangover the next day when he spotted a brief newspaper report on the incident, allegedly captioned 'Kinks Hijack Plane!' It did not go down well with the management. "Robert Wace phoned and he was not happy," Dalton recalls.

Whenever the Kinks visited Los Angeles, their partying reached an unholy crescendo. In Hollywood, they discovered the delights of cheap champagne cider, groupies and silly costumes. They bought face masks at a local novelty store and Dave Davies found his inner cowboy after purchasing a fake gun, complete with caps. Clubs offered them free entry, but soon came to dread the sight of the marauding Londoners, who invariably turned up drunk. At one venue, Dave sat watching Black Sabbath while pinpricking their satanic, heavy-rock image by shouting out "Play 'Temptation' or 'Albatross'." On another night, the entourage bumped into Peter Asher who, since splitting from Peter and Gordon, had established himself as a manager and producer. He was keen to introduce them to his protégé James Taylor, but the meeting went badly. Dave pulled out his fake gun and threatened to shoot the singer-songwriter who turned away in apparent disgust. Later they were thrown out of a club for acting like inebriated school-boys. An exasperated Grenville Collins called a meeting urging restraint, but it was disrupted by the late arrival of Gosling in full Viking regalia, blowing a horn and reducing everyone to laughter.

Ray usually absented himself from the bad-boy action, partly because he knew that they would enjoy themselves more without his overbearing presence. He preferred his excesses in smaller doses, and seldom found pleasure in partying. Everyone agreed that there was greater fun to be had if the brothers were kept apart. By now, 'Lola' was in the US Top 10, re-establishing the kinky image originally associated with the group. Ray, ever inquisitive, shamelessly visited nude bars that made Soho's London seem tame and furtive by comparison. It was as if he was finding a new persona.

In England, a more highbrow image was maintained. During October, the BBC had premiered the Philip Savile-directed *The Long Distance Piano Player* on their *Play For Today* slot, with Davies in the lead role as Marathon Man, driven to break the record for non-stop piano playing by his callous promoter/manager. The drama, which included two new songs – 'Marathon' and 'Got To Be Free' – features a solid performance by Davies, who even attempts a Yorkshire accent. "I don't play the piano, the piano plays me," he says, while reminiscing about a childhood friend who died of tuberculosis. He quotes Shakespeare, by way of William Faulkner: "The sound and the fury – signifying nothing". Finally, he abandons his trial of endurance. "Leave me be," he cries, staggering into the arms of his beloved Ruth (played by Lois Daine). The performance was strange, but intriguing. Alas, the few notices that appeared were poor. Critic James Thomas carped: "If this was a play for today, heaven help us tomorrow . . . It could take the prize as one of the most palpable non-events to be seen on TV in a long time."

On 27 November, the new single 'Apeman' appeared. Written on a Spanish guitar during the Davies' summer family holiday in Mullion, it was catchy enough to reach the Top 5, somewhat belatedly, in the New Year. The song had strong novelty appeal, accentuated by Ray's cod West Indian accent. Many listeners were convinced that he was actually singing "the air pollution is fucking [not foggin'] up my eyes" but the BBC generously gave him the benefit of the doubt. In America, Reprise Records were not so accommodating and insisted he re-record the line. It was like the 'Coca-Cola' controversy all over again. "My diction is terrible," Davies demurred with a mischievous glint, but dutifully amended the offending word.

The first Kinks album of the Seventies was the confusingly titled *Lola Versus Powerman And The Moneygoround Part One*. A transitional work of mixed intent, it had a hard-rocking edge in keeping with the times, but also included some reflective songs, alleviated by dashes of comedy and a sustained satire on the music industry. While *The Village Green Preservation Society* and *Arthur* were retrospectively applauded, particularly by Sixties' enthusiasts, the bleaker aspects of *Lola Versus Powerman* . . . remain largely unexplored. Nevertheless, as an insight into Davies' psyche at the turn of the decade, it is as revealing as anything he would ever compose. In retrospect, it may be the Kinks' most underrated album.

The work is laced with arsenic cynicism and bitter disillusionment about the current state of his career, with only 'Lola' and 'Apeman' providing light relief. Subdued reflections on all that has been lost ('A Long Way From Home') and what awaits in the future ('This Time Tomorrow') underline how detached he has become from the present. Instead, he offers a veritable history of the Kinks, detailing their interminable financial and business problems for an audience largely unfamiliar with the workings of the music business. In doing so, he also provides his greatest satire, exposing the process of pop fame in lacerating fashion. With the possible exception of the Fifties play and film *Expresso Bongo*, nobody had dared to comment on the British pop industry from the inside with such impudence, amused contempt and scornful insight.

The suite of songs that dominate side one of the album could have provided the basis of a great stage musical or scabrous television documentary. 'Denmark Street' attacks uncaring musical publishers ruled by monetary motivation yet devoid of any aesthetic appreciation of the product they are exploiting. Davies pictures Tin Pan Alley as a hustler's paradise in which songs and artistes are bartered and bought like shares on the stock market. 'Top Of The Pops' bites deeper, simultaneously deriding the BBC's chart programme and the feeding frenzy that attracts *Melody Maker* and the *New Musical Express*, along with screaming fans, false friends and even a dinner invitation from "a prominent queen". The drama ends with the song reaching number 1, followed by Ray imitating a Yiddish voice straight out of central casting, with the avaricious aside: "This means you can earn some *real* money."

'Get Back In Line' sounds like a reactionary attack on union power, understandable considering the 'ban' resulting from the American Federation of Television and Radio Artists' complaint against the Kinks in 1965. Davies provides a cinematic touch, inspired by one of his favourite films, *On The Waterfront*, in which Marlon Brando is cast as Terry Molloy, a former boxer pursuing a personal crusade against the corrupt practices employed within the longshoremen's union. Even Brando's most famous line ("I could have been a contender") provides the introductory, scene-setting track 'The Contender'. What makes 'Get Back In Line' different from the other satirical barbs is Davies' abandonment of vocal affectation in favour of a vulnerable and moving lamentation. As he admitted, the song went beyond the environs of Tin Pan Alley to include memories of his own experiences of the print union when working at a magazine long before the Kinks, and his father's humiliation after signing on the dole.

There are no such nuances in 'The Moneygoround', his greatest and most powerful satire. In 'Denmark Street' and 'Top Of The Pops' he had mentioned specific places and institutions, but here he goes further, breaking the barrier between fiction and reality by daring to name his three managers. He could have used pseudonyms, composite characters or teasing allegories but risked further litigious rancour by placing his managers in the dock in what was surely the most explicit and personal attack yet heard on record about anybody in the music business. The song takes the form of a music hall romp, its manic pace and speedy, frenzied execution mirroring Davies' own psychological state in 1966 when, close to a 'nervous breakdown', he had emerged from a sick bed and ran from Fortis Green to Denmark Street to confront his imagined detractors. The tragi-comic elements are effectively conveyed, not least because Davies does not spare himself from criticism for being so green and trusting. He criticizes foreign publishers and overseas affiliates for creaming off 50 per cent commission after which the home publisher legally deducts their own 50 per cent of what remains before passing on the monies to the songwriter. Of course, as Larry Page points out, that was "standard publishing procedure" in the Sixties and would not be challenged in court until the succeeding decade.

Davies does not name Eddie Kassner in his list of rogues, instead concentrating solely on Page, Collins and Wace. The aggrieved participants said nothing publicly, but seethed in private. It was particularly tough on Wace and Collins whom Davies had always described as his friends and who were still trying to function as his managers while he was lampooning them in song. His gleeful diatribe fails to mention that they had long since relinquished their contractual right to receive any commission from his publishing. Hearing 'The Moneygoround' for the first time must have been akin to a personal betrayal, however witty the words. "I didn't see the funny side of that at all," Wace grimaces. "Grenville and I were very upset about some of the lyrics on the album because, by and large, they were untrue. The fact was that Grenville and I never earned a dime from his songwriting. There's no doubt that that album severely soured our relationship with Ray. There are deep-seated things that lurk and linger. The opening lines of 'The Moneygoround' are funny and amusing – but they don't happen to be true. I accept that part of the song is about Denmark Productions' placing rights on publishing. But we never saw *anything* from his bloody songs."

Apart from Davies' tribulations, the album also includes a couple of contributions from brother Dave whose songwriting on recent B-sides ('This Man He Weeps Tonight' and 'Mindless Child Of Motherhood') had been impressive. He offers two strikingly contrasting compositions: the poignant, philosophical 'Strangers' and the grotesque and acerbic 'Rats'. If this suggested a subtle shift in the power structure or a new willingness to share, then it was little more than a sad delusion. It would be another eight years before the younger brother would be allowed to contribute a song to a Kinks album. Even more remarkably, over the next 19 years, right up until the commencement of *UK Jive*, only three of his compositions would be deemed suitable for inclusion.

Dave had good reason to feel rejected and excluded from the Kinks' own moneygoround. As the years passed, he looked back to this period with envy, sometimes wondering if he had been naive in not pushing for greater credit. The big-selling 'Lola' was one song that stuck in his mind. He remembered the composition emerging during a jamming session at Ray's home in Fortis Green. "I was messing around on guitar and the actual riff was my idea. I'd played it at the house, just messing around, and it evolved into a song. Ray had this quirky idea about some lyric. It didn't seem a big deal at the time. It was just collaborating, like you do in a band." Whether his contribution was worthy of a co-credit was quite another matter. "I think that Ray would admit that if push came to shove," he adds. This proved fanciful. When questioned, the elder brother was adamant that Dave had been credited correctly on Kinks' songs and deserved nothing more. A friend once asked Dave if he had ever considered suing his brother, a notion that seemed beyond his imagination. "I'm so used to being in the collaborative mode that it didn't seriously bother me until I started thinking about it. It's stimulating to feel that you've helped someone think up another idea. That's what collaboration is. I wasn't thinking of publishing. It just seemed natural to be supportive . . . The problem I had business-wise was that money was never a criterion for me, whereas with Ray it was much more on his mind."

Indeed, Ray had addressed the issue of money on the album's penultimate track: 'Powerman'. This imperious abstraction, a rapacious, all-consuming symbol of greed, is portrayed in a David and Goliath struggle against the narrator whose idealism and humanity are his only salvation. Davies sings of a girl who keeps him sane. However, the dichotomy between work and family had never been easy to resolve and remained a source of unstated tension in his personal life. While his brother was surrendering to booze and drug excesses, Ray couched his emotions, burying himself in work as an avoidance tactic. A few days before Christmas, he acquired a £300 return ticket from London to Los Angeles, incarcerating himself in the clouds solely to complete some lyrics for the next Kinks album. It was a great story testifying to his eccentricity, but also indicated where his priorities lay. "I don't really like flying but I can't concentrate on the ground. There are too many distractions like strikes and things. The only way I can finish these songs is in the air. I'm not sure when I will be coming back but I certainly will be back for Christmas to see Walt Disney on television . . . When you are flying you are nowhere at all – and that's the best place to be for concentration." If this was partly a publicity stunt then there was no doubting its success. The festive edition of *Melody Maker* featured his face on the front page under the headline, 'Kinky Way To Welcome Christmas!'

CHAPTER TWENTY-SEVEN

MORTE D'ARTHUR

By 1971, the Kinks resembled a band peculiarly out of time. Their recent singles success with 'Lola' and 'Apeman' had proven a mixed blessing, nailing them in many people's perceptions as a novelty group. What Ray Davies craved was albums success, a desire heightened by a minor breakthrough in the USA. Over the past year, changes in the rock marketplace had been swift and decisive. The Beatles had broken up and the Rolling Stones and the Who were close to abandoning the singles market which had previously served as the lifeblood of their existence. Both 'Brown Sugar' and the forthcoming 'Won't Get Fooled Again' were the equivalent of last hurrahs. Neither band would fashion 45s to change the world as they had done with '(I Can't Get No) Satisfaction' or 'My Generation'. Henceforth, singles would become, both for the Kinks and their leading contemporaries, little more than an afterthought, a promotional device or advertising board for their increasingly 'important' albums and money-making tours. There was no profit to be made in creating mini-masterpieces like 'Shangri-la' in the hope that quality alone would triumph and invigorate an aesthetically weakened format. Instead, Davies wanted to join his great peers in the American pantheons of worship. He knew he could never match the sexuality of Jagger or the physical presence of Daltrey, but he had the instincts of a showman in the Max Miller mode, a persona that would evolve over the next few years.

At home, Davies was dangerously detached from current and

emerging musical trends. He was never seen as a confessional singer-songwriter like Cat Stevens or Al Stewart, nor had he anything in common with the American masters of the genre, Crosby, Stills, Nash & Young and their various offshoots. The Kinks were not part of the progressive or heavy-rock scene, nor were they likely to be accommodated amid the ranks of the younger glam-rock exponents whose product would enchant British teenagers over the next few years. In short, their options were limited.

Ray Davies needed to be alert to opportunities and artistic developments, but all too often he blinkered himself. Just as he had avoided listening to the Beatles' greatest albums, so he had resisted hearing the work of his closest rival, Pete Townshend. "To this day, I haven't heard *Tommy*," he told an *NME* journalist in February 1971. Three years later, he was saying the same thing to an American reporter. "That's where I fall down. I don't listen to other things. And I'm not going to hear *Tommy*. I don't see why I should." Davies' insularity meant that he tended to make questionable decisions. Among his recent irksome commitments was the completion of a soundtrack for the film *Percy*, a sub-*Carry On* comedy about the consequences of a penis transplant, starring Hywel Bennett (of *The Virgin Soldiers*) as the lucky recipient who discovers that the organ's deceased donor was a philanderer whose former female conquests are keen to be reunited with their treasured 'member'. "We had 'Lola' number 1 in the *NME*," Davies recalls, "and somebody came up and asked us to do the film. I'm sure they looked down the charts and thought, 'Well, who's in the charts this week? We'll get them to write a film score for us.' I don't know if these people ever heard my work. I doubt it." Of course, all they needed to hear was 'Lola', whose novelty and risqué sexuality were enough to convince them that Davies was perfect for the job.

Instead of rejecting the offer, Ray pushed ahead in bad faith. "I did the film and treated it with what it deserved." That was not the entire truth. Although the soundtrack was pretty dismal, with instrumental filler, a thematic rerun of 'Apeman' ('Animals In The Zoo') and a funny cameo vocal by John Dalton on the country & western pastiche 'Willesden Green', there was also strong evidence of Davies' songwriting talent. In an inspired decision, four of the songs were plucked from the soundtrack and issued on a 33 rpm EP. If the film-makers were expecting a series of saucy songs about seduction and penile jokes, Ray's contributions must have seemed puzzling indeed. Lead track 'God's Children', a spellbinding melody, beautifully enhanced by Stanley Myers' orchestral arrangement, was a plea for Edenic innocence and a warning against the dangers of technology. 'The Way Love Used To Be', another enticing melody, was followed by the tender 'Moments' (". . . to remember all our lives", a paraphrased 'Days') and 'Dreams' (reputedly part of some vaguely conceived, imaginary or abandoned musical about football). Both the soundtrack album and EP (neither of which was issued in America) failed to sell in any quantities at home. Regrettably, completed versions of the songs were not featured in the film *Percy*, but inserted piecemeal between breaks in dialogue and rendered barely audible in the process.

On 30 March, the same week that *Percy* was released, the Kinks appeared at New York's Philharmonic Hall, a prestigious performance that ended in chaos. Ray was unsteady on his feet from the moment he took the stage, a caricature of the stumbling drunk. He suspected that his drink had been spiked, but nobody knew for sure. At the beginning of the fifth song, 'Apeman', he tottered towards his brother who sashayed like a matador, leaving Ray grasping thin air, after which he plummeted into a stack of amplifiers. "Dave just stepped out of the way," Avory remembers. "It was a spectacular moment." The younger brother was unrepentant. "Ray was out of it – we all were, actually. His legs were giving way under him, and he moved back towards me, thinking he could lean on me, and I fell out of the way, and he went over my amps. The audience loved it. For anyone else, it would have been a disaster, but with the Kinks it was like a peak in people's lives."

Several fans climbed onstage to assist the fallen vocalist, who was still on his back, pathetically attempting to sing into a half-dead microphone. Ever resourceful, Davies could yet turn helplessness to his artistic advantage. "I realized then, they could see I was in trouble and they wanted to help me. That taught me quite a lot. People like you for your weaknesses too; you don't have to go up there and be in control of everything." After recovering his poise and completing the set, the drunken showman was rewarded with a stage invasion. Not that everyone was amused. The *New York Times'* visiting critic was tolerant enough of the "above average band" singing about "the bankruptcy of British middle-class life" but registered a Swiftian disgust at the 'sordid' reaction of some hard-core fans standing at the front "smoking marijuana and turning to shout obscenities at anyone who asked them to be seated". A final revolting image of a man "walking up the main aisle spitting into a seat" summed up the desecration. The Philharmonic threatened to ban future rock gigs if there was ever a repetition of such disgraceful behaviour.

Oblivious to the consequences, the group continued drinking the following night in advance of a late show in North Attleboro, Massachusetts. Safe from media scrutiny, Ray was keen to have more fun and announced, "Let's open the show with 'Shoe Without A Lace'." He was greeted by puzzled looks. The song was a comically banal blues pastiche invented by John Dalton to amuse the troops. "We thought he was joking," Dalton recalls, "but he insisted, even though it was terrible. The Americans thought the song was really deep because it started with the words, 'Shoe without a lace, banana without a skin.'" Later in the set, Ray became so loose that he momentarily attempted the same song twice, prompting a rebuke from his brother that could have ended nastily. "It's so emotional onstage," Ray later said. "You hate yourself for hitting each other, but you do it." On this occasion, they resisted, but the show still ended in a mass stage invasion with Ray reportedly falling into the drum kit during the finale.

If Ray Davies was over-indulging, that was as nothing compared to his brother who had been unsettled since the start of the tour. An aversion to flying, slight at first, had built up over the years into a genuine fear. Alcohol anaesthetized apprehension, but there was always a cost. That terrible dread would return alongside sobriety, demanding the comfort of oblivion once more. Dave's ill-advised combination of acid and alcohol worsened his mental state, fuelling his imagination with nightmarish scenarios. A welcome four-day break awaited the group after arriving on the West Coast, but Dave was already frazzled. Desperate for quietude, however uneasily achieved, he locked himself in his hotel room and conducted a chemical experiment on his body, mixing wine and mescaline, like some alchemist in search of equilibrium. He almost succeeded, but after the next date, in San Diego, he fell ill and was forced to return to the UK. With the remaining shows cancelled, the other Kinks followed suit – except Ray.

While hanging around Warner Brothers Studios in Burbank, Davies became sexually entwined with one of the girls he had met on his excursions to the city's nude bars. He spent the night with her in the Hollywood Hills, a liaison that threatened to reach closer to home when she later made a brief appearance in London. His wife Rasa learned of the adulterous amours, but was spared the tawdry details. "He had an affair with somebody in America for a while, but I don't know about anyone in the UK . . . Ray did it in America. I remember that was a bad time. The band was on tour there and Ray didn't come back. He stayed out there having an affair. I knew he was up to something – it was either drugs or women. He was going through another downward spiral, again."

Sex and alcohol had been close companions in the fall of Dave Davies, but few would have guessed that same combination would have overwhelmed his brother. Equally surprising was the panacea. Both found instant salvation in that other proletarian pastime: football. The brothers had been Arsenal supporters since childhood, following the family tradition. Alas, there had not been much to crow about of late. Arsenal had last won the League Championship in 1953 and the FA Cup in 1950. They had started the season the previous August as 14-1 outsiders for the championship and many considered even those odds generous. Leeds United manager Don Revie was not among them and predicted they would emerge as his greatest threat. The Gunners boasted a relatively young team under astute manager Bertie Mee and while the Kinks were away in America the championship had turned into a two-horse race: Leeds and Arsenal. Improbably, Arsenal were also still in the FA Cup, a task made less daunting when Leeds were knocked out by lowly Colchester. Suddenly, there was an outside chance of winning the 'double'. Not even the 'titty bars' of Hollywood could compete with that fantasy epoch.

Ray Davies arrived back in London on Friday 16 May and was still jet-lagged the next afternoon when he and Dave set out for Highbury to see Arsenal beat Newcastle in an Easter fixture. Far more significant was the news from Elland Road, summed up in the doom-laden headline: 'Sheer Tragedy For Don Revie and Leeds'. Referee Ray Tinkler had overruled a linesman's flag to allow a blatant offside resulting in a goal which threatened to rob the Yorkshire team of their second League title. But it was not quite over. In another twist, guaranteed to shred the nerves of the Davies brothers, Leeds defeated Arsenal during the run-in and completed their programme a point clear of the Londoners who still had one match left to play. The Gunners went on to win the title at north London rivals Spurs; five days later they overcame Liverpool at Wembley to lift the FA Cup and secure the coveted 'double'. It was enough to distract attention from marital troubles, cancelled tours, management problems and record company disputes – but not for long.

Three weeks after the FA Cup final, the Kinks were corralled aboard a plane bound for Australia, their first appearance on that continent since the eventful tour of 1965. It was an oddly organized tour, a mere seven concerts spread over a week, which hardly seemed worth the travel or expense. Considering Dave's recent problems on the road, such a long-haul flight was tempting disaster. It soon emerged that there was an even more nervous passenger on board: John Gosling. The keyboardist coped by downing a cocktail of sedatives and alcohol which did little to improve his mood. After arriving in Sydney, the group were immediately despatched to Brisbane for their opening show at the city's Festival Hall. During the flight, Gosling threw an empty can at an air stewardess, a gesture which the local press translated into the sensational headline: 'Pop Star Attacks Air Hostess'. It was a novel experience to read a Kinks controversy that, for once, did not directly involve the Davies brothers.

After the Brisbane show they flew to Adelaide to see sister Rose and her family. This was the first time Ray had confronted his brother-in-law Arthur since the release of the album he had inspired. Such visits were always a poignant combination of celebration and regret, stirring memories of what might have been if the family had stayed in England. If Ray was wary of meeting Arthur then he was soon put at ease. In an uncharacteristic show of emotion his brother-in-law confided: "I loved that album you did about me." Arthur's reassuring words may well have had deeper connotations. He was not a well man and probably suspected his time was limited. Incurable cancer was already ravaging his lungs. Sixteen months later, he would be dead.

The remainder of the tour was a catalogue of gripes. Why were they playing in the only country in the civilized world that had actually banned their hit 'Lola'? Why did their speaker cabinets and amplifiers keep blowing up during shows at Newcastle, NSW, and Canberra? What was the point of the trip? Their penultimate date at Perth's Aquatic Centre on 5 June summed up their frustrations. "We played in an open-air swimming pool there," says John Gosling. "The stage blew down, so we ended up playing on the steps. It was ridiculous. Kids were jumping in the pool. It had rained for the first time in about nine years. Overall, they didn't have a clue how to set up rock gigs. It was disastrous – the worst tour I ever did. We vowed never to go back there."

There was one final indignity the next day when they appeared at the Sydney Showgrounds in Moore Park. Poor weather rendered the occasion a fiasco. Risking electrocution, the band played part of the set in heavy rain, but halfway through police intervened, curtailing proceedings at 5 p.m., much to the audience's disappointment. Frustrated and disillusioned, Dave flew back to London in advance of an ABC television special that the others were unable to complete in his absence. Robert Wace's diplomatic skills were required to fend off legal reprisals for breach of contract. The Kinks would not return to Australia for another 11 years.

By now, Ray Davies was reassessing his future, seemingly transforming himself into the 'powerman' he had warned the world about on his last album. That record had sold poorly in the UK despite the inclusion of two major hits, 'Lola' and 'Apeman'. From Davies' perspective, this was evidence enough that Pye Records could not market the Kinks adequately as an albums band. A change was needed. Surprisingly, he was also willing to leave US label Reprise Records despite their sterling promotional work. Emboldened by recent successes stateside, he seemed determined to sell the Kinks to the highest bidder. Two major corporations, CBS and RCA, were keen to sign the group to a worldwide deal so Davies and Wace returned to the US in July to commence negotiations. CBS president Clive Davis, an artiste-friendly businessman with an enviable reputation, had risen through the ranks during the Sixties, a period during which the label had established itself internationally with such acts as Johnny Cash, Bob Dylan, Simon & Garfunkel, the Byrds, Barbra Streisand and Janis Joplin. RCA Victor – still most famous for marketing Glenn Miller and Elvis Presley – had a more stolid image but equally deep pockets and a newfound determination to invest heavily in available talent, old and new. Their president, Rocco Laginestra, accompanied by legal representative Steve Fisher and A&R head Mike Everett, proved a formidable team, evidently willing to accommodate Davies' demands and pay for the privilege. Ray enjoyed being wooed, carefully noting the number of free meals he enjoyed as the negotiations continued.

At the beginning of August, the Davies brothers found time for their annual holiday but, on this occasion, there was no big family reunion in Cornwall. Dave preferred sunnier climes and headed for Spain where he grew a beard and attempted to unwind after the recent touring traumas in America and Australia. Rasa, meanwhile, persuaded Ray to splash out and take a family break in Cyprus, but he proved a reluctant traveller. "It was quite difficult on holiday because Ray doesn't know how to relax. To him a holiday is a complete waste of time. What's a holiday? I remember when we were in the hotel in Famagusta and he lost his temper about something. He smashed a chair and threw it over the balcony. Ray was an absolute nightmare on holiday. Occasionally, I used to say to him: 'Can't we get away somewhere for the weekend?' Never, never, never. We had a few holidays in Cyprus and that was it. The rest was working."

Davies seemed much more comfortable back in north London – writing, recording and people-watching. One of his favourite haunts was the Archway Tavern at the bottom of Highgate Hill. The Irish pub regularly featured live bands in their capacious hall – and, even better, there was no entrance fee. The music consisted of popular covers songs, mixed with country & Irish, a subgenre originally popularized by acts such as Big Tom & The Mainliners and Larry Cunningham & The Mighty Avons. Ray loved the maudlin ballads, evergreen pop tunes and old-fashioned rock 'n' roll songs that were the staple fare of the pub's musicians, several of whom had played in Irish showbands during the Sixties.

The showband had been a phenomenon in Ireland since the mid-Fifties, spearheaded by the Clipper Carlton, the Royal

Showband, the Dixies, the Freshmen, the Capitol, Dickie Rock & The Miami, and Joe Dolan & The Drifters. They had earned a lucrative living, appearing at the countless, newly constructed dance halls scattered across the island. Although the venues had no drinks licences, they could still attract audiences numbering 3,000 or more. During Lent, when the dance halls closed, the musicians travelled to England to play at similar venues in the emigrant Irish communities of London, Manchester, Liverpool and Birmingham. The showband scene was in decline by the early Seventies, killed off by a combination of changing musical fashions, poor facilities and the attendant popularity of lounge bars which offered seating and alcohol. In London, several of the big halls stayed open, but dancing was no longer popular enough to attract mass audiences. It was all too reminiscent of what had happened to the ballrooms of romance once frequented by the Davies sisters decades before.

The Archway Tavern at least retained some of the esprit associated with old Ireland and most of its habitués would have attended the dance halls, one of which still operated nearby. Drinking alongside the regulars, Davies could watch the band and drift nostalgically into a parallel world of old-fashioned music. The sentimental country songs reminded him of the weekend get-togethers at his parents' home in Denmark Terrace, another tradition that was in decline as family members moved out of the area. Gradually, almost imperceptibly, the country & Irish influence infiltrated his musical imagination, sparking ideas for a series of songs completely different from any he had previously written or recorded.

Davies had good reason to feel an edge of uncertainty during his visits to the Archway Tavern that summer. He would later describe the forthcoming album as a political statement centring on the destruction of his community by a heartless government more concerned with redevelopment than people. Although he still did not vote, Davies was affected by such local issues which, in turn, stemmed from wider political developments. One evening, he witnessed somebody burning a flag at the Archway Tavern, an atypical event that would normally have appeared shocking. But these were not ordinary times. Fears of an escalation of troubles in Northern Ireland had persuaded the British government to

introduce internment. Under the Special Powers Act, the authorities were able to arrest, detain and imprison members of the
public indefinitely without trial or recourse to legal representation.
As a means of defeating terrorism, the policy backfired spectacu-
larly. The heavy-handedness of the forces provoked much bitterness, made worse by the realization that the arrests were sectarian
in intent. Significantly, not one loyalist paramilitary or Protestant
was detained during the operation. Two days later, a priest was
shot dead by British soldiers while giving the last rites to a dying
man. Worse followed when 5,000 Catholics had their homes razed
during four days of violence. In Dublin, the Irish PM, Jack Lynch,
decried the "deplorable poverty of Ulster's politics". On London's
Oxford Street, 1,500 marchers turned out to protest about British
involvement in Northern Ireland. At the centre of the crowd John
Lennon could be seen carrying a placard which read: 'For the
IRA Against British Imperialism'. What hardened opinion on the
left were details of police brutality which resulted in the European
Commission of Human Rights finding Britain guilty of "inhuman
and degrading treatment". The "brutal techniques", seemingly
designed to unhinge detainees, also provoked condemnation from
several unexpected commentators, including novelist Graham
Greene, who wrote: "'Deep interrogation' – a bureaucratic phrase
which takes the place of the simpler word 'torture' and is worthy
of Orwell's *Nineteen Eighty-Four* – is on a different level of
immorality than hysterical sadism or the indiscriminate bomb of
urban guerrillas. It is something organized with imagination and
a knowledge of psychology, calculated and cold-blooded . . ."

Frequenting the Archway Tavern during a flag-burning risked
drawing attention to Davies' Englishness but he never complained
of any anti-British sentiments. In any case, an affection for his
songs would have been the perfect talisman. Unlike Lennon on
Ireland or Jagger on Vietnam, Davies avoided the big political
issues of the era. There was no 'Revolution' or 'Street Fighting
Man' in his repertoire. Personal politics and the plight of the 'little
man' were his favoured field. Questioned about his political stance
during the Seventies, he said: "I don't know which side I'm on.
There's things I hate about liberalism, extreme socialism and
obviously the National Front. I'm a rock 'n' roll singer, which is
a good cop-out. There's Left and there's Right, and there's rock

'n' roll." Strangely enough, the apolitical stance echoed the words of his perennial rival and fan, Pete Townshend. That same summer, the Who were back in the UK Top 10 with the evasive 'Won't Get Fooled Again', a passionate and powerful performance that thrilled fans but left its composer dissatisfied. "We consciously kept out of politics," Townshend admits, "and 'Won't Get Fooled Again' was an anthem for the apolitical. It's a terrible song. It's saying, 'There's no point in having anything to do with politics and revolution, because it's a lot of nonsense.' It's like the anthem of the ex-Nazi general, 'I was just following orders.'" That perspective was unduly harsh, an inflation of what a pop or rock singer could contribute to culture and politics. Ray Davies would never admit such shortcomings.

By early November, he had completed mixing the new album, masters of which were passed on to his new record label. After lengthy negotiations, Davies had finally signed with RCA, which issued an effusive press release crowing: "This is a triumphant day for RCA – it is the biggest deal the company has been involved in since becoming independent five years ago. We are delighted to welcome the Kinks to RCA." The five-year agreement, covering six albums, included a key clause which was of crucial importance to Davies. Rather than owning their Kinks' recordings in perpetuity, as Pye Records had done, RCA agreed that all rights would revert to Davies after 1986. It was a major concession. Asked why he'd chosen RCA, Davies deadpanned, "I always wanted to be on the same label as Chet Atkins."

That same month, *Muswell Hillbillies* was released on both sides of the Atlantic. The work was a surprise departure for the Kinks with a stripped-down sound in striking contrast to their last album. In a peculiar melange of seemingly contradictory musical styles, Davies fused the aforementioned country & Irish influences with American country rock, Dixieland, British music hall and folk, complete with conventional brass imitating Salvation Army cadences, courtesy of the Mike Cotton Sound. It was a bizarre concoction carefully assembled by Davies, assisted by engineer Mike Bobak. Their first trick was to speed up the arrangements of fast songs, then drag the tempo of the slower numbers to create a particular ambience. Vocals were recorded live, but Ray still expressed frustration at the slick studio sound. In an inspired moment, they replaced the sensitive studio microphones with old radio models that had not been used since the early Sixties. The PA system was then set up outside the studio with Davies using a separate microphone for his vocal. This double-feed effect produced the distinctly dated sound that made the album so unusual.

At one point, Davies fantasized about expanding the work into a two-LP set and filming a television special before admitting that he did not have enough time. RCA would doubtless have vetoed both plans for practical and financial reasons. A semblance of *cinéma vérité* was used on the gatefold album sleeve with its unflattering portrait of the group drinking in the Archway Tavern and overlooking the corrugated iron fencing of north London's Retcar Street. In the background stands Archway's Whittington Hospital and the green trees of the barely visible Dartmouth Park Hill. The stark effect captures a moment in time, like a scene from an early Seventies documentary. It matches perfectly the bleak characterization and hardships described in several of the songs.

Almost every track on the album deals with the lives of ordinary people struggling to survive – from the alcoholic who has deserted his wife to the anorexic girl and the Muswell Hillbilly boy lost in fantasy. "It was very much based on real-life characters," Dave Davies says. "It was the Kinks' roots and it also explained a lot of our musical influences, including country & western. We were big fans of Lester Flatt and Earl Scruggs and Leadbelly. There were folk elements too. Families getting together, having a laugh, getting drunk, and writing songs. There are lots of magic moments in *Muswell Hillbillies* that are drawn from the culture of that time when they were pulling down all those lovely terraced Victorian cottages and rebuilding Holloway."

Ray had already satirized urbanization and the lure of the New Towns in 'Shangri-la' on *Arthur*, but when discussing *Muswell Hillbillies* his tone was angrier. "There are all these people who've been taken out of the East End of London and put into these places where they don't really exist as they did before. They're trying to keep things the same as when they lived together in London, but they have to break down eventually. You can't just live on memories. The government think they are taking them into a wonderful new world but it's just destroying people. The album is a condensed version of all these ideas."

This was the closest Davies came to uttering a political broadcast, but most of his concerns on the second half of the album were endearingly parochial and personal, centring on events from the lives of his parents' generation. By contrast, the first side, he explained, was about "trying to live in this world". The dual structure enabled him to combine the serious and the comic in a single package. Side one is a catalogue of black humour overflowing with misfits whose problems are intended to provoke laughter rather than sympathy. The raucous '20th Century Man' rails against modern writers and painters, grey bureaucrats, prying civil servants and the evils of technology, while fantasizing about Blakean "green pleasant fields of Jerusalem". 'Acute Schizophrenia Paranoia Blues' tackles mental illness in a flippant tone, replete with a knowing reference to fear of the tax man; 'Holiday' mocks the city escapee who suffers sewage pollution and sunburn on his vacation retreat; 'Skin And Bone' portrays a friendless 16-year-old anorexic, turning her plight to comedy in the fashion of 'Bony Moronie'; 'Alcohol', a mock-serious singalong, is predominantly a drinks list; and 'Complicated Life' (originally titled 'Suicide') lampoons neuroses in an affected American accent.

The second side is more personal because it deals specifically with family issues, traditions and the 'old world' of Ray's lost childhood. 'Here Come The People In Grey' laments heartless bureaucracy and was inspired partly by the fate of his displaced grandmother, a matriarch diminished by a changing world. "My gran used to live in Islington in this really nice old house, and they moved her to a block of flats, and she hasn't got a bath now. She's got a shower because there isn't room for a bath. And she's 90 years old, she can't even get out of the chair let alone stand in the shower. They haven't taken that into consideration. And they knew she was going to move in because it's a new block and they took her around and showed her where she was going to live and she didn't have any choice. They didn't think to help her in any way. It's just a lack of consideration for people." The grandmother reappears in 'Have A Cuppa Tea' which includes delightful vignettes of Ray's childhood in Denmark Terrace when tea was regarded as the perfect social emollient and panacea for every imagined ailment, including his own insomnia. 'Uncle Son', an undisguised tribute to his mother's brother, captures the sensitivity of a much-loved figure in the Willmore household who never saw his nephews grow up. 'Oklahoma USA', a Hollywood fantasy, takes us back to his sisters' era when he accompanied them to watch musicals at the cinema. *Oklahoma!* (1955), starring Gordon Macrae (namechecked in the song) was a favourite of theirs, as was *Calamity Jane* (1955) in which Doris Day sang "take me back to the Black Hills . . . of Dakota", a line borrowed in part for the album's finale, 'Muswell Hillbilly'. Here, several themes converge – the family migration from King's Cross to Muswell Hill, the fantasies about a fictional, cinematic America, and a celebrated cameo appearance from Rosie Rooke, the ultimate embodiment of an era lost in time. "She used to be my mother's best friend when they were about sixteen," Ray reveals. "They used to walk up the Holloway Road, and all the boys whistled at her because she was very big and well-endowed and nice and shapely. She had a very sad life, and she never felt fulfilled as a person. On the original demo for the album there was a whole song called 'Rosie Rooke'. Leaving Rosie Rooke behind is like leaving everything behind. She symbolized all that for me . . . and I didn't even know her."

Excited by the album, RCA launched their new signing with a lavish party at the exclusive L'Etoile restaurant in New York. Music journalists were flown in and enjoyed an expenses' paid stay at the city's Plaza Hotel. An estimated 500 people attended the launch, including such luminaries as Andy Warhol, Lou Reed, Alice Cooper, Keith Moon, John Entwistle and the cross-dressing troupe the Cockettes, whose camp cavorting secured additional publicity. For Ray Davies, it seemed that the Seventies had finally arrived.

CHAPTER TWENTY-EIGHT

CHANGES

New beginnings coincided with further ructions in the group's business structure as Ray Davies established total control. The RCA signing concluded with the departure of Grenville Collins who, according to one former associate, elected to "manage his wife's estate" rather than the Kinks. There had been several frustrating moments on the road which stretched his patience and some of the antics associated with the group had become tiresome. The decision seriously affected Dave Davies, who had come to rely on Collins as a psychological ally and confidant. "I spent a lot of time with Grenville. We became really close just before he left. He showed me yoga and knew about people that did meditation, and I was curious. If we hung out together, it was more me and Grenville, and Ray and Robert. Robert was more into Ray, although we all loved each other. It was really close knit." Collins travelled extensively after resigning from the Kinks, at one point living near Bodrum in southern Anatolia. His keen interest in the Ottoman Empire saw him amass one of the most comprehensive postcard collections of Turkey in the world. He also established himself in the antiques business for a time, a welcome departure from his previously hectic occupation.

The RCA signing was followed by an American tour, including a memorable performance at New York's Carnegie Hall, featuring the return of 'Shangri-la'. "We were presented with these plaques," Gosling remembers with pride. "I kept mine on the mantelpiece – it's still there." Just as it seemed the group were settling into a routine, there was another bombshell when Robert Wace officially quit on 30 December 1971.

Wace had grown weary of Ray's obduracy, particularly in the aftermath of 'The Moneygoround' which he considered an unwarranted attack. It was difficult simply to laugh it off as an example of Davies' whimsy. The final insult occurred after a delay in payment of outstanding monies, a tactic seemingly guaranteed to rile Wace. Indignant, he walked away. The timing was unexpected, given that the Kinks had just signed a new record deal, but Wace stuck to his convictions. It had never been the easiest of business relationships, largely due to Davies' unpredictability and uncertainty of purpose. Psychological conundrums, mind games and career crises all played their part in the story, as did Davies' tendency to retreat at inopportune moments. "The Kinks as a group never worked as hard as the Who or the Rolling Stones," Wace maintains. "I mean *graft*. This was part of Ray, I suppose. They were unreliable in those days, cancelling tours and all those sort of things. There was too much worrying, bickering and infighting . . . Ray once described the group as being like a football team that's always on the brink of relegation to the second division but somehow just does enough to avoid the drop by getting a hit record. They never wanted to be as big as the Beatles or the Stones. They could have been, but they ran away from it."

Collins and Wace had been lampooned by Larry Page as neophytes but his perspective only covered their first 18 months as managers. By the end of the Sixties, the duo had been involved with a number of acts, including Marianne Faithfull and the Small Faces, and Wace later put that experience to sterling use by catapulting Stealers Wheel and Sailor into the charts. There was even a return to harder rock with Terraplane, but Wace eventually retreated from the music business, finding more suitable employment working in the War Office.

By now, Ray Davies had dismantled and rebuilt the Kinks in his own image. The successive departures of Larry Page, Shel Talmy, Pete Quaife, Collins and Wace, along with publishers, agents, road crew and record company, had each taken their toll in different ways. "I don't know how I'm going to survive," Davies said at the time. "I just can't see it because these people know me, and they've got inside of me, they know I worry about it."

In what sounded like another run on 'The Moneygoround' he complained about unnamed associates who had betrayed his trust: "I'm in a business where I think up something in my little dream world. I put it down on paper, or a piece of tape, and I play it for people who are outside of that world, and they judge it by the world they live in. And the whole thing gets destroyed for me . . . I know that if Sir Lew Grade [head of ATV] or [agent/impresario] Harold Davison doesn't like something I do, I can understand that. It's the kind of people who get inside me and manipulate me because they know my work is everything I do. If I have a bad time writing it affects me, and if they can get inside that little world and find a niche for themselves, they're sitting there forever. And then you suddenly turn around and look expecting to see them in the world that I've got, and they're outside, and all along they've been there, and they've been using what's there; it's kind of disturbing."

What followed was a long spell of uneven recordings, a lack of managerial guidance and an almost monomaniacal attempt by Ray to impose his arcane musical-theatrical experiments upon an increasingly sceptical audience. History would prove a harsh judge. "It's like we died in 1972," says Dave Davies, "like the world ended. In the early Seventies, we started to break America and we worked so much. When you look back we had so many down points in our lives and career. It was like we were always gasping for breath – and then it was all right again. I don't know what happened in the UK. I fell asleep in the Seventies."

Success in the US was now paramount and the Kinks enjoyed some wild nights, notably at New York's Carnegie Hall (2–3 March), which was recorded for inclusion on a live album. "All the Warhol people were there," Ray Davies remembers, "people like Jayne County and Holly Woodlawn. They were in front all standing up . . . They were the only people I could actually see." Warhol's crowd rapidly latched on to the Kinks, and transvestite Candy Darling (James Lawrence Slattery), along with colleague 'Tinkerbelle', later spoke to Davies for their mentor's art magazine, *Interview*. The opening question, "Are you married?" was met with a paragraph of obfuscation, including the ominously past tense observation, "Everybody *was* married". According to Ray, his initial encounter with Candy Darling was on a blind date during which he assumed the transvestite was a woman until he noticed some telltale stubble. "I got my payback after the 'Lola' incident," he declared, as life imitated songwriting art. Candy Darling was not the only transvestite who picked up on the 'Lola' allusion. John Gosling recalls "Dave Davies fleeing in terror down a corridor pursued by this huge, coloured man dressed in suspenders and a wig. It was a frightening sight. A lot of transvestites claimed they were Lola – and even believed it."

Some of these incidents were captured on film as Ray had decided to make a home movie, which was soon transformed into a documentary of the US tour. Mick Avory, a keen observer of transvestite behaviour, summed up the shenanigans and backstage posing with a prescient one-liner, "Everybody wants to be a star".

In Hollywood, RCA attempted to outdo the New York office by throwing another launch party, this time at Gene Autry's Continental Hyatt House on Sunset Strip. Cashing in on the English image, they festooned the lobby with Union Jacks, served fish and chips in newspaper and hired a couple of security guards who were dressed like London 'bobbies', the type so beloved of Roger Miller in 'England Swings'. The following night, the Kinks appeared at the Hollywood Palladium, where Davies' dress and deportment were much commented on. "Ray, in an ill-fitting green satin jacket and his customary floppy bow tie, was delightfully uninhibited, camping it up like crazy alternately in the manner of a sultry torch songstress and a giddy schoolgirl at her high school talent show." His showmanship reached new levels of camp excess as he wiggled around the stage, hands on hips, pouting at the crowd and celebrating the structural beauty of his backside. Some critics castigated the Kinks for treating their treasured catalogue of hits with irreverence. 'Sunny Afternoon' was transformed into an applause-baiting singalong, while other classics were swamped by the Dixieland brass accompaniment of the Mike Cotton Sound. While burlesquing his own material, Davies added several camp cabaret pastiches such as 'You Are My Sunshine', 'Banana Boat Song' and 'Baby Face'. The latter emerged after he heard Mike Cotton playing the song backstage. "Ray started singing it and said: 'We'll do it tonight!'" recalls trombonist John Beecham. "With Ray Davies anything could change at any time. That was something that wasn't even Ray's idea. It just appealed."

At one show, he began crooning an impromptu version of Connie Francis' 1958 chart topper 'Who's Sorry Now?'. Forgetting the words, he suddenly turned to John Dalton and said, "Sing it, Nobby!" It was small wonder that one reviewer suggested that Davies might be better advised to record a *Live At The Talk Of The Town* album.

This was the career dilemma that Davies faced for much of the early Seventies. His work, onstage and in the recording studio, divided critics like never before or since. Some reviewers surrendered their preconceptions and simply enjoyed the show with all its music hall trappings. Others, usually those more steeped in pop and rock's cultural revolution during the peak years of the Sixties, felt short-changed – or betrayed. "From the start Ray Davies presents a foolish image," one critic announced after witnessing the Kinks play in Berkeley, California. "There followed the most pitiful display of squandered talent it's ever been my misfortune to regret seeing . . . Like a former star mugging it up for the crowd, Davies refused to take seriously either his music or the crowd's capacity to enjoy it . . . He comes across compulsively campy. I never before gave thought to his sexuality. I personally don't care if he's homosexual or not, but whether he's acting out some inner confusion of roles or perhaps trying to cash in on the success met of late by such champion andromorphs as David Bowie, Marc Bolan and Alice Cooper, I find such affectations as his mock striptease act and his treatment of 'Lola' extremely annoying." This was the rockist perspective at its most acerbic and bewildered. It must have seemed as if Davies was reverting to a pre-Presley world of light entertainment.

American audiences, starved of the Kinks for so long, responded enthusiastically to the theatrical aspects. They also appeared happy to join in the fun. Some fans came armed with confetti, paper planes and cans of beer, transforming the show into a carnival. Davies responded in kind with an elongated version of 'Alcohol' during which he would spray himself and the front audience with a shower of beer. During one derring-do performance, he climbed up the stage scaffolding followed by a white spotlight as he tiptoed his way between the monitor speakers. "I'm not necessarily drunk onstage," he insisted. "I drink very little. I'm not a great drinker, that's why I get drunk. I have one drink and I get tipsy . . . I guess you could say that the stage is my kind of pub."

The recruitment of the Mike Cotton Sound transformed the Kinks' show in audacious fashion, puzzling commentators more accustomed to hard rock or heavy metal. Instead of attempting to compete with Led Zeppelin or the Rolling Stones, Ray Davies seemed intent on turning back the clock to the vaudevillian era. This effectively neutered Dave Davies' contribution as lead guitarist. Ray took additional perverse delight in introducing his sibling with the demeaning epithet: Mr 'Death Of A Clown' Dave Davies. Witnessing his career reduced to a spiteful soundbite infuriated the younger brother, but that was nothing new in the Kinks' story. Other members sympathized, but kept their counsel. John Gosling never fully understood or appreciated Ray's latest musical policy. "I didn't think the brass was right. The sound of a three-piece brass section playing 'You Really Got Me' didn't gel. It was almost like a travesty. We used to laugh a lot about being like the Billy Cotton Band Show."

By May, the Kinks were back in the UK promoting their new single, the calypso-tinged 'Supersonic Rocket Ship'. This would prove their last Top 30 hit of the decade, a sad statistic for such a once-formidable singles group. The decline was symptomatic of the times. With glam rock dominating the charts, the Kinks looked and sounded old, while Davies was concentrating almost exclusively on albums. Without a producer or manager to offer guidance and support, there was no longer a sounding board or critical ear to challenge his opinions. As the exiled Robert Wace perceptively noted: "The personal motivation of the artiste is to come up with the right song. But it's also a question of spotting it and making sure he locks on to the potential of the song that has the special magic that maybe twenty others he's played haven't got. 'Lola', for example, was recorded three times until it was done to my satisfaction. If you've got somebody who's not in the group but has a relationship with them, he becomes an outside arbitrator. He's able to say 'that's good' or 'that's terrible'. Ray needs that because not everything he does is good. Some of it is really awful. He's with a bunch of musicians who are not enthusiastic about what he does. They couldn't give a toss. You need somebody there who's an enthusiast, who'll say 'that's terrific' – so that he's almost making a record for you. At least I was able to make reasonable criticisms that he would accept."

The Kinks performed their minor hit single on *Top Of The Pops* at the end of which teenage dancers undulated uneasily to Don McLean's Van Gogh tribute 'Vincent'. T. Rex's 'Metal Guru' had just been displaced at the top; Osmond mania was in the ascendant; Gary Glitter was enjoying his first success; Slade were heading for number 1 with another poorly spelt composition, 'Take Me Bak 'Ome'; and Procol Harum's reissued 'A Whiter Shade Of Pale' was back in the charts five years after its original release. It was a pop firmament in which the Kinks looked decidedly uncomfortable. Ever the outsider, Ray Davies transformed this mundane television spectacle into a conflict between old and new pop values. Rumours of a bust-up in the BBC bar involving Davies and an unnamed group reached the gossip columns of the national press, much to his astonishment. The contretemps featured Slade, their manager Chas Chandler and bassist Jim Lea, who was doused in a pint of beer by the disgruntled Davies. This hardly compared with the casual violence perpetrated by the Kinks in their heyday but the knockabout was deemed worthy of column inches. "It was an absolute joke," Davies complained. "People don't realize what happens. Within five minutes I'd had somebody come over and say they didn't like my record. Somebody else said, 'Oh, we're suing you for a lot of money' and then somebody else came over and touched me up. Five minutes later, I find myself being throttled by some manager. A week or so later I read that I've attacked a group of people. All right, I'm six foot and a bit and I might look quite strong, but I'm not capable of beating up five or six people. I don't think I could even beat up their manager. Then all those ridiculous stories come out and I wouldn't say anything because it was all so ridiculous."

Concert reviews and interviews suggested that this was a fun period for the Kinks, but the partying and stage banter disguised darker moments. Occasionally, Davies revealed his mournful side in an unexpectedly flippant remark passed off as rock-star armchair philosophy. "I think life is a series of peaks and pinnacles. The ultimate pinnacle is when you go. Well, I hope it's a grand day when I go. Although I did write in my diary the other day, 'I hope it will be soon . . . and alone.' I was very upset . . .

People think that I'm strong, and I'm not. I'm weak. If I hadn't done all this I think I would have gone to the other extreme and gone to the Outer Hebrides to live, and become a sculptor or a painter and hid under a pullover . . . a big pullover." Was this a cry for help or an attention-seeking soundbite? It depended on which Ray Davies you believed – the one who told us "I'm mentally too strong to have a nervous breakdown" or the 'weak' vulnerable figure portrayed here.

If Ray was feeling brittle, his brother seemed on the edge of a complete breakdown. Two years before, a combination of sleeping pills, alcohol, mescaline and LSD had almost proved his undoing. Despite taking up yoga and seeking spiritual salvation, he had continued drinking heavily and was in poor psychological shape as the Kinks embarked on a grand summer stadium tour supporting the Beach Boys. They ended the season headlining their own show in New York's Central Park, a performance greeted by rave reviews and rioting fans. Nobody knew that Dave had fallen into some psychic netherworld and was consumed by paranoiac imaginings. Returning to the hotel where the group were staying, he felt he was channelling the voices of weird creatures who were urging him to leap out of the window. "I want to jump," he told himself, before slowly retreating. On this occasion, he did not confide in Ray who remained oblivious to his brother's demons.

Years later, when asked to name the sloppiest show the Kinks had ever played, Ray nominated a performance in Owings Mill, Maryland, which took place less than a fortnight after Dave's psychotic episode. "It was a revolving stage. During the first song, I jumped in the air, fell on my head, knocked myself out and was carried off stage." Later, Ray saw this as the symbolic moment when Dave might have asserted his authority and "taken over the band", at least for one evening. Instead, he sat slumped in a chair too drunk to stand. It was left to Mike Cotton to take centre stage performing 'You Really Got Me' on harmonica. Ray was so aghast that he fought with the ambulance crew, reasserted his position and completed the set with a bandaged head.

This was Dave's second epiphany and upon returning to London he determined to curb his drinking, cease experimenting with hallucinogens and become a vegetarian. So began the next stage of his spiritual journey, one from which his brother was conspicuously alienated. As he sobered up, Dave was consumed by rhetorical questions. "I was asking, 'Why do people lie? Why do people behave like they do? Why is one person kind and the other the opposite?' Astrology showed me how and why. Then I was learning about occultism, mystical stuff and tarot and how they worked together. After Robert and Grenville went, it felt very insecure and then all the mystical stuff started awakening in me. I thought that maybe this was a way to work out our everyday life and career."

Suffice to say, Ray was not of similar mind. Over the next two decades, a new dynamic emerged. The more that Dave delved into spirituality, the more his brother turned towards materialism to solve life's problems. Dave loved discussing metaphysics with an almost child-like wonder, but Ray was left cold by such musings. "I've spoken to my sisters about it over the years," Dave says. "I think he was afraid of it, and I could never find out why. It was a pivotal problem." Ray found whatever spiritual solace he required in his songwriting, which remained prolific. There had always been a significant discrepancy between the brothers' respective earnings, but by now this had widened into a chasm as Dave's contributions to the Kinks' canon all but ceased.

Before the next album was released, Dave was questioned about his brother's increasingly dominant creative role. All he could do was put on a brave face. "It's by no means a dictatorship. It's just that he has a lot to say. When it comes to recording, most of the songs are his, and when he writes a song he obviously knows how he wants it to sound. To work with him, you must respect his ideas. You've got to be flexible. He can get upset, but he will compromise, otherwise there would be no working relationship at all." There would be few such 'compromises' over the succeeding years.

Completing the new album presented Ray with unexpected problems. He had conceived the work as a film with an accompanying soundtrack, an idea that baffled the RCA hierarchy. Unable to secure additional finance, he had gone ahead and filmed the US tour using a 16mm camera. After returning to the UK, he reconnected with his art school friend and film-maker Paul O'Dell who could only sympathize with his plight. By the summer Davies had 6,200 feet of celluloid totalling six hours, which was eventually edited to 45 minutes for a documentary that would never be released. "I shot the film then wrote the songs but RCA said to me: 'We're not in the talent business, we're in the music business. We'll buy your film stock but we don't want to put any more money into it.' I didn't quite understand that."

It made perfect sense to RCA whose executives assumed Davies should be recording albums rather than directing film documentaries. By now, they must have been wondering about the sagacity of their investment. *Muswell Hillbillies* had only reached number 100 in the *Billboard* album charts and was an obvious departure from the group's previous work. After hearing selections from the new record, one A&R representative took Davies aside and politely suggested: "It would be great if you could make two albums that were similar so that people could say, 'Ah, it's the Kinks.'" Davies seemed puzzled by the notion of brand identity. "I treated [the albums] like you treat films. You wouldn't expect someone to make the same film time and time again. I treated it more as a special; each album is a special project. Of course they were unprepared for anything I was prepared to give them."

On 2 September, a week after its US premiere, the Kinks' *Everybody's In Show-biz, Everybody's A Star* (retailing at a bargain £2.98) was released in the UK. A sprawling double album – featuring a disc of live selections from Carnegie Hall and another recorded in the studio – it was predictably erratic. Rather than emphasizing past Kinks hits, the concert selections concentrated on the vaudeville tunes, including a 30-second snatch of 'Mr Wonderful', a one-minute singalong of 'Banana Boat Song', and the Mike Cotton-inspired 'Baby Face', complete with a Louis Armstrong-like vocal. As one reviewer observed: "No one, absolutely no one in rock, could get away with doing these numbers but the Kinks." A disproportionate number of songs from *Muswell Hillbillies* (five in total) weakened the live set, although Davies' transformation of 'Alcohol' into a melodramatic comedy with Prohibition-era brass was inspired. The accompanying studio album featured a series of songs inspired by life on the road, including three ('Maximum Consumption', 'Hot Potatoes' and 'Motorway') that dealt specifically with food. The opening 'Here Comes Yet Another Day' had a quirky horn arrangement, far removed from traditional jazz. As if anticipating a negative critical reaction to his new material, Ray threw in a riposte to music writers: 'Look A Little On The Bright Side'. There were also two potential classics: 'Sitting In My Hotel', a stark, piano-led reflection on rock-star isolation, and 'Celluloid Heroes', which several critics applauded as his finest song of the Seventies. Its strong melody was complemented by a thoughtful lyric analysing the complex ambiguities of movie stardom. Namechecking a litany of Hollywood stars, Davies contrasts their mythical status on the silver screen with the human frailties of the flesh and blood actors. Even while acknowledging this dichotomy, the narrator cannot escape the overwhelming allure of stardom or resist envying the fantasy Hollywood existence with its Faustian promise of celluloid immortality.

'Celluloid Heroes' was an obvious choice as a single but, despite its enduring popularity, failed to chart on either side of the Atlantic. More than one reviewer pointed out its melodic similarity to Tim Hardin's 'The Lady Came From Baltimore', but it never garnered the number of cover versions associated with that modern standard. The parent album climbed to number 75 on *Billboard*, a modest success at best but way below what RCA had hoped. Reviews were also lukewarm – "good but not great" being the most common reaction. *Rolling Stone* complained that it was "inconsequential" while the underground magazine *Us* uncharitably declared: "*Everybody's In Show-biz* is abysmal beyond belief, a totally worthless album from the same group that was responsible for so many rock 'n' roll masterpieces of the Sixties."

Davies still felt burdened by his back catalogue. Pye Records were sporadically issuing greatest hits collections such as *Golden Hour Of The Kinks*, which crammed 20 songs on to a single album with no respect for sonic fidelity. A second volume would soon follow. In America, Reprise had issued *The Kink Kronikles*, a collection of hits and relatively rare B-sides, including the previously unreleased 'Did You See His Name'. They were now preparing another archive collection, *The Great Lost Kinks Album*, featuring discarded masters and leftover tracks. Despite vociferous objections from its composer, these songs would remain in Reprise's catalogue for a further two years.

As Christmas 1972 approached, Davies was enlivened by an invitation to contribute to a 'Fanfare For Europe', a cultural jamboree celebrating Britain's long-anticipated entry into the

Common Market. This had been part of the political agenda since the days of Macmillan and was finally pushed through under the stewardship of Prime Minister Edward Heath. It was to be accompanied by the introduction of a new tax: VAT. Considering Davies' vignettes of a lost England on both *The Village Green Preservation Society* and *Arthur*, it might have been assumed that he was at least ambivalent about European fiscal union but, if so, he made no comment on the matter. Instead he greeted the 'Fanfare' as an opportunity to fulfil – at least in miniature – his long-standing and nearly forgotten dream of a *Village Green* musical. This, in turn, kick-started another concept album, prompting a songwriting flurry over the festive period. Against the odds Davies completed the musical in time for its allotted showing at London's Drury Lane Theatre on 14 January. In addition to the Kinks and their Mike Cotton Sound compatriots, six brass players and a further six singers were recruited to embellish the sound. Considering the speed with which the show was completed, the results were impressive. Davies presented a potted history of his musical career with a selection of hits including 'You Really Got Me', 'All Day And All Of The Night', 'A Well Respected Man', 'Sunny Afternoon', 'Waterloo Sunset', 'Victoria' and 'Lola'. *The Village Green Preservation Society* was represented by its title track, 'Picture Book' and 'People Take Pictures Of Each Other', enhanced by a backdrop of images projected on to a screen. Among the new songs premiered, 'Where Are They Now?' offered nostalgic memories of a wealth of Sixties' icons. The show won rave reviews in the music press, boosting Davies' confidence at a crucial time. He spoke of a more elaborate show that he hoped to perform in New York and even suggested a tour of small halls across England based around *The Village Green Preservation Society*. Critics and fans were thrilled by the news, but misinterpreted the meaning. Davies was, in fact, referring to an entirely new project with a similar name: *Preservation*.

CHAPTER TWENTY-NINE

THE LEAVING OF RASA

While Davies was plotting his most ambitious and overreaching theatrical production to date, his marriage was in deadly trouble. Extended periods on tour were often the bane of rock-star marriages, particularly if wives were left at home to look after the children. Some adapted, like the stoical spouses of sailors or servicemen, establishing a long-term routine and enjoying the excitement of reconciliation following their husband's return. That had been the case with Ray and Rasa during the first flush of marriage, but over the years his attentiveness had dwindled. It was an insidious process that he could not quite articulate, even to himself. "The classic thing people say about any sort of relationship is 'I don't know what went wrong' and the fact that you're saying that says it all. If you knew, it probably wouldn't have happened." Increasingly, homecomings became short-lived grand reunions as Ray reverted to type and buried himself in songwriting projects and other professional obligations.

Arguments and recriminations, previously unheard of, were becoming frequent. "We were rowing," Rasa admits. "We weren't getting on. I was becoming really dissatisfied at the way he was and the fact that I was isolated. He was always working and I wasn't first any more. I was taking second or third place. We had two children but he didn't really want to be a father. They didn't call him 'Dad'. They weren't allowed to. They had to call him 'Ray'." This was another of Davies' quirks that did not go down well with Rasa, who grew weary of his eccentric, unpredictable behaviour. "I just wanted what I thought was a proper marriage and I wasn't happy. I think I'd probably fallen out of love with him by that stage. He'd been quite mean to me. We were always short of money. I never knew what he was going to be like in the mornings when he woke up. When he used to go out, I never knew what time he was coming in. I just got fed up with it, to be honest. I thought there must be something better than this. This isn't right."

In the background, of course, was Ray's recent illicit liaison in America. "When I lived in Los Angeles, just off Sunset Boulevard. I was in a relationship," he admits. "I guess you could call it that." He was more forthcoming about the adulterous affair in his semi-fictional memoir *X-Ray*. Therein, he identified the woman using the sobriquet 'Savannah Molloy', supposedly a redhead from the South, who'd once had an Eskimo lover and was now dancing naked in a club he called the Rat Trap. He described their sexual antics while also insisting that he still wanted to save his marriage. This was 'rock-star privilege' – the belief that it was perfectly acceptable to cheat on a wife during a tour provided the affair remained distant and discreet. Davies normalized his behaviour by citing the amorality or immorality of the time. If he required a wayward moral compass, Ray needed to look no further than his brother whose definition of marital fidelity was conveniently fluid when temptation beckoned.

By the early Seventies, American tours seemed synonymous with groupies and cocaine. It was a hedonistic pleasure zone in which girls and women were frequently treated with the same casual disregard as a plate of sandwiches provided by room service. Such behaviour was particularly prevalent among the hangers-on. One critic wrote of attending a wild 'Kinks party', minus the group members, but featuring acolytes and 'liggers' who were all too willing to take advantage of the free booze provided by record companies or promoters. "They took this girl and they got her totally undressed and these two roadies held her upside down and spread her legs and somebody poured champagne on her cunt while somebody else took pictures."

Conversely, the emergent feminism of the time inspired a greater desire for women's independence. Since marrying Ray as a teenager and raising two children, Rasa had become more self-sufficient. Over the years, she had established casual friendships with other young mothers in Muswell Hill. In addition, she remained close to her own family. Her sister Dalia had married a French restaurateur, Guy Gelineau, who, at one point, was managing the famous Chelsea Drugstore in the King's Road. Occasionally, Rasa would attend a dinner party thrown by the couple. It was there that she was first introduced to Colin O'Donnell, the owner of a 'steel fabrication company' who had designed and installed the fittings at the Drugstore. Accompanied by a business colleague, he spent much of the dinner talking shop with Guy but later proved an engaging personality. "That's how I got to know him and he actually became a friend," says Rasa. When Ray learned that Colin had become part of Rasa's social circle, he became suspicious and possessive. One weekend, she took their daughters to a pop festival that several of her friends were attending. Ray discovered that O'Donnell was part of the entourage, lost his temper and accused his wife of having an affair. Then and now, Rasa denies that she and Colin were anything other than platonic pals at the time. Given his own recent transgressions, Davies' outburst about infidelity was rich indeed. Perhaps there was an element of self-sabotage in his protestations, a trait which his brother recognized of old. "If something good happens, Ray will construct a situation to make it go wrong. It's safer when things are uncomfortable."

Davies distracted himself from negative thoughts by feverishly completing the next Kinks album in advance of a US tour. He described the work as "an extension and modification of *The Village Green Preservation Society*". Conceived as a double album, it reached the mixing stage by March but, after listening to a playback, Ray concluded that it was not strong enough to release and deferred the project until later that year.

Some of the recording had been completed in the warehouse of a former biscuit factory in Tottenham Lane that the Davies brothers had purchased for £70,000. Konk Studios, which would be launched officially in the spring, was intended to save the group from spending excessive sums on outside studio hire. It was hoped that the financial outlay might be offset by leasing the studio to other musicians during the Kinks' absence. An impressive arsenal of equipment was ordered including a 16-track control desk, a 16-track tape recorder, a noise reduction unit, microphones, speakers and a baby grand piano. Completing deliveries was not always easy. Dave remembers pursuing his brother to countersign cheques for down payment on a Neve mixing board as akin to pulling teeth. Special lighting was also installed, along with a snooker table and later a bar. It seemed an eminently practical project, testifying to Ray's business acumen, but his brother had grander ideas. "I wanted us to have a career and I wanted us to help people, and not just superficially. When we first got the Konk building, I used to go down there on my own with the keys and open it up. I'd go in with incense and try and purify the vibes of the place. I wouldn't tell anyone because if you did something like that in those days people thought you were off your head. I was always called the crazy one because of my beliefs and it was a very difficult period." Later, the Kinks discovered the extent of Dave's dabblings when someone noticed a pentagram chalked on the studio floor.

On 27 March 1973, the Kinks set out on a six-week tour of North America, commencing three days later at Fordham University in the Bronx where the support act was future hard-rock superstars Aerosmith. The highlight of the visit was the penultimate show at the Hollywood Palladium which ended with Ray abandoning his trousers and being carried across the stage by the burly John Gosling. This was probably Davies' final fun moment of the entire year.

In mid-April, he returned to Fortis Green, jet-lagged and hungry for sleep. Oddly, the house was empty. Uncharacteristically, he slept for most of the day, awakening late in the evening to the sound of silence. The girls had returned and were in bed, but there was no sign of Rasa. Then he found a note saying that she had popped out to meet some friends. Indignant that she had not waited for him to wake up, he decided to find her. Visiting her favourite haunts, he tracked her down at Patricia's, the French restaurant in Fulham owned by her brother-in-law, Guy Gelineau. Ray saw her sitting with a group of friends, one of whom was Colin O'Donnell. Rasa was startled by his unexpected arrival. "I said, 'Oh my God, Ray's here' and I moved quickly out of the way." Davies later claimed that he mortified everybody within hearing distance by graphically explaining the plot of *Deep Throat*, the pornographic film featuring Linda Lovelace that was currently causing a sensation in America. "What?!" Rasa now says in disbelief. "No. I don't know anything about that. He had an argument with somebody and was hit over the head with a flowerpot, then thrown out. That's what it was." Ray recalls visiting a hospital, accompanied by Rasa, and having his head X-rayed, after which he was discharged. His wife was embarrassed by the sad spectacle, and frosty on the way home.

On 8 June, the Kinks played at the Royal Festival Hall and were well received. Twelve days later, on the eve of Ray's 29th birthday, Rasa left Fortis Green along with their two daughters. The decision seemed spontaneous rather than calculated. "I had one bag with some of my belongings and the children's – the rest I left behind." Rasa's destination was Cheltenham, the home of her elder brother Aleksandras Napoleanas and sister-in-law, Mirdza. Back in Fortis Green, Ray was disorientated as everything in the house looked more or less the same, but there was an emptiness at its heart and a surreal quietness where there had previously been the noise of children. Oddly, his initial reaction was one of relief, even elation, that he was now free, single and able to pursue his own agenda. That brief surge of ersatz ecstasy was rapidly replaced by a feeling of deflation as he realized all that had been lost. Dave, whom he had by now told of Rasa's sudden disappearance, arrived on the evening of his birthday only to be greeted by what he described as "a sad lost child". This was Ray at his most vulnerable – and sympathetic.

The story of Rasa's leaving had an eerie quality, which left Dave angry and puzzled. It did not seem in character. "I couldn't blame her, but running off like that was cruel. I felt sorry for him." Years later, Rasa wrote an impassioned letter expressing her emotional confusion about the incident while simultaneously confronting several conflicting issues surrounding her leaving:

I agree, in retrospect, with Dave Davies when he says the way in which I left my husband on [the eve of] his birthday was cruel. Will people understand when I say that I was young, inexperienced, unhappy, afraid and confused? I didn't know who or where I was, or in which direction I was heading. I had nowhere to turn to.

In a strange way, I thought that by not confronting the hurt I felt over the way I had been treated, it would somehow all go

away if I just left. And that by telling Ray, I would hurt a person
that I loved too much. That seems totally illogical now, but to this
day I'm left with unresolved guilt and sadness. It was the hardest
thing I've ever done and an experience I don't ever want to repeat.

The timing of her leaving, as Ray Davies later acknowledged,
probably had more to do with avoidance of emotional confrontation than malice. It could just as easily have happened at Christmas
or on a wedding anniversary, always – in his mind – a time when
it was impossible to disguise or feign emotion. Evidently, she did
not have the stomach to face a day of enforced jollity. That, at
least, was Davies' perspective. His wife had no such easy explanation. Even now, she cannot distinguish between emotion and
logic when trying to unravel her thought processes at that time.
"The decision that I made was very hard. I can't even tell you
why it was on his birthday. I don't know how that happened.
For the life of me I don't know why it happened on 20 June or
the 21 June. For goodness sake: why? It was devastating and I
didn't know if I'd done the right thing."
The Davies family quickly rallied around Ray during that final
week of June. Gwen, the youngest sister, offered tea and sympathy
at Fortis Green, while Dave and Joyce decided to confront Rasa
and persuade her to return. They drove to Bradford, heading for
her parents' house in Howard Street, but were greeted by a steely
silence. Clearly, she was not there and nobody knew of her
whereabouts.
In the end, they found her through a combination of investigative skill and luck. After arriving in Cheltenham with only a single
bag of possessions, she had decided to sell her prized yellow
Volkswagen Kharmann Ghia in order to raise some funds. "I
advertised my car in the local paper and that was the route that
brought Dave (and Gwen, I believe) to the address at my sister-
in-law's house." It is likely they were assisted in the search by a
private detective employed by Ray.
During the drive to Cheltenham, Dave was still hopeful that
he could appeal to Rasa. They had always had a close relationship, and never fallen out. The meeting proved frustrating. He
found her distant and unreachable, as if she had been 'brainwashed'. Afterwards, he suspected that she had been 'got at' by

her sister Dalia or other family members. For Rasa, of course, this was another example of the interfering influence of the Davies family, something she had experienced through much of her marriage. Being confronted by Dave *and* Gwen was not a pleasant experience, irrespective of their good intentions. "They tried to persuade me to return. I was pressurized but wasn't able to agree and wanted time to decide."

Days later, Rasa left England. Her destination was Switzerland, a safe haven beyond the reach of any in-laws. There, she stayed with a female friend who was married to a cousin of Colin O'Donnell, who had arranged the trip. This was the man whom Ray suspected of having an affair with his wife which, no doubt, coloured his opinion of her motives.

By now, Davies was in a seriously conflicted state, drinking heavily and self-medicating. He was mixing champagne and valium, in an attempt to stabilize his mood swings which oscillated between elation and depression. Later, he wrote of a strange night out during which he encountered a group of homosexuals in a pub and was invited to a party in the course of which someone attempted to stick a finger up his arse. The assailant was felled by Davies, who then rushed from the scene pursued by the words, "Bye bye, Kinky!" The tragi-comic melodrama continued when Ray was discovered asleep in a bath by his assistant Marion Rainford and taken to a nearby hospital to have his stomach pumped. He was advised not to mix alcohol and barbiturates again.

Amid his emotional confusion, Davies decided that music – in reality, work and creativity – was the monster that had destroyed his marriage. If he was to save his family, a drastic decision was required. He would break up the Kinks, retire from the music business and reinvent himself as the ideal husband. In mid-July, the group were due to play an outdoor gig – the Great Western Express Festival – at White City, which would provide the perfect platform for such an announcement. This would be the ultimate sacrifice and perfect proof of his familial love. In his fantasies, he pictured Rasa, Louisa and Viktoria in the audience, no doubt moved or overjoyed by his grand act of atonement.

Davies' heightened state was exacerbated by an amphetamine-related prescription designed to combat his recent valium consumption. Unfortunately, he continued to mix the drugs with alcohol and became increasingly contradictory and irrational. He vainly sought out 'Savannah Molloy', the mystery woman with whom he had conducted the affair that had already damaged his marriage. For a man who wanted to win back his wife and children this was extraordinary behaviour. Equally oddly, he ended up inviting one of her pals (whom the press called 'the American girl') to stay at his house and hinted that their relationship might not be entirely platonic. In his overwrought imagination, she became a strange mixture of guardian angel and temptress.

The events of Sunday 15 July are enshrined in the Ray Davies story. This was the day of destiny – the end of the Kinks, the end of his career, and possibly the end of his life. The Great Western Express Festival at White City offered an eclectic bill featuring the JSD Band, Barclay James Harvest, Lindisfarne, Canned Heat and Edgar Winter's White Trash. The Kinks were no longer hip enough to secure top billing which was reserved for funk/soul fusionists Sly And The Family Stone. It was a day of cemetery weather, befitting Ray's mood. Tentative as a sparrow in a lion-filled coliseum, he was ushered into a dressing room, while the backstage area buzzed with ominous rumours. Unexpectedly, the doom merchants were the two people serving as his guardians: personal assistant Marion Rainford and the ever present 'American girl'. Backstage, *Melody Maker*'s Roy Hollingworth was intrigued by the whispered revelations. "Have you heard that Ray is quitting tonight?" said the American girl to anyone within hearing distance. "They're really going to split tonight." Standing outside Davies' dressing-room door, Rainford confided: "He's in a dreadful state . . . He feels that tours and concerts have split his married life." Rainford then revealed that Rasa and the children had 'disappeared' less than three weeks before. "They could be dead for all he knows," she added. "He doesn't know what he's doing." These were obviously words of concern but so uncharacteristically indiscreet that a cynic might conclude there was an element of political spin in the subtext. It was unlikely that a spokesperson as dedicated and accomplished as Rainford would comment on his marriage without his approval.

Onstage, Davies looked drained and haggard, but performed the set with consummate theatricality. Everything about him bespoke the embattled clown – the outsized bow tie, the shirt emblazoned with fiery red symbols, the bottle of light ale perched precariously on his head of wild hair. Standing nearby, Dave Davies was far from happy. "The White City gig was terrible. I didn't want to play anyway and Ray was acting really oddly. I didn't know he'd been popping lots of pills all day long. It was so sad, it was hilarious. He was totally white onstage and he decided he was going to end it all." The set seemed sprightly enough, commencing with 'Victoria', 'Brainwashed' and 'Dedicated Follower Of Fashion'. It was at the start of the fourth song, 'Lola', that Hollingworth noticed Ray swearing into the microphone, followed by the line, "I'm sick up to here with it." Mick Avory smiled enigmatically and continued drumming, while Dave assumed the words were a joke. This was a not unreasonable assumption. The line "I'm sick, sick, sick up to here" was the catchphrase of the popular television comedian Freddie 'Parrot Face' Davies and anybody could be forgiven for concluding that Ray had merely borrowed the words of his namesake as part of his music hall routine. Towards the end of the set, guitarist Phil Palmer (Ray and Dave's nephew) joined the group. Ray then gently kissed his brother on the cheek and informed the crowd: "I just want to say goodbye and thank you for all you've done." According to *Sounds*' correspondent Jerry Gilbert, he uttered the more emphatic: "This is goodbye forever." Davies then returned to the microphone to reveal more, only to be drowned out by the PA system. It was an anti-climactic epitaph, unheard by most of the audience, but coherent enough to inspire music press headlines. 'Ray Quits Kinks' were the words blazoned across newsstands amid confirmation that Davies "had done a Bowie". Twelve days before, at London's Hammersmith Odeon, Bowie had announced to the audience: "This is the last show that we'll ever do". It was the end of Ziggy Stardust and his band the Spiders From Mars, but Bowie himself would return with a new persona. It was hoped that Davies would do the same but, in the meantime, what of the Kinks?

"The Kinks are dead," began *Melody Maker*'s valediction. "Long live the Kinks! Ray Davies should never have been at London's White City Stadium, on Sunday. Physically, and more important, mentally, Davies was in no fit condition to play. And in no fit condition to stand on a stage and say that he was quitting. He was a man neck-high in troubles, and when he shouted 'I quit,' he should have shouted 'Help!' Then, for once, and for the most important time in his life, he would have seen just how much he is loved. And he needs to see that." Roy Hollingworth ended his rhapsodic report with a poignant plea: "If you are going to go, Ray, and if you really want to, then thank you for the days. Nobody will press you to stay. Those who love you will let you make whatever decision you wish to make. But you must believe that if you leave, then there's precious little left. Think again, Ray. Think again."

Other reports were more hopeful. After the show, Marion Rainford spoke to the *New Musical Express*, warning: "One has to understand that Ray is in a very emotional, confused state. Two-and-a-half weeks ago his wife Rasa left, together with Ray's two children – and she hasn't been heard from since. Ray is naturally a very worried man. He hasn't eaten since she left, he hasn't slept – it's a miracle he got through the gig. He feels that touring and gigs have contributed to the situation . . . But I must say that neither the Kinks nor I believe for one moment that Ray will really quit the business. He's a grieving man and he made an emotional statement."

It was *Sounds'* Jerry Gilbert who picked up the biggest scoop of the day when he learned of Davies' 'drugs overdose', a detail which was mentioned without additional comment or analysis on the paper's front page the following week. It was a few hours after the White City debacle that the eternally vigilant 'American girl' noticed Ray was acting peculiarly with nervous tics that she recognized as drug-related. He then hesitantly produced an empty bottle of uppers. Years later, he offered an endearingly absurd excuse for consuming them all. "The doctor gave me pills and said, 'Take one of these when you feel a bit down, it'll make you feel better.' I was doing what I thought was my last show and I felt down every ten seconds, so I just kept taking them." Road manager Ken Jones acted quickly, driving Davies to Archway's Whittington Hospital where even his admittance was a comedy of confusion. At reception, he declared: "I'm Ray Davies . . . and I'm dying." A nurse responded by asking for an autograph. "It was funny," he recalls, laughing at the memory. "It was even funny at the time. When you're that down, everything is funny." After collapsing in the hospital hallway, he was rushed to a nearby room to have his stomach pumped. "I'd taken a whole bottle of pills and I should have died. And a part of me *did* die that day onstage in White City. I realized a lot of the mistakes I made. I should never have got married, but then I wouldn't have had those two wonderful kids. Unfortunately, my encounter with myself took place in front of fifteen thousand people."

It was the early hours of Monday morning when Dave discovered his brother's plight. By the time he arrived at the Whittington, Ray was lying in bed looking like "a pathetic sad lost boy". They found mutual cheer by joking about a junkie who had been admitted to the hospital the previous night. His abandoned cowboy boots stood incongruously beside an adjacent bed. The humour turned considerably darker when they learned that he had died during the night. It was a grim reminder of how close Ray had come to suffering the same fate.

"I did try to kill myself that day," he confirmed, a decade later. Thereafter, he was more coy, preferring to avoid the subject. Later still, he would make light of the harrowing event. "I was emotionally run down. I have this theory that people who want to commit suicide manage it. And I didn't. Calling it a suicide attempt makes me look like a 'survivor'. It was a mishap, let's call it that. If I did talk about it as a suicide attempt it was like boasting about it in the pub so everyone would buy you a pint."

Davies may well have used the 'suicide' story to cadge some free drinks, but he was clearly in a wretched state. Dave helped collect his belongings and moved him into his own house where Lisbet became a surrogate matron and nursemaid. They even surrendered their own bedroom so that the patient would feel more comfortable. At first, Ray seemed numb to everything but, while lying in bed, he remembered discovering Gustav Mahler via his college friend Paul O'Dell. Classical music soothed his troubled mind during those short weeks of convalescence. The brothers also rekindled some of their childhood camaraderie via memories of favourite blues records and performers. Soon, the guitars came out and they started playing Chuck Berry riffs, just like the old days. Rousing Ray from his bed, Dave suggested they should take a break abroad. That experience was enough to make Ray want to get back onstage again. "I *was* going to give it up, but I went on holiday with my brother to Denmark to see a bunch of shows in the clubs. The experience washed away all my tedium. That White City concert did give the Kinks a new life in a way."

'New life' was preceded by a lengthy period in limbo for the subsidiary Kinks who remained uncertain about Davies' intentions and knew better than to ask for an update. "It was a funny atmosphere," Gosling recalls. "He suddenly said he was retiring . . . I don't know whether it was a stunt but I took it seriously. I was quite upset that it happened that way . . . We could have done it as a big farewell gig . . . I don't know to this day whether he meant it. It was a mystery to me."

It was only at the end of August that Gosling and the others were told via a phone call that the Kinks still existed. The following week, the music press printed a statement from Ray officially retracting his retirement:

> Several weeks ago I wrote a letter to the world; it turned out to be a letter to me. But I do feel that I made a decision, whether emotionally motivated or not, to change the format of the band. The White City was not a good place to say goodbye. The sun wasn't shining, my shirt was not clean, and anyway rock festivals have never held many happy memories for me, personally. The Kinks are close enough to be able to work as a team in whatever they do, and anyone who thinks they are only my backup band is very mistaken. There are still things to extract from the Kinks on an artistic level – whether or not it turns out to be commercial remains to be seen.

Conspicuously missing from the statement was any mention of Rasa. Instead, he sent her a coded message via a new single, 'Sweet Lady Genevieve', a self-confessed apologia which failed to reach the charts or change her mind. Amid all the drama, she had stayed in Switzerland while regularly receiving music paper reports and alarming snippets of gossip about Ray's state of mind. "There was stuff about him saying, 'If she wants me to be a road sweeper, I'll do that' and a problem about him being dressed like a clown and going into hospital." The public revelation about the overdose was particularly painful. "I said to my sister, who came over to

Switzerland, that I thought I should go back. She said, 'Don't go back to him!' I was really torn. I didn't know what to do." It was never easy deciding whether to respond to her husband's needs or look to her own.

"I felt so guilty, thought about all the hurt which was affecting me and Ray, and seriously considered a return. My sister was adamant that I should leave Ray and she persuaded me to file for divorce saying I would be 'better off'. *I did not return.* It is easy to say, in retrospect, I should not have been influenced by my sister's opinion. However, ultimately I decided that I could not return to a life of being alone much of the time, feeling unworthy as a wife, having to deal with Ray's mood swings, constantly worried about money and having to face the anger and opinions from Ray's family regarding my leaving him . . . I am sure a return would have further coloured their opinion of me and any forgiveness."

Her reading of the Davies family's reaction was largely correct. Ostracism was immediate and permanent. It was hardly surprising in the circumstances, especially among such a close-knit unit. Dave Davies was angry and upset about the effect her departure had on his brother. "I think when Rasa left it was like a chasm opening before him. She had grown up through our success . . . like an extra member of the band really. She brought me and Ray together a lot, working out vocals and harmonies. We were close in those years when Rasa was around." Dave also knew that the group would never be the same. Every time someone left the Kinks' orbit, Ray retreated inwards and became even more single-minded. Suddenly, he announced a new routine. He would start the day at 7 a.m., following a breakfast of raw eggs, complete some work, then retire to bed for several hours. "Then I get up again and have a little worry and cry and get that out of my system and try to do a bit more work. The day goes very quickly." This was the sensitive, vulnerable Ray, a figure that needed to be treasured and emotionally contained. Hereafter, his attitude hardened as he buried himself in his project, doubly eager to complete a revised version of *Preservation* as soon as possible.

In November 1973, the perplexing *Preservation Act 1* was released as Davies prepared to launch a stage version which the Kinks would play on the university/college circuit early in the New

Year. The album introduces the work's three main characters – the Tramp, Flash and Mr Black – plus the slight return of Johnny Thunder from the *Village Green* days. Davies allocates the finest songs to the enigmatic Tramp, an allegorical figure who represents freedom and what Orwell once called "the golden country". The Tramp roll-calls a cast of Swinging Sixties characters on 'Where Are They Now?', mourns lost love on 'Sweet Lady Genevieve' and re-enacts the lazy feel of 'Sunny Afternoon' and 'Sitting By The Riverside' on the languid 'Sitting In The Midday Sun'. 'One Of The Survivors' offers a more rounded, naturalistic portrait of Johnny Thunder, demythologized into a greying rocker, stuck in the world of Jerry Lee Lewis and Johnny And The Hurricanes. 'There's A Change In The Weather', 'Money & Corruption'/'I Am Your Man' and 'Demolition' appear overtly theatrical, while 'Cricket', which introduces the Vicar character, offers a strained analogy between sport and religion, no doubt baffling American audiences with its cricketing terminology: 'LBW', 'googly' and 'bowling a maiden over'. Brother Dave is allowed a couple of dramatic cameos, 'Here Comes Flash' and 'Demolition', but is otherwise under employed. His contribution to 'Daylight' – a striking Indian blues in open tuning – caused some lingering resentment when he failed to receive a writing credit. Despite the recent cordiality between the brothers, fraternal tensions obviously remained intact.

Critics were cagey and perplexed by the album. It was self-evidently an incomplete work, diffuse and difficult to categorize in any genre. At best, it felt like reviewing the first act of a three-act play with no knowledge of what might follow. The aesthetic problems it posed meant that several commentators preferred to reserve judgement until the release of *Preservation Act 2*. The public voted with indifference. Nobody was surprised by its commercial failure in the UK but a chart placing of number 177 in *Billboard* was an appalling statistic and a major setback. Davies pushed ahead in the studio while attempting to suppress his disappointment. "It didn't run up massive sales. I suppose I was disgusted – I worked really hard on it but maybe that's a reward in itself. I was unhappy when people hadn't heard it. That's all I care about really . . . I'm not concerned that people buy it, they don't have to walk around with a copy under their arms. But I would like them to *hear* it."

Davies' troubled marriage had seriously affected the Kinks' morale in 1973. The various disruptions and delays meant that money was scarcer than usual. John Dalton, usually so complacent and uncomplaining, dared question the financial arrangements but ended up feeling like Oliver Twist, humiliated for demanding more. "I can remember at one of the meetings saying, 'We aren't earning enough' and Dave said to me: 'You should be looking at your music rather than what you're earning.' I said, 'You better tell that to the gas man – he's coming around to cut me off!' So that didn't help."

CHAPTER THIRTY

DIVORCE AND PRESERVATION

A new, granite-hard Ray Davies emerged during the fallout of his separation from Rasa. The fragility, so evident during the summer of 1973, was vanquished by a relentless work rate and a seeming willingness to consider any new project. Granada Television promptly commissioned a musical which Davies described as 'an experimental dream'. The storyline featured an ordinary man in a split-personality relationship with a pop star. It sounded promising.

In addition to television and film proposals, Davies was expanding his entrepreneurial empire. The establishment of Konk Studios was followed by Konk Records, an independent label whose first signings were Claire Hamill, Andy Desmond and Café Society. Davies also spoke confidently of directing films, a long-term ambition since his art-school days. While all this was occurring, the *Preservation* project was progressing, both in the studio and on the road. "All these people were backstage working for Ray," Gosling recalls. "Half of them didn't know what they were doing. It was chaos."

These myriad ventures served as the backdrop to Davies' reconstructed life as a divorcee. Almost immediately after Rasa's leaving, he had vacated 87 Fortis Green, which was first rented to road manager Ken Jones and his wife and later purchased by Ray's sister Gwen and her husband Brian Longstaff for £25,000. The matriarch Annie Davies later resided there in her final years. Ray bought a new, capacious home in Effingham, Surrey, the grounds of which included a cottage where the classical composer Mendelssohn had once worked. It was there that Davies awaited the dreaded divorce proceedings which he vainly hoped might win him custody of Louisa and Viktoria. It was an unrealistic expectation, the more so considering his amorous exploits in America. Rasa had by now moved into a flat in Streatham with the children. It was owned by her friend Colin O'Donnell, reason enough apparently for Ray to maintain a watchful eye on the property. "Ray used the services of a detective agency," Rasa reveals. "He really did! The 'detective' sat in an orange Marcos sports car outside watching my every move and who came in and out of the flat." Emboldened by the sheer absurdity of the situation, she eventually approached the private investigator and asked him if he'd like to come into the flat and join her over a pot of tea. "He had the shock of his life when I approached him and I never saw him again. He did not take up the offer of tea."

The divorce proceedings did not go well for Davies, who failed to win custody of the children. Rasa was awarded a settlement of £50,000. "That's the sum my solicitors had suggested and that's what I got." Ray also had to face one additional horror. During the close of proceedings, the judge announced that all costs in the action were to be paid by the singer. At that moment, he stood up in court and slowly clapped his hands in ironic appreciation. It was like a footballer showing his contempt for a penalty award – only worse. "That's Ray, isn't it?" Rasa concludes, with a wry smile.

Lingering resentment was revealed in occasional asides, including one comic encounter where Ray attempted to transform his wife into 'Wicked Annabella'. "One of the girls said to me, 'Mummy, are you really a witch?!' I said, 'What? No, I'm not a witch. Why?' She said, 'Well Ray says you *are* a witch.' Oh, right. OK!'" As Rasa stresses: "It was only later on when we were divorced that he used to say some nasty things about me."

Davies saved his sharpest barbs for his memoir *X-Ray*, which was generally sympathetic in tone up until their breakup. At that point, he portrayed his ex-wife as a calculating pragmatist who no longer believed he could make hit records and was keen to start afresh while he was still solvent. "Oh for goodness sake," she retorts, unaware of his reasoning. "That's Ray being really annoyed and upset and angry – and it's rubbish! How would I know he wasn't able to make any more hit records? It had nothing to do with that – or the money. It was just the years of emotional abuse . . . him having affairs, sometimes dismissing me and making me feel unimportant and not wanting the kids calling him dad – and *all* that stuff. It was just too much. And in the end I'd just had enough. It was nothing to do with money. And I didn't actually leave him for somebody else. I'd just had enough."

After the divorce, Rasa and the children visited her sister Dalia in Vancouver, then bought a house in Streatham. Over time, she grew closer to Colin O'Donnell and they became a couple, no doubt convincing Ray that his previous suspicions about their relationship were sound. Rasa had two more children: Kaz and Camila (born in 1977 and 1980, respectively). Her connections with the Davies family were severed. "The divorce was awful because they all turned against me. Apparently, it was all my fault. Well it wasn't, was it? But that's how they looked upon it. I was actually banished from the family. They didn't want to know me after that." Passing time and the arrival of grandchildren later led to a thawing of relations. "Mrs D was OK a few years down the line. We communicated quite well then. As people get older they change. I was still in contact with Ray's mum. Tor [Viktoria] even lived with her for a while. I invited Mrs D to Sunday lunch one time, but she didn't come, but I found she communicated with me better than she had in the beginning."

Amid the year of divorce, the double album *Preservation Act 2* was released. Over 67 minutes long, it stretched Davies' concept to breaking point. Rather than concentrating on one figure as he had done with *Arthur* and Pete Townshend had attempted with *Tommy* and *Quadrophenia*, Davies continued to present poorly sketched pasteboard characters. Figures such as Johnny Thunder and the Vicar, who had been allocated key songs in Act 1, were written out of the script in order to focus on the central clash between the socialist reformer Mr Black and his wide-boy adversary, Mr Flash. The simplistic plot line and conclusion were straight out of George Orwell's *Nineteen Eighty-Four* with a dash of Anthony Burgess' *A Clockwork Orange* – complete with brainwashing, rehabilitation and ultimate surrender to a totalitarian dystopia, with no hope of change. In the past, in songs such as

'A Well Respected Man' and 'Sunny Afternoon', he had created characters that the listener could laugh at or show sympathy towards, even though they were unnamed. In others, like 'Do You Remember Walter', he captured the essence of nostalgia in a moving statement about the losses experienced simply in growing up. Walter didn't need an opera written about him. His wistful presence and dramatic function were perfectly encapsulated in miniature. Paradoxically, in enlarging his creations to accommodate the needs of a concept album, Davies could only diminish their importance. What remained in *Preservation* were wooden figures, difficult to believe in, let alone care about. None of this would have mattered if the songs had been of sufficient quality, but they too were generally unarresting. Trade reviews were dispiriting. Ian MacDonald, the *New Musical Express'* most musically erudite critic, exposed the limitations of *Preservation* in a devastating overview, concluding: "The plot's obvious, the method is at best hit-and-miss and the words are a shade on the schlocky side, as well as being badly sewn together . . . Finally, we come to the music. Or rather we don't – since there's hardly any here . . . Davies' facility for creating beguiling tunes dies the death in the face of his doggedly unimaginative lyric requirements and ponderously low-profile dramatic aims . . . in attempting a rock equivalent of *The Threepenny Opera*, Ray Davies has merely created a drawn-out sequence of socio-political platitudes couched in the tritest lyric formats and supported by music of little overall cohesion, and no individual personality whatsoever. In short, what started out as a worthy project has failed on every conceivable level – which must at least be some sort of record in consistency."

Of course, it could be argued that *Preservation* transcended the standard critical criteria since it was never intended solely as an album but as part of some audio/visual package. Of all the writers to emerge from the rock field, Davies seemed the most likely to produce a full-blown theatrical work, accompanied by a soundtrack album of memorable songs, but that combination appeared a challenge too far at this point.

In many respects, *Preservation Acts 1 and 2* was a solo outing released under the banner of the Kinks. Onstage, the group dressed as if they were actors, but the costumes could not hide their inexperience. Jazz singer Maryann Price was part of the troupe and contributed lead vocal parts on 'Nothing Lasts Forever' and 'Scrapheap City'. Among the singles taken from the album was the effervescent 'Mirror Of Love', the first release of which was effectively a Ray Davies solo on which he played piano, acoustic guitar and drums. Apart from Dave on mandolin, the other Kinks were noticeably absent. After it flopped, a second rendition featuring the full line-up was issued, but it also failed to reach the charts. The only consolation for Davies was an unexpectedly rave review in *NME* which made 'Mirror Of Love' their 'Record Of The Week'. The reviewer was named Chrissie 'Hynd', a 23-year-old from Akron, Ohio, who was then dating the paper's star writer, Nick Kent. Championing the Kinks was courageously unhip but the American had seen them play live in 1969 and it had left a lasting impression. She'd always had a soft spot for Ray Davies and hoped to meet him someday.

Preservation Act 2 was not only unheralded in the UK but did not even enter the *Billboard* US Top 100. It was difficult to avoid the impression that Davies was stubbornly pursuing a bad idea gone stale. "A lot of people think I'm completely on the wrong track these days," he admitted at the time. "They think I should never have stopped writing three-minute story songs like 'Waterloo Sunset', 'Autumn Almanac' and 'Dead End Street'. But I've written so many of them, I've lost count. You can't keep doing that. People lose interest in you if you just keep doing the same thing over and over, which is what I felt I was doing. The magic goes. It did for me, anyway . . . I know I'm upsetting a lot of people who want something else from me. Some of them are in my own band. One of them is my brother."

Such single-mindedness was admirable, if frustrating, for fans and band members alike. Nevertheless, there was a quixotic quality to Davies' approach, as if he was defying both his record company and universal critical opinion by doggedly persisting with the theatrical experiments. The recent commission from Granada Television, by contrast, bore unexpected fruit. While touring America, Ray fell ill in Chicago and was briefly confined to bed. During the afternoons, he watched television soap operas and was struck by the plastic perfection of the actors. This inspired the creation of the silver-suited 'Starmaker', who sets out to transform the most boring person in the world into a superstar.

The idea spawned an entire album of songs written with extraordinary rapidity.

In September 1974, less than two months after the UK release of *Preservation Act 2*, *Starmaker* was screened nationally. The teleplay, written and co-starring Davies alongside actress June Ritchie, combined dialogue and song in a fashion pre-empting Dennis Potter's *Pennies From Heaven*. Its storyline was deceptively simple, yet extremely complex: a suburban accountant named Norman, believing himself to be a rock star, decides to write a concept album based on his mundane lifestyle. Or is he really a rock star assuming the role of an accountant? Filmed onstage, as if it were a theatrical performance, complete with an audience, Norman's dilemma is presented as a 'play within a play'. As the drama progresses, dream and reality are increasingly confused. "I feel a whole concept album coming on!" Norman says, apparently morphing into the 'real' Ray Davies. Quoting reviews from *Melody Maker* and *Rolling Stone*, he concludes: "I'm a star and I've got the press cuttings to prove it." His 'wife' Andrea then tears up the cuttings. In several psychologically revealing asides, Davies appears to confront his own fears and anxieties with exchanges that sound like extracts from the final days of his own marriage.

"All you think of is your work," Andrea complains.

"You know how important this project is to me!" Norman retorts.

There are several bitter exchanges. "Why don't you accept reality?" his wife cries. "Just who do you think you are, anyway? I can't talk to you when you're in this mood." In a final attempt to persuade Norman that he is not a pop star but a "dull ordinary and insignificant bloke", his wife catalogues a history of previous delusions. But what they document is nothing less than Ray Davies' biography from football-playing adolescence, through art school to the present. "Why don't you be yourself? First it was a footballer, then a painter, and then since 1965 you've had this fantasy of being a pop star."

Towards the end, 'Norman' (or Davies) admits defeat: "Maybe I'll be an ordinary person until something better turns up." The 30-minute play concludes with Norman wandering into the audience eating crisps and watching the Kinks, led by Dave, close the show. The symbolism is almost overwhelming.

Unsurprisingly, Dave was the member least impressed by Ray's psychological autobiography which he regarded as monumentally egotistical, "totally pointless and stupid". He felt humiliated and sidelined by the television production which had reduced the Kinks to an anonymous backing band seen, if at all, through a fish-eye camera lens. Ray, by contrast, was so pleased with his conceit that he promised an album based on *Starmaker* in the New Year. It was enough to convince Dave that the Kinks had virtually ended as a creative unit. He complained about Ray's 'vampiric' intensity. Ray seemed detached and uninterested in listening to any advice, let alone collaborating. Dave recalls receiving a telephone call from an unnamed individual who claimed to be Ray's psychiatrist. "He said to me, 'If you don't get away from Ray, he's going to destroy you. Not deliberately, but in a way he can't help himself.'" Dave heard the warning but failed to act on it.

Ever unpredictable, Ray suddenly became entwined in a new romance. Like the subject of *Starmaker*, Davies seemed attracted to the notion of stolid solidity and down-to-earth goodness. Rasa had been the teenage fan who became a pop star's wife and, given Ray's level of fame, her successor was similarly modest in terms of glamour. It was soon after moving to Effingham that Davies met a 22-year-old domestic science teacher named Yvonne Ann Gunner, who was living not far away at Shirley Road in Croydon. Their casual friendship rapidly deepened and it was very soon after his divorce that they were married at Croydon Registry Office on 1 November 1974. The nuptials were not reported in the press. In a remarkable attempt at subterfuge, the groom actually changed his name by deed poll, dropping his surname. As a result, two marriages were logged in the official register under the names 'Raymond Douglas' and 'Raymond Davies'. He did not refer to himself as a 'musician', preferring the term 'Company Director'. Although he had celebrated his 30th birthday four and a half months before, he registered his age as 29. Unravelling the logic of such eccentric behaviour is no easy task. Perhaps after all the publicity surrounding Rasa's departure and his subsequent breakdown and overdose, he was desperate for privacy and felt the need to control the flow of personal information. "I wanted to be anonymous," he now says, without much further explanation.

"Why Raymond Douglas? Well, [publisher] Freddy Bienstock always called me 'Raymond Douglas Davies'." As a result, Yvonne remained a closely guarded secret as far as the public was concerned. No pictures of them together have ever been published in any magazine or journal, nor are any registered with a photo agency.

The 'secret' marriage came as shock to those who knew about it. Rasa was perplexed by the timing, as the divorce papers had barely been signed. If Ray felt so dejected by the outcome of his settlement, why was he so eager to re-enter the entangled emotional and financial commitments of marriage? "People are different," his brother reflects. "Ray came from a terrible trauma trying to top himself, then living with me for weeks to recover. When you've gone through an emotional trauma you always look for something to help hold you up, emotionally. I suppose Yvonne came along as a pretty attractive, sophisticated woman, and that's what he needed. That type." Evidently, it was not a 'type' that appealed to Dave. "Yvonne and I didn't get on that well," he says. Their first meeting took place at a restaurant in Surrey, near Ray's Effingham home. The wine flowed as Dave and Lisbet toasted the newly-weds. Alas, cordiality deteriorated when Dave ventured beyond small talk to describe his esoteric interests in religion, spirituality, yoga and philosophy. Yvonne listened patiently, but not uncritically, while challenging his airier notions with a school teacher's scepticism and tidy logic. Dave became so exasperated and indignant that he stormed out of the restaurant. Later that night, he dismissed her as a middle-class suburbanite from the straight world, a type that he had rebelled against all his life. It was the ever-accommodating and even-tempered Lisbet who maintained the peace. "Lisbet and Yvonne got on and that kind of helped to move the thing together *a bit*," Dave says, like some commentator discussing the nuances of a Cold War summit. Subsequently, they learned to "tolerate each other". She even surprised him with a nugget of psychological insight that he felt was both cogent and intuitive. Casually reflecting on their contrasting personalities, she noted: "If Ray was a bit more like you and you were a little more like him, then both of you would have been better off." This anticipated Ray's own theory that both brothers were somehow psychologically 'incomplete'.

Nineteen seventy-four closed with an upsurge of positivity for Davies who took the *Preservation* tour to the East Coast of America. The improved show included several segments of film shot in England, additional songs and special screen projections. Realizing that the entire recording of *Preservation* would run for approximately two hours, Davies edited the show to an hour and a half, concentrating on the Mr Black and Flash confrontation and jettisoning the Vicar's sermon about cricket and other less relevant material. The new production required a significant expansion in the ranks with newly recruited brass players, a larger lighting crew, set designers and a total of six backing singers: Pamela Travis, Shirlie Roden, Debi Doss, Anna Peacock, Lewis Rich and Trevor White. Choreographers Dougie Squires and Carole Todd were hired and film producer Dennis Woolf accompanied the ensemble throughout the tour. Ray's wife, Yvonne, was also invited.

During the lengthy auditions and rehearsals, Davies had adopted the persona of a Hollywood music mogul. When Shirlie Roden applied for the position of backing singer, Ray informed her: "I'm looking for a star. Are you a star?" Uncertain how to respond, she sat at the grand piano and performed Laura Nyro's 'Poverty Train'. Davies was cannily sparing with his compliments, but she was deemed acceptable. She left Konk Studios feeling starstruck by Davies' charisma. "I got on fine with Ray and I had a great deal of respect for him. Over the years, I gradually realized what a huge thing he was taking on. He was the frontman and all the responsibility fell on him. He was brilliant and his heart was really in the music. Even singing something silly like 'The Banana Boat Song', the energy he had at a performance was fantastic."

Understandably, given the size of the crew, Ray ran a tight ship. Only the Kinks flew first class, while the rest travelled in economy. "There were lots of restrictions," Roden recalls. "We were allowed only one phone call home per week and our washing had to be done at the hotel once a week too." Other expenses were covered by a modest daily stipend provided by Davies' chief lieutenant Ken Jones, who enforced his master's rules with slavish loyalty. "We were constantly running after Ken trying to get our per diems," Roden reminisces. "He never wanted to pay you. I think there was a lot of pressure from Ray to keep the costs down."

The US tour opened on a celebratory note, preceded by a hearty drinking session. Backing singers Roden and Doss both recall swaying on a rickety stage at New York's Colgate University at Hamilton (on 23 November), then slowly sobering up during the set. They also received an early taste of the misogynistic antics favoured by the male members. Shirlie Roden recalls: "The first night I went out onstage to sing 'Mirror Of Love' in *Preservation*, Dave came up behind me with a pint of beer and poured it over my head. I carried on singing. The next night he was lying on the floor playing guitar and looking up my skirt. I didn't know why the audience were laughing. Every night he'd try to do something to detract from my performance and I didn't understand why. Now, he'd probably laugh about it and say, 'I was pissed off with Ray and I took it out on you.' At the time it just seemed strange."

Part of the reason for Dave's mischief was a lingering resentment about being forced to play what resembled a stage musical. It soon became apparent to the backing singers that they were the only ones, apart from Ray, who appreciated the theatrics. When the backstage buffoonery became tiresome, Roden pointedly asked Dave: "When are you going to grow up?" Always ready with a riposte, he informed her: "I was born grown up, I've been growing *down* ever since."

While Ray retained a professional distance, Dave was always involved in the drinking bouts and backstage drama. Roden admits that there was a flirtatious frisson between herself and Dave from the first tour onwards. "While I just got on with Ray, Dave and I had this love/hate passionate relationship. There was this ongoing attraction between us, I suppose. I was very drawn to him because he was so wild and so tortured and he was drawn to me because it seemed I could understand his spiritual side . . . He'd get very frustrated and angry with me and quite violent sometimes. It was also difficult because *Preservation* brought quite a lot of stuff up."

The chief antagonist in the *Preservation* wars was John Gosling who made little effort to disguise his disdain for the new recruits. "Baptist seemed to take an instant dislike to me," says Debi Doss. "That was just because we were girls, I think. Thirty-five years later he apologized for pouring beer over my head. We left a bar once and he jumped on me in a lift and Shirlie had to pull him off." The 'lift incident' threatened to turn even uglier after Roden's intervention. "Baptist was so rude to Debi that I poured a tequila sunrise over his head and he chased me. We were going up and down in the lift fighting, and this elderly couple were trying to step over us and get out. Typical stupid stuff. Sometimes it wasn't very nice."

"From day one, they didn't want us there," Debi Doss concludes.

Momentary tensions and minor spats were eclipsed by the thrill of playing before large American audiences who clearly revered the Kinks. Roden and Doss had never experienced this level of fame and were at first awestruck by the spectacle. "It was an amazing experience to go on the road and we really enjoyed it," says Roden. "It was great fun doing *Preservation* and it went down really well. What hit me most were the fans and how deeply loved the Kinks were. In 1974, they weren't really happening that much in England but the fans in America absolutely adored them. I think the *Preservation* shows were the best thing we ever did."

While staying at New York's Warwick Hotel, there was tomfoolery aplenty. On one occasion, Mick Avory played the mischief maker by commandeering a limousine outside the hotel and taking everyone to the Gaylord Indian restaurant on Lexington Avenue. Upon arrival, he informed the driver: "Take the rest of the evening off." The chauffeur was unaware that Avory was not his actual client. Baptist joined in the fun by eating the restaurant bill, a trick which surely would have impressed Davies, had he joined them. When Pamela Travis did the same at another eaterie, she was sternly reprimanded by Ken Jones. "Only members of the band can do that," he warned.

After the troupe arrived in Los Angeles, the backing singers, by now used to Davies' frugality, received an unexpected reward. Amid the rush, they were inadvertently ushered into a white limousine reserved for 'the Great Raymondo' and driven to their hotel. Pamela Travis was so excited that she stood up and stuck her head out of the roof window, shrieking in triumph at passers-by.

Following a performance at the Santa Monica Civic Auditorium, the group concluded the US tour with shows in St Louis, Chicago and Cleveland. Debi Doss, a St Louis native, was thrilled when Ray introduced her onstage at the Ambassador Theater as the 'local girl'. Afterwards, the entire ensemble visited her home for a pre-Christmas celebration where Baptist disgraced himself and was hastily ejected in a taxi. "They liked to drink," says Roden, stating the obvious. "It was crazy. I'd never toured America. For me, it was a like a big party from beginning to end."

Festivities concluded back at the hotel in the so-called 'noisy room' where every available drinks bottle was collected and consumed in a climactic shindig. Ray seldom got drunk in such circumstances but observed proceedings with a crooked smile, like a teacher dutifully attending an end-of-term school disco.

Davies' sense of humour was enigmatic rather than obvious and frequently laced with unexpected innuendo. Shirlie Roden recalls being in a car with Ray when he uttered one of his mischievous one-liners. He was perusing a collection of paper plates that fans had thrown onstage during the Kinks' set. They contained scribbled song requests and goodwill messages, the traditional means of communication between aficionado and star. "Ray was reading these paper plates. Then, he turned to me in the back of the car and said, 'It's the only kind of plate I get these days.'"

The year ended in glory with a memorable three nights at London's Royalty Theatre during Christmas week. Reviews were kind and, despite some reservations, the *Guardian*'s Robin Denselow felt there was still hope for a revised staging of *Preservation*. "It has been an uphill struggle," he wrote, "but with *Preservation* it seemed he would at last produce a significant work. The tragedy is that he has, but it ran so briefly, and the lack of promotion was matched by the shambling, cheap production. And yet *Preservation* has all the makings of a major success, if only it was carefully staged and put on at, say, the Roundhouse for a couple of months."

Instead, Davies prepared his theatrical troupe for a new project: *Soap Opera*. Based on the *Starmaker* television programme, this live spectacle featured the participants in Afro wigs, surrounded by props, including a vertically placed bed and gigantic ducks to accompany 'Ducks On The Wall'. Despite its overt Englishness and parochial allusions, the musical was premiered in America during the spring of 1975. Audiences were no doubt puzzled by some of the references, but appreciated the humour. In the original play, Ray Davies had pleaded to the TV audience, "I'm not Norman, am I?" This became a panto call and response with spectators yelling, "No! No! You're Ray Davies!" The new songs were leavened by the usual selection of classic Kinks' hits and the tour was brief enough to prevent any serious conflicts. Not that everyone was happy.

The female backing singers were generally treated like 'lads' which meant they were subject to sexist insults. "They all jumped on the bandwagon," Roden says. "We got called terrible things like the Old Trouts. If we walked into a bar after a gig, they'd say: 'Oh, go away, you old trouts'. Unlike Pam, Debi and I weren't very large-breasted and we got called the Titless Wonders. Ray introduced us onstage once as the Pointless Sisters. It didn't worry me that much because I had a fairly healthy sense of self-worth. I thought 'Oh, it's just them'." Their chief tormentor, John Gosling, continued to long for the streamlined rock group he had joined before Ray had turned them into a theatrical troupe.

Dave Davies was similarly disillusioned, dismissing *Soap Opera* as a veritable solo project from which he felt excluded. "Dave was tormented anyway," says Shirlie Roden. "Back then, I didn't understand where all this anguish came from. He was a passionate, fiery, intelligent guy, full of verve and go, but a tortured soul. Ray played on that as perhaps only a brother can. You always know your brother's weaknesses. At the same time, Ray adored Dave, but he would still torment him."

Dave's frustration soon turned to consternation as he pondered his brother's motives. Even the set list was subject to suspicion. There was still a sprinkling of *Preservation* songs including 'Mirror Of Love', during which Ray left the stage for a short break while Shirlie Roden sang her part. "Dave got really angry and upset with me," she recalls. "He said, 'What are you trying to do in this band?' I was just doing as I was told. I was employed by Ray and if he said, 'Sing this song', I sang it. Obviously, to Dave, it was like I was upstaging him in some way because he wasn't being given a big solo number to do, but I was. I don't know why Ray did that. It seems strange. One night, he asked Dave to sing 'Death Of A Clown' and Dave forgot the words." At the end of the song, Ray took mischievous pleasure in telling the audience: "Now you know why he doesn't sing it very often."

Overall, the tour went well, partly because Ray was accompanied by his wife Yvonne, who distracted him from conflicts within the band. Apart from an occasional tirade against the Kinks' road manager and whipping boy Ken Jones, Davies was in deceptively good spirits. Jones knew his place and accepted Ray's caprice without visible complaint. Unfortunately, the subsidiary Kinks picked up on the roadie's vulnerability and delighted in subverting his authority. "All the lads used to take the piss out of Ken," Roden acknowledges. "He had a little moustache and people would do Ken impressions. You'd put your finger under your nose and say: 'You've got to get up at five a.m. to catch a plane.' Nobody took him seriously, really. I think he was scared of Ray who could be so damning. You never really knew where you stood with Ray. He can be absolutely charming but you've got no idea what's going on [in his head] . . . Ken tried his hardest but he was never given full rein and, as you say, he was very much the whipping boy. He wasn't allowed to be the manager, but if anything went wrong it was absolutely his fault. That was Ray's thing. I don't think he really wanted management. Ray wanted to be calling the shots and he could control and manipulate Ken."

After the shows, Davies would socialize with his wife, leaving the others to indulge in the usual drinking sessions. On tour, Yvonne served as wardrobe mistress, preparing the props and assisting the backing singers with their various costume changes. "I think Ray likes to get his girlfriends or wives involved in some respect on tour," says Debi Doss. "She was a quiet, shy and friendly girl." Others concurred. "I really liked Yvonne," adds John Beecham. "I always thought she was classy."

Such positive traits were welcomed, but her status as Ray's wife meant that the musicians remained guarded in her presence. "Yvonne was lovely, but she was a cookery teacher," Roden notes. "She had no idea about life on the road. There were long journeys in Greyhound buses and Yvonne had never done that before. So she was completely out of her depth, really. Imagine you're a teacher and suddenly you're married to this rock star travelling around America going from hotel to hotel. It was very difficult for her. Yvonne was fine with the girls, but she didn't mix much with the boys. She found the arguments very distressing. It was difficult. Ray tried to shelter her from it. She would giggle and laugh about all these groupies throwing themselves at him and the boys. She knew the band in England but, of course, put a band on the road and they become animals, basically. She didn't like that. They had to be careful as well because she knew the wives. Not that everyone was messing around but there were always girls in people's rooms. You couldn't keep them out."

The hell-raising Dave Davies curbed none of his excesses for Yvonne's benefit. He had already expressed disdain for her middle-class trappings, so simply chose to ignore her presence most of the time. "I don't think I ever saw him speak to her," Roden considers. "She was very sweet, so I don't know why he wouldn't get on with her. But then, he used to say to me: 'You're a posh cunt.' Once, we were staying in some hotel and they had a fish tank with a beautiful tropical fish that had a little turned-up nose. He called me over and said, 'Look it's a posh cunt fish, like you, Shirl.' So, he probably thought Yvonne was a 'posh cunt' as well."

In May 1975, the album *Soap Opera* was released. The critical response was muted as, amazingly, the UK's two biggest music papers – *New Musical Express* and *Melody Maker* – failed to print a review. Whether this was editorial apathy or, more likely, record company negligence in failing to send sufficient review copies, was never ascertained. The album featured three UK singles – 'Holiday Romance', 'Ducks On The Wall' and 'You Can't Stop The Music' – none of which charted. Nine of the songs, previously premiered on *Starmaker*, sounded rushed or written to a deadline. 'Rush Hour Blues' and 'Nine To Five' document the tedium of the rat race, while 'When Work Is Over' and 'Have Another Drink' celebrate escape into alcohol. There are some funny moments such as the mock poignant 'You Make It All Worthwhile' in which Norman placates his wife after rejecting her shepherd's pie. Two recently composed songs are shoehorned into the album: 'Holiday Romance' includes Ray's familiar Noël Coward vocal imitation, while the Caribbean-style 'Underneath The Neon Sign' is a predictable dystopian lament. Davies saves the best two songs for last. '(A) Face In The Crowd', a strong melody whose lyrics document Norman's abdication of stardom, has the pathetic resonance associated with the better material on *Arthur*. Finally, 'You Can't Stop The Music' allows Dave an opportunity to play some hard electric guitar, suggesting that a more convincing fusion of theatre and rock might yet be forthcoming.

Soap Opera fared better in the US charts than either of the *Preservation* releases, but a number 55 placing in *Billboard* could hardly be described as a major breakthrough. The group returned to the UK for a short tour of universities before Davies 'retired' the *Starmaker/Soap Opera* saga with a well-received performance at London's New Victoria Theatre on 14 June. "It's a step in the right direction and I'm going to get there eventually," he said, defiantly. This was bad news for the other Kinks, who were tired of the concept albums and wanted only to play straightforward rock. Dave admitted that *Soap Opera* was his least favourite Kinks album, a view that none of the others, bar Ray, contradicted.

"I didn't think the music was that good," John Dalton adds, "and we all had to dress up in those stupid suits and wigs. It would probably have been better if he'd tried to do it as Ray Davies instead of as the Kinks. He should've got a backing band to do it. It wasn't the Kinks really." Gosling concurred, adding that he now felt he was in an amateur dramatics society rather than a rock band.

"Ray was always trying to write these wretched rock operas," concludes Robert Wace. "Part of the problem was that he always thought he was a better writer than Pete Townshend and, subconsciously, he started trying to compete with him." Of course, Davies' vision was more centred on the mundane than the mythical. "We kept in touch with our subject matter a little more," he counters. "Maybe if I had written about psychedelic kids in Shepherd's Bush who took drugs. . . . but I didn't want to write *Quadrophenia*."

Davies was beginning to feel rejected in his homeland, misunderstood by his record company, patronized by critics and rebuffed by his own band. "Especially in Britain, they didn't really understand what we were trying to do. I think that whole period was very underrated. We got some great performances out of that band – maybe the tightest rhythm section we ever had. I felt we were doing something genuinely experimental – our equivalent of doing fringe theatre, in a way. But the mainstream people in the music industry had no idea what we were doing, or why."

On 3 July 1975, a few weeks after the final *Soap Opera* show,

Ray received the shock news that his father had died. Fred and Annie Davies had been staying at Ray's home in Effingham at the time while the singer was temporarily working from a base in London. A lifelong smoker, Fred had been diagnosed with emphysema. Weakened by breathing problems, he enjoyed staying in suburban Surrey, tending his son's garden. His death was sudden. Unable to breathe, he had collapsed on the kitchen floor, knocking himself unconscious, after which he expired.

The family congregated in Effingham. Dave was among the first mourners, still mulling over the last time he had seen his father. A week before, Fred had visited his home, parading around the garden and imitating the sound of chirping birds like a seasoned ornithologist. Cheerful and vivacious, despite his condition, he suggested they should adjourn to the pub for a summer pint, but Dave excused himself. Declining that final drink would always be remembered as a lost opportunity and was an enduring source of regret. Dave's musings were interrupted when Ray arrived alongside sister Gwen and her husband Brian Longstaff, who had driven them from London. It was a grand reunion of the Davies family, full of memories of the uproarious father whose 'Minnie The Moocher' routine had enlivened so many parties over the decades and generations.

Family memories were uppermost in Ray's mind when he announced his new project, due to commence almost immediately after Fred Davies' funeral. There were stifled groans in the Kinks' camp as he proposed another album based on *Preservation*. This time it was to be a prequel, reconstructing the origins of his favourite character Flash, commencing with his schooldays. The good news for Dave was that the entire treatment was to be based on the story of his adolescence, culminating in his expulsion from William Grimshaw after impregnating his young girlfriend. This was the closest Ray came to offering an olive branch and Dave accepted it with grace. Honoured that his most traumatic life experience was to be immortalized on record, he was equally pleased to learn that the musical direction would be more hard-hitting, with a strong emphasis on electric guitar rather than brass.

The Kinks Present Schoolboys In Disgrace was released in November 1975 in America, a full two months before the UK issue. With its pastiche cartoon cover, rear shot of the Kinks dressed in school uniform and liner notes beginning "Once upon a time there was a naughty schoolboy . . .", the project looked decidedly unhip. Instead, it turned out to be the most fully-fledged group recording of all the Kinks' theatrical forays. The opening 'Schooldays' sets the scene with its nostalgic longing for a return to the harsh innocence of school life, with Dave prominent on backing vocals and guitar. In keeping with the time period, the Davies brothers use rock 'n' roll arrangements on several songs: the amusing, crowd-pleasing 'Jack The Idiot Dunce' references Jerry Lee Lewis' 'Great Balls Of Fire' and the genre's fascination with dance crazes; 'The First Time We Fall In Love' sounds like a doo-wop imitation with echoes of the Poni-Tails and Danny And The Juniors. These retro influences were far from unfashionable in 1975. Earlier that year John Lennon's acclaimed album *Rock 'n' Roll* had been released, while the 1973 movie *American Graffiti* – a tribute to a more innocent, romanticized era – was still fresh in the memory. The remainder of the album features a more contemporary sound, with Dave relishing the extended solos, particularly on those songs documenting his caning and expulsion. The centrepiece 'Education', over seven minutes long, prefaces side two's impregnation revelation, 'I'm In Disgrace'. 'Headmaster' chronicles the boy's confession of his sex crime, ending with the poignant plea, "Please don't take my trousers down"; 'The Hard Way' emphasizes school rules, its anger encapsulated in Dave's fierce guitar soloing. 'The Last Assembly', performed as a country/gospel death-row take-off, offers a solace of sorts, concluding with 'No More Looking Back', one of Ray's most reflective songs of the period, detailing obsessive retrospection and its attendant dangers.

The album peaked at number 45 in America, a modest success by recent standards, but nothing to excite either Ray Davies or RCA Records. Tours in support of the album were an unexpected hoot, with the Kinks portrayed as schoolboys and Avory receiving the lash of a whip during 'The Hard Way'. Ray was given a ceremonious caning by Debi Doss, who was dressed as the headmaster while still in her stockings. She remembers Ray's whispered aside ("Harder! Harder!") as the mock punishment was administered. Pam Travis played the pregnant schoolgirl, a 'leading lady' role that wasn't entirely flattering. "Pam had this inflatable stomach," Roden recalls. "While she was singing she had to press this [button] and her stomach got bigger under her gymslip. She hated being big and fat onstage like that." Debi Doss had no such qualms, having been allocated the role of the dervish Jack The Idiot Dunce. Her mother had once run a dance school in St Louis, so she was a fairly accomplished hoofer. "It was choreography, silly gymslips and hats," she remembers. "Maybe the tour was more fun for me because I got to be Jack The Idiot Dunce. My mother came to a show. I had to dance around with a cane in stockings and suspenders and beat Ray Davies in front of my mother. Fabulous. I loved it."

Completing the effects was a backdrop of film footage shot in the grounds of Kenwood House, the scene of Dave's teenage sexual encounter and the original inspiration for the album. Shirlie Roden was both amused and surprised by the musical's fantasy element, not yet realizing that it was so closely based on Dave's adolescence. "I thought it was all bizarre. When we were touring, especially in New York, all the English bands' road crews knew about us being in stockings and suspenders. Word got around and the roadies would come to watch us onstage simply because we were dressed like schoolgirls. It shows you how pervy the English boys were."

The first leg of the *Schoolboys In Disgrace* tour included Steve Harley's Cockney Rebel as support act. The group had topped the charts earlier in the year with the infectious '(Make Me Smile) Come Up And See Me' and Harley was a known admirer of Davies' songwriting. One evening he invited the Kinks' scantily clad backing singers for a drink. Champagne flowed, but the next day there were repercussions. Ken Jones dutifully dictated a warning: "You're not to go out with Cockney Rebel again." Shirlie Roden interpreted the message as another exercise in headmasterly control. "Ray didn't want to buy us a drink, but he didn't want anybody else to buy us a drink either. We belonged to him. I can count on the fingers of one hand the amount of times Ray bought a drink."

Although Roden still respected Ray Davies, she was no longer the awestruck girl entranced by his rock-star presence. Successive tours had exposed his more irritating traits, eccentric ways and scheming mind games. "We used to call Ray the manipulator. He manipulated people and he knew he manipulated people, but he pretended he didn't. I got so pissed off with him once that while we were doing the soundcheck I was miming. He said, 'There's something wrong with your microphone – sing it again.'"

Such petty vengeance was born of exasperation. During the *Schoolboys* tour, Davies had been pestering Roden about her then partner John Miller, who had been working on Café Society's second album at Konk. "Ray's a strange man. He never confronts you directly with something. It's always going around the whole situation. Ray was continually trying to find out from me what John was doing in the studio. 'How's he getting on? Have you phoned John this week?' 'No, Ray, I haven't had my *one* allowed phone call this week.' John was trying to get agreement from Ray to put strings on the album and Ray was trying to find out if John had put strings on without his agreement. It was so manipulative. In the end I said: 'Phone him yourself.'"

Ray's circuitous scheming often worked to his disadvantage. In private moments when he exposed his tender side, some reacted suspiciously or cynically, uncertain of his motives. "Part of his manipulation is being charming," Roden reminds us. "He once came up to me in the dressing room. I'd just bought a new perfume in New York and was putting it on. He said, 'That's a nice perfume, what's it called?' I said, 'It's called "fuck off and stop bothering me".' It was a terrible thing to say because he was actually being very nice. The trouble was there were so few occasions where he'd actually pay you a compliment. I was so thrown that he was being pleasant to me that I immediately countered with something awful. That's what you learn from Dave, really – just be lippy back!"

Ray's need for control continued to ruffle feathers, not least with another support act, the Pretty Things. Even more than the Kinks, the Pretties were renowned as Sixties' bad boys with a file of news clippings detailing exceedingly long hair, violence and an anti-authoritarian attitude. They also showed a keen interest in R&B and were far better practitioners of the genre than most of their rivals. Coincidentally, they had also pioneered the 'concept album', releasing *S.F. Sorrow* within a month of *The Village Green Preservation Society*, and the best part of half a year in advance of the Who's *Tommy*. The parallels with the Kinks may have suggested common ground, but that does not necessarily bode well for a support act. The Pretties had only limited chart success and temporarily broke up before 'reforming', somewhat tentatively, in the early Seventies. Founder Phil May felt fractious at the time and touring with the Kinks hardly helped. There was "a lot of animosity" made worse by perceived belittlement from the headliners. May had little fondness for the Kinks' theatrical excursions and regarded the 'Schooldays' show as an embarrassment. Privately, he lampooned Ray Davies as 'Max Bygraves'. Never a lover of rules, May took exception to Davies' restrictions about lighting and reluctance to sanction the use of a grand piano onstage rather than plain keyboards. Ken Jones was called upon to lay down the law on such matters, much to May's chagrin. "Davies would get his manager to do the dirty work, he had the job of telling us all this – and he hated it – stabbing us in the back. Davies was a horrible geezer – a cunt." May's angry assessment arguably said more about his own disgruntlement than Davies' despotism. Interestingly, his choice of insult ('cunt') echoed Dave Davies' favourite putdown of his brother, and others.

The Kinks Present Schoolboys In Disgrace had mollified Dave who was energized about playing rockier material again. Even John Gosling conceded there was some improvement, but was it enough? "The dressing up was good fun," he admits. "It was in the Kinks' character. We dressed up in clubs as clowns, gangsters and schoolboys. We all liked theatre and the movies, but it went too far. It was a hassle to do these things. At one stage, we did two shows in Los Angeles. We'd get to the theatre at two in the afternoon, and leave at two the next morning. A twelve-hour shift for one gig! After that we still got cries of 'rock 'n' roll' from the audience. They didn't take it to their hearts as Ray had hoped. I suppose we were all upset. We all had our say but Ray was hellbent on doing it."

Davies was already threatening a sequel to *The Kinks Present Schoolboys In Disgrace*, documenting Flash's late adolescence and fall into crime, but eventually conceded that the seemingly never-ending *Preservation* saga had run its course. Reflecting on the 'theatrical years' provided a salutary insight for both Davies and RCA Records. Despite numerous American tours, no Kinks album had cracked the Top 40 and all of their singles had failed to chart.

The statistics made dismal reading. In Britain, of course, they were even worse. Reluctantly, Davies was ready to admit defeat and revise his thinking. During a visit to the UK, he was already speaking of his theatrical concepts in the past tense. "In a way I think I neglected the music and concentrated too much on the lyric form, but I don't think it was overdone. To me the albums were musical plays. I don't think I'm being big-headed when I say that it worked."

It was time for a fresh start.

CHAPTER THIRTY-ONE

THE RETURN OF VIOLENCE

In 1976 Ray and Yvonne Davies relocated to Manhattan, moving into an apartment on the Upper West Side. It was a practical decision designed to assist their respective careers. Yvonne had given up teaching and was keen to pursue her interests in art, design and photography, while Ray was now committed to breaking the Kinks in America on a grand scale. Being at the centre of the New York music industry was empowering – in terms of both business and creativity. His songwriting would alter as he immersed himself in American life. Before long there would be songs about tax exile, gasoline shortages, US disc jockeys and iconic American comic-book superheroes. The Village Green had never seemed so far away.

On 23 June, the Kinks signed to Arista Records, the label formed by Clive Davis in 1974 after his departure from CBS. Davis had previously attempted to sign the Kinks – in 1966 and 1971 – and was convinced of their potential as a stadium act. News that Ray was willing to tour incessantly and stay away from theatrical musicals inspired corporate confidence. The singer gave a witty speech at the signing ceremony, concluding: "Arista seems to be an exciting new company and the emphasis on the Kinks' music is on the future." In order to show his commitment, Ray disappeared into the newly renovated 24-track facility at Konk and spent most of the next six months preparing the group's debut album for Arista. Although the return to straightforward rock was welcomed, there was still unease and tension among the participants. The sessions were stifling, clinical and lengthy as Davies tinkered with ideas, equipment and arrangements in a quixotic quest for perfection. There was also a ghost in the ranks.

John Dalton, that loyal, pacific player whom Davies had twice recruited in 1966 and 1969, was intending to quit. He had made the decision prior to the Arista signing but elected to complete his bass work on the new record, not realizing that it would take most of the year. "I told Ray first and he asked me to stay. He thought I was joining another band." Davies' suspicion proved unfounded. Dalton had no intention of playing with anyone else, or even continuing in the business. He was burned out and wished nothing more than to spend time with his wife Valerie and their three children. Financial disappointment also played a part. "I had all these promises of a quarter of the company but nobody in the band, apart from Ray and Dave, had any money. We were all on the breadline. It was hard work, and we were away from home a lot. I think it might have been different if there was a future there with the promise of earning some money. It's a bit silly when you can come out of a band like that and earn more money on a building site. People think you must have earned some money, but no. I never got any royalties."

Dalton never regretted his decision to leave. Indeed, he believes it was fated. Not long afterwards, his youngest son was diagnosed with leukemia, which would later take the boy's life. "I wouldn't have been able to continue with the band anyway, so it was meant to be." He subsequently opened a transport café with a friend, then returned to the building trade as a carpenter. Even then, there was no escaping Davies' bargain basement clutches. Dalton was subsequently hired to rebuild the bar at Konk, which he ran for a time. He also did some building work on one of Ray's houses, presumably for mate's rates.

Dalton's replacement was Andy Pyle, a respected pro who had previously played in the Alvin Lee Band, Savoy Brown and Blodwyn Pig. Having toured the Luton circuit as a kid in the Wages Of Sin, he knew John Gosling, but it was former Savoy Brown tour manager Brian Wilcock, then working for Ray, who alerted him to the vacancy. His audition was unusual. At first, he was invited to contribute bass to a couple of tracks, one of which, 'Mr Big Man', would appear on their next album. "Ray would say, 'Go on, Andy, play loads of things – anything you like', and then he snipped all the best bits together. It was a very funny approach, recording with the Kinks – and not always in a jocular way."

Pyle felt a certain trepidation. The tense atmosphere and mournful mood were unlike anything he had ever encountered working as a professional musician. "I couldn't understand why, whenever we were in the studio Dave, Mick and Baptist [Gosling] would be there with their heads down all day. Not a word would be spoken by anybody. The minute we'd finish, we'd go to the pub, Dave, Mick, Baptist and myself, and it'd be pints and a good laugh. Then we'd go back to the studio the next day and not a word would be spoken. I'd say, 'Come on, boys!' I was feeling really up – working with the Kinks seemed wonderful. I used to like the Kinks. But Mick and Baptist kept warning me: 'You'll find out when your time comes!'" Pyle paid little attention to their warnings and failed to discern any reason for their discontent. It would be several months before he discovered the true meaning of their words.

While Pyle was completing his 'audition', Ray made a rare public appearance at London's Nashville Rooms where the newly formed Tom Robinson Band was appearing. A fortnight before, Robinson had quit Café Society, the Konk-signed group, whose career had come to a frustrating halt. Their second album had been stymied by constant prevarication from Davies, who was fatally distracted by protracted work on his own project. "He didn't realize how difficult and how much time it would take to run the Konk label," drummer Nick Trevisick maintains. "Ray gets these ideas and then he gets bored with them." When Robinson saw Davies in the audience, he performed 'Tired Of Waiting For You' as a sarcastic riposte. Fierce words were exchanged. "I was in the middle," says Trevisick who often worked with Dave Davies. "I took no sides. Ray came down to see what Tom was up to and they started their slanging match and I walked off stage and refused to come back until it had died down." Davies concluded matters by aiming V-signs at Robinson, then storming off. Afterwards, John McCoy, the first manager of Café Society, catcalled: "Davies couldn't run a luggage label, let alone a record label."

Konk had failed to sign any new batch of acts since its inception and no further releases would be forthcoming. It was not entirely surprising. Larger vanity labels such as Rolling Stones Records and Led Zeppelin's Swansong had been launched with noble, expansionist intentions, only to devolve into single artiste enterprises. Davies realized his mistake too late. "When you get involved in business, the music stops. It happened to the Beatles when they tried to get Apple together. Certainly with the Who. It took over the Beatles and it started to take over with me. You should do what you're good at, what can feed your 'art'." Robinson defected to EMI, which was forced to buy out his contract with Konk. However, Davies retained Robinson's publishing and benefited financially from hits such as '2-4-6-8 Motorway', 'Don't Take No For An Answer' and the anthem, 'Sing If You're Glad To Be Gay'. Eddie Kassner would have been very impressed.

In February 1977, the Kinks released *Sleepwalker*. The album had undergone a long gestation with Davies completing 30 demos and recording around 20 songs which were finally whittled to nine. The PR hype and initial critical reaction suggested a veritable Kinks' renaissance but, overall, the results sounded somewhat soulless and antiseptic, features associated with the many mainstream AOR (adult-oriented rock) bands then dominating American radio.

Thematically, *Sleepwalker* combines songs of isolation and alienation. On 'Sleepless Night', Dave is allowed his first lead vocal on a Kinks' album since 1972. 'Brother', a comment on the world's lack of brotherhood rather than Dave, features a closing string accompaniment suggested by Clive Davis in the vain hope that a suitable single might be forthcoming. 'Life On The Road' presents a compendium of Davies touchstones – the country runaway adrift in London; the teasing gay reference; the parochial fascination with London place names. 'Juke Box Music' offers sweet relief, the female narrator's musical fantasies recalling the escapism of *Starmaker*. The album closes with 'Life Goes On', partly a song of marital abandonment, rescued by Davies' mordant humour. At the end, he imagines a darkly comic scenario, reminiscent of a Tony Hancock sketch. The protagonist attempts to gas himself only to fail as the utility company has cut off the supply following non-payment.

Strong publicity, a decent promotional budget and the novelty of a return to rock roots sent *Sleepwalker* to number 21 in the US, with sales around the 350,000 mark, their best showing since the mid-Sixties. The title track was also a minor hit with a lyric that appeared tantalizingly autobiographical. "It's about a vampire, but not the bloodsucking kind. It's more somebody who feeds off of people's lives rather than people's blood – somebody who feeds off their stories. It's like a writer going around getting people to talk in their sleep and then coming out with all of the things they say in their subconscious."

Davies was not entirely convinced by the success of *Sleepwalker*. One year later, he admitted: "There wasn't the commitment, the conviction in that album that is the absolute essence of what the Kinks are really about." There were no such reservations at the start of 1977 when the group set out on the first of four American tours that year. Despite their new image, they were still accompanied by three brass players and two female backing singers keen to play a well-rounded set.

Pamela Travis was the singer relieved of duty, a decision guaranteed to instil doubt about the future in the minds of her colleagues. Shirlie Roden believes Davies played on such fears in his usual mischievous way. "I fired the wrong girl," he bluntly told her, some weeks later. The comment was tantalizingly vague. "Of course, he didn't say whether he meant he should have got rid of Debi or he should have got rid of me. I was left feeling, 'Is it me?' Typical Ray manipulation."

On 1 February, the Kinks played at the Palladium in New York. For part of the show, Dave and Andy Pyle cavorted onstage in a provocative dance routine while playing their guitars. For the new boy, it was a harmless jape and perhaps an indicator that he was being accepted by the younger brother. Ray, however, was not happy. During 'You Really Got Me', he glared disapprovingly at Dave. Ray returned for the encore with some reluctance, this time fixing his stare on the whole band while performing the provocatively titled 'Money Talks'. After the gig, Ray locked himself in his dressing room. Nobody seemed entirely sure what had caused his bad mood, but blaming Dave seemed the best bet. The negative feelings passed just as suddenly as they had arrived, and cordial relations were restored by the following evening.

Andy Pyle had almost forgotten the Cassandra-like warning ("You'll find out when your time comes") that Avory and Gosling had voiced during the Kinks' pre-Christmas sessions. He assumed they must have been indulging in some private joke at his expense. Their words made no sense when applied to the apparently affable group leader who, thus far, had gone out of his way to make Pyle feel welcome. Ray did not reveal himself to others, not so much because he was obsessed with his own privacy, but, rather, due to a preference for allowing people to unravel his motives, to solve that enigma that betrayed itself only occasionally beneath that diastema smile and courteous handshake.

Pyle was impressed, still heedless of the cynical smiles emanating from his fellow Kinks as Ray allowed praise to fall from his lips. Nine dates into the tour, Pyle learned the unpalatable truth. "My time came in Chicago. Then I knew what it was all about. When it came my time to be accepted as a member of the band, I received this devastating attack on my person from Ray. Absolute devastation. He gave me a real belittling speech. 'Who the hell do you think you are, cunt?' It was completely out of the blue whereas an hour before it had been 'Another pint, Andy?' I can remember this real tirade in the dressing room in Chicago. At first I thought the bloke was joking. I'd seen him do this before with other people, airline pilots and people like that. For no reason at all he'd pick on me and lay into me in not a very nice way. I didn't think he could be serious because I hadn't done anything. I picked the bass up, clonked down the stairs and went back to the hotel. We didn't speak to each other for another fortnight. The boys all went, 'There you go – told you.' They had *all* experienced it."

"Andy Pyle, bless him, came in and was just crucified," says Shirlie Roden. "Psychologically, he couldn't understand it. He'd say, 'I've never been in a band like this. All I want to do is play.' He'd been asked to play bass and was being beaten left, right and centre." Davies offered no explanation for his verbal outburst beyond the suggestion that Pyle was 'dispensable' and not a proper Kink, whatever that meant. Perhaps private matters contributed to the drama. That same Chicago evening, Ray's wife Yvonne flew in to join the tour – and there were PR commitments ahead.

Over the next week, Ray conducted a series of interviews with the US media while Dave and the band went clubbing on their few days off. During a St Valentine's Day visit to the Whisky on Sunset Strip, Dave spotted a girl barely out of her teens with whom he became instantly infatuated. Her name was Nancy Evans. The intense attraction seemed to connect with fantasy memories from the distant past. It was surely no coincidence that she bore more than a passing resemblance to his great lost teenage love, Susan Sheehan. They talked into the night, stirring up emotions which Dave found both exhilarating and disturbing.

Heightened romance did little to assuage his temper though. Just as Ray had suddenly turned on Andy Pyle, Dave's 'Mr Hyde' personality re-emerged a few days later. Both brothers showed their violent tendencies during a three-night stint in Santa Monica. "You can have all this chaos going on but there is a certain wonderful feeling when you're onstage and twenty thousand people are singing along with you," Pyle says. "You feel good for five minutes until you get another kick in the shins. Drums are kicked over and people are spat on. Dave went around and spat at everyone in the band. This was at the Santa Monica Civic Auditorium. We came off, got an encore, and Baptist said, 'I'm not going back on with that cunt!' And Ray said, 'Either you go back there or I'll knock you out.' And then, 'Bop!' – he was out! Ray ran on all smiles and played the keyboards. But Ray's clever because after a while, for some reason, you think, 'Ah, it's not so bad after all.' But it *is*."

The violence was especially disconcerting, not least because they had only recently arrived in America. It was expected that tempers might fray during a long tour, but not usually at the beginning. If knockout blows were being delivered during the first leg of their tour, what awaited them on the next three?

The Santa Monica debacle was serious enough to prompt a meeting behind closed doors during which the conflict between Dave and Mick was briefly discussed. It also emerged that the punch that laid out Gosling may have been prompted by his supposedly sloppy playing that night. The participants failed to communicate coherently about the tensions onstage or offer any lasting solution. Nobody addressed the Pyle problem or came to his defence, apart from Roden and Doss, who privately sympathized, but had no say anyway. Wary of challenging either of the Davies brothers, the subsidiary Kinks simply shrugged and carried on.

In an unlikely turn of events, several group members sought solace from the two backing singers who offered tea and sympathy. At one point they joked about placing a sign on their door saying: 'Psychiatrist. Hours open: 10–12'. But it was no laughing matter. "Andy was terribly upset," Roden recalls. "Mick, Dave and Baptist also came to our room and they were so miserable. They were complaining, saying the fun had gone out of it. I was worried about Dave because he was so violent. I was worried about Baptist as well because he's a nice guy who wanted to play. For him to be playing in the wrong key when he's such a gifted musician and dragged off the keyboard and punched . . . . I don't know what happened. Everything was knocked out of him . . . That was the worst." Roden's closeness to Dave meant that he opened up emotionally, even hinting that the Kinks might not continue. "I remember Dave falling into my arms in the wings and crying, 'Why am I doing this? The soul's gone out of it.' It was a seminal moment, and terribly sad."

Arista Records, unaware of the inner politics, had no cause for complaint and there was a general air of back-slapping triumphalism the following week when the group appeared on the prestigious, high-rating NBC programme *Saturday Night Live* performing five songs, including a medley of four classic Sixties hits. This was proof positive that they were on the way back to mainstream popularity in America. What awaited them on their return to England was less predictable. Over the past year there had been a seismic shift in the UK music scene with punk proselytizers dominating the headlines and subverting the rock hegemony. Punk was the new rage with the Sex Pistols branded the scourge of the nation. Goaded by the establishment, banned from performing and even thrown off their record label, the Pistols had become the great cause célèbre of the era. Initially, they had been greeted with cynicism, even in the letters pages of the more radical UK music press, but as one outrage followed another, support grew. When the Kinks returned to the UK in March 1977 to perform at London's Rainbow Theatre, it was only three months before punk's high water mark with the banning of 'God Save The Queen' during the Jubilee celebrations.

The attitude towards the Kinks was ambivalent and uncertain. In certain ways, 'You Really Got Me' was the template of the punk sound, but Ray Davies was also associated with pop operas, theatrical shows and, worst of all, a new mainstream American album, *Sleepwalker*, which had been largely ignored in his home country. Even those among the punk fraternity who liked the Kinks would probably have preferred that they had broken up in the Sixties like the Small Faces. History was seen as a burden amid 1977's intense, ageist glorification of the present. The punk ethos lampooned the rock aristocracy, deriding their achievements and pricking the pomposity of everyone from the Rolling Stones to Led Zeppelin. If the Kinks escaped much of the fiery rhetoric it was not because they were more loved – it was simply a testament to their irrelevance. Suddenly, they just looked old.

Their Rainbow concert inspired a full-frontal assault from the *New Musical Express*' leading tastemaker Nick Kent, who described the spectacle as "the pits of mediocrity" and complained of "Davies' oafish self-satisfied clowning, the band's corporate facelessness, their utterly facile professionalism, and above all the dire choice of material". In a scathing summation, he lamented the decline of a once great group into self-parody: "When a band who've been around for ten years or more fail to present their audience with new inspired material then that's one problem. But when said band is seemingly incapable of handling even their own established masterworks with any dint of respect or authority then that's just too much."

Warily or wisely, the Kinks did not undertake a full UK tour, restricting themselves to television promotion on *The Old Grey Whistle Test*. Ray, meanwhile, could be seen on ITV's *Supersonic* playing alongside an all-star line-up including Marc Bolan, Elkie Brooks, Dave Edmunds and John Lodge. Interviewed about the current music scene, he sniffed: "Well, it's not new is it?", cautiously adding, "there's some amazing talent around, but a lot of bands seem manufactured and out to make a quick buck." As for the iconic Johnny Rotten, Davies was succinct. "He's a cunt, he's not real." Later, he was equally bullish about Rotten's first lieutenant: "If Sid Vicious ever came up to me, I would've killed him."

The Kinks took some of the punk attitude back with them across the Atlantic during the next leg of their US tour. On 3 May 1977, in Washington, DC, old hostilities between Mick Avory and Dave Davies were reignited, culminating in a brawl after which the pair stormed off stage, leaving Ray to face the consequences. "At the end of the show I was just standing there. Mick got fed up and kicked his drum kit over. There I was strumming my guitar saying, 'Well, I'd like to play this number' realizing that it would have to be a solo job. I was about to go into 'Juke Box Music'. I thought, 'No, I can't do it without a group.'"

The violence between Mick and Dave was real enough, but it also helped to distract attention from the ongoing, unresolved conflict between the brothers. The other members sometimes got caught in the crossfire, but that was merely considered collateral damage. "We had fights onstage," Gosling notes plainly. "It was part of the Kinks thing. It was almost expected of us. Dave and Ray never really saw eye to eye on anything. It was very difficult to take sides with either of them. Mick was always the middleman. It was an awkward situation, not always easy to work with."

Five days later, the second leg of the tour concluded in Tampa, Florida. This turned out to be the final appearance of long-term backing singer Shirlie Roden. Dissatisfied since the start of the *Sleepwalker* tour and weary of the internecine strife between band members, she needed a fresh challenge. "I was bored," she admits. "When we started *Preservation* we were singing, acting and dancing and I had a solo song and that continued in *Soap Opera*. When we got to *Sleepwalker* it wasn't challenging. We were doing television in America, and Debi and I were hidden behind screens, not on camera."

During the tour, Roden had been asked by a musician friend to audition for a musical, *Sailing Down Everest*, to be staged at London's Roundhouse. It was a welcome opportunity. "I needed to grow and I wanted to get into theatre. I'd done the Kinks, but that wasn't 'acting' or spoken word. I was really torn because I still loved the Kinks, the music, and the glamour of it all, and Ray's a brilliant man." Roden hoped that she might be invited back on tour after the Roundhouse musical, which was only a short-term project scheduled to last four to six weeks. Road manager Ken Jones soon divested her of such illusions with a pithy and perceptive comment: "If you leave, you know Ray will *never* take you back – you can't walk away from Ray." The truth of that statement was confirmed as she was preparing to return to London. "Ray wouldn't say goodbye to me. We were in a taxi, and I was crying. I said, 'Please, Ray, I'm only doing this because I need to do something else . . .' But, Ken was right, you can't walk away from him." Debi Doss was instructed to find a replacement, Kim Goody, closely followed by Linda Kendrick, but by the end of the year the backing singers were phased out.

The Kinks returned to Europe in May 1977 but shrewdly avoided performing in England for another six months. Public antipathy towards punk had intensified as the Jubilee celebrations approached, ultimately ending in violent attacks on its leading perpetrators, the Sex Pistols, and their retinue. This radicalized the music press even more. Headlining at Holland's Pink Pop Festival, the Kinks were still geographically close enough to receive a critical mauling, largely predicated on their advancing years. "They're not only over the hill, they're down the valley and into the ditch . . . Ray Davies was inevitably charismatic and nobody's denying that he has been one of the most important figures in British rock 'n' roll, but his day seems to be finished."

Ignoring the ambivalent and hostile reactions in the UK, the group resumed their ongoing US tour. By now, Nancy Evans, the girl Dave had met in February, was accompanying him on the road, a complication that caused underlying tensions. Ray had always retained a soft spot for Dave's wife Lisbet, so his response was unsurprisingly cool at best. Suppressed sibling antagonism manifested itself vicariously onstage. Whenever Dave was irked by Ray's attitude, he was liable to release his anger on either Avory, Gosling or Pyle. The bass player was barely beginning to understand the group dynamics when he found himself caught in the middle of the psychic crossfire. "In tandem with Ray asserting his control, you had Dave asserting his. There were periods when Dave would say, 'Come out to the mike and sing the choruses.' One of the reasons I got the job in the first place was because I could sing – which I can't! Dave would say, 'Come out and join me on the choruses of 'Lola',' but he'd say that to me without Ray knowing. So I might venture out, and then at the next soundcheck there would be a monitor put in front of me to prevent me going out again. Dave would say something to me and Ray the opposite. At other times I'd be encouraged by Ray to play what I liked because I think he had a certain respect for me as a bass player. But while I was playing, Dave would come up and I'd feel this belt in the shin and this screaming in my ear, 'What are you doing, cunt?' We'd be playing a song in C and he'd scream in my ear, 'Give me an E flat *now*.' And this would be in front of an audience. The band were merely pawns in a little game that Ray and Dave were having among themselves."

When he returned home to Tring, Pyle would tell his wife about the various tribulations on the road, the intense relationship between the brothers and the difficulty of dealing with Ray. She assumed the singer must be some ogre, but when they met he was charm personified. It was enough to make her doubt her husband's judgement. As Andy well understood, Ray's extreme changes of personality from the polite gentlemen to the iron-fisted dictator were somehow disorientating enough to quell the unrest. Over time, Pyle found he was not only excusing but normalizing the brothers' extreme behaviour, as if it was perfectly acceptable. His once enthusiastic attitude towards the Kinks was also changing. In every other group he had been associated with, the evening gig was always the highlight of his day. That feeling should have been heightened with the Kinks whose audience was far bigger than those of either Savoy Brown or Blodwyn Pig. Instead, that familiar build-up to the show, followed by the buzz of performance and pleasant wind down, appeared to be happening in reverse. Almost every night, Pyle, Gosling and Avory, usually accompanied by the horn players and backing singers, would return to their hotel and play rock 'n' roll standards with the house band in attendance. If there was no band in the bar, they would find a local club, get up onstage and perform some Kinks songs. "We had some fun," Pyle stresses, "you mustn't assume it was all bad, but it was never when the brothers were together. With the Kinks, the gig was the *low* point of the day. The attitude was 'Let's get it over with, let's get it done.' Onstage at the hotel – *that* was the high point. I remember once we played four gigs in a day and that was our compensation. It was sad . . . The crux of it is that you've got two blokes who are extremely talented. I've got a great respect for both of them as writers and musicians. If only they could work together. The reason they're not up there with the Beatles, the Stones and the Who is because of their silly arse games . . . and that pisses me off."

By the fourth leg of the 1977 US tour, Mick Avory was suffering road fatigue and threatening to quit. At the beginning of the year, he had married girlfriend Joan Lyons and was looking towards starting a family and settling down. Nobody took his threats seriously. "Every tour was Mick's last tour," Pyle remarks. "Every tour. Baptist's first tour was meant to be Mick's last. Once a week he would put his sticks down and say, 'Right, I'm not having any more of this.' Now, if you're a painter and decorator and you have two bosses and one tells you to do something and another comes in and says, 'What are you doing that for, cunt? Go back to where you started and do it again,' you'd say, 'Stick this!' But when you're a musician living on the road with these people, it gets difficult. You finish the gig, go back to the hotel and you get a call from one of them at five in the morning."

There was a sense of doom in the ranks as the group prepared to record their next album, a contractual necessity, irrespective of their touring schedule. During one interview, Davies suggested that he might release a solo record in the New Year, which some took as a couched admission that the Kinks were close to breaking up. Avory's disenchantment was by now a serious concern. His humour and easy-going attitude had always stabilized the group and made life tolerable for the subsidiary members when fraternal squabbles threatened to spill over into general warfare. Now, he could barely stomach returning to the studio for an extended spell.

Andy Pyle, still the relative newcomer, attempted to appeal to Avory's instinctive musical professionalism, but was ultimately rebuffed. "I said, 'Let's be the best rhythm section, let's get good, let's get tight.' And Mick would say, 'All right, we'll try . . . ah, but it doesn't matter, does it?' And he was right. It *doesn't* matter with the Kinks. Mick's got a good feeling for the drums and he's a good listener. He listens to what other people do and plays accordingly. He could have been a good musician, but he'd been there too long. Heaven help them if a drummer's drummer had been in there instead of Mick. Mick wasn't allowed to play drums. He was a mediator – the Henry Kissinger of drums."

Reluctantly, Ray turned to session musicians to fill Avory's spot midway through the sessions. Nick Trevisick, still working on separate recordings with Dave Davies, deputized on three tracks. "Mick was a bit disillusioned," Trevisick remembers. "Basically, the whole band was in disarray. Ray called me to do some tracks. It wasn't behind Mick's back – he was there all the time. After I'd done those tracks Mick told me he'd asked Ray to include my name on the record." Trevisick intended to finish the album, but a clash of commitments meant that famed sessioner Clem Cattini, who had previously played Avory's parts on *The Kinks Kontroversy*, was recruited for one song, 'Live Life'.

Avory was not the only problem facing Ray. Gosling was grumpy and the previously enthusiastic Pyle suffered the equivalent of an identity crisis. "I suddenly realized that there I was getting up in the morning, driving to the studio and sitting in silence until it was the end of the day and we'd go to the pub. I'd *become* like the others. Within the space of a year my enjoyment of going to work and playing had gone. It was gradual. Everything else was fine, but I didn't like playing. If it wasn't for the fact that I knew I was getting worse as a bass player, I'd probably still be there. You either accept that, or you get out."

It was already clear from the interminable sessions that the next album would not be completed until the New Year. Frustrated and disillusioned, Pyle proffered his resignation. Davies was irritated by the timing. Unbeknownst to Pyle a short US tour had been pencilled in for December and Ray was not keen on finding a replacement bassist at short notice. Pyle knew that if the tour was cancelled the other Kinks would be deprived of a much-needed Christmas bonus. "They were my mates, and still are, but Ray put me in that position." Reluctantly, Pyle agreed to stay till the end of the year.

With no album forthcoming, Arista were keen for the group to release a 1977 Christmas single. The challenge seemed to enliven Davies who responded with a quickfire, almost punkish statement titled 'Father Christmas'. Its anti-festive lyric about a gang of kids mugging a department-store Santa Claus was funny, while the arrangement was fast and furious. It must have come as blessed relief after all the studio tinkering on the still uncompleted album. The single's B-side, 'Prince Of The Punks', a thinly veiled satirical attack on Davies' former protégé and nemesis Tom Robinson, gained some additional publicity, but it was not enough to transform the single into a chart hit. At least there was a memorable promotional video of 'Father Christmas' with Ray dressed as

Santa and the other Kinks playing the gang of kids. When instructed to enact the line "we'll beat you up", they laid into Ray with such aggression that it was feared he might be seriously hurt. They ended up desperately restraining Dave, whose relish for the role was unquenchable.

As promised, the Kinks did complete an 11-date North American tour in December, but the band's Christmas bonuses, which had occupied Pyle's thoughts when deciding to continue, turned out to be of superficial significance. "It was nothing like what it turned out to be. What you get depends on how Ray feels on the last day at the end of the tour. What bonus you get depends on what side of the bed he got out of. The bonuses varied so much from tour to tour it was a joke. The basic wage was about the same as I'd get as a motor mechanic, which is what I used to be. I earned a lot more money with other bands. Alvin Lee was paying me twice as much as the Kinks paid me. In fact, I got twice as much from Savoy Brown five or six years before. But I don't do this thing for money. Even if I was making a fortune with them I'd still have gone. If I got ten times the amount, it would [only] have been compensation for all the shit I had to put up with."

The finale to an over-active year in Davies' career occurred at London's Rainbow Theatre (23–24 December). He had promised a Christmas show with a difference. It was intended to be a 'History Of The Kinks', including guest appearances from former bassists Pete Quaife and John Dalton. This prompted further rumours that the Kinks might be breaking up. In the end, the ex-members did not appear but the 'historical' aspect was strongly in evidence. Disc jockey Alan Freeman served as master of ceremonies, addressing the audience like a history teacher chronicling the passage of an empire. Re-enacting their past, the Kinks appeared in red hunting jackets at the start of a 28-song set commencing with songs not heard in years: 'Little Queenie', 'Beautiful Delilah' and 'Louie Louie'. A formidable selection of hits followed. There was a palpable sense of celebration and finality from Davies, who teased the audience with hints that they were witnessing the final act of a two-decade drama. Some reviewers half expected a White City-style retirement announcement at the close, but the two performances ended on a note of tantalizing uncertainty. "The whole evening was a very odd affair," the *NME* noted of the first show, "and at the end of it you weren't sure whether you'd seen the last – but one – show by the Kinks. Just before they performed 'Alcohol', Ray Davies insisted that it'd be the last time they ever played it. At the end of the show . . . Davies grabbed the mike and sang, 'This could be the last time.' Maybe I've been fooled by Davies' sense of humour, but there was something very final about this Kinks concert." Looking back, six months later, Davies reflected: "You could say it was the last gig the band did as it was. There were changes to be made because I'd gone as far as I could with that particular group. It was the end of a certain era."

CHAPTER THIRTY-TWO

MR MISFIT

After the Christmas Rainbow shows, Andy Pyle never saw Ray or Dave Davies again. It was a fate similar to that of former members John Start and Mickey Willett. Technically, Pyle remained a Kink until as late as April 1978 but he was not invited back to the studio where session bassists Ron Lawrence and Zaine Griff took his place. John Gosling was working independently with Pyle, a union that bothered Davies who insisted he should sign an exclusive contract with the Kinks, outlawing extracurricular work. Having never signed anything before, Gosling declined. He had returned to Konk in January 1978, evidently under duress, drowning his sorrows in the studio bar while Davies prevaricated and tinkered with the final list of songs. "Ray knew what he wanted," Gosling says. "If you're a writer you know exactly how the song is going to sound. Certain writers will compromise their ideas in order to make it a group sound. But with Ray, I don't think he was willing to compromise. He was producing the stuff as well and it all became a little wearying. He couldn't see the wood for the trees. Dave used to get quite frustrated. Often Ray would end up telling him the solo note for note."

It was the same for the others. Even on an innocuously simple song such as 'Hay Fever', Davies had pushed them beyond the bounds of reason. "We did that song over and over again," Gosling remembers. "We did it with John Dalton on bass, and then Andy on bass. We did it in *E,* we did it in *C,* we did it with backing vocals, without backing vocals. It was incredible."

Davies' perfectionism was insidiously destabilizing the Kinks from within. Dave's spontaneity had been squashed by demands for regimented reproductions of his melodies; Avory had been reduced to watching proceedings from a booth while a session drummer took his place; Pyle found himself playing four notes on a different finger at one point and Gosling was systemically drained of inspiration.

Baptist's final session as a Kink took place at the end of January. Davies introduced a new composition, 'Get Up', intended as the finale to the completed album. A tribute to the common man, it included the memorable rallying cry, "Get off your arses, men". After a dozen hours in the studio and seemingly infinite re-recordings, Gosling would have preferred to lie down. It felt like water torture. "In the end, I don't think Ray knew which was the best version. I counted sixty-three takes of the one song. He went back the next morning and said: 'Do you think we could try that song once more?' I just exploded. I was worn out – I'd had enough. It seemed that certain songs got washed and dried of their original melody and emotion because we'd done them so many times. To me, the last three albums sounded like a lot of bored people – the spark had gone."

Turning to Davies, Gosling shook his head and said: "This isn't the Kinks any more." After eight years in the group, he felt his departure was long overdue. "I left the Kinks for the same reason as others have; it's not easy working with a megalomaniac, and I got tired of being used and abused just to satisfy Ray's unreasonable and selfish demands."

Davies may have sounded autocratic, but he was emotionally fragile and fearful that the Kinks were fracturing before his eyes. Exhausted by the constant need to write new songs, he returned to New York and stagnated in his Manhattan apartment, desperate for a holiday that he would never take.

The overdue album *Misfits* finally came out in May 1978. After the emotional vacuity and chilliness of *Sleepwalker* it was a surprisingly warm collection of songs with occasionally sharp lyrics. The title track, a plea for individuality with a lyrical theme strongly reminiscent of Pete Townshend's 'Substitute', prefaced a series of compositions in which Davies commented on a number of contemporary issues. In an era characterized by extreme political divergence and dogmatic sloganeering, he introduced multiple points of view into his songwriting. "I'm not saying I'm going with any one side," he insisted, reiterating a familiar apolitical posture. "I want the truth to come out, and you can't get the truth if you adopt that one-legged attitude, if you're that rigid . . . I do get angry about things. I want to say things and my music is my vehicle for saying them. But I won't put myself on a platform and tell people to do this and to do that and have control over them." It was a stance unlikely to impress the socialist wing of the British music press, but Davies was happy to vacillate. 'Live Life' attacked fascists and left-wing militants in the same line, while 'Black Messiah' targeted white racists but concluded with a plea for the sole 'honky' trapped in a black ghetto. There were also songs of light comedy, such as 'In A Foreign Land', a tale of tax evasion made funnier by knowledge of Davies' own frugality and 'Hay Fever' which lampooned neuroses. 'Permanent Waves' equated punk/New Wave with the ephemeral thrill of a new haircut; while 'Out Of The Wardrobe' revisited the 'Lola' theme with the story of a burly husband whose cross-dressing turns him into a princess. 'A Rock 'n' Roll Fantasy' was arguably the album's centrepiece and later a US Top 30 single. Its first verse was an open plea to brother Dave not to break up the band but look to the future, even though Ray's vision was predicated on a fantasy. Part of the song had been written the previous summer following the news of Elvis Presley's death. From his Manhattan apartment, Davies had observed someone in an adjoining block who spent entire evenings listening to records. This inspired the creation of Dan the Fan, the archetypal Kinks' follower, who never loses faith in the mythology of rock 'n' roll. It was an important symbol of commitment at a time of fragmentation within the group.

Dave Davies welcomed the prospect of a 'new' Kinks. Secretly, he regretted that Avory had not followed Gosling and Pyle through the exit door. Ray was equally eager to finalize the next tour and audition musicians. The new recruits were an oddly contrasting pair. Bassist Jim Rodford, a former member of Argent and Phoenix, had once been part of the Mike Cotton Sound, several of whom had swelled the Kinks' ranks during the early Seventies. Rodford was steady, reliable, sensible and even-tempered. Keyboardist

Gordon Edwards was a different species entirely. A poodle-permed journeyman whose main claim to rock fame was involvement with a latter-day version of the once riotous Pretty Things, he seemed born to a life of Holiday Inns, Jack Daniel's, Marlboro cigarettes and studiously rolled marijuana joints. Dave regarded him as a kindred spirit. "He was a genuine rock star – who never became a rock star."

Ray was so keen to blood the new line-up that dates were announced before they even had a chance to rehearse. As a result, shows in Birmingham, Manchester and Liverpool were swiftly cancelled. Davies offered profuse apologies in a prepared statement, punctuating his mea culpa with the promise of a benefit concert in aid of the famed London venue the Roundhouse. "As we're an English band I feel it's only right that we should debut here in England so when I discovered that the Roundhouse had a free day [19 May], I felt it was an ideal opportunity to play a concert which would also help the theatre." An 800-capacity audience attended the show and reviews were pleasing. Davies' apparent magnanimity was applauded although suspicions linger that the idea was largely a pre-planned publicity stunt. A full month before the release of *Misfits*, Arista's Andrew Bailey had despatched a memorandum to his colleagues with the revealing line: "Interest in London will be stimulated by faking a sudden decision to do a one-off club date during the week of the LP's release."

Arista's London office was aware that elements within the UK music press were hostile toward the Kinks simply because of their age and attitude. This prejudice even spread to record dealers and the company's own marketing department. One internal memo noted: "As discovered in the past, there's a problem with the Kinks because they have such a long recording history that at every level – from dealer to critic to fan – there's a degree of difficulty in distinguishing one LP from the other." Their answer was to market Ray Davies' enigmatic image, as if he was a solo singer-songwriter. "That is what we must get over, so that Ray is once again a figure of controversy, a voice to be listened to, relevant to 1978," Bailey reiterated. If Davies could be rebranded as an angry young man with a social conscience, then it might convince the punk-loving commentators to look more kindly on his work.

The Stalin-style diminution of the Kinks was executed with an advertiser's dark art. Their record was to be referred to as 'The *Misfits* Album' and never as 'the Kinks latest LP'. Arista's most brazen concept was to transform Davies into a cartoon character named Mr Misfit. Teaser stickers and mock adverts were produced with instant aphorisms borrowed from the album, including 'You don't have to be a chick to wear suspenders' ('Out Of The Wardrobe') and 'You don't have to be white to be God' ('Black Messiah'). "A posse of students" were to be hired to "instantly blanket the London underground system". It was hoped the cartoon might be used in mainstream magazines such as *Time Out* and *Private Eye* as well as the music press and could be revived long after the album's release. Andrew Bailey was already working with Davies on the concept while politely explaining to his superiors: "Mr Misfit is really Ray Davies in thin disguise . . . he doesn't like movements, he's a rebel without a cause, a loner, a suitable hero for the Seventies." This was nothing less than an attempt to market Davies' apoliticism as some sort of radical commentary on the state of modern Britain. An open memorandum between executives at Arista welcomed the idea wholeheartedly:

> The existence of Mr Misfit gives Ray a specific topic to base his approach on. Ray will become known as the spokesman for the misfits of today, the people who don't want to be labelled as punks or left-wing protestors, but who still don't feel like giving up the fight. Ray believes this whole idea is strong enough to pass on to the US office for them to consider using it as the basis of back-up advertising for the LP over there. One could imagine the cartoon strip appearing in magazines like *Rolling Stone* and *Creem*.

The Americans proved less keen on the idea. Unlike their UK counterparts they had no problem with the Kinks' brand identity which they regarded as an asset rather than a burden. Marketing Ray Davies separately made little sense. There may have been a slight shiver of disappointment in the New York office when *Misfits* peaked at number 40, a disconcerting dip following the much publicized *Sleepwalker*, but it was assumed that extensive touring with the new line-up would rectify that blip. Davies had recently appointed an American business manager, Elliot Abbott, whom he pointedly notes was "a synagogue cantor's son from Chicago", who had previously represented Randy Newman. Abbott was an engaging figure, ready and eager to plot the Kinks' ascension to stadium-sized venues. All that was required were commitment and hard work.

It was a different scenario in the UK where punk ideology still held sway. When Arista issued the politically ambivalent 'Live Life', the single received a scathing attack from former Sex Pistol John Lydon. "What can you say about patronizing, prattish, ill-conceived, calculated token gestures of 'understanding the scene maaan' like this? Just hear the thing and find out for yourself because I can't put into words readable my disgust with this and would it be worth the effort?"

One month after this diatribe, Davies received a much-needed boost in Britain when the Jam hit the Top 30 with a revival of 'David Watts'. Singer Paul Weller, a connoisseur of Mod culture, was a big fan of Ray Davies and his allegiance gradually alerted a new generation to the wonders of the Kinks' back catalogue. Converting the music press was more difficult. A cameo appearance at London's Hammersmith Odeon saw them dismissed as "a second rate heavy-metal band" and "a travesty of rock 'n' roll". Davies' apolitical ideals of individuality on songs like 'Misfits' were derided as "selfish, insular and thoroughly reactionary". The review seemed to confirm Arista's worst fears about the Kink's 'uncool' image.

There were no such problems in America. Earlier that year, Van Halen had secured a minor hit with a heavy-metal reworking of 'You Really Got Me' which reconnected the Davies brothers with a younger audience. Taking advantage, the Kinks toured and toured, often with upcoming 'New Wave' acts including Blondie, Cheap Trick, Tom Petty & The Heartbreakers and the Cars. They seemed revitalized by the competition and the enthusiasm of the new line-up.

"I relate it a lot to sport," Jim Rodford explains. "It's teamwork. A bit like a football team. You have to have the right person in the right place. He needn't be a virtuoso. Musically, the Kinks represented England at the highest level. It was fantastic. To be in the Kinks you've got to be a rock 'n' roller – and I am. So were John Dalton and Pete Quaife. I'd seen the Kinks in their different incarnations and understood the total appeal of the band. They'd been the hardest rocking band on the planet, then they became more versatile with the rock operas, but the element of their hard rock beginnings was always there. Dave's guitar was integral to the beginning of the band and I think it was integral to the third coming. Ray understood that without having to say anything."

Old conflicts were still present but accommodated. Asked about the incendiary relationship between the brothers, Ray suggested it had improved of late. "I wouldn't want to destroy him or anything," he observed charitably. "He sees bits of me that he hates, and it just starts. I don't know how much of it is serious from his side. Me, I try to look at it light-heartedly and say it's a joke. I get the feeling from him that it's real. Dave is a real tight guy, and he can turn just like that."

Mick Avory could testify to Dave's volatility. Simmering tensions between the two boiled over that summer when Avory stormed off stage, barely able to suppress a desire to annihilate the guitarist. Backstage, they had to be separated. Avory relieved his tension by smashing some bottles and hurling a chair through a window. It seemed to help.

Gordon Edwards witnessed proceedings with a weary eye. "The animosity had been building up over a long period of time. Mick just flew off the drums and tried to strangle Dave. We managed to get Mick into the dressing room. He was pacing around like a raging bull. It took me half an hour talking to him before he calmed down. Mick was really having a bad time in the band."

Ray remained aloof from the carnage, rightly figuring that it would all blow over, just like before, but the dissension was now spreading. Edwards was becoming creatively frustrated and disillusioned. "I was only using half my talent, just playing the piano and singing backing vocals. I couldn't play the guitar because Dave would get pissed off. Ray would criticize me occasionally because I was singing louder than he was. It was driving me crazy. Some nights I had to have half a glass of whisky to be able to go on and do the gig." Those small measures would increase with each successive tour.

If Edwards was finding it difficult adjusting to the Kinks, the opposite was the case with Jim Rodford. Less concerned about his status in the band, which remained uncertain in this probationary period, he was simply enjoying the tours and hoping all would be well. Career strategies, long-term plans or business matters were never discussed, at least not with the new members. "Nothing's ever said," Rodford reflects. "There were never any discussions about what we could do. The best songwriters work with what they've got and work to the strengths of whoever is there. The intermediary band with John Dalton, John Gosling and the horn players had its strengths and that's what brought the best out of that era."

Rodford was unsure whether he was merely a touring musician or something more until the weekend of 12 August 1978. After completing two legs of a US tour promoting *Misfits*, the group were set to appear at a music festival in Bitzen, Belgium. Rodford was taking a stroll outside the hotel when he bumped into Ray on one of his constitutionals. As they walked together, Davies enquired: "Could you make it permanent, then?" Effectively, he was confirming that Rodford would work on all subsequent Kinks recordings. "Do you mean that?" the bassist asked. "Yes," Ray concluded. Rodford was now a fully-fledged Kink. "That's how Ray operates. There was no big meeting. That was all he said. I didn't talk to Dave or Mick. Ray made the decision and I went along with it. You use your instinct. He does – all the time. And I never signed anything. It was just man to man. An understanding. It didn't bother me at all that nothing was signed. My feeling was that if this doesn't work I'm just back where I am."

Between visits to America, Ray Davies had been approached to co-write and contribute songs to a modern adaptation of Aristophanes' *The Poet And The Women*. The playwright was 33-year old Barrie Keeffe, whose most recent credits were the televised *Gotcha*, the story of a school leaver holding his teachers hostage, and the controversial *A Mad World My Masters*, which had included satirical sketches featuring several media figures including newscaster Angela Rippon and members of the Royal Family. Keeffe clearly had an affinity with popular music, evident enough from the very titles of previous plays such as *Here Comes The Sun* and *Gimme Shelter*. Earlier in his career, he had even written a television drama titled *Substitute*. The collaboration with Davies looked promising. A staging at the National

Theatre, Stratford, was mooted, but they eventually passed on the script.

Keeffe and Davies promised to revisit the project and the script-writer paid his friend the ultimate compliment by writing a play in his honour. On 29 January 1979, *Waterloo Sunset* was broadcast on the BBC's prestigious *Play For Today* slot. Set in south London, the drama focuses on an elderly woman, Grace Dwyer (played by Queenie Watts), coming to terms with racial tensions in the community. It opened with her playing 'Waterloo Sunset' on the piano, a flattering touch which must have pleased its composer.

There was more good news only weeks later when the Pretenders entered the charts with a surprise cover of 'Stop Your Sobbing', then considered a relatively obscure track from the Kinks' first album in 1964. Lead singer Chrissie Hynde had previously penned that flattering review of 'Mirror Of Love' which had appeared in the often hostile *New Musical Express*. A devotee of the Kinks since her teens, she was still keen to meet Ray, an ambition that would have to wait for another year. "She tried to meet me two or three times and I just avoided it, and not because I disliked her in any way. I just couldn't face it because I'd heard that she said nice things about me. I thought, 'Oh God, when she meets the real person and sees what a conner I am.'"

In a determined effort to crack America, Davies insisted that the Kinks temporarily relocate to New York using the Wellington Hotel as a base. By now he had already written a batch of new songs and was eager to record them quickly. Sessions had begun at Konk but it was felt the album could be completed promptly and achieve an edgier feel if they recorded in New York. It meant that Davies could not tinker endlessly or prevaricate too much. Privately, the others joked that the studio costs would ensure a speedy resolution. There was one problem. Pianist Gordon Edwards was in emotional turmoil back in England and about to break up with his long-term girlfriend. "I really felt a lot about the relationship and got really depressed. I was drinking a bottle of whisky a day to get completely smashed and to blot everything from my mind." That included any ongoing commitments to the Kinks. Without explanation, Edwards failed to turn up for the flight to New York and, not surprisingly, was immediately fired.

Ultimately, his drug and alcohol excesses would defeat his ambition.

Rather than seeking a replacement, Ray assumed keyboard duties during the forthcoming sessions, which proved positive and productive. "That was one of the happiest periods of my life," he said, on numerous occasions. "I could walk over to Clive Davis' office, play him some songs and then we'd go and record them with the Kinks. It was wonderful."

Low Budget was released in America on 10 July 1979, two months before its appearance in the UK. The album sounds like Davies' answer to the New Wave, a sleek, spontaneous and refreshing record. It includes the composer's familiar snapshots of urban life, laced with a lacerating, droll wit. Lyrically and musically lean, the songs generally favour energy in place of finesse. The opening 'Attitude' is a statement of intent, a wake-up call to the approaching Eighties sung in a heavily accentuated London voice like the war cry of a young punk. Its intensity is amplified on 'Catch Me Now I'm Falling'. Powered by a Stones-inspired guitar riff caught somewhere between 'Jumping Jack Flash' and '(I Can't Get No) Satisfaction', it presents Marvel Comics' Captain America as a superannuated superhero confronting an ungrateful public. That theme is partly repeated in '(I Wish I Could Fly Like) Superman', inspired by the movie starring Christopher Reeve. The witty story of a nine-stone weakling imagining himself as DC Comics' caped crusader fits the tradition of Davies' compositions celebrating ordinariness and fantasy. If these songs seem tailored for American stadium audiences, then there are others that look to Britain. The title track comments obliquely on the state of the economy with a self-mocking portrayal of a penny pincher, justifying his frugality with the priceless line: "Don't think I'm tight if I don't buy a round". The roll call of subjects extends to over-population ('In A Space'), the oil crisis ('A Gallon Of Gas'), nervous tension ('National Health'), depression ('Misery'), suppressed feelings ('A Little Bit Of Emotion') and the catch-all 'Pressure', a frantic complaint about modern living. "I thought if people get a bit of pressure and talk to somebody about it then somebody else would go off and worry about it. I thought it would be a nice idea for a play – somebody has a bit of pressure and it gets passed on and eventually gets to the president. It's like a disease. The first verse could be about VD." The album ends with 'Moving Pictures', an evocation of life seen as an impermanent film, like an undeveloped 'Celluloid Heroes'.

Low Budget was a spectacular success in America, climbing to number 11 on *Billboard*, their best selling studio album ever. "It was a curious time," Davies remembers, "because we were starting to make it in America, which was still Styx and big hair and perfect guitar phrases. It was a fine balancing act between being British and doing something suitable for US stadium shows." With extensive tours now booked, Davies urgently needed a new keyboardist.

It was just before his 27th birthday that Ian Gibbons was asked to join the Kinks. Having played in such bands as Life, English Assassin, Tonight and, more recently, the Records, he already had a reputation as an emergency substitute accompanist for live shows and recordings. When Jim Rodford, whom he had known from the Argent and Phoenix days, phoned to ask, "Do you want an audition?", Gibbons was ready. "It was a Saturday afternoon," he remembers. "They were all there and Ray was trying to finish mixing *Low Budget.* I just ran through a few things like 'Celluloid Heroes' with Mick Avory on congas and Dave playing acoustic guitar. I sang a bit and Ray said 'You've got the job. Jim will give you a tape and you can learn it. Bring your passport because the American tour is starting next week.'" Five days later, Gibbons was in New York.

The Kinks toured unrelentingly hereafter, milking the success of *Low Budget* with high-energy shows from their leaner line-up. Only the presence of Nick Newell on saxophone was a reminder of the once extended cast list. "That was a fantastic period," Jim Rodford says. "Playing with Ray, Dave, Mick and Ian felt great. I was on cloud nine. At soundchecks Ray would start riffing . . . and in about six months that would be a song. Something was happening here. I could feel the groundswell." Two months into the tour, their album was belatedly issued in the UK. Surprisingly, the most effusive review was in the *NME*. Charles Shaar Murray, a severe critic during the theatrical years, reckoned it was "the first great Kinks album in eight years" and "a miracle". Intrigued, he joined the tour soon after for a major feature that helped rehabilitate the Kinks' reputation in their home country. The most amusing part of the article was the opening paragraph which celebrated Davies' common-man persona, detailing his frustrations when attempting to purchase a round of milkshakes. After fumbling in his pockets, he was forced to ask manager Elliot Abbott to lend him $10. Murray made Davies sound like an absent-minded professor, but the truth was more prosaic. Those who knew him of old, such as Larry Page, Robert Wace and Sam Curtis, could testify to similar examples of miserliness 15 years before.

Despite all the enthusiasm surrounding *Low Budget* and the freshly dynamic live performances, Davies had not changed radically. Apart from a new haircut, skinny trousers and the occasional namedropping of artistes such as the Residents, Devo and Pere Ubu, his views were still old school. The socialist-orientated *NME* was still interested to hear his political comments, particularly in a year when Margaret Thatcher had been elected Prime Minister. What emerged was nothing new. "I was a socialist," Davies said. "I was brought up to think that way, and then I had success and it made a lie out of what I was. I made a gesture and it wasn't accepted so I left it physically and emotionally, but I didn't become a capitalist. I hate ultra-capitalism and ultra-socialism, but I'm not a liberal. I believe in anarchy with order." Stripped of the obfuscating rhetoric and fashionable reference to 'anarchy', this was the same apolitical mantra that Davies had been uttering since the Sixties. "I'm not really extreme about anything except getting my work done," he continued. "I don't want the world to be overrun by the National Front, but I don't want it overrun by the Socialist Workers' Party either."

In common with his 'Mr Misfit' image, Davies cleverly played the rebel card, stressing those aspects of his personality that most differentiated him from international jet-setters such as Mick Jagger and Rod Stewart. Interviewers were amused to hear that he still travelled by Tube, forgot to pay his television licence and refused to take taxis because they were too expensive. "I've never been into the celebrity trip," he stressed. "I did go into Studio 54 in New York once, and I actually asked Bianca Jagger to dance. She told me to clear off. I'm a fairly anonymous person, and hardly anyone ever recognizes me. I've stood at the bar at places where the band have been playing and I've heard people talking about the Kinks but, to them, I'm just a guy having a drink."

Success might have brought Davies stability and confidence but, in the background, his marriage was unravelling and he was not sure entirely why. "Maybe that's why I was a bad husband," he now considers. "I just thought that I was alone. I was doing my work. I remember walking around in New York on New Year's Eve looking for someone to go into the studio with me to work and mix. I was there a lot, alone. That's what resonates with me – the isolation I had there. I could write a whole book on Manhattan, the West Side."

During summer 1980, a live double album, *One For The Road*, exceeded expectations by selling over half a million copies and climbing to number 14 in America. Its 20 tracks featured a reasonable selection of Kinks' classics, albeit with a strong emphasis on the recent *Low Budget*. The album was evidence enough of the calculated shift to hard rock in recent years. Cannily, Davies added 'David Watts' and 'Stop Your Sobbing' to the group's repertoire to remind younger listeners of the group's pedigree. The timing was apposite.

The first number 1 single and album of the new decade were both by the Pretenders ('Brass In Pocket' and *The Pretenders*). Their fans would soon become aware of the name Ray Davies as Chrissie Hynde had finally tracked down her quarry and arranged a meeting at Trax, a New York nightclub. According to Ray, there was an ominous miscommunication from the outset. "This sounds daffy, but she said 'Hello' and I thought she was really saying, 'Help me'. She couldn't take the sudden fame that had come to her, and I think she saw me as someone who had done all that rock 'n' roll stuff and understood it. It was a good friendship for a few weeks, but that should have been it." Hynde accompanied Davies on a trip to France that summer, but the music and tabloid press missed the story. What started out as an innocent meeting of pop minds was about to blossom into a full-blown affair.

As was often the case, sudden changes in Ray's life were paralleled by similar upheavals in his brother's state of mind. In 1973, they had both gone through dark times together, now they were experimenting with new loves, irrespective of the consequences. Dave's relationship with Nancy Evans had deepened to such an extent that she had moved to a flat in Highgate, much to the disapprobation of his family. His sisters were upset by his licentious behaviour and Peggy Davies even considered placing a spell on his American girlfriend, a threat he took extremely seriously. It was particularly tough on his wife Lisbet who, only a year before, had given birth to their fourth son, Russell. When Dave tentatively suggested the possibility of a *ménage à trois*, even her patience was stretched to breaking point. By the end of the year, Dave and Nancy had moved in together amid news that she was pregnant. Characteristically, Dave accomplished the transition without undue trauma. Unlike Ray, he always retained close contact with his former wife and children.

Dave's domestic drama did not inhibit his creativity. One month after the release of *One For The Road*, he finally issued his long overdue solo album, *AFLI 3603*, which sold 150,000 copies in America. "He wanted to make the ultimate heavy metal album," says drummer Nick Trevisick. "At one point he hired a massive drum kit and put it in the stone hall at Konk. It was even heavier than the old John Bonham Led Zeppelin sound." The album sounded as far removed from the work of his brother as any listener could imagine. RCA Records were impressed by the sales figures, which eclipsed those of several Kinks albums they had released. This should have been the start of a successful solo career for Dave. A follow-up, *Glamour*, was issued exactly one year later, but performed less well in the marketplace. Dave subsequently switched labels, signing to Warner Brothers for 1983's *Chosen People*, arguably his best solo album, but found himself subject to diminishing sales returns. Industry interest in Sixties' survivors was in decline among major labels and it was only the Kinks' brand name and touring prospects that kept the younger brother solvent.

Although they were far more efficient and professional in their approach to live performances, Kinks' shows were still subject to bizarre moments. During an appearance at the Seattle Center Arena on 3 October, a gatecrasher plummeted through the roof of the auditorium into the 6,000 crowd, injuring three fans who were subsequently hospitalized. The intruder walked away unscathed. There was even more drama two days later when Ray was detained at the airport in Portland, Oregon, on an alleged fraud charge. Airport police suspected that he might be a San Francisco swindler who had been hiring limousines, borrowing money and running up unpaid bills in hotels under the name 'Ray Davies'. According to one report, the malefactor had even secured an advance from an unnamed record company with the vague promise of completing some future album. "It was surreal," remembers Ian Gibbons. "It's not very often police get on a plane. We were asked to remain seated. Ray was in the first two seats with Elliot Abbott and they took them both away for questioning. It was then proven that Ray *was* Ray Davies! They caught the other guy, eventually, but I'm not sure what they did with him."

Back in New York, Davies enjoyed a similar ease with celebrity and was seldom, if ever, bothered on his early morning jogs to Central Park. On one occasion, he slipped on some ice and was rescued by a small group of concerned college students who clearly had no idea he was a major rock star. Continuing his run, he noticed a familiar looking woman standing beside a traffic light near the Dakota Building. It was Yoko Ono. Davies was struck by the absence of her husband. He had seen John and Yoko several times on the streets of New York, always together, seemingly inseparable. They were about to release *Double Fantasy*, Lennon's first new recording in five years. A series of major in-depth magazine and radio interviews had been commissioned to promote the record and Davies was impressed by Lennon's articulacy and positive stance on life. The former Beatle spoke with enthusiasm about the new record and his optimism was contagious. "If John Lennon can do it, so can I," Davies mused as the Kinks embarked on a European jaunt, taking in the Netherlands, West Germany, Belgium and France. On the morning of 9 December, Davies was interviewed by a French journalist in Paris and asked his opinion about the Lennon/Ono single '(Just Like) Starting Over'. "I think it's a good record," he said. "I'm glad he's having success, but it's not as good as the stuff he's done on his own." At that moment, the journalist noted, almost in passing, that Lennon had just been shot dead in New York. "I felt cheated, bitter, foolish – and ambushed by the reporter. I thought back to when I was a student in the recreation room at art college [in spring 1963] and heard John sing 'Twist and Shout' on the record player, and how I was blown away by his directness.

How his voice cut through all the nonsense and sent a message to me that said, 'If I can do it then so can you, so get up off your backside and play some rock 'n' roll,' as if to throw down a musical gauntlet."

Still angry with the journalist, Davies followed a troupe of people to Notre Dame Cathedral. He and Lennon had never been close or fraternized, beyond some sarcastic words, but a sense of bereavement was nevertheless present. "I lit a candle for him. It was the only thing I could do in the circumstances. It was a big sense of loss. You know sometimes rivals are closer to you in life than friends."

Three days later, the Kinks returned to England for a one-week tour, supported by Pimlico-based band the Gas. Davies was in bad spirits, now drained of the optimism inspired by Lennon. He was needled by the negative reaction of music press reviewers and complained about disc jockeys and radio stations deliberately ignoring the group. It was not the best time to be touring, particularly with a pop/rock act with New Wave associations. Donnie Burke, lead singer of the Gas, had appreciated the Kinks as a teenager and hoped that the Davies brothers might display some friendship towards his group, who had recently signed to Phonogram. He was rapidly divested of such fantasies and instead met with the hierarchical aloofness that younger musicians, brought up on the aesthetics of 1976–7, often found infuriating.

"They seemed paranoid about their position and paranoid about their future. We were denied access to their kitchens and told that we had to cater for ourselves. You couldn't even walk into a soundcheck. They were like schoolkids. The most entertaining thing was watching the evening's argument. It was like a soap opera. I saw guitars being thrown across stage and Ray giving Dave the two fingers. It seemed like Ray and Dave were always on the verge of exploding. There seemed to be a lot of jealousy, as if they still had the same argument going on after twenty years. You could understand this in 1964, but in 1980 they were still like sixteen-year-olds. I don't see how you can run a group like that with the kind of love-hate relationship that was going on between the brothers. The rest of them seemed to be pandering towards their whims. But what's Mick Avory going to do? Get up and say, 'Look, I've had enough of this'." In fact, Avory had uttered those very words on any number of occasions but, like a child caught in the middle of a dysfunctional family, found it almost impossible to break free.

The tour ended in Nottingham on 19 December, with all parties happy to return home in time for Christmas. Attendances had been reasonable, but not spectacular. Burke felt disillusioned and full of disdain. "They should have stopped. Those guys for their own dignity should have stopped ten years ago and Ray should have carried on as a solo and become an enigma in his own right. That band were, quite frankly, going onstage and living on their name. Bringing their dirty washing out in public is perhaps excusable in the gossip columns, but onstage? I was embarrassed. I was embarrassed I ever liked the Kinks."

Such casual scorn underlined the ambivalence felt towards the Kinks in their homeland at a time of shifting musical fashions. Respect for Sixties icons was at a premium at the turn of the decade and the Kinks were not the only veterans on the UK rock circuit suffering poor returns. In his last ever interview, conducted on the day he was assassinated, John Lennon had offered new words of hope to his generation. "I was visualizing all the people of my age group . . . being in their thirties and forties now, just like me, and having wives and children and having gone through everything together. I'm singing for them . . . I'm saying, 'Here I am now. How are you? How's your relationship going? Did you get through it all? Wasn't the Seventies a drag, you know? Here we are. Well, let's try to make the Eighties good because it's still up to us to make what we can of it' . . . We were the hip ones in the Sixties, but the world is not like the Sixties. The whole world's changed and we're going into an unknown future, but we're still all here."

CHAPTER THIRTY-THREE

STATE OF CONFUSION

Ray Davies remained defiant when faced with criticisms of the Kinks' relevance in the post-punk music scene of the early Eighties. He was not ready to consign his group to the nostalgia circuit and took pride in their continued success in America where arena audiences and music critics treated them with greater respect. Ageism, a fashionable prejudice among his contemporaries back in the Swinging Sixties, he now considered unfair. "I think people should give groups like the Stones and the Who more credit and not write them off as being the tired old men of rock. These bands started in the Sixties and are still going . . . Our rock music is still regarded as the best in the world. America and Europe always look to Britain for the new influences. We are an export."

Concert receipts confirmed Davies' boasts but the auteur within was not content with treadmill touring. He still wanted to extend himself and such ambition was not sated by working with the Kinks whose albums were now geared towards an American mass market. There were still elements of quirkiness and eccentricity in his songwriting but little that could be described as experimental or adventurous. What he most desired was an opportunity to employ those talents in other areas – notably theatre and film.

During early 1981, much of his time was spent working with playwright Barrie Keeffe on a revamped version of the aforementioned Aristophanes adaptation. Since their first meeting in 1978, Keefe had written scripts for *Bastard Angel*, *Black Lear* and *She's So Modern* (yet another song title reference) and, most famously, the acclaimed film *The Long Good Friday*. This time around, East Stratford's National Theatre gave the Keeffe/Davies collaboration the go-ahead and *Chorus Girls* opened on 6 April for a limited run. With its strong feminist subtext and references to unemployment and royalty, the musical drama was both topical and funny. It was also far removed from the standard 'rock musical'. "That's just like putting on make-up," Keeffe observed. "This is the real thing. You can tell the difference." Davies, in another of his pressure runs, managed to complete 12 songs for the production, including 'Everybody's Slagging Off England', sung by actor Marc Sinden. *Chorus Girls* proved a cathartic experience for Keeffe whose girl-friend Verity lay in hospital dying of cancer during its completion. Ray agreed to serve as his best man when the couple married only weeks before her death. Davies also attended her funeral at which 'Days' was played as a touching valediction.

With film ideas still swimming in his imagination, Ray commenced talks with RCA Video about transforming the next album into an audio-visual release. It was a concept slightly ahead of its time made no easier by touring and recording commitments. Initial work at Konk was interrupted by the police who warned of an impending riot nearby and suggested that the studio should be blocked off with wooden boards. Davies subsequently spray-painted the wall with the words 'Give The People What They Want', creating an album title and lead track in the process. Assisted by engineer Ben Fenner, he also erected a corrugated metal surround on the studio walls in an attempt to create an arena-style wall of sound. While on the road, he continued writing, assimilating ideas from myriad sources. During a drive to Scotland, he learned that Pope John Paul II had been shot, a news story that dominated headlines internationally. It reminded him of the recent assassination of John Lennon and, in turn, all the publicity surrounding the trial of the Yorkshire Ripper, Peter Sutcliffe. "I saw his parents being interviewed on television. Imagine what Sonia Sutcliffe, his wife, must have gone through, not knowing he was a murderer. There's this madness, this attention people want in the Sunday papers. 'Sonia's Terrible Torment'. But they don't give a shit about Sonia Sutcliffe, she's just good copy." All three events percolated in his imagination to create 'Killer Eyes', another key track on the forthcoming album.

If Davies' imagination was aflame, then there was good reason. His wife Yvonne had just filed for divorce, naming Chrissie Hynde, her senior by one year, as co-respondent. The legal proceedings would culminate in the autumn when his 'secret' romance with Hynde became a matter of public record and tabloid sensation. He turned the divorce to his songwriting advantage by composing a song of hope for the future: 'Better Things'. Issued as a single in June, it climbed into the UK Top 50. Many felt it deserved to do even better.

Give The People What They Want, released in America in August 1981, did not appear in Britain until the following January. The time lapse confirmed the general feeling that the Kinks were now an 'export brand'. Sales figures confirmed as much. The album sold over 500,000 copies in the US, and reached number 15 in *Billboard*. As usual, it did not chart in the UK. In common with *Low Budget*, the work offered assured, high-energy rock, leavened by Davies' flights into social commentary and relationship issues. 'Around The Dial' (a tribute to American DJs), the title track (a cynical comment on US television), and 'Back To Front' (a comic play on the Misfit theme) were all powered by heavy riffs, ideal for American arenas. 'Predictable' (later issued as a single) was a wry commentary, sung in a slight West Indian accent. 'Destroyer' combined the chord sequence of 'All Day And All Of The Night' with a lyrical allusion to the character Lola, which even Davies felt might be too self-referential. Momentarily, he considered removing the track. It was only after remembering David Bowie's 1980 number 1 hit 'Ashes To Ashes', in which the character Major Tom had been resurrected, that he felt vindicated. Elsewhere, there were fleeting character sketches and issue songs of varying quality. 'Yo Yo' chronicled a suburban marriage gone sour; 'A Little Bit Of Abuse' documented domestic violence and 'Art Lover' offered an ambiguous portrayal of a lonely man watching little girls in a park. As ever, Davies was inspired by journalistic observation, creative biography and childhood memories. "I used to live down the block from this woman in Muswell Hill, where I grew up and her face always used to be cut. I was too young to realize what it was. Her husband came home pissed every night and they were always shouting and fighting, but she stayed with him, until one day she couldn't take it any more."

When discussing songwriting themes, Davies often provided revealing insights into his emotional life. An interviewer's reference to 'Art Lover', for instance, prompted a brief meditation on his own family. "I run in Regent's Park and it's lovely and I believe in beautiful things and I'm divorced – I have two little girls who I don't see. I'm not allowed to contact them, but I can write to them. So I have a lot of feeling for people in that situation."

This was Ray at his vulnerable best but was he also being disingenuous? Nobody dared question why he was prevented from seeing his children. Had access been denied by the judge at the time of his first divorce? Evidently not. "The children *were* able to see Ray on a regular basis when he wanted," Rasa confirms, "usually for a 'one time a month' period. But he was often away and the access was spasmodic. He was very *distant* and had no idea how to interact with them. He was unkind about me, and the children were often upset when they came home. It was Ray's choice whether or not he wanted to see them. He did not keep in regular contact regarding this. I am certain the breakup of the marriage was the significant reason."

Davies admitted as much in one of his maudlin asides. "I feel that I've fucked up my life so much. I've failed as a person . . . Maybe I should have made an effort to contact them, but I've kind of hardened myself against it. I made a promise to myself I wouldn't become one of those weekend parents." Part of his notion of a 'weekend parent' was someone who always bought their children "expensive gifts", which he clearly regarded as anathema. "You must never let them see that it affects your lifestyle. Don't do extraordinary things. If you have to play a game of football on a Sunday morning, you play it. They'll have to come along. Once they see you pandering to them and breaking up your lifestyle, it turns them off, turns them away from you." Whether his daughters would concur was a moot point.

The summer of 1981 saw more revelations. On 31 August, Davies appeared at a Pretenders' show in Santa Monica, duetting with Chrissie Hynde on a cover of Jackie Wilson's 'Higher And Higher'. It was akin to a declaration of love. The tabloid press were soon demanding quotes, and Hynde obliged. "Obviously, I'm besotted with him," she cooed. "It's a major part of my life. I've got the band and then I've got my relationship, or whatever you want to call it, with him. Did you see that movie *Last Tango In Paris*? You know how he met that girl and they had that affair, and they never spoke to each other for a long time? It was a little like that."

The fairy-tale aspect of the romance failed to impress Dave Davies who felt it was doomed from the outset. His initial impressions of Hynde were caustic. He remembers calling her a 'Virgo slut' to her face and concluded that she was a self-regarding personality, even using the word 'vampiric', an adjective he usually reserved for his brother. At the time, Dave and Nancy were living quietly in Maida Vale so it came as a shock when "Ray and Chrissie bought a house about two hundred yards away [in Sutherland Avenue]". What could have been intrusive actually worked to everyone's favour. On the first day she moved in, Hynde claimed that she had detected a phantom presence and Ray was called upon to play the indignant ghostbuster. "I went upstairs into the attic on that first day to tell the ghost that it no longer had any place in the house, but Chrissie was still terrified." The mischievous spirit supposedly later brushed past Davies on one of its nocturnal walkabouts. Evidently, there was only one solution – an exorcist. Rather than bothering the priesthood, Ray sought advice from his psychic sister Peggy who, not unexpectedly, turned to their supernatural-loving brother for assistance. "I got a phone call from Peggy asking me to come down to Ray's house because they'd had some kind of visitation. I was ready because of my investigations and research over the years. I used to do magic in my basement." A makeshift service was performed, although even Dave suspected that it was not a ghost at all but some 'psychic energy' created by the ferocity of the Davies v. Hynde feuds. Already they were known for their passionate squabbles.

The 'ghost' incident was an ice-breaker in the fractious relationship between the parties. Ray had never previously shown any interest in Dave's spiritual beliefs but, indirectly thanks to Hynde, some small acknowledgement had at last been forthcoming. It augured well. Dave was further softened by female camaraderie. Previously, Lisbet had smoothed tensions between himself and Ray's second wife Yvonne. Now Nancy was doing the same with Chrissie Hynde. "They got on well being Americans and from the same culture," he acknowledges. His attitude towards Hynde was best described as ambivalent. At times he thought she "brought me and Ray together a bit", but he was still wary of her influence in Kinks' matters, creatively or otherwise. In such circumstances, the rage of 'Mr Hyde' would be unleashed.

On 25 September 1981, there was a surprise reunion with Peter Quaife when the Kinks appeared at the Maple Leaf Gardens in Toronto. "We asked him to come and do 'You Really Got Me', and he couldn't handle it," Ray recalls. "The last time he played with us we had AC-30s and we carried our own PA. We'd never even worked with monitors when Pete was in the band." Quaife actually played on 'Little Queenie', but the results were little short of a fiasco. Later, he claimed that he was drunk, playing the wrong chords and unable to follow Dave's instructions.

The newer Kinks were bemused by his presence. "He was a bit of a storyteller," Ian Gibbons remembers. "He turned the bass up full, which was ever so loud, and whizzed up and down all over the place. I had difficulty following because it was so messy. He was all over the stage, and then he wouldn't get off. We were trying to do an encore. It was quite funny. It went down well with the fans, seeing the old line-up, but it was a very odd situation, almost tongue-in-cheek. Ray and Dave didn't seem to take him seriously at all." More than anything, it demonstrated the fantasy element in any notion of the original Kinks reforming or recording.

Nonetheless, Quaife's strange return brought back memories of past triumphs and conflicts. In an echo of the Cardiff debacle, there was a clash between Dave and Mick a week later in Nassau Coliseum. At the end of the set, Avory threw his sticks at his adversary and stormed offstage. "I think our drummer's just had a phone call," Ray informed the audience. He found him at the back of the auditorium, sitting in a car, still seething. That night, there was a 'curry fight' in the dressing room between the brothers which somehow alleviated the tension. The next performance (3 October) was at New York's Madison Square Garden, which Ray regarded as a career milestone. Annie Davies was flown over from England to join the celebrations.

There were further felicitations the following month when a relatively obscure Ray Davies composition climbed to number 7 in the UK charts. 'I Go To Sleep' had never been released by the

Kinks, although it had been covered (without chart success) by many, including Peggy Lee, the Applejacks, Cher, Truth, Lesley Duncan and Adrian Pride. Chrissie Hynde resurrected the song for the Pretenders, as if determined to remind the world of Davies' songwriting genius. It was a fine compliment.

Ray had good reason to be satisfied with the Kinks' standing, at least in America, but new challenges were beckoning. Channel 4 was interested in commissioning a play or television drama and, following a meeting, Davies presented a short treatment based on a train journey from Guildford to Waterloo Station. "I sat opposite this man and began to fantasize what his life may have been about." The incident had already inspired an incomplete song, 'Return To Waterloo', which Davies submitted as a likely title. The executives at Channel 4 urged him to write something daringly experimental and, in a remarkable display of commitment, agreed that he could direct the film. Davies was so thrilled that he immediately phoned his friend Ned Sherrin, who voiced a single note of caution. Was Davies prepared to devote the time and energy to complete the project? It was sage counsel. Over the next two years, Ray would have to juggle filming, touring and recording commitments, business and personal affairs connected with the Kinks, and the unravelling of a potentially toxic relationship.

If Ray ever assumed that he had his brother's full commitment during this period then he was sorely mistaken. Dave was keen to pursue his own projects, the more so after an extraordinary epiphany that took place in a hotel in Hampton, Virginia, on 13 January 1981. He later claimed that he was visited by five 'intelligences', two of whom identified themselves as his spirit guides and bestowed life-changing esoteric knowledge. Suffice to say, he was never the same again. Wisely, he kept these revelations private, fully aware that they would be dismissed as delusions by both his brother and the other Kinks. What mattered was that he believed – and would continue to do so.

Ray, in any case, had other problems pressing on his mind. He was planning to marry Chrissie Hynde. It was a great tabloid press story. Supposedly, there was an argument at Guildford registry office, a change of heart, then "we talked some more and we decided we would go through with it after all". By then it was too late. "The registrar wouldn't marry us because we'd missed our wedding time." Shortly afterwards, Davies announced: "Now we've decided that we don't need to be married to stay together and be happy." Years later, he added: "It wasn't through want of trying. But the gods were up there. Somebody did *something* right."

Hynde and Davies were both busy touring with their respective groups, but arranged itineraries so that they could meet as often as possible. "If you care about somebody who's in a shell," Hynde said, "wouldn't you have the ambition to pull him out and smash the shell so he can't go back? Because it's not like he's happy in there." If this made Davies sound like the more vulnerable of the two, music press headlines told a different story. On 14 June, the Pretenders completed a world tour, punctuated by the firing of bass player Pete Farndon, a former boyfriend of Hynde, whose alcohol and drug abuse had made him a liability. Within a year, he would be dead. Two days after Farndon's sacking, Pretenders' lead guitarist James Honeyman-Scott died from a heroin/cocaine overdose in London. Hynde took a flight to Philadelphia to be reunited with Ray at what was clearly an upsetting moment. The Kinks appeared at the city's John F. Kennedy Stadium on the 19th on a bill featuring Foreigner, Joan Jett & The Blackhearts and Huey Lewis & The News. Towards the end of the Kinks' set, Ray introduced the audience to the "greatest female music rock 'n' roller in the world". Hynde did not sing with the Kinks but her physical presence onstage infuriated Dave, who reportedly spat in her face or, more likely, simply shoved her away. "There was conflict," Ian Gibbons recalls. "Dave didn't want her onstage because it was a Kinks show and he was a bit upset about that. There was some pushing and shoving, but I don't think any punches were thrown. That did put a strain on things because it was quite a difficult relationship anyway. That was a very strange period." Ray showed remarkable restraint in the circumstances, but it was an ominous sign of another growing rift between the brothers.

Another source of tension was the *Return To Waterloo* project. Ray initially wanted to involve the entire Kinks as part of the eventual score but Dave immediately baulked at the idea of being used as a session player on an extracurricular excursion. He had not used Ray on his solo recordings, nor any of the other current group members. "Dave wanted to be as far away from the Kinks as possible," Ian Gibbons says. Although Ray later complained vociferously about Dave's attitude, it was difficult to argue that *Return To Waterloo* had anything to do with the Kinks. Far from being abandoned by Dave, Ray initially seemed almost pleased to be rid of his brother on a project that required a mono-maniacal focus. "I don't like working with him very much," he acknowledged while preparing the script of his 'fantasy musical'. "Obviously you love your brother and all that crap, but I would prefer to work with other people for a bit rather than with him, simply because I would like him to explore his own personality and playing. Sometimes I've got such a strong idea for my songs it doesn't give anybody else a chance to improvise. I say to the guys all the time: 'This is the definitive way this song should be played, you can't do it any other way because it's my original song.' They don't quite see that because they feel that maybe they can contribute to it."

Despite touring and recording commitments with the Kinks in 1982, Davies never lost sight of *Return To Waterloo*. Its importance was magnified because it followed so many thwarted attempts on his part to combine film and music. Ever since the 'Dead End Street' black and white promotional film back in 1966, Davies had dreamed of developing these ideas. He would have loved to have made a film based on *The Village Green Preservation Society*, if only the album had been more successful. Its follow-up, *Arthur*, originally intended as a Granada Television musical play, had been killed off before going into production. *Muswell Hillbillies* was a movie idea that never got beyond wishful hoping; film stock existed of a documentary based around *Everybody's In Show-biz*, but it was never released – and so the list went on. *The Long Distance Piano Player* and *Starmaker* were major break-throughs by comparison, but these small-screen triumphs now seemed fleeting achievements. A *Time/Life* release of the live concert *One For The Road* as a videocassette was another false dawn. A full-scale video based on the recent *Give The People What They Want* was merely the latest setback in a frustrating list of unrealized celluloid dreams.

Davies kept the faith, spurred on by the upsurge in promotional music videos. There had already been many memorable examples of number 1 hits associated with acclaimed productions over the past decade from Queen's 'Bohemian Rhapsody' to the Boomtown Rats' 'I Don't Like Mondays', Buggles' 'Video Killed The Radio Star', Pink Floyd's 'Another Brick In The Wall', David Bowie's 'Ashes To Ashes' and the Specials' 'Ghost Town'. In every case, the video supplemented the hit, rather than vice versa. The unexpected game changer for the music business occurred on 1 August 1981 with the launch of MTV (Music Television) in America. Its effect on British pop, in particular, was profound.

For years, it had been a truism that the only way to crack the US market was constant, almost mindless, touring. The Kinks were a good example of that familiar process. Household names in the UK charts and music press – the Sex Pistols, Echo & The Bunnymen, the Jam, the Boomtown Rats, Madness and Adam And The Ants – were virtually unknown in mainstream America. Entire movements from punk to Two Tone (Specials, Beat) and Futurist/New Romantics (Spandau Ballet, Visage, Ultravox) were virtually ignored and considered immune to US radio play. A cultural chasm between the US and UK youth markets had grown so wide that some commentators felt that it might never be bridged again. The launch of MTV, with its non-stop broadcast of pop videos, enabled UK record companies to overcome the insular programming of American radio stations and the endless slog of loss-making concert tours by reaching younger purchasers through a previously unexploited medium. That Christmas, the number 1 single in the UK was the Human League's 'Don't You Want Me', which was accompanied by a clever video which enhanced the listening experience. When the MTV-promoted song emulated its chart performance in America, it kick-started what some dubbed a second 'British Invasion'. Suddenly acts as diverse as Culture Club ('Do You Really Want To Hurt Me') and Dexys Midnight Runners ('Come On Eileen') were overnight 'transatlantic' stars.

Ray Davies had neither the youth nor sex appeal of the latest British invaders, but he had a fondness for video and a technical knowledge superior to that of his younger contemporaries. He established an excellent working relationship with director Julien Temple, who had won his spurs working alongside Malcolm McLaren on the Sex Pistols' movie *The Great Rock 'n' Roll Swindle*. His first venture with the Kinks was an hilarious promo for 'Predictable', featuring Ray in a series of comic calamities, dressed variously as a hippie, a Teddy boy and a Mod. Unfortunately, that single only appeared in the UK – a wasted opportunity. It seemed the same fate might await its follow-up, 'Come Dancing', issued in November 1982.

A winsome evocation of the Davies sisters' dancing youth, the song captured the innocent thrill of ballroom romance and the power of memory to re-enact treasured experiences. Its narrative consistency made it perfect for video. Temple and Davies constructed a brilliant period piece, filmed at the Ilford Palais, with Ray adopting the persona of his Uncle Frank to remarkable effect. The single got lost in the 1982 UK pre-Christmas rush and, despite Davies' protests, Arista's president Clive Davis vetoed an American release. He insisted the song was too parochial for radio airplay, made more so by Ray's London accent. The label owner had evidently forgotten his pop history. In the mid-Sixties, acts such as Herman's Hermits ('I'm Henry VIII, I Am') and the New Vaudeville Band ('Winchester Cathedral') had played the 'English card' to profitable perfection. Two of Ray Davies' quintessentially English songs ('A Well Respected Man' and 'Dandy') were also among his best known hits in the USA. Perhaps Arista felt such scenarios could never happen again, but MTV made all things possible. They latched on to the brilliant 'Come Dancing' video, creating a thriving market for import copies of the single. Clive Davis finally threw up his hands and belatedly sanctioned its release. Before long, it was in the US Top 10, peaking at number 6, their best chart position since 'Tired Of Waiting For You'. The London branch of Arista reissued the song a few months later and it became a summer success. Only students of ancient history would have known that the Kinks' last UK Top 20 entry was 'Supersonic Rocket Ship' 11 years before.

The international success of 'Come Dancing' was not the only surprise package that year. On 22 January 1983, Chrissie presented Ray with a daughter, Natalie Rae. Her arrival momentarily resurrected the 'marriage question' in his mind. While waiting to register the birth, he saw an announcement of a forthcoming wedding and winced. The groom was only 18. "What chance has he got at that age"? he thought. Ray was suddenly reminded of Rasa and Yvonne, failed marriages, divorces and legal arguments. "I don't think I'm very good marriage fodder," he concluded.

The hoopla surrounding 'Come Dancing' assisted the passage of the Kinks' 1983 album, *State Of Confusion*. Solid rather than spectacular, it was a decent addition to the Kinks' canon, boosted by the presence of 'Come Dancing' and its companion piece, 'Don't Forget To Dance'. Structurally, Davies mingled anthemic rockers like the title track with more pensive reflections in his now familiar fashion. Painful meditations on marriage and its aftermath ('Labour Of Love' and 'Property') and clumsy social commentaries ('Young Conservatives', 'Clichés Of The World') were all part of the mix. If the stylistic pot-pourri seemed over-familiar the strike rate was reasonably impressive. Even 'Long Distance' and 'Noise' (both included on the cassette version) were surprisingly good as outtakes. Davies' favourite track on the album was 'Heart Of Gold', a Pretenders'-style ballad partly inspired by Princess Anne's celebrated 'naff off' rebuke to the paparazzi. "I wrote about it imagining I was a photographer, but really it was about Chrissie having her first baby. Both she and Princess Anne seem to be quite anonymous people at times."

State Of Confusion, in common with the last four Kinks albums, reached the Top 15 of the US charts. The metronomic exactitude emphasized an almost mechanical quality to the Kinks' progress at this point. After years of erratic, self-destructive development, they had locked into the repetitive album/arena tour/album cycle so loved by American concert promoters and record companies. This enabled Davies to compartmentalize his activities. He could mentally switch off the Kinks and turn his attention to *Return To Waterloo* for weeks or months, if necessary. It was all work and no play, but that was what brought him the greatest satisfaction and security. He found an ally in producer Dennis Woolf, whom he had previously worked with on *Starmaker*. Soon, they would form Waterloo Films to oversee *Return To Waterloo* and Kinks-related videos. Davies' television drama had already made considerable progress towards the screen. After seeing the first draft, Channel 4 felt confident enough to invest £200,000. On completion of the script, in May 1983, RCA injected a further £160,000 advance to secure the retail video rights. The £360,000 budget enabled Woolf to recruit a formidable crew including art director Terry Pritchard (*The French Lieutenant's Woman*), director of photography Roger Deakins (*Another Time, Another*

Place), production manager Paul Sparrow (*Nelly's Version*) and assistant director Selwyn Roberts (*Give My Regards To Broad Street*). Actor Kenneth Colley (the tramp in Dennis Potter's *Pennies From Heaven*) was selected for the main part. Filming commenced on 4 September and was completed exactly three weeks later with footage shot on a real train at Horsley. During post-production, Davies was required to write the score and attend to various administrative and technical matters. Meanwhile, the Kinks were preparing to tour once more.

In October 1983, Dave Davies was at a low ebb. That month his third solo album, *Chosen People*, had been issued in the UK, but the sales were so bad that there would be no fourth for a major label. With credits to the 'Mystical Order of St Peter' and a dedication to Sir George Young, founder of the Aetherius Society who, like Dave, had also heard alien voices in his head, it was hardly surprising that some reviewers ridiculed the guitarist. Others thought it was his best work to date, but he was still angry and disillusioned. There was even resentment over the credits to *State Of Confusion*. Years later, Dave insisted that he had arranged four songs on the record and accused Ray of deliberately excising the information from the liner notes or album artwork. They were barely talking at the time. It came as a great shock when Dave announced that he was pulling out of their New Year American tour. Whether it was petulance, bloody-mindedness, revenge, depression – or a combination of all four – nobody was entirely sure. Ray was incensed and reportedly threatened to go ahead "with or without Dave". Rumours spread that the younger brother was officially leaving the Kinks, to be replaced by the talented journeyman guitarist Chris Spedding. One paper reported: "Dave Davies has checked into a mental institution for treatment of a 'serious mental illness', the details of which have been kept mum. It's not known if the hospitalization was voluntary and brother Ray was unavailable to shed further light on the situation." When contacted later that month, road manager and spokesperson Ken Jones told me that Dave was suffering from "fatigue" but insisted that the other rumours, including the strange Spedding story, had no foundation. Soon after, it was agreed that Dave should take six weeks off and the lucrative tour was back on. It did not bode well for the New Year.

CHAPTER THIRTY-FOUR

NINETEEN EIGHTY-FOUR

The year 1984 had always held a lingering fascination for Ray Davies. He was not alone. Anyone who had been moved or influenced by George Orwell's vision of a totalitarian future during their youth could not resist wondering what might await the world in that far-off year. It had a similar numerical charm to 1999 and the prospect of a new century, begging the questions: What will society be like then? Where will I be? What will I be doing? Davies had been asked those very questions at the very start of his pop star odyssey and answered them with the naive confidence of an idealistic, crusading young man. "In 1984 I shall be fighting what I fight now. The same kind of petty authority and pocket-sized tyrants I resent now will be around in 1984."

In 1964, he could scarcely have imagined that the Kinks would not only still be together 20 years later, but also receiving gold disc awards and selling out stadiums in America. Pop groups were supposed to last a few years, not decades. Who could have anticipated that a band as unstable and volatile as the Kinks would emerge as the great survivors of the British beat boom, and beyond? If the idea of 1984 was once laden with prophecies of doom in Davies' mind, then he had evidently escaped such a fate. 'Come Dancing' was still alive in the public's imagination and fans were hoping for a Kinks' bonanza of books, records and retrospectives to celebrate the group's 20th anniversary. It promised to be a great year but, in keeping with Davies' tendency to snatch Icarian self-destruction from victory, everything swiftly unravelled.

If Davies was searching for a bad sign to confirm the augurs of 1984, then he did not have long to wait. On 7 January, at a concert in Hampton, Virginia, he fell awkwardly onstage, breaking his kneecap. For the remainder of the tour, he was reduced to performing while hobbling around with a brace attached to his leg. The itinerary included an unappetizing series of dates across the Midwest which drained everyone's enthusiasm. "That was when it really started to get difficult for Mick Avory," Ian Gibbons recalls. "He really hated it. It was horrible weather, drizzly and depressing and Mick was pissed off. He'd been doing it for 20 years and had definitely had enough. He just wanted to get back on the golf course." If the most phlegmatic and easy-going member of the Kinks was complaining, then they were surely in severe trouble.

Dave, always an antennae for Avory's apathy or anger, responded disdainfully, accusing the drummer of not caring enough about the group and acting the buffoon. While everyone else loved Mick's sense of humour, Dave grimaced at his downbeat witticisms. "His attitude was changing. He didn't seem interested. It was like he wasn't there or concerned about what we were doing." Wary of interfering, Ray quietly despaired of the poisoned relationship. "The situation between Dave and Mick had gotten so bad that I couldn't bear to be in the same dressing room with them. I was always afraid that they were going to fight . . . It was clearly apparent to me that it was just two people who had reached the end of their journey together."

Once they all returned to England, Ray distracted himself with extracurricular work. He was still immersed in editing *Return To Waterloo*, a project he found engrossing, even though it was having a detrimental effect on his domestic life and relationship with his brother. It could have been worse. Ray had recently agreed to appear in Julien Temple's adaptation of Colin MacInnes' novel *Absolute Beginners*, and it was only when that project ran into financial problems and was postponed for a year that he found some free time.

A half-hearted, ten-date UK tour at the end of March did little to improve the Kinks' reputation at home. Even the group's staunchest fans were showing impatience with the predictability of their repertoire. Critic Robin Denselow, a long-time supporter, accurately pinpointed the dilemmas faced by the Kinks' leader in his 'anniversary' year. "Ray Davies has had a brilliant, if uneven, career, but always seems to sell himself short . . . A master of melody, sentiment, nostalgia and crowd control, with his throwaway music hall showmanship, Davies still has to match these skills against the heavy metal wailing guitar style of brother Dave. This has long been one of the Kinks' many contradictions, and one that has actually helped them in America, but in the cheerful dance hall atmosphere of the [Hammersmith] Palais it seemed particularly wrong."

The clash between Dave's hard-rock playing and Ray's graceful vignettes had by this point degenerated into an artistic tug of war. In concert, the younger brother adamantly refused to perform any of the songs from *Return To Waterloo*. He was the only member of the Kinks not to appear on the sessions, a fact that now irked Ray who realized that its commercial value as a soundtrack might be compromised without the group brand name. The frostiness between the brothers was best summed up in Ray's casual admission that their primary method of communication was conducted vicariously through their respective solicitors.

"Self-destruction is quite dominant in Ray's life," Ian Gibbons adds. "He'd been so involved with *Return To Waterloo* and Dave didn't want it to be called a Kinks album or have anything to do with it. I don't think Ray and Dave talked to each other for months while that was going on. But there wasn't anything predominantly guitar-like on the album anyway."

The coldness between the brothers was the least of Ray's problems. Domestic disharmony was now uppermost in his mind. Over the past year, the once idyllic fan/star relationship with Chrissie Hynde had deteriorated into open hostility. To paraphrase Davies, their romance had turned from a fairy tale into a Hitchcock horror movie. Broken furniture and trashed rooms testified to the intensity of their passions. During one memorable argument, the volatile Pretender had smashed the keyboard on which Davies had composed 'Come Dancing'. Ray kept the pieces as a memento of her frustration. No third party has suggested or even hinted (certainly not in any printed interview) that Davies ever physically abused Hynde. Oddly, Hynde spoke, or was quoted, as if such rumours were commonplace, rather than unstated. "Other people have said that he beat me up, I never did. He had some problems, let me put it that way. But I gave it a good run. And being beaten up is not the same thing as having some pretty nasty fights. We had nasty fights and if there was alcohol involved, things got broken. Let's leave it at that." Their troubled partnership reached a final impasse when Hynde embarked on an extensive tour with the Pretenders, leaving Ray still mulling over the *Return To Waterloo* script. It should have provided them with breathing space, but the bickering continued. "There were terrible long-distance fights," he says. "The phone was our worst enemy." Their relationship was effectively over by this point, but there was to be no comfortable period of drifting apart.

On 5 May 1984, Hynde married Simple Minds' vocalist Jim Kerr in New York. Davies seemed overwhelmed by the sudden news and the very public nature of the event. "It was a sunny day, brilliant and all of a sudden everything went black and white. It was a bad day because I felt lied to – obviously – but there's more going on. It's really difficult. The reason I can't talk about it is because I really don't understand where it started or ended. I'm a very quiet person who doesn't like to talk about his personal life, usually. Obviously, a relationship ended and all that came to a head on one day. And also it was something else in my past that I definitely won't talk about that came to a head at the same time."

It would be an understatement to suggest that Ray Davies does not take rejection well. When Rasa left him, he was almost driven to suicide and although Hynde's abandonment was hardly unexpected given their arguments, his reaction was excessive. According to Dave, he had a round-the-clock psychiatric nurse in attendance for a brief spell, which must have been frighteningly expensive, assuming it was privately funded. Dave dutifully attended his brother's bedside to offer support, just as he had done after the split with Rasa, but this time there was an angry exchange. Ray railed unmercifully, as if Dave was the author of his woes. Evidently he had not forgotten those moments, onstage and off, when Dave had clashed with Hynde. Passing some of the blame on to Dave evidently made Ray feel slightly better. Unsurprisingly, the other Kinks

Dedicated followers of Carnaby Street fashion. (© Chris Walter: www.photofeatures)

Posing with car. (© Chris Walter: www.photofeatures)

Ray's promotional photo
for RCA Records.
(Courtesy of RCA Records)

(*Above and below*) John Dalton and John Gosling
in the line-up during the RCA years.
(Courtesy of RCA Records)

Ray onstage. (Courtesy of RCA Records)

His dramatic appearance at
White City 15 July 1973 when
he announced his 'retirement'.
(© Debi Doss)

Backing singers Debi Doss, Pamela Travis and Shirlie Roden.
(photo: Colin Fuller. © Debi Doss)

The Kinks promo photo for Arista Records.
(Courtesy of Arista Records)

Ray relocates to New York, 1976.
(Courtesy of Arista Records)

A rare photo of Ray's second wife, Yvonne. (© Debi Doss)

This certificate confirms that Ray had already changed his name to 'Raymond Douglas' when he married Yvonne Gunner on 1 November 1974. (© Crown copyright)

19.74... Marriage solemnized at..............
District of ...Swindon...

Columns:—	1	2	3
No.	When married	Name and surname	Age
236	First November 1974	Raymond DOUGLAS formerly known as Raymond Douglas Davies	29 years
		Yvonne Ann GUNNER	22 years

Married in the .....Register Office.....
This marriage was solemnized between us, { Raymond Douglas. / Yvonne Gunner. }

Ray at airport security, followed by his wife, Yvonne. (© Debi Doss)

Ray and his third wife, Patricia Crosbie. (© Neal Preston)

| 1986 Marriage solemnized at The Register Office | | | | | | | | in the |
| District of Surrey South-Western | | | in the County of Surrey. | | | | | |

No.	When married	Name and surname	Age	Condition	Rank or profession	Residence at the time of marriage	Father's name and surname	Rank or profession of father
25	Twenty fifth January 1986	Raymond DOUGLAS Name changed by Deed Poll	41 years	Previous marriage Dissolved	Musician	Slaters Oak Effingham Common Road Effingham	Frederick George DAVIES (Deceased)	Gardener
		Patricia May Eva CROSBIE	27 years	Spinster	Dancer	Slaters Oak Effingham Common Road Effingham	George Frederick CROSBIE	Newspaper Director

Married in the Register Office by Certificate before me,

This marriage was solemnized between us, { Raymond Douglas / Patricia Crosbie } in the presence of us, { K. J. Winn / B. C. Winn. } G. K. Swaby, Superintendent Registrar G. A. Pickett, Registrar

Ray marries Patricia Crosbie, 25 January 1986. The certificate confirms that he is still known as Raymond Douglas, having changed his name by deed poll.
(© Crown copyright)

Ray and his fourth daughter, Eva, pictured at Buckingham Palace where he received his CBE from the Queen on 17 March 2004. (© Rex)

The original Kinks, photographed together at the UK Music Hall of Fame at London's Alexandra Palace, 16 November 2005. (© Rex)

Ray with
Karin Forsman,
the Swedish singer
who was his
companion for
several years
during the first
decade of the
new century:
7 September
2010. (© Rex)

A photo for
the ages. Ray, on
12 February 2014,
flanked by his
current partner
Alma Karen Eyo
and model/
photographer
Jill Kennington
whom he first
met while working
on an uncompleted
film in December
1963. (© Rex)

refrained from commenting on Hynde in public, but hoped that Davies' darker moods would not engulf them in further problems. Surprisingly, Davies found a distant ally in his former adversary Tom Robinson, who casually opined: "Ray's all right. The way Chrissie treated him stinks." No further comment was forthcoming.

Ray later offered a more realistic evaluation. "It's a human thing falling in love, you go with it. If you step back it's a whole different relationship. They say the thing you hate about the person you just broken up with is what attracted you to them in the first place, and that's quite true." Gradually, Davies' wrath dissipated, only to be replaced by a lazy petulance, summed up in the spiteful aside, "I'd like to do something to piss her off, but I never want to see her again. Why bother?" Hynde's successor in his affections would be a very different proposition.

In a familiar pattern of 'on the rebound romance', Davies soon found himself in a new relationship. While recovering from the broken kneecap he had sustained in Virginia back in January, Ray had unwisely decided to resume his daily two-mile jogging routine. Troubled by torn ligaments, he was attending a physiotherapy centre where he met a beautiful ballerina, 14 years his junior, who was being consulted for a broken ankle. Despite the age difference, they shared a similar sense of humour and dedication towards their work.

Patricia May Eva Crosbie was a scion of one of Ireland's most famous families. Her father George was the owner of the *Cork Examiner* and a renowned golfer who had played at international level for Ireland during the Fifties. His eight children had inherited his love of work and sport and each achieved success in their own right. Patricia had always wanted to be a ballet dancer and at the age of seven enrolled at the celebrated Joan Denise Moriarty School of Ballet where she studied for 11 years while completing her formal education at Cork's Regina Mundi College. Moriarty was a legend in Irish dance, having founded the Cork Ballet Company in 1942 before forming her own schools. Under her tutelage, Crosbie learned lessons in humility as well as dance instruction. If Moriarty was attending to another student, then Patricia was expected to remain standing in silence until she had finished, regardless of how long it took. She was also obliged to bow demurely in thanks to Moriarty at the end of every lesson.

Summers were spent avoiding the sun as even the slightest tan might provoke the famous Moriarty reprimand to her *Swan Lake* students: "There is no such thing as a brown swan."

Crosbie continued working with her mentor during her time with the Irish National Ballet Company. Aged 19, Patricia appeared as Widow Quin in the ambitious ballet production of Synge's *The Playboy Of The Western World*, which was staged in Dublin, New York and London's Sadler's Wells. With music provided by the Chieftains, whose folk background and instrumental virtuosity enhanced the spectacle, the production was innovative and daring, inspiring Crosbie to experiment beyond the confines of classical ballet. Davies was fascinated, not least because some of this narrative echoed his own multi-media attempts to fuse music, film and theatre. The more he saw of Pat Crosbie, the closer they became. Suddenly, he discovered a surprising interest in dance, informing reporters of his intention to produce a documentary on the state of modern ballet. He even threatened to incorporate a dance motif in the Kinks' set and wanted to feature a ballet dancer on the cover of the group's next album.

With the Chrissie Hynde split exposed in the press, his relationship with his brother strained and his group uncertain of their future, Davies decided to take stock. As usual, work offered a reprieve from past worries, so he concentrated on producing a summer single. The A-side 'Good Day' extracted something positive from the Hynde breakup while its flip side, 'Too Hot', used his gym workouts as a metaphor for the state of the nation. Unfortunately, the recording was marred by further conflict between Dave and Mick, with Ray cast in the role of the unhappy mediator. "There were terrible fights, and I got to the point where I couldn't cope with it any more." Reluctantly, Davies decided to use a drum machine in place of Avory. It was another humiliation, but even that was insufficient for the younger brother who was determined to vanquish the drummer once and for all. "Dave said he wanted to replace Mick, and Mick had an important sound. Mick wasn't a great drummer, but he was a jazz drummer – same school, same era as Charlie Watts."

"There was something in our natures that didn't gel," Avory says, referring to the ongoing conflict with Dave. "I'm slow and laid-back and that probably frustrated him. He's the opposite –

he's quick and wants to get things done. The other thing is the relationship with Ray. If you get too close to Ray, Dave doesn't like that either. It wasn't a good atmosphere."

While Avory pondered his fate, there was another person at the session whose presence was nothing less than startling. Both sides of the single featured a cameo vocal appearance from Ray's 19-year-old daughter Louisa, who had recently moved into the 'Mendelssohn cottage' in the grounds of his Effingham home for an extended stay. Coincidentally, her mother was also reviving her singing career, which had been dormant since those early appearances on Kinks' records. Rasa had formed a songwriting team with musician Noel Durdant-Hollamby, working at a studio near London Bridge. "His scores were brilliant," she says. "I was the lyricist and he did all the background music." After setting up a company, they entered the Eurovision Song for Europe, finishing just shy of tenth place. In another strange twist of history, she found herself in the offices of her former husband's great nemesis Eddie Kassner. The publisher oozed charm and finesse along with those vulpine instincts that had always marked him out as an exceptional businessman. "He was very pleased to see me," Rasa remembers. "He was going to give me money. He was interested in my work but the thing he was most interested in was Ray. He said: 'Have you got any lyrics of Ray's hidden away? I'd be very interested in those.' It was really funny. Wasn't that a typical thing he would say?"

Rasa was not alone in revisiting old memories and former colleagues. One afternoon, Larry Page was sitting in his office when the phone rang. "It's Ray," the caller announced. "Ray, who?" Page replied. The entrepreneur nearly fell from his chair at the realization that Davies was about to end their ancient falling out. "I didn't even know who it was – it was weird." Soon after, they met at a pub in Surrey and, after some pleasant banter, Page discovered what was on offer. Davies urgently needed a UK-based manager to oversee the Kinks' affairs, revitalize their career and allow him the chance to rediscover his muse. As he noted at the time: "Most days I'd get up and say, 'I can't write a note to the milkman'. I couldn't write a thing." Page was soon to discover that Ray's joke about the milkman was not far from the literal truth. On their next appointed meeting at Ray's house,

Larry received an amusing call from the anxious Kink imploring, "Er, could you bring a bottle of milk with you? I haven't got any milk."

"Well, it'll save him nineteen pence," Page said to himself as he set out. Their exploratory conversations proved cordial enough and Page was rapidly reinstated, albeit in a less powerful role than he had enjoyed in the mid-Sixties. "It was completely different because they were now established. When you launch something from square one you can take control, which I've often been accused of. But in a situation like this you couldn't take *complete* control because the patterns had already been laid down. They'd been existing for years. It was weird because there were certain things we just didn't discuss, like the court case. That was never mentioned." Page was obliged to play the diplomat, not least because Davies already had a long-term US-based business manager, Elliot Abbott, and a frustrated road manager, Ken Jones, who still remained in a lowly position. "Ken had been a loyal roadie for over twenty-five years and obviously wasn't keen to have me on board, nor was Elliot, so it was difficult. All I knew about Elliot was that he'd done a good job in America. Whatever had been said in the past, I think Ray knew that I was honest when it came to opinions on music and anything else. He was surrounded by people who maybe worshipped him, but that's not always constructive."

The traditional svengali manager may have seemed an anachronism in the Eighties rock business, but Page was frequently called upon to play the paternal mediator. Over the next year, he was astonished to find himself in a mental time warp, witnessing a fraternal battle that still raged two decades on. "It's like being back in 1965," he told me, shortly after his reappointment. "They're worse than ever."

Much of Page's time was taken up acting as intermediary, refereeing imaginary disputes between the brothers, fending off paranoid phone calls and trying to fathom the peculiar group dynamics that made the Kinks one of rock's most famous underachievers. Dealing with Davies was never a part-time job. "When you're involved with Ray, you're involved with *everything*. If it's a leaky roof, you're involved – if he's letting a house you're involved." Even when the Kinks were away in America, Page was fielding calls at all hours of the day. On one occasion, Ray phoned asking his manager to contact his brother about some minor issue. "Where is he?" Page asked. "In the hotel room, next door," Ray replied. "Well, why don't you go and ask him yourself?" Page said, concluding the call. On other, rarer occasions, there were emotional outpourings. "I used to have Dave on the phone crying one night and Ray on the phone crying another night about Dave, and this and that. I tell you, he's not a happy man."

Intriguingly, Page's arrival coincided with the most significant shake-up in personnel since the departure of Pete Quaife. In July 1984, fans were still celebrating the Kinks' 20th anniversary when it was announced that Mick Avory was no longer a member of the group. The drummer had been disappointed about being left off 'Good Day'. This, followed by another bitter confrontation with Dave Davies, convinced both him and Ray that enough was enough. Nineteen years before, he had been ostracized after almost killing Dave onstage at Cardiff, only to be dramatically reinstated when Page forced the group back on the road. This time round, Page was barely back in the camp himself and lacked the influence to reverse a decision that had been on the cards since 1965. In truth, Page felt Avory was better out of it and secretly marvelled that the drummer had shown the fortitude to stomach 20 years of psychological and sometimes physical abuse.

Ray deeply regretted Avory's departure as the two had grown close over the years. When Mick's father had died, the drummer went through an uncharacteristically dark phase which Ray felt able to respond to sympathetically. At one point, he found Avory in tears and coaxed him out of his sadness with a mixture of ironic humour, tea and sympathy. Avory appreciated the gesture. "It seemed to help," he admitted. Although Ray might have intervened in this decisive confrontation between Mick and Dave, he was too absorbed by his own problems to influence the outcome. Worn down by the incessant feuding, Ray finally capitulated. Although Avory assumed he had already resigned, Davies maintains that the axe actually fell during an inebriated evening at a pub in Guildford. "I took Mick out and we got very, very drunk after about five pints of this wonderful scrumpy. Mick said that if any other band offered him a tour he wouldn't take it because he didn't want to tour. I remember him getting the train back – because he was banned from driving; it was a very bad year for Mick – and he walked to the station and disappeared into the mist. I'd never fired anyone before." Perhaps the cider affected both their memories, but if Avory was sacked then it was only a statement confirming his own decision. "Mick had had enough and was happy to go," Page insists. "It wasn't like he was kicked out. The idea then was to bring new blood into the Kinks." It was agreed that Avory would continue working for the Kinks, as token manager of Konk Studios. He also remained a director of their companies, but later lost that standing as his role in their organization diminished. Outwardly, Avory seemed content with the arrangements and, stoical as ever, announced his intention to spend more time with his family, while improving his golf handicap.

Avory's replacement was Bob Henrit, a former Cheshunt Grammar pupil who had played with John Dalton in the Blue Jacks back in the Fifties, served as a member of Adam Faith's Roulettes, recorded for Pye Records, and appeared as a session player on Unit Four Plus Two's number 1 hit, 'Concrete And Clay'. In 1969, he had been a founding member of Argent, along with Jim Rodford, whom he also collaborated with as part of the trio Phoenix. With all those historic connections he was, in short, the perfect replacement. Born barely a month before Ray, he even had age on his side. Henrit had also appeared on a couple of Dave's solo albums and was obviously the younger brother's first choice as drummer. Unlike Avory, whose interest in drumming technique had stopped sometime in the Seventies, Henrit had kept up with recent technological developments and regularly updated his equipment. His larger kit was perfectly suited to the arenas and stadiums that regularly accommodated the Kinks in America. While his induction proceeded smoothly, he soon discovered some eccentricities typical of the Davies duo. Shortly after joining, he was backstage at a gig when the road manager announced that he was getting some food and requested various orders. Henrit innocently suggested that he would like a pizza, a request that prompted an unexpected tirade from the brothers. Larry Page was both amused and aghast. "They were saying, 'You fucking cunt, you come out here and think you can do that.' There was nearly a punch-up over the pizza. I couldn't understand it, and Bob certainly couldn't understand it. The roadie was just asking who wanted to eat what and Ray and Dave went apeshit when they found out he wanted a pizza."

Like his predecessors, Henrit quickly learned the art of keeping his head down and avoiding the fraternal mind games. Page claims he offered to negotiate a better pay deal for the subsidiary members at this point, but was warned off. "I think everybody was a bit worried that they might lose their jobs. I was told not to discuss it with Ray, but I did anyway. I felt they should have been getting a bit more. You've got to realize that those boys weren't getting the royalties. It was wages."

By the autumn, the group were working on a new album, while adapting to recent changes. "It was just a completely different style," says Gibbons, "and the first album Ray had done without Mick. Bob's style is a lot different from Mick's – it's more rock and that changed the feel. It was more settled in the studio because there wasn't anything going down between Dave and Mick. This was almost like starting again. The different style of playing altered the sound of the band quite considerably."

In November, the long-awaited *Return To Waterloo* received its television screening and was warmly greeted by most British critics. Although the *New Statesman* mischievously dismissed the work as "an updated version of the *Magical Mystery Tour*", other publications saw merit in Davies' directorial debut. His ambitious and highly imaginative portrayal of a commuter caught in mid-life crisis was adroitly dramatized in a series of set pieces, weaving fantasy and daydream sequences, similar in style to Dennis Potter's *Pennies From Heaven*. In common with Potter, Davies' drama had dark undertones, leaving the viewer uncomfortably uncertain whether the central character might be a rapist, paedophile or simply a lonely fantasist blighted by the loss of his daughter. Larry Page was concerned about the subject matter. "It worried me. At the time the Surrey rapist was still on the loose and this was all about a rapist. But it was well received and you welcome that."

The journey into the commuter's consciousness was accompanied by some striking new Davies compositions on which the Kinks (*sans* brother Dave) guested. In an obvious tribute to Hitchcock, Ray even made a cameo appearance, playing a busker in his own film. What could easily have been an overreaching effort from Davies as a writer, director and composer instead proved immensely engaging. Its promise was best summed up by the *Listener*'s Miles Kington – admittedly a long-time Davies supporter – whose highly sympathetic review concluded: "There was very little dialogue. Instead, the film images fitted very tightly together like a satisfying jigsaw, and Ray Davies' own songs provided ample commentary – from time to time the characters even burst into song with him or danced briefly before resuming their real identity. It could have been a load of rubbish; instead it was like a long and very good poem."

During the same month as the *Return To Waterloo* TV premiere, Arista issued the new Kinks' album, *Word Of Mouth*. Davies cleverly played to his strengths, including just enough high-quality songs to satisfy his committed following. The opening 'Do It Again' reminded the world of the group's pre-eminence as purveyors of Sixties melodic pop. Arguably their last great single, its sales were muted despite another inspired Julien Temple-directed video which poignantly featured Mick Avory as Ray's assistant busker, promoting a song on which he did not play. Critics searching for key references to the breakup of Ray's relationship with Chrissie Hynde were struck by the wistful 'Good Day' and the bitter 'Word Of Mouth'. The title track, bolstered by a riff inspired by the Rolling Stones' 'Start Me Up', showed Davies at his angriest, bemoaning the evil voice of rumour. The quality of the album was enhanced by the inclusion of three songs from *Return To Waterloo*: 'Going Solo', 'Sold Me Out' and 'Missing Person'. There was even room for a couple of Dave Davies compositions, notably 'Living On A Thin Line' in which he covered his brother's terrain by attempting a song alluding to the death of England's past glories. Dave had vainly hoped that Ray might sing lead on the track, thereby promoting his worth as a songwriter, but that was a concession too far. Having found a common lyrical theme with his brother, Dave was frustrated by Arista's refusal to release the song as a single. He even put forward a conspiracy theory claiming that there was a clause in his brother's publishing contract which insisted that the first two or three singles from a Kinks' album had to be Ray Davies compositions. "I can't remember the exact details but it was something like that, so 'Living On A Thin Line' missed the boat because Ray was under a contractual obligation and I didn't find that out for quite a long time after." No paperwork has ever emerged to confirm or contradict Dave's contention.

A major publicity coup for the album came via an appearance on NBC's *Saturday Night Live* on 17 November. Two songs were performed: 'Word Of Mouth' and a scintillating 'Do It Again'. The following weekend, they flew to Frankfurt via London for a filmed concert at the Festhalle which was also broadcast on radio. Leading German group BAP had been eager to appear on the same bill as the Kinks and their solicitations proved crucial in securing the booking. Larry Page initially met resistance from Ray, who was in two minds about whether the visit was a good idea. "What does Dave think?" he asked. "Dave? He's not keen on it at all," Page replied. "Oh, we'll *definitely* go then," Ray responded, his mind made up. Nevertheless, there were still signs of Davies' wavering commitment even after their arrival in Frankfurt. "When we got to Germany the promoter was saying, 'Only Larry Page could have done this. You are wonderful. You've brought Ray Davies back to Germany.' Within a couple of hours, Ray was asking the roadie to take him back to the airport and the promoter was panicking." When Page confronted Davies he was told: "I can't sleep in the beds over here. I've got to sleep in my own bed." Ray left with Larry's final words ringing in his ears: "Don't let us down on this – it's a biggie." Page feared the worst, but was pleasantly surprised. "He didn't let us down. He flew home that night, went to sleep, then came back the following day!"

Unfortunately, the eagerly awaited performance proved anti-climactic. The Kinks took the stage after the Klaus Large Band only to find themselves in complete darkness when the lights failed. Initially, there was much jostling at the front of the stage but, after a handful of songs, a large proportion of the audience drifted to the bar, preferring to save themselves for the arrival of BAP. The Kinks' enthusiasm understandably waned. Even some older fans described the set as perfunctory, complaining that it was virtually identical to a performance on *Rockpalast* two years before. The German press were equally unenthusiastic, observing: "The Kinks acted like copies of themselves. Songwriter/singer Ray

Davies offered the same gestures and the same jokes as on earlier occasions here in Germany and, of course, the veterans of rock let the audience sing along with their greatest tunes. Depressing."

Undeterred, the Kinks returned to America four days later for a lengthy East Coast tour stretching from New Orleans to New York. The nightly song list was predictable, including the usual set pieces such as the false start to 'Lola' and the call and response 'Banana Boat Song'. What some found stale and unimaginative was lapped up by others as camp ritual. Overall, it was very successful. The tour ended at New York's Madison Square Garden on 21 December, the perfect excuse for a Christmas party. Larry Page flew in from London and was impressed. "It was an excellent gig. Whatever anybody says about Ray, when he gets out there he does his thing." Also in attendance was Patricia Crosbie who had decided to spend Christmas with Ray. He seemed thrilled by the prospect. "It's wonderful," he gushed. "It's great! I'm really happy. I think I'm in love." It had been a tempestuous year, even by the Kinks' standards, but somehow they had survived their 20th anniversary. For all that, Davies could not help thinking that he should have taken the opportunity to do something different. "I wish I could have taken a break from recording in 1984. I would have liked to have dropped out to do films. But I went ahead with making records anyway and I didn't like myself for it."

CHAPTER THIRTY-FIVE

THE THIRD MARRIAGE

In January 1985, Larry Page placed an advertisement in the UK trade paper *Music Week* announcing that the Kinks' Arista deal had expired and inviting offers from other interested parties. With the exception of 'Come Dancing', Davies had enjoyed little commercial success in his homeland for many years. The last Kinks album to reach the charts (bar compilations) had been *Something Else*, back in 1967, a statistic completely out of synch with their stateside success. Page soon discovered how far Davies' star had fallen in the eyes of the British music industry, and even their own record company. Two days after taking the job as Kinks manager, Page had phoned Arista to arrange a meeting to discuss plans for the future. The response was devastating. "When I mentioned, 'it's about the Kinks', the MD said, 'I don't give a fuck about the Kinks' – and that was just for openers! Later, after I'd only walked into his office, he told me, 'If you've got any problems, talk to Clive Davis because I don't give a fuck.' Needless to say, he didn't get away with that. I'll take someone saying 'fuck' to me three times, and then they're over a desk." However, the more he learned about the transatlantic record company politics, the more Page appreciated some of the anger and frustration he had witnessed. It seemed that the Kinks were now regarded as an American-signed band and their promotion in the UK had been weakened as a result. Whatever budget was spent on them, the profits ultimately went back to the parent company in New York. At least that was what Page had been told. "Even if the

UK got a number 1 record, they were still on to a loser according to the MD," he maintains. Such nuances aside, it was clear that the marketing people at Arista were less than happy and the Kinks were no longer a priority. It seemed a good time to switch labels.

While Page set up meetings, Davies was seriously rethinking his strategy in America. His relationship with Arista's Clive Davis had been exemplary, but there was good reason to assume that a new company could do better. The recent *Word Of Mouth* had only reached number 57 in *Billboard*, a worrying sign in itself, reinforced by a dip in concert receipts. If the marketplace was starting to turn against them then it made sense to look further afield before their commercial reputation weakened. Davies was even more concerned when he found himself under financial threat from his former wife, Yvonne Gunner. Oddly, they had retained a joint checking account in New York from which Gunner withdrew $125,000. Davies responded indignantly by suing for $375,000, then there was a countersuit. By February 1985, newspaper reports estimated that she was suing Davies for between $4.5 and $5 million. In papers filed at Manhattan Supreme Court, she claimed that although Ray had offered assurances that he would "provide for me financially" he had failed to do so. In addition, he had allegedly "harassed and abused" her. Davies disputed the claim, insisting "I have paid defendant thousands of dollars since the settlement." The case came before Judge Bruce Wright, whose credentials had a fortuitous ring. After receiving his law degree, he had worked for the law firm Proskauer Rose, where he represented such jazz legends as Billie Holiday, Miles Davis, John Coltrane and Max Roach. However, his knowledge of the music business did not work to Davies' advantage. Surveying the evidence, he suggested that Ray had been "extraordinarily casual and negligent" about the joint account. He duly froze $62,500 of Yvonne Gunner's assets – half the amount she'd withdrawn, to which he said she was entitled – after which the case continued. In the end, a settlement was reached between the parties that was not made public. Gunner remains discreet and modest about her contribution to Ray's development in the Seventies. "I was a very small part of a very talented life."

Davies was disheartened by the mounting legal fees and felt obliged to point out how he had helped Gunner's budding career as a photographer by securing her access to rock concerts. He might have had a point if she had achieved wealth and fame as a rock 'n' roll snapper, but this was clearly not the case. Subsequently, she worked for several years as a photographer for Sygma News Agency, then established her own design company before working for the management consultant Stern Stewart & Co. Thereafter, she resumed her photographic career, but her clients were as far removed from the world of pop and rock as could be imagined. Her speciality was CEOs and later international political figures including presidents Bill Clinton and Nelson Mandela, US Deputy Secretary of State John Negroponte, Mayor of New York Michael Bloomberg and UN Secretary General Kofi Annan. If she learned anything from Davies, it was probably a keener understanding of the dual persona of the performer and the private man. "We all give out a persona to the world," she says. "That doesn't mean that's what we really are. We all have two sides, one we show to the world and one we keep to ourselves. I'm trying to bring the other side out in people."

Davies was also attempting to engage with the other side of his personality. Away from the legal wrangling and business deals, he was engrossed with his 27-year-old girlfriend. Patricia Crosbie seemed to bring out a sensitive nature so familiar in countless Davies' songs, but more rarely seen in his everyday encounters. His colleagues could not fail to be struck by the contrasts between his new love and recent partner. Whereas Chrissie Hynde had been volatile, outspoken and loud, Crosbie was mild-mannered, even-tempered and quiet. Even Dave Davies, a seasoned critic of wives and girlfriends, could find nothing wrong with his brother's latest choice. "I really loved Pat. I thought she was really a good person, but she got messed up by Ray in the end anyway." That, of course, was in the future. At this point, they still resembled love's young dream. In the past, Davies' workaholic tendencies had blighted relationships, but living with a ballet dancer almost made him appear lazy by comparison. Although Crosbie had not even started school when Davies formed the Kinks, their hit singles had been part of the soundtrack of her early life. The couple's backgrounds could hardly have been more contrasting and yet there were odd little similarities. They both came from large families – Pat was the fifth of eight children, with three elder sisters, Anne, Jean and Susan. Ray, who had been surrounded by older sisters since birth, could empathize. There was even a reverse symmetry in their father's respective names: Frederick George Davies and George Frederick Crosbie. Maybe something was written in the stars.

As summer approached, Dave Davies was keen for the Kinks to appear at the epochal Live Aid extravaganza scheduled for 13 July. Singer Bob Geldof had promised to assemble the cream of rock's commercial elite for a marathon twin concert in aid of Ethiopian famine to be televised simultaneously at London's Wembley Stadium and the JFK Stadium in Philadelphia. Dave, ever eager, rang the organization's office but was deflated to learn that they only wanted 'famous acts'. "I guess the Kinks just are not as big as the Boomtown Rats," Ray later quipped. Further humiliation followed when they learned that their immemorial rivals the Who were among the stellar cast list.

That same month, Arista issued the soundtrack to *Return To Waterloo* in America, but there was no outlet for the record in the UK. A big-screen version of the television programme was also shown at selected independent cinemas, but it was considered a bomb. Oddly, the accompanying album only featured eight songs, omitting 'Ladder Of Success' and 'Good Times Are Gone' which had been included in the film. Davies watched disconsolately as his prized project faded from memory. Without the Kinks' brand endorsement, sales had evidently suffered. Characteristically, Ray casually blamed his brother. "If he had worked with me on it, it would have been a *great* record, but he let me down."

Davies may have been fooling himself about the current viability of the Kinks. Back in Britain, it seemed their reputation had hit a new low. Response to Larry Page's advertisement in *Music Week* had been derisory. Nobody seemed interested. It was rather like travelling back to late 1963 before the Pye deal. Page's first port of call had been Polydor Records whose A&R representative curtly retorted: "We're not interested in geriatrics!" Virgin, usually a label with a fresh approach, seriously upset Davies by keeping him waiting in reception as if he was a novice in search of a deal. When he walked out in disgust, Page felt sympathy rather than frustration. "Ray, like all artistes, wants to feel that the company is one hundred per cent behind him and willing to show that in every way." Clearly, Virgin was neither. Hope was reignited when EMI International voiced interest but their reaction rapidly cooled after hearing the material that Davies presented. They passed, as did CBS. Perhaps the most jaw-dropping suggestion came from Phonogram. After listening to the latest compositions from a performer generally considered to be one of Britain's most accomplished songwriters, their representative took Page aside and impudently enquired: "Couldn't you get someone to work on the lyrics with Ray?" According to Page, the audacious suggestion was not as insulting or ignorant as it sounded. "The girl who said it was quite intelligent, and she wasn't talking rubbish. She actually told Ray and he took it very well, although we didn't do the deal. I knew then we had a tough job on our hands." The matter would remain unresolved for the remainder of the year.

With Mick Avory stripped of his partnership, the Davies brothers formed a new company, Kinks 85 Ltd, which Dave assumed would allow him greater power in the organization. Nevertheless, the shares were divided 60:40 in Ray's favour. Dave appeared to have little or no say in the pursuit of a new record label in America. That was left to Ray and Elliot Abbott. The younger brother's anger and frustration were manifest during a show at the West Point Military Academy on 21 September. It was the penultimate night of their US tour and insults were traded onstage with much finger pointing and snide asides between the brothers. Ray was so exasperated that he dropped his trousers and displayed his backside to the audience. Afterwards, Ray assaulted Dave in the corridor. "All of us heard it from the dressing room," Ian Gibbons recalls. "There was definitely a punch thrown. I was asked afterwards by Dave if Ray had said anything to me about it and I told him, 'No'. Dave seemed to think that Elliot was stirring stuff between them, but I don't know the outcome as the next day [at the end of tour party] everything was back to normal."

Although Dave hoped the Kinks might stay with Arista, MCA eventually won their hand with a substantial offer. A contract was signed in January 1986, the last meaningful act under Abbott's stewardship. "Elliot subsequently went into film music, quite successfully," Page reveals. With Abbott gone, Page had even greater responsibilities worldwide. Davies was still a free agent in the UK as the MCA deal only covered America. "We were trying to avoid the Arista problem and do a separate deal for Europe." Page quickly contacted MCA officials in London with the assertion: "We've done the deal with MCA America for the Kinks. Are you interested?" They acted as if they had never heard of the group. "It was pass, pass, pass – everywhere. We just couldn't get a deal going." Eventually, Page found a sympathetic voice at London Records, where Roger Ames – who fully understood Davies' importance as a songwriter – brokered a deal. "He was enthusiastic and London were a hot, energetic label at the time. It wasn't a silly advance but a substantial one and, if they did the job, they were in a position to recoup . . . I thought it was a good deal but, then again, I thought the Pye deal in 1964 was a good deal. It's relative. If you go to all the record companies and they pass and someone comes up with a deal, then, hey, it's a good deal!"

As Page well knew, Davies often prevaricated over contracts. Twenty-one years before, he had emptied a fountain pen of ink in a comic attempt to avoid signing a document. Now he was feeling under stress, not least, one assumes, due to the recent litigation with his former wife, Yvonne. As a result, the new agreement would not be signed until some months later. "I hate contracts of any kind," Davies admitted at the time. "And now record companies impose more restrictions than ever before – it's a labyrinth of do's and don'ts and reading page fifty-eight. You have to get out the manual just to make music. When I got out of college and went into rock 'n' roll, it meant freedom. Now it's an assembly line of musicians writing songs for their album commitments. Music should be art."

Page offered an alternative explanation. "He went to see a doctor. He had problems. It may have had to do with the contractual situation. He was told, 'If that's the way you feel you shouldn't really sign a contract', at which point, of course, he signed the contract." The whole affair sounded like another of Davies' whimsical dramas – or was it? "That boy doesn't miss a trick," Page laughed, clearly convinced that Ray was up to something. In his imagination, Page envisaged Davies placing the 'sick note' in a safe and later retrieving it in case he needed a get-out clause in the event of a renegotiation. That never happened, and may never have been Davies' intention, but Page was always cynical enough to assume that his charge had some devious plot in the back of his mind.

On 25 January 1986, Ray married Patricia May Eva Crosbie at Surrey South-Western Registry Office. There was mystery surrounding the event right up until the final moments. Family members were alerted but, as far as Page knew, it was simply a party in a Guildford pub. "But Ray doesn't do parties," someone said. Before long, rumours intensified that he really was planning a wedding celebration. "Well, don't buy a bloody wedding gift until you see the certificate," Page warned anyone in earshot, "otherwise he'll take away the presents, and that'll be it." Everyone was gathered in the pub when the couple arrived. "We've just got married," Ray announced. Page was amazed that they'd gone ahead without any of the family present. Ray explained that they had plucked a couple of witnesses from the street to complete the ceremony. The marriage certificate identified them as 'K. J. and B. C. Winn'. Page was even more astonished when Davies suddenly conjured a Danish pastry from his pocket, placed a small candle on top and put it on the table. "That was the wedding cake, I suppose! He then ordered a takeaway curry – and that was the wedding dinner."

Music was provided by the noted jazz pianist Bruce Boardman, who had once worked with the Davies brothers' guitar hero Tal Farlow, among many others. Also in attendance was clarinettist Terry Lightfoot, whose presence ensured that the band could play both jazz funk and "New Orleans stuff". According to Dave, his eldest son Simon joined in on drums, accompanied by Ray's daughter Viktoria (Tor) on vocals. A few days later the tabloid press learned of the wedding rumours and sought confirmation from Page who feigned ignorance. After investigating further, they discovered that the groom had married using the name 'Raymond Douglas'. The certificate confirmed his occupation as a musician, as opposed to 'Company Director' which he had used at his last wedding. The name change provided a funny story, which was trumpeted by the *Sun* as evidence of Ray's eccentricity. No further explanation was sought. Dave Davies never even bothered to speculate, let alone enquire, about his brother's name change. "I don't know. There came a point when I became immune to Ray's eccentricities. I wouldn't waste my energy on it." Larry Page was convinced that the newspaper had missed a more intriguing scoop. He suspected that Davies, still recoiling from his last settlement, may have chosen to marry under a different name as insurance against alimony in the event of divorce. Of course, this would never have worked in law. As a conspiracy theory, it was ultimately unconvincing. Page had been innocently unaware that Ray had already changed his name by deed poll a decade previously, just before he married Yvonne Gunner. He really *was* 'Raymond Douglas'.

Immediately after the wedding Davies began preparing demos for the next Kinks album. Soon after, the long-awaited *Absolute Beginners* was finally premiered. The film was almost universally panned by high-brow critics but received extensive publicity in the national press. Almost everyone agreed that Davies' role as the father was surprisingly impressive while his song 'Quiet Life' was an understated highlight of the soundtrack. In retrospect, it was regrettable that Ray was not featured more heavily in the film, although it is doubtful he wanted a major role. "They'd cut the dad's part down from the book. I took the part because it was pivotal to the book. So 'Quiet Life' was filmed months before the rest. I said, 'Once you've got the money, cut me out.' But because of contractual things, they had to include me. I went along and did a few other scenes, but I didn't enjoy it." One crucial scene that ended up on the cutting-room floor featured the song 'She's So Contrary' which Davies had written for the Max Miller character in the film who was to be played by Keith Richards. Unfortunately, that sequence was shelved, so Ray missed the chance to hear a Rolling Stone sing one of his compositions.

At the end of March, the Kinks reconvened at Konk to commence rehearsals for their first MCA album. It was a troubled time for the band, made worse by Davies' lack of new material. His head was still full of potential projects including a treatment for a movie based on his involvement with Hamilton King's Blues Messengers. Back in 1963, they had incorporated blues, ska and trad influences in a musical pot-pourri that was to be all but swept away by the beat boom. Whatever its merits as an idea, it remained undeveloped. While at Konk, Davies appeared distracted and unable to focus on the sessions. His insomnia was particularly bad at this time and the pressure of work merely increased his irascibility and tension. Page recalls seeing him chasing an engineer down the road at one point, hammer in hand. Evidently he was just letting off steam.

After several fruitless rehearsals, Davies reluctantly decided to take a break. Not for the first time, Larry Page was called upon to busy giddy minds with foreign quarrels. He persuaded the group to undertake a brief tour of Portugal and Spain, a trip intended to ease them back into working mode. Of course, it might also tear them apart. The Kinks had not played in Spain since the mid-Sixties so nobody could be sure precisely how audiences would react. If nothing else, it promised to be an adventure.

The tour proved more enjoyable and entertaining than expected. Nearly 3,000 people turned out for a show in Cascais, Portugal, where Davies played the showman, encouraging the crowd to sing along at every opportunity. The evening ended with a moving version of 'Waterloo Sunset'. Five gigs in Spain followed, two of which took place in bullrings. "You went down in the morning and the bulls were all on the job, mating," Page remembers. "Then they'd clear the ring and the concert went ahead in the afternoon." One performance, at La Maestranza in Seville, began dramatically when a truck entered the bullring to spray water on the ground to prevent dust from swirling around the arena. As it neared the stage, the vehicle became entangled with a cable connecting the mixing and lighting desks. Spectators watched in amazement as the driver inadvertently toppled a large spotlight from the tower while trying to break free. He then made a hasty exit before being collared by the lighting engineer. That show ended with the loss of a tour manager. "There was a punch-up and Ray whacked him one," Page remembers. "So we left without him."

The highlight of the tour was a performance at Madrid's prestigious San Isidro Festival. For the Davies brothers it must have seemed like a flashback to the mid-Sixties when singers and groups were constantly shuttled across Europe to appear at festivals alongside continental stars unknown outside their country of origin. Larry Page, of course, was more than familiar with the scene, having published a variety of minor European hitmakers, notably Los Brincos. Unlike the infamous US tour of 1965, Page's presence abroad eased everyone's nerves. During the soundcheck in San Sebastián, Davies persuaded his colleagues to play several Troggs songs, a mischievous reminder to Page of the group he had championed after the Kinks. "The funny thing was Ray had never mentioned the Troggs before. We'd never discussed it. And after the soundcheck, it *still* wasn't mentioned."

Davies added to the sardonic nostalgia by sending up Pete Townshend in an otherwise faithful version of 'My Generation'. The fun continued later when the support group Los Santos ended their set with a cover of 'Victoria'. The Kinks were in excellent form playing before such a large crowd of well-wishers. Their efforts might have reached an even wider audience but for Davies' strict stipulations. "The silliest thing of all was that Ray refused to allow the Kinks to be filmed because he wanted to own all the footage. Looking back, it must have been one of the greatest concerts they'd ever done". Overall, the Spanish sojourn provided a welcome opportunity for everyone to reconnect and the group went home satisfied, accompanied by some goodbye plaudits from the Barcelona press.

The Portugal/Spain tour revitalized the Kinks and they even agreed to travel overseas again for the Midtfyns Festival in Denmark. There they appeared on an incongruous bill alongside Jethro Tull, the Fall and the Dubliners. Davies seemed more positive, having alleviated his insomnia after consulting an acupuncturist. While discussing writing technique, his practitioner had suggested that he should visualize his thoughts. This rekindled the idea that all his work was essentially pictorial. That notion gave birth to the working title of a new album, *Think Visual*.

Davies was so carried away with his latest recording that he announced he was writing a book about the experience. He promised to analyse his ongoing conflict with Dave while detailing the growth of the new album from conception to completion. What possessed Ray to chronicle such a barren period in the Kinks' history remains a mystery. *Think Visual* was hardly likely to be another *Sgt Pepper's*, or even a *Village Green Preservation Society* or *Arthur* for that matter. When asked by one puzzled journalist why he felt this particular album deserved a book, Ray coyly changed the subject. Larry Page remembers the singer keeping a diary in which he surreptitiously wrote entries, none of which were revealed to anyone.

The release of *Think Visual* in November 1986 was a frightful anti-climax at a time when the Kinks urgently needed a high-quality record. In the past, a move to a new label meant a fresh and innovative approach, but *Think Visual* merely sounded like another average album. The dominant theme was the evils of a dehumanized, over-mechanized society in which people are robbed of the need to think or the ability to feel. Pop stars are reduced to factory fodder, city workers are portrayed as the "living dead", the urban unemployed are seen as lobotomized couch potatoes and virtually everyone else appears to be subject to mindless repetition. The sole victors in this bleak scenario are the video shop owner who offers instant gratification to the bored masses and a market-crazed merchandiser obsessively spouting slogans such as "better get computerized" and "think visual".

Overall, the album testified to Davies' disillusionment with the music business. The bitter 'Working At The Factory' acknowledged how pop music had provided hope in 1963, only to be corrupted by corporations that had turned musicians into assembly-line automatons. Similar sentiments were offered in the cynical title track. Having heard such tirades before, Larry Page was unconvinced by his charge's latest sentiments. "It's trendy to be bitter about the world. Ray's got nothing to be bitter about. He's a very wealthy man. But he's always been bitter – look at 'The Moneygoround'. The problem is: why is he bitter? There are people in the world starving and dying and there he is, a wealthy guy, who's professionally making money out of being bitter. It doesn't make any sense."

One of the grand ironies of *Think Visual* was that Davies approached the album very much like a market-minded corporate thinker. The production was calculatingly crisp and synth heavy as if in pursuit of a contemporary feel. Davies sounded oddly resigned when promoting the record. "My philosophy for this record was 'Nothing is as bad as I think it is.' That's what pulled me through it."

In many respects, *Think Visual* is even more acidic than *Lola Versus Powerman* . . . but less interesting as a document of its time, lacking the locale of Denmark Street and the familiarity of *Top Of The Pops* as touchstones. It includes some memorable melodies, notably 'How Are You?' and 'The Video Shop'. However, all too often Davies allows the work to subside beneath the weight of an extended metaphor on the iniquities of corporate power. Characterization is also worryingly sparse. Figures like the unnamed underachiever in 'Natural Gift', the unsketched video shop owner and the listless couple in 'Killing Time' seem even less defined than the minor pasteboard figures of the soap opera days. The album as a whole cried out for a more visualized character – a Walter, an Arthur, a Johnny Thunder, a Rosie Rooke – instead of portrayals of everyman as a factory employee. Davies might argue that this was the point of the album, but its abstractions, platitudes and musical lack of adventure make sometimes painful listening, even accepting possible ironic undertones.

The album's final track, 'When You Were A Child', a reflective comment on childhood innocence sung by Dave, stands in striking contrast to Ray's acerbic observations on modern life. If this suggested a cessation of hostilities, artistically or personally, then it was mere illusion. "I don't think it's been anything other than difficult," Ray said at the time. "But I have to do what I have to do creatively, and I can't let anyone lead their own creative life through me. It's not right. And I could never write with him. But he defines what I was after on this record, and he's an important part of it. It's a very hard relationship and I don't know how long it can go on professionally."

When riled, either brother could bite hard. They each knew the other's weak spots and there was little that was out of bounds when they were in full flow. Dave had successfully – inasmuch as such things are possible – compartmentalized his life so that he was seeing all his children. He would still visit Lisbet but was also a family man with Nancy. They now had two children, Daniel and Lana. Whether Ray envied or objected to his brother's domestic arrangements was difficult to ascertain, but he was not above using them as convenient weapons of abuse. When Nancy joined the tour, she became an easy target. "Ray could be a right arsehole," Larry Page says. "He used to call her everything. He'd say to Dave in front of her: 'Are you going home to the wife tonight, or are you going to stay with the slag?'" Perhaps he was taking psychic revenge, but such exchanges had a nasty, provocative edge that did not reflect well on anybody.

CHAPTER THIRTY-SIX

80 DAYS

Since his marriage to Patricia Crosbie, Ray Davies had spent much of his time living in the coastal town of Kinsale, 16 miles southwest of Cork. With a population only slightly over 2,000, the fishing port, with its Georgian terraces and medieval streets, was a favourite spot for wealthy tourists keen to sample its culinary treats. Although Davies sometimes craved the familiar bustle of a major city, he enjoyed his time in the 'Rebel County', frequenting pubs and listening to the conversations of the locals. People-watching remained both a favourite pastime and a continued inspiration for his songwriting. There were also some unintentionally comic moments, including a long-running dispute with a local builder that over-exercised Davies' indignation. He was also at loggerheads with his own solicitors about specific professional fees, the details of which remain privileged. In the background, of course, was the costly 'Yvonne Gunner business' which no doubt impacted on his spending habits.

Ray's thriftiness reached fresh heights of ingenuity during this time. While promoting *Think Visual*, he was adept at suddenly remembering he was supposed to buy some perfume or similar gift for his spouse. A record company representative would dutifully complete his shopping spree to keep him on schedule. The singer's 'forgetfulness' became a profitable trait. "He ended up with a load of presents from that," Page remembers. In New York restaurants, his wife was mortified by the looks or quips of disgruntled waiters indignant about the size of their gratuity. Page, of course, was well used to such behaviour. "If you were with him, he'd either lose the bill or make things so embarrassing that you'd pay. I remember him asking a waitress for a bill and she said, 'But I just brought you one!'" Ray was so proud of one scam that he could not resist revealing the trick to a journalist. "I was at an Indian restaurant, and I was seated in the corner and getting no service. So I started taking notes and later told the waiter I was the restaurant critic for *Time Out* magazine in London. They were very nice to me after that. In fact, I don't think I even paid the bill." At other times, he would play the poor mouth. Page always brought a winter coat to any meetings at Ray's home, ever aware that the radiators would probably be switched off. "When we were on tour abroad I remember Ray saying he was a travelling troubadour who lived out of a suitcase. He'd got a house in Effingham, a place in Ireland, two homes in London and another in New York!" In a questionnaire for *Q* magazine, the singer was asked to name his most unpleasant characteristic. "My generosity," he responded.

The Irish retreat enabled Davies to spend additional time on his latest project, a musical reimagining of Jules Verne's *Around The World In Eighty Days*. Canadian director Des McAnuff had originally been commissioned to adapt the work for the Radio City Music Hall, but they cancelled the undertaking. Undeterred, he extended the project into a full-scale musical, recruiting writer Barrie Keeffe, who suggested Davies as composer. The proposal appealed to McAnuff, once a member of the band Isaac, whose views on theatre were progressive and egalitarian. "In the Fifties when the American musical could have taken rock 'n' roll in, it made another choice. You got some brilliant people coming out of that like Stephen Sondheim. But musical theatre stopped producing songs on charts." McAnuff was a great proselytizer of theatre as popular art and had already worked with popular entertainers, most notably Roger Miller on the Tony Award-winning *Big River*. After his conversations with Keeffe, McAnuff was convinced that Davies could make a major contribution. He duly despatched a telegram asking: "Would you like to write a musical based on *Around The World In Eighty Days*? Broadway needs you."

At this point, Davies may well have felt that he needed Broadway too, but he was initially sceptical of the project. Never a fan of Jules Verne's book, he concluded, with good reason, that the travelogue would probably translate into a mediocre musical. In Ray's mind the book was inextricably linked with Michael Todd's 1958 film in which the suave David Niven plays the intrepid Phileas Fogg who, following a wager with the Reform Club, attempts to circumnavigate the world within 80 days. Twenty years before Todd's version, Orson Welles had produced an epic circus adaptation, while an earlier show in Paris had featured a live elephant. Coincidentally, after receiving the proposal for the Verne musical, Davies was also drawn to the idea of using circus elephants in a musical adaptation of *Babar The Elephant*. "From what I can gather the elephants were going to be talking and things like that," Larry Page confirms. "We had several meetings about it, but it went by the wayside."

Instead, Davies was drawn back to the Verne concept and rapidly changed his views about its merits after learning more of its sociological history from Des McAnuff. Verne's satire on English Victorian class mores appealed to Davies as he realized the script would enable him to compose songs that obliquely commented on the zenith of the British Empire. He then committed himself to the musical which would dominate his life for the best part of two years. No doubt in his mind it was an opportunity to return to the spirit of *Arthur Or The Decline And Fall Of The British Empire*, albeit from the standpoint of a Victorian.

In common with many musical productions, the newly titled *80 Days* suffered various delays, rewrites and negotiations. Eventually, competing commitments forced Keeffe to leave, but McAnuff persevered, bringing in another British playwright, Snoo Wilson, whose credits included *The Number Of The Beast* (the life and times of black magician Aleister Crowley) and *The Grass Widow* (a black comedy about Californian marijuana dealers). Keeffe's departure must have been a blow to Davies but he stuck with the project.

Davies was momentarily distracted by an American tour to promote *Think Visual*. The first leg of the itinerary concluded at New York's Beacon Theatre, followed by a party at the Hard Rock Café, with guests including Robert De Niro and Jeff Beck. Dave even donated a guitar for the patrons to hang on the wall.

After returning to the UK in April for an appearance on *The Tube*, the Kinks were soon back on the road, travelling across Germany before returning to the US for a summer tour. It was at this point that Ray fulfilled his ambition of introducing ballet into the Kinks' stage act courtesy of his wife, Patricia. Along with dancer Annie Cox, she incorporated 'It (I Want It)', a so-called 'rock ballet' into the set. Initially, Dave was aghast at the suggestion, while Larry Page also voiced concern. "It worried me when I saw the dancing segments in the middle of a heavy rock set. But, then again, if that's what Ray wants to do, that's what he does. He controlled the situation artistically. Pat was involved. Dave's attitude was 'If she dances past me, I'll whack her one.' But Dave always gets the short straw. The problem is that he's never consulted about things, and then they happen."

The other Kinks also had the dance segment thrust upon them, but dared not complain or express their reservations directly to Ray. "Everyone was a bit unsure of what it had to do with the Kinks," says Ian Gibbons. "When you're in our situation you accept what's going on and just do it. I remember Dave was not keen on the idea! He felt it was going back to the era when there were loads of brass players and backing singers onstage. He doesn't have fond memories of that. But it was something different and Ray's always been interested in putting theatre into the Kinks. I'd never experienced it before; it was all new to me. I didn't know how to take it, so I just kept my head down really, the same as Jim and Bob. We tried not to get involved in the inner politics. It wasn't anything to do with us anyway. That was between Ray and Dave."

As the tour progressed, the dancers were also featured on 'Clichés Of The World (B Movie)', 'Think Visual' and 'Welcome To Sleazy Town'. Dave resisted any temptation to 'whack' anybody largely, one suspects, because he was disarmed by Patricia Crosbie's sweet nature. "It's true that I didn't like 'It'," he admits, "but I really loved Pat." The feeling was reiterated by others on the tour, including Larry Page. "Pat's a nice girl," he confided at the time. "It must be very difficult for her being married to someone like Ray, but I think she's good for him. I don't know how much she can influence him, but she's there."

On 19 June, the Kinks appeared at Ontario's Kingswood Music

Theatre where they were greeted backstage by the spectral Peter Quaife. He was not invited to appear onstage but joined them back at the hotel for an evening of reminiscences and tall tales. Ray listened with amused detachment, never sure what to believe. Quaife regaled them with reports of his new life as an inventor, artist, ecologist and newspaper man. He claimed to have developed a technique by which he was growing tomatoes underground, something that he insisted would transform the food industry. "There was talk of him running a newspaper or the advertising section, but then it turned out to be a free paper," Gibbons remembers. Supposedly, he was contributing political cartoons or free-lancing as an airbrush artist, but nobody seemed entirely certain.

Quaife's history had become a life of fragments – a strange mixture of the prosaic and the fantastic. After his fairy-tale pop star marriage to Denmark's Annette Paustian, he was suddenly divorced and living in reduced circumstances in a bedsit. He stayed in Denmark, working sporadically as a freelance graphic artist, then met his wife-to-be, Hanne. In the spring of 1980, he popped up in London long enough to marry her. "Pete was working as a swimming pool attendant at the time," his brother reveals. Former drummer, John Start, who hadn't seen Quaife in years, was amazed to be asked to serve as his best man. They never saw each other again. The wedded couple swiftly relocated to Canada, initially living in Toronto and later in Belleville, where Quaife changed his name to 'Peter Kinnes', supposedly to avoid fans finding him in the phone book. This implausible justification disguised the truth – Kinnes was his actual birth name and his American serviceman father was still in North America some-where, which partly explained his destination. They never did reunite. There were extended periods where Quaife disappeared completely from everybody's narrative. His brother Dave recalls gaps of three years where there was no contact and he could not even be reached by phone. Then, he would suddenly reappear with only the vaguest of explanations. It was a familiar pattern that could be traced back to his split from the Kinks.

By July 1987, the Kinks had recorded enough concerts for Davies to piece together a live album. MCA were less than enthused by the suggestion, but reluctantly supported the idea. Ray, mean-while, retreated to New York's Alcott Hotel where, for the best part of two months, he collaborated with McAnuff and Wilson on the ongoing *80 Days*. The discipline stretched his abilities and adaptability as a composer, much to McAnuff's appreciation. "One reason Ray was such a good choice is that he's a master of hopscotching from genre to genre. He's very difficult to nail down. He's very comfortable taking marches and nineteenth-century music hall tunes and welding forms together. We really needed a composer who could go from Calcutta to Yokohama to America and be comfortable using period influences and still make it sound like contemporary music."

One crucial change in the musical was the imaginative introduction of Jules Verne as a character in his own drama. Wilson decided that Verne should function as an alter ego to Phileas Fogg, chasing his creation around the world and desperately attempting to complete the play within the 80-day deadline. "Our musical is about Jules Verne inventing the world," Wilson enthused. "It's the imagined voyage in his head. Verne is a character who's able to talk to the audience but is pursued by a typewriter on his journey. What he does is create his complete opposite. Verne is this housebound man running out of money with a family to support, who then creates this ramrod stiff, reticent, unattached, independently wealthy Englishman. The whole thing about masters and servants reversing roles is a Renaissance gag. Although Verne is actually making them up as they go along, none of the characters take him seriously."

The surreal touches and comedy of English manners appealed to Davies who was amazed how far the project had progressed from its prosaic beginnings. Using Verne as a character enabled him to employ his satirical pen to greater effect, although he remained faithful to the Victorian setting. "I wanted my score to establish a feeling of the time. There is Verne, who I see as a timeless character. He can sing anything in any style. But, basically, I didn't want British members of the court running around with electric guitars. The music had to serve the play – which is basically a period piece."

Ray's head was still spinning with ideas for *80 Days* as he travelled to Switzerland in September for a Kinks show with the Toy Dolls and Triffids. It may have been a lack of concentration that night that contributed to an unfortunate head injury. During the encore, an over-enthusiastic fan threw a Kinks' single onstage which he hoped Davies might sign. Instead, the disc sliced through Ray's scalp like a parodic imitation of Avory's high-hat cymbal in the 1965 Cardiff story. Fortunately, Davies was not seriously hurt and after receiving several stitches took the plane back to London.

During November, Ray returned to New York to undertake more work on *80 Days* and complete some remastering for a live album intended for the Christmas market. It was a troubled time for the Davies brothers as their 82-year-old mother had recently undergone a stomach operation at Archway's Whittington Hospital to arrest the advance of a cancer that ultimately proved inoperable. She was looked after by her daughter Gwen and son-in-law Brian at the house in Fortis Green. Dave and his ex-wife Lisbet were among the visitors, along with several other family members. There was a degree of resentment from some quarters at Ray's seeming reluctance to leave New York and attend her bedside, but he remained in regular telephone contact and, according to Dave, wrote a moving letter testifying to her enormous impact on his life. Annie was thrilled by the missive, but also concerned for the future of her younger son, who seemed almost naively perplexed by her misgivings. "I should have listened to my mum. Three weeks before she died she said to me, 'Make sure you get something for yourself because your brother's never going to help you.' I was thinking, 'We're family, we look after each other.' But I don't think that now."

Ray learned of his mother's death on 23 November and made immediate arrangements to fly back to London the following day for the funeral. He provided a eulogy which even Dave acknowledged as being exceptionally powerful and poignant. Interestingly, Annie chose 'My Way' as her funeral anthem in preference to one of Ray's songs. He had half expected to hear 'Waterloo Sunset'.

After the funeral, the brothers lost themselves in work. The Kinks continued touring Europe in December 1987 when *Live – The Road* was issued in Germany. The album was an adequate representation of the group's current live set but nothing more. Essentially, it was aimed at die-hard fans or those in search of a concert souvenir. At least it enabled Davies to include the theatrical 'It' on a Kinks album, plus the studio-recorded title track, a jaundiced mini-history of the group. It was intended that the album would be issued in various territories at precisely the time the Kinks arrived on tour. Predictably, that plan would soon be scuppered by unforeseen events.

After Germany, the Kinks made a once in a lifetime appearance in Italy, where they played the Rolling Stone Club in Milan on 13 December. Their equipment had to be driven from Austria, but the roadies arrived punctually only to find that they could not gain access to the venue. "There was a kids' disco in the place," Ian Gibbons recalls. "It was totally sold out, but we weren't allowed to take equipment in until the evening and couldn't go on till late. There was a lot of hanging around. We never went back to Italy again. I wonder why."

Five days before Christmas, the group appeared at London's Town and Country Club where they were videoed by MTV. As a festive treat, Mick Avory was invited to appear on drums for 'A Well Respected Man'. All went well, but the following day Davies felt ill. Over the Christmas holidays, his condition worsened. He complained of chest pains and initial reports erroneously suggested that he had collapsed from a heart attack. It was not that serious but he did require an angiogram. A small blood clot was discovered and he was told that his arteries would have to be cleared immediately.

The prospect of a genuine heart attack was increased when Ray realized that if he stayed in England much longer he would forfeit his status as a tax exile. This so terrified him that he decided to leave his sick bed and fly to Ireland. Aer Lingus employees were intrigued by the sight of Davies in a wheelchair, covered in blankets with his face hidden behind a large hat. "It was so over the top he only drew attention to himself," one steward noted. Ray had hoped to avoid press attention but his driver, Terry Draper – who had previously worked for high-profile comedian Jim Davidson – was a familiar face to tabloid reporters. "When Terry got on the plane, the press were onboard," Larry Page remembers. "They knew that all they had to do was follow him to find Ray, so there was a lot of chasing around."

There were also some priceless quotes. Ray's mother-in-law Joan Crosbie summed up the melodrama in an unintentionally comic remark that betrayed her son-in-law's true priorities: "It was serious enough having a heart attack, but the thought of being thumped with a massive tax bill while lying in hospital meant he had to get out of Britain very quickly."

Having successfully escaped the claws of the taxman, Davies was happy enough to be taken to Dublin's Blackrock Clinic where he reportedly underwent an operation for both a blood clot and fluid on his lungs. Other journalists were deflected by euphemistic explanations of 'exhaustion' or 'bronchitis'. These sounded credible enough considering his work rate. While Ray lay in a hospital bed, Dave sent a message – tellingly through an intermediary – stating that he would happily agree to the dissolution of the Kinks if his brother wanted to quit. Ray made light of the suggestion and promised to be back on tour by the spring. His stay in hospital at least provided an unexpectedly erotic moment. "I thought it was amazingly sexy on the life support machine watching these nurses. It's the way they move, they don't have restraints."

While Ray was convalescing at his in-laws' home in Cork, two of his old songs unexpectedly hit the UK charts. The Stranglers' faithful reworking of 'All Day And All Of The Night' and the Fall's similarly orthodox reading of 'Victoria' indicated that there was still a market for his classic compositions. Exploiting newer material was more problematic, a point underlined by the January release of the Kinks' live album in America. With the group unavailable for promotion, its appearance was a wasted opportunity. By the time they rescheduled their tour for late March, the album was consigned to history. It was not released in the UK until as late as May and its impact was again negligible. Davies was deflated but appeared to take some pleasure from driving record and television companies to distraction. MTV had been keen to screen the pre-Christmas show at the Town and Country Club, but could not persuade Ray to sign a waiver agreeing to its broadcast. After perusing the document, he took exception to the wording and insisted on drafting an alternative. "He wrote his own and then, of course, he refused to sign that," laughs Larry Page. As a result, the MTV film was never shown.

By the spring of 1988 it was painfully clear that Davies had lost faith in his record company. The disappointing reception afforded *Think Visual*, the live album fiasco and the tiring touring schedule made him again consider whether it was worth persevering with the Kinks. "I didn't think that physically I could go on," he says. "We were scheduled to do a tour and it was post-poned because I got sick and so the whole emphasis was on going through the motions. I did the best I could, but I didn't believe in the tour and I didn't want to go through that again." *The Road* tour crawled towards its conclusion in June with a handful of UK dates and a couple of festival appearances in Denmark. The shows in England were poorly publicized and passed virtually unnoticed by critics. If these were to be the last ever performances by the group it seemed that few cared.

The Kinks had lost the power to invest drama into their longevity. Minus a hit single or top-quality album, their appeal seemed limited to a golden age past. Countless mid-price compilation albums reinforced that notion, particularly in the UK. Their reputation had cemented into apathy. Unlike the Who or the Rolling Stones, a world tour would not be seen as some last hurrah. Their stature had been insidiously reduced by their very availability and even their illustrious history had not proven potent enough to receive an invitation to appear at Live Aid, thereby depriving them of global attention.

What Davies urgently required was a new challenge to arrest the stagnation. His plight was not made easier by continued uncertainty about the group's future. "We were always available for the Kinks," recalls Ian Gibbons who, like the other subsidiary members, was kept on a retainer. "But there were long blank periods of not knowing what was going on. We weren't involved in the business end of the Kinks, so it was a bit frustrating because we didn't know what was going to happen next. There's nothing worse than sitting around waiting for the phone to ring."

Increasingly, Ray Davies sought fulfilment away from the Kinks, but still lacked the confidence to surrender the brand name. By the summer of 1988, he was back in New York sifting through various film treatments. These included *Medication Abuse In Middle America* (a black comedy detailing drug usage in America), *Playing The Crowd* (a musical about the music business) and *Man Of Aran* (a thriller about an IRA man on the run, with a title inspired by Robert Flaherty's celebrated 1934 documentary, but a plotline reminiscent of Carol Reed's 1947 film, *Odd Man Out*). Like so many of Davies' plans, these projects did not reach the screen. What he was experiencing was the perennial frustration of the film-maker: the shelved project. For a composer used to seeing his ideas immediately translated into recorded performance it must have been particularly tough to witness enthusiastic ideas defeated by sudden reversals of policy or financial obstacles.

One dream that was finally realized was the staging of *80 Days* which opened at San Diego's La Jolla Playhouse on 28 August for a six-week run. The show received cautious commendation but critics were in universal agreement about its vitality. With 400 costume changes, 173 masks and 40 scene changes, the musical had the power to dazzle. As a spectacle it was impressive, but some commentators detected bathos beneath the bombast. One critic nearly fell over himself with praise before readjusting his critical spectacles for a telling observation: "*80 Days* is a dizzy, complex, glittering pageant of stagecraft, an encyclopaedia of tricks and gimmicks, a fancy mechanical marvel in the spirit of Verne's own baroque sense of technology. The trouble is that there's no soul to the show."

What Davies brought to the musical was many years of working in the constantly mutable arena of popular music. Although the Kinks had never been the most self-consciously experimental of groups among the pop elite, they had straddled various musical genres and delved heavily into music hall and Variety during their long career. The ever-changing geographical locations in *80 Days* provided a grand challenge to Davies who was called upon to introduce a similarly eclectic range of styles with show tunes embracing pop, rock, ragtime and even a touch of raga. For avid Davies followers there were subtle comparisons to be made between the songs in *80 Days* and several familiar Kinks songs. The title 'Well Bred Englishman' obviously recalled 'A Well Respected Man', although the satire was necessarily more exclamatory in tone with a mock jingoism that perfectly fitted the plotline. 'It Could Have Been Him' was reminiscent of 'She Wore A Hat Like Princess Marina', a slight song that betrayed clear music hall echoes. Davies even returned to the spirit of *Muswell Hillbillies* for the country-tinged 'A Place In Your Heart'. The plaintive 'Be Rational' was another of Ray's more vulnerable songs, while 'Let It Be Written' with its fear of the empty page, echoed the songwriter's own neurosis. Despite the Victorian setting, 'Just Passing Through' sounded daringly modern with a brooding, synth backing and a cutting lyric about 'poverty tourism'. Other songs suffered some of the weaknesses associated with his Seventies' theatrical efforts. While *80 Days* had its share of functional singalongs, these were arguably necessary in a carefully structured theatrical format. Davies was never likely to produce a song of the transcendent power of 'Waterloo Sunset' in such circumstances, although that was the ultimate challenge for a writer of great musicals.

Regional critic Gregory Sandow politely concluded that "Davies is, by Broadway standards, an amateur lyricist . . . as a composer he's modestly professional at best." Despite these shortcomings, and doom-laden scepticism that the musical could never reach Broadway, Sandow acknowledged: "The music does have one great virtue. When it works, it's clear, concise and never strays from its point. The songs come at infallibly right moments too, a success I'd credit jointly to all three collaborators, and which is rarer than anyone who hasn't examined dozens of failed musicals might imagine."

Davies remained hopeful, if not confident, that *80 Days* would play in New York and continued reworking the musical over the next year. Along the way there were rumours of possible runs in San Francisco, Hollywood and Portland but, as the months and years passed, such promises grew thinner. In the end, *80 Days* was akin to another great unrealized project, heard by few, appreciated by fewer. It left several memorable songs lost to history. As a final, unintended rebuff to Davies, director Des McAnuff went on to achieve Broadway success working with Pete Townshend on a new $6 million production of *Tommy* which won five Tony Awards.

CHAPTER THIRTY-SEVEN

THE WHIP HAND

Ray Davies began 1989 back at Konk Studios where work was progressing on another Kinks record. He spoke enthusiastically about a new song 'The Million-Pound Semi-Detached', a mild satire on the Eighties property boom. He had intended to develop the lyric into a film script but now it was to be the backbone of the album. Sessions for the track proved interminable with Gibbons and Henrit endlessly reprogramming a drum machine set against a keyboard accompaniment. "That's how Dave heard it and he wasn't impressed," Gibbons recalls. "It was getting more and more tense and I felt fried. I don't know whether Ray was going to use a drum machine on the final track but he wanted it to be like New Order. It was still a Kinks/Ray Davies song, but he felt a different approach might make it harder." Dave was not the only person to dismiss the song outright. MCA also failed to discern its charm and the song was eventually removed from contention, unheard by most fans until its appearance on *The Songs Of Ray Davies* in 1997.

As preliminary work continued on the new album, relations between the brothers worsened. Dave showed little enthusiasm for the new material and felt both frustrated and angry with his current status in the band. Not for the last time, Ray also showed scant interest in his songwriting contributions. The younger brother was currently enthusing about a new song, 'Perfect Strangers', which was near completion. "It meant a lot to me, Ray knew that. I went away for the weekend when he was mixing, but came back early. The engineer played me the mix and I realized Ray had taken out great chunks of my guitar playing." In despair, Dave accused his sibling of acting like a vampire. "How am I supposed to express myself when all you do is take my energy?" he implored. "What do you want?" If Dave's memory is correct, then Ray's response reached new levels of haughtiness. "He said, 'I can do what I want because I'm a *genius*.' I said 'You're not a genius, you're an arsehole.'" The verbal sparring ended in a fistfight which spread to the roof of the studio. Their loyal road manager Ken Jones, who had been in the front line of countless disputes over the years, attempted to intervene, but ended up in tears. "I've never seen two human beings go at each other like that," he said.

The toxic atmosphere soon spread to more sensitive souls. Even their easy-going keyboardist Ian Gibbons could not escape the fallout from this latest flare-up. At the end of March, he informed Ray that he was leaving. "It was getting too much. The tension gets on top of you after a while. You try and keep an even keel and not bring all that crap home with you. But the album was very hard work and we were taking a lot of time to do things. I didn't feel as if I was wanted. It's difficult to take sides [with the brothers]. You never knew what the conflict was *really* about. I knew Dave wasn't happy and at that point I felt I was in the middle of the argument. Ray wrote me a letter asking me to reconsider and I replied saying I wasn't comfortable, that I'd been offered other work and felt the need to take it. I couldn't do it any more, so I stopped. I needed a break! When they finally put the album out they didn't credit me, but I couldn't give a toss at the time."

Such sentiments were all too familiar to Larry Page, who had witnessed more conflict in the Kinks' career than any reasonable person could stomach. Within days of Gibbons' departure, he also took his leave. Predictably, it was another financial argument that caused the rift. Page had recently negotiated a £50,000 advance from Penguin Books for the first volume of Davies' memoirs. After the deal was struck, Ray disputed his manager's commission claiming that there had been an earlier discussion about the book prior to his involvement. In the end, Page was so disgusted by what he regarded as Ray's parsimony that he declined to continue.

The argument over commission was the catalyst, but it was clear that their business relationship had already run its course. "I couldn't do anything for him," Page admits. "We didn't have any contracts. We'd agreed at the start that if it didn't work out that we would just shake hands and that would be it. We met for coffee one morning and agreed it wasn't working. If people don't want to work or are not creating material that you think is doing the job then you're just hitting your head against a brick wall. Plus, I don't need to argue over silly deals. It's very difficult. I set up that Penguin deal, got £50,000 up front and he didn't want to give me anything!"

For his part, Davies later observed that Page was still playing the archetypal parental manager who always needed to be in control. "He's right," Page admits. "I can't really change. I am what I am. I really believe that if somebody phones you and says, 'We want the Kinks for this show', you have to say, 'You got 'em!' The minute you say, 'I'll speak with the band' – you've got problems. If you phone Ray he'll say, 'Have a word with Dave' and if he's up for it it'll be, 'No, I don't fancy doing it', and you're in the middle of the thing." Even after announcing his departure, Page would still find himself involved in the psychodramas for several months more as tensions between the brothers escalated.

With a German tour forthcoming, the Kinks urgently required a new pianist. Tour manager Ken Jones found a promising candidate in Mark Haley. A former solo artiste with RCA, Haley was something of a journeyman, having played with Billy Fury just prior to his death and, more recently, with the Monkees on their comeback tour. He arrived after the new album was completed but was allowed to add keyboards to 'Down All The Days'. He quickly learned never to take the Kinks on trust when the German tour was abruptly cancelled.

Larry Page's final actions as Kinks' manager involved helping Dave, rather than Ray. The younger brother had run into money problems, which would worsen over the succeeding months. With his numerous family commitments, he suddenly found himself stretched financially and under scrutiny from the tax authorities over liabilities of which he was unaware. There was even the looming threat of bankruptcy. According to Page, Ray's reaction was phlegmatic to the point of cruel. "I think that would be good for Dave," he allegedly said, adding that it might teach him a valuable lesson. More than anything, Dave needed songwriting income, so it came as a double blow when he learned that two of his compositions – 'Bright Lights' and 'Perfect Strangers' – had been removed from the track listing of their forthcoming album. Violence erupted in a London hotel over the weekend of 24–25 June, culminating in another fraternal fistfight. On this occasion, even Dave was convinced that the Kinks were dead. He phoned the recently estranged Larry Page, asking "What are we going to do?"

"We'll do what we always do when this happens," Page counselled. "Nothing. Ray always leaves before the release of a new album. Just wait and see." Page was correct. Tempers cooled and a compromise of sorts was reached. Dave's two compositions were not included on the vinyl version of the new album, but were tagged on to the end of the CD release. At least it improved his revenue stream. Eventually, Dave would appoint a financial adviser, sell some real estate and various valuable artefacts, including, several years later, a rare Bo-Weevils acetate from 1963. It proved enough to keep him solvent.

Although the new album was still several months away from release, Ray undertook some promotion during July. His timing was opportune as Kirsty MacColl's striking version of 'Days' was currently scaling the UK charts. During his round of press interviews, Davies revealed that he was working on another television script based on events leading up to the death of his mother. It was to be titled *Breakfast In Berlin*. The project sounded intriguing but, once again, little more was heard of it after this point. Music press readers could be forgiven for feeling even more sceptical about *Goodbye Pork Pie Hat*, a documentary about the life of Charles Mingus. On this occasion, though, Davies' perseverance was rewarded and the programme went into production early the following year. "Mingus was an insomniac, and so am I, which is possibly why he had so many problems," Davies observed. The film was finally screened in the summer of 1993 under the title *Weird Nightmare* with guest appearances from several prestigious names, including Keith Richards, Charlie Watts and Elvis Costello.

During autumn 1989, the Kinks were due to set out on an extensive US tour. Ray was less than entranced by the prospect and spoke with a jaundiced air, which suggested that he might have been better advised to stay at home. "With this new tour, I might not be able to do the first few shows, because it will be a miracle to get onstage at all. Not because we can't play, but there are a few problems I want to work out with the guys. As we go through the tour I hope to evolve new things like I did with the ballet 'It' . . . I'd like to take six months off and work on a whole stage show." This was less than encouraging news for the other Kinks, but they had long since learned not to take Davies' protestations too seriously. When he coyly added, "I'd like to do an album of instrumental music," it was quite likely that he was targeting Larry Page, who had done precisely that with the orchestral *Kinky Music*. He also found time to attack some familiar rivals. "Putting out a record involves a thought process. It's not a gift from heaven. For twenty-five years, the Kinks have done that work and consistently supported our records with tours. Then I realize the Who are touring without a record – and the Rolling Stones only have one because they'd lose millions without it. To me, these aren't really bands at all any more. The essence of the Who died with Keith Moon. To my mind, the Who are a support act to us like they were twenty-five years ago when they were still called the High Numbers."

The tour eventually opened on 9 September at the Mann Music Center in Philadelphia. Even before the Kinks set foot onstage the event was rendered a fiasco. Their album was still not available and would remain unreleased until after the tour had been completed. To make matters worse, Castle Communications, which had acquired a sizeable chunk of the Kinks' back catalogue, chose this very moment to issue a well-publicized compilation, *The Ultimate Collection*. The Kinks found themselves in the unenviable position of promoting old product while their new work remained unheard. The final insult for Davies was hearing someone from MCA's marketing department suggest, "Maybe we should come out on the back of the Castle record." As he wearily concluded, "That's how much belief they had in the album." It was all too reminiscent of similar instances at Pye when back-catalogue compilations watered down the impact of several major Kinks albums.

Despite recent problems, Ray avoided any serious conflict with his brother on tour, but still felt their relationship was strained. "He plays the same tricks. People don't lose those fundamental things they've always had. It saddens me a bit when the same tricks start going down, and it's ten or twenty years later." At least Dave had come to terms with playing the balletic 'It', despite his previously violent objections. Perhaps he saw divine retribution at work in Binghamton, New York, when 'It' was followed by a fire in the auditorium. Nearly 3,000 fans were evacuated after an overloaded circuit box ignited. The fire was rapidly quenched but it took one and a half hours to clear smoke from the gymnasium. Outside the venue, the crowd grew irritable, and police were called to restore order. After 11 p.m., the doors reopened and the Kinks returned for a 30-minute set which was greeted with a mixture of enthusiasm and relief. The group included a new song 'Aggravation', an appropriate summation of the evening's entertainment. 'You Really Got Me' ended the show at the stroke of midnight.

The tardy new album *UK Jive* finally received a transatlantic release in October 1989. Like most Kinks' records from this period it was patchy overall, but Davies still managed to include some of his better pop melodies as timely reminders of a once supreme songsmith. 'Down All The Days (Till 1992)', easily the best Kinks' single since 'Do It Again', took its title from Christy Brown's evocative autobiographical novel, but the song was not about Ireland but, rather, a celebration of impending European unity. Davies' exultant vocal, prefaced by the pealing of bells (a reminder to old fans of 'Big Black Smoke') and cheering crowds was arguably his most positive statement of the decade. Its strength was matched by 'Loony Balloon', a complex composition full of downbeat social observations rescued by a rousing chorus. Both its theme and title clearly echoed the subject matter of *80 Days*, indicating a more disciplined approach to songwriting, typical of his industrious working relationship with Des McAnuff over recent years. Davies cutely played the Swinging Sixties card to ambivalent effect, where necessary. The title track was the catchiest song on the album, laced with doo-wop harmonies and an *Alfie*-influenced cockney accent, complete with austerity era references to the 'tallyman' and the 'never never'. It even closed with a snatch of the Who's 'My Generation', accompanied by distinctive Beach

Boys-inspired vocals. 'War Is Over' (with its John Lennon-inspired title) was a pretty Beatle-influenced tune redolent of past glories. 'Aggravation', by contrast, was a more formulaic number, whittled down from a 15-minute Daveathon guitar workout. In common with previous one-word diatribes like 'Pressure' and 'Repetition' it veered towards the histrionic.

The remainder of *UK Jive* was structurally sound. At its centre were three more Davies meditations: 'How Do I Get Close' (decrying designer feelings); 'Now And Then' (a solo piece thematically reminiscent of 'God's Children') and 'What Are We Doing?' (a rhetorical reflection on ecology with a synthetic brass band accompaniment). The sole oddity was 'Entertainment', a lumpy outtake from *Give The People What They Want* which sounded strangely out of place. The CD closed with three Dave Davies compositions, as if Ray could not bear to see them attached to the main body of the album. 'Dear Margaret' damned the Prime Minster while commenting on her enigmatic sexual attraction. 'Bright Lights' was a predictable hard-rock workout while 'Perfect Strangers', the best of the three, was probably worthy of the fistfight that had secured its inclusion. By detaching these songs, Ray had effectively created a distinctive mini-album for fans of his brother's work. It was evidence enough of their separation throughout this period.

The ructions of the previous year caught up with the Kinks on *UK Jive*. Its untimely arrival, over halfway through an American tour, derailed effective promotion. As the weeks passed, any lingering hopes of a breakthrough were quashed. In the end it stiffed at number 122 in the US album charts, faring even worse than *Think Visual*. "I don't think *UK Jive* was given a fair shot," Davies complained, not entirely unreasonably. "The problem is the music industry has this terrible two-week cycle. If you don't get airplay within two weeks, all the record company people lose confidence. They have to keep their BMWs on the road and they think, 'Oh, we'd better move on to something else.' It was a huge disappointment to me what happened to that record. I'm very proud of some of the songs on it. It could've knocked me sideways and stopped me wanting to work in the music industry ever again."

Davies was not exaggerating. By the end of 1989, rumours

were circulating that he was on the brink of dissolving the Kinks. The commercial failure of *UK Jive* appeared to make all effort purposeless. Instead of promoting the album in the UK, Davies fell into a maudlin slump. His troubled state of mind was revealed in the tabloid press where, uncharacteristically, he opened up about his feelings for his 'lost' daughter Natalie, who had remained with Chrissie Hynde after their breakup. "I was never even daddy to her," Davies reflected, in a series of mawkish asides. "I only saw her for about eighteen months then I was given the option of being a weekend parent . . . I know it's accepted now as part of the modern world we live in. But you can't change the natural instincts of a child simply because society now accepts it. So I thought it was better not to see my daughter at all. I felt I had to make that choice . . . I've really been disturbed by it all. I don't think I'll ever recover. I used to wonder all the time what she was doing and it nearly drove me mad. Now I just hope she's happy. If you can't actually be with the person you love, at least you can wish them happiness wherever they are." Whether this was chocolate box sentimentality or a genuine cry of anguish was difficult to ascertain. Reminded of his current happy marriage and the prospect of further children, he added, only partly in jest, "I'd like to have a boy play cricket for England."

The Kinks concluded the decade with a short tour of Germany. Four days before Christmas, they appeared at the Nuremberg Jurahalle. It was a sad spectacle. Here they were, one of the most important and celebrated groups of their era, playing in a spartan, non-seated venue with a capacity of 2,200. Drenched with rain and suffering from flu, Davies cheered himself up by running through some old favourites during the soundcheck, including the Crickets' 'That'll Be The Day', Duane Eddy's 'Ramrod' and Don Gibson's 'Sea Of Heartbreak'. Against the odds, the evening performance went well, but afterwards Ray hinted that there was "nowhere else to go". He seemed to be drifting with each successive performance, sometimes staying up till 6 a.m. drinking beer. "Drink a lot and try not to get too much sleep" was his perverse motto for survival. He brightened somewhat when talk moved to the Kinks' forthcoming induction into the Rock 'n' Roll Hall of Fame. "We've never won anything in our lives," he said, wistfully. If nothing else, the ceremony was something to look forward to in the New Year. It might even provide the opportunity for another relaunch.

Since the departure of Larry Page, Davies had been without a manager which partly explained his deteriorating relationship with MCA. An intermediary was clearly necessary and there were at least two candidates. Gene Harvey, who represented Whitney Houston, impressed Dave Davies when they met for a cordial meal in New York. The manager even complimented him on his song 'Perfect Strangers'. That may have been enough to dissuade Ray who ultimately appointed Kenny Laguna, a former member of Tommy James & The Shondells, who would last for less than a year. In the background was the forlorn figure of Ken Jones who must by now have realized that he would never be trusted or respected enough to rise above the lowly position of tour manager. Like Mick Avory, years before, he was regularly threatening to hand in his notice, only to be reined back at the last moment. At the worst of times, he suffered the whip hand of Ray Davies whose haughty pronouncements resembled those of some medieval prince. One handwritten letter concluded with the imperious demand: "I would like to have some sort of explanation to your decision to say that you were 'quitting' . . . You knew that I had been seriously ill . . . and yet you failed to respond to my telephone calls for over a week which caused me unnecessary stress at a time when my doctors were telling me to rest."

On 17 January 1990, the Kinks were inducted into the Rock 'n' Roll Hall of Fame at New York's Waldorf Hotel by Graham Nash. The former Hollie recalled the landmark 1964 package tour when they had first met, then acknowledged their achievements, adding: "They were from the street and that's where their fans live and breathe." Dave then took the stage, complaining that it was difficult to read his brother's writing on a prepared script. "Don't fuck up," Ray chided, while Nash pleaded: "I don't want to see the brothers fighting again". "Speak, dummy, speak!" Ray told his brother, who responded, "Thanks for the award – we really do deserve it!"

Although hunting jackets might have been appropriate garb for the occasion, the Kinks favoured the standard tuxedo and dinner jacket. Davies, who had to be coaxed from his room by new manager Kenny Laguna, expressed his reservations in a sparky acceptance speech. "My name's Ray Davies and I'm the Beatle of the group," he began. He then read what sounded like a fictitious memo supposedly sent to the A&R department of Pye Records just before the release of 'You Really Got Me': "This is the third release by the Kinks on our label and as you know sales of the first two records failed to live up to expectations. We all know that the Kinks are a very unique band but are difficult to promote. I recommend that if this new Kinks record is not a success that we drop the Kinks from our label and not renew our option."

After winning a laugh from the crowd, he continued: "This is a very posh event and we're all tarted up to be here tonight. I'm looking at the picture on the wall over there of the Kinks and we're still wearing the same band suits. We're a very thrifty band. We had to be." Downplaying his creativity, he noted: "I just wrote lyrics to get out of the house and get out of college and make a living . . . and seeing everybody here tonight, it makes me realize that rock 'n' roll has become respectable. What a bummer." Reflecting on his American experience, he concluded: "I was very intimidated by this country but now I've learned to admire these very strange people that eat pizza and pump iron. I wanted to serve my country as a musician. I don't think it would have been possible if it hadn't been for America because it was this country that realized you could build a career on rock 'n' roll whereas in England it was just disregarded. So that's why I'm here tonight, not for the so called respectability, because [to] anyone who knows anything about us that would be a joke . . . More than anything else I'm dressed in this ridiculous way for my fans who stayed with the Kinks when our records sold twenty-five thousand copies." At that point he tore up the paper containing his speech. Unable to resist some last-minute humour at his former drummer's expense, he quipped: "And if they need any help building the Rock 'n' Roll Hall of Fame in Cleveland, Mick Avory's not doing anything. He's quite good with the bricks. Thanks a lot. Good on you, America, and keep it going for another twenty-five years."

Davies no doubt had mixed feelings about his once great rivals the Who, themselves inducted by U2 later that evening. Ray praised them in his speech while reminding the world that they had once been a support act to the Kinks when performing as the High Numbers. His kindest words were reserved for Keith Moon, "the

craziest drummer I ever saw" who "changed the sound of drumming". When the Who played 'Substitute' and 'Won't Get Fooled
Again', Dave joined in, but his brother was not around. Ray's
sole musical concession to the evening was an all-star jam with
the Kinks, Sting and Rickie Lee Jones on a medley of 'You Really
Got Me', 'Mack The Knife' and 'Set Me Free'. Thereafter, he was
conspicuous by his absence.

The Kink who hogged the limelight was erstwhile bassist Pete
Quaife. At one point it seemed unlikely that he would attend, but
he was persuaded to accept his place in rock history by long-time
Kinks fan Doug Hinman, who even paid for his rented tuxedo.
Quaife brought a touch of the old Kinks' truculence to the proceedings. At the end of his brief speech, he complained, "I just have
one question. What kept you?" Perhaps he failed to realize that
you have to wait 25 years to be elected into the Hall of Fame.
Unlike Ray, Quaife was not put off by the presence of the Who.
During the grand finale, he turned to John Entwistle, looked at
his bass guitar, and cheekily exclaimed: "Why don't you give that
to a real bass player?" As Quaife remembered: "That really pissed
him off."

For the rest of the evening, Quaife was seldom absent from the
television cameras. He even took mischievous pleasure in
attempting to upstage several stars, including Bruce Springsteen.
During a shaky version of 'Substitute', Quaife deliberately whispered the wrong chords to his new partner just to watch the
calamity. After the Who's set, Quaife was still locked beside
Springsteen for a version of 'Long Tall Sally' and was there again
alongside Dave backing Simon & Garfunkel on 'The Boxer'. For
a guy who had walked away from pop music two decades before,
it was quite a comeback.

"It was funny," Dave remembers. "Pete was exactly the same.
He was playing guitar with Springsteen and it wasn't even plugged
in. I could still sense that same spirit that we had when we first
started."

The other big surprise of the evening was the emergence of
Mick Avory as an orator of beguiling charm. Among the speech-
makers, it was Avory who provided the witty rejoinders and
self-effacing asides, pointing out that he had turned down a function at his golf club to attend the ceremony. He seemed far more

relaxed than either of the Davies brothers and revealed a knowing irony that signalled him out as the perfect host for any future Kinks convention.

A surprise guest among the retinue was Jim Rodford, whom Avory had invited using his absent wife's ticket. Although he did not appear onstage, Rodford was thrilled by the occasion during which he met Gerry Goffin, Carole King, Springsteen and the Four Tops, among others. By this point, Rodford was the longest serving member of the Kinks, bar the Davies brothers and Avory, so his presence at the event was fitting.

Three months after the Hall of Fame induction, the Kinks received another accolade when they were presented with the Ivor Novello Award For Outstanding Service To British Music. For Ray, these public acknowledgements of the Kinks' importance came as a welcome boost at a low point in their career. "I've always said that if I felt it was psychologically not the right thing to do, then I would stop. The Hall of Fame came as a surprise to me. We were inducted, then I sat down and thought, 'Well, this is a nice thing.' I was always sceptical of awards of any kind, but that wasn't an award. It was kind of a 'Welcome, you actually exist.' It's strange, I've always felt an outsider. I think it was after that, realizing what we had contributed and the body of work that we'd made, that I thought, 'Well, let's try and do this because I do like playing.'"

With no recording commitments during 1990, the Kinks spent one of their quietest years undertaking low-key tours in America and Europe. One of their most memorable shows that summer was at the Marktrock in Leuven, Belgium. Fifteen thousand people attended the free festival despite torrential rain. Ray watched from the stage and found himself strangely moved by the audience's dedication. Once again, he had found a good reason for believing in the longevity of the Kinks and was quick to praise the suffering spectators. "We got drenched and the crowd got drenched, but they wouldn't go home. For an encore we went out and did 'Twist And Shout' which we hadn't played for years. That was a wonderful moment . . . I was amazed that I still got the same thrill out of it." Davies may also have felt a thrill later in the year when he made a fleeting appearance as the guest of honour at the first official 'Kinks Konvention' in Muswell Hill. Impressively, all the present line-up attended, and new boy Mark Haley hung around at the end of the evening to join fans in a singalong 'Waterloo Sunset'.

Ray Davies was keen to sign a new record contract, but felt conflicted about the state of the music business. "It's infested with attorneys, sociologists and marketing managers. I really think they should go to work in the Third World and leave us all alone. They're not doing Britain any favours. We're a wild tribe of people. We're a classy race here, and they're turning us into mindless robots who follow a pattern laid down by a corporation. That's not our natural way of going about things. British people debate, they argue, they question things . . . I've still got a lot of hopes for this country." The Churchillian tone sounded strangely out of place amid the politically correct rock rhetoric of the early Nineties. While even the most chauvinistic rock stars were making some concessions to feminism, Davies was hinting that things had already gone too far. His latest target was inverted sexism, symbolized by that over-publicized figure the 'new man'. Bristling with reactionary indignation, he declared: "I have nothing against feminists but you know what I dislike now more than anything? Male feminists. Pussy-whipped men. They're not women, why should they be feminists? They're married to a woman who wears the trousers. I can't stand that. We're going into an era with sexism being reversed . . . it worries me a bit."

Besides the occasional vexed interview, Davies busied himself with quixotic rewrites of *80 Days* and made progress filming his documentary on Charles Mingus. He celebrated his 47th birthday with a performance in Oxford at Magdalen College's Commemoration Ball. The Kinks had played the university back in the mid-Sixties, so this was a chance to revisit old memories. Two thousand students in full evening dress gave the Kinks a stirring welcome as Ray announced, "It's good to be back in Cambridge." Opening with the familiar 'The Hard Way', the group quickly moved into 'UK Jive', which gave Ray a chance to show off his Stars and Stripes jacket, with a Union Jack on the back. The garb summed up the duality of the Kinks – a quintessentially British pop group, now better known and appreciated in America. In generous mood, Davies gave the students what they most desired – a catalogue of Kinks hits. 'Come Dancing', 'Sunny

Afternoon', 'Dead End Street' and 'Till The End Of The Day' were followed by a medley of 'Dedicated Follower Of Fashion', 'Lola' and 'All Day And All Of The Night'. The encores included 'Days' and 'Waterloo Sunset' before the thundering 'You Really Got Me' brought proceedings to a close. At dawn, the students drank champagne and looked back woozily on what was undoubtedly one of the most sustained sets of Kinks classics heard in years.

The prospect of a new Kinks album was confirmed in July 1991 with the news that they had signed to CBS/Sony. Label president Don Ienner, who had previously worked with the group as promotions head of Arista, was convinced, like many before him, that he could entice a classic album from the Davies brothers and reinvent the Kinks for a contemporary audience. On the recommendation of publisher Freddy Bienstock, the brothers also appointed a new manager, Nigel Thomas, who had once repre- sented the tempestuous Joe Cocker and was currently working with the mercurial Morrissey. With Ray Davies and Morrissey in his stable, Thomas could reasonably boast that he was managing two of the most challenging and neurotic figures on the pop landscape. Like Larry Page, Thomas was old school and had the ability to relate to both Davies brothers independently. "I liked Nigel, he was very bright and funny," Dave recalls. "Ray also liked him because he reminded him of Robert Wace. It was a bit like the early days. Nigel kind of looked down on everyone in a humorous way. He had that condescending air that Robert had. I think Ray found that attractive. Nigel had been a stand-up comic when he first started, a bit of a rebel. He grew up in a military family and his father wanted him to be an officer in the army and he refused all that. We had a lot in common in some ways. We never wanted to fit in with the showbiz club either."

As a stop-gap, CBS/Sony sanctioned the release of a five-track single in America on 24 October. 'Did Ya' was an exuberant pastiche, complete with allusions to 1966's summer chart topper 'Sunny Afternoon'. The tone was satirical rather than celebratory as Davies waded through the debris of idealistic Sixties imagery to express his own peculiar nostalgia, laced with sardonic glee. "It's about me taking a walk down King's Road, which I was never part of. I went there occasionally but, to me, the Sixties was a youth club in Muswell Hill, being up there in our red hunting jackets. All our friends were in the audience. In fact, the most vivid memory to me of the Sixties is before we had the hit. We were playing 'You Really Got Me' but it hadn't been recorded yet. It was in Nottingham, in a club, and I was watching two little Mod girls, after the club had closed, dancing to 'I Get Around'. Images like that are interesting to me. Not all the pomp and circumstance of *Oz* or Mick Jagger getting arrested. That doesn't mean anything to me."

In an inspired move, the Davies brothers promoted 'Did Ya' by performing as an acoustic duo for the first time since 1960. The occasion was a benefit show at the Boston Garden. 'Low Budget' opened a varied acoustic set, which also featured 'Alcohol', 'Dedicated Follower Of Fashion', 'Celluloid Heroes', 'Days', 'A Well Respected Man' and 'Apeman'. Dave was then handed a black Stratocaster and launched into 'Sleepwalker'. Towards the close of 'Lola', the curtain rose to reveal support group the Smithereens, who assisted the brothers for a raucous finale of 'You Really Got Me'. The evening ended with Ray leaping in the air, scissors fashion, just like Pete Townshend. The notion of the Kinks' 'Unplugged', with the brothers facing each other onstage and singing in unison, was an intriguing experiment, never to be repeated.

Tour manager Ken Jones was conspicuously absent during the promotional activities. Increasingly disillusioned and with little work on the horizon, he was preparing to leave the Davies' employ having served them loyally since 1968. It would prove a bitter parting. Insiders suggest that, in addition to the contretemps with Ray, Jones was angry about the appointment of Kenny Laguna and also had a prickly relationship with new manager Nigel Thomas. Tensions reached a head when Jones was due to fly out from Heathrow to New York with Davies and Thomas. At the eleventh hour, he was told that the manager and star were flying first class while he, for budgetary reasons, was reduced to economy status. Humiliated, he refused to fly, hoping, against all logic, that Ray might intervene and put his hand in his pocket. Jones walked away in frustration knowing that he had placed himself in a situation from which he could never return. Davies made no attempt to persuade him otherwise, reinforcing Jones' view that he had been effectively fired. The lingering indignity for Jones was that he had never once been considered as a managerial candidate after years of faithful service. In a strange twist, he contacted Larry Page for advice. Although he had previously resented Page's reappointment as Kinks' manager in 1984, they had become closer over the years and established a reasonable professional relationship. "Ken was a good worker and, if you kept on top of him, as good as anybody in the business. When they got shot of Ken – and they did get shot of him – there was talk about redundancy money. I told him he should go all the way on it." Jones betrayed his lack of negotiating skills when confronted and accepted a timid settlement. "Ken Jones was with them for twenty-five years and they paid him off with £2,000," Page remarks. "There's gratitude for you. And he may even have saved Ray's life when he almost topped himself [in 1973]."

Davies spent much of 1991–2 preparing the new Kinks album. When CBS/Sony president Don Ienner enquired about a working title, Ray deadpanned: 'The Next Nirvana'. The press were subsequently informed that it would be named 'Don't' after a grandiose nine-minute track, an idea abandoned when the song devolved into a more modest Kinks' ballad. At least there were positive signs that Dave's lyrics would be accommodated. Among the first songs attempted was 'Close To The Wire', one of the younger brother's more spiritual reflections. The big question was how long the album would take to complete. Ray endlessly tinkered, remixing, rewriting, editing, then extending the track listing, while driving his impatient brother to distraction. "There was this genuine undercurrent of 'You bastard, what are you trying to do?'," Dave recalls. He managed to curb his frustrations, while acknowledging, "I like to think that I'm more tolerant of Ray than he is of me, but he would probably say the opposite." Alcohol sometimes brought out Ray's darker side, even when working in the studio. By his own admission he was "rat-arsed drunk" on the eve of recording 'Only A Dream' and was "still shaking" the following morning when he attempted the vocal. On another evening, while downing a bottle of wine, he wrote his brother a vicious note, with the words: "Why don't you drop dead and never recover?" Later, he reflected on their fractious ways and decided to transform those negative feelings into a more positive statement about their relationship. 'Hatred' was designed as a therapeutic exorcism of decades of suppressed bitterness. It began as an interior monologue, interrupted by different voices in Davies' head arguing opposing points of view. Suddenly, it made sense to record the vocal as a duet. Slyly, Ray added Dave's voice to the track without informing him of the song's theme, an inspired idea intended to provide a combustible edge. "I set out to write the complete hate song, but it's so violent that it's laughable, so it's obvious that it's not meant seriously. It's just two guys who are driven to such lengths of despair and frustration with one another that they sound like clowns in a circus." Although not considered commercial enough to be released as a single, 'Hatred (A Duet)' was tailor-made for the media, the perfect song on which to launch a juicy discussion about their ongoing family feud. It would play a key part in the promotion of the album.

During the autumn of 1992, Davies took time off to host a songwriting workshop at Fen Farm in Suffolk. Among the budding composers were several established pop musicians, including Lene Lovich and a member of Katrina And The Waves. Davies assigned his pupils various writing projects and conducted one-to-one tutorials. Those in attendance found him surprisingly supportive and eager to assist with songwriting ideas. "That is the *real* Ray Davies," acknowledges one of his former colleagues. "In that environment, you'll see Ray at his very best, helping creative people to find their way. Each of us has got a path and Ray has a formula for writing and constructing songs which is very precise. It's beautiful to see someone with so much talent helping future songwriters. That's the true magic of Ray Davies. It's moments like those that will keep Ray going for a very long time because in that scenario he can give and share, whereas in other areas he cannot."

Probably the highlight of the five-day Fen Farm workshop was a jamming session in the local pub where Ray entranced his audience by playing requests including 'Wonderboy', 'See My Friend', 'Mister Pleasant', 'When I Turn Off The Living Room Light', 'Moments' and 'Rosemary Rose'. The experimental workshop was so gratifying that it became a regular occurrence and one of Davies' more endearing enterprises.

CHAPTER THIRTY-EIGHT

BEYOND BRITPOP

Nineteen ninety-three was intended as the year of the great Kinks' comeback, backed by a major label and established management. It all started to go wrong barely a week into the New Year. In advance of the next album, Davies was under pressure from his manager and CBS/Sony Records to sanction the release of 'Scattered' as a single. However, MCA Records argued that they owned the rights to the song under the Kinks' previous contract and were threatening to file an injunction to halt its release. While driving home for the weekend, Davies became embroiled in an angry exchange on his mobile phone with manager Nigel Thomas whom he felt had failed to deal with the matter. That same night, he composed a letter requesting his resignation. The next morning, 9 January, he rang Thomas' home to confirm his fax number, intending to send the letter. He was astonished to discover that his 45-year-old manager had died in his sleep, the victim of a heart attack brought on by a stroke. "It was awful," he recalls. "He didn't actually get the fax. They told me he was dead. I didn't want him to die. It was quite chilling."

The Davies brothers attended their manager's funeral and each paid private tribute to his brief but positive influence on their career. At the graveside, Ray joked with Dave about the possibility that Thomas had faked his death just to get away from them. Later, he told a journalist, "I have considered the possibility that Nigel died rather than taking another call from me. I hope he's actually somewhere in the Bahamas laughing at me." The gallows humour was reiterated by Larry Page, who also wondered to what extent stress had played a part in the manager's demise. "That's what Ray will do to you," he warned. "He'll kill you!"

On 3 February, Ray sent Dave a birthday card with the enigmatic message: "Why do I love you?" Later that day, the brothers entertained the personnel of CBS/Sony with a concert in the California company's cafeteria in Santa Monica, performing an engaging eight-song set. Whether they were any closer as brothers was debatable, but they were certainly focused, playing the love/hatred angle in numerous media encounters. Tellingly, they were frequently interviewed together and remained civil and unruffled when faced with provocative questions. Committed to promotion, they spent the remainder of February traversing the Continent, taking in France, Holland, Denmark, Sweden, Germany and Belgium.

Extensive touring plans were announced and this time the brothers were determined to avoid any backstage arguments. Ray even agreed to appoint Eugene Harvey, whom Dave favoured, as their temporary manager. It seemed that after years of conflict the siblings were at last learning the art of compromise and accommodation. Now all they needed was a best-selling album.

Phobia was released in March 1993 and, despite its uneven quality, received generally favourable reviews. With 17 tracks spread over 76 minutes, there was no denying the album offered value for money. Heralded as a personal and musical reconciliation between the brothers, the work also revealed their fundamental aesthetic differences, marked by wildly varying stylistic shifts. For all that, it was unarguably the most widely discussed Kinks albums for many years, not least by the brothers themselves, who offered the music press a veritable track by track analysis.

Dave Davies was a big fan of *Phobia*, understandably so, given his brother's willingness to sanction his hard-rock workouts on the bombastic title track and elsewhere. 'Surviving', 'It's All Right (Don't Think About It)', 'Drift Away' and 'Wall Of Fire' testify to his heavy-metal leanings, often with overwrought results. "He's got the right to express himself," Ray countered. "Part of being in a band is to actually let the soloist solo . . . Dave's a wonderful player but unless you get him first time, it takes a couple of days to get anything out of him. I always say to engineers, 'Whenever he's playing, press the button', because you never know what you're going to get. I ended up sampling his solos on 'Wall Of Fire'."

Among the album's highlights are two older songs: 'Still Searching' (previously demoed during 1977's *Misfits* sessions) and 'Scattered' (a powerful lyric, partly inspired by Annie Davies' death and once an outtake from *Word Of Mouth*). The mid-section of the album features some reflective moments: 'Don't', the original title track, dramatizes a near suicide; 'Babies' offers an amusing parable of the insecurities of the still unborn; 'Only A Dream' (the final song written for the record during a plane trip to London) tells of an 'executive goddess' won and lost within the space of a couple of lift rides; 'Over The Edge' documents a neurotic love affair set against a backing reminiscent of the Beatles' 'Dear Prudence'; 'Somebody Stole My Car' playfully references the Fab Four's 'Drive My Car'; and 'Hatred (A Duet)', a fraternal psychodrama, provides some unexpected comedy. 'The Informer', inspired by Davies' stay in Kinsale, Co. Cork, is a cinematic account of a character who betrays his comrades. "It has IRA connotations," Davies admits, "although I'm never that obvious as a writer. It doesn't mention the word assassination, but there's a subtext to the song that I've crafted into it." Unlike its American counterpart, the European CD issue of *Phobia* ends with the bonus track 'Did Ya', a suitably sardonic yet upbeat coda to an ambitious but flawed record.

Phobia served its purpose as a conceptual sampler offering something for everybody, but, without Ray's strongest songwriting, chart success was never likely. Despite a media blitz, extensive touring and high hopes, the album spent only a week in the US charts at the embarrassingly low position of 166, their poorest showing since *The Village Green Preservation Society* at the tail end of their American exile. In the UK, the sales figures made even grimmer reading. One newspaper report revealed that *Phobia* had shifted only 5,000 copies, a frightening statistic, even by the Kinks' declining commercial standards.

After the failure of *Phobia*, it seemed that the Kinks were left with nowhere to go. Even their record company had turned against them as if fully recognizing their bad investment. While the group were touring Germany, label president Don Ienner was quoted in a New York newspaper promising to "ditch dinosaur rock" from CBS/Sony. Davies was furious. One month later, at the Royal Albert Hall, he was railing against the public perception of the Kinks as superannuated has-beens. "If there are any journalists here, don't review this show," he announced. "I'm tired of reading that the Kinks are a Sixties band. Our songs are part of Britain's heritage, and that heritage is being thrown away."

Davies' plea was prescient considering the quiet explosion about to revolutionize British pop music. There had been a long, almost unbroken, strain of Englishness in chart pop whose lineage stretched back to the early Kinks and forward to embrace any number of acts from the Jam to Madness, XTC, the Smiths and beyond. Generally, these groups eschewed American influences in favour of a lyrical landscape filled with English place names and suburban locales in which low-key dramas were played out without glory or epic resolution. The Jam borrowed openly from the Who and the Kinks, covering Davies' 'David Watts', while also echoing his class-consciousness (*All Mod Cons*), social commentaries (the urban violence of 'Down In The Tube Station At Midnight') and colonial concerns (*Setting Sons*); Madness matured from ska-copyists into subtle observers of working-class life on 'Embarrassment', 'Grey Day' and 'Our House'; XTC combined conformity and condescension in 'Making Plans For Nigel', while documenting the stultifying 'Shangri-la'-like uniformity of small-town life in 'Respectable Street'; the Smiths' lyrical territory was largely set in Manchester, but they also had several 'London songs' and even one that immortalized the loss of a bag in Newport Pagnell ('Is It Really So Strange?').

The UK music press, lately enthralled by American grunge, as exemplified by Nirvana, had found a great white hope of Englishness in Suede, who had achieved front-cover status even before issuing a single, then went on to live up to the hype. During the spring of 1993, their singer Brett Anderson saw his image superimposed over a Union Jack flag by *Select* magazine alongside the call to arms, 'Yanks Go Home!' It was too early to talk about a movement, but *Select* cobbled together a handful of acts – Pulp, the Auteurs, St Etienne and Denim – as evidence of a vague collective whose roots, sensibility and songwriting were peculiarly English in tone. Pulp singer Jarvis Cocker appeared as the chief flag waver and mentioned one crucial influence: "When British pop is great, it's great because of the personality of the music. The sense of the romantic in the everyday. Ray Davies finding the poetic in the sun going down on 'Waterloo Sunset'. You don't get that much in American rock."

While music press readers were still pondering *Select*'s patriotic call (subtitled in *Dad's Army*-style: 'Who Do You Think You Are Kidding, Mr Cobain?') the incumbent Prime Minister John Major gave a speech, part of which sounded like some crazed sequel to Ray Davies' 'The Village Green Preservation Society'. "Fifty years from now, Britain will still be the country of long shadows on county grounds, warm beer, invincible green suburbs, dog lovers and pools fillers and, as George Orwell said, 'old maids bicycling to Holy Communion through the morning mist' and, if we get our way, Shakespeare will still be read, even in school. Britain will survive unamenable in all essentials." That Major and Davies both owed inspiration to Orwell was telling. Still, it was a delightful irony that the origins of 'Britpop' and 'Cool Britannia' – later so closely associated with the rise of Tony Blair – could also be located in the sepia-tinted predictions of his Conservative predecessor.

On 29 March 1993, the same day *Phobia* had been released, Suede's first album was issued. *Suede*, one of British pop's greatest debut albums, sold 20 times more copies in its first week of release than *Phobia* achieved in its lifetime. Brett Anderson presented an enclosed world of small-town hopes, bored teenagers, conscious-ness-numbing drugs, sordid sex and tarnished glamour. It closed with 'The Next Life', a fantasy that included the memorable image of retiring to Worthing to sell ice cream. The album's swift ascent to number 1 appeared to vindicate *Select*'s dream of a Brit-based resurgence, but it was not that straightforward. Although Anderson's lyrics were filled with council houses and images of suburban unrest, he was also over-keen on Americanisms – notably gasoline and trash in place of petrol and rubbish. He objected to being lumped in with any Brit list and was even more upset by Union Jack symbolism. Only a year before, Morrissey had sparked a *New Musical Express* frenzy when he was pictured with the flag at a concert in front of a battalion of Madness fans. Anderson's ire no doubt increased after hearing about John Major's pro-England speech which took place only 22 days after the release of *Suede*. The singer retorted with the arch suggestion that he was intending to move to America. "We were superimposed in front of flags and stuff, and it got a bit nasty," he told me. "We were being offered this baton which said: 'You are the spearhead of British music', and I didn't want to be categorized in such a nationalistic way. So I just wound people up and said 'I don't want anything to do with Britain, I want to live in America.' That whole Little England thing, which later became Britpop, was offered to us. It was thrust upon us to such an extent that we didn't want anything to do with it. Suede had got a lot more scope than just wanting to be some silly Little Englanders that other bands wanted to be."

It was not too difficult to identify those "silly Little Englanders" that Anderson had in mind. Oddly enough, Blur had not been included in *Select*'s round-up of Anglophiles, but they were about to grasp the 'baton' that Anderson had declined. The group had recently undertaken a dispiriting US tour during which singer Damon Albarn's only cheer was listening to the Kinks' 'Waterloo Sunset'. After returning to the UK, he was even more determined to pursue a musical policy in which Englishness was the predominant theme. In May 1993, *Modern Life Is Rubbish* was released, its contents featuring British music hall elements and songs like the London-based 'For Tomorrow', the overtly English 'Sunday Sunday' and 'Colin Zeal', an allegorical character who sounds like a first cousin to some of the personalities on the Kinks' *Face To Face*.

Ray Davies was acutely aware of Blur's progress and embraced Albarn like a canny patriarch in search of a protégé. Within a month of the release of *Modern Life Is Rubbish*, Blur were supporting the Kinks in Stockholm. Nine days later, the Kinks headlined at the Glastonbury Festival. Across at the *NME* stage, the previous night, Suede were parallel headliners, as if bridging the generations.

Davies may have been slightly irked by the way the Kinks were seen as some kind of heritage act, while secretly flattered about his own ascension to the soon-to-be familiar title 'Godfather of Britpop'. He spoke of an urge to complete a solo album, even while stressing that the Kinks was still a democracy. "I'm very interested in taking my music in new directions now, but maybe

I should do that somewhere else. I've got this new bunch of songs that have been written since this album, and they're all me and I'm not afraid of them at all. It may sound odd coming from someone who's been around for as long as I have, but suddenly I'm not afraid of showing my emotions. In the past, I've always written a lot of observations about other people, but I haven't written very often about myself and that's going to be the idea behind my next project." Despite these hints, there was no evidence of any such solo venture nor any indication that Davies was ready to abandon the security of the Kinks. If anything, he seemed drawn back into their past. That summer of 1993, a Boston theatre company staged a version of *Preservation Act 2*. Although it was only a minor production, Davies was flattered that there was still cult interest in his oft-maligned work. He even spoke of re-recording the songs and rewriting the script, hoping to breathe life into the old musical. "It's kind of my lost lifelong project, the thing that I constantly find myself going back to, just like Rembrandt kept painting his self-portrait. It's about lost innocence and lost friendship, and things that can never be recaptured which are things that have always interested me."

In Europe, the Kinks increasingly found themselves playing summer festivals, dominated by oldies acts and ageing legends. They shared billing with such luminaries as Chuck Berry, the Beach Boys and Bob Dylan. It was telling that they had been specially chosen for the Glastonbury appearance only after those supergroup ancients Crosby, Stills & Nash had pulled out. All this was gratifying but also frustrating, as if confining them to rock history like some museum piece. It was a different challenge in America where the neologism Britpop was irrelevant and the Kinks were still considered a hard-rocking stadium act, whose Sixties heritage was incidental rather than self-defining. Despite the US public's rejection of *Phobia*, Davies was still ready to mine their favourite constituency, like a once popular politician in search of lost voters.

A couple of weeks before departing for America, Davies confirmed that Ian Gibbons had returned to the line-up. He had been invited to their recent show at the Royal Albert Hall, alongside Mick Avory. Backstage, Gibbons spoke to Dave Davies for the first time in four years and found him in cordial, almost exuberant, mood. It soon transpired that keyboardist Mark Haley was about to tender his resignation following a furious argument with the guitarist after a show in Switzerland the previous evening. Clearly, Gibbons was being headhunted and, days later, received a call from tour manager Dave Bowen requesting his presence in America. "I didn't assume I'd ever come back. I didn't think I'd be asked. I thought about it for a while and told myself, 'It's just a tour. I'll see how it goes from there. I'll play like a freelancer and keep my head down.' That's the best way of dealing with them really."

The US tour was accompanied by the usual instances of low drama, including injury and comedy in equal measure. A show in Pittsburgh coincided with a boisterous regatta which was taking place on an adjacent riverbank. At one point, the performance was interrupted by a fireworks display. "Ray did one of his instant composing tricks," Gibbons recalls. "We had a break for the fireworks and he came back with a song called 'Regatta My Arse' and got all the crowd singing along." Alas, he also broke a couple of toes that evening, placing the remainder of the tour in jeopardy. Five days later, there were amusing scenes at the Mann Music Center in Philadelphia where the Kinks enjoyed a rare stage invasion. At one point a proud parent thrust a five-year-old child into Ray's arms as if she were offering a sacrifice to a pagan god. Support act Aimee Mann also got caught up in the excitement, joining in the encore of 'You Really Got Me'. The tour ended with the grandly titled 'Jurassic Jam' in Somerset, Wisconsin. "That was a farce," says Gibbons. "Some guy decided he was going to put on a terrific festival at an amusement park in the middle of nowhere. All sorts of things seemed to go wrong and there weren't many people in attendance. If he'd promoted it in a major city it might have been a great gig. But it ended the tour on a downer, plus Ray wasn't feeling too good about his foot."

The remaining US dates were cancelled but, after a month's convalescence, Davies was ready for a two-week tour of Japan. The Kinks had played there in 1982 and, second time around, the reception was far better. Ray was amazed at the audience's knowledge of his more obscure material and flattered that so many young fans attended the shows. The other Kinks were also impressed. "Everybody went crazy!" Gibbons recalls. "The audience was wonderful. It was as if a veil had been lifted over the youth of Japan. The last time we were there they'd sat very politely. They obviously enjoyed it but there were a lot of restrictions. This time they were up out of their seats before we even came on. A great tour and very well organized."

The year of Ray Davies' 50th birthday, 1994, was a time of reflection. While editing his memoirs and recalling past incidents, he received some sad news. On 14 March, Rasa's mother had died. Ray had always got on well with his first mother-in-law, who liked to call him her 'golden boy'. He was sufficiently moved by the sad tidings to respond with a display of affection and respect which took Rasa by surprise. "Ray sent a beautiful bouquet of white flowers, signed: 'From your Golden Boy, Ray'. I cried, and my mother would have been overwhelmed. This gesture of Ray's provided deep thinking for me regarding his heart and his deeper feelings of empathy and love, so hidden away from others, rarely visible from the man, however, written and audible in so many of his songs." This was the Ray Davies recognizable from the lyrics of 'Waterloo Sunset', an observer of the human condition with feelings of empathy untouched by cynicism. As his brother acknowledges, that same person was visible whenever he spoke about his feelings for his own parents. At other times, the shield of emotional distance was usually an easier option.

On a less personal note, Louis Benjamin passed away three months after Rasa's mother and, during the same period, the former Davies family home at 6 Denmark Terrace was sold. These passing epochs had no positive effect on the brothers' relationship which, if anything, had grown chillier of late. With Dave, Nancy and their two children having moved to America, communication between the brothers was now taking place mainly via the fax machine. Ray sounded distant when discussing their interaction. "You go through a lot with people, and you are too tense to have dinner together. We just can't be that civilized about it any more. It's got to be done by fax. I think the music's the only thing that's held us together, quite frankly."

Others suggest that Ray may have been encouraged or persuaded by a couple of his sisters to ensure that Dave was not cut adrift from the Kinks. There was little doubt that Dave's influence over the group had been systematically weakened over the decades by economic as well as creative differences. "They have a love/hate relationship, but you've also got to remember that Ray holds the money card," Larry Page told me in 1994. "Without the Kinks, what has Dave got? He's in trouble. Power? It's domination. If Ray finished the Kinks tomorrow, I don't know what Dave would do. It would affect him very much, financially."

For all the sibling squabbles, the Kinks continued touring. Ray's wife Patricia, long a part of the show, remained a pacific presence onstage and off. Remarkably, she had survived seven consecutive years on the road during which a long list of dancing partners – Annie Cox, Robin James, Brenda Edwards, Suzie Thomas and Louise Wodwell – had been and gone. Although there was uncertainty about how long the Kinks might survive, the passing plaudits Davies was receiving from younger British groups offered some small hope of a resurgence of interest, even after the *Phobia* sales debacle.

Davies' affiliation with the new gods of Britpop was reinforced in the spring with the release of Blur's *Parklife*, featuring more songs of suburban strife and Damon Albarn's mockney makeover, complete with Fred Perry shirt, Doc Marten boots and, in one famous photograph, a Great Dane. The singer even announced a love of dog-racing and 'Essex girls'. While *Parklife* was topping the charts, Albarn went through an uncharacteristically dark period, not dissimilar to Ray's famous setbacks in 1966. Again, the major problem was insomnia, while the solution was straight out of Davies' medical textbook: acupuncture and regular games of football.

That summer of 1994, Blur's chief rivals, the recently feted Oasis, released *Definitely Maybe*, another chart-topping album. Coincidentally, the CD shared its title with a Davies song, but that was not the main comparison with the Kinks. If Blur were reprising Davies' quirky class commentaries, then Oasis were more familiar with the riffs immortalized on 'You Really Got Me' and 'All Day And All Of The Night'. The most newsworthy connection, of course, was the fraternal friction between Oasis' Noel and Liam Gallagher. In documenting their exploits, commentators invariably mentioned that the 'battling brothers' from Manchester appeared to be re-enacting the immemorial conflict between Ray and Dave Davies. Later in the year, at *Q* magazine's annual prize-giving, all three groups were honoured: Blur for Best Album (*Parklife*), Oasis for Best New Act and the Kinks for the Inspiration Award. Also present was the Prime Minister-in-waiting Tony Blair, whose opening speech paid tribute to Ray Davies by employing an Oasis song to emphasize the point: "The great bands that I used to listen to – the Stones and the Beatles and the Kinks – their records are going to live forever."

Davies had good reason to feel pleased with himself as he accepted his award. That same autumn, *X-Ray* – subtitled 'Unauthorized Autobiography' – was published by Viking/Penguin to critical acclaim. By using two narrators Davies overcame his characteristic reticence about his emotional life to offer an unflinching insight into his troubled psyche in what was a welcome panacea to the traditional anodyne showbiz memoir. In interviews, Davies testified to the book's veracity, indicating that his 'unreliable narrator' may have been far more trustworthy than some readers assumed. Still, it was a confessional with caveats, depicting a reality in which the differences were so subtle and seemingly inconsequential that they actually drew attention to themselves. There were various misspellings of names, including heroes and villains from the Davies story – Allen Klein ('Alan Klein'), John Stephen ('John Steven'), Mickey Willett ('Mickey Willet'), Jon Lord ('John Lord'), Freddy Bienstock ('Freddie' 'Beinstock'), Jo Durden-Smith ('Jo Derden Smith') and Marion Rainford ('Marian Rainford'). Even family members were not exempt: grandmother Catherine Willmore ['Kate Wilmore'] was an error carried forward into Dave's autobiography. The unfortunate Davies family dog ended up with two names, 'Alfie' and 'Georgie', within the space of three pages. "It's my brain," Ray now admits. "A combination of mischief and *bad spelling*." Road manager Sam Curtis, a caustic and frequently hilarious critic of the Davies brothers, became 'Sam Levy'. According to Ray, the road manager had once revealed that his birth name was Samuel Ben Hitchcock Halevy. "He shortened it, then changed it again." Few, if any, readers would have known that, after adopting the name Gurvitz, he had then anglicized his name in the Fifties to radiate the glamour of heart-throb actor Tony Curtis. By rechristening him 'Sam Levy', Davies was reminding the world of his disguised Jewish origins. A more blatant example of Davies' arch humour was the transformation of Mick Avory into a beleaguered sex beast, eagerly sought after by rapacious transvestites. On one occasion, the drummer was described in sexual congress with a showgirl only to be interrupted by an unnamed disc jockey who thrusts four fingers up his backside. Other scenes had the feel of a modern Restoration comedy. Avory was stoical about his portrayal, telling me that it was "Ray's way" and "quite funny". Whether his immediate family agreed was never ascertained.

The book was launched at Ronnie Scott's jazz club in Soho with guitar accompaniment by Pete Mathison and a surprise appearance from Ray's 26-year-old daughter Viktoria (now known as Tor), who sang along on 'Tired Of Waiting For You' and 'No Guarantees'. Just as Louisa had re-entered Ray's life for a cameo vocal appearance on *Return To Waterloo*, so Tor sought his countenance before forming and fronting a band, Pout. Their name resulted from a fortuitous accident at a punk gig where Tor was elbowed in the face and left with a swollen lip ("a big pout"). Oddly, Ray spoke about his second daughter as if she was a stranger from another planet. "When she first came to me, she was from a marriage years ago, and I had not seen her for many years. She sort of landed on the doorstep with a demo of songs." Davies was impressed enough to invite Pout to accompany the Kinks on a six-week tour of the UK and Ireland, starting on 16 October 1994. This low-key excursion was to promote *To The Bone*, an impressive part acoustic/part electric live album, issued via Konk Records in collaboration with the independent label, Grapevine.

Pout's short set included two Davies' compositions 'I Need You' and 'Heart Of Gold', then Ray would play some songs, before the full Kinks' line-up took their places. Dave was less than enthusiastic about Ray's mini-set and scornful of his sudden elevation to solo star. Clearly, the elder brother was unsubtly testing the waters for his first major tour without the Kinks. 'An Evening With Ray Davies', with accompaniment by guitarist Pete Mathison, was launched the following spring. This five-date tour would later develop into the 'X-Ray World Tour', a two-hour performance in which Davies would read selections from his book, play Kinks' classics and incorporate less familiar compositions from his song catalogue. Dave remained unimpressed. "Obviously I do love Ray very much but he is such a manipulative sod. That's a part of his craft as an artiste but in his personal life he uses it as well. John Gosling, and other band members, were often saying that when Ray wants to leave or go solo that he 'wouldn't be able to get onstage without you.' That always surprised me because it's hard to be objective about yourself. I think this insistence that he had to do this 'one-man show' has been a big thing for Ray. Personally, I can't think of a more boring evening out, but he had to prove that to himself."

Davies' confidence was boosted by the continued rise of Britpop. In February 1995, Blur received an unprecedented four Brit Awards – Best Band, Album, Single and Video – while their emerging rivals Oasis scooped the Best Newcomer Award. The Mancunians were presented with their statuette by Davies with the words "Truly wonderful – Oasis". That same month, Ray appeared on Channel 4's *The White Room*, duetting with Blur's Damon Albarn on 'Waterloo Sunset' and 'Parklife', as if they were father and son. "I was in love with him for that hour," Albarn later acknowledged. He even wrote a song in his mentor's honour titled 'Dear Ray', which subsequently emerged in completely different form as 'It Could Be You', a satire of money-conscious Lottery winners. The Blur singer could also be seen discussing Davies on the television documentary series *My Generation*. Ray readily associated his work with that of Blur and Oasis, perhaps out of politeness rather than conviction. "Fashions come in and out and I think what they are doing is writing songs about things they know about, which is where they come from and the local stories. I think that's where the similarities with the Kinks is because our early records were like that. For a long time, particularly in the 1980s, English bands were writing about American experiences or drawing on things out of their own experience and knowledge and that tends to make the music sound different. I think lyrically Blur and Oasis are very similar in that respect."

Summer 1995 saw Britpop reach its apogee with the heavily hyped chart battle between Oasis' 'Roll With It' and Blur's 'Country House'. What might usually have been a tabloid pop story was elevated to television news amid reports of the biggest chart rivalry since the Beatles and the Rolling Stones. Unlike their

Sixties counterparts, who always staggered record releases to avoid a clash, Oasis and Blur were issuing singles on the same day in the ultimate battle for chart supremacy. The story was perfect media fodder with the simplistic subplot of northern, working-class Oasis pitched against their southern, middle-class competitors. Although neither song was among their best, it was Blur's 'Country House' that reached number 1. Ray Davies could not help observe that the lyrics of the victor's song repeated the title of his 1966 composition, 'House In The Country'.

History records that Blur won the battle of Britpop, but Oasis ultimately won the war. In September, Blur's fourth album *The Great Escape* was initially acclaimed by critics; less than two months later it would receive the annual Best Album Award from *Q* magazine. It included several Davies-inspired suburban vignettes, most notably 'Stereotypes', while some of the song titles betrayed a knowing nod to Sixties antecedents – 'Ernold Same' (Pink Floyd) and 'The Universal' (Small Faces). Two months later, Oasis released *(What's The Story) Morning Glory?* which sold in phenomenal numbers and even catapulted the Mancunians into the US Top 10. Its title track included lyrical references to "another sunny afternoon" recalling the Kinks' 1966 hit. Davies seemed to be embracing his 'godfather' role and noting all sorts of connections with his Britpop successors. "I listen to the current [Oasis] album, and I hear every song and I say, 'Yes I know when I went through that.' I see a lot of myself, and I can relate to it. It's very much the attitude of the Kinks – a gritty, edgy attitude . . . 'Don't Look Back In Anger', for example, is like a Kinks song . . . Blur is more similar in the text, similar to the way I would write – sort of an observation. And in an odd way, Pulp have the look that the Kinks had with fashion."

Davies was canny enough to use the Britpop connection as leverage in the hope of securing a major record deal either for himself or the Kinks, but some believed he was pricing himself out of the market. "Ray's asking for silly money," Larry Page confided at the time. "He keeps pissing everybody off. He was lucky to get the deal with Sony. That only happened because of Don Ienner." The Kinks remained active, although their tours were now like relay events, embracing Ray's solo outings. The group appeared at the opening of the Rock 'n' Roll Hall of Fame Museum in Cleveland in September 1995 on a bill that included such greats as Bob Dylan and Bruce Springsteen. Ray acted like some Anglo-American diplomat that evening, resplendent in his Union Jack/Stars and Stripes jacket. The event was followed by a two-month solo tour during which he acknowledged the Kinks' legacy by performing seldom heard songs such as 'Animal Farm', 'Village Green', 'Two Sisters', 'Rosy, Won't You Please Come Home' and 'Shangri-la'. It begged the question: how much longer could he continue to perform and record as both Ray Davies and the Kinks?

CHAPTER THIRTY-NINE

END OF THE CENTURY

In 1996 Ray Davies made his long-awaited escape from the shackled security of the Kinks into an unknown future as a solo singer-songwriter. The year began, appropriately enough, with the appointment of a new manager. Deke Arlon, in common with Larry Page, had first recorded during the late Fifties, but fell from public favour at the start of the Sixties beat boom. He moved into acting, appearing regularly on the soap opera *Crossroads*, then joined several of Van Morrison's showband colleagues in the Silhouettes. By the late Sixties, he had moved into music publishing and personal management. One of his first clients was producer Ned Sherrin, who had already worked with Ray Davies on *The Virgin Soldiers* and *Where Was Spring?*. After Larry Page resigned in 1989, Davies contacted Sherrin about the possibility of appointing a new manager who was as experienced in theatre and film as he was in pop music. Sherrin dutifully set up a lunch meeting between Davies and Arlon which ended cordially but without resolution. It was several years later before Ray picked up the phone and decided that Arlon should be appointed. With Ken Jones long gone, the burden of administration had increased for Davies and there was an urgent need to co-ordinate back-catalogue re-releases and, where possible, negotiate better terms. It was also hoped that Arlon's involvement in theatre might assist Davies' various unrealized stage projects, including future musicals.

During February, Davies was in New York for a series of solo shows at the Westbeth Theatre Center Music Hall billed as '20th Century Man – An Evening With Ray Davies In Concert'. The TV cable channel VH-1 were so impressed that they filmed a performance for broadcast later in the year using the title *Storytellers*. Deke Arlon, who had chosen the venue, had good reason to feel very pleased with himself, but any celebrations proved short-lived. That same week, Dave Davies' forthcoming memoirs were serialized in the *Daily Mail*. The timing was co-incidental, but Dave could not have chosen a better week to spoil Ray's moment of self-congratulation in New York. Days later, the oracular Larry Page was on the phone predicting that the Kinks would never play together again. "I think if they meet, there'll be an almighty punch-up," he suggested. "The extract in the *Daily Mail* mentions words said by the mother on her death bed. Forget Dave's book – just look at the headline in the newspaper. It says – 'Get Away From Ray – He Will Destroy You'. It's heavy stuff. I know the atmosphere without being there. Even if Ray says: 'No, everything's all right – let's go ahead with a tour', he'll either refuse to do it or wait till he goes onstage and fucking go for Dave like mad. Deke Arlon is about to earn his money. No doubt about it!"

After digesting Page's comments, I interviewed Dave in London three days later. He was accompanied by an assistant, Kate, who also appeared to be serving as his publicist and manager. It later became apparent that they were romantically involved and, after setting up home in Devon together, she became his long-term partner and manager. Dave seemed chirpily oblivious to any notion that his book might cause offence to his brother. Did he therefore think that all the mind games over the years had been exploited by Ray to maintain his interest in particular projects? "Of course," Dave responded. "He's often used my emotions as a device to get things done. He knows that I'm the sort of person that if someone does something, then I will react. He's obviously used that and I've fallen for it many a time and realized why he does it but, at the same time, it still comes under the heading 'abuse'. I've forgiven him an awful lot, and I'm sure I'll continue to forgive him, but our relationship has been built and grown on abuse." Far from contemplating the end of the Kinks, Dave spoke confidently about them recording a new studio album and promised a summer tour.

Two years before, Larry Page had suggested that Dave would be in serious trouble if the Kinks folded and now Dave was willing to admit the same. "The fact is that I do have to rely on the Kinks for income. We can romanticize about the wonderful business we're in, but the bottom line is money. With the Kinks, we can sell out arenas and the rest. I'd be a liar if I said that wasn't part of it." His prospects of surviving without the group looked bleak, at best.

Ray was still intending or hoping to launch his daughter's group, Pout, partially on the back of the Britpop boom. "There is that parallel there with Blur, and the band Menswear. Oddly enough, because of the dynamic sound of their rhythm section, they have more of a Seattle sound. I feel their future is in the United States. The songs are very suburban, about living in the Nineties and being young, but instrumentally and sonically, its roots are very American."

With the exception of Elastica, whose potential was never fully realized, Britpop remained a predominantly male preserve until the unexpected arrival of the Spice Girls, whose summer single 'Wannabe' climbed to number 1 in the UK. Over the next two years they would achieve international success on a scarcely believable scale, albeit with a much younger audience. Tor Davies was more interested in pursuing a harder edged style. "The sensitive Britpop around right now is thin," she declared. "Not to slight them, but many British bands are afraid to let loose. We're much more spiky – much more wrapped in barbed wire . . . We want to give the people what they've been cheated out of. We want to move away from the Britpop pack – we want to progress, to move forward."

Pout barely survived the millennium and never did record that elusive CD for Konk Records or tour America. Ray later offered them one of his best and most acerbic compositions on the state of modern Britain, 'Yours Truly, Confused, N10', but they felt it was inappropriate and declined to record the song. "They were a good band," Davies concludes. "They made some demos at Konk. Tor was close to getting signed by EMI but they wanted her to be the front person. It was that old thing. She said: 'I'm not a front pretty blonde, it's a band.' They didn't get signed and they stopped making music. Simple as that."

While Pout were struggling, the Kinks' career was in stasis. After a couple of Scandinavian shows on the oldies festival circuit in the summer of 1996, they effectively ceased performing as a live entity. The final show at the Norwegian Wood Music Festival in Oslo (15 June) was uncommemorated, its historic significance only realized years later as a statistical footnote. The only Kinks record that year was an extended two-CD reissue of *To The Bone* featuring several selections from *The Village Green Preservation Society*, including an amusing 'Bavarian version' of 'Do You Remember Walter' and two 'new' songs: 'Animal' (an account of an abusive relationship ending in divorce) and the Eastern-flavoured title track. Despite Dave's prediction, there would be no new studio album.

The sense of an ending was punctuated by the news that former tour manager Ken Jones had died from cancer on 12 October. After accepting his meagre settlement from the Davies brothers, Jones had moved to America, briefly working for Kiss, after which he had fallen on hard times. At one point, he was reduced to cleaning hotels in order to make ends meet. Ironically, it was the Who's John Entwistle who proved his saviour, allowing him to stay at his Gloucestershire home and offering him work on the road. On his death bed, Jones was visited by Mick Avory, who read out a letter from Ray Davies which moved the roadie to tears. The funeral took place at London's Islington Cemetery on 18 October and was attended by a number of musical colleagues, including the subsidiary members of the Kinks. Even Larry Page, once a bitter rival but later a respected adviser, was present. "I didn't see a wreath from Ray and Dave," he confided, "but the Who sent one." Page had another funeral to attend soon after when Davies' old nemesis Eddie Kassner expired on 19 November, aged 76.

Ray still resisted any suggestions that the Kinks were finished. There was even hope of a rapprochement between the brothers on the evening of 3 February 1997. The occasion was Dave's 50th birthday which, fittingly, took place at the Clissold Arms, his father's favourite drinking haunt and the place where he and Ray played as the Kelly Brothers back in 1960. Dave was thrilled by the celebration at which several of the latter-day Kinks appeared (Avory was understandably absent), alongside numerous family members. "Ray had the money and I didn't, so he offered to throw it for me." When he saw his brother, Dave went over and kissed him on the cheek. Ray reacted as if he had just been kissed by Judas Iscariot, his body stiffening, then flinching in embarrassment. "It was like he really wanted to do something for me, but it irritated him to do it." The gathering initially brought out Ray's sensitive side and he even spoke about a fantasy Kinks concert at which all the past members might reunite for one grand evening. That reverie was broken when he realized it could never work economically. The event culminated in the presentation of a 50th birthday cake, at which point, as Larry Page had correctly predicted, Ray took playful vengeance on Dave, who later accused his brother of ruining the party. "As I was about to cut the cake, Ray jumped on the table and made a speech about how wonderful he was. He then stomped on the cake." This was the evening when Ray and Dave should have been at their closest, but they ended the evening more distant than ever. Dave subsequently returned to America and began performing with his own band. It would be some time before he saw his brother again.

Ray's connection with the Britpop movement gradually unravelled as the fascination with retro England reached its peak. The previous summer, he had appeared at the 'Poetry Olympics' (aka 'A Hip Mass: The Super Jam'), a culturally reactive accompaniment to the Olympic Games, staged at London's Royal Albert Hall. Poet and organizer Michael Horovitz had promised a "different spirit to that of the zealously competitive modern Olympics", but social historians were well aware that the event was effectively a re-enactment of the 1965 'International Poetry Incarnation' (captured on film as *Wholly Communion*) which had been staged at the same venue. The original poetry reading had featured American Beat heavyweights Allen Ginsberg and Lawrence Ferlinghetti, plus a selection of British poets including Horovitz himself, Adrian Mitchell, Pete Brown, John McGrath, George MacBeth, Christopher Logue and Harry Fainlight. The 1996 version included James Fenton, Paul Durcan and Brendan Kennelly but this time there were representatives from the pop and rock communities: Patti Smith, Kylie Minogue, John Cooper Clarke, Moondog, Ray Davies and Damon Albarn. Davies ended the nine-hour marathon with a nine-song set, including the now familiar duet with Damon on 'Waterloo Sunset' and 'Parklife'. However, on this occasion the joining of hands between the generations looked more forced. Albarn had by now denounced Britpop, along with 'New Labour', and the next Blur album would feature the tellingly titled 'Look Inside America'.

Over the next few months, Davies also distanced himself from the Britpop tag despite its still popular appeal. In November 1996, *Newsweek* announced: "London reigns. Hot fashion, a pulsating club scene and lots of new money have made this the coolest city on the planet." The tone of the piece was remarkably similar to John Crosby's aforementioned 1965 piece on the 'Swinging' capital. The recycling of hoary myths would continue but at least *Newsweek* ended their reverie with a cautious footnote: "The fun won't last, of course. London swings violently between booms and busts."

The boom reached an apogee in February 1997 when Geri Halliwell, of the all-conquering Spice Girls, appeared at the Brits clad in a Union Jack minidress. The following month, *Vanity Fair* published the ultimate celebration of Britpop culture under the title 'London Swings! Again!'. The magazine spoke of an "epic scale youthquake" proclaiming: "As it was in the mid-Sixties, the British capital is a cultural trailblazer, teeming with new and youthful icons of art, pop music, fashion, food and film. Even its politicians are cool. Or, well, coolish." Bizarrely, this echo of *Newsweek*'s story reflected *Time* magazine's 1966 commemoration 'London – The Swinging City', itself a follow-up piece to John Crosby's 1965 article on Swinging London. Many of the personalities featured sounded like modern-day equivalents of former icons, including designers, authors, photographers and painters. The front cover of *Vanity Fair* featured Liam Gallagher perched on Union Jack pillows and encased in a duvet of the same design. Beside him, dressed in a provocative black see-through bra, was his girlfriend and soon-to-be-wife "the internationally acclaimed film actress, Patsy Kensit". They resembled nothing less than a modern incarnation of Mick Jagger and Marianne Faithfull. Inside, the 'coolish' politician was identified as Tony Blair, who courted pop stars with an opportunism reminiscent of vintage Harold Wilson. The only disappointment was the supporting cast of Britpop's supposed new elite: Cast, Kula Shaker and Ocean Colour

Scene. As in 1966, the Americans were celebrating a scene that was all but over.

The summer of 1997 was the 30th anniversary of *Sgt Pepper's Lonely Hearts Club Band*, a time when Noel Gallagher, his wife Meg Mathews and Creation Records label owner Alan McGee were invited by the new PM Tony Blair for drinks at 10 Downing Street. It was also the season of *Be Here Now*, the new Oasis album which was almost universally acclaimed at the time of release, only to be derided months later as an example of bloated cocaine-induced excess. It was the end of the party.

Ray Davies continued to tour with guitarist Pete Mathison playing the role of the 'Storyteller' in an autobiographical acoustic revue which disguised grander ambitions. Far from being over-whelmed by the rise and fall of Britpop, Davies was attempting to transcend the entire genre with the creation of a musical history of the twentieth century. It was his friend Ned Sherrin who had come up with the idea of *See My Friends*, partly inspired by Noël Coward's 1931 three-act play and later film *Cavalcade*, itself a panorama of English life from the eve of the previous century through to the beginning of the Thirties. Coward's opus had employed historical events, including the death of Queen Victoria, the sinking of the *Titanic* and the outbreak of the Great War, as the occasion for such songs as 'Keep The Home Fires Burning', 'I Do Like To Be Beside The Seaside' and 'Take Me Back To Dear Old Blighty'. Sherrin's production was similarly audacious with an even longer timescale covering seven decades. Over recent years, the producer had been busy familiarizing himself with Davies' entire catalogue and had sketched a rough treatment which was tantalizingly ambitious.

See My Friends was intended to commence with the title track accompanied by images of famous people projected on a back screen. Originally, the leading lady was to be Bertice Reading, who had played Bessie Smith in the 1955 all-black revue, *The Jazz Train*. She was "a wonderful, big busty, black woman who would have been magic coming on as Victoria, and later Winston Churchill," Sherrin concludes. Her sudden death in 1991 at the age of 57 scuppered that plan, but the musical's structure remained intact. The Edwardian era was to be documented in 'Village Green' and 'Picture Book' before the onset of war, at which point, "all hell was going to break loose with 'All Day And All Of The Night'". War's end was to be recalled by 'Some Mother's Son', after which the mood changed for the Twenties with 'Autumn Almanac' and 'A Well Respected Man'. A pivotal song for 1929, leading into the Hungry Thirties, was 'Dead End Street'. 'Drivin'' and 'She Bought A Hat Like Princess Marina' conjured the inter-war years. As Sherrin explained: "People were only starting to get motorcars so 'Drivin'' would have taken one into that time", while "Princess Marina summed up the cheek and elegance of the Thirties". The Forties was represented by the call to arms 'Mr Churchill Says' before "another explosion of war" with 'You Really Got Me'. The pacific calm of post-1945 ushered in the reflective 'Waterloo Sunset'. Sherrin chose 'Where Have All The Good Times Gone' and 'The Last Of The Steam-Powered Trains' for the Fifties, even though there were arguably better candidates. For the Sixties, emigration was explored in 'Australia', young photographers like David Bailey via 'People Take Pictures Of Each Other', Swinging London in 'Dedicated Follower Of Fashion' and the prospect of economic gloom in 'Sunny Afternoon'. Androgyny and 'gender bending' through the Seventies was to be explored courtesy of 'Lola' and the entire production was due to end with the leading lady singing 'Young And Innocent Days', while looking back at the past century. It was, by any estimation, an intriguing project, with a scope far beyond anything Davies had previously attempted. It also required a hefty budget and a large cast which stretched even Sherrin's powers of persuasion. Originally, he had hoped to raise £4–5 million, but even that figure seemed insufficient and backers could not be found for such an elaborate project. Despite boasts of a stage production before the millennium, Sherrin was forced to admit defeat, while Davies transferred his attention to a more modest musical which would eventually emerge under the title *Come Dancing*.

In January 1997, Patricia and Ray registered the birth of their daughter, Eva Carol Davies, at the Mid Surrey registrar. She was Ray's fourth daughter. After lengthy stays between Cork, New York and Effingham, Surrey, the family were spending more time in Highgate where Ray always felt at home. He was now a dedicated gym rat and could often be seen undertaking his 35-minute aerobic programme, completing 75 press-ups or using weights to maintain upper body strength. That same year, Davies honoured his publishing commitments to Viking/Penguin but not, as originally intended, with a second volume of memoirs covering the Seventies onwards. Instead, he produced a modest collection of short stories, *Waterloo Sunset*. Unlike *X-Ray*, the book contained no experimental tricks in narration or structure but was a well-received attempt by Davies at working in a new format. Its publication was accompanied by a Kinks compilation, *The Singles Collection*, which included a bonus disc titled *The Songs Of Ray Davies – Waterloo Sunset*. As well as remixes of 'Voices In The Dark' and 'Art Lover', it boasted three previously unreleased tracks: 'The Shirt', an outtake from the first Arista album about a second-hand purchase; a satire on real-estate prices, 'The Million-Pound Semi-Detached'; and the reflective 'My Diary' with its plea "my life is empty".

The 'Storyteller' shows were still popular throughout this period and spawned an album of the same name, released in March 1998. Here, some of the Kinks' best work was presented in a largely acoustic format, augmented by amusing anecdotes. The set included a Delta blues version of 'You Really Got Me', boasting the presence of drummer Bobby Graham, who had played on the 1964 Pye version. For those familiar with the Kinks' story, the humorous tales of Mick Avory's induction and the impressions of Larry Page, Grenville Collins and Robert Wace were very entertaining. Even the new songs – the sumptuous 'The Storyteller', 'Art School Babe', 'The Ballad Of Julie Finkle' and 'London Song' (a cast list of famous Londoners through the ages) – sounded impressive in this context.

Over the next two months, fans were entertained with extended reissues of their Pye-era albums from *Kinks* to *Percy*. Instead of the usual addition of a few bonus tracks, the early works were completely transformed by the inclusion of hit singles, B-sides and EP tracks. Their first album included 12 additional songs, while their second, *Kinda Kinks* – one of the weakest in the canon – was remoulded into a tour de force thanks to the bonus tracks which eclipsed the original material. Ironically, it was the more celebrated *The Village Green Preservation Society* and *Arthur* that contained the fewest surprises, testifying to a time when the group's singles-only policy was superseded by more elaborate album concepts. In the USA, Velvel mined the RCA/Arista catalogues for a parallel set of re-releases. Although the reissue campaign focused interest on the Kinks, there was still no sign of them playing or recording together again.

In May, Pete Quaife travelled from Canada to New York in the hope of igniting some interest from the Davies brothers, who were both playing separate shows on alternate nights. At the Bottom Line, Quaife appeared onstage with Dave for a lively 'You Really Got Me'. The following night, the bassist turned up in Atlantic City, New Jersey, where Ray was playing, but remained seated at the venue. He was not acknowledged from the stage and afterwards failed to secure an audience with his former colleague who seemed oddly unapproachable. Within a year, possibly from hurt pride, Quaife himself was decrying the likelihood of any reunion. "That will never happen. The antagonisms between Ray and Dave are so colossal. Can you see those two in the studio together? Peace would reign for about twenty seconds [then] everybody off to the nearest hospital. I don't want to do that. Music has never been a source of violence for me, it's always been something I've liked and something I'd love to get into." Ray and Dave remained tantalizingly vague on the reformation issue. Companies House told the real story, though: at the end of 1998, Kinks 85 Ltd was dissolved, the firmest indication yet that the brothers were now separate business entities with no intention of trading under the group name in the future.

Ray was still working on various projects in sporadic fashion. Among these was *Flatlands*, a 50-minute choral piece about St George and the Dragon, commissioned by the Norwich and Norfolk Festival, featuring the Britten Symphonia. Prior to the performance, he was contacted by his former headmaster Charles Loades, who had retired to Norfolk. Although Dave never forgave the head for the caning he had received on his last day at school, Ray held no such resentment. "It was lovely to hear from him. He told me how much he liked my work. I think of him fondly." Davies' wife was also involved in composing a classical piece during this period in the form of a balletic poem, *Eva*, in honour of their daughter. Adapted to music by Van Morrison it was, according to one later reviewer, "a tantalizing hint of what Ireland could contribute to ballet if it managed to harvest its immense musical talent".

As he entered the millennium, Davies' third marriage was falling apart. As before, touring and recording had taken its toll. "You can't whip the road," Ray told me. "The road whips you in the end. I don't know anybody that's beaten it." More pertinently, as Dave predicted, he had 'messed things up', an assessment that Ray conceded was largely correct. "I haven't had that many relationships in my life but they've all been catastrophic." The breakup derailed him at the time, although he was later philosophical about male/female differences. "Women like you to be a hundred per cent exactly the way they want you to be. But a lot of men, particularly creative men – we like gaps. We like the fact that there's space in a character. There's a nothingness about me. There's a lot of nothing in me . . . It allows the admirer to look at you romantically. If you saw what we were really like, you wouldn't want us." The dichotomy between his working and home lives was cited as part of his ongoing problem, but that was ever so. Later he recalled a tendency in certain of his partners to see themselves in his songs. "They say, 'You wrote about this, you wrote about that.' I said to one woman, 'That was a song. That's not the real world.' She said, 'But the songs are the only real part about you.'"

Patricia returned to Ireland to continue her career in ballet, but harboured no ill feelings when questioned about the end of their relationship. "He was eccentric. It was never dull being married. I had a very exciting life with him." As always, Ray attempted to bury himself in work, channelling his upset into several new compositions, the first of which, 'After The Fall', confronted his failings. "I started writing 'After The Fall' after my marriage broke up and I was in Ireland visiting my daughter; it was about retribution and guilt and life changes and how you've got to be responsible for your own actions . . . My personal life went through chaotic times. The only enduring thing that's come through is that I've got a beautiful daughter . . ."

Throughout this period, Ray was determined to retain regular contact with Eva and frequently visited Cork between engagements. Eva also stayed at his home in Surrey, where he put on a deliberately exaggerated London pronunciation, as if claiming part of his daughter's psyche on Britain's behalf. Patricia was comically exasperated after hearing Eva's accent upon her return to Cork. She wryly accused Ray of attempting to turn their daughter into a cockney. For a time, it seemed that Davies might succeed as a commuting parent. However, familiar patterns soon began to repeat themselves. In common with his interaction with Louisa, Viktoria and Natalie, Ray sacrificed regular access and remained a distant presence hereafter. "It was a decision. 'Am I going to pursue a solo career, or shall I just go and live in Ireland where my daughter was?' I chose the career. And in some respects I regret it . . . It was a big decision, because I had to reinvent myself . . ." The reinvention would not happen overnight. It would be the best part of six years before Davies completed his first studio album as a soloist, a tortuous journey that would involve a shift of locale, a crisis in confidence, and a postponed date with the Grim Reaper.

CHAPTER FORTY

THE SHOOTING OF RAY DAVIES

In the aftermath of his separation from Patricia Crosbie, Davies' public profile slipped, as did his sobriety. "Not many people know this but I was living alone in 2000–2001. I was living in an isolated place and drinking heavily. I watched the same film over and over for three weeks. It comforted me, because I knew every line. I'm not going to tell you what it was . . . it was a foreign movie . . . But alcohol did get the better of me. I was having sleep problems. But drink doesn't cure sleep."

Davies had been stockpiling demos with the intention of completing a solo album for Capitol Records, but was reluctant to allow them access to the songs. "I totally lost my confidence on how to make records. When you go in the studio without the usual musicians around and it's you and a click track, it's frightening. I was so nervous I couldn't even tune my guitar properly. I was going through tremendous personal and psychological issues. I had to justify what I was doing to myself again. Why couldn't I just retire and get a day job?" Ray had voiced similar questions after Rasa left him in 1973 but, even at his lowest ebb, he had never doubted himself creatively. It was an ominous development.

In August 2000, Davies premiered some of his new material at New York's Jane Street Theatre for an audience that included several representatives from Capitol Records. Frustrated by his continued prevarication ("I didn't trust them") they eventually lost interest. The shows were nevertheless a minor revelation. Backed by guitarist Pete Mathison and the New Jersey group Yo

La Tengo (who had recorded 'Big Sky' on their 1986 debut album, *Ride The Tiger*) Davies was encouraged to delve into the more obscure areas of his back catalogue for 'No Return', 'This Is Where I Belong' and 'This Strange Effect'. The Capitol contingent listened patiently to the new songs, including 'The Deal', 'Empty Room', 'Vietnam Cowboys' and 'Otis Riffs'. There was also 'Things Are Gonna Change (The Morning After)', ostensibly a reflection of his current emotional state, but equally applicable to traumas from the past. When he spoke of "resurrecting the clown", it recalled the description used in later reports of his 1973 trauma onstage at White City. Similarly, the ambiguous "your girls left – never to return" (with the mysterious missing apostrophe in the printed lyrics) could be applied autobiographically (as singular or plural) to Rasa or Patricia or Louisa and Viktoria. As Davies said of another new song, the wry 'All She Wrote': "People have come and gone in my life and 'All She Wrote' is a combination of *all* the breakups." In short, he was writing some of his most personally revealing songs, but fusing memories of disparate incidents and relationships to disguise the autobiographical origins. Referring to another new composition, 'Next Door Neighbour', he advised: "If you listen to the characters, I've been through all of it myself. I ran off with an Essex blonde, threw the television through a window. It's all me really."

While Davies was poring over new songs and pondering his relevance, Sanctuary Records issued the long-awaited archival collection, *BBC Sessions 1964–1977*, in March 2001. A couple of months later, there was a shock report that founding Kinks member Pete Quaife had suffered a heart attack. It later transpired that the 'attack' was actually a heart spasm brought on while he was undergoing dialysis, having been diagnosed with kidney failure back in 1998. Dave Davies, meanwhile, was busy touring and at the end of July played a concert at New York's World Trade Center. Six weeks later, the building was reduced to rubble in the terrorist attack enshrined forever by its American dating: 9/11.

Ray had been scheduled to return to the States at this time but instead of cancelling the dates he elected to push ahead. Due to internal flight restrictions, Davies' ensemble were forced to drive long distances. "I saw bits of America that I'd missed before and I started writing a whole new batch of songs on that trip.

Eventually, I ended up going down to New Orleans to write more songs." Davies was catapulted back to his youth, invigorated by memories of Hank Williams, Big Bill Broonzy and all the American music that had inspired him to play guitar.

The trip to New Orleans, where he would stay on and off for the next three years, provided the key to his 'reinvention'. Although the decision to relocate seemed a sudden one, it had been germinating in his mind for a couple of decades. While promoting *Low Budget* in the summer of 1979, he had promised: "The next album I'm going to do will be a blues album. I'm going to go to New Orleans, live there for a bit and write it there." What had seemed a flippant remark at the time was evidently deadly serious. Three months before his showcase gigs at the Jane Street Theatre, he had undertaken a reconnaissance trip to New Orleans with the intention of sparking his songwriting muse. He had even completed a meditation on his recent marriage, 'The Art Of Moving On', followed by other songs such as 'Wings Of Fantasy', 'The Fields Are On Fire' and 'Run Away From Time'. He continued touring, working on demos (including some unsuccessful run-throughs with his brother). There were even attempts to launch a musical, *Come Dancing*, a project that would not reach fruition for several more years. But his real inspiration was New Orleans. "I found the place to be quite haunting, its mystery, its folklore; voodoo and magic."

Davies had also (at least temporarily) fallen out of love with England. The brash affluence of the Britpop years had left him cold, even when he was being courted as an honorary member by its more celebrated participants. He had always been cynical about the Swinging Sixties and critical of Harold Wilson, but the promises of New Labour sounded far more hollow. Having professed an apolitical attitude throughout his adult life, he now expressed an almost nostalgic affection for the old Labour Party, whose values had been eroded in the name of capitalism and market forces. It was the reverse of 'The Village Green Preservation Society', a song that sounded antediluvian in its sentiments, while also betraying a psychological need to cling to the familiar. Radical and reactionary views served an equivalent purpose in Davies' new world. "Another reason I wanted to move to New Orleans was to escape Tony Blair. I'm a socialist, and Labour is not socialist any more. The working man is still downtrodden and unheard. Blair came in and it became uncool to be working class. Everybody aspired to be something a little better. Nothing wrong with wanting to better yourself, but when you forget your origins – that's bad . . . I don't fit into this culture any more." Whether Davies had ever fitted into any culture was a more pertinent consideration.

During his stay in New Orleans, Davies befriended two established members of the local arts community: Robert Cary Tannen and Jeanne Nathan. Seven years older than Davies, Brooklyn-born Tannen, an architect, artist, sculptor and urban planner, had settled in New Orleans two years after a consulting assignment in the aftermath of 1969's Hurricane Camille. He and his wife Jeanne became founding members of the New Orleans Contemporary Art Center. Davies, with his art school background, was intrigued by Tannen's conceptual ideas, not least, one assumes, because Robert was a true original. Al Nodal, former president of the Los Angeles Cultural Affairs Commission, noted with arch humour: "Even in New Orleans, which is a city of eccentrics, he's seen as a major eccentric. I think the brilliance of his ideas will become clear as the problems facing the country become increasingly pressing."

Tannen and Nathan were articulate, passionate about art and keen activists in the local community. They were also generous hosts, regularly inviting Ray to dinner at their large colonial house on Esplanade Avenue. They knew a number of local musicians, including Alex Chilton, the vocalist/guitarist who had enjoyed Sixties hit success with the Box Tops ('The Letter', 'Cry Like A Baby') and cult status the following decade with Big Star. Chilton had rented a cottage on the Tannen/Nathan property for many years, which was occasionally sublet to girlfriends or relatives when he was away. Eventually, he moved to a farmhouse in Tremé, but retained close links with Tannen. Like Davies, Chilton was socially shy, if not reclusive, but the pair did meet and established a passing friendship.

It was through one of Chilton's friends that Davies secured a two-roomed garage apartment on the Esplanade property. There was also an important woman in his life, Suzanne Despres. Clearly a music aficionado, Despres was also friends with Davies' New York associates Yo La Tengo and later managed Ambrosia Parsley, the maverick singer-songwriter from alternative Americana pop trio Shivaree. Despres was a valuable companion during a period of uncertainty and readjustment in his life, but the relationship would not survive his time in the Big Easy.

Davies enjoyed the company of Tannen and Nathan who regarded him as an abstract thinker with an insatiable curiosity. "He was delightfully intelligent," says Jeanne Nathan, "a little nutty, and it was great to have him here." Tannen was equally impressed. "Thinking back, he had an interest in all of the arts. Visual arts, parades, the culture of New Orleans in all of its manifestations. The Indian marching groups and the costumes of the Indian tribes. His interest was very broad. He had a great deal of curiosity [as if he was undertaking] an almost sociological study of this indigenous place and culture. We shared a similar point of view on art being accessible, inclusive and collaborative, that it not be just ivory-tower-in-the-studio activity. He became very interested in the street culture of New Orleans and Tremé, and was very curious about everything that was going on."

It was not long after moving into Esplanade Avenue that Davies was struck by the sound of a marching band emanating from the John McDonogh High School, a mere block away. Racially integrated since 1967, the school was known for its sporting achievements, but it was the band that intrigued Davies. As Jeanne Nathan says: "It's a wonderful thing around four in the afternoon to listen to them rehearsing in the streets around your house."

With Robert Tannen as his intermediary, Davies set up a meeting with the principal and cast himself in the role of a cultural attaché, suggesting an exchange programme by which students might visit White Hart Lane School in north London, bringing a smidgen of their jazz and blues heritage to Wood Green. Tannen recalls Ray attending a class and filming students as they spoke about their daily lives in the community.

Over the succeeding months, Davies connected with the heads of both schools, armed with a light political agenda promoting British culture. He had even started to sound like a character from *Arthur*. "I used to go to school and sing hymns," he said of his upbringing in north London. "I'm not saying people from Croatia or Afghanistan should sing songs by William Blake. I'm not suggesting morris dancing in the mosque. But it would be interesting for people to realize we have a culture here [in Britain] too. We don't ask people to swear an oath of allegiance in this country . . . We had an empire and we lost the empire. That's fine. This is all a question of compassion. We are not alone. In America, and Europe even, there are places where the culture is changing with immigration."

Davies attempted to keep himself busy in New Orleans, largely oblivious to a series of violent incidents, sporadically chronicled in the press. A brutal kidnapping and homicide had occurred only a few blocks away from Davies' apartment, but he still felt safe in his cosseted world. On 14 April 2003, tragedy struck John McDonogh High School at the very moment when Davies was attempting to forge his cultural exchange and promote the marching band. At 10.30 a.m., two assailants armed with an AK-47 and a semi-automatic pistol, entered the school gymnasium and fatally shot a 15-year-old pupil, Jonathan 'Caveman' Williams. The slaying was connected to a previous shooting in another school only a week before. Thereafter, the body count multiplied. Although Williams' killers were apprehended, their families were subsequently targeted. Two more deaths occurred on 27 October, summed up by a headline in the *Times-Picayune*: 'Student's Death Sparks Crescendo Of Revenge'.

Davies made no mention of these killings, either at the time or later when he wrote a memoir dealing with his stay in New Orleans. By his own admission, it was a period of personal disorientation and uncertainty. Universal Records were about to reject his proposed solo album and he still seemed fragile after the breakup of his marriage and absence from his youngest daughter. He recalled feeling that he was somehow living in "a fake world", having become "a lost, clumsy imitation of a person". That description was uncannily similar to the sense of unreality he had experienced as an adolescent in the immediate aftermath of his sister Rene's death in 1957. Back then, he had described life as a 'reproduction', like some fake oil painting. "It wasn't real," he thought. Suddenly, those suppressed anomic impressions were re-emerging in New Orleans. He was sufficiently concerned to visit a church and consult a priest who sat with him for an hour, offering counsel. Was that feeling of 'unreality' directly comparable with the Rene episode? "Yes," he admits. "It's like a curse. When you go through teenage years and you think you have a fault and in later life you think you've escaped it, it brings it all back to that traumatic feeling. That's when I was lost, talking to the preacher."

Davies returned to Ireland for Christmas 2003 to see his daughter Eva, but the homecoming was fraught with danger. A notoriously poor driver, he was left stranded atop a cliff near Kinsale and had to be rescued by the local gardai who phoned for a recovery vehicle on his behalf. A week later, Davies was back in New Orleans for a rather subdued New Year's Eve. Still, there was reason to believe that better things lay ahead. He had recently learned that he was to be named in the Queen's Honours as a CBE (Commander of the Order of the British Empire). Amusingly, the official letter from the Palace had lain unopened at Konk where staff assumed it was probably a tax bill. Nobody had the courage to inform Ray that he might owe money to the Revenue, so the dreaded document was studiously avoided for several days. Davies was pleasantly surprised by the news, recalling that historic moment when the Beatles had been awarded MBEs back in 1965. The notion that a member of the Kinks might one day be offered an even higher honour would have been regarded as an impossible fantasy during the Sixties or Seventies. In the new millennium, however, even pop stars with criminal convictions were invited to become knights of the realm.

The year 2004 was also the fortieth anniversary of the Kinks' formation and the occasion of Ray's 60th birthday. In different circumstances, this might have been a time of double celebration. Unfortunately for the Davies brothers, 2004 was to be their *annus horribilis*. It started to go wrong on the evening of Sunday 4 January when Ray and his 39-year-old girlfriend Suzanne Despres were in New Orleans' French Quarter, having just enjoyed a meal at the Japanese restaurant, Wasabi, on Frenchmen Street. It was close to 8.30 and dusk was falling. Rather than hailing a cab, the pair decided to walk home while there was still sufficient light. The streets were deserted and police time was largely taken up with the well-publicized Sugar Bowl football game between Louisiana State University and Oklahoma. While sauntering along the 1400 block of Burgundy Street near the intersection of Esplanade Avenue, Davies and Despres were tailed by a white

Pontiac Grand Am. A passenger alighted from the car and, with deliberate clumsiness, bumped into Ray, then punched and pushed him to the ground. The assailant then turned on Suzanne, pulled out a gun and fired into the pavement to prove the firearm was loaded. He demanded her handbag which she surrendered, but more drama soon followed.

Earlier that evening, Davies had placed his cash and credit cards in Suzanne's bag and now the thief was getting away with the entire stash. Instinctively, Ray gave chase, desperate to retrieve his money at any cost. By now the robber had reached the getaway car but before speeding away he turned and shot his pursuer in the right leg. Davies recalls veering to the left, narrowly avoiding what might otherwise have been a fatal bullet. While he lay bleeding on the ground, police were called on a mobile phone and Despres was astute enough to jot down the licence number of the assailants' vehicle. A medical team immediately arrived on the scene and started cutting Davies' trousers in order to examine the wound. "But, they're new trousers!" he exclaimed, as the medics ignored his complaints. Now he had lost both his money and his trousers. If Ray was hoping for some form of accolade as a 'have-a-go hero', the words of Police Chief Superintendent Eddie Compass merely stressed his foolishness. "He put himself in harm's way. You really don't confront individuals participating in those type of activities. Anything that's taken from you can be replaced, but your personal safety is paramount."

On reflection, Davies accepted Compass' harsh judgement. "It was a ridiculous thing to do, but a person never knows how they'll react until they've been put in a situation like that. I should have said, 'I'll just go the hell in the opposite direction and get out of here', but on that particular day and the circumstances of the moment, I chose to go after the guy . . . It makes you thankful for what you still have. You become more cautious afterwards, and react differently with certain instincts, but it did make me feel thankful for being around."

Davies was taken to the nearby Charity Hospital on Tulane Avenue which proved a chastening experience in itself. "I saw a lot of sad and damaged people in there." Within 48 hours, the shooting was international news. The reporting was surprisingly upbeat with English newspapers stressing that Davies remained in good spirits and was well on the way to recovery. Evidently, doctors were keeping him in hospital purely for observational purposes. Ray's distant representative Deke Arlon informed BBC News: "It's not really serious. He should be up and around in a day or two." There was also news of an arrest which had occurred only a few hours after the mugging. Police had located a car with the number plate jotted down by Suzanne Despres. The suspect was 25-year-old Jerome Barra, who was duly charged with armed robbery and aggravated burglary.

As it turned out, almost every aspect of the reporting proved overly optimistic. At first, Davies had been told that his wound was clean and sank into a morphine-induced sleep, tormented by evanescent snatches of song that ran through his head. Fearful about the possibility of a revenge attack from someone connected with the shooting, he told hospital staff to inform anonymous callers that he had been discharged and was already back in England. It rapidly became clear that he would not be leaving New Orleans anytime soon. Doctors were concerned about his dangerously slow heartbeat, a more worrying issue than any leg wound. It later transpired from additional X-rays that Davies had broken his thighbone – the strongest bone in the human body. Now, he required a titanium rod to be inserted in his leg to mend the fracture. "It's not like in the westerns where you get up and carry on," he says. "Bullets really hurt."

Davies was subsequently moved to University Hospital which meant better conditions but continued psychological stress. His insurance status remained unresolved for some time, and the fear that he might be deemed responsible for some of the mounting hospital and medical fees preyed on his mind. It was almost worrying enough to bring on a heart attack. Even after his operation, Davies was unable to leave the country and, like Blanche DuBois in *A Streetcar Named Desire*, appeared increasingly reliant on the kindness of strangers. "That was a scary time," he says. "Here's someone who usually travels with an entourage where insurance and credit cards are taken care of. Everything is taken care of. But when everything is taken from you, you've got no identity. So I did feel helpless."

After his discharge from hospital, Davies stayed at Robert Tannen and Jeanne Nathan's capacious home while convalescing.

This time he was discreetly placed in a second-floor apartment, previously occupied by Jeanne's mother. "He wanted as much privacy as possible," Tannen adds. "There were a lot of people here that were not only concerned about him but curious about his state of mind and condition."

Suzanne Despres was in frequent attendance, sometimes staying in an adjoining room. It took a while for Davies to adjust to crutches and his mobility was limited, but gradually his condition improved. His spirits were further heightened when his insurance company confirmed that his medical bills were covered. Still on crutches, he was nevertheless able to attend the New Orleans Athletic Club where he worked hard on strengthening his upper body in preparation for his return to England. The arduous routine ensured that he was able to fly home in time to collect his CBE from the Queen on 17 March 2004. Photographed in a dark suit, offset by a walking stick, Ray was accompanied by his seven-year-old daughter, Eva. His sister Joyce was the only other family member at the ceremony.

The recent shooting inevitably soured Davies' connections with New Orleans, putting paid to any fantasies about settling there in the future. One year later, the city would be devastated by Hurricane Katrina. By then, the case against Jerome Barra was still unresolved, having been subject to unexplained delays. Within the space of a year, court hearings were postponed 13 times and the police had yet to arrest Barra's alleged accomplice. Barra had cooperated with the authorities from the outset, implicating himself as the driver while maintaining his innocence of the shooting. During an audio-recorded interview he claimed that he had been driving around, accompanied by his cousin Kawan Johnson, who briefly left the vehicle. Barra then recalled hearing gunfire and seeing a man lying on the ground, after which Johnson returned to the car and Barra drove off. Johnson was never arrested and it was Barra alone who stood in court one year later on 20 April 2005. Despite assurances that he would attend as a witness, Davies did not appear for reasons never properly explained. At one point, he claimed that he was unaware that he had to attend in person, which sounded disingenuous.

Barra was freed, but District Attorney Eddie Jordan insisted that was not the end of the matter, promising to pursue the case until they could get Davies to appear in court. "We do need victims in order to prosecute an armed robbery case," Jordan explained. The DA was as good as his word and Barra was re-indicted on 23 March 2006. Four months later, he was back in court. Once again, Davies did not show. This time, the case was thrown out and Barra walked free. When contacted, Davies expressed his disappointment, claiming that he had only learned of the impending trial a few days before, while insisting that such scant notice made it next to impossible to schedule an appearance. However, court records clearly show that the prosecution, defence and Judge had each committed to the trial date as early as 17 May. Either Davies was the victim of a preposterous administrative blunder or he had simply forgotten the key details when interviewed. Perhaps there was an issue of psychological avoidance in Davies' odd comments and failures to attend the proceedings. By his own admission, the entire episode was traumatic.

Davies subsequently admitted that he had deliberately not travelled to New Orleans for the trial, preferring to complete the final mixdown of his latest solo album. "I was supposed to be in court in Louisiana, but I realized it was futile because the DA was going to let the guy off, because they lost his confession in the Hurricane. So I thought, 'Well, am I going to mix these tracks or am I going to go there and let it ruin my life again?'" Whether there was any truth in Davies' contention about the 'lost confession' was never ascertained. It was certainly not mentioned in any reporting of the case.

Four years later, he was busy preparing an account of his time in New Orleans for a memoir in which he promised to unravel the *true* story of the shooting. "What I'm trying to get to is the reason why it happened. That real reason. I'll have to be really honest. There was a lot going on at the time . . . two days before it happened somebody threatened to have me killed. That's what I like to believe." When journalist David Cavanagh asked if he was saying it was a 'contract killing', Davies demurred: "No. They don't do it that way. It's just 'Will you shoot this guy for me if I give you some drugs?' . . . That guy should not have been walking down that street. I've walked down that street a thousand times and you don't see people dressed that way. He was dressed like 50 Cent. It was the wrong neighbourhood for him to be walking in . . . But if I'm really honest about what I'm writing, it will all come out."

In 2013, the memoir titled *Americana* was published with details of his time in New Orleans. Contrary to his comments three years before, there was evidently no longer a conspiracy to address. According to the book, someone had 'threatened' his life a week before the shooting, but this turned out to be a drunk in a New Orleans bar who had snarled, "I'll kill you." Davies could find no connection between the verbal outburst and the shooting. Nor did he offer any suggestion at any time as to why anyone would wish him harm. He also admitted that if anyone in New Orleans really wanted to kill him, he would already be dead. As for the seemingly paranoid musings of 2010, Davies now suggests, somewhat obliquely, that they may have been stress-related. "There was a lot of eerie significance going on at the time. When you're in a heightened state of tiredness, I think you read into things. I maybe read into things. But the psychic world is quite heightened."

Davies did return to New Orleans when he played at the Voodoo Experience in 2011. "I was nostalgic," he says. "I had lots of friends there and I get nostalgic about a place. A great town, but for my epiphany, it was not happy. I would not live there again. I still love the music. That will endure. There were a lot of sketches for tunes. I just wish I'd done that marching band project."

CHAPTER FORTY-ONE

DAVE'S STROKE

On 30 June 2004, five months after Ray's shooting, his brother, now aged 57, suffered a stroke. Dave was promoting a new album, *Bug*, and had just completed a radio interview on *The Danny Baker Show* when he collapsed in a lift at BBC Broadcasting House. Still conscious, but unable to speak and with his entire right side frozen, he was taken away in an ambulance, accompanied by his son, Christian. Only three weeks before, he had suffered what sounded like a mini-stroke with similar, less serious symptoms, including stiffening of the right hand and a sudden loss of speech. Dave described the first incident as a transient ischaemic attack, possibly brought on by stress, extensive touring and an excessive lifestyle. When Ray heard the news, he concluded the same. "I could tell he was going to get sick. He kept turning up out of breath at doorways. He was doing too much. Not looking after himself. It came as no surprise to me that he got ill."

Doctors concluded that the stroke had probably been brought on by high blood pressure. Dave blamed it on his overuse of amphetamines as a young pop star. Whatever the cause, the road to recovery would be a long one. It seemed doubtful that Dave would ever play onstage again, but he proved a determined and resilient patient. "I knew I was going to have to work very hard if I was to get better, and I started using meditation and visualization. I thought if I could visualize myself running, walking and playing the guitar, it might prompt my brain to remember how I used to be." His therapist told him about 'muscle memory' and how the body automatically performs familiar tasks without having to think through the movements. Dave even took his guitar to bed and placed his hands on the strings, hoping that his non-conscious mind might do the rest. Extensive physiotherapy dominated his life over the next couple of years, with impressive results. As he admitted: "Now, I appreciate my slower pace of life. I feel I have discovered an inner strength which I know will see me through any adversity."

As had happened in the past, serious illness brought the Davies brothers together again, but their happy reunion was short-lived. Dave was lacerating about his brother's bedside manner and cynical about his motives. "I'm undecided whether he was pleased I was ill or jealous I was getting the attention. I stayed at his house afterwards. I was ill in bed and could barely move, but he started saying, 'I'm sick, I'm sick.' He was screaming in pain from his stomach. A doctor from Harley Street came around at 3 a.m. and said, 'There's nothing wrong with your stomach.' He just wanted attention." Even by their standards, this was a cynically low blow which failed to take account of Ray's psychological and physical condition. He had nearly been killed only months before and was still in considerable pain from the titanium rod that had not yet been removed from his leg. For the moment, it seemed that non-communication was probably the brothers' best stress-free option.

With the passage of the Kinks' 40th anniversary, Dave was inevitably asked if there was any likelihood that the group might reconvene in the future. "No," he stated, later joking that he could barely stand an hour in his brother's company so any 'reunion' would be necessarily short. In more reflective mode, he added: "I wouldn't know what sort of band it was. I'm not a great person for nostalgia. When they do those tours – like the 'final' Who tour – they look a bit sad to me. I can't help it. I think it would be a bit sad if the Kinks got together like four silly old men playing. The music was then, not now. I'm more interested in my life now than the Sixties. I don't know why people harp on about the past so much. The Sixties were OK but surely we should be more concerned with what's going on in the world around us today." The only 'Kinks reunion' of 2004 occurred in parodic fashion when Pete Quaife performed alongside his 'replacement'

John Dalton on 12 September at a Kast Off Kinks get-together for their Dutch fan club.

Over the next year, Ray continued tinkering and remixing his elusive solo album, a work that had been interrupted by his hospital stay and convalescence. His live appearances were less frequent, although there was a high-profile outing at London's Alexandra Palace on 16 November 2005 where the Kinks, the Who, Joy Division and New Order were inducted into the UK Music Hall of Fame. Among the performers that evening were the Pretenders. Acknowledging the occasion, singer Chrissie Hynde played two Ray Davies compositions, but there were no reunion hugs or kisses. "She only sang," Ray stresses. "I didn't have to talk to her. I was quite uncomfortable, but I thought it was a nice moment. Love ends, but the songs are for ever. They capture a moment and an emotion. You can have two human beings who should not be in the same house, or possibly even the same country, but the music tells you that it really could have been for ever. In those three minutes there are no hard feelings."

All this nostalgic talk was making Dave Davies rather grumpy. He was riled after reading a second-hand quote about how Ray was supposedly helping him relearn the guitar. "What a load of bollocks," he retorted. "That is so Ray. He likes to think he's the good guy. He was very sympathetic when I became ill, of course, but I've had great therapists. Ray's not been part of that. My whole family have been immensely supportive. Ray did make me egg and chips one night, though."

After what seemed an age, Ray finally issued his long overdue solo album for V2 Records in February 2006. Remarkably, it was his first full work of new songs since 1993's *Phobia*. *Other People's Lives* featured compositions dating back to the previous decade, long before the incident in New Orleans. Indeed, several tracks had been premiered as part of his showcase with Yo La Tengo at New York's Jane Street Theatre in August 2000.

The work begins with a ring of feedback leading into the vibrant 'Things Are Gonna Change (The Morning After)', the first of several breakup songs on the album. The same theme is re-examined on 'All She Wrote', 'After The Fall' and 'Over My Head'. Davies' tone is sometimes sardonic, but also poignant and heartfelt. That old Kinksian humour is most evident on 'Is There Life After

Breakfast' which offers the perfect panacea for a fractured romance: "take the pills and drink your tea". While coyly admitting that these songs were largely autobiographical, Davies advised caution in applying them to any particular person. The self-doubting 'Creatures Of Little Faith', for example, deals with fears of marital fidelity but, when examined, its lyrical content could apply to any or all of his past marriages. Adding tonal variety, Davies throws a Spanish cantina into the title track, abetted by guest vocalist, Isabel Fructuoso. There is some familiar social satire on 'The Tourist' with its vulgarian observer assimilating images of the Mardi Gras, the Blarney Stone and the Wailing Wall, while 'The Getaway' and the hidden bonus track 'Thanksgiving Day' document Davies' initial experiences after visiting New Orleans. Completing the set are a couple of songs echoing his music hall roots – 'Next Door Neighbour' and the live favourite 'Stand Up Comic'. The latter introduces the mischievous 'Max' character (in memory of Max Miller), who, rather alarmingly, began to infiltrate Davies interviews of the period in which he would suddenly announce that the words he had just spoken were those of his uproarious doppelgänger. "Max is always there waiting to humiliate me," he now says when reminded of this troubling alter ego.

Other People's Lives climbed to number 36 in the UK charts. It was a decent song selection, certainly no worse and arguably better than several later Kinks albums, but the mannered production and musical orthodoxy left some critics wanting more. The work was clearly not adventurous enough for radical tastes and the lack of a hit single ensured that it escaped the notice of many mainstream listeners. Davies' songwriting was still strong but his potential audience was dwindling. The album emphasized the perennial problems facing a performer who has surrendered a classic group brand name in search of a solo identity. Relaunching a career on such terms was seldom easy but in the post-digital record business it became more difficult than ever.

In assuming control of his own career, Davies was also limiting the power of any managerial or authority figure in his orbit. He had dispensed with Deke Arlon (manager of Sanctuary Music) and briefly appointed Peter Rudge (of Octagon Music) whose role appeared to be restricted to music publishing rather than organizing any career strategy. Davies subsequently appointed American

Chris Metzler, a former promotions person and owner of Décor Records. His powers were similarly constrained. Davies did not even appear on his personal management roster, but could be found in a subsection with the carefully worded caveat: "We manage individual release projects, promotion, merchandise, websites for Ray Davies and the Kinks." It was all a long way from the days of Larry Page, Grenville Collins and Robert Wace.

V2 Records were keen for Davies to release a follow-up album at the earliest opportunity. He had already stockpiled approximately 35 songs, many written during his spell in New Orleans, and was ready to undertake an extensive tour which augured well. Responding enthusiastically, Davies contacted producer Ray Kennedy, who had previously expressed interest in working on *Other People's Lives*. Kennedy insisted he could complete the initial recordings in the space of a fortnight, using top-notch Nashville musicians. Having agonized over his previous album for years, Davies convinced himself that a more spontaneous approach might vitalize the project. Amazingly, everyone adhered to the tight schedule and *Working Man's Café* became the second fastest album ever recorded by Davies (beaten only by *Kinda Kinks*). Among the backing musicians was Swedish singer Karin Forsman, who had already joined Davies' touring troupe and would emerge as his steady girlfriend over the next few years. With her striking blonde hair, Forsman was already well known in Scandinavia, singing alongside her identical twin Maria in the Pilgrim Sisters. Davies would later produce an album for Karin at Konk titled *Harbour Girl*, credited to Pilgrim. The relationship remained cordial but Davies hinted that geographical distance was a problem. "It's difficult," he said. "She goes to Sweden a lot." He also admitted that his own isolation may have proven significant. "I'm a lonely adult. I was a lonely child. When I'm busy I have tunnel vision. I give off signals that I don't want to see people, but all they have to do is knock on the door. That's what they should be doing. They think I don't want to talk to them, but they're wrong."

While scheduling the release date of *Working Man's Café*, V2 Records came up with a bold idea. With CD sales in decline, there was much talk in the music industry of a future dominated by internet downloads and giveaway promotional tracks. On 15 July

2007, a veritable revolution occurred when the *Mail On Sunday* offered Prince's new CD *Planet Earth* free to its readership. The paper sold over 2.8 million copies that weekend, with the CD accounting for an estimated 600,000 extra copies. Industry observers were divided about the experiment and its potential benefits to the performer and the newspaper. The *Mail On Sunday* pointed out that its year-on-year circulation had risen by 4.4 per cent, irrespective of the Prince giveaway.

In theory, Ray Davies' reputation as an elder statesman whose songs were much loved by the public made him a suitable candidate for newspaper rehabilitation. V2 began negotiations with the *Times* newspaper group and it was agreed that, following the Prince model, a copy of *Working Man's Café* would be included in the *Sunday Times* on 21 October. It would be preceded the week before by a free download of the opening track, 'Vietnam Cowboys', an arch observation on globalization and economic meltdown. Media sales and marketing director Katie Vanneck announced: "This is a first for the *Sunday Times* and Ray Davies and continues the changing trend in the music industry for artistes showcasing their new work."

Evidently, Davies had given his full blessing to the project and insisted he was "truly excited that 1.5 million copies will be distributed to people who'll hear it organically . . . the way it was intended. It's an exciting opportunity I couldn't resist. Personally, it's about reaching as many people as possible." Coincidentally, Radiohead launched their new album *In Rainbows* that same week via their website. In a deal that might well have struck fear into Davies' soul, they were allowing their fans to pay whatever they thought the album was worth. Suddenly, the former Kink seemed at the cutting edge of music media experimentation.

On 21 October, the *Sunday Times'* readership were presented with a 10-track version of *Working Man's Café*, which was certainly a bargain and included several songs that ranked alongside his best of the past two decades. The title track mourns the death of the working man from Fred Davies' generation, a world now displaced by encroaching Americanization. Even the narrator's cockney accent is compromised as he uses words like 'pants' (instead of trousers) while lamenting the loss of the 'fruit and veg' man. There is even an echo of another meditation on the past,

'Do You Remember Walter', with Davies repeating one of its key lines: "I knew you then, but will I know you now?" Davies' London voice is also present on the insolent 'You're Asking Me' which sounds uncannily like a Kinks song. Similarly, the Neville Chamberlain refrain 'Peace In Our Time', an anthem with a descending chord progression, could have been a lyric suitable for *Arthur*. Davies' fascination with personal identity is dramatized in 'Imaginary Man', one of his most reflective songs of recent years. From the material composed in New Orleans, the neurotic 'No One Listens' alludes to his frustration over the handling of his court case. The chilling 'The Voodoo Walk' captures the spirit of the Big Easy, a considerable achievement considering the work was produced in Nashville. 'Morphine Song', arguably the standout track on the album, is one of Davies' most morbidly comic compositions. Set in the Charity Hospital ward where he was scribbling song notes while connected to a morphine drip, it has a surreal air, enhanced by some delicately observed character sketches of the mullet-haired Nelson with his 10 grandchildren, and Brenda, an alcoholic for whom nobody grieves. The backbeat sounds like a soundtrack produced by Davies' own slow heartbeat which is suddenly interrupted by the arrival of a full marching band. It resembles an hallucinatory scene out of Dennis Potter's *The Singing Detective*.

Twenty-four hours after its appearance in the *Sunday Times*, *Working Man's Café* was available for purchase. With only two extra tracks, 'Hymns For A New Age' and 'The Real World', it was largely ignored by the record-buying public. With thousands of copies lying around abandoned on shelves or thrown in the rubbish with yesterday's papers, its fate in the UK was sealed. Davies briefly held hopes that something good might come of the newspaper giveaway. "I've had calls from old friends saying, 'It's great to have access to your music again.' Maybe a lot of people who don't read the *Sunday Times* will buy this record. We'll have to see what evolves."

Davies' views hardened after reviewing the poor sales figures and learning that the V2 label was terminating future releases. Thereafter, he insisted that he had been kept in the dark about the plan to offer virtually the entire album to the *Sunday Times*. "I thought they were only going to give away five tracks, but they put the whole bloody lot on it," he complained. "I'm still destroyed by that." Elsewhere, he qualified that statement claiming that he expected the paper to use tracks from both *Other People's Lives* and *Working Man's Café* so that it would serve as a sampler of his solo work. Assuming either statement was true, it underlined a terrible lack of communication between record company, management and performer. For someone as controlling as Davies, it was hard to believe that a decision as important as releasing an album via a national newspaper was not thoroughly scrutinized beforehand.

Despite all the creative liberation that his solo work provided, Ray still felt ambivalent about the loss of the Kinks. As if realizing this, his brother posted a mischievous message on his website, lambasting any lingering notions of another get-together. "Ray has been doing Karaoke Kinks shows since 1996. 'Phobia . . . what you got . . .' What is he talking about? I wouldn't mind or rather consider doing some shows with Ray purely in respect of the Great body of work we have been fortunate to have been involved in over the years. And for the fans of course. And the money, don't forget the money, Reg . . . But to sit in a room or studio with him and have my brain and heart slowly sucked out . . . no friggin' thank you. Got the T-shirt, overcoat, bruises, psychiatrist, warts, scars, lumbago and somnambulistic gaze to prove it . . . It would be like a poor remake of *Night Of The Living Dead* . . . There is nothing wrong with the old songs or new songs that we have been writing on our own; but no more torture, please. No more Hannibal Lecter. The swansong Ray and Dave tour should be called 'The Kinks Are the Fractured Mindz Preservation Society'. Preserve in Peace."

Ray responded almost immediately, employing similar words to Dave, but with a more positive message. "I really would like to get together if we had new music. Otherwise it's just 'Karaoke Kinks'. The chemistry is still important. I wrote for those characters and they all had an influence on what I did. I know I wrote a lot of the stuff, but they were my muse. They were what I was writing for and I couldn't have done it without knowing they'd be there. I really hate being a solo artiste. But there's no other way to get my songs sung." Elsewhere, he reiterated those points, as if he was using the media to communicate with his brother.

They had not spoken on the phone for some time and it seemed that only business matters kept them in contact via desultory fax and email messages. "I would like to work with him again," Ray confessed. "It's something I really look forward to, as irksome and painful as it can be at times. But it's the spark that made the union function in the way it did. I miss that opposition. I'm not saying that what I do now is unopposed, or that I don't do a certain amount of self-criticism, but I do miss that continually having to prove the point. People would say, 'If only Ray Davies would do a solo album, get away from the Kinks.' But I've done that and I miss them. I miss the playing, casting music for them. We'd make records like *Village Green* somehow knowing that it might be a flop, but it was a cause we all believed in . . . A band can make that statement. It's much more difficult as a solo performer. You go, 'I'm alone at last' and what happens? You can't write. A lot of the good stuff is written on the back of newspapers you're carrying around, anyway. But I'm really bad at taking that handwritten scrap and typing it into a computer. In a strange way, it loses its innocence if you do. It's not as tactile, you can't feel that moment in a restaurant when you wrote it on a napkin . . . I'm uncomfortable being a solo artiste – it really is awful."

Such words hardly inspired confidence in the likelihood of a thriving independent career, but they were typical of Davies' sentimentality when questioned about his past. In many ways, it could be argued that he was the biggest impediment to any reunion of the Kinks, even though it seemed easier to cite Dave's disaffection and anger. Providing a business model that would work creatively and economically for each brother remained an insurmountable hurdle. It would have been more difficult than reinstating a failed marriage.

Davies liked to portray himself as an innocent abroad, a misfit doomed to wander between conflicting social circles, never entirely comfortable with himself or the world. "Inside I'm just this confused eighteen-year-old walking around," he mused at the end of 2007. "I'll go for a quiet drink and when I leave I'll hear someone say, 'That was Ray Davies, miserable bastard, he didn't even buy a round. Ha! Ha!'" For his brother, that persona sounded genuine enough. "I quite like being Dave Davies. I'm just not sure

Ray likes being Ray Davies. I'm not sure he knows who Ray Davies is."

In 2008, the elder brother was drawn farther back into the past when, after nearly a decade of missed opportunities, the musical *Come Dancing* was finally staged at Stratford East's Theatre Royal. Inspired by the song of the same name, the production expertly evoked the Fifties, with authentic stage costume and a clever setting with the front seats replaced by table and chairs, breaking down the gap between audience and performer. Even the onstage bar was available during the interval for refreshments, with spectators mingling alongside members of the cast. Davies' tale of Palais romance took on a new dimension to those familiar with his early life. For this was nothing less than a psychological re-enactment of the great tragedy of his childhood – the death of his beloved sister Rene. Instead of naming her, he creates a composite character, Julie, whose story also incorporates those of Gwen (at her first dance) and Peggy, the sister who had an inter-racial romance. That other great emotional event of his early life – the emigration to Australia of his sister Rose and brother-in-law Arthur – serves as a parallel subplot, with their real names unchanged. Using major events from the Davies family history was made doubly poignant by the inspired idea of employing Ray as the omniscient narrator. After starting with a stark rendition of 'Tired Of Waiting For You', he re-introduces us to the world of the Palais, whose combined aroma of "Brylcreem, cigarettes, cheap perfume and beer" was the "best smell in the world".

Overall, the musical was well received and provided an exuberant spectacle. Although no trained actor, Davies sounded authentic in his role as narrator and his performance was almost unbearably moving at times. Slender and aged, he appeared almost ghost-like, wistfully looking back at a treasured time and place that he could now only recapture via memory. And yet, there he was, inches from the action, an invisible dimension away from that fantasy world of his sisters' youth when, as an impressionable boy, he experienced the vicarious thrill of their Palais preparations and dreamboat romances. A psychological frisson was added to the drama by the telling absence of Dave Davies from the narrative. Although he was ten at the time of Rene's death and could vividly recall that epoch, there was no place for him in this script. It was almost as if Ray was recreating a prelapsarian world of idealized youth, made more tolerable by his brother's non-involvement.

At the end of the musical, Ray revealed to the audience that his entire songwriting career was a response to the death of his sister in that dance hall and effectively a tribute to her memory. Although all of Davies' musicals could be obliquely linked to aspects of his life, this one was the touchstone for everything. Never before had he been this revealing or more endearingly human. Onstage at Stratford East, his more puzzling, petty and negative personality traits were consumed by the emergence of Davies the humanitarian. Were he a great actor, this would be one of the most astonishing performances of his life, but the knowledge that he was effectively playing himself made the spectacle even more moving. This was the Ray Davies of songs such as 'Waterloo Sunset', a fragment of a more complex persona but, for fans and idealists, the true essence of the man.

CHAPTER FORTY-TWO

THE CUSTODIAN

Two months after the Stratford East season ended, Davies oversaw the release of the Kinks' box set *Picture Book* in December 2008. The six-CD set featured 137 songs from every stage of the group's career, including many rarities. The general consensus among reviewers was respect for the Kinks' golden era. Familiar hits and B-sides were supplemented by collectors' items such as 'Lavender Hill' and 'Misty Water' from *The Great Lost Kinks Album* and other rarities. Seemingly, everyone adored the first three discs, but felt less enthusiastic about the remainder. While the Kinks' post-Sixties' recordings could have been cherry-picked to produce a seamless work, Davies included a number of unreleased items on Volume Five which would normally have been welcomed were it not for their poor recording quality and sketchy structure. In a curious way, the erratic quality of the box set testified to the Kinks' peculiar career trajectory over the decades.

While fans and critics debated the merits of *Picture Book*, hopes were still high that *Come Dancing* would secure a transfer to the West End in the New Year. Sadly, it never happened. A nationwide tour was booked for late 2009, then cancelled, without explanation. Industry rumour pointed to differences between Davies and the celebrated theatre producer Bill Kenwright. Ray supposedly wished to retain the original Stratford cast, even though several were no longer available. There were also alleged differences over money and musical content. Kenwright had hoped Davies might consider adding some Kinks hits to the musical to boost ticket sales. It cannot have escaped Kenwright's attention that several reviewers had already suggested subtle changes in the script to improve its chances of opening in the West End. "*Come Dancing* needed somebody like Bill to tighten it up," says one observer, who worked with both parties. "He knows what he's doing. I felt it was a clash of personalities. Bill likes to control everything, and Ray likes to control everything about his work." It was a regrettable conclusion to one of Davies' most memorable projects.

Early in 2009, Davies received an unexpected request from Kinsale, Co. Cork, in connection with his daughter, Eva. The 12-year-old was attending Ballinadee National School, a small institution situated between Kinsale and Bandon with 100 pupils and only five teachers. Fundraising issues for improvements had frequently proven challenging for the principal, Alice Kingston, who could only call upon the 77 families whose offspring attended the school. At the time of Eva's enrolment, Davies had said that he would be willing to assist in some way and now that favour was being called in. It was requested that he play a short benefit concert at Kinsale's 400-capacity White Lady Hotel where estimated ticket sales and prize raffles were likely to raise up to €18,000. "I never wanted to ask," says Kingston, "but I did call him. He agreed to it with no fuss or bother. He didn't do it for publicity."

Eva was progressing well at school. Shy and self-effacing, she was not about to follow either of her parents on to the stage. "She's done some dancing," her mother explained, "but she's not as passionate about it as I was. She's still finding her thing. Among other interests, she's a very good writer."

The low-key concert took place on 19 June in picturesque surroundings. Accompanied by Cork guitarist Bill Shanley, Davies arrived onstage just after 9 p.m. for a 90-minute concert during which he performed a varied selection of Kinks' hits ('All Day And All Of The Night', 'Tired Of Waiting For You', 'Set Me Free', 'Dedicated Follower Of Fashion', 'Sunny Afternoon' and 'Lola'), interspersed with more recent material like 'The Getaway' and 'The Tourist'. At one point, someone requested 'Waterloo . . .', which prompted Ray to sing a few lines from Abba's 1974 Eurovision winner instead of the expected 'Waterloo Sunset'. He remained in good spirits, clearly thrilled by the presence of his daughter, whom he frequently talked to from the stage between numbers. This was the first time Eva had seen her father perform and her response was politely measured. "It was interesting," she said, when he asked her opinion. She was equally unassuming when Ms Kingston consulted her about what her father might like for a small present. "He likes Galaxy bars," she suggested. Later, the principal recalled that they had completed a short film about the school the previous year in which Eva was included. It seemed the perfect gift.

Eight days after the Kinsale show, Davies appeared at Kenwood, the former stately home on Hampstead Heath whose grounds had always played a key part in his life story, from Dave's sexual exploits in its high grass to the filming of *Veronica* and the rear cover artwork of *The Village Green Preservation Society*. Those hoping for a sunny summer concert instead encountered torrential rain, leavened slightly by the curiosity of witnessing Davies' latest venture, the Crouch End Festival Chorus. He had previously worked with the 65-piece ensemble on his *Flatlands* project and performed alongside them at 2007's BBC Electric Proms and in the studio for 'Thanksgiving Day', the bonus track on *Other People's Lives*. All this culminated in *The Kinks' Choral Collection*, an album of the group's classic songs, reimagined for a full-scale choir. Cynics could easily accuse Davies of milking his old hits, but the truth was more complicated. He had always imagined the Kinks beyond the confines of a four-piece group and, as early as 1967, was telling journalists, "We would very much like to do an LP with a big orchestra," adding, "we would probably do some of our old hits."

The Kinks' Choral Collection divided fans and critics, many of whom could see little point in adding a choir to such hard-edged songs as 'You Really Got Me' and 'All Day And All Of The Night'. Conversely, some considered the delicate 'Waterloo Sunset' too precious to be augmented by a 65-piece chorus. It was generally agreed that the singers worked best embellishing key selections from *The Village Green Preservation Society*, notably its title track, 'Do You Remember Walter', 'Picture Book', 'Johnny Thunder' and 'Big Sky'. *The Kinks' Choral Collection* included only one new composition, 'Postcard From London', later issued as a download single. The song's most remarkable quality was the shock presence of Davies' former girlfriend Chrissie Hynde. Davies was typically evasive about her presence, at first suggesting that he did not attend the session. "Chrissie came into the studio and did her part brilliantly. I wasn't there at the time and, of course, our relationship history adds yet another texture to the song. But it wasn't recorded around a log fire or anything. We weren't toasting marshmallows and cracking nuts. My girlfriend Karin [Forsman] sang on the demo and, with Chrissie, it was clear what the vocal parts were. Some artistes are happy to let the writer direct things. There was no real discussion, which surprised me." In another interview, he claimed that he was in the studio for the recording, but remained hidden behind a one-way mirror, adding that he and Hynde had not spoken since their breakup in the early Eighties. That version of events was later contradicted, and it was clear that he felt uncomfortable talking about Hynde, let alone using her on the recording. "That was difficult," he coyly concedes. "She wasn't my first choice, I have to say. I wanted Dame Vera Lynn . . . but yeah, Chris. We just got it over and done with quickly. She was very professional. She wouldn't have done it if she didn't like the tune. It was nice to know that. The edgy bit was sitting down and getting the best takes. I said, 'That's the best way you sing it.' She said, 'No, it's not.' I said, 'Oh, do it the way you want then.' Then, when she left, I did it the way I wanted."

Instead of concentrating on a new solo album, Davies was seduced into further Kinks-related projects. On 4 July 2009, Alex Chilton had visited Konk in London and recorded a couple of Kinks songs with Ray: 'Set Me Free' and 'Till The End Of The Day'. Alas, Chilton would not live long enough to see their release. When Davies took the demos to Universal Records, they advised him to transform the idea into a covers project titled *See My Friends*. Over the next year, he collaborated with a series of international artists who offered their own selections and interpretations. There were several surprises along the way. Lucinda Williams chose 1970's 'A Long Way From Home'; Bruce Springsteen covered 'Better Things', although at one point he had nominated the controversial 'Art Lover'; Mumford & Sons presented a medley of 'Days' and 'This Time Tomorrow'; and Jackson Browne daringly tackled 'Waterloo Sunset', a song considerably less well known in California than it was in London. Most of the recordings were done face to face, with Davies travelling to New York for the Jon Bon Jovi/Richie Sambora union ('Celluloid Heroes') and to Oslo for the collaboration with Metallica ('You Really Got Me'). By contrast, Billy Corgan's contribution ('All Day And All Of The Night'/'Destroyer') was achieved through online file sharing. Davies particularly enjoyed seeing younger performers attempting songs that were hits before they were born, notably Paloma Faith ('Lola'), Amy McDonald ('Dead End Street') and Gary Lightbody ('Tired Of Waiting For You').

Inevitably, news of the tribute collaboration prompted stale questions about whether the original Kinks might tour or record again. That fantasy ended on 23 June 2010 when Pete Quaife died from renal failure in Denmark, aged 66. He had been struggling with kidney failure for many years and had even written a short book of sketches on the subject, *The Lighter Side Of Dialysis*, published in Canada. During 2004–5, Quaife had moved back to Denmark and, following his divorce from Hanne, began a new relationship with Elisabeth Bilbo. They had been planning to marry at the time of his death.

On 27 June, Davies appeared at the Glastonbury Festival and paid tribute to his fallen colleague. Bizarre as it seemed, he had retained fantasies of involving Quaife in some reunion, even in the months before his death. Davies spoke of the possibility of completing some tapes, transferring them to his hard drive and flying to Denmark where Quaife could contribute some bass. Considering Dave Davies had not been consulted, let alone agreed to any such idea, this was a project that existed largely in Ray's imagination. He had spoken to Quaife by phone, but the idea was nothing more than a mutual fantasy, despite the bassist's apparent acquiescence. "Pete wouldn't have been able to do it," says his brother. "He wouldn't want to do it. I couldn't understand it. I spoke to Pete about three months before and he mentioned something about reforming the Kinks. I asked him if he would do it and he said, 'No way!' He was very sceptical. I know he was upset about that. It happened a few times."

On 13 July, Pete Quaife's funeral took place in Denmark, after which there was a private memorial service. "There wasn't a single wreath or anything from the Kinks at the funeral," claims David

Quaife. "Nothing. It was as if they'd written him off. There was only about ten people who turned up anyway." This sounded harsh but was indicative of some of the emotional detritus that followed Pete's demise. That same month, Ray posted a message on his Facebook page: "Because so many people were unable to make the trip to Denmark for Pete's funeral, Mick [Avory] and myself have spoken and decided to put on a memorial night for Pete in Muswell Hill where the Kinks first formed. We are currently talking with others and looking into venues and will hopefully announce information soon." Soon after, Ray added a postscript. "Hopefully, Dave can attend as well."

The younger brother was incandescent. Not for the last time, he sensed manipulation. Although Ray's comment sounded like a polite invitation, Dave suspected that more mind games were afoot. Ray appeared perplexed and hurt by the response. "I'm going to do a memorial concert for Pete somewhere in Muswell Hill, and I'd like to involve Dave, but he won't do it. Dave's a very proud man. I don't know what his problem is, apart from pride. But that's so trivial when someone has died. If fiction is anything to go by, even the Mafia get together and make up when someone dies. If only for the funeral."

Dave was in no mood for any polite or pleading gestures. Ironically, the proposed memorial for Pete Quaife – an event that should have brought concord – was instead reaping a whirlwind of abuse. Dave defended his stance, explaining: "After Pete died, I had my own private service for him on my website. I asked Elisabeth, Pete's girlfriend, and his brother David to join me in sending Pete our love and they were happy to. I wrote a few prayers and made my peace with Pete. I wasn't going to get involved in using Pete as a PR exercise to bolster Ray's vanity."

Although there was nothing to suggest that Ray was exploiting Pete's memory in any way, Dave could not restrain his anger and his abrasive words rapidly reached a froth of tabloidese vituperation. "You've heard of vampires? Well Ray sucks me dry of ideas, emotions and creativity. It's toxic for me to be with him. He's a control freak. I hate to say it, but it's got worse since he met the Queen [in 2004]. In his mind, it's given him even more validity, more 'I'm better than you', more 'I'm superior'. With him it's 'me, me, me'. He thinks he is the Kinks. When I think of all the beautiful music we made, it wouldn't have been the same if I or Pete hadn't been there." Dave even offered some instant psychoanalysis, arguing: "Ray's a narcissist. I walked into a bookshop a month ago and picked up Tony Blair's autobiography. I looked at the picture and felt sick. I thought, 'Hello, he's got the same thing as Ray.' It's some sort of grandiose disorder." As usual, the diatribe burned itself out with a conciliatory coda: "Oh no, I don't hate him. It's impossible . . . I could never not love Ray. He's my brother."

When confronted with his brother's words, Ray turned them back on his accuser. "Emotional vampire?" he considered. "I think that's unfair. I'm not an emotional vampire at all . . . My brother made it rivalry rather than being in a team. He just got envious for all the wrong reasons. We had some good times." Their mirrored reactions were telling, including the somewhat strained positive afterwords.

The well-intentioned memorial for Pete Quaife soon ran into problems. Davies felt obliged to clarify the position for his Facebook followers. "First off I would like to state it is not a Kinks reunion and will not be a concert. It will be a memorial with some family, friends, fans and a celebration of Pete's life with a few songs. We will probably be able to fit around a hundred and fifty fans." This proved over-optimistic and, although there were tentative plans for a get-together at Konk, the moment passed.

Complicating matters, David Quaife was in the process of setting up the Pete Quaife Foundation, a charity whose aim was to provide support for children undergoing dialysis treatment. Having already been snubbed by Dave Davies, he expected more from Ray but became frustrated and embittered by the constant prevarication.

"I wanted Ray to donate £350 to a blue plaque and he came out with a sob story. I mean £350. That upset me quite a lot. We had people who'd bought tickets in Spain to go to a memorial in the cellar of Konk Studios. Ray didn't want more than thirty people and was willing to pay £10 a head. I nearly said to him: 'I'll tell you what, I'll get a hot dog stall outside and a marquee from the local Scouts. Would that be better?' It didn't happen. I do feel bad about that because Ray keeps coming back and giving the impression that he misses Pete and all that stuff, but there's nothing real in it. A public relations thing. That's all it is."

Others felt David Quaife's expectations were presumptuous and unreasonable and praised Davies for providing signed CDs and memorabilia for the Foundation when asked. More pertinently, and unknown to the public and possibly David Quaife, Ray was in poor health. As Christmas 2010 approached, his condition worsened. Doctors confirmed that residue from the 2004 bullet wound had caused a blood clot on his lungs. He was briefly hospitalized and persuaded to cancel a forthcoming US tour. Despite his condition, he agreed to assist Julien Temple who was busy shooting footage for *Imaginary Man*, a television documentary on Davies' life. Ray was not well enough to appear in every scene and Temple masqueraded as his double for some faraway shots. Broadcast the following year, Temple's sympathetic portrayal had an elegiac quality, reinforced by Davies' remark when discussing his nervous disorder back in 1966: "Compared to the way I feel now, having a nervous breakdown was a jaunt."

Davies' psychological condition had been subject to erroneous speculation after his name had been added to a list of famous bipolar personalities in an exhibit on the brain at Boston's Museum of Science in 2007. The libellous diagnosis was casually picked up by internet profilers, much to Davies' mystification. "Why did they put me there?" he asked. "I'm not [bipolar]. Like everybody, I get depressed from time to time, but I get depressed when I can't do my work. I'm a frustrative-obsessive." With health scares mounting, Davies was in urgent need of a relaxing haven.

A few weeks before Christmas, he moved to the house of his north London neighbour Marjorie Wallace, CBE, founder member of the mental health charity SANE. A former mistress of Princess Margaret's ex-husband, Lord Snowden, Wallace was married to the Polish psychoanalyst Count Andrzej Skarbek. Through her work with SANE, she had helped many people during times of stress. Six months after his festive sojourn at her house, Davies repaid her hospitality by playing a benefit concert for SANE at London's Purcell Room, backed by the Leisure Society. The highlight of the evening was a fascinating new composition, 'Depressed I Am Not', which concluded with the rallying cry: "I'm not finished yet!" Subsequently, he spoke about mental health awareness, lamenting government cutbacks to social services. "I'd like to high-light that cause because it's something that's riddled throughout society. I was with a fourteen-year-old last night who's been excluded from school because he doesn't fit the formula, and the services that would normally help that kid have been cut. Then there are the people who are going through stressful economic times. It's such a devastatingly austere world we're living in now, and people need a point of contact . . . Our society is very fractured."

During 2011, Davies settled into his role as the official curator of the Kinks' legacy. His recent collaborative work *See My Friends* had climbed to number 12 in the UK charts, his best placing since *Face To Face* in 1966. Davies was so pleased that he promised to consider a *See My Friends Volume 2* in the future. The work had divided his fan base and critical reaction was equally sniffy. *Mojo* magazine, traditionally a great supporter of his work, offered the album a derisory one-star review. Nevertheless, the chart statistics confirmed that there was a bigger market for the Kinks than there was for Ray Davies as a soloist. This was reflected in the seemingly never-ending reissue campaign of remastered, re-imagined works. In May, the first three Kinks albums were re-released, their contents barely recognizable when compared to the originals. They each included a bonus CD featuring contemporaneous singles, B-sides and EP tracks. Even *Kinda Kinks* won a four-star review from *Uncut*, an evaluation that only made sense with the caveat: "the real glories are on the second disc." The deluxe treatment would continue relentlessly. Thanks to modern marketing, the Kinks history was being systematically rewritten.

Davies' status as rock icon cum national treasure was underlined by an invitation to curate the 18th Meltdown Festival at the South Bank. The event also celebrated the 60th anniversary of the Festival of Britain, a cherished moment from Davies' childhood. From 10 to 19 June, he presented an impressively diverse series of acts, acknowledging the achievements of his Sixties contemporaries, alongside some harder edged New York acts. Among the performers were the Crazy World Of Arthur Brown, Geno Washington & The Ram Jam Band, the Alan Price Set, Nick Lowe, Madness, New York pals Yo La Tengo, the Sonics, Wire, Lydia Lunch and Canadian Ron Sexsmith. Other highlights included Peter Asher's 'Musical Memoir Of The Sixties And Beyond' and an endearing evening recreating the spirit of the seminal television show *Ready, Steady, Go!* with Ronnie Spector, Sandie Shaw, the Manfreds, Nona Hendryx and Paloma Faith.

The Festival closed on Sunday 19 June with Davies appearing alongside the London Philharmonic Orchestra and the Crouch End Festival Chorus in a carefully constructed set that included Kinks' hits, selected solo material and most of *The Village Green Preservation Society.*

One of Davies' personal highlights at Meltdown was the presence of the Great Preservation Hall Jazz Band, who had been flown in from New Orleans. "They said, 'We always felt your songs were appropriate to New Orleans.' That was a big compliment. They made me aware of my work and where my music comes from. I never thought that 'Acute Schizophrenia Paranoid Blues' and 'Alcohol' would be street music in New Orleans. Now I'm aware where my influences come from. The Highgate Jazz Club. Dixieland. Good time music."

Davies sounded rejuvenated throughout the month of Meltdown. Inevitably, he was asked about the current state of his relationship with his brother and entertained interviewers with some sardonic observations. Although goaded by reporters quick to rehash some of Dave's most acerbic putdowns, Ray preferred to play Mr Magnanimity. "I love him to death," he gushed. "He's my little brother. What can I say? Some people say he's a jumped-up upstart, but I say: take him as you find him. He feels it's his duty to have a swipe at me occasionally and that's all right. We've come a long way from the crib." This was Davies at his mischievous best: conciliatory and condescending in the same breath.

He was also surprisingly forthcoming about his love life. "I'm in between girlfriends. I'm easy to love, and impossible to live with. There's nothing like having a partner. You want someone you can go home to and say, 'I had a crap day.' It doesn't help the day, but you've got someone to say it to. I'm rationing relationships in the sense that I want the next one to be a good one, a sincere one." It was only his interaction with his daughters that caused some momentary wistfulness. "That's the one thing I really regret about my career, not having been with my kids more. I have a daughter in Ireland. She's fourteen. I speak to her when I can. I haven't seen her in nearly a year, which is terrible. I was going to go at Christmas, but then I got sick. I miss her. I could see her if I wanted to, it's just . . . [his voice trails off] I wish I could have sustained a normal married relationship . . ."

Davies was determined to keep busy hereafter and seemed ready to take on any new project. In September, he directed a school musical, *Child's Play*, which had been commissioned by Grazdale Arts in the Lake District. "It took me a weekend to write it," he casually noted, "and it was really good fun."

On 16 October, the long promised blue plaque memorial for Pete Quaife was finally unveiled by the Heritage Foundation at Fortismere School (formerly William Grimshaw Secondary Modern). Ray Davies' presence brought a combination of gravitas and humour to the presentation, marked by a comic repartee with Mick Avory. Former Searcher Frank Allen (part of the introductory party) unwittingly astonished the audience by mistakenly assuming that Dave Davies had just arrived in the building. It transpired that the younger brother had merely sent a goodwill message from Cornwall.

"I've always had a thing about people doing the right things for the wrong reasons," Dave later told me. "I've spent most of my life working behind the scenes with my yoga and my magic trying to lift the vibration and energy of a gig or recording. I've been very happy being a mystic, if you like. Some of these charity things – like that Facebook campaign – everybody's a good guy. It's like: I was at this and I was at that. Again, it's people doing the right things for the wrong reasons. We're put here to cultivate our spiritual lives and we can't cultivate our spiritual lives by pretending. I'm afraid that's not the way to advance spiritually. Going to Pete's memorial just to be seen is doing it for the wrong reasons. I don't want his memory to be exploited by possibly dubious notions from people projecting their private agendas about how they want to be seen. I'm not interested in that. I want to remember him as a dear and close brother and friend. I don't need to show some flimsy bullshit thing in public."

Others simply saw the unveiling of the blue plaque as a commemoration worthy of attendance. Ray, dressed in his familiar brown jacket and scarf, paid tribute to his former band, pointing out how each member assumed a specific role: "Dave, the mad one, the intellectual one (that's me) and a strange one (that's

Mick). Pete was important to our chemistry." Mick Avory offered his impressions upon first meeting the Kinks, acknowledging that Pete was "the most friendly one" and recalling his madcap antics and love of practical jokes. "If he saw that today," he said, pointing at the plaque, "he'd take it down and put it on his scooter" and drive away. Avory remembered one occasion where Quaife shaved a single eyebrow prior to a television show. "Yeah, it was your eyebrow!" quipped Ray from the wings. After the blue plaque unveiling, there was a reception and meal with music provided by the Kast Off Kinks. Ray made a surprise appearance later that afternoon, accompanied by his former girlfriend Karin Forsman. Coaxed onstage, he did not sing but offered further tribute, stating: "Pete made everyone mix together – it was critical to the band." Recalling the class divide of the Fifties and Sixties, he remembered his former headmaster Charles Loades advising, "Don't mix with him!", as if living in a council flat in Steed's Road was the ultimate symbol of working-class deprivation. Ray then reiterated and parodied his previous speech about the characteristics of the Kinks, offering the ironic inversion: "The drummer [Mick Avory] was the intelligent one – he's not as dumb as he looks." A fundraising raffle followed along with a reading from Quaife's privately published novel, *Veritas*.

Davies ended 2011 with short tours of the UK and USA but also found time to enter the studio briefly, accompanied by Mick Avory. A handful of new songs were attempted, but this was nothing more than a casual reunion. The drummer was sceptical about ever recording with Dave Davies given their volatile history. Ray sounded similarly pessimistic. "I don't know what my brother's current plans are, other than making my life as miserable as possible. He kind of revels in that, really. It would be great to do another couple of great tracks with him, not a whole album. He's a great player, a powerful player, and I can write stuff that brings him out. I like writing for Dave. It's unlikely right now. But you just never know the way the world changes." When contacted, Dave sounded as distant as ever. "About an hour with Ray's my limit, so it would be a very short reunion."

Amid great secrecy, Ray Davies was booked to appear at the closing ceremony of the 2012 London Olympics on 13 August. In an extravaganza titled 'A Symphony Of British Music' he took his place on a cast list that included Madness and a surprise reunion of the original Spice Girls. Davies was allowed only one song and most viewers would have correctly predicted his choice: 'Waterloo Sunset'. He arrived onstage in a black taxi cab, looking slightly frail and uncertain. At the soundcheck his earpiece was malfunctioning and he was still concerned that he might not be able to hear his own voice when he sang. When he emerged from the taxi, the harsh stage lights transformed the colour of his hair into bright orange, like that of some hired clown. Although his vocal performance was slightly faint, the emotion of the night carried him through.

The evening ended with the Who – Townshend and Daltrey, abetted by brother Simon Townshend and Zak Starkey – performing 'See Me Feel Me' and 'My Generation' (minus the 'hope I die before I get old' line). Even after all these years, it seemed that Davies was still in danger of being upstaged by his old rivals. This was an event that cried out for a Kinks' reunion of sorts, but it was the Who, Madness and the Spice Girls that spoke of reformations. Ray sang alone.

Over the decades there had been much speculation about the rivalry between the Who and the Kinks, and especially between Davies and Townshend. Occasionally, Ray and Dave had made some stinging comments about the Who, but these were balanced by more generous appraisals, acknowledging that both groups were following parallel paths. For his part, Townshend had always been a great supporter of Ray Davies. "He's a great eccentric English genius," he acknowledges. "We were just thinking alike." Of course, during the Seventies, the Who's main rivals in the States were the Rolling Stones and Led Zeppelin, while the Kinks were the equivalent of an aspiring cult band. Perhaps Townshend might have been less magnanimous if *Arthur* had eclipsed *Tommy* but, over the years, his appreciation of the Kinks had increased, amid puzzlement at their inability to reconcile festering differences. Prior to Quaife's death, he had been urging a reunion. "They're more than they were," he pointed out. "I feel differently about the Kinks than I did at the beginning: adoration, love, affection and respect. When I was young, I wouldn't have talked to Dave about how good he was. I wouldn't have given him five bob. It wasn't about competition – it was just, 'We're in a band, you're a guitar player. Fuck off.' But today I look back and I think these guys were extraordinary. We didn't expect to be looking at such a lineage of music that has spawned so much other stuff."

Townshend even went as far as suggesting that Ray Davies deserved to be crowned Britain's Poet Laureate. Part of Townshend's affection and admiration for Davies can probably be explained by their mutual emotional distance. After decades of supposed rivalry, they remain virtual strangers. "I've always respected him," Townshend ponders, "but I've never really had a chance to get into a deep conversation with him and yet so many people that I know very well, like Chrissie Hynde, who had a long relationship with him, have managed to really get inside his head and I've never managed to do that. And on the stage I think you see the complete Ray. In the early days you saw the man, his music, what he loved, who he was, where he came from, and most of all you saw somebody who was carrying and building and developing the leading edge, the pressure wave of post-war British writing which in pop has reinvented everything. Absolutely everything. Not just music but clothes, fashion, ideas, television, everything . . . Ray was one of the first three, four or five people who took this language of ours and defined, refined and purified it, and made it what it is today. He was one of the people who wrote the rules and I work with the Ray Davies rulebook to this day. I wish I could get more out of myself like he does and observe characters as lovingly and as clearly and precisely with the kind of scrutiny that he does, but I always tend to inhabit my own music. He's really one of the rule makers and groundbreakers and Dave is one of the great guitar gods of the Sixties."

After the Olympics, Davies again took stock of the Kinks' catalogue and attempted another reappraisal of his past. Over the years, the group's reputation as albums artists had rested increasingly on the classics, *The Village Green Preservation Society* and *Arthur*. Davies argued that greater focus needed to be placed on the succeeding *Lola Versus Powerman And The Moneygoround Part One* and *Muswell Hillbillies*. On 27 November 2012, he appeared on BBC Radio 4's *Front Row* for a memorable interview with the impressively interrogative John Wilson (son of Arsenal goalkeeper Bob Wilson). Among the highlights were acoustic renditions of 'Here Come The People In Grey', 'Muswell Hillbilly' and 'This Time Tomorrow'. This paved the way for the release of deluxe versions of those albums, with *Muswell Hillbillies* boasting such notable rarities as 'Lavender Lane', 'Mountain Woman', 'Kentucky Moon', 'Nobody's Fool' and 'Queenie'.

At the beginning of 2013, Ray and Dave Davies found themselves in the same room for an unexpected family reunion. Their aunt Dorothy (Dolly) was celebrating her 100th birthday and there was a gathering of the clans with representatives from at least three different generations of the Davies family. Ray's daughter Louisa was amused to see her father hiding behind a video camera filming the event. For the first half-hour he hardly said a word to anybody and seemed happy to fade into the background. This was not a time to discuss the Kinks and he and Dave maintained a cordial distance.

For much of the year, it seemed that Ray Davies was being usurped in the news headlines by his third daughter, Natalie Hynde. First, she became involved in a protest about a link road between Bexhill and Hastings, complaining about the "bloody dangerous" burrowing. She was removed by police. "I feel sorry for the trees," she pleaded, ahead of a court date. "The protest is not over. The trees have been chopped down, but this is not the end. The trees are symbolic of what is being done to our society and we cannot let that happen."

By the summer, Hynde was back in the news, this time protesting against fracking. Described as a 'green activist', Hynde played a prominent part in the campaign whose battle ground was the picturesque village of Balcombe in West Sussex. One newspaper solemnly reported: "Ms Hynde, 28, and her boyfriend, veteran eco-warrior Simon 'Sitting Bull' Medhurst, 55, are on bail facing charges related to another campaign earlier this year – a failed attempt to prevent the building of a road linking Bexhill-on-Sea and Hastings. They said they were quite prepared to go to prison for the anti-fracking cause." Hynde was pictured emerging from a blue tent with a Salman Rushdie novel and a banana. "Ms Hynde describes herself as an anarchist and lives with former RAF photographer Mr Medhurst in a low-rent Hastings flat," the *Mail Online* noted, without further comment.

Ray was in the national press himself, though, following the news that Elton John had an attack of appendicitis and had to withdraw from a headlining show at London's Hyde Park. The organizers were forced to offer refunds and transform the day into a Free Festival with Davies elevated to headlining act. It was quite a coup but also a challenge as Ray was obliged to entertain a large audience without the benefit of backing singers. At 69, his vocal range was stretched severely, but his stagecraft was as impressive as ever. With a veritable songbook of hits at his command, he coaxed the audience into a community-style singalong.

Davies appeared more relaxed of late, an impression reinforced by an autumnal romance. His current intimate was Alma Karen Eyo, who soon became involved in every aspect of his life, from co-ordinating family get-togethers to officiating art exhibitions and events at Konk Studios. Ray made no mention of her to the media, but he always liked to keep his personal life private. Coincidentally, Dave was also involved in a new relationship. He had recently broken up with his long-term partner Kate and taken up with Rebecca Gwyn Wilson, a 43-year-old freelance journalist. Unlike Ray, he saw no reason to be discreet and announced their union on his Facebook page on 24 July. Those close to both brothers could not help wondering whether the arrival of new partners might lead to a cessation of fraternal hostilities, if only for a time.

In October 2013, Virgin Books published Ray Davies' memoir *Americana*. Less an autobiography than a meditation, it attempts to understand a country that he had loved, feared and ultimately conquered, only to be shot and almost killed while walking its streets. The book is part odyssey, a search for what Davies calls the 'Perfect Riff', the source of the music that had enraptured his imagination over the past 60 years. Although he chronicles some of the Kinks' adventures in America, these are presented in snapshot form, serving as a backdrop to more pressing concerns about aspects of identity and the nature of the creative process. The book conveys, in stark fashion, his helplessness as he lies in a New Orleans hospital ruminating on his songwriting and pondering his mortality. Certain episodes in the text are tantalizingly elliptical. "I wrote until I thought I'd be bored, then moved on," Davies admits. "It was a difficult book to write in terms of what happened to me. It became a bit of a trauma."

As a storyteller Davies is arch, allusive and evasive. Several people in the book are transformed into well-disguised 'composite characters'. There is even a guardian angel in the form of 'Travis Davis', an alter ego who functions as a spiritual guide. "Travis is three people," Davies confides. "The real guy's dead. I had a great falling-out with my editor about Travis. Some people have an air of mystique. You don't want to know where they live, you don't want to know they have children, you don't want to know about their past life. They just exist in the moment."

Given the book's American angle, Davies tells us frustratingly little about the time he spent living in Manhattan with his second wife, Yvonne. Indeed, her name does not even appear once in the text. There is a similar reticence throughout. The imprint page includes, in very small print, the defensive caveat: ". . . the names and identifying characteristics of certain individuals have been changed to protect their privacy, dialogue has been reconstructed to the best of the author's recollection, and some time frames have been compressed." This was not so much a legal notice as a testament to Davies' evasion and need to direct his own life story.

Overall, the book offers an intriguing insight into the creative inner workings of one of popular music's most talented songwriters and mercurial characters. Many previously unseen song lyrics and notebook entries illuminate the text, like coded commentaries on his psychological state. In common with Bob Dylan and Neil Young, Davies prefers the abridged memoir to explicate his life and work. In this format, he can cherry-pick specific scenes or time periods for close focus analysis, then move on, leaving the promise of additional reflections and revelations later down the line. Whether he will ever open up fully about his personal relationships and marriages with equal vividness remains a tantalizing question.

In 2014, the Davies brothers were feeling the hand of history on their shoulders. Fifty years after their formation, there was still ongoing interest in some kind of Kinks' reunion. Broadsheet newspapers and the music press were full of such stories, fuelled by news that the brothers were speaking again and had even had some cordial meetings to discuss a possible get-together. Given previous grievances, financial safeguards were uppermost in Dave's mind. If there was to be any reunion he wanted a lawyer present from the outset with a strict list of terms. He had no interest in working with any of the Kast Off Kinks, least of all Mick Avory. Dave's dream was for a family affair, featuring his sons, Russell and Daniel. Ray, conversely, had no wish to play or record with any of his nephews and, in keeping with the anniversary mood, saw the Kast Off Kinks as the perfect celebrants.

This latest impasse was complicated by the launch of a critically acclaimed musical *Sunny Afternoon*, which made a successful transition from Hampstead to the West End. It focused more attention on the history of the group, but Dave objected to the way his character was presented, citing inaccuracies online, then audaciously suggesting that Ray might consider amending the script. His comments did little to assist fraternal relations.

On 21 June, Ray celebrated his 70th birthday at his north London home. A grand gathering of family and friends was present, including his three eldest daughters. It was a bittersweet occasion, not least because his sister Joyce had passed away on 28 May, aged 83. The longevity of the Davies family had been remarkable but this was now a time of funerals. Soon after, Rose – the mother figure with whom Ray had lived during his teenage years – died on 2 July in her 90th year.

These events made Davies more aware of his own mortality. It was no longer likely that he would be able to complete all the projects that inhabited his imagination. Increasingly, he was thinking in terms of collaboration, referring to the Renaissance painter Raphael who employed assistants to complete his later art projects. On the horizon was a feature film, *You Really Got Me*, produced by Jeremy Thomas, directed by Julien Temple and written by the great British comedy team Ian La Frenais and Dick Clement. Further ahead lay the prospect of an opera – not a 'rock opera', Ray cautions, but a real one. "There's a story I want to tell. I think it's really important. I need to have meetings with opera people about it. I wrote the outline after I did *Come Dancing*. I've done some musical sketches for it. It's a collaborative thing. I'm not Puccini. Directors are so important in opera and I'd really like to write this one."

In the midst of this creative activity there remains the perennial question about working with Dave and producing a Kinks'-related work. At present, the younger brother appears the more resistant to the idea, blowing hot and cold whenever the topic is mentioned. During our last interview, he was more concerned about touring solo and promoting his latest solo album. "The Kinks music is going to last for ever anyway," he concludes. "For it to go down in history as these poor oldsters getting together and falling over to make a few bob would really upset my mum and dad, and it upsets me. With Ray, it's like a ravine between us. It's only because Ray wanted to pursue a solo career that the Kinks disbanded. I realized in Ray's mind it's all about him, and I should really not go down that road. I'm not going to go out and do a Kinks tour for Ray's sake. If you want a quite blunt answer, I don't need that day-to-day madness . . . I know where I'm going." As ever, just as the tape recorder is about to be switched off, Dave cannot resist one final qualification. "A little footnote at the end," he declares, like a crime writer in search of a surprise twist. "It's not beyond the realms of possibility for me and Ray to do something again. What, I don't know. Just don't put a nail in the coffin yet."

EPILOGUE

There was no Kinks reunion during 2014 and, despite further fanciful predictions in newspapers and rock monthlies, there was no get-together in 2015. Contrary to Ray's comments at the 2013 'Kinks Konvention', he did not collaborate with the Kast Off Kinks either. Not that anyone close to the former members of the group would have been surprised. Forecasting events based on Davies' capricious comments was never advisable.

Consolation came via the surprise success of *Sunny Afternoon*. Previous Davies musicals, notably *80 Days* and the brilliant *Come Dancing*, had never reached the large audience that their creator craved. By contrast, *Sunny Afternoon* transferred to the West End's Harold Pinter Theatre in October 2014 and went on to win four Olivier Awards. The musical may have lacked the sustained emotional resonance of *Come Dancing*, which was illuminated by Davies' role as onstage narrator, but it provided some classy entertainment, enhanced by classic Kinks' hits, including 'You Really Got Me', 'Dedicated Follower Of Fashion', 'Dead End Street', 'Waterloo Sunset', 'Days', 'Lola', and many more. But this was no mere jukebox musical nor a wholly sanitized version of the Kinks' story. It dramatized some of the low moments as well as the highs, most powerfully the vignette in which Davies is forced to his bed on the verge of a nervous breakdown. As he rightly observes, that scene was painful to reimagine but crucial to the narrative. "I am such a secretive person and I was showing one of the most difficult times in my life. But it had to be done to tell the complete story." A soundtrack album followed, featuring 29 songs from the cast. "The songs lend themselves to the theatre," Davies stresses. "They have a dark side that makes them useful in storytelling."

This was all a long way from the *Preservation* and *Soap Opera* years when Davies' theatrical yearnings stoked conflict among the subsidiary Kinks and heightened tensions with his brother. Dave was not entirely happy with *Sunny Afternoon* either but was mollified by subtle changes in the script. Away from the band, Ray has been able to avoid the problems associated with taking a concept on the road. It was very telling that, once the Kinks ceased touring, the fiery fraternal conflicts of old receded. While the Kinks' tale was one of unrelenting drama, there is little evidence of Ray encountering similar difficulties in his solo career or theatrical collaborations. And that period now covers over 20 years.

Perhaps Ray the dramatist simply chose the wrong vehicle for his art. As former backing singer Shirlie Roden acknowledges, it was only years later that she fully appreciated the enormity of the task that Davies undertook in choosing to present his musicals while working with the Kinks. Her respect for his willingness and determination to shoulder that burden remains to this day. While certain key members have questioned the sagacity of that decision, the shows were generally enjoyable. "Certainly, things like *Soap Opera* I felt were absolutely brilliant," says former Kinks' trombonist John Beecham. "The fact is that he could do that every night on stage. As you can imagine, there were a lot of Kinks fans and perhaps members of the Kinks themselves who were a bit surprised but at least he *did* involve his band. He could have gone away and done that with a bunch of actors and strangers."

Such are the contradictions of this complicated man. Part of him still misses the camaraderie of the Kinks and perhaps some of the artistic conflicts, too. The once bitter encounters with his brother may have dissipated of late but a lingering dispute about the sonic origins of 'You Really Got Me' can still produce some disproportionately strong reactions, particularly from Dave. Each of them retains fond memories of their family history, a subject that peppers media quotes more frequently than ever. Ray can still be an evasive interviewee but, in this author's experience, he comes across as charming, gracious and wistful.

The year 2016 promises a new solo album, *Americana*, which may or may not be adapted as a musical. Further off is the opera mentioned on page 633, a project that is largely dependent upon Davies' longevity. More promising is the filming of *You Really Got Me*, which finally received a green light when Ray and Dave signed off on the script. Financing is currently in place. "It wasn't an easy process," says director Julien Temple. "It's taken eight years. It was always going to be difficult to get to a point where they both said 'Yes'. A lot of shifting sands were involved. We're talking about real people's lives. It's a delicate thing and it's quite brave for Ray and Dave to allow a fictional film to be based on their lives."

At the time of writing, actors Johnny Flynn and George MacKay have been cast as Ray and Dave, respectively, with Temple's daughter Juno set to play Rasa. Although the film inevitably repeats part of the storyline of *Sunny Afternoon*, the treatment will be very different. "They're different genres really," Temple points out. "Musical theatre has broad strokes. Hopefully this is going to be a darker, psychological, more raw and real film, with a lot of humour in it as well." Contrary to media reports suggesting that the biopic will cover the entire career of the Kinks, it is set to end in 1973 after the White City incident, detailed at length in Chapter 29. "It's a natural place to make a break," Temple says. "We do indicate that they go on but I don't think there was a Kinks after that – not for much longer." Indeed, Temple is such a purist that he feels the group were never the same after Quaife left, let alone following Avory's departure in the early Eighties. "There is no Kinks without Mick Avory. Come on!"

Temple's belief in the film is deeply personal as well as professional. His connection with the Davies brothers actually stretches back to his youth. Just over two months before his twelfth birthday, he first heard 'You Really Got Me' on the radio and the Muswell Hill quartet immediately became his favourite group. As a teenager, he was transferred to St Marylebone Grammar School and happily discovered that the Kinks frequented a nearby pub. "We used to bunk off school to watch them drink outside the Flask. They would sit long into the afternoon and we were like schoolboys in disgrace. As a kid that was really informative."

In an accident of history, the 13-year-old Temple was privy to one of Ray's emotional epiphanies. "I had this amazing day when I saw Ray on Hampstead High Street in tears. I couldn't believe that pop stars had issues. I just thought that they were happy to be pop stars. This guy was top of the charts and there he was walking down Hampstead High Street in tears. I don't know what I was thinking but I followed him. I just kept wondering what could be making this guy so upset. Then he went into a café and sat down. He saw me and I think he knew me from watching him at the Flask. But that always struck me. Why was Ray Davies crying in broad daylight?" If Temple's chronology is correct, this would have occurred in early 1966 around the time of Davies' quasi-breakdown, one of the worst moments of his life.

After attending King's College, Cambridge, Temple elected to study film and enrolled at the National Film and Television School in Beaconsfield, Buckinghamshire. While there he planned to work on a film "about understanding the world through the Kinks, but I never really made it". Instead, he stumbled upon the Sex Pistols who were rehearsing 'I'm Not Like Everybody Else' in a warehouse in Bermondsey. "I asked them if they'd do the music for this student film which was really about the Kinks and these other bands and growing up with that music." This connection ultimately led to Temple working on the Sex Pistols-related films *The Great Rock 'n' Roll Swindle* and *The Filth And The Fury*.

It was not until 1981, at the start of the MTV boom, that Temple finally got a chance to work with Ray Davies exclusively on the video of 'Predictable'. This was followed by the acclaimed 'Come Dancing', whose strong visual narrative proved an MTV hit and brought the Kinks back into the Top 10 singles charts on both sides of the Atlantic. Temple worked extensively on several other Kinks' videos and was even mentioned by name in the lyrics of 'Too Hot'. In common with previous non-Kinks associates like Barry Fantoni and Ned Sherrin, he dextrously avoided the inter-group conflicts and enjoyed a close working relationship with Ray Davies. The results were fruitful, but it would be naïve to suggest that it was always easy-going.

"Nothing's easy with Ray, as you know. If it was easy it wouldn't be worth persevering. The guy's a one-off and he has good days and bad days. As I do. I understand that he's a human being.

He's not some godlike genius but he's an endlessly fascinating person who's very honest and very like a fox that covers his tracks. Maybe that's deceitful at the same time – I don't know. There's an openness but an incredible sense of wanting to dig your shit deep into the ground. He's an unusual human being that's for sure. I've met several in my life and he's one of them. And you are fascinated by someone who is more than what you expect. There's a lot going on with Ray. I've never had any other feeling but enthusiasm in terms of working with him, and the other way round."

Temple was perfectly placed to work as director alongside producer Jeremy Thomas when the proposal for the Kinks' film *You Really Got Me* was first mooted. Matters became more complicated in 2010 when Alan Yentob, editor of BBC Four's *Imagine* series of documentaries, announced that Ray Davies was to be the subject of a programme titled *Imaginary Man*. Yentob secured Temple's services as producer/director, but it was a controversial commission. Julien was obliged to discuss the proposal with Jeremy Thomas who advised him against getting involved. "I was telling him: 'It's better if I do it, then we can control what's different in the movie.' " The argument made sense, but it almost scuppered the chances of making *You Really Got Me*. Unwittingly, Temple had triggered Dave Davies' wrath. The younger brother felt betrayed by his decision to work with Ray on a separate project and told him bluntly "the movie is off!". Desperate to make amends, Temple approached Yentob about directing a documentary devoted entirely to Dave's life and career. Titled *Kinkdom Come,* it was broadcast the following year, albeit on a smaller budget. "Alan found me the money to do it. I enjoyed it. I was really into it, but the BBC were not." The programmes complemented each other remarkably well and re-established concord between Temple and the Davies brothers. "I really love both of them in equal measure," Temple now says, echoing almost verbatim the sentiments of the brothers' childhood friend and former roadie Peter 'Jonah' Jones, whose relationship with the Davies's meant negotiating far more complex mind games.

The major players in the Kinks' story have all learned the art of dealing, successfully or otherwise, with the ongoing sibling rivalry. As a film director, Temple is no exception. "You have to remember which button you're pushing when you send the email," he jokes. "It's a complicated business being stuck in the middle of these two brothers because it is love and hate – and very extreme versions of those things. If you're in the crossfire of either of those, it's like virtual bullets hitting you in the stomach. There's lots of skills involved. Psychology and diplomacy. That's what makes them unique. There's something deeply at stake for both of them, far more than with Mick [Jagger] and Keith [Richards]. I see them becoming more like Ray and Dave as the years go by with the same kind of psychological stratagems emerging. It's quite funny. They're effectively brothers in a different way but Ray and Dave are brothers of the blood. The full flowering of this is the Kinks' sibling rivalry. You can't duplicate that. It's on a level that's fascinating. And that's what the film is about. There's this incredible love and hate dynamic. The build-up with all the antagonism, rivalry and jostling is, to me, about creating the songs in the end . . . Ray's got a thing with Dave that goes both ways. I'm not really capable of explaining why that is. Other than that I've found him great to work with. But other people have told me he's a nightmare to work with [and that's] on other projects recently."

Temple could not resist mentioning another of Ray Davies' more exasperating traits. "He's legendarily mean. *Everybody* will tell you that. But he finds it very funny that people don't understand that it's a great laugh that he won't pay for a meal. Though, sometimes he does. It's a wonderful thing when Ray Davies pays for a cup of coffee. I have to say it tastes a lot better."

Raconteurs still love tales of his frugality. In reviewing the hardback edition of this book, *The Times*' Will Hodgkinson wrote: "When I met Ray Davies in Highgate, north London, in 2013, he relayed gloomily his fears of being made homeless and asked whether I was OK with paying the restaurant bill. It was terrible to see the man who wrote 'Waterloo Sunset' in such dire straits. It was only when I took the Tube home, and he wandered off to his mansion around the corner, that I realized this multimillionaire pop star, who had written any number of classic songs, had spun me a hard-luck story for the sake of a free meal."

These are wonderful after-dinner tales made all the more remarkable for the small amounts of money involved. Other pop luminaries speak of great rock 'n' roll swindles, drugs binges or business deals involving millions. Reminiscences of Davies more usually centre on pennies or the price of a pint. Such stories are reassuringly innocent and often hilariously funny. More than anything, they testify to Ray's enduring connection to the frugality of the Fifties, as if part of his consciousness is still imprisoned in that twilight time of post-war rationing. Of course, you cannot help concluding that Ray is also playing a game with himself and the world and perhaps rather enjoying the surprised and baffled reactions to his thriftiness.

A biography like this is never quite exhausted. Post-publication there are always belated bulletins and bit players with fresh tales and perspectives. One of Ray's former flames wrote a moving and revealing account of her coming to terms with the break-up of their relationship, but still declined to be interviewed or quoted, at least for the present. Colin Huggett, the mature student with the glass eye described on page 76, recounted fond memories of Ray and John Philby at Hornsey Art College. Whereas Philby and his attractive girlfriend Kate Herbert stood out, Ray "was rather nondescript, a gangly youth in one of those Fair Isle sleeveless jumpers, short hair, an air of insecurity, even shyness about him". They would often mess about playing football in the college's corridors. Later, Ray asked Colin's girlfriend Audrey to intercede on his behalf in pursuit of a tall, dark-haired student, Jo Fathi, who showed not the slightest interest. The non-romance might have provided a memorable pop lyric had Davies been writing at the time.

In terms of Kinks' history, there was also a crucial and previously unheard postscript to their greatest and most dramatic episode. After the infamous 1965 'Cardiff Incident', where a provoked Mick Avory attacked and bloodied Dave Davies onstage with a high-hat cymbal or pedal, a replacement drummer was sought. The candidate, Paul Ainsley Morgan, was a jazz drummer from Mumbles, Swansea, the same town where manager Larry Page's father, Gordon, was born. Precisely how this connection was made is lost to the mists of time but Page was quick to act even though Avory's future as a Kink appeared all but over. "Dave said he would not go onstage with Mick again," Morgan remembers, "and, unbeknownst to Mick, I was auditioned to take his place as drummer a few days after the fracas in Cardiff. I was doing recording work in London one night when I had a phone call from the band's manager Larry Page asking to meet him and Ray Davies in a pub in New Oxford Street the next morning. Ray, Larry and I had a brief chat before going up to a large room with a drum and a piano. Ray played piano and I the drums while Larry sang the songs – one of which was 'You Really Got Me'. Ray shook my hand and said he'd see me soon and Larry told me to call his office at 2 p.m. the next day to finalize things. But I took a phone call from Larry in Swansea the next morning saying it was his job to keep the band together and he'd managed to patch things up. The rest is history."

Such testimony indicates how important it is to appreciate the nuances of events when relating a biography as complicated as this one. Ray's complex personality adds psychological layers to every aspect of his life and work. Davies is refreshingly aware of his shortcomings but also recognizes the process by which these foibles can be transformed into art. "My life is defined by my music," he says, in a revealing inversion.

There is something about the subconscious aspect of Davies' songwriting that proves intriguing and adds to his mystique. For Temple, part of the secret lies in Ray's lifelong insomnia. "Most people spend a third of their life asleep. If you don't have that option and can't sleep, you're living longer, you're weirdly wiser and you're boring into who you are much more every night. I think there's something about that with Ray. He just has more experience about who he is and he has his dark thoughts about what other people think. It's like that weird time in the night when you're paranoid about getting up tomorrow. If you live your life like that, all these stupid worries take over a bit more. It's night terrors . . . It's Thomas Nashe [the sixteenth-century pamphleteer who wrote the treatise *The Terrors Of Night*]. I think Ray is very attuned to that."

Like many Elizabethans, not least those of the School Of Night, Nashe understood the power of darkness and solitude in playing upon our subconscious. While Davies' insomnia seems like a curse, it is also a profound asset. "I think creativity happens when you're half awake and half asleep and you're not sure who you are," Temple argues. "Ray's the master of that. I believe 'I

Go To Sleep' is the key song to understand the whole nature of Ray's connection with the world which, on the one hand, is natural and realistic, and on another level it's very surreal, filtering experiences through dreams. This half-awake state is where the power of his lyrics come from."

The last words should be left to the songwriter. "I think the songs will be remembered," he says. "I might just disappear."

NOTES

Preface

"Are you OK . . ." email to Anna Green: 13 September 2013.

"I wonder if Larry is still with that girl Jade? . . ." Ray Davies, interviewed by the author. London: 1 October 2013.

"That's good! . . ." ibid.

"A lovely man . . ." ibid.

"great characters . . ." ibid.

"Veronica turned up . . ." ibid.

"Did you meet him? . . ." ibid.

"It was the beginning and the end . . ." ibid.

"His father was half North American Indian . . ." ibid.

"I always write for the extras . . ." ibid.

"I don't really know my brother . . ." ibid.

"Ray does talk a lot of shit . . ." Dave Davies, interviewed by the author. London/Cornwall: 3 October 2012.

"It was obvious . . ." Rasa Didzpetris, interviewed by the author. London: 4 March 2013.

"I've got special plans . . ." Ray Davies, onstage at the 'Kinks Konvention', Boston Arms. London: 17 November 2013.

"Can I have that as an affidavit? . . ." ibid.

"My work is better than I am . . ." Ray Davies, interviewed by Len Brown. *Without Walls – My Generation: The Kinks*. Channel 4: 18 March 1995.

Chapter One: The Family

". . . Catherine Emily Bowden . . ." Oddly, in his autobiography *Kink*, Dave Davies consistently misspells 'Willmore' as 'Wilmore'. Perhaps he picked this up from Ray whose book *X-Ray* does exactly the same. As countless birth, marriage and death certificates confirm, Willmore is correct. There is not a single mention of 'Wilmore' on any certificate. Dave also repeats various family legends that are unverifiable, including the suggestion that his mother was one of 21 children (a factoid featured in early Kinks interviews), a rumour that his grandfather Albert was a disinherited toff and that his maternal grandmother Catherine (whom he spells as 'Katherine') was a foundling.

"The girls were babies . . ." Dave Davies, interviewed by the author. London: 1 March 1996.

". . . complications arose when Annie Davies, almost 42 . . ." In his narration on the 1998 CD *The Storyteller*, Ray Davies incorrectly suggests, in passing, that his mother was 45 at the time of Dave's birth.

". . . David Russell Gordon Davies . . ." The younger brother took his middle names from his brothers-in-law, Russell Whitbread and Gordon Arthur Anning.

"When Dave was born . . ." Ray Davies, interviewed by Penny Valentine. *Disc*: 12 August 1967.

"Are you OK? . . ." Dave Davies/Rogan. London: 1 March 1996.

"It's symbolic of our whole relationship . . ." ibid.

"I was quite a happy kid . . ." Dave Davies, interviewed by Len Brown. *Without Walls – My Generation: The Kinks*. Channel 4: 18 March 1995.

"Differences in the evolvement . . ." Peter B. Neubauer, MD, 'The Importance Of The Sibling Experience' in *Psychoanalytic Study Of The Child* 38; pp. 325–6. Whether Ray perceived his younger brother's more gregarious personality as a threat to his own standing in the family unit is debatable, but Dave saw no signs of favouritism. "Of course he was loved equally, but as the years went by he became more shy and withdrawn, and many hidden jealousies and resentments would surface, unleashing themselves in cruel and abusive ways." Elsewhere he added: "I think Ray loves me very much, but he only loves me in the way he wants me to be loved."

"The elder child . . ." Sigmund Freud, *1900a*, p. 250.

"I'm not a psychologist . . ." Ray Davies, interviewed by Carla Hay. *Music Connection*: 10 November 1996.

"At a very early age . . ." Ray Davies, interviewed by Richard Green. *New Musical Express*: 13 February 1970.

"Then I trained myself . . ." Ray Davies, interviewed by James McNair. *Independent*: 19 June 2009.

"I picked up . . ." Ray Davies, interviewed on the documentary *Imaginary Man*. Broadcast BBC 1: 21 December 2010. This may be a fusion of two memories from school. A 'demobilization suit' was worn by Davies' Maths teacher, Mr Lill, at William Grimshaw Secondary Modern.

"I think I saw Max Wall . . ." Ray Davies, interviewed by Peter Doggett. *Record Collector* 169: September 1993.

"When I was five . . ." Ray Davies, interviewed by Margaret Rooke and Ruby Wellington. *Telegraph Magazine*: 1997.

"I was just an infant . . ." Ray Davies quoted in *Music Week*: 23 March 2011.

"It's poignant to me . . ." Ray Davies speech on opening of Meltdown Festival. June 2011.

"Let us – like the good Home Service types . . ." J. B. Priestley. *Listener*: June 1951.

"Homosexuality is an unpleasant subject . . ." Douglas Warth. 'The Evil Men'. *Sunday Pictorial*: 25 May–8 June 1952.

"I have watched it growing . . ." ibid. Warth was, of course, thinking of 'decadent' pre-war Germany but the allusions to "Hitlerite corruption" were oddly out of place considering the Führer's own detestation of homosexuality and imprisonment, even extermination, of those considered guilty of such activities.

"When you were the youngest . . ." Dave Davies, interviewed by Johnnie Walker. Broadcast BBC Radio 2: 30 December 2010.

"I can't explain . . ." *Imaginary Man* documentary. Broadcast BBC 1: 21 December 2010. Ray's miscalculation about the number of sisters in the household was not unique to this broadcast. When discussing his family in print similar such errors were evident. Even in the self-penned 'unauthorized autobiography' X-Ray, he describes Rene as "the eldest of my six sisters" (p. 35), even though she was born two years after Rosina (Rose). Considering his closeness to Rose and the years he spent living at her house, the error is, to say the least, peculiar. Later in the book, Rose is correctly referred to as his eldest sister (p. 51).

"No disrespect . . ." ibid.

"My sisters used to take turns . . ." Ray Davies, interviewed by Ira Kaplan. *Magnet*: 1 June 2008.

"During the time . . ." Dave Davies, writing in *Rave*: 11 November 1965.

Chapter Two: 'The Negro's Revenge'

"Frank was an old school kind of cockney . . ." Dave Davies/Rogan. London/Cornwall: 3 October 2012.

"I can't remember talking to him . . ." Ray Davies, interviewed by Janis Schacht. *Circus*: February 1972.

"He drew me a picture . . ." ibid.

"I would have known him . . ." Dave Davies/Rogan. London/Cornwall: 3 October 2012.

"At the time . . ." ibid.

"These people had lived . . ." Ray Davies, interviewed by Rob Fitzpatrick. *The Word* 113: July 2012.

"It was then . . ." Ray Davies. *The Times*: 6 May 2006.

". . . a weak tea . . ." ibid.

"My father instilled in me . . ." ibid.

". . . by retiring to the sanctuary of his allotment . . ." The Allotment Act of 1922 provided that "Every citizen who is able and willing to cultivate an allotment garden is legally entitled to be provided with one."

"I had no way . . ." Ray Davies, interviewed on *The World Of Ray Davies And The Kinks: I'm Not Like Everybody Else*. Broadcast BBC 2: 21 December 1995.

". . . the stuff you used to put down the sink . . ." Ray Davies/Rogan. London: 1 October 2013.

"I drank a bottle of that . . ." ibid.

"Gwen inspired the song . . ." ibid.

". . . the inner world of an only child . . ." Prophecy Coles, 'The Importance Of Sibling Relationships' in *Psychoanalysis* (London: Karnac, 2003), p. 6.

"I called Rosie 'Mum' . . ." Ray Davies, interviewed by Ken Sharp. *Goldmine*: March 1996.

". . . a big brother transference . . ." S. A. Sharpe and A. D. Rosenblatt, 'Oedipal Sibling Triangles' in *Journal of American Psychoanalysis Association* 42; pp. 491–523.

"Siblings have easier access . . ." ibid.

"I often got chased . . ." Dave Davies. *Rave*: 11 November 1965.

". . . new girl in the class . . ." Dave Davies/Rogan. London: 1 March 1996.

"I really fancied Gillian . . ." ibid.

"I was absolutely terrified . . ." ibid.

"I never had sex at the age of seven . . ." ibid.

"All of a sudden . . ." Peter 'Jonah' Jones, interviewed by the author. London/Montreal, Canada: 8 May 2013.

"A couple of days later . . ." ibid.

"He was tipped off . . ." David Kassner, interviewed by David Taylor. *Independent*: 9 June 2008.

". . . soldier would shoot him . . ." Larry Page, interviewed by the author. Avoca Beach, New South Wales, Australia: 18 May 2011.

"How Lucky You Are" . . . Kassner co-wrote 'How Lucky You Are' under the name Eddie Cassan.

"My sisters bought be-bop . . ." Ray Davies/Rogan. London: 1 October 2013.

". . . . an animated golliwog . . ." *New Musical Express*: 18 January 1957.

"It is nothing more . . ." Sir Malcolm Sargent, quoted in Pete Frame, *The Restless Generation* (London: Rogan House, 2007), p. 190.

"It has something of the African tom-tom . . ." *Daily Mail*: 4 September 1956.

"It is deplorable . . ." *Daily Mail*: 5 September 1956.

"Viewed as a social phenomenon . . ." *Melody Maker*: 5 May 1956.

"Are We Turning Our Children Into Little Americans?" *Everybody's Weekly*: 3 July 1957.

"I became concerned . . ." Ewan MacColl, quoted in Robin Denselow, *When The Music's Over* (London: Faber & Faber, 1989), pp. 25–6.

". . . most of the customers . . ." Richard Hoggart, *The Uses Of Literacy: Aspects Of Working-Class Life* (London: Chatto & Windus, 1957).

"That was the 'People's Music' . . ." Ray Davies/Rogan. London: 1 October 2013.

"The music hall is dying . . ." John Osborne, *The Entertainer* (London, 1957), p. 7.

Chapter Three: Rene And Rose

"We'd played a few songs . . ." *Imaginary Man* documentary. Broadcast BBC 1: 21 December 2010.

"It was her decision . . ." ibid.

"She died . . ." ibid.

"It was poignant that it was on [the eve of] my birthday . . ." Author's parenthesis. Although Ray Davies has consistently said she died on his birthday, it was actually the night before, as confirmed by her death certificate. The death was registered on 22 June by her husband Russell Whitbread. A post-mortem without inquest was conducted by G. Thurson, the Coroner for the County of London.

"I remember waking up . . ." Dave Davies, *Kronikles: Mystical Journey* DVD; detune films: 2009.

"He'd come from a time . . ." ibid.

"Clearly, I couldn't cope . . ." Ray Davies, interviewed by Peter Silverton: RX: 23 November 1997.

"Ray sat in front of me . . ." Rita Lack, letter to *Daily Mail*: 23 February 1996.

"I wasn't a rebel . . ." *Imaginary Man* documentary. Broadcast BBC 1: 21 December 2010. In their study *Separate Lives: Why Siblings Are So Different* (New York: Basic Books, 1990), professors Judy Dunn and Robert Plomin examine how a negative life-changing event can affect siblings in different ways, both psychologically and physically. "Uncontrollable life events are thought to drive people crazy to a greater extent than controllable events," they maintain. "Uncontrollable events include illness or death of a family member . . . When individuals feel that they have no control over what happens to them, they begin to behave in an increasingly 'helpless' way – they learn to be helpless. This helplessness can lead to depression and to a breakdown in immune system functioning and thereby can cause physical illness."

"Life was like a reproduction . . ." Ray Davies, *X-Ray* (London: Viking, 1994). The same point was repeated to the author by Davies. London: 1 October 1996.

"The *Sunday Pictorial*'s showbiz correspondent, Jack Bentley . . ." Bentley confronted Page after the show, convinced that he was the best man at Tommy Steele's wedding. The fact that Steele was still a year away from announcing his engagement did not deter Bentley. "It was very heavy," Page recalls. "He was saying, 'Now, I know Tommy's married. I can make or break you.' It scared the bloody pants off me because it was a real threat job. I said I knew nothing about it." Larry Page, interviewed by the author. London: 24 June 1983.

"capable of performance . . ." Memo from the BBC's Director General titled 'Popular Songs And Music By British Composers', quoted in Pete Frame, *The Restless Generation* (London: Rogan House, 2007), p. 290.

"We should look . . ." ibid. The xenophobic attitude towards American rock 'n' roll recordings was based on avarice rather than aesthetics. It was a familiar practice in the music industry then and later, and the Americans could hardly claim any moral high ground. In their own country they had been systematically siphoning 'negro' R&B talent for years, passing over regional hits to white-bread singers for reinterpretation. It was simply the way of the world.

"It won't be released . . ." Page/Rogan. London: 24 June 1983. Newell's hopes were undone as soon as Coral elected to release the Crickets' original in the UK. It rapidly climbed to number 1 rendering Page's version irrelevant.

"It was the biggest . . ." ibid. Page quickly learned the value of publicity, but some of it was fortuitous. During rehearsals for a television spot, the make-up department noticed the floor lighting exaggerated the fairness of his hair, so he was provided with a dark tint. After the programme, Page was scheduled to appear onstage and there was no time to rinse out the dye. Under the harsh theatre lights, the blue tint was accentuated, instantly creating a new image. The press even fabricated a feud between the blue-rinsed Page and his orange/pink-haired contemporary, Wee Willie Harris.

"It was a really bad injury . . ." Ray Davies/Silverton: RX: 23 November 1997.

"It turned out . . ." Ray Davies, interviewed by Fred Schruers. *Rolling Stone:* 4 February 1982.

"This wonderful person . . ." Ray Davies, interviewed by Ken Sharp. *Goldmine*: March 1996.

"A lot of people . . ." Ray Davies, interviewed by Jeff Tamarkin. *The Aquarian/Manhattan*: 7–14 October 1981.

"Ray went into hospital . . ." Dave Davies/Rogan. London: 1 March 1996.

"It was about three o'clock . . ." ibid.

"It wasn't life-threatening . . ." Ray Davies/Rogan. London: 1 October 2013.

"I needed to get out . . ." *Imaginary Man* documentary. Broadcast BBC 1: 21 December 2010.

". . . 'You Really Got Me' and an instrumental titled 'South' . . ." In various interviews, Ray Davies has claimed that these songs were first conceived when he was 15 years old, which would date them between 1959–60. However, in a later interview published in *Mojo* 148, in March 2006, Davies, while discussing the origins of 'You Really Got Me', informed Mark Paytress: "I'll tell you *exactly* when I started writing that song. I was sixteen or seventeen, and at art college, way before the Kinks were formed. I'd fractured my jaw, had it reset, and I was in a brace and at my sister [Rose's] house. And I was just picking a country blues song, Chet Atkins-style, a simple slide-down from *F* to *G* but I played open chords because I was a lazy guitar player." These comments testify to Davies' tendency to concertina events either for brevity or obfuscation. Note how the word '*exactly*' is immediately undermined then contradicted by the following sentence in which he cannot actually remember his precise age at the time. The further claim that he was at college is also chronologically awry. He did not enter art school until the autumn of 1962 when he was eighteen years old, not "sixteen or seventeen". The precise date of the 'jaw fracture' and subsequent stay in hospital is also uncertain. Dave believes it happened when Ray was fifteen, around 1958–9. In other interviews Ray has also shifted the time frame, but he told me he was fourteen, which again indicates 1958.

". . . a horrifying, discordant set . . ." Dave Davies, interviewed by Keith Altham. *New Musical Express*: 9 April 1965.

"Mike was from an older generation . . ." Dave Davies/Rogan. London: 1 March 1996.

"I consider myself . . ." Long John Baldry, quoted in Pete Frame, *The Restless Generation* (London: Rogan House, 2007), p. 350.

"It was an archive documentary . . ." *The First Time . . . With Ray Davies*. BBC 6 Music: 3 April 2011.

"It didn't matter . . ." *The Davies Diaries*. BBC Radio 2: 23 November 2000.

"I was quite shrewd . . ." *The First Time . . . With Ray Davies*. BBC 6 Music: 3 April 2011.

"This was a big step forward . . ." Dave Davies. *Rave*: 11 November 1965.

"I saw it best . . ." Ray Davies, interviewed by Johnnie Walker. Broadcast BBC Radio 2: 30 December 2010.

". . . Picker also took the brothers to see their first gig, featuring Duane Eddy . . ." In the BBC programme *The First Time*, Ray Davies was asked about his first gig and confirmed it was one of Duane Eddy's London shows. However, he claimed that Little

Richard was on the same bill, which was not the case in 1960 where the supporting acts comprised Frank Ifield, Kathy Kirby, the Four Playboys and Alan Randall, with Des O'Connor as compere. As with some of his other early reminiscences, Ray was possibly combining different memories. Eddy and Little Richard, along with the Shirelles, did appear in London three years later in November 1963, but it seems unlikely that this was the *first* gig Ray ever saw as he would have been 19 by then. Little Richard performed at the Regal, Edmonton (9 November), the Granada, Woolwich (10th) and the Granada, Harrow (11th) after which he retired from the tour citing an injured ankle. Dave told me that he was 13 when he attended the Duane Eddy show, confirming that it was 1960. He remembers thinking Frank Ifield "old-fashioned". Two years later, Ifield would become a dominant figure in UK pop with three consecutive number 1 hits: 'I Remember You', 'Lovesick Blues' and 'The Wayward Wind'.

". . . the Clissold Arms . . ." Dave Davies/Rogan. London: 1 March 1996.

"It was in the [Bald Face] Stag . . ." Ray Davies/Margaret Rooke and Ruby Wellington. *Telegraph Magazine*: 1997.

"I always thought . . ." Annie Davies, interviewed by Michael Aldred. *Fabulous*: March 1965.

"Maybe it was an England . . ." Ray Davies, interviewed by Neil Rosser. Unedited interview despatched to author: 30 November 2005.

"I think that my problems . . ." *Imaginary Man* documentary. Broadcast BBC 1: 21 December 2010.

"One of my favourite characters . . ." Ray Davies/Rosser. Unedited interview despatched to author: 30 November 2005.

Chapter Four: The Ray Davies Quartet

"I decided . . ." *Imaginary Man* documentary. Broadcast BBC 1: 21 December 2010.

"I did quite well . . ." Ray Davies, interviewed by Keith Altham. *New Musical Express*: 16 April 1965. School friend Peter 'Jonah' Jones confirms that Davies was in the William Grimshaw cricket team in addition to his other sporting achievements.

"Ray was really competitive . . ." Peter 'Jonah' Jones/Rogan. London/Montreal, Canada: 8 May 2013.

"Ray pinned me down . . ." ibid.

"It took me a long time . . ." ibid.

"Annie, the mother . . ." ibid.

"They used to have seances . . ." ibid.

"There was such a weird energy . . ." ibid.

"He wanted me . . ." Ray Davies, interviewed by Kate Bohdanowicz. *Times Educational Supplement*: 18 October 2013.

"I first heard Pete . . ." David Quaife, interviewed by the author. London: 27 February 2013.

"Although we were the same age . . ." Pete Quaife, interviewed by the author. London/Copenhagen: 3 July 2006.

"The teacher wanted to know . . ." ibid. Oddly, Pete Quaife sometimes referred to the teacher as Mr Gill, but others, including Ray Davies and Rod Stewart, confirm that the class was run by Bruce Wainwright.

"Pete wasn't very happy . . ." John Start, interviewed by the author. Haslemere, Surrey: 25 September 2012. Quaife's relationship with his stepfather was not confrontational. "Mum and Dad were very easy," says David Quaife. "Dad actually helped him find a guitar with a pickup and made amplifiers and things. Dad built our television set when I was four years old. He was a bit of an electronic genius, Dad."

"He was quiet and aloof . . ." ibid.

"I had no idea . . ." ibid.

"Pete used to come . . ." Dave Davies. *Rave*: 11 November 1965.

"I can't even remember . . ." Start/Rogan. Haslemere, Surrey: 25 September 2012.

"I was a great fan of the Ventures . . ." Dave Davies/Rogan. London: 1 March 1996. The Ventures' influence can be heard clearly on several Kinks' originals from 'All Day And All Of The Night' through 'Rosy, Won't You Please Come Home' and 'Brainwashed'.

"I was basically threatened . . ." Pete Quaife, interviewed by Neil Rosser. Unedited interview despatched to author: 30 November 2005.

"I was terribly embarrassed . . ." Start/Rogan. Haslemere, Surrey: 25 September 2012.

"Ray was a tetchy, difficult, almost bad-tempered person . . ." ibid.

"I'm not sure . . ." Pete Quaife, interviewed by Johnny Black. *Mojo* 82: September 2000.

"It was a very loving environment . . ." Start/Rogan. Haslemere, Surrey: 25 September 2012.

"Dave and Ray always saw my parents . . ." ibid.

"I don't think Ray liked me . . ." ibid.

"I did more singing . . ." Dave Davies/Rogan. London/Cornwall: 3 October 2012.

"The biggest mistake . . ." Peter 'Jonah' Jones/Rogan. London/Montreal, Canada: 8 May 2013.

"Rod looked like a beaten animal . . ." Start/Rogan. Haslemere, Surrey: 25 September 2012.

"I don't think any of us . . ." ibid.

"Rod was very aloof . . ." ibid.

"The comparisons you make . . ." Pete Quaife/Rogan. London/Copenhagen: 3 July 2006.

"I could see Ray thinking . . ." Pete Quaife/Paytress. *Mojo* 148: March 2006.

"No . . ." Pete Quaife/Black. *Mojo* 82: September 2000.

"I was real cocky . . ." Rod Stewart, internet bio.

"He was there *before* . . ." Start/Rogan. Haslemere, Surrey: 25 September 2012.

"That was Sue Redmond! . . ." ibid.

"She was a nice girl . . ." ibid.

"It got to the point . . ." ibid.

"My father was a bit mean . . ." ibid.

"Sue was introduced to me . . ." Dave Davies/Rogan. London: 1 March 1996.

". . . Mr Loades, who administered corporal punishment . . ." Loades always regarded himself as a progressive, idealistic headmaster. If his memoirs are veracious and Dave Davies' account is correct, then the caning was very significant. Loades recalls: "I had only used the cane once in my teaching life, and that was a long, long time ago. In fact, I was so disgusted with myself that I took the cane back to my room and broke it up.

It was a serious offence that I had dealt with, but I vowed that I would never lose my temper again with staff or pupils." Charles Loades, *Born Teacher* (Bury St Edmunds: Arima Publishing, 2009), p. 183.

"If I hadn't had such a big family . . ." Dave Davies/Rogan. London: 1 March 1996.

"I was totally emotionally devastated . . ." ibid.

Chapter Five: Hornsey

"It was a clearing house . . ." Pete Townshend, interviewed by Pete Hamill. *New Yorker*: 18 October 1982.

"That was the remarkable thing . . ." Lisa Tickner (née Warton), interviewed by the author. London: 28 June 2012.

". . . neither good industrial designers . . ." quoted in Lisa Tickner, *Hornsey 1968 – The Art School Revolution* (London: Francis Lincoln, 2008).

"Most people were pleased . . ." Lisa Tickner (née Warton)/Rogan. London: 28 June 2012.

"I got thrown out . . ." Pete Quaife/Rosser. Unedited interview despatched to author: 30 November 2005.

"We were Mods . . ." Patricia Thomas, interviewed by Michael Aldred. *Fabulous*: March 1965.

"She lent us her Anglia . . ." Start/Rogan. Haslemere, Surrey: 25 September 2012.

"Art school was still a place . . ." Lisa Tickner (née Warton)/Rogan. London: 28 June 2012.

"I remember one girl . . ." ibid.

". . . a strange guy called Colin . . ." ibid.

". . . a Maltese guy . . ." ibid.

"There was a real social mix . . ." ibid.

"What Ray is talking about . . ." Paul O'Dell, interviewed by the author. London/Arnace la Poste, France: 19 November 2012.

"At art school . . ." Ray Davies/Paytress. *Mojo* 148: March 2006.

"The teachers were quite radical . . ." Clive Tickner, interviewed by the author. Darsham, Suffolk: 2 October 2012.

"Where's all the tits then? . . ." Ray Davies, interviewed by Julien Temple. London: BFI South Bank: 18 June 2011.

"I was only thirteen . . ." John Philby, interviewed by Monica Porter. *Daily Mail*: 1998.

"John Philby was a familiar sight . . ." Lisa Tickner (née Warton), email to author: 1 February 2013.

"I was quite often carted off . . ." O'Dell/Rogan. London/Arnace la Poste, France: 19 November 2012.

"My guardians felt . . ." ibid.

"We used to go . . ." ibid. O'Dell was taken under the wing of these tutors as a cultural protégé. The English teacher, an American named Norm Fruchter, introduced him to non-syllabus poets, while fellow expatriate Jim Kitses worked and wrote articles for the British Film Institute. The intellectual socializing provided an esoteric education, enabled by the limited requirements of art school for which he only needed to study three O-levels, plus A-level Art.

"Apart from the cracked lens . . ." ibid.

"Paul was the leading light . . ." Clive Tickner/Rogan. Darsham, Suffolk: 2 October 2012.

"I'm certain Ray would be happy . . ." Lisa Tickner (née Warton)/Rogan. London: 28 June 2012.

"He was the *real* film buff . . ." ibid.

"We were very keen . . ." Paul O'Dell, email to author: 23 October 2012.

". . . *Captain Video* . . ." "I was really proud of that," O'Dell stresses. "A lot of the tutors who came took me to task. They thought it was just children's Saturday morning pictures, which in fact it was. That's what it was made for. I thought it was a struggle between right and wrong with some interesting subtexts, but it didn't go down terribly well with everybody."

"I was usually taking the money . . ." Lisa Tickner (née Warton)/Rogan. London: 28 June 2012.

". . . Tottenham-born Geoff Prowse . . ." There are darker aspects to the story, too detailed for the main text. According to Davies in an ancient interview, one of his best friends committed suicide around this time, but he never elaborated on the subject. Oddly, neither his brother nor art school colleagues of the period recall hearing about any such trauma. Whether it was a real or imagined event was never ascertained. In one Davies-related book it was stated as fact that the suicide Ray described was that of his Hornsey friend Paul O'Dell. This highly irresponsible assertion was conjectural nonsense as even a glimpse at a reputable website would have revealed. After completing his course at Hornsey, O'Dell became a successful television producer and film editor. In 1972, he worked with Clive Tickner as film editor on the Christopher Mason directed *All The Advantages*. In 1998, after a long career in film, O'Dell retired to France to become a full-time painter. So who was the mysterious person who committed suicide? When I confronted Ray Davies on this, he claimed that it was Geoffrey Prowse, but then admitted that his friend had not taken his own life. "It wasn't suicide. He got poisoned by sucking a pen. He died of lead poisoning." Even if this is true, the death did not take place while Ray was at Hornsey. Prowse died in 1972, aged 30.

". . . bass player, Stuart 'Maciejewski' . . ." The surname, I regret to say, is a best-guess phonetic representation. I asked Ray Davies for a correct spelling but he could only pronounce the name which he assumed was Polish.

"He was into clarinet playing . . ." Dave Davies/Rogan. London: 1 March 1996.

"I seem to remember . . ." *The Davies Diaries*. BBC Radio 2: 23 November 2000.

"You're fine . . ." Lisa Tickner (née Warton)/Rogan. London: 28 June 2012.

"Alexis arrived . . ." *The Davies Diaries*. BBC Radio 2: 23 November 2000.

"There was a collision of styles . . ." Tom McGuinness, interviewed by Neil Rosser. Unedited interview despatched to author: 30 November 2005.

"I saw the energy . . ." Ray Davies, interviewed by Phil McNeill. *New Musical Express*: 16 April 1977.

"I don't know how we got the gig . . ." Start/Rogan. Haslemere, Surrey: 25 September 2012.

"Sadly I didn't go . . ." O'Dell/Rogan. London/Arnace la Poste, France: 19 November 2012.

"Ray was quite reticent . . ." ibid.

"Would you like to make a film? . . ." ibid.

"It was about a guy . . ." Ray Davies, interviewed by David Fricke. *Rolling Stone*: 27 May 1985.

"It was made over six months . . ." O'Dell/Rogan. London/Arnace la Poste, France: 19 November 2012.

"It was about somebody coming back . . ." ibid.

"We were so noble . . ." Ray Davies/Temple. London: BFI South Bank: 18 June 2011. Recently, footage emerged of a 1964 film *Bridge*, directed by Paul O'Dell while he was a student at Hornsey. He stars in the short alongside Charlotte Womersly. The black and white film is shot on Hungerford Footbridge and Charing Cross Station, pre-empting 'Waterloo Sunset' by several years. Alas, *Veronica*, the short film O'Dell made with Ray Davies, has been "sadly lost except for some fuzz frame enlargements".

Chapter Six: The Boll-Weevils

"It is impossible . . ." Christopher Brooker, *The Neophiliacs* (London: William Collins, 1969; London: Pimlico, 1992), p. 190.

"The pianist played 'Honky Tonk Train Blues' . . ." Ray Davies, interviewed by Richard Green. *New Musical Express*: 13 February 1971. In the interview Davies is quoted as referring to them as 'Bob Cosby And The Bluecats'.

"He's the one who told me . . ." Ray Davies/Rogan. London: 1 October 2013.

"I felt a lot more comfortable . . ." Peter 'Jonah' Jones/Rogan. London/Montreal, Canada: 8 May 2013.

"It was strange . . ." Ray Davies/Rogan. London: 1 October 2013. Dave Davies confirms as much, adding, "Ray learned a hell of a lot from Hamilton King, more than he would care to admit."

"Hamilton King was this West Indian . . ." Peter Bardens, quoted in *Trouser Press*: October–November 1976.

"No, there weren't any . . ." Dave Davies/Rogan. London: 1 March 1996.

"I was amazed . . ." *The World Of Ray Davies And The Kinks: I'm Not Like Everybody Else*. Broadcast BBC 2: 21 December 1995.

"Dave and I weren't playing . . ." *The Davies Diaries, Part 1*. BBC Radio 2: 23 November 2000.

"Ray didn't take over . . ." Dave Davies/Rogan. London: 1 March 1996.

"We used to go to the Marquee . . ." Start/Rogan. Haslemere, Surrey: 25 September 2012.

"We played in the West End . . ." ibid.

"This was 1963 . . ." Ray Davies, interviewed by Jeff Tamarkin. *The Aquarian/Manhattan*: 7–14 October 1981.

"I had other things going on . . ." Start/Rogan. Haslemere, Surrey: 25 September 2012.

"I picked that up somehow . . ." ibid.

". . . no reason to conclude that Mr Philby . . ." Foreign Secretary, Harold Macmillan, speaking in the House of Commons: November 1955.

". . . disclosures which have shocked the moral conscience of the nation . . ." Harold Wilson, speaking in the House of Commons: 17 June 1963.

"... Dave ... changed their name from the Ramrods to the Boll-Weevils ..." Although he thought of the name 'Boll-Weevils', Dave Davies erroneously refers to the group in his autobiography *Kink* as the 'Bo Weevils'. An existing calling card of the period with the title 'Robert Wace And The Boll-Weevils' confirms the correct spelling.

"... a government post at the Ministry of Defence ..." I have heard several rumours over the years that Robert Wace may have been connected with MI5 or MI6 before managing the Kinks. It seems an extraordinary proposition. That said, when I last spoke to Wace he was working at the former British War Office, arguably a fitting post for a manager who had gained vast experience dealing with the Davies' battles over many years.

"I think they were looking ..." Ray Davies/Rosser. Unedited interview despatched to author: 30 November 2005.

"... some try-out demos were recorded with engineer Bill Farley ..." The specific details of these remain unknown, but Mickey Willett's testimony has credibility. While working with Tommy Bruce he gained record studio experience and later co-produced a couple of songs at Southern Music in Denmark Street for the Cortinas, a band from St Albans who won a local beat group contest.

"... lots of Grenville and Robert's friends ..." Dave Davies diary entry: 15 September 1963.

"I know this really good group ..." Robert Wace, quoted in John Mendelssohn, *The Kinks Kronikles* (New York: Quill, 1985), p. 29.

"We were merely considering ..." Grenville Collins, email to the author: 23 September 2012. Collins adds, somewhat obliquely: "The 'overt' reason that attracted Mr Epstein to Raymond Davies was because he thought he had an interesting voice and possibly also he thought that he looked a little different to the 'scousers' he was having to deal with on a day to day basis."

"... courteous and pleasant ..." ibid.

"He turned them down ..." John Mendelssohn, *The Kinks Kronikles* (New York: Quill, 1985), p. 29.

"... to get rid of the group ..." Grenville Collins, email to the author: 23 September 2012.

"It is always valuable ..." ibid.

"On Saturday 28 September, the group ended an eventful week supping champagne ..." Four days later, Dave's diary reveals that the group rehearsed at a "school in Summers Lane, Finchley. Robert bought new Vox amplifier. Very good, successful practice." The next entry for 3 October notes: "Good job at Grocer's Hall, Prince's Street, London ... hope to get plenty of good jobs out of it."

"Ray and Dave were singing R&B numbers ..." Robert Wace, interviewed by the author. London: 15 October 1982.

"It was probably one of the first ..." Dave Davies/Rogan. London/Cornwall: 3 October 2012.

"A separate document dated 29 October was produced for drummer Mickey Willett ..." A pure coincidence, but the day after Willett was officially signed, Dave's diary reveals that they played "Brady's Club, East End, for Bobby Graham (a favour) being paid for expenses." Graham, arguably Britain's premier session drummer, later played on the first five Kinks' singles.

"I don't think Pete knew ..." David Quaife/Rogan. London: 27 February 2013.

"**Instead, they settled on the Ravens . . .**" The Ravens made their debut under that name at the 'Northbank' on 23 November 1963. Dave's diary provides a leaflet advertising "A Raving Rhythm And Blues Session With 'The Boll-Weevils'." However, by the time the ticket was printed the group name was altered to 'The Ravens'.

"**. . . one of the most vivacious party-goers . . .**" Andrew Alderson. *Telegraph*: 31 August 2008.

"**Countess Cowley is some cookie . . .**" Suzy Knickerbocker, 'Smart Set' column. *Montreal Gazette*: 2 November 1971.

Chapter Seven: The Power Players

"**How they became their personal managers . . .**" Sam Curtis, interviewed by the author. Brownhills, Walsall: 24 August 1982.

"**They had a circus fairground . . .**" Peter 'Jonah' Jones/Rogan. London/Montreal, Canada: 8 May 2013.

"**I was about thirteen . . .**" David Quaife/Rogan. London: 27 February 2013.

"**. . . it's all over now . . .**" Reported in *Guardian*: 23 November 1963.

"**There are times in life . . .**" Prime Minister Alec Douglas-Home, BBC Television broadcast, printed in *Guardian*: 23 November 1963.

"**. . . this young, gay and brave statesman . . .**" ibid.

"**One afternoon the vicar invited us . . .**" Ray Davies/Margaret Rooke and Ruby Wellington. *Telegraph Magazine*: 1997.

"**The only sore point . . .**" Mickey Willett, interviewed by the author. London: 4 November 1982.

"**I had a word with the boys . . .**" ibid.

"**It wasn't Aristotle Onassis' party . . .**" Robert Wace, interviewed by the author. London: 25 June 1983.

"**This agreement shall be determinable . . .**" Contract between Willett and Collins dated 29 October 1963.

"**When I confronted Ray . . .**" Willett/Rogan. London: 4 November 1982.

"**Instead, they hired an even older drummer than Willett . . .**" In his 'unauthorized autobiography' *X-Ray*, Ray Davies refers to him as 'Johnny Green', but given his penchant for misspelling names and the fact that there was an earlier drummer named Johnny Bremner, this could be a convenient invention. Nobody else from the period recalls Green by name.

"**It wouldn't be proper . . .**" Philip Solomon, interviewed by Donal Corvin. *Spotlight* magazine. Additional information, Solomon interview with author, Dublin: 15 April 1982.

"**This food isn't fit for a pig! . . .**" Solomon quote, as recalled by Larry Page to the author. London: 24 June 1983.

"**Then he refused . . .**" ibid. Page was almost bamboozled by the presence of Solomon and Kassner during the meeting. "Every time I went to the bathroom one of them would follow and say, 'Come and work with me in London, my boy.' It was a bit heavy but a good position to find yourself in."

"**. . . the shrewdest of them all . . .**" Dick Rowe, interviewed by the author. London: 5 May 1983.

"Solomon had Dick Rowe in his pocket . . ." Larry Page, interviewed by the author. London: 12 July 1994.

"Kassner had Dick Rowe . . ." Larry Page, interviewed by the author. London: 26 November 1996.

"Rowe placed Talmy with Doug Sheldon . . ." Sheldon had already lost out to Dion with a cover of 'Runaround Sue' but scraped into the Top 30 with 'Your Ma Said You Cried In Your Sleep Tonight'. Talmy produced the unsuccessful single, 'Lollipops And Roses'.

"Britain's Answer To The Crystals" . . . Dental surgery was arranged for one of the girls following an accident with a hockey stick. They had already gained some publicity with their September 1963 debut, 'Gonna Make Him Mine'.

". . . clutching an acetate of the Ravens . . ." Shel Talmy, interviewed by the author. London: 17 September 1982.

". . . looking for a producer . . ." ibid.

"Philip Solomon is a winner . . ." Rowe/Rogan. London: 5 May 1983.

". . . an absolutely super group . . ." Page/Rogan. London: 24 June 1983.

"Larry was recruited . . ." Wace/Rogan. London:15 October 1982.

"Kassner was very good news . . ." Page/Rogan. London: 24 June 1983.

"Decca, Philips and EMI . . ." Larry Page, interviewed by the author. London: February 1995.

"He was obviously drawn towards the theatre . . ." John Turney, interviewed by the author. London: November 1983.

"By then he was already playing . . ." ibid.

"I didn't think it would last . . ." Ray Davies/Rosser. Unedited interview despatched to author: 30 November 2005.

"Freddie Crooke was the sort of man . . ." Turney/Rogan. London: November 1983.

"I always thought . . ." Freddie Crooke/Aldred. *Fabulous*: March 1965.

"The Arthur Howes connection . . ." Wace/Rogan. London: 15 October 1982.

Chapter Eight: Kinky Boots

". . . a new Britain . . ." Harold Wilson, speech at Birmingham Town Hall: 19 January 1964.

"1964 is the year . . ." ibid.

"This is the time for a breakthrough . . ." ibid.

"On the island . . ." *Time* magazine: March 1963.

"'How To Spot a Homo' . . ." *Sunday Mirror*: April 1963.

". . . perverted sex orgies . . ." *Lord Denning Report*: September 1963.

"I seem to remember . . ." Robert Wace, *The Story Of The Kinks*. Original unedited film footage. Courtesy of Cyriel Van den Hemel.

"After 26 episodes Hendry . . ." Ian Hendry, interviewed by the author. London: October 1981. Hendry told me that he felt the programme became successively 'sillier' after his departure and its move away from a crime series. However, most consider the golden years of Honor Blackman and Diana Rigg as *The Avengers* at its peak.

"I'm a first for television . . ." Contemporaneous newspaper quote, reprinted in Dave Rogers, *The Avengers* (London: ITV Books, 1983).

"The leather thing . . ." ibid.

"It was thought up . . ." Robert Wace, *The Story Of The Kinks*. Original unedited film footage. Courtesy of Cyriel Van den Hemel.

'All I want for Christmas . . .' Cartoon caption. *Daily Mail*: 24 December 1963.

"I sat down with Ray . . ." Page/Rogan. London: 7 August 1982.

"I thought it was a waste of time . . ." Page/Rogan. Avoca Beach, New South Wales, Australia: 18 May 2011.

"You've got to get in there . . ." Arthur Howes quote, as recalled by Larry Page to the author. London: 7 August 1982.

"I thought it would be a good idea . . ." Talmy/Rogan. London: 17 September 1982.

"Drummer. Young, good kit . . ." Advertisement, placed by Mick Avory. *Melody Maker*: 25 January 1964.

"They were rehearsing for the Marquee . . ." Mick Avory, interviewed by the author. London: 8 November 1983.

"Some posh la-di-da gent . . ." ibid.

"Ha, he's just got out of prison . . ." Dave Davies/Altham. *New Musical Express*: 9 April 1965.

"I was wearing . . ." ibid.

"It was actually Pete's fault . . ." Dave Davies/Rogan. London: 1 March 1996.

"Poor old Mick! . . ." Ray Davies/Rosser. Unedited interview despatched to author: 30 November 2005.

"Mick would do anything . . ." Page/Rogan. London: 7 August 1982.

"I don't think Dave thought . . ." Mick Avory, interviewed by Neil Rosser. Unedited interview despatched to author: 30 November 2005.

"He was the best drummer . . ." Dave Davies, interviewed by Johnny Black. *Mojo* 82: September 2000.

"Dave was very excited . . ." David Quaife/Rogan. London: 27 February 2013.

"I said, 'If I'm going make it . . .'" Ray Davies, *The Story Of The Kinks*. Original unedited film footage, dated 7 November 1984. Courtesy of Cyriel Van den Hemel.

"It's the most important decision . . ." Ray Davies, interviewed by Mick Watts. *Melody Maker*: 23 January 1971.

Chapter Nine: March Of The Mods

"Dave would have been better . . ." Ray Davies, interviewed by Peter Doggett. Author's transcript: summer 1996.

"There weren't three managers . . ." Page/Rogan. London: 7 August 1982.

"Our managers were conservative . . ." Ray Davies/Rogan. London: 1 October 2013.

"And just for the record . . ." Wace/Rogan. London: 15 October 1982.

"I would say that is wrong . . ." Page/Rogan. London: 24 June 1983.

"'One Fine Day' is just a chorus . . ." Dave Davies/Rogan. London: 1 March 1996.

". . . with a knitting needle (according to Ray) . . ." The 'knitting needle' versus 'razor blade' debate has become part of the Kinks' mythology. In some interviews, Dave has taken umbrage at the suggestion a knitting needle was ever used. However, in at least one interview, he mentioned the knitting needle himself. Speaking to Peter Doggett, Dave claimed: "We hadn't found the right sound for 'You Really Got Me' until I experimented with the guitar using a knitting needle to pierce the casing of the speaker, which produced this incredibly distorted sound." In another interview, he claimed the knitting needle was just a figment of Pete Quaife's over-active imagination. "He used to make up stories. I'm glad I didn't use knitting needles because they wouldn't have been half as effective." Ray Davies has tended to prefer the 'knitting needle' anecdote, most notably in his quasi-fictional memoir, *X-Ray*. Reconciling myriad accounts, it seems most likely that both instruments may have been used over time, with the razor blade ultimately providing the desired effect.

"I based the act on 'Louie Louie' . . ." Page/Rogan. London: 7 August 1982.

"I taught Ray and Dave . . ." ibid.

". . . relied too much . . ." Reviewer Richard Green. *New Musical Express*: 3 April 1964.

"Leave them alone . . ." Graham Nash quote, recalled by Mick Avory to author. Broxbourne, Hertfordshire: 9 October 1994.

"I made a right idiot of myself . . ." Dave Davies, interviewed by Cordell Marks. *New Musical Express*: 28 August 1964.

". . . a lot of trouble . . ." Malcolm Cooke, interviewed by Neil Rosser. Unedited interview despatched to author: 30 November 2005.

"They actually cut . . ." ibid.

"I did not want that . . ." Talmy/Rogan. London: 17 September 1982.

"'You Still Want Me' and 'Long Tall Sally' . . ." Dave Davies/Rogan. London: 1 March 1996.

"It has a similar chord progression . . ." ibid.

"So that was the first major rip-off . . ." ibid.

"It used to have a very abrupt ending . . ." Dave Davies/Marks. *New Musical Express*: 28 August 1964.

"It used to blow away people . . ." Dave Davies/Rogan. London: 1 March 1996.

"The record company . . ." *The Davies Diaries*. BBC Radio 2: 23 November 2000.

"If you like the 'Rolling Stones' . . ." billing at Wallington Public Hall: 5 June 1964.

"Ray was just finding himself . . ." Peter 'Jonah' Jones/Rogan. London/Montreal, Canada: 8 May 2013.

". . . these long-haired, mentally unstable, petty little hoodlums . . ." Dr George Simpson, quoted in the *Daily Express*: 19–20 May 1964.

"We were still an amateur band . . ." Pete Townshend, interviewed by Neil Rosser. Unedited taped interview despatched to author: 30 November 2005.

"Probably in the days of the Mods . . ." ibid.

"It was the only song . . ." Ray Davies, interviewed by Jon Savage. *Ugly Things* 90: summer 2010.

"On the day they went to Australia . . ." Ray Davies/Rogan. London: 1 October 2013.

"What's your name? . . ." Rasa Didzpetris, interviewed by the author. London: 12 May 2004.

Chapter Ten: The Mystery Of 'You Really Got Me'

". . . Time dissolves in his many retellings . . ." Even towards the end of 2014, Davies was adding another anecdote to an over-familiar history. "The inspiration for the lyrics and title came to me one night while playing with Dave Hunt at the Scene Club in Soho. During our set, I looked out in the darkness about ten feet from the stage and saw what appeared to be a 17-year-old girl moving better than anyone else on the dance floor. She had ash-coloured hair set in a beehive style popular then. When we finished, I went off to find her, but she was gone and never returned to the club. She really got me going." Ray Davies interviewed by Marc Myers. *Wall Street Journal*: 29 October 2014.

"There has to be an acetate . . ." Dave Davies/Rogan. London: 1 March 1996.

"I don't know where the tape is . . ." Ray Davies/Rosser. Unedited interview despatched to author: 30 November 2005.

"When I played the song . . . " Ray Davies/Myers, *Wall Street Journal*: 29 October 2014.

"I remember when we previously did it . . ." Dave Davies/Rogan. London: 1 March 1996.

". . . slower and more R&B influenced . . ." Talmy/Rogan. London: 17 September 1982.

"We did it about twenty-five per cent slower . . ." Shel Talmy, interviewed by Danny McCue. *Goldmine*: 13 July 1990.

"I became obsessive . . ." Ray Davies/Rosser. Unedited interview despatched to author: 30 November 2005.

"When I played the song . . . " Ray Davies/Myers, *Wall Street Journal*: 29 October 2014.

"I'd already demoed those songs . . ." Page/Rogan. London: 7 August 1982.

". . . would have been a number 1 hit . . ." Talmy/Rogan. London: 17 September 1982.

"Ray was so sure . . ." Wace/Rogan. London: 15 October 1982.

"It could have been our last shot . . ." Dave Davies/Rogan. London: 1 March 1996.

"That moment before his solo . . ." Ray Davies/Walker. BBC Radio 2: 30 December 2010.

"When that record starts . . ." Ray Davies/Green. *New Musical Express*: 20 February 1971.

"Glyn Johns was the engineer . . ." Talmy/Rogan. London: 17 September 1982. On reflection, Talmy may have been confusing this session with some later album recordings while discussing the personnel.

"Avory was not involved . . ." ibid.

"My brother Dave hasn't got much . . ." Ray Davies, interviewed by Vic Garbarini. *Musician*: August 1983.

"It was amazing hearing it . . ." Dave Davies/Rogan. London: 1 March 1996.

"The song was replaced at number 1 by the Rolling Stones' cover 'It's All Over Now' . . ." Albeit not on every chart. It remained at number 2 for four consecutive weeks on the *NME*'s Top 30, but its success on the other listings meant it reached number 1 on *Top Of The Pops*.

". . . caveman-like quartet . . ." *New Musical Express*: January 1964.

". . . one of them looked . . ." *Daily Mirror*: 22 April 1964.

"They look like boys . . ." *Daily Express*: 28 February 1964.

"They've done terrible things . . ." Columnist Maureen Cleave. *Evening Standard*: 21 March 1964.

"Never have the middle-class virtues . . ." Columnist Maureen Cleave. *Evening Standard*: 11 May 1964.

"Gum, dark glasses and hair . . ." letter of complaint to *Daily Mirror*: summer 1964.

"The Duke of Marlborough . . ." Dale Parkinson, solicitor for Mick Jagger, addressing the court in Tettenhall, Staffordshire: 27 November 1964.

"OK, so we've got the hair . . ." Ray Davies, interviewed by Ray Coleman. *Melody Maker*: 19 September 1964.

"I like going to Indian restaurants . . ." Ray Davies, interviewed by Chris Roberts. *Melody Maker*: August 1964.

"We are still trying hard . . ." ibid.

"Can I borrow your song list . . . ?" John Lennon quote, recalled by Ray Davies, interviewed by Michael Small. *People Magazine* Vol. 28, issue 1: 6 July 1987.

"He meant that as a criticism . . ." ibid.

"It seemed to bring something new . . ." Townshend/Rosser. Unedited interview despatched to author: 30 November 2005.

"He wasn't very loud . . ." ibid.

"I'm going to be better . . ." Pete Quaife. *Brothers In Arms*. Broadcast BBC 1: 2 May 2005.

"Mick and Pete . . ." Townshend/Rosser. Unedited interview despatched to author: 30 November 2005.

"What did I feel? . . ." Start/Rogan. Haslemere, Surrey: 25 September 2012.

"You're right . . ." Ray Davies, interviewed by Peter McGill. *Pop Weekly*: 26 September 1964.

"The first album . . ." Dave Davies, interviewed by Steve Peacock. *Sounds*: 7 October 1972.

"We certainly had time to finish . . ." Talmy/Rogan. London: 17 September 1982.

Chapter Eleven: Love And Marriage

"For a first album . . ." Talmy/Rogan. London: 17 September 1982.

"I didn't see them as a blues band . . ." Chris Dreja, interviewed by Neil Rosser. Unedited interview despatched to author: 30 November 2005. Additional information author's interview with Dreja (London: January 1999 and 1 February 1999).

". . . we used to call them the Cricketers . . ." ibid.

"It blew me away . . ." ibid.

"'You Really Got Me' was a different record . . ." Ray Davies, interviewed by Colin Larkin. *Dark Star* 21: July 1979.

"I don't think we were taken very seriously . . ." Ray Davies, interviewed by Dave Hinkley. *New York Daily News*: 13 September 1989.

"I remember Mick Jagger's jaw . . ." Ray Davies, interviewed by Harold DeMuir. *Pulse!*: May 1993.

". . . rather nasty little boys . . ." Pete Quaife/Rosser. Unedited interview despatched to author: 30 November 2005.

"I really admired Billy J. Kramer . . ." *The Davies Diaries*. BBC Radio 2: 23 November 2000.

"I didn't feel a sense of solidarity . . ." ibid.

"Burt Bacharach wrote a review . . ." Ray Davies, film documentary. *The World From My Window*, Isis/Sanctuary: 2003.

"I thought I was being put down . . ." Ray Davies in Jon Savage, *The Kinks: The Official Biography* (London: Faber & Faber, 1984), pp. 39–40.

"They could get very close to number 1 . . ." Reviewer Derek Johnson. *New Musical Express*: 22 October 1964. The single reached number 3 in the *NME* chart.

"I watched them . . ." Jim Rodford, interviewed by the author. St Albans, Hertfordshire: 21 May 2014.

"The Kinks were very gothic . . ." Marianne Faithfull with David Dalton. *Faithfull* (New York: Little, Brown, 1994), p. 35.

"We were in awe . . ." John Beecham, interviewed by the author. London/Weston-super-Mare, north Somerset: 2 June 2014.

"He was the one . . ." ibid.

Rasa Pupyte Emilija Halina Didzpetryte. As Rasa explains: "The Dicpetryte ending ('yte') applies to female members of family who are not married. The male (Dad) is Mr Dicpetris. When married to Mr Dicpetris, the wife/mother becomes Mrs Dicpetriene. Males: brothers and uncles remain Dicpetris. The daughters before marriage are name endings 'yte' or 'iate'. It is male-dominated. I found my birth certificate, having mislaid it for months. It is German, of course, as I was born in Blomberg and my family were living in a refugee house. So, my surname of DIDZPETRIS now is spelt the German way! My brother in Germany sent the original birth certificate to me and pencilled all of the translation into English. My Father named me: Rasa Pupyte Emilija Halina. Interestingly, 'pupyte' means 'darling'. I had forgotten this and when I looked at this certificate, I have to admit that I cried, knowing that my father called me 'darling'."

"He's romanticizing . . ." Rasa Didzpetris, interviewed by the author. London: 4 March 2013.

"Thereafter, Sue began dating drummer Mick Avory . . ." Surprisingly, neither Rasa nor Mick Avory could recall Sue's surname when I asked them both. Since Sue took Rasa to Sheffield, it could be argued that it was Mick Avory who was partly responsible for connecting Rasa and Ray. When I reminded Avory of this, he provided one of his best one-liners. "She can't blame that on me!" In other accounts, including Dave's autobiography and innocently repeated by Hinman, it was suggested that Eileen Fernley, another of Rasa's friends, accompanied her to Sheffield. However, she did not make this trip, although she dated Dave Davies later that year.

"I basically fell in love . . ." Rasa Didzpetris/Rogan. London: 4 March 2013.

"She wasn't very happy . . ." ibid.

"That was my first experience . . ." ibid. Additional details from author's interview. London: 12 May 2004.

"Behind the front door . . ." Rasa Didzpetris/Rogan. London: 4 March 2013.

"Ray has been hoping . . ." Aleksandras Dicpetris, interviewed by Judith Simons. *Daily Express*: November 1964.

"He really needed somebody . . ." Pete Quaife/Rogan. Copenhagen: 3 July 2006.

"I don't think I should have got married . . ." Ray Davies, film documentary. *The World From My Window*, Isis/Sanctuary: 2003.

"I've got tickets to South America . . ." This anecdote was cited in several articles, broadcasts and alluded to in Ray Davies' *X-Ray*.

"Dave, taking the honours as best man, was already there, talking to Eileen Fernley . . ."

Eileen, another Bradford connection, later became involved in a paternity suit with Dave Davies. The details are too convoluted to discuss herein. Suffice to say, the entire affair does not reflect well on the guitarist.

"I'd driven Ray overnight . . ." Page/Rogan. London: 7 August 1982.

"It was all very dramatic . . ." Rasa Didzpetris/Rogan. London: 4 March 2013.

Chapter Twelve: Australia

"It's slap . . . Don't you wear any? . . ." Bryan Burdon quotes, recalled by Malcolm Cooke, interviewed by Neil Rosser. Unedited interview despatched to author: 30 November 2005.

"Dave's feminine looks attracted attention . . ." The increasing importance of looks in the youth-obsessed mid-Sixties should not be underestimated. Cultural historian Arthur Marwick pinpoints 1964 (tellingly the time of the Kinks' first hit) as a pivotal moment in western society's re-evaluation of the definition of beauty. He sees an acceleration from that year onwards as "the triumph of the 'modern' view of beauty, of physical beauty, detached altogether from moral judgements, wealth and class . . . This 'modern' conception of beauty, of beauty as 'an autonomous status characteristic', did not of course fill the hearts and minds of every single individual . . . but as never before it dominated society at large, in its public mores, its newspapers, its advertisements, its television programmes, its social, cultural, and political behaviour. More and more people behaved as if they recognized that 'mere' physical beauty had a particular value of its own. Male beauty was increasingly recognized as having something of the same significance that had always . . . attached to female beauty. In the middle and later 1960s beauty was universally praised and sought after; it had achieved a kind of parity with wealth and status, and certainly was no enemy to either." Arthur Marwick. *The Sixties* (Oxford: Oxford University Press, 1998), p. 406.

"He was one of those poofy . . ." Pete Quaife, interviewed by Danny Kirby. *Now And Then* 8: 1994.

"It didn't seem strange to me . . ." Dave Davies/Rogan. London: 1 March 1996.

"My biggest problem with him . . ." Larry Page, interviewed by the author. London: March 1996.

"I don't think we were allowed . . ." Ray Davies/Rosser. Unedited interview despatched to author: 30 November 2005.

"It was certainly a brave departure . . ." And it was appreciated as such by the *NME*'s ever discriminating Derek Johnson: "Change of character for the Kinks . . . from their raucous broken-beat approach . . . it's a more rock ballad with a slow shake-shuffle. Very nice it is too!" *New Musical Express*: 15 January 1965.

"We were supposed to do *Top Of The Pops* . . ." Dave Davies/Rogan. London: 1 March 1996.

"I couldn't sleep . . ." Ray Davies/Rosser. Unedited interview despatched to author: 30 November 2005.

"The audience were marvellous . . ." Dave Davies, quoted in *Rave*: 11 November 1965.

"Rose, I don't want to go . . ." ibid.

"I was terrified of flying . . ." Ray Davies/Rosser. Unedited interview despatched to author: 30 November 2005.

"Yes, I'm *Honey Lantree*! . . ." ibid.

"We were vying with each other . . ." McGuinness/Rosser. Unedited interview despatched to author: 30 November 2005.

"It was Stones, Stones, Stones . . ." Dave Davies, interviewed by Chris Welch. *Melody Maker*: 20 February 1965.

"We were in the same hotel . . ." McGuinness/Rosser. Unedited interview despatched to author: 30 November 2005.

"While in Sydney, they were photographed on Bondi Beach . . ." Davies provided a sociological explanation for such hostility to the UK music press. "The blokes in Australia try to give out the rock-hard image. Much the same as in the north of England. Naturally the girls are downtrodden and they look forward to a chance to let off steam at a beat show. Their blokes don't like this. They threw sand and stones at us on the big beaches, so when we tried surfing we had to use a little beach. It wasn't used much because the sewers opened out there. We didn't discover that until we were swimming about. Most unpleasant." Ray Davies, interviewed by Norman Jopling. *Record Mirror*: 17 April 1965.

"We spent thirty-six hours in Singapore . . ." Dave Davies, quoted in *Rave*: 11 November 1965.

"I got a bottle of champagne . . ." Ray Davies, interviewed by Barbara Charone. *Sounds*: 7 June 1975.

"We all came to a halt . . ." Ray Davies, interviewed by Keith Altham. *New Musical Express*: 24 December 1965.

"I suffered when he went to Australia . . ." Rasa Didzpetris/Rogan. London: 4 March 2013.

"It's got a great night life . . ." Dave Davies/Welch. *Melody Maker*: 20 February 1965.

"Ray didn't want to do it . . ." Avory/Rosser. Unedited interview despatched to author: 30 November 2005.

"We would like to very much . . ." Dave Davies, quoted in *Melody Maker*: February 1965.

"We came back from a world tour . . ." Ray Davies/Doggett. *Record Collector* 169: September 1993.

"When they supported us . . ." ibid.

"I broke up the rhythm . . ." Townshend/Rosser. Unedited interview despatched to author: 30 November 2005. Recalling 'I Can't Explain' to Bob Edmands (*New Musical Express*: 3 April 1975), Shel Talmy said: "I heard that as a one minute thirty-second demo. Just a collection of chords stuck together. I rearranged the whole thing for them and brought in Nicky Hopkins. And again I tried for that guitar sound I was experimenting with. And it really was as simple as that. It was a conscious advance on the Kinks . . . I established a sound for the Kinks and 'I Can't Explain' is certainly the format, the same general ballgame as the Kinks. I freely admit it . . . I went to Decca in the States which has nothing to do with Decca over here, except that Brunswick was distributed by them. And I realized that if the Who came out on Brunswick, Decca over here would have to release it to live up to their contract, and not say anything about how the Who were promoted or anything. That way I could beat the system."

"All right, boy . . ." Rasa Didzpetris/Rogan. London: 4 March 2013.

"I had no idea about English cooking . . ." ibid.

"It was difficult . . ." ibid.

"I was married . . ." Ray Davies, interviewed by Richard Smith. *Gay Times*: October 1994.

"Well, he was young . . ." Rasa Didzpetris/Rogan. London: 4 March 2013.

Chapter Thirteen: Ray's Conspiracy Theory

"We did a show in London . . ." Sam Curtis, interviewed by the author. Brownhills, Walsall: 24 August 1982.

"Were the audience aware of his bollocks . . . ?" ibid.

"The Hooray Henrys . . ." Page/Rogan. London: 7 August 1982.

"I can't do it! . . ." Ray Davies, interviewed by Charles Shaar Murray. *Q* 36: September 1989.

"Don't be stupid! . . ." ibid.

"I feel very sorry for Rasa . . ." Ray Davies/Altham. *New Musical Express*: 16 April 1965.

"I'm hopeless around the house . . ." ibid.

"I'm a collection of loose ends . . ." ibid.

"He was great, Robert . . ." Dave Davies/Rogan. London: 1 March 1996.

". . . teaching the Davies brothers . . ." Wace/Rogan. London: 15 October 1982.

"What's that? . . ." Page/Rogan. London: 24 June 1983.

". . . and it was all creeds and colours . . ." Curtis/Rogan. Brownhills, Walsall: 24 August 1982.

"They [Ray and Dave] came from a very bad home . . ." ibid.

"It was a pig-sty family . . ." ibid.

"Sam was one of the great characters . . ." Ray Davies/Rogan. London: 1 October 2013.

"That's where 'Ev'rybody's Gonna Be Happy' came from . . ." Ray Davies/Doggett. Author's transcript: summer 1996.

"It didn't help . . ." Mick Avory interview. *Now And Then* 2: 1991.

"Oh, I loved the song . . ." Rasa Didzpetris/Rogan. London: 4 March 2013.

"We were disappointed . . ." Dave Davies/Jopling. *Record Mirror*: 17 April 1965.

"I wandered into the dressing room . . ." Pete Quaife/Jopling. *Record Mirror*: 17 April 1965.

"'Ev'rybody's Gonna Be Happy' was a single . . ." Talmy/Rogan. London: 17 September 1982.

"I don't know what caused it . . ." Pete Quaife, interviewed by Mike Ledgerwood. *Disc*: 3 April 1965.

"I'd see a drop of blood . . ." Pete Quaife/Kirby. *Now And Then* 8: 1994.

"He said he fainted . . ." David Quaife/Rogan. London: 27 February 2013.

"It was total chaos . . ." Ray Davies, interviewed by Connor McKnight. *Zigzag* 27: December 1972.

"Come along, David . . ." Dave Davies/Rogan. London: 1 March 1996.

"We wrecked a lot of places . . ." Ray Davies/Fitzpatrick. *The Word* 113: July 2012.

"That night . . ." ibid. Peter Quaife, who later lived in Denmark, provided a more piercing overview to Neil Rosser. "Danes are quite conservative and they appreciate art and design. And the whole of the Tivoli Gardens is very pristine and modern and you don't stub your cigarette out on the floor. That applied to the theatre as well. We were appearing that night and we went into 'You Really Got Me'. En masse, they [the audience] came at the stage. In Denmark, in those days, it was considered awful for somebody to do that and they called in the guards . . . then the police came and started beating everybody with their truncheons . . . Alex [King, the road manager] said, 'Get off, get out of here.' In the dressing rooms we could hear the place explode upstairs. Alex came in and said, 'We're getting out.' The police followed us to the hotel and they came in and dragged Brian [Longstaff] off to jail. The next day we were allowed back to have a look and they took that theatre apart. We were escorted out of the country and told not to come back." No one disputes Quaife's account, although Dave substitutes a different road manager, Jay Vickers, in his retelling. Interviewed by Charles Shaar Murray in *Q* 36 (September 1989), Ray Davies added: "The police were beating the kids up and the kids smashed the theatre up, and they locked us up in a room. The people were very abusive to us as if they thought we'd brought the devil with us. It was very frightening, but if it had happened to the Beatles it would've been a fun experience. They would have been smuggled out in an ambulance . . . It was things like that which caused a lot of insecurity with the other guys, and the famous fights started between Dave and Mick."

"I was drunk . . ." Dave Davies/Rogan. London: 1 March 1996.

"Ray flipped . . ." Quaife/Black. *Mojo* 82: September 2000.

Chapter Fourteen: The Cardiff Incident

"In Soho . . ." Article by John Crosby. *Weekend Telegraph*: 16 April 1965.

". . . the happiest and most electric city in Europe . . ." *Epoca*: summer 1965.

"It's jealousy . . ." Wayne Fontana, music press clipping, dated 20 April 1965.

"At that time . . ." Page/Rogan. London: 7 August 1982.

"We thought it would be great . . ." Pete Quaife, interviewed by Penny Valentine. *Disc*: 1 May 1965.

". . . the best club of its kind . . ." cited by Robert Chalmers. *Independent*: 27 March 2011.

"It's hard to imagine . . ." ibid.

"Robert Wace was dancing . . ." Ray Davies/Smith. *Gay Times*: October 1994. Davies offered a variant of this story a few years earlier to *People* magazine's Michael Small (issue date 6 July 1987, Vol. 28, issue 1): "One night I was dancing with this really attractive woman till dawn. Then she said, 'Come on back to my place,' and I said, 'OK.' It wasn't until we got in the daylight that I saw the stubble on her chin. So I blew that one off."

"You didn't think of it . . ." ibid.

"Their heads went down . . ." Ray Davies/Rosser. Unedited interview despatched to author: 30 November 2005.

"At this moment . . ." Derek Johnson, writing in *New Musical Express*: 30 April 1965.

"We hated the sight . . ." Dave Davies, interviewed by Norrie Drummond. *New Musical Express*: 8 April 1966.

"In those days . . ." Ray Davies/McKnight. *Zigzag* 27: December 1972.

"Whatever you wanted to do for them . . ." Curtis/Rogan. Brownhills, Walsall: 24 August 1982.

"We did a show . . ." ibid.

"Ray and Dave had nothing in common . . ." ibid.

"It was the brothers against Mick . . ." ibid.

"These guys could provoke the Pope! . . ." ibid.

"For the first two years . . ." Dave Davies/Rogan. London: 1 March 1996.

"It actually started . . ." Pete Quaife/Black. *Mojo* 82: September 2000.

"The mood was dangerous . . ." Pete Quaife/Rogan. London/Copenhagen: 3 July 2006.

"That's it! . . ." ibid.

"The stage hands . . ." Curtis/Rogan. Brownhills, Walsall: 24 August 1982.

"I remember that night . . ." Ray Davies/Doggett. Cited in Kinks' box set *Picture Book*: December 2008. Original interview, author's notes: *c.* June 2004.

"He was getting on my tits . . ." Dave Davies, interviewed by Neil Rosser. Unedited interview despatched to author: 30 November 2005.

"Mick picked up his high-hat cymbal . . ." Curtis/Rogan. Brownhills, Walsall: 24 August 1982.

"I was standing in the wings . . ." Dreja/Rosser. Additional information author's interview with Dreja (London: 30 January 1999 and 1 February 1999).

"Mick picked up a cymbal . . ." Pete Quaife/Rogan. London/Copenhagen: 3 July 2006.

"My brother! . . ." Quaife/Black. *Mojo* 82: September 2000.

"Dave was lying on the floor . . ." *The Davies Diaries*. BBC Radio 2: 23 November 2000.

"Mick thought he'd killed him . . ." Curtis/Rogan. Brownhills, Walsall: 24 August 1982.

"Finally, I found him . . ." ibid.

"They wanted to do Mick . . ." Ray Davies/Doggett. Cited in Kinks' box set *Picture Book*: December 2008. Original interview, author's notes: *c.* June 2004.

"This looks like the end . . ." Sam Curtis, press clipping: May 1965.

"There was no way . . ." Page/Rogan. London: 7 August 1982.

"Everything was a bit upside down . . ." Pete Quaife, interviewed by Jean-Pierre Morisset. *Jukebox Magazine* 230: May 2006. For the remaining dates of the tour, the Kinks were replaced by the Walker Brothers, a risky substitute as the American trio had yet to achieve national fame, having just registered their first, lowly hit with 'Love Her'.

"That song was commissioned . . ." Ray Davies, interviewed by John Wilson. *Mastertapes*. BBC Radio 4: 3 December 2012.

"As you can imagine . . ." Page/Rogan. London: 7 August 1982.

"It was part of a new routine . . ." An even more unconvincing account appeared in *Disc*, where Avory recalled how "Dave is leaping around and ends by whirling his guitar round his head and pretending to throw it to the audience. It was then that my 18-inch crash cymbal was knocked over and fell on him. It's untrue that we had rowed and are going to break up."

"There was nothing left . . ." It should be noted that every other witness to the Cardiff incident – Ray, Dave, Pete Quaife, Sam Curtis, Mitch Mitchell and Chris Dreja all state, without hesitation, that the instrument of assault was the actual high-hat cymbal. Ray adds, "Mick got the cymbal and hit him over the head with it, *with the sharp edge*."

"I'm sorry about my brother . . ." Ray Davies, newspaper clipping, May 1965.

"I would have been hurt . . ." Dave Davies, interviewed by Keith Altham. *New Musical Express*: 11 June 1965. Larry Page concurred, adding: "I think we would have been defrauding the public to have included a substitute."

"There wasn't a single hotel . . ." Curtis/Rogan. Brownhills, Walsall: 24 August 1982.

"I'm ashamed of that song . . ." Ray Davies, interviewed in Sweden. *Expressen*: August 1965.

Chapter Fifteen: The Great American Disaster

"I think that during the first year . . ." Dave Davies, interviewed by Brenda Tarry. *Disc*: 8 July 1970.

"He was being hit from all sides . . ." Page/Rogan. London: 7 August 1982.

"I'm sure Ray saw us as money . . ." Wace/Rogan. London: 15 October 1982.

". . . probably have jacked it in . . ." ibid.

"If we ever discussed it with the Kinks . . ." Page/Rogan. London: 7 August 1982.

"They were extraordinary . . ." Dave Davies/Rogan. London/Cornwall: 3 October 2012.

". . . we had the relationship . . ." Wace/Rogan. London: 15 October 1982.

"I was very, very close to Ray . . ." Page/Rogan. London: 24 June 1983.

"It might have been a bit different . . ." Curtis/Rogan. Brownhills, Walsall: 24 August 1982.

"We got the contracts sent from America . . ." Page/Rogan. London: 7 August 1982.

"The incident with Dave and Mick . . ." Ray Davies, interviewed by Chris George. *Independent*: 27 August 1994.

"One thing worries me . . ." Dave Davies, interviewed by Laurie Henshaw. *Disc*: 23 June 1965.

"I think I'd like to meet President Johnson . . ." Pete Quaife, interviewed by Peter Sands. *Disc*: 19 June 1965.

". . . a fashionable spiral staircase . . ." According to Rasa, the 'spiral staircase' claim was an exaggeration. "It had a staircase going up to a tiny landing, with the bathroom behind, a bedroom facing the front and a bedroom at the back. There were two rooms on either side of the roof, attic rooms, so there was a little staircase that had to bend slightly, but it wasn't a spiral staircase. We also had a lounge, a beautiful backroom which had an extension. Later, we had a bigger kitchen built and there was a downstairs loo, a kitchen diner, a garage and a decent sized garden. We bought it from a couple who'd designed it in a very modern way. The front room was painted orange, and it was beautiful; a real Sixties style. It had lights in the ceiling. With the sash windows you could pull out the side panels and there were wooden shutters. Beautiful. It was the best house ever."

"The 'advance', approximately six times or more the average wage . . ." It is possible Davies misremembered this figure, although he was very clear about the £9,000 advance in his book *X-Ray*. He could have bought several houses outright for this money – surely he only needed a deposit, a few hundred pounds would be more than enough. Average house prices were £3,418 according to Nationwide BS House Price Index, 1952–2009.

"I was paying for my cheese on toast . . ." Ray Davies, 'Guitars And Greasy Spoons'. *Daily Telegraph*: 22 February 2001.

"It took Ray five years . . ." Wace/Rogan. London: 15 October 1982.

". . . made Rod Stewart look like a philanthropist . . ." Shel Talmy, online interview.

"When I hear 'The Moneygoround' . . ." Page/Rogan. London: 7 August 1982.

"He was miserly . . ." Dave Davies. *Kink* (London: Boxtree, 1996). There is some evidence to suggest that Dave was cadging cigarettes at the very start of the group's career when they were travelling with road manager Hal Carter, but once money came in, he spent freely and recklessly entertaining old and new friends, in contrast to his brother.

"You can't rationalize the actions . . ." Curtis/Rogan. Brownhills, Walsall: 24 August 1982.

"The money? . . ." Rasa Didzpetris/Rogan. London: 4 March 2013.

"Some years earlier . . ." Giorgio Gomelsky liner notes from the Yardbirds' *Train Kept A-Rollin': The Complete Giorgio Gomelsky Productions* box set. Charly: 1993.

". . . an outlandish experiment . . ." ibid.

"It didn't turn out too bad . . ." ibid.

"It makes you sick . . ." Ray Davies, interviewed by Richard Green. *Record Mirror*: 19 June 1965.

". . . ponderous boring guitar work . . ." Letter from M. Harding quoted in Peter Jones' article 'Now Elvis Fans Slam the Kinks'. *Record Mirror*: 3 July 1965.

". . . run of the mill records . . ." Letter from Derek Finlayson. ibid.

"These pop music veterans . . ." Letter from R. Phillips. ibid.

"We feel only pop stars should get MBEs . . ." Ray Davies. *The Clay Cole Show*: 20 June 1965.

"What's plating, Ray? . . ." As recalled by Larry Page. Page/Rogan. London: 7 August 1982.

"We were very conservative . . ." Ray Davies/Rosser. Unedited interview despatched to author: 30 November 2005.

"We didn't have the savvy . . ." *The First Time . . . With Ray Davies*. BBC 6 Music: 3 April 2011.

"It was very emotional . . ." Page/Rogan. London: 7 August 1982.

"There were birds in the cupboards . . ." Curtis/Rogan. Brownhills, Walsall: 24 August 1982.

"I want that song! . . ." Larry Page, interviewed by the author. London: March 1996.

"The whole tour was problematical . . ." Page/Rogan. London: 7 August 1982.

"That way they'll get it . . ." ibid.

"I had to gee them up . . ." ibid.

"Is this what you want? . . ." Curtis/Rogan. Brownhills, Walsall: 24 August 1982.

"Well, don't phone her . . ." ibid.

"It was a school armoury! . . ." ibid.

"This woman booked a stadium . . ." ibid.

"The Kinks didn't play . . ." Ray Davies/Walker. Broadcast BBC Radio 2: 30 December 2010.

"The Beatles were refined . . ." ibid.

"We were getting situations . . ." Page/Rogan. London: 7 August 1982.

"Among his new contacts were Charlie Greene and Brian Stone . . ." Details provided by Charlie Greene, interviewed by the author. London/New York: 20 March 2000.

"I thought some of the songs . . ." Page/Rogan. London: 7 August 1982.

". . . in a mixed-up state . . ." Ray Davies/Rogan. London: 1 October 2013.

"Sam could have been due . . ." Page/Rogan. London: 7 August 1982.

"I used to stand there . . ." ibid.

"I used to have to count my underpants . . ." ibid.

"We were doing a Dick Clark show . . ." Ray Davies, interviewed by Valerie Wilmer. *Hit Parader*: 1965.

"One of the guys working there . . ." Curtis/Rogan. Brownhills, Walsall: 24 August 1982.

"I'm not going on . . ." Recalled by Larry Page. Page/Rogan. London: 7 August 1982.

"At that stage . . ." ibid.

"I didn't have a passport . . ." Rasa Didzpetris/Rogan. London: 4 March 2013.

"I must have had some money . . ." ibid.

"I spent all day pleading . . ." Page/Rogan. London: 7 August 1982.

"Nobody abandons the Kinks . . ." Quote recalled by Sam Curtis. Curtis/Rogan. Brownhills, Walsall: 24 August 1982.

"I'd had enough . . ." Page/Rogan. London: 7 August 1982.

"I could see no reason . . ." Curtis/Rogan. Brownhills, Walsall: 24 August 1982.

"I thought it would be spoilt . . ." Ray Davies/Cott. *Rolling Stone*: 10 November 1969. Davies adds: "The song just didn't come off really. I didn't like a lot of the lines."

"Waikiki was like a second honeymoon . . ." Rasa Didzpetris/Rogan. London: 4 March 2013.

"Larry could not make them perform better . . ." Curtis/Rogan. Brownhills, Walsall: 24 August 1982.

"The point is that management is about relationships . . ." Wace/Rogan. London: 15 October 1982.

"That group were capable of anything . . ." Wace/Rogan. London: 25 June 1983.

"Larry Page blew his stack . . ." Wace/Rogan. London: 15 October 1982.

Chapter Sixteen: A Legal Matter

"He and Rasa spent some time at the Imperial Hotel . . . and began furnishing their new home in Fortis Green . . ." The move again exposed Davies' shortcomings as a handyman. Jonah Jones visited the house and was amused to see a door left lying around. "They had this big, thick carpet laid. Ray took the door off but he couldn't organize cutting it so that it could open and close properly. It was just left there for I don't know how long."

"Contrary to later reports, there was no official 'ban' . . ." Both the Davies brothers and their management were remarkably vague about the Union ruling. "Basically the Kinks were bad news," says Larry Page. "Everybody knew that if they booked the Kinks they were in for problems. And the word goes round and no doubt they have their reasons for banning. That was it." Ray Davies was equally unclear, explaining that the group had been 'banned' by "some sort of union for alleged things we were supposed to have done on tour, just asking for our pay."

"As their publisher . . ." Page/Rogan. London: 24 June 1983.

"We had no power . . ." ibid.

"Page! . . ." Talmy/Rogan. London: 17 September 1982.

"That was appalling! . . ." Ray Davies, interviewed by Chris Twomey. *Strangled*: December 1990.

"I was out to boost him . . ." Page/Rogan. London: 7 August 1982. *Kinky Music* was released on Decca, the label that had originally turned down the Kinks. It sold poorly.

"The song is about homosexuality . . ." Ray Davies, interviewed by Maureen Cleave. *Evening Standard*: Summer 1965.

"It's patently obvious . . ." Ray Davies/Smith. *Gay Times*: October 1994.

"It isn't about sex . . ." *Imaginary Man* documentary. Broadcast BBC 1: 21 December 2010.

"He was a great guitarist . . ." Talmy/Rogan. London: 17 September 1982.

"I wanted a droning sound . . ." Ray Davies, film documentary. *The World From My Window*, Isis/Sanctuary: 2003. Previously, Davies told Jonathan Cott (*Rolling Stone*: 10 November 1969): "I always like the chanting. Someone once said to me, 'England is grey and India is like a chant.' I don't think England is that grey but India *is* like a long drone. When I wrote the song, I had the sea near Bombay in mind."

"I'm of fairly average intelligence . . ." Ray Davies/Rosser. Unedited taped interview despatched to author: 30 November 2005.

". . . a very cheap Framus 12-string guitar . . . quite bad sound . . ." Ray Davies, *The Story Of The Kinks*. Original unedited film footage, dated 7 November 1984. Courtesy of Cyriel Van den Hemel. Ray was more critical of the song in this programme, as he was about many things during the interview. "Everyone thought it was a really great sound but it was basically quite bad," he insisted.

"It had a great quality . . ." Ray Davies/Doggett. Author's transcript: summer 1996.

"Artistes are very jealous . . ." Wace/Rogan. London: 25 June 1983.

"Even as their publisher . . ." Page/Rogan. London: 7 August 1982.

"I said, 'Get out of the studio . . .'" Ray Davies, testimony in *Denmark Productions Ltd v. Boscobel Productions Ltd*. Royal Courts of Justice. London: 25 May 1967.

"The package worked . . ." Page/Rogan. London: 7 August 1982.

"They copied all the thoughts . . ." Ray Davies, interviewed by Chris Welch. *Melody Maker*: 21 August 1965.

"I could outsing . . ." ibid. Davies added: "Tony Bennett is not as good as Andy Williams. I feel that Andy Williams is much more sensitive in his singing. Tony Bennett always gives me the impression he's trying to impress his friends when he's singing." Twenty-four years later, Davies recalled this interview, albeit confusing Tony Bennett with Frank Sinatra. "I'd just had enough of doing publicity. I'm not very good with the press and I don't like my pictures in the paper. I'd said that I thought I could sing 'You Really Got Me' better than Frank Sinatra, and somebody asked, 'Who is this guy who thinks he can sing better than Sinatra?' I'd had all the praise for the first three records and I was getting the backlash and I didn't want to do it any more."

"It's Andrew Oldham . . ." ibid.

"[It's] the only one . . ." Ray Davies, interviewed by Norman Jopling. *Record Mirror*: August 1965.

". . . being in Marianne Faithfull's flat . . ." Barry Fantoni, interviewed by Neil Rosser. Unedited interview despatched to author: 30 November 2005.

"I was a bit shattered . . ." Ray Davies, interviewed on *The World Of Ray Davies And The Kinks: I'm Not Like Everybody Else*. Broadcast BBC 2: 21 December 1995.

"You talk to someone . . ." Ray Davies/Welch. *Melody Maker*: 21 August 1965.

"He was protected . . ." Screaming Lord Sutch, interviewed by the author. London: 16 September 1989.

"Cobblers . . ." Curtis/Rogan. Brownhills, Walsall: 24 August 1982.

"We received your letter . . ." Letter from Michael Simkins to Denmark Productions, dated 14 September 1965.

"I said, 'I'm not going to play . . .'" Ray Davies/Tamarkin. *The Aquarian/Manhattan*: 7–14 October 1981. In an interview with *Record Mirror*, printed on 8 January 1966, only a few months after the song's release, Davies explained: "I was staying in a hotel, a hotel which was a bit snobbish. I felt a bit sick – even though I was paying the same money as the businessmen who were also there. But I was wearing old jeans. So the way I felt, I wanted to be respected, which is nothing to do with money. I wrote a song . . . 'A Well Respected Man'."

"Robert was a big influence . . ." Dave Davies/Rogan. London/Cornwall: 3 October 2012.

". . . a composite character . . ." Ray Davies/Doggett. Author's transcript: summer 1996. Davies also spoke to me about his use of 'composite characters' in his book, *Americana* amid a discussion about the nature of personal identity.

"I always create characters . . ." ibid.

"There is no more sombre enemy . . ." Cyril Connolly. *Enemies Of Promise* (1938).

"on a journey . . . rock roots . . ." *The Davies Diaries*. BBC Radio 2: 23 November 2000.

"The Sixties was a lie . . ." Ray Davies/Tamarkin. *The Aquarian/Manhattan*: 7–14 October 1981.

"Everyone I knew seemed . . ." ibid.

". . . the world has taken a step backwards . . ." Prime Minister Harold Wilson: November 1965.

"As they began . . ." *South Wales Argus*. Review of Kinks' appearance at the Sophia Gardens, Cardiff: 27 November 1965.

"Every time we come to South Wales . . ." ibid.

"I get sick of it sometimes . . ." Ray Davies/Altham. *New Musical Express*: 24 December 1965. Another project mentioned that December was a song specially written to tie in with Thom Keyes' book *All Night Stand*, published by Talmy/Franklin. 'All Night Stand' was passed on to the Thoughts, another act produced by Shel Talmy, who released the Davies' composition as a single, without success. Ray's original demo appears on the 2008 Kinks' box set *Picture Book*.

"The 'World Group' section . . . the Kinks were nowhere to be seen . . ." The listing and votes for 'World Group' read: 1. Beatles 9,320; 2. Rolling Stones 6,002; 3. Everly Brothers 2,334; 4. Seekers 1,759; 5. Animals 1,543; 6. Jordanaires 1,307; 7. Walker Brothers 1,284; 8. Beach Boys 701; 9. Manfred Mann 693; 10. Shadows 670; 11. Bachelors 622; 12. Sonny & Cher 434; 13. Byrds 387; 14. Supremes 380; 15. Peter, Paul & Mary 351; 16. Hollies 322; 17. Searchers 317; 18. Four Seasons 269; 19. Yardbirds 245; 20. Dave Clark Five 230. It was a revealing snapshot of the times.

"The David Hemmings–and–Veruschka scene . . ." Jill Kennington, interviewed by Philippe Garner. *Vanity Fair*: 15 April 2011.

". . . excited whispers . . ." ibid.

"I've been halfway . . ." Ray Davies/Altham. *New Musical Express*: 24 December 1965.

Chapter Seventeen: England Swings

". . . alive with birds and Beatles . . ." *Time*: 15 April 1966.

". . . the wind of today . . ." *L'Express*: 2–8 May 1966.

"The song came about . . ." Ray Davies/Tamarkin. *The Aquarian/Manhattan*: 7–14 October 1981.

"I had a slight flare . . ." Ray Davies/Brown. *Without Walls – My Generation: The Kinks*. Channel 4: 18 March 1995.

"We had a punch-up . . ." ibid.

"He's always been a control freak . . ." Pete Quaife/Paytress. *Mojo* 148: March 2006. Quaife elaborated on this point in an interview with Russell Smith and Bill Orton (printed in the special edition of *The Official Kinks Fan Club Magazine*: 25 June 1999). "This is Ray's biggest problem – we could have helped him had we known. He was trying to get this sound at the beginning of 'Dedicated Follower Of Fashion' – dang, dang, dang, dang, dang. He couldn't get it and he was fighting, but he wouldn't say anything to us about what he was looking for. So it was one of those times where you sat in the studio for hours doing nothing but listening to Dave play the beginning part, and then Ray would say, 'No, No' and go running down and play the guitar and say, 'Like this'. That didn't work and then Dave took it up again and it went back and forth and eventually Ray burnt all the tapes . . . All he had to do was say, 'You are the guys that I work with, you're musicians, this is what I'm trying to get. Can you hear that sound?' And we all would have said, 'Yes' and then somebody could have suggested 'Why don't you do it with that guitar instead' or 'I know someone who has that guitar.' And then it would have been done – accomplished. But, again, Ray was keeping it to himself so we had to sit there and suffer." Davies, while not denying a lack of communication, felt he had good reason not to listen to Quaife. "He didn't have anything to say," he told Johnny Black (*Mojo* 82: September 2000). "I think Pete got everything he wanted out of it early on. He got on TV, met a few interesting people. Got into a set he liked. As time went on, his mind wasn't in it. I think Pete went into it because he wanted to grab a piece of the swinging whatever it was, and then it becomes a job."

"At least Mick Avory made some belated capital . . ." He was not the only one to benefit from the song. A more enduring artefact was a 1966 colour film which would be used in Kinks retrospectives and documentary programmes on the era. As Barry Fantoni recalls: "William Rushton's cousin Tony was into fashion and got cameraman Nat Crosby and director John Cromer. We went around Carnaby Street, all the boutiques."

"My love . . ." Rasa note, allegedly written in Ray Davies' diary, cited in his fictional memoir, *X-Ray*, page 272. In the book, Davies quotes from supposedly 'diary entries' some of which are said to be written in Rasa's hand. Did she loan Ray any diaries? "No I didn't," she confirms. "But I did have a Biba diary . . . . [in 1973]. I obviously left some stuff behind because I couldn't take everything with me." Ray suggests that the 'diary quotes' are taken from one volume, as if they were written in a joint diary. "I wouldn't be writing in the same diary," Rasa insists. As for the accuracy of the 'diary' quotes, which may have been invented by Ray, Rasa acknowledges their emotional veracity. "I was very dejected about my marriage because I was very isolated. To be honest with you, the words sound like something I would say if I was depressed. I don't recall writing those words, but I think I was at a bad point in my marriage and if I was feeling depressed it's the sort of thing I could have written."

"Ray went bananas . . ." Dave Davies/Rosser. Unedited interview despatched to author: 30 November 2005.

"We weren't getting on . . ." Rasa Didzpetris/Rogan. London: 4 March 2013.

"We had a big black phone . . ." ibid.

"Maybe I was downstairs . . ." ibid.

"My art was the world . . ." *Imaginary Man* documentary. Broadcast BBC 1: 21 December 2010.

"I'm not a weak person . . ." *The World Of Ray Davies And The Kinks: I'm Not Like Everybody Else*. Broadcast BBC 2: 21 December 1995.

"I understand every bloody word . . ." Avory/Rosser. Unedited interview despatched to author: 30 November 2005.

"Dave – *he's* not Ray! . . ." Dave Davies/Rogan. London: 1 March 1996.

"To say the least . . ." Ray Davies/Brown. *Without Walls – My Generation: The Kinks*. Channel 4: 18 March 1995.

"There was nothing unusual about that . . ." Page/Rogan. London: 7 August 1982.

"For all I know . . ." Curtis/Rogan. Brownhills, Walsall: 24 August 1982.

"I was a zombie . . ." Ray Davies/McNeill. *New Musical Express*: 16 April 1977.

"I couldn't listen . . ." ibid.

"It sort of cleaned my mind . . ." Ray Davies, interviewed by Bob Dawbarn. *Melody Maker*: 10 April 1966.

"I walked across the street . . ." Ray Davies, interviewed by Penny Valentine. *Disc & Music Echo*: 9 April 1966.

". . . communication within the family . . ." Arthur Marwick. *The Sixties* (Oxford: Oxford University Press, 1998), p. 313.

"There is little conjunction of truth . . ." R. D. Laing. *The Politics Of Experience And The Bird Of Paradise* (Harmondsworth: Penguin Books, 1967).

". . . that dark and sinister Kink . . ." Ray Davies, interviewed by Bob Farmer. *Disc & Music Echo*: 11 June 1966.

"I really need . . ." ibid.

"If I lie down . . ." ibid.

"I'd Hoover . . ." ibid.

"I've always liked . . ." ibid.

"the Indian look . . . all these recent records . . ." Stanley Adams, interviewed by Bob Farmer. *Disc & Music Echo*: 11 June 1966.

"We'll call it the sitar jacket! . . ." ibid.

"I worry about everything . . ." Ray Davies/Valentine. *Disc & Music Echo*: 9 April 1966.

"I keep thinking . . ." ibid.

"When you look . . ." Fantoni/Rosser. Unedited interview despatched to author: 30 November 2005.

"I just thought . . ." ibid.

"If you flatter Ray . . ." Rasa Didzpetris/Rogan. London: 4 March 2013.

"I didn't really understand . . ." Avory/Rosser. Unedited interview despatched to author: 30 November 2005.

"I was learning how to write . . ." Ray Davies/Doggett. Author's transcript: summer 1996.

"I hope England doesn't change . . ." Ray Davies/Dawbarn. *Melody Maker*: 10 April 1966.

Chapter Eighteen: Sunny Afternoon

"The first song . . ." Ray Davies, film documentary. *The World From My Window*, Isis/Sanctuary: 2003.

"If that had been . . ." ibid.

". . . one of our most atmospheric . . ." Ray Davies/Rogan. London: 1 October 2013.

"I still like to keep tapes . . ." Ray Davies/Cott. *Rolling Stone*: 10 November 1969.

"I played the intro . . ." Ray Davies/Doggett. Author's transcript: summer 1996. Reflecting on Hopkins' contribution, Davies informed the *New York Times* (1 January 1995): "When we recorded 'Sunny Afternoon', Shel insisted that Nicky copy my plodding piano style. Other musicians would have been insulted but Nicky seemed to get inside my style, and he played exactly as I would have. No ego. Perhaps that was his secret."

"That was the most annoying thing . . ." Pete Quaife/Rogan. London/Copenhagen: 3 July 2006.

"What is happening? . . ." Pete Quaife press cutting, uncredited. *c.* spring 1966.

"I have been offered . . ." ibid.

"There was a lot of jealousy . . ." Dave Davies/Rogan. London: 1 March 1996.

"There was a lot of resentment . . ." Pete Quaife, interviewed by Russell Smith and Bill Orton. Printed in the special edition of *The Official Kinks Fan Club Magazine*: 25 June 1999. Rasa later contacted Quaife through the Kinks fan club and received an apology about his outburst. It was evidently insincere. Six years later, he repeated the same complaints in more vociferous fashion, telling Jean-Pierre Morisset: "I didn't like her and felt that she was just a jumped up groupie that had no right to be there." Quaife may have had ulterior motives for these words, the facts of which remain confidential and were unknown to his interviewers. They certainly cast him in a less favourable light. "I think Pete was very frustrated," adds Rasa, by way of vindication following his apology. "For Pete, it wasn't the right role for him. I don't know what talents Pete had. I think he was probably dissatisfied. Maybe he had a bit of insecurity or jealousy going on. Who knows?" Dave Davies concurs. His memories of the recording sessions with Rasa are contrastingly positive. "I really liked them." "That was the other element: *Rasa*. Rasa and I were really good friends and she and Ray were very much in love so when they were together there was that nice feeling. She was important. She was also a fan and had a certain musical intuition herself. She acted as a catalyst between me and Ray. Not necessarily musically, but in feeling, inspiration, keenness, excitement and love."

"What do you think? . . . It's great . . ." Rasa Didzpetris/Rogan. London: 4 March 2013.

"That was the only one . . ." ibid.

"Pye Records was a great company . . ." Ray Davies, *The Story Of The Kinks*. Original unedited film footage, dated 7 November 1984. Courtesy of Cyriel Van den Hemel.

"Membership was seven guineas, meals (including wine) 30s. and miniatures a hefty 12/6d . . ." I would never dream of insulting the reader's intelligence by condescendingly converting these figures from LSD into decimal coinage. It would only prove misleading and give the incorrect impression that they were more reasonably priced than they actually were. Equivalent prices, taking inflation into account, are almost impossible to compute without looking at many other variables, involving wages and particular prices of related consumer goods. While other books often print say ten shillings (50 pence) or 30s. (£1.50), the parenthetical addition is not merely distracting, confusing and misleading, but largely meaningless.

". . . a wonderful person . . ." David Quaife/Rogan. London: 27 February 2013.

"I still remember her . . ." ibid.

"The atmosphere in London . . ." Anthony Lewis. *New York Times*: 8 June 1966.

"It was a bit like me . . ." Ray Davies, film documentary. *The World From My Window*, Isis/Sanctuary: 2003.

"By then, I had a one-year-old daughter . . ." Ray Davies, interviewed by Will Hodgkinson. *Songbook*. Sky Arts: 24 December 2009.

"a load of rubbish . . ." Ray Davies' review of *Revolver*. *Disc & Music Echo*: 29 July 1966.

". . . sounds like they're out to please . . ." ibid.

". . . a cross between the Who and Batman . . ." ibid.

". . . too predictable . . ." ibid.

". . . not up to the Beatles' standard . . ." ibid.

". . . not my sort of thing . . ." ibid.

". . . it'll be popular in discotheques . . ." ibid.

". . . I don't want to be harsh . . ." ibid.

"I could never choose . . ." Peter 'Jonah' Jones/Rogan. London/Montreal, Canada: 8 May 2013.

"Dave wore his heart on his sleeve . . ." ibid.

"He kicked me in the head . . ." ibid.

"But that was on the spur of the moment . . ." ibid.

"Pete was a happy-go-lucky person . . ." ibid.

"I was working with the Kinks . . ." ibid.

"Ray was going absolutely crazy . . ." ibid.

"Ray said 'That fucking bastard . . .'" ibid.

". . . most of the windscreen . . ." Pete Quaife/Rogan. London/Copenhagen: 3 July 2006.

"Pete was so frightened . . ." Ray Davies/McNeill. *New Musical Express*: 16 April 1977. Pete Quaife expanded upon this incident to Jean-Pierre Morisset in November 2005 (published in *Jukebox Magazine* 230: May 2006). "That accident had smashed me up quite badly. I thought that I was able to continue playing and touring but, after a few trips here and there, I realized that I needed to recuperate properly! I was in a lot of pain and unable to concentrate properly. So I went to Denmark to stay with my girlfriend for a long awaited holiday. It worked and when I felt better I rejoined the band." Quaife told me that the holiday was taken under doctor's orders, although I always suspected that he was grateful to be away from the pressures and tensions associated with the Kinks. "I flew to Denmark, hobbling along and I stayed there for a while. I thought it was best if I left the band because nobody knew what was going on, least of all myself. I officially left so that John Dalton could take my place and everybody knew where they were."

"I hadn't slept for about four days . . ." Peter 'Jonah' Jones/Rogan. London/Montreal, Canada: 8 May 2013.

"He was in a terrible state . . ." Pete Quaife/Rogan. London/Copenhagen: 3 July 2006.

"Ray didn't come . . ." Pete Quaife/Black. *Mojo* 82: September 2000.

Chapter Nineteen: The Seduction

". . . play a scale in *D-Minor* . . ." John Dalton, interviewed by the author. Broxbourne, Hertfordshire: 9 October 1994.

"It was the first time . . ." John Dalton, interviewed by the author. Hoddesdon, Hertfordshire: 4 August 1982.

"It sounded like a honky-tonk piano . . ." Pete Quaife/Rogan. London/Copenhagen: 3 July 2006.

"We eventually got to Oslo . . ." Curtis/Rogan. Brownhills, Walsall: 24 August 1982.

"'The Day It All Stopped'" . . . Headline in the *Observer*: 24 July 1966.

"I have very little time . . ." Ray Davies, quoted in *Beat Instrumental*: July 1966.

"They are a touchy people . . ." *Observer*: June 1966.

"Pay may be frozen . . ." *Observer*: 31 July 1966.

"We were very pleased . . ." Ray Davies, interviewed by Dick Tatham. *Valentine*: 21 October 1967.

"Louis Benjamin is a shit . . ." Talmy/Rogan. London: 17 September 1982.

"On a personal level . . ." Wace/Rogan. London: 15 October 1982.

"Our deal got extended . . ." Wace/Rogan. London: 25 June 1983.

"We neither made nor lost . . ." Wace/Rogan. London: 15 October 1982.

"I don't look on myself . . ." Ray Davies, music press cutting titled 'They All Want A Kinky Song': 2 July 1966.

"I had no idea . . ." Ray Davies/Doggett. Author's transcript: summer 1996. Davies adds: "When I discovered that I could come up with my own material, I suppose I broke away from a lot of the influences that I'd had – R&B, folk-blues, people like Big Bill Broonzy. I felt I needed to come up with something more commercially-minded."

"Ray is one of the most prolific writers . . ." Talmy/Rogan. London: 17 September 1982.

". . . Dave Davies noticed that Watts was wearing pink socks . . ." Elsewhere, Ray suggested that the socks were white, although that too would have been considered outré, in common with white polo necks.

"I felt that would be the right thing . . ." Ray Davies/Smith. *Gay Times*: October 1994.

"Everyone was acting in a camp way . . ." Dave Davies/Rosser. Unedited interview despatched to author: 30 November 2005.

"There was an awful row . . ." ibid.

"What stuck in my mind . . ." Dave Davies. *Kink* (London: Boxtree, 1996), p. 96.

". . . provided Davies with a song title . . ." Reflecting on the song in 1994, Ray remarked to Richard Smith (*Gay Times*: October 1994): "I must clarify one thing. I totally admire David Watts. I do wish I could be like him. About two years ago I went up in the car to try and find him. I searched and searched. Finally I found this guy, and he's dead. I cried. He added so much in my life. I really did admire him. It wasn't mocking. I think people misinterpret things a lot of the time. It's going back to this sly wit, you know, cynicism? I never betrayed my subjects."

Chapter Twenty: *Face To Face*

"When Pete came home . . ." David Quaife/Rogan. London: 27 February 2013.

"We'd been friends . . ." Ray Davies/Doggett. Liner notes to the Kinks' box set *Picture Book*: December 2008. Original interview: *c.* June 2004.

"That's the trouble . . ." Start/Rogan. Haslemere, Surrey: 25 September 2012.

"The cancellations were very tedious . . ." Wace/Rogan. London: 15 October 1982.

"That's what parents do . . ." Ray Davies/Walker. Broadcast BBC Radio 2: 30 December 2010.

"We were inventing rock 'n' roll . . ." Dave Davies, interviewed by Rebecca Hardy. *Daily Mail*: 30 October 2010. "But he got a kick out of grinding me into the ground," Dave adds.

"You could tap into all cultures . . ." Ray Davies/Paytress. *Mojo* 148: March 2006.

"When we realized . . ." Ray Davies, interviewed by Adam Forrest. *The Big Issue*: 13–19 June 2011.

". . . 'partly inspired' . . . 'something classy' . . ." Ray Davies acknowledged these in a tribute to Nicky Hopkins printed in the *New York Times*: 1 January 1995.

"It was at a time . . ." Ray Davies in Jon Savage, *The Kinks: The Official Biography* (London: Faber & Faber, 1984), p. 80.

". . . to find work as a coalman . . ." According to Dalton, neither of the brothers had the courtesy to inform him that his services were no longer required. Instead, Dalton was called into their managers' office where he learned the bad news. He vaguely recalls being told that Quaife was a quarter of the company and therefore could not be over-ruled by the management. Dalton was seemingly unaware that Quaife had officially resigned from Kinks Productions two months before. The fairest view of this was that Collins and Wace were attempting to soften the blow to allay any disappointment or embittered feelings.

". . . two bass guitars . . ." In common with several songs on *Face To Face*, there has often been confusion over who played the bass on 'Dead End Street': Quaife or Dalton? "That period is hazy," Quaife concedes. "I'm sure it's me on 'Dead End Street'. John Dalton says he played on it. OK, I'll give it to you, take it, it's yours." In his book, *Kink*, Dave Davies credits Quaife, whereas Ray in *X-Ray* reckons it was Dalton. Doug Hinman, a keen student of Kinks' sessionography, is also convinced it was Dalton. In interviews over the years, Dalton – a subject never known for exaggeration or unreliability – has described the session in detail, including information on the night they went back into the studio to re-do the song after Talmy left the building. That said, Dave Davies also claimed back in 1980 that there were "two basses" on the song. It may be that Dalton and Quaife were both featured on the disc. Alternatively, Quaife may have appeared on an earlier take.

"That was the beginning . . ." Ray Davies/Doggett. Author's transcript: summer 1996.

". . . written by professional tunesmiths, Geoff Stephens and John Carter . . ." Geoff Stephens, along with his other songwriting associate Peter Eden, managed Pye artiste Donovan as well as Davies' arty pal Barry Fantoni.

"a book about the life . . ." . . . "very similar to those . . ." Ray Davies, press cutting in colour titled 'That's Life'. Uncredited: late 1966.

"I wanted to write about the cold reality . . ." Ray Davies/Brown. *Without Walls – My Generation: The Kinks*. Channel 4: 18 March 1995.

"Beatlemania is at an end . . ." *Sunday Times*: 13 November 1966.

"There was no water . . ." *The Times*: 29 August 1963. Such descriptions were far from unique. Social historian Dominic Sandbrook quotes figures presented by the homeless charity Shelter revealing that 12,000 people had seen in the New Year at a hostel for the homeless. He also mentions "a house in Church Road, Birmingham, occupied by 27 people, with one family to a room, sharing one toilet, two cold-water taps, and the company of innumerable rats" (from *White Heat*, London: Little Brown, 2006), p. 566.

"It showed slums and poverty . . ." Ray Davies, quoted in Johnny Rogan, *The Sound And The Fury* (London: Elm Tree Books/Hamish Hamilton, 1984), p. 74.

"I don't think it's sick . . ." Dave Davies, interviewed by Keith Altham. *New Musical Express*: 3 December 1966.

"Our roadie, Stan [Whitley] . . ." Dave Davies, interviewed by Peter Doggett. *Record Collector* 200: April 1996.

"I now look upon making a song . . ." Ray Davies. *Music Maker*: December 1966.

"We were trying to put out two good songs . . ." Talmy/Rogan. London: 17 September 1982.

"Once you've had . . ." Ray Davies, interviewed by Keith Altham. *New Musical Express*: 3 December 1966.

"I'm worried about Dave . . ." ibid.

"Can you use the word 'cunt'? . . ." Dave Davies/Rogan. London: 1 March 1996.

Chapter Twenty-One: Liverpool Sunset

"I'd like to own the group . . ." Ray Davies, interviewed by Penny Valentine. *Disc & Music Echo*: January 1967.

"According to Oldham, Wace had actually witnessed this incident . . ." Details provided in author's interview with Andrew Loog Oldham. London: 8–10 September 1995. Additional information about Arden's encounter with Stigwood were conducted in various interviews between the author and Arden, most notably on 29 July 1997 and 4 February 1999.

"The Small Faces cost us money! . . ." Wace/Rogan. London: 25 June 1983.

"[It] was one of the happiest times . . ." Ray Davies/McNeill. *New Musical Express*: 16 April 1977.

"I didn't see a lot of Swinging London . . ." Rasa Didzpetris/Rogan. London: 4 March 2013.

". . . imaginary schemes was mentioned in interviews . . ." A press release from March 1966 announced a fascinating five-track EP featuring 'Two Sisters', 'Mr Reporter', 'Village Green', 'And I Will Love You' and 'This Is Where I Belong', a brilliant idea that was soon forgotten.

". . . derailed by his breakdown . . ." Although Ray Davies would never lose the intensity of old, there were signs of serenity that even his brother acknowledged. "It's really difficult to talk about Ray as a person because he changes so much," he said that spring. "He's more introvert than anything else, and a very deep person. But since the nervous breakdown he had a year ago, he's been much better as a person. He used to flog himself workwise unmercifully, but not any more. He's eased up and become less tense."

"I wanted to write something . . ." Ray Davies, *The Story Of The Kinks*. Original unedited film footage, dated 7 November 1984. Courtesy of Cyriel Van den Hemel.

"That's where I've differed . . ." Ray Davies/Hay. *Music Connection*: 10 November 1996.

"There were two recorded . . ." Talmy/Rogan. London: 17 September 1982.

"I knew it was going to be a special record . . ." Ray Davies/Hodgkinson. *Songbook*. Sky Arts: 24 December 2009.

"It started as a real personal song . . ." Ray Davies/Sharp. *Goldmine*: March 1996.

"I was almost making a little documentary . . ." Ray Davies/Brown. *Without Walls – My Generation: The Kinks*. Channel 4: 18 March 1995.

"It happens a lot . . ." Ray Davies, interviewed by Keith Altham. *New Musical Express*: 20 May 1967.

"I wanted a place . . ." Press cutting: *c.* early 1967.

"I knew it was going to be . . ." Ray Davies, interviewed by Mark Breyer and Rik Vittenson. *Crawdaddy*: 1976.

"It *was* going to be called . . ." Ray Davies/Paytress. *Mojo* 148: March 2006.

"If you look at the song . . ." Ray Davies/Altham. *New Musical Express*: 20 May 1967.

"Ray's never been very good . . ." Dave Davies, interviewed by Nick Hasted. *Independent*: 26 August 2011.

"Terry and Julie . . ." Ray Davies. Interviewer uncredited. *Uncut* 140: January 2009.

"I imagined it . . ." *The World Of Ray Davies And The Kinks: I'm Not Like Everybody Else*. Broadcast BBC 2: 21 December 1995.

"It doesn't mean anything . . ." Ray Davies, quoted in Johnny Rogan, *The Complete Guide To The Music Of The Kinks* (London: Omnibus Press, 1998), p. 57.

"'Waterloo Sunset' is an accumulation . . ." Ray Davies/Walker; BBC Radio 2: 30 December 2010.

". . . wasn't a great advance . . ." Ray Davies/Doggett. Author's transcript: summer 1996.

"I can't see it . . ." Press cutting, *c.* early 1967. Composer Geoff Stephens had formed the New Vaudeville Band. He also co-wrote 'Semi-Detached Suburban Mr James' for Manfred Mann.

". . . absent from the 'Best British Disc This Year'. . ." The 'Best British Disc This Year' featured: 1. 'A Whiter Shade Of Pale' – Procul Harum. 2. 'All You Need Is Love' – the Beatles. 3. 'Massachusetts' – the Bee Gees. 4. 'The Day I Met Marie' – Cliff Richard. 5. 'Penny Lane' – the Beatles. 6. 'The Last Waltz' – Engelbert Humperdinck. 7. 'Release Me' – Engelbert Humperdinck. 8. 'Eveybody Knows' – the Dave Clark Five. 9. 'I'll Never Fall In Love Again' – Tom Jones. 10. 'Hole In My Shoe' – Traffic. The poll confirmed the popularity of old-fashioned ballads even among the predominantly teen readership of *NME*. The Rolling Stones were notable by their absence and none of these ten songs could reasonably be described as rock. Fascinating.

"**After four years . . .**" Talmy/Rogan. London: 17 September 1982.

"**This producer doesn't know . . .**" Ray Davies/Wilson. *Mastertapes*. BBC Radio 4: 3 December 2012.

"**No disrespect . . .**" ibid. In other interviews, Davies has been more respectful and kinder about Shel Talmy. In 1980, he told *Hot Press*' Jack Lynch: "He was good for us because I'm the sort of person who will do things time and time again, past the point where I think it's good, and Shel would always say, 'That's it, that's the first take, that's what this band is all about', so I learned a lot from him."

"**The Kinks had their sound . . .**" Wace/Rogan. London: 25 June 1983.

"**I went out with Grenville and Robert . . .**" Ray Davies, *The Story Of The Kinks*. Original unedited film footage. Courtesy of Cyriel Van den Hemel.

"**I still intend to sing . . .**" Ray Davies/Altham. *New Musical Express*: 20 May 1967.

"'**Ray Davies Quitting The Kinks?**'" Headline. *New Musical Express*: 20 May 1967.

"**It is difficult . . .**" Statement by Ray Davies under the title 'Changes Mind' included as addendum to Keith Altham's interview. *New Musical Express*: 20 May 1967.

Chapter Twenty-Two: High Court Drama

"**I had to spend three to four hours . . .**" Page/Rogan. London: 7 August 1982.

"**The Kinks on the witness stand . . .**" Page/Rogan. London: 24 June 1983.

"**I said, 'Do you by any chance . . .**'" Page/Rogan. London: 7 August 1982.

"**I could have been vindictive . . .**" ibid.

"**I hated him . . .**" Ray Davies, testimony in the High Court. London: 25 May 1967.

"**The crux of the case . . .**" Wace/Rogan. London: 15 October 1982.

"**. . . unfounded and not justified at all . . .**" His Honour Justice Widgery. *Denmark Productions Ltd v. Boscobel Productions Ltd*. Royal Courts of Justice. London: 5 June 1967.

"**It was not until I saw the four members . . .**" ibid.

"**I was always told . . .**" Page/Rogan. London: 7 August 1982.

"**They always spoke to people . . .**" Curtis/Rogan. Brownhills, Walsall: 24 August 1982.

"**There, they were greeted by Ursula Graham-White . . .**" Information on the Kinks' visit to Belfast provided to the author by Ursula Graham-White. East Grinstead: 17 November 1993.

"**Whenever the Beatles came on . . .**" Rasa Didzpetris/Rogan. London: 4 March 2013.

"**He's a really good singer . . .**" Ray Davies/Valentine. *Disc*: 12 August 1967.

"**Well, why don't you let him sing . . .**" ibid.

"**Robert would sometimes tell me things . . .**" Dave Davies/Rogan. London: 1 March 1996.

"**I think if it had been . . .**" Dave Davies, interviewed by Alan Walsh. *Melody Maker*: 12 August 1967.

"**I do feel responsible for Dave . . .**" Ray Davies/Valentine. *Disc*: 12 August 1967.

"**When it was mentioned . . .**" Dave Davies/Rogan. London: 1 March 1996.

"... a weird song ..." Dave Davies, interviewed by Keith Altham. *New Musical Express*: 12 August 1967.

"I was twenty [something] and married ..." *The World Of Ray Davies And The Kinks: I'm Not Like Everybody Else*. Broadcast BBC 2: 21 December 1995.

"I wish all his money ..." Dave Davies remembers his sister Peggy at first mishearing the lyrics and assuming that Ray was singing: "Wish I could be like David *was*" which sounded strangely appropriate considering the presence of 'Two Sisters'.

"It's about a cricket player ..." Ray Davies/McNeill. *New Musical Express*: 16 April 1977.

"The song just didn't come off really ..." Ray Davies/Cott. *Rolling Stone*: 10 November 1969.

"I must say I'm pleased ..." Ray Davies/Tatham. *Valentine*: 21 October 1967.

Chapter Twenty-Three: The Cabaret Season

"... reviewers appreciated 'Autumn Almanac' ..." The only reservations expressed were fears of repetition. The *NME*'s Derek Johnson said: "There are few groups more capable of painting vivid and descriptive verbal pictures than the Kinks. This follows the tradition of 'Waterloo Sunset' by latching on to everyday happenings and giving them an absorbing lyrical quality ... I wouldn't class it as one of their very best discs, if only because the melody has a certain similarity with past releases. But a big one for sure." Over at *Melody Maker*, Nick Jones was more impatient: "Is it time Ray stopped writing about grey suburbanites going about their fairly unemotional business? One feels Ray works to a formula, not a feeling, and it's becoming boring."

"That was the real step forward ..." Ray Davies, interviewed by Peter Doggett. *Mojo* 111: February 2003. Davies elaborated on the importance of place in his songs during his BBC interview with Johnnie Walker. "Everything I wrote about in the early days I was inspired by American blues music but the subject matter I wrote about subsequently was inspired by things I saw happening within a hundred yards of where I lived ..."

"As I got to know him ..." Ray Davies/Hodgkinson. *Songbook*. Sky Arts: 24 December 2009.

"We are a nation ..." George Orwell: 'England Your England', first published: *The Lion and the Unicorn: Socialism and the English Genius* (London: Secker & Warburg, 1941).

"I'm going off meat ..." Ray Davies, interviewed by Keith Altham. *New Musical Express*: 4 November 1967. Elaborating on Ray's conversion to vegetarianism, Rasa notes: "He chopped and changed. He was going to be a vegetarian, then he was a bit vegetarian, then he ate meat. He was verging on being a full vegetarian around the divorce time but he wasn't when we were together. He is now, but he does eat prawns."

"Suzanah's Still Alive" ... The song is titled 'Suzanah's Still Alive' on the original UK single and referred to as such in Dave Davies' autobiography.

"... about a bird ..." Dave Davies, interviewed by Bob Dawbarn. *Melody Maker*: 9 December 1967.

"I want people to know what's in me ..." Dave Davies, interviewed by Richard Green.

New Musical Express: 3 August 1968. When I threw those words back at Dave in 1996, he replied: "I don't remember the quote. I'm sure I said it, but I'm not sure why. I did like that record. It said a lot about my influences. That song is Leadbelly and Eddie Cochran to me musically, mixed with my own feelings. It was really important to me, personally, the riffs and the musicality."

"I didn't really want the responsibility . . ." Dave Davies/Rogan. London: 1 March 1996. Dave went on to tell me: "I lost heart in it. We were in the studio for two to three days and I just didn't want to do it. It just petered away. The spirit went. The most enjoyable track we did and still one of my favourites is 'Creeping Jean'. I loved the feel of that but some of the other songs I didn't like. Especially the ones I dragged out from a long time ago like 'Crying'. Maybe, I didn't like the direction."

". . . Jeannie Lamb . . ." Coincidentally, Lamb had previously appeared with a precursor of the Mike Cotton Sound, whose membership always had close associations with the Kinks. Trombonist John Beecham recalls: "Jeannie was lovely but we'd parted company when we were still a traditional jazz band before we became a rhythm & blues band. We discovered Jeannie in a club called the Two Red Shoes in Elgin. She left her home in Inverness and came down to London to be in our band."

"I'm still trying to justify that album . . ." Ray Davies/Larkin. *Dark Star* 21: July 1979. *Live At Kelvin Hall* had been released in America the previous August under the title *The Kinks Live*. The US release, which was largely ignored, was even less impressive than its UK counterpart as the tracks were banded rather than sequenced together.

"I read up quite a bit . . ." Ray Davies, interviewed by David Griffiths. *Record Mirror*: 31 August 1968. The chronological list of Davies' contributions to *At The Eleventh Hour* read: 'You Can't Give More Than What You Have' (30 December); 'If Christmas Could Last Forever' (6 January); 'We're Backing Britain' (13 January); 'Poor Old Intellectual Sadie' (20 January); 'Could Be You're Getting Old' (27 January); 'Just A Poor Country Girl' (10 February); 'The Man Who Conned Dinner From The Ritz' (17 February); 'Did You See His Name?' (24 February); 'This Is What The World Is All About' (2 March). Davies completed nine of the ten songs commissioned, missing only the 3 February broadcast.

"We don't want to push ourselves . . ." Pete Quaife 'Pop Think In'. *Melody Maker*: 27 May 1967.

"To be honest . . ." Pete Quaife/Paytress. *Mojo* 148: March 2006.

"I couldn't take the way . . ." Pete Quaife/Rosser. Unedited interview despatched to author: 30 November 2005.

"I had a party . . ." Ray Davies/Hodgkinson. *Songbook*. Sky Arts: 24 December 2009. Davies assumed the Max Miller album was *You Can't Help Liking Him* but that was not released until 1979 as part of the 'Golden Hour' series. What he would have played his guests in that spring of 1968 was either *Max At The Met* or *That's Nice, Maxie*, both of which were available on Pye Records (the former on their budget label, Marble Arch). Davies as a fellow Pye artiste no doubt received his copies gratis.

"Where Larry Page made his mistake . . ." Wace/Rogan. London: 25 June 1983.

". . . the bitter end of the tour . . ." His Honour Justice Widgery. *Denmark Productions Ltd v. Boscobel Productions Ltd*. Royal Courts of Justice. London: 5 June 1967.

". . . that would only produce an outburst of temperament . . ." ibid.

"I find it very strange . . ." Lord Justice Salmon, Court of Appeal, High Courts of Justice. Strand, London: 28 June 1968.

"I think that almost anything . . ." ibid.

". . . bask in the sun . . ." ibid.

"You don't talk about respect! . . ." Wace/Rogan. London: 15 October 1982.

"No fucking way! . . ." Page/Rogan. London: 24 June 1983.

"I thought it would be a boy . . ." *The Davies Diaries*. BBC Radio 2: 23 November 2000.

"'Wonderboy' was horrible . . ." Andy Miller, *The Kinks Are The Village Green Preservation Society* (London: Continuum, 2004), p. 29.

"It should never have been released . . ." Ray Davies, interviewed by Keith Altham. *New Musical Express*: 31 August 1968.

"I like to think that story's true . . ." *The Davies Diaries*. BBC Radio 2: 23 November 2000.

"The Kinks seemed sadly out of place . . ." Reviewer David Hughes. *Disc & Music Echo*: April 1968.

"They were the 'new faces of '68' . . ." Dave Davies, interviewed by Julie Webb. *New Musical Express*: 8 July 1972.

"She just liked me . . ." Ray Davies/Savage. *Ugly Things* 90: summer 2010.

". . . wasn't talented enough . . ." Philby/Porter. *Daily Mail*: 1998.

"He offered no explanation . . ." ibid.

". . . an affair . . ." Ray Davies/Savage. *Ugly Things* 90: summer 2010.

"I didn't want to be her lover . . ." ibid.

"Well, thanks for all the good times . . ." ibid.

"That's got nothing to do . . ." David Quaife/Rogan. London: 27 February 2013.

". . . little bits . . ." ibid.

"That was a shock . . ." ibid.

"That is so not true . . ." Pete Quaife/Rosser. Unedited taped interview despatched to author: 30 November 2005.

"I went, . . ." Pete Quaife/Russell Smith and Bill Orton. Printed in the special edition of *The Official Kinks Fan Club Magazine*: 25 June 1999.

"The reason I wanted to move . . ." Rasa Didzpetris/Rogan. London: 4 March 2013.

"I was upset about the dog . . ." ibid. In *X-Ray*, Davies erroneously implies that the dog had been stolen. Weirdly, he also changed the dog's name from Alfie to Georgie, the same name as the mystery woman with whom he was having his 'chaste assignation'. Amusingly, Davies appears to become confused by his own fictional machinations. On page 357 of *X-Ray*, Georgie the dog momentarily reverts to his real name, Alfie, for the one and only time. Despite these discrepancies, Davies evidently enjoyed the dog's company. He later admitted to *New Musical Express* (13 October 1973): "I wrote a little poem for my dog before it ran away. I was writing one night and my dog was asleep having a nightmare and I really couldn't talk to him. That was the most upsetting thing. I couldn't talk to my dog and he couldn't talk to me, which was worse . . . I think if they could talk to us it would really be interesting because they really get kicked around. Let's face it, it's a hard life for a mongrel."

"I finished the song . . ." *The Davies Diaries*. BBC Radio 2: 23 November 2000.

Elsewhere, Davies credited keyboardist Nicky Hopkins' contribution to the song. "Nicky, unlike lesser musicians, didn't try to show off; he would only play when necessary. But he had the ability to turn an ordinary track into a gem – slotting in the right chord at the right time or dropping a set of triplets around the back beat, just enough to make you want to dance . . . He managed to give 'Days', for instance, a mysterious religious quality without being sentimental or pious." (*New York Times*: 1 January 1995). Speaking to Peter Doggett, Davies added: "The trick in that song was summing up the whole feeling in five words: 'thank you for the days'. That's the wonderful thing about being young – you have that built-in editorial quality . . . We used a mellotron for the strings, while I played piano."

"We landed . . ." Ray Davies/McNeill. *New Musical Express*: 16 April 1977.

"Rasa is a very sore point . . ." Pete Quaife/Morisset. *Jukebox Magazine* 230: May 2006.

"By then I was suffering from claustrophobia . . ." Pete Quaife/Rogan. London/Copenhagen: 3 July 2006.

"Memoirs of Ray Davies . . ." Reviewer Keith Moon. *Melody Maker*: 28 June 1968.

"I still have a lot of faith . . ." Ray Davies, interviewed by Lon Goddard. *Record Mirror*: 3 August 1968.

"We've been doing cabaret . . ." Dave Davies/Green. *New Musical Express*: 3 August 1968.

"You have to get into a new field . . ." Mick Avory, press cutting: *c.* late 1968.

Chapter Twenty-Four: *The Village Green Preservation Society*

". . . a lamentable petty bourgeois cry . . ." Richard Merton, *The New Left Review*: issue 59. Autumn 1968.

". . . are deliberately safeguarding . . ." quote cited in Johnny Rogan, *Lennon* (London: Calidore, 2006), p.79.

"That record was no more revolutionary . . ." 'An Open Letter To John Lennon' by John Hoyland. *Black Dwarf*. Vol 13, number 7: 27 October 1968.

". . . on a destruction kick . . ." John Lennon, letter to *Black Dwarf*, printed in issue dated 10 January 1969.

"I don't worry . . ." ibid.

". . . A bunch of crackpots . . ." Editorial comment in *Wood Green, Southgate and Palmers Green Weekly Herald*: 27 September 1968.

"I just immersed myself . . ." Ray Davies/Walker; BBC Radio 2: 30 December 2010.

"I didn't think . . ." Ray Davies/Sharp. *Goldmine*: March 1996.

"There were student riots . . ." Ray Davies/Doggett, original file for liner notes to the Kinks' box set *Picture Book*: December 2008. Courtesy of author.

"The origins . . . Dylan Thomas' *Under Milk Wood – A Play For Voices* **. . ."** *The Village Green Preservation Society* has a history of false leads, compounded by Davies' conflicting and occasionally flippant comments about its gestation. Over the years, it has also been the subject of misinformation and misconceptions that continue to be trotted out in retrospective reappraisals, interviews, articles and sanctioned liner notes. Although Dylan Thomas' poignant musings on passing time appealed to Davies' sensibility, the poet's comedic characters appeared unsuitable for his purpose. Nevertheless, the 'Village' idea was retained and developed. However, any lingering plans to adapt *Under Milk Wood* ended with 'Polly', a composition that name-checked Polly Garter, but otherwise bore no relation to Thomas' promiscuous, Mother Earth character. Davies' composition 'Polly' lacks the depth of the poet's 'Polly Garter Song', a poignant elegy to her many lovers and the memory of 'Little Willie Wee' who is "dead dead dead". In the end, Davies removed 'Polly' from contention, relegating the song to the B-side of 'Wonderboy'.

"Rehearsals took place . . ." Pete Quaife/Rogan. London/Copenhagen: 3 July 2006.

"The only way . . ." *The Davies Diaries*. BBC Radio 2: 23 November 2000.

". . . elaborately titled *The Kinks Are The Village Green Preservation Society* . . ." In addition to the many contradictory aspects of the album, one thing that nobody talks about is the confusion over its actual title. It may be pedantry and false exactitude that finally caused the record to become known as *The Kinks Are The Village Green Preservation Society*. That title was, of course, part of the album's artwork and also on the original label, but there was *no* separate artiste credit, thereby causing confusion. Should it have been called *The Kinks Are The Village Green Preservation Society* or simply *The Village Green Preservation Society* by the Kinks? It seems clear enough from the artwork's lettering and font size that 'The Kinks' was detached from the rest of the title. Who was responsible for inserting 'Are' (instead of the expected 'By') has never been ascertained. For many years, the album was generally known as *The Village Green Preservation Society* (in keeping with its opening track). In concerts, interviews and his own writings, Ray Davies has *always* referred to it as *The Village Green Preservation Society*. On the CD reissue, which departed from the original release, the label separately credited 'The Kinks' in large letters, followed by the title, *The Kinks are The Village Green Preservation Society*, changing history in the process. Nobody has yet been pedagogical or literal enough to suggest that it should 'correctly' be called, however illogically, *Are The Village Green Society* by the Kinks!

"The Village Green . . ." *Imaginary Man* documentary. Broadcast BBC 1: 21 December 2010.

"It's a shame . . ." Ray Davies, interviewed by Derek Boltwood. *Record Mirror*: 10 May 1969.

"against the menace . . ." *Observer*: 17 March 1966.

"The band played . . ." *The Davies Diaries*. BBC Radio 2: 23 November 2000.

"Walter was a friend . . ." Ray Davies, interviewed by Bob Dawbarn. *Melody Maker*: 30 November 1968.

"I wrote this song . . ." Ray Davies/Sharp. *Goldmine*: March 1996.

"I was just . . ." George Orwell, *Coming Up For Air* (Harmondsworth: Penguin Modern Classics, 1939), p. 219. The first person to spot the George Bowling connection in print was Andy Miller in his mini-book on the album.

". . . on two people . . ." . . . **"someone I didn't want to fall out with . . ."** Ray Davies/ Hodgkinson. *Songbook*. Sky Arts: 24 December 2009.

"What are you rebelling against, Johnny?" . . . **"What have you got?".** From the film *The Wild One*: 1953.

"'The Earth Without A Justice League'" . . . *Justice League Of America* 37: April 1965.

"I can't for the life of me . . ." Ray Davies/Doggett. Draft of liner notes to the Kinks' box set *Picture Book*: December 2008. Original interview: *c*. June 2004. According to

Pete Townshend, he received a telephone call from Davies suggesting that the Who should cover 'Johnny Thunder'. Unfortunately, Townshend could not recall precisely when this occurred, but it seems likely that it was some time after the release of *The Village Green Preservation Society*. In an interview with *Rolling Stone*, published in November 1969, Ray Davies said of 'Johnny Thunder': "Johnny Thunder lives on water, he don't eat food, he feeds on lightning (laughter). Frankenstein. It's not a cowboy song. It would be nice to hear the Who sing it."

"I'd rather have the actual things . . ." Ray Davies/Boltwood. *Record Mirror*: 10 May 1969. In 'England Your England', George Orwell wrote: "Yes, there *is* something distinctive and recognizable in English civilization . . . It has a flavour of its own. Moreover it is continuous, it stretches into the future and the past, there is something in it that persists, as in a living creature. What can the England of 1940 have in common with the England of 1840? But then, what have you in common with the child of five whose photograph your mother keeps on the mantelpiece? Nothing, except that you happen to be the same person." The incidental origins of 'People Take Pictures Of Each Other' were recalled by Davies in a 1976 interview in *Crawdaddy* conducted by Mark Breyer and Rik Vittenson: "I was at a wedding . . . in the country . . . We walked back from the church. The guy was in the navy . . . and he put a flag up in the back garden . . . and they all stood there and they took a picture. And then she got the camera and took a picture of him . . . and he got the camera and took a picture of her . . . and that's strange. That's where that came from."

"There's an element of lost youth . . ." Ray Davies/Rosser. Unedited interview despatched to author: 30 November 2005.

"That was just me . . ." Ray Davies/Dawbarn. *Melody Maker*: 30 November 1968.

"The reason why it worked . . ." Pete Quaife/Kirby. *Now And Then* 8: 1994.

"No, it's not about God . . ." Ray Davies/Dawbarn. *Melody Maker*: 30 November 1968.

". . . a being somewhat bigger . . ." notes in CD *This Is Where I Belong; The Songs Of Ray Davies & The Kinks*: 2002.

"I'm always wary . . ." Ray Davies, interviewed by Danny Holloway. *New Musical Express*: 13 May 1972.

"It was an R&B concert . . ." Ray Davies/Dawbarn. *Melody Maker*: 30 November 1968.

"If I'd done that song today . . ." Ray Davies/Doggett. *Mojo* 111: February 2003.

"It's about a prostitute . . ." Ray Davies/Dawbarn. *Melody Maker*: 30 November 1968.

"I think I explained it . . ." Ray Davies/Mark Breyer and Rik Vittenson. *Crawdaddy*: 1976.

"Meher Baba is the Avatar . . ." Pete Townshend, interviewed by Hugh Nolan. *Disc & Music Echo*: 30 November 1968.

"John thought . . ." Neil Aspinall, quoted in Philip Norman, *Shout!* (London: Elm Tree Books/Hamish Hamilton, 1981), p. 340.

"I don't like to think . . ." Ray Davies/Mark Breyer and Rik Vittenson. *Crawdaddy*: 1976.

"Phenomenal Cat went to Singapore . . ." Ray Davies/Jonathan Cott. *Rolling Stone*: 10 November 1969.

". . . easily their best LP . . ." Ray Davies/Dawbarn. *Melody Maker*: 30 November 1968.

". . . words of wisdom . . ." *Disc & Music Echo*: 22 November 1968.

"Ray Davies has written a song picture . . ." Reviewer Judith Simons. *Daily Express*: November 1968.

"Pye wouldn't give us any money . . ." Ray Davies/McKnight. *Zigzag* 27: December 1972.

"They said we *could* have the money . . ." ibid.

"It was strange . . ." ibid.

"It's the most talked-about record . . ." Ray Davies/Cavanagh. *Uncut* 163: December 2010.

"I wanted a record . . ." Ray Davies/Sharp. *Goldmine*: March 1996.

"'an embarrassment' . . ." Andy Miller, *The Kinks Are The Village Green Preservation Society*. (London: Continuum, 2004), p. 5. If subjective speculations such as the 'handful of people' are allowable, then perhaps I should add as a personal footnote that, as a 15-year-old in 1968, I knew several people who owned the album (at least two were in my class at school) and I purchased a copy myself. There was no sense among us that the album was obscure or a poor seller. It was prominently displayed in record shops in London. Nor do I recall seeing copies available at a reduced price which, presumably, might have occurred if the work had been the sales disaster of modern myth.

"If we're talking about . . ." Ray Davies, quoted in Neville Marten & Jeff Hudson, *The Kinks* (London: Sanctuary, 2001), p. 97.

"The decision to do the album . . ." Ray Davies/McKnight. *Zigzag* 27: December 1972.

". . . it's a beautiful record . . ." Dave Davies/Rogan. London: 1 March 1996.

"I should have left . . ." Ray Davies/Doggett. *Mojo* 111: February 2003.

"It was more of a band effort . . ." Mick Avory, quoted in Andy Miller, *The Kinks Are The Village Green Preservation Society* (London: Continuum, 2004), p. 7.

"Making that album . . ." Pete Quaife/Morisset. *Jukebox Magazine* 230: May 2006.

"His denunciation of city life . . . tallied with the new ecology movement . . ." Three years before, the Kinks had been part of the white hot technological revolution and were famously photographed at Centre Point, that towering edifice on the corner of Tottenham Court Road and Oxford Street. Now the concrete jungle was itself under threat. Six months before the release of *The Village Green Preservation Society*, London had been rocked by a gas explosion at the Ronan Point tower block in Newham. The prosaic details – a middle-aged woman innocently turning on her gas cooker for a cup of tea – were almost as frightening as the horrific images of devastation unseen in the capital since the Blitz. Davies' pleas for preservation and bucolic bliss were not as reactionary as many later commentators assumed.

"It seemed that Dylan too was seeking salvation in old wisdom . . ." That same mood could be detected in the Band's *Music From Big Pink* and the Byrds' *Sweetheart Of The Rodeo*, both of which seemed designed to cleanse rock music of its recent indulgences by seeking refuge in a golden age of dustbowl America in which images of pastoral bliss co-mingled with tales of hardship, alcoholism and prison life.

Chapter Twenty-Five: End Of The Sixties

"His debut single, 'My Father' . . ." Jonah P. Jones' recording career continued with 'It Ain't Us Who Make The Wars' b/w 'Sunrise Highway', both songs written by Ronnie Dante and Gene Allan. Dante was a bubblegum pop specialist, who had sung lead on the Archies' million seller 'Sugar Sugar' as well as fronting the Cuff Links. By then, Jones had become disenchanted with the musical direction favoured by his management. "I didn't want to be a teenybopper. I wanted to blow my brains out on mescaline, LSD and all the psychedelics and play acid rock and blues. They didn't want me to do that. We were at complete loggerheads. I got so heavily into drugs at that point that I completely blew it and gave up singing." For a time, Jones worked in pre-production on an off-Broadway musical drama, *Billy*, but it was never staged. He had no work permit and was staying in America on an extended tourist visa. Eventually, he was deported.

"A terrible moment . . ." Rasa Didzpetris/Rogan. London: 4 March 2013.

"It's so enormous . . ." Ray Davies, interviewed by Derek Boltwood. *Record Mirror*: 29 March 1969.

"I find that . . ." ibid.

"I think he wanted . . ." Ned Sherrin, interviewed by Caroline Boucher. *Independent On Sunday*: 25 February 1996.

"Why don't you use Ray Davies? . . ." Ned Sherrin, interviewed by the author. London: 15 March 1988.

"My knowledge of Sixties' pop . . ." ibid.

"Ray's music really interested me . . ." Sherrin/Boucher. *Independent On Sunday*: 25 February 1996.

"rather wooden . . ." ibid.

"Acting didn't really interest me . . ." Ray Davies/Boucher. *Independent On Sunday*: 25 February 1996.

"Ned was very good . . ." ibid.

"I witnessed the tension . . ." Sherrin/Rogan. London: 15 March 1988.

"Ray may have had a reputation . . ." Sherrin/Boucher. *Independent On Sunday*: 25 February 1996.

"After one meal . . ." ibid.

"I'd heard songs he'd written . . ." Dave Davies/Rogan. London: 1 March 1996.

"I made attempts at writing . . ." Pete Quaife/Rosser. Unedited interview despatched to author: 30 November 2005.

"flawed liberal . . ." Martin Priestman, 'A Critical Stage: Drama In The 1960s' in *Cultural Revolution? The Challenge Of The Arts In The 1960s*, edited by Bart Moore-Gilbert and John Seed (London: Routledge, 1992) p. 135.

"Bond's ghastly cannibal heaven . . ." ibid.

"Nothing happens . . ." Julian Mitchell, liner notes to *Arthur Or The Decline And Fall Of The British Empire: 1969*.

"I thought it would be a nice idea . . ." Ray Davies, interviewed by Jerry Gilbert. Press clipping: November 1969.

". . . few found any great merit in 'Plastic Man' . . ." Ray Davies informed Peter Doggett: "The golden age had died by then. We had journalists from the *Observer* over analysing what we were doing. DJs who were getting better than the records they were playing. But it was really a rebellion against commodities, like a first step to '20th Century Man' and then *Preservation*."

"This record has outgrown . . ." Ray Davies, quoted in *Melody Maker*: 12 April 1969.

"It's probably not the greatest song . . ." ibid.

"It's ridiculous . . ." Ray Davies/Boltwood. *Record Mirror*: 29 March 1969.

"I don't know why . . ." Pete Quaife, interviewed by Mike Ledgerwood. *Disc & Music Echo*: April 1969.

"I'm sick of standing onstage . . ." ibid.

"That was his personality . . ." Dave Davies/Rogan. London: 1 March 1996.

"Pete had a big flip out . . ." David Quaife/Rogan. London: 27 February 2013.

"Ultimately, the reasons for Quaife's departure . . .". "It was the infighting the whole time, the drudgery," he recalled to Smith & Orton of *The Official Kinks Fan Club Magazine*. "I was a lowly session musician that's all I was and I didn't like that . . . I wanted to be a part of it and enjoy it and be able to talk about it, and with the Kinks, especially with Ray, you can't talk, there is no way you can, you can't discuss something, he'll take it as a criticism, then he would get angry and everything blows up . . . Ray wouldn't listen to anybody . . . he wanted full control from day one, whatever suggestions anybody came up with were automatically dismissed, which meant he got into a habit of doing that. He dismissed everything, he went his own way, but it was wrong . . . he was treating the whole thing as if it were him personally, he totally forgot behind him was the group."

"Pete Quaife was the true amateur . . ." Ray Davies/McNeill. *New Musical Express*: 16 April 1977.

"It never happened . . ." Dalton/Rogan. Broxbourne, Hertfordshire: 9 October 1994.

"I was so pissed off . . ." John Dalton, interviewed by Russell Smith & Bill Orton. *Bass Lines* booklet: March 1996.

"Learning to drive . . ." Ray Davies/Cavanagh. *Uncut* 163: December 2010.

"He was a nightmare . . ." Rasa Didzpetris/Rogan. London: 4 March 2013.

"I believe that once . . ." Ray Davies, *The Story Of The Kinks*. Original unedited film footage, dated 7 November 1984. Courtesy of Cyriel Van den Hemel.

"It embodied all my thoughts . . ." Ray Davies/Hodgkinson. *Songbook*. Sky Arts: 24 December 2009.

"I tried living . . ." Ray Davies/Cott. *Rolling Stone*: 10 November 1969.

"I'm not laughing . . ." ibid.

"But there's nothing . . ." Ray Davies, interviewed by Ian Middleton. *Record Mirror*: 13 September 1969.

"We got the director . . ." Ray Davies/McNeill. *New Musical Express*: 16 April 1977.

"*Arthur* was designed . . ." Ray Davies, interviewed by Pat Gilbert. *Mojo* 226: September 2012.

"*Arthur* is by all odds . . ." Reviewer Greil Marcus. *Rolling Stone*: 1 November 1969.

"with a very seductive English chick . . ." Internal Memo, undated, from Warner Brothers/Seven Arts' editorial assistant, John Mendelssohn. Oddly, he is called 'Mendelsohn' on the Warners' document.

"Arrange for the group . . ." ibid.

"Davies' lyrics . . ." Review of Fillmore East performance, 17 October 1969. *Billboard*: November 1969.

". . . seemed content to play rhythm guitar . . ." Pete Senoff. *Music Now!*: November 1969. In his book *Kink*, Dave Davies remembers walking off stage midway through a set on the opening night at the Whisky and returning to his hotel. Fortunately, this was not reported in the press. He also claimed that the remaining shows at the Whisky were cancelled. The printed reviews clearly suggest the contrary.

"My dad put his pint down . . ." *The Davies Diaries*. BBC Radio 2: 23 November 2000.

Chapter Twenty-Six: Lola

"I thought maybe I could . . ." Ray Davies, *The Story Of The Kinks*. Original unedited film footage, dated 7 November 1984. Courtesy of Cyriel Van den Hemel.

"I used to take Ray . . ." Ray Davies/Brown. *Without Walls – My Generation: The Kinks*. Channel 4: 18 March 1995.

"Who are they? . . ." John Gosling, interviewed by the author. Berkhamsted, Hertfordshire: 29 July 1982.

"The Kinks! . . ." ibid.

"That was the one they used . . ." ibid.

"panicked . . ." ibid.

"The Kinks from England . . ." Reviewer Peter Crossley. *Winnipeg Free Press*: June 1970.

"That fool will fall in . . ." Ken Jones, interviewed by the author. London: November 1982.

"Ruin and misery . . ." David Frost and Antony Jay, *To England With Love* (London: 1970).

"I had the cameraman . . ." Ray Davies, interviewed by Lon Goddard. *Record Mirror*: 23 July 1970.

"Lola is a real person . . ." Undated press cutting titled 'Will The Real Lola Stand Up?'

"I like writing songs . . ." Ray Davies/Goddard. *Record Mirror*: 23 July 1970.

"I continued to deal with everything . . ." Rasa Didzpetris/Rogan. London: 4 March 2013.

". . . 'Lola' had climbed to number 1 in the *NME* **charts, dislodging Free's 'All Right Now'. . ."** This news was no longer the momentous event it would have been 18 months before. From 1952 to February 1969, the *New Musical Express* had been the country's most influential chart. That era ended on 13 February 1969 when BMRB (British Market Research Bureau) took over the compilation of the charts for the BBC's *Top Of The Pops*. Neither 'Lola' nor indeed Free's 'All Right Now' topped the 'new' chart. The *NME*, in common with other music papers, continued compiling their own charts but they no longer had the influence they'd wielded during the Sixties.

"This is a hijack . . ." Dalton/Rogan. Broxbourne, Hertfordshire: 9 October 1994.

". . . allegedly captioned . . ." I use 'allegedly' as I never located the newspaper article mentioned by Dalton. It may have appeared in a local paper or gossip column.

"Robert Wace phoned . . ." ibid.

"If this was a play for today . . ." Reviewer James Thomas. Press notice: October 1970.

". . . the confusingly titled *Lola Versus Powerman And The Moneygoround Part One* **. . ."** As with *The Kinks Are The Village Green Preservation Society* it has never been entirely clear whether 'Kinks' was part of the title or not. The album was alternately known (especially on CD release) as *Kinks Part One Lola Versus Powerman And The Money-goround*, which makes less sense. The cover artwork hardly helps to resolve the issue with its puzzling layout in which even the word 'Powerman' is detached from the main title. At least the name 'Kinks' is in purple and the remainder in black lettering which suggests that the group name was not part of the title.

"... standard publishing procedure ..." Page/Rogan. London: 7 August 1982.

"I didn't see the funny side ..." Wace/Rogan. London: 25 June 1983.

"I was messing around ..." Dave Davies/Rogan. London: 1 March 1996.

"I think that Ray would admit ..." Dave Davies/Doggett. *Record Collector* 200: April 1996.

"I'm so used to being in the collaborative mode ..." Dave Davies/Rogan. London: 1 March 1996.

"I don't really like flying ..." Ray Davies, uncredited interview in *Melody Maker*: 26 December 1970.

Chapter Twenty-Seven: Morte D'Arthur

"To this day ..." Ray Davies/Green. *New Musical Express*: 20 February 1971.

"That's where I fall down ..." Ray Davies, interviewed by Scott Cohen. *Circus*: 1974.

"We had 'Lola' ..." Ray Davies, interviewed by Andrew Tyler. *New Musical Express*: 13 October 1973.

"I did the film ..." ibid.

"Dave just stepped out ..." Ray Davies/Small. *People Magazine* Vol. 28, issue 1: 6 July 1987.

"Ray was out of it ..." Dave Davies/Doggett. *Mojo* 111: February 2003.

"I realized then ..." Ray Davies, interviewed by Michelle Hush. Undated press cutting.

"above average band" ... "bankruptcy of British middle class" ... "smoking marijuana ..." Reviewer Mike Jahn. *New York Times*: 1 April 1971.

"Let's open the show ..." Dalton/Rogan. Hoddesdon, Hertfordshire: 4 August 1982.

"We thought he was joking ..." ibid.

"It's so emotional ..." Ray Davies/Small. *People Magazine* Vol. 28, issue 1: 6 July 1987.

"He had an affair ..." Rasa Didzpetris/Rogan. London: 4 March 2013.

'Pop Star Attacks Air Hostess' *Truth* [Melbourne]: 5 June 1971.

"I loved that album ..." Ray Davies/Tamarkin. *The Aquarian/Manhattan*: 7–14 October 1981.

"We played in an open-air swimming pool ..." Gosling/Rogan. Berkhamsted, Hertfordshire: 29 July 1982.

"It was quite difficult on holiday ..." Rasa Didzpetris/Rogan. London: 4 March 2013.

"'Deep interrogation ...'" Graham Greene letter to *The Times*, reprinted in *New York Times*: 12 December 1971.

"I don't know which side ..." Ray Davies, quoted in Robin Denselow *When The Music's Over* (London: Faber & Faber, 1989), p. 95.

"We consciously kept out of politics ..." Pete Townshend, quoted in Robin Denselow *When The Music's Over* (London: Faber & Faber, 1989), p. 97.

"This is a triumphant day ..." Ken Glancy, RCA official statement on signing the Kinks: 12 November 1971.

"I always wanted ..." Ray Davies, comment on signing to RCA. London: 12 November 1971.

"It was very much based . . ." Dave Davies/Rogan. London/Cornwall: 3 October 2012.

"There are all these people . . ." Ray Davies/Schacht. *Circus*: February 1972.

"My gran used to live . . ." ibid.

"She used to be . . ." ibid.

". . . the Cockettes, whose camp cavorting . . ." The *NME*'s John Wells, recalling the lavish launch, noted: "The more liberal might have called it a raving transvestites/homosexuals/sex maniacs jamboree. I'm not sure what the hell it was." As for the Cockettes, Wells revealed that they were "a group of female impersonators", currently appearing in *Pearls Before Shanghai* at Broadway's Anderson Theatre. "Whether they were genuine transvestites or simply out to shock I hadn't the stomach to find out."

Chapter Twenty-Eight: Changes

". . . manage his wife's estate . . ." Talmy/Rogan. London: 17 September 1982.

"I spent a lot of time . . ." Dave Davies/Rogan. London/Cornwall: 3 October 2012. Dave adds: "Yoga and magic were amazing. Then I came across Dion Fortune, a wonderful mystic and cabbalist and occultist. She lived at the bottom of Glastonbury Tor and had a little cottage there. I was mesmerized by her writings. That brought me into the Eastern teachings. From a mystical standpoint, I was just learning about occultism, mystical stuff and yoga, tarot and astrology."

"We were presented . . ." Gosling/Rogan. Berkhamsted, Hertfordshire: 29 July 1982.

"The Kinks as a group . . ." Wace/Rogan. London: 15 October 1982.

"I don't know how . . ." Ray Davies, interviewed by Lisa Robinson: *Disc*: 15 April 1972.

"I'm in a business . . ." ibid.

"It's like we died in 1972 . . ." Dave Davies/Rogan. London/Cornwall: 3 October 2012.

"All the Warhol people . . ." Peter Doggett, liner notes to 1998 CD edition of *Everybody's In Showbiz, Everybody's A Star* (Velvel 63467-79720-2).

"Are you married?" . . . "Everybody *was* married . . ." Ray Davies, interviewed by Candy Darling, Tinkerbelle and Glenn O'Brien. *Andy Warhol's Interview*: January 1973.

"I got my payback . . ." Davies spoke about the 'Candy Darling' encounter in several interviews during the Seventies and later, including 1995's filmed *The World Of Ray Davies And The Kinks*. Some commentators have mistakenly assumed that the song might have been inspired by the meeting, but it was written long before Davies had even heard of Candy Darling.

"Dave Davies fleeing in terror . . ." Gosling/Rogan. Berkhamsted, Hertfordshire: 29 July 1982.

"Ray, in an ill-fitting green satin jacket . . ." Review of Hollywood Palladium show (9 March), press cutting dated: 25 March 1972.

"Ray started singing it . . ." Beecham/Rogan. London/Weston-super-Mare, north Somerset: 2 June 2014.

"From the start . . ." Greg Shaw, review of the Berkeley Community Theatre show: 27 February 1972.

"I'm not necessarily drunk . . ." Ray Davies, interviewed by Lisa Robinson: *Disc*: 22 April 1972.

"I didn't think the brass was right . . ." Gosling/Rogan. Berkhamsted, Hertfordshire: 29

July 1982. "I agree, quite honestly," John Beecham adds, when confronted with Gosling's words. "I thought what Ray did with horns on the original material was interesting and I thoroughly enjoyed playing, but to add horns on to 'You Really Got Me' was not just gilding the lily but superfluous to requirements. I think at the time Ray felt we ought to be onstage for it."

"The personal motivation . . ." Wace/Rogan. London: 25 June 1983.

"It was an absolute joke . . ." Ray Davies/Tyler. *New Musical Express*: 20 October 1973.

"I think life is a series of peaks . . ." Ray Davies/Lisa Robinson: *Disc*: 22 April 1972.

". . . their own show in New York's Central Park . . ." John Beecham has fond memories of this show. "I'd never been in Central Park before and had never seen anything like it. I have a photograph of us rehearsing in the afternoon, then we went along in the evening to play the concert. Touring America in those days was more like being in Germany. The people were surprisingly upfront. I loved that you could walk through the lobby late at night and there'd be all these Kinks fans there. These people knew each other, not because they all lived in the same part of New York or New Jersey but because they were Kinks fans who were used to hanging around lobbies or at stage doors. That was something I don't remember seeing in the UK. In the 1964 period, we got chased and screamed at simply because we were on the show, but that loyalty was quite moving." Beecham/Rogan. London/Weston-super-Mare, north Somerset: 2 June 2014.

". . . I'm mentally too strong . . ." *Imaginary Man* documentary. Broadcast BBC 1: 21 December 2010.

"I want to jump . . ." Dave Davies/Rogan. London: 1 March 1996.

"It was a revolving stage . . ." Ray Davies, interviewed by Austin Scaggs. *Rolling Stone*: 23 February 2006.

"I was asking . . ." Dave Davies/Rogan. London/Cornwall: 3 October 2012.

"I've spoken to my sisters . . ." ibid.

"It's by no means a dictatorship . . ." Dave Davies, interviewed by Julie Webb. *New Musical Express*: 8 July 1972.

"I shot the film . . ." Ray Davies, *The Story Of The Kinks*. Original unedited film footage, dated 7 November 1984. Courtesy of Cyriel Van den Hemel.

"It would be great . . ." ibid.

"I treated . . ." ibid.

"No one . . ." Review of *Everybody's In Showbiz, Everybody's A Star. Melody Maker*: 5 August 1972.

"The opening 'Here Comes Yet Another Day' . . ." John Beecham remembers saying to Dave at the playback: "This sounds like the Band – with quirky horns!" He adds: "If anyone is interested in what Ray Davies could do with a horn section, check out 'Maximum Consumption' on *Everybody's In Showbiz*. It's full of the bluesy licks that horn players love to play – and at the end of the chorus he had me playing an ascending figure alternating between tuba and trombone."

"*Everybody's In Show-biz* is abysmal . . ." Reviewer Mike Saunders. *Us* magazine: 1972.

". . . *The Great Lost Kinks Album*, featuring several solo demos and leftover tracks . . ." Among the rarities was 'Lavender Hill' which Davies described as "a complete piss-take about the hippies. Sometimes, to ease the tension in the studio, I used to present horrible material and see how long everyone could keep a straight face. I tried putting in as many production clichés and as much grotesque instrumentation as I could think of, and some studio people actually thought I was being imaginative. Hearing it now makes me melt with shame. There are a few good moments, though. Even this debacle had sincere beginnings – 'lavender memories' . . ."

Chapter Twenty-Nine: The Leaving Of Rasa

"**The classic thing** . . ." Ray Davies, interviewed by Fred Schruers. *Rolling Stone*: 2 November 1978.

"**We were rowing** . . ." Rasa Didzpetris/Rogan. London: 4 March 2013.

"**I just wanted** . . ." ibid.

"**When I lived in Los Angeles** . . ." Ray Davies, interviewed by Alan de Perna. *Guitar World*: January 1997.

"**They took this girl** . . ." Victor Bockris, *NYC Babylon, From Beat To Punk* (London: Omnibus, 1998), p. 207. Bockris doesn't confirm who the roadies represented. It is quite likely that there were hangers-on from other bands staying at the same hotel where this event occurred. That said, later backing singer Shirlie Roden told me: "They used to have this photograph album at Konk of these groupies which we had a glimpse of. The groupie stuff was really quite sordid. They always made sure that wedding rings on hands in the wrong places were obliterated."

"**That's how I got to know him** . . ." Rasa Didzpetris/Rogan. London: 4 March 2013.

"**If something good happens** . . ." Dave Davies, interviewed on *The World Of Ray Davies And The Kinks: I'm Not Like Everybody Else*. Broadcast BBC 2: 21 December 1995.

"**. . . an extension and modification** . . ." Ray Davies/Tyler. *New Musical Express*: 20 October 1973.

"**I wanted us to have a career** . . ." Dave Davies/Rogan. London: 1 March 1996.

"**I said, 'Oh my God** . . .'" Rasa Didzpetris/Rogan. London: 4 March 2013.

"**What?!** . . ." ibid.

"**I had one bag** . . ." ibid.

"**. . . a sad lost child** . . ." Dave Davies/Rogan. London: 1 March 1996.

"**I couldn't blame her** . . ." Dave Davies/Hardy. *Daily Mail*: 30 October 2010.

"**I agree, in retrospect** . . ." Rasa Didzpetris, letter from London, SE25. *Daily Mail*: 23 February 1996.

"**The decision that I made** . . ." Rasa Didzpetris/Rogan. London: 4 March 2013.

"**I advertised my car** . . ." Rasa Didzpetris, email to author: 5 March 2013.

"**They tried to persuade me** . . ." ibid.

"**. . . taken to a nearby hospital to have his stomach pumped** . . ." This 'first overdose' was underplayed in later years. Even Dave Davies made no mention of it in any interview or biography. The original source of the story was a reference on the front page of *Sounds* on 21 July 1973. The 'first overdose' was also mentioned in Jon Savage's 'official biography', albeit without a supporting quote from anybody. Ray Davies' *X-Ray* elaborates on the story at greater length and he also refers to it in *Americana*.

"**Have you heard** . . ." Reported by Roy Hollingworth. *Melody Maker*: 21 July 1973.

"**He's in a dreadful state** . . ." ibid.

"**They could be dead** . . ." ibid.

"The White City gig was terrible . . ." Dave Davies, *Kronikles: Mystical Journey* DVD; detune films: 2009.

"I'm sick up to here . . ." Reported by Roy Hollingworth. *Melody Maker*: 21 July 1973.

"This is goodbye forever . . ." Reported by Jerry Gilbert. *Sounds*: 21 July 1973.

"The Kinks are dead . . ." Reported by Roy Hollingworth. *Melody Maker*: 21 July 1973.

"If you are going to go . . ." ibid.

"One has to understand . . ." Marion Rainford, quoted in news section ('Upset' Davies Quits Onstage'). *New Musical Express*: 21 July 1973. Included in the statement were the words "And don't forget Rasa had a nervous breakdown . . . and Ray knows all about nervous breakdowns." There is no evidence that Rasa ever had a breakdown. It is not mentioned in any of Davies' writings nor in any interview with him or anybody else. "No, I never had a breakdown," she confirms, puzzled by the suggestion.

"The doctor gave me pills . . ." Ray Davies/Paytress. *Mojo* 148: March 2006.

"It was funny . . ." Ray Davies, interviewed by Chris George: *Independent*: 27 August 1994.

"I'd taken a whole bottle . . . 15,000 people . . ." Ray Davies/Paytress. *Mojo* 148: March 2006. Or 30,000 or 10,000 – reports of the crowd size vary.

". . . a pathetic sad lost boy . . ." Dave Davies/Rogan. London: 1 March 1996.

"I did try to kill myself . . ." Ray Davies in Jon Savage, *The Kinks: The Official Biography* (London: Faber & Faber, 1984), p. 129.

"I was emotionally run down . . ." Ray Davies/Silverton. *RX*: 23 November 1997.

"I *was* going to give it up . . ." Ray Davies, interviewed by Tom Ward and Mike Hammer. *RockBill*: May 1988.

"It was a funny atmosphere . . ." Gosling/Rogan. Berkhamsted, Hertfordshire: 29 July 1982.

"Several weeks ago . . ." News Desk feature titled 'Kinks Resume British Dates But Ray Davies Hints At Upcoming Changes'. *New Musical Express*: 1 September 1973.

"There was stuff . . ." Rasa Didzpetris/Rogan. London: 4 March 2013.

"I felt so guilty . . ." Rasa Didzpetris, email to author: 5 March 2013.

"I think when Rasa left . . ." Dave Davies, *Kronikles: Mystical Journey* DVD; detune films: 2009.

"Then I get up again . . ." Ray Davies/Tyler. *New Musical Express*: 20 October 1973.

"It didn't run up massive sales . . ." Ray Davies, interviewed by James Johnson. *New Musical Express*: 11 May 1974.

"I can remember . . ." Dalton/Rosser. Unedited interview despatched to author: 30 November 2005.

Chapter Thirty: Divorce And Preservation

". . . willingness to consider any new project . . ." At one point, Davies had been approached to play the lead part in a drama based on the life of the aesthete Aubrey Beardsley. There was further talk of a television play inspired by *Muswell Hillbillies* with a revamped treatment centring on a schizophrenic country & Irish singer resident in Camden, who falls victim to his stage persona and ends up in a *High Chaparral*-style shoot-out with London policemen.

"All these people were backstage . . ." Gosling/Rogan. Berkhamsted, Hertfordshire: 29 July 1982.

"Ray used the services of a detective agency . . ." Rasa Didzpetris, email to author: 5 March 2013.

"He had the shock of his life . . ." ibid.

"That's the sum my solicitors had suggested . . ." Rasa Didzpetris/Rogan. London: 4 March 2013.

"That's Ray, isn't it? . . ." ibid.

"One of the girls said . . ." ibid.

"It was only later on . . ." ibid.

"Oh for goodness sake . . ." ibid.

"The divorce was awful . . ." ibid.

"Mrs D was OK . . ." ibid.

"The plot's obvious . . ." Reviewer Ian MacDonald. *New Musical Express*: 3 August 1974.

"A lot of people . . ." Ray Davies, interviewed by Allan Jones. *Melody Maker*: 21 September 1974. Text revised/rewritten for *Uncut: The Kinks The Ultimate Music Guide* issue 12 (undated).

". . . *Starmaker* was screened nationally . . ." Nine songs were broadcast on *Starmaker*: 'Starmaker', 'Ordinary People', 'Rush Hour Blues', 'Nine To Five', 'When Work Is Over', 'Have Another Drink', 'You Make It All Worthwhile', '(A) Face In The Crowd' and 'You Can't Stop The Music'. The subsequent album, *Soap Opera*, featured all of the above, plus 'Holiday Romance', 'Underneath The Neon Sign' and 'Ducks On The Wall'.

". . . his brother's 'vampiric' intensity . . ." Shirlie Roden counters: "Well Dave vampires as well in his own way. Dave vampires with his excesses because he drains you with his excessive behaviour. You can't control him. He just goes completely mad. And that, in a way, is attention seeking and vampiric energy, but he doesn't see that."

"He said to me . . ." Dave Davies/Paytress. *Mojo* 148: March 2006.

"I wanted to be anonymous . . ." Ray Davies/Rogan. London: 1 October 2013.

"People are different . . ." Dave Davies/Rogan. London/Cornwall: 3 October 2012.

"Yvonne and I . . ." ibid.

"Lisbet and Yvonne . . ." ibid.

". . . tolerate each other . . ." ibid.

"If Ray was . . ." ibid. Davies used the same words in his autobiography and in his interview with Peter Doggett in *Record Collector*.

"I'm looking for a star . . ." Shirlie Roden, interviewed by the author. London: 16 January 2014.

"I got on fine . . ." ibid.

"There were lots of restrictions . . ." ibid.

"We were constantly running . . ." ibid.

"The first night . . ." ibid.

"When are you going to grow up? . . ." ibid.

"I was born grown up . . ." ibid.

"While I just got on with Ray . . ." ibid.

"Baptist seemed to take an instant dislike . . ." Debi Doss, interviewed by the author. Walton-on-Thames, Surrey: 23 January 2014.

"Baptist was so rude to Debi . . ." Roden/Rogan. London: 16 January 2014.

"From day one . . ." Doss/Rogan. Walton-on-Thames, Surrey: 23 January 2014.

"It was an amazing experience . . ." Roden/Rogan. London: 16 January 2014.

"Take the rest of the evening . . ." Quote recollected by Debi Doss. Doss/Rogan. Walton-on-Thames, Surrey: 23 January 2014.

"Only members . . ." Quote recollected by Shirlie Roden. Roden/Rogan. London: 16 January 2014.

". . . concluded the US tour with shows in St Louis, Chicago . . ." By the time they reached Chicago, the theatrical aspects were in greater evidence. During 'Money & Corruption' pictures of leading political figures were flashed on the screen followed by an image of Ray in his Mr Black disguise. With Dave Davies striking up the chords of 'Here Comes Flash', backed by the full chorus, Ray appeared in his Mr Flash outfit, followed by his cronies Mr Twitch (Dave), Mr Lugs/Big Knob (John Dalton) and Big Ron (Mick Avory). During Flash's assault on society various landmarks were projected on the backdrop including the Empire State Building and the White House. Another clever touch was the inclusion of Victorian pornographic photos during the puritanical tirade, 'Shepherds Of The Nation'. The Kinks also included a new song, 'Slum Kids', backed by a film showing scenes of poverty in contemporary Britain.

"They liked to drink . . ." Roden/Rogan. London: 16 January 2014.

"Ray was reading . . ." ibid.

"It has been an uphill struggle . . ." Reviewer Robin Denselow. *Guardian*: 23 December 1974. John Beecham was also impressed by Ray Davies' commitment during the *Preservation* shows. "I knew that Ray was in charge and everybody followed his lead, but what he took on was quite remarkable. That's what I admire. Whether the music was approachable or not, whether it was a success or a failure, it was an achievement in itself. Why would anybody want to take that on unless they were driven by what they wanted to do? I suppose the answer is he wanted to do it – and he did do it . . . The one thing that I thought was awkward was when *Preservation* started on stage and the two male singers came on singing 'Daylight' and they were standing in front of Dave Davies. I didn't feel comfortable with that. This was the Kinks. What's Dave doing standing behind somebody?" Beecham/Rogan. London/Weston-super-Mare, north Somerset: 2 June 2014.

"They all jumped . . ." Roden/Rogan. London: 16 January 2014.

"Dave was tormented . . ." ibid.

"Dave got really angry . . ." ibid.

"All the lads . . ." ibid.

"I think Ray likes . . ." Doss/Rogan. Walton-on-Thames, Surrey: 23 January 2014.

"I really liked Yvonne . . ." Beecham/Rogan. London/Weston-super-Mare, north Somerset: 2 June 2014.

"Yvonne was lovely . . ." Roden/Rogan. London: 16 January 2014.

"I don't think . . ." ibid.

"In May 1975, the album *Soap Opera* was released . . ." Once again, the actual title of the album was not entirely clear. On the cover it says '*The Kinks present a Soap Opera featuring Norman and the Starmaker*'. The words *Soap Opera* appear solely in large type.

"It's a step . . ." Ray Davies, interviewed by Barbara Charone. *Sounds*: 7 June 1975.

"I didn't think . . ." Dalton/Smith & Orton. *Bass Lines* booklet: March 1996. John Beecham offers an alternative view: "There were a lot of Kinks fans and perhaps members of the Kinks themselves who were a bit surprised but at least he *did* involve his band. He could have gone away and done that with a bunch of actors and strangers."

"Ray was always trying . . ." Wace/Rogan. London: 25 June 1983.

"We kept in touch . . ." Ray Davies, interviewed by Dan DeLuca. *Philadelphia Enquirer*: 24 October 1996.

"Especially in Britain . . ." Ray Davies/Doggett, original, pre-edited notes to the CD box set *Picture Book*: 2008. Courtesy of author.

"*The Kinks Present Schoolboys In Disgrace* . . ." This was the full title of the album, both on the front cover and the vinyl label.

". . . 'Jack The Idiot Dunce' . . ." Recalling the genesis of the song, Ray reveals: "It was based on a real person in England who failed all his entrance exams but didn't try to commit suicide – he just got kicked out of home. I was amazed when I heard that; I didn't think people did that any more. He turned up at a relative's house. He said: 'Can I stay here? My father's thrown me out.' Like Victorian times. His father had big ambitions for him and he just didn't make it. The guy was a dummy in school but ended up a rock 'n' roll dancer and a world famous *character*."

"Harder! Harder! . . ." Doss/Rogan. Walton-on-Thames, Surrey: 23 January 2014.

"Pam had this . . ." Roden/Rogan. London: 16 January 2014.

"It was choreography . . ." Doss/Rogan. Walton-on-Thames, Surrey: 23 January 2014.

"I thought it was all bizarre . . ." Roden/Rogan. London: 16 January 2014.

". . . Steve Harley's Cockney Rebel . . ." In various profiles, it has been erroneously stated that Steve Harley is Ray Davies' cousin. "I don't believe so," Ray cautiously told me in 2013, "but there is a part of the family in Hertfordshire. Not direct cousins, but second cousins that probably married someone. I'm not sure. I can't state categorically, but it's been raised in the past. I don't know the direct bloodline." Further research confirms that Harley has no blood relation to the Davies clan. Steve Harley's aunt Olive is the mother of Tony Palmer's wife Jackie. Tony's uncle, Ken Palmer, is married to Joyce Davies, sister of Ray and Dave. That is the extent of the tenuous link.

"You're not to go out . . ." Quote recollected by Shirlie Roden. Roden/Rogan. London: 16 January 2014.

"Ray didn't want to buy us a drink . . ." Roden/Rogan. London: 16 January 2014.

"We used to call Ray . . ." ibid.

"Ray's a strange man . . ." ibid.

"Part of his manipulation . . ." ibid.

"a lot of animosity . . ." Phil May, quoted in Alan Lakey *The Pretty Things: Growing Old Disgracefully* (London: Firefly Publishing, 2002), p. 140.

"Davies would get his manager . . ." ibid.

"The dressing up was good fun . . ." Gosling/Rogan. Berkhamsted: 29 July 1982. Gosling appears to be referring to the final *Preservation* shows in the latter part of this quote.

"In a way . . ." Ray Davies, interviewed by Rosalind Russell. *Record Mirror & Disc*: 7 February 1976.

Chapter Thirty-One: The Return Of Violence

"Arista seems to be . . ." Davies added a witty anecdote: "This all came about because Clive Davis, Elliot Goldman and myself were having lunch. I was having a simultaneous conversation with both Clive and Elliot – Clive asked me if I wanted to sign the contract and Elliot asked me if I wanted any tossed salad. I said, 'yes'. As a result, I have made my first and only decision of 1976. I met Clive Davis on two or three occasions during our career and always felt that some phase of our recording career would be spent with his company." Davis responded with a painfully tautological comment: "I couldn't be happier that they've chosen Arista as their new home and am confident that the future of the Kinks lies very much in front of them."

"I told Ray first . . ." Dalton/Smith & Orton. *Bass Lines* booklet: March 1996.

"I had all these promises . . ." Dalton/Rosser. Unedited interview despatched to author: 30 November 2005. Dalton's testimony requires slight modification. Mick Avory was still a partner in the Kinks' enterprise and was thus on a higher income than the subsidiary members. There is no evidence that he was ever "on the breadline", or anything similar.

"I wouldn't have been able . . ." ibid.

"Ray would say, 'Go on . . .'" Andy Pyle, interviewed by the author. Tring, Hertfordshire: August 1982.

"I couldn't understand why . . ." ibid.

"He didn't realize . . ." Nick Trevisick, interviewed by the author. London: July 1982.

"I was in the middle . . ." ibid.

"Davies couldn't run a luggage label . . ." John McCoy, quoted in *National Rock Star*: 18 December 1976.

"When you get involved . . ." Ray Davies, *The Story Of The Kinks*. Original unedited film footage, dated 7 November 1984. Courtesy of Cyriel Van den Hemel.

"In February 1977, the Kinks released *Sleepwalker* . . ." Considering the time and effort expended in production, one might reasonably have expected a work of lyrical density and musical complexity. Instead, Davies favoured commercial minimalism. "Basically, I've tried to say something in one line and then use the next three for repetition instead of using four lines and saying something different in every one." As a result, several of the songs were lyrically sparse. There was nothing here that came close to equalling his finest work, though perhaps that was too much to ask for a decade on. Most fans and critics were pleased enough to see the group working as a streamlined unit once more, devoid of the brass players and backing singers. The Kinks were back, but this was not the group that so many had loved during the Sixties.

"It's about a vampire . . ." Ray Davies, interviewed by Paul Nelson. *Rolling Stone*: 24 March 1977.

"There wasn't the commitment . . ." Extract from Arista Records press release: May 1978.

"You'll find out . . ." Pyle/Rogan. Tring, Hertfordshire: August 1982.

"My time came in Chicago . . ." ibid.

"Andy Pyle, bless him . . ." Roden/Rogan. London: 16 January 2014.

"You can have all this chaos . . ." Pyle/Rogan. Tring, Hertfordshire: August 1982.

"Andy was terribly upset . . ." Roden/Rogan. London: 16 January 2014.

"I remember Dave . . ." ibid.

". . . *Saturday Night Live* . . ." The show was good news for the Kinks. As John Beecham recalls: "Ken Jones said, 'We're not staying in the Warwick Hotel, we're staying in the Plaza. There's no per diem, you sign for everything because the TV company's paying for it tonight.' So I had a slap up dinner in my room!"

". . . the pits of mediocrity . . ." Reviewer Nick Kent. *New Musical Express*: 2 April 1977.

"Davies' oafish self-satisfied clowning . . ." ibid.

"When a band . . ." ibid.

"Well, it's not new . . ." Ray Davies, interviewed by David Brown. Article titled 'Dreaming On A Sleeping Afternoon'. *Record Mirror*: 9 April 1977.

"He's a cunt . . ." ibid.

"If Sid Vicious ever came up to me . . ." Ray Davies/Ward & Hammer. *RockBill*: May 1988.

"At the end of the show . . ." Ray Davies/Larkin. *Dark Star* 21: July 1979.

"We had fights onstage . . ." Gosling/Rogan. Berkhamsted, Hertfordshire: 29 July 1982.

"I was bored . . ." Roden/Rogan. London: 16 January 2014.

"I needed to grow . . ." ibid.

"If you leave . . ." ibid.

"Ray wouldn't say goodbye . . ." ibid.

". . . Doss was instructed to find a replacement, Kim Goody . . ." Goody undertook some European dates but was not available for the forthcoming tours of America where Kendrick appeared. Goody returned for the year-end concert at London's Rainbow Theatre.

"They're not only over the hill . . ." Review of 'Pink Pop Festival'. *Sounds*: 11 June 1977.

"In tandem with Ray . . ." Pyle/Rogan. Tring, Hertfordshire: August 1982.

"We had some fun . . ." ibid.

"Every tour was Mick's last tour . . ." ibid.

"I said, 'Let's be the best . . .'" ibid.

"Mick was a bit disillusioned . . ." Trevisick/Rogan. London: July 1982.

"I suddenly realized . . ." Pyle/Rogan. Tring, Hertfordshire: August 1982.

"They were my mates . . ." ibid.

"What you get depends . . ." ibid.

"The whole evening . . ." Reviewer Tony Stewart. *New Musical Express*: 30 December 1977.

"You could say it was the last gig . . ." Ray Davies, interviewed by Tony Stewart. *New Musical Express*: 24 June 1978.

Chapter Thirty-Two: Mr Misfit

"Ray knew what he wanted . . ." Gosling/Rogan. Berkhamsted, Hertfordshire: 29 July 1982.

"We did that song . . ." ibid.

"In the end . . ." ibid.

"This isn't the Kinks . . ." ibid.

"I left the Kinks . . ." John Gosling, letter to *Record Collector* 346: February 2008.

"I'm not saying . . ." Ray Davies/Stewart. *New Musical Express*: 24 June 1978.

"He was a genuine rock star . . ." Ray Davies/Rogan. London: 1 October 2013.

"As we're an English band . . ." Ray Davies, press apology following show cancellations: April 1978.

"Interest in London . . ." Andrew Bailey, Arista Records internal memo: 27 April 1978.

"As discovered in the past . . ." Arista Records, internal memo from Andrew Bailey to Charles Levison: 1 May 1978.

"That is what we must get over . . ." Andrew Bailey, Arista Records internal memo: 27 April 1978.

"A posse of students . . ." ibid.

"Mr Misfit is really Ray Davies . . ." Arista Records, internal memo from Andrew Bailey to Charles Levison: 1 May 1978.

"The existence of Mr Misfit . . ." ibid.

"a synagogue cantor's son . . ." Ray Davies, *Americana: The Kinks, The Road And The Perfect Riff* (London: Virgin Books, 2013), p. 157.

"What can you say . . ." John Lydon, reviewing the Kinks' 'Live Life'. *New Musical Express*: 22 July 1978.

". . . a second rate heavy-metal band . . ." Reviewer Graham Lock. *New Musical Express*: 7 October 1978.

". . . a travesty of rock 'n' roll . . ." ibid.

"I relate it a lot to sport . . ." Rodford/Rogan. St Albans, Hertfordshire: 21 May 2014.

"I wouldn't want to destroy him . . ." Ray Davies, interviewed by Ira Kaplan. *Soho Weekly News*: 15 June 1978.

"The animosity had been building up . . ." Gordon Edwards, interviewed by Terry Coates: 7 January 1995. Published in *S.F. Sorrow* 67: 1996.

"I was only using . . ." ibid.

"Nothing's ever said . . ." Rodford/Rogan. St Albans, Hertfordshire: 21 May 2014.

"Could you make it . . ." ibid.

"Do you mean that? . . ." ibid.

"That's how Ray operates . . ." ibid.

"She tried to meet me . . ." Ray Davies, quoted in John Mendelssohn, *The Kinks Kronikles* (New York: Quill, 1985), p. 188.

"I really felt a lot . . ." Edwards/Coates. *S.F. Sorrow* 67: 1996.

"That was one of the happiest periods . . ." Ray Davies/Paytress. *Mojo* 148: March 2006.

"I thought if people get . . ." Ray Davies, interviewed by Ed Sciaky for *The Low Budget Interview* disc: July 1979.

"It was a curious time . . ." Ray Davies/Pat Gilbert. *Mojo* 226: September 2012.

"It was a Saturday . . ." Ian Gibbons, interviewed by the author. London: 4 July 1994.

"That was a fantastic period . . ." Rodford/Rogan. St Albans, Hertfordshire: 21 May 2014.

"the first great Kinks album" . . . "a miracle . . ." Reviewer Charles Shaar Murray. *New Musical Express*: 8 September 1979.

"I was a socialist . . ." Ray Davies, interviewed by Charles Shaar Murray. *New Musical Express*: 6 October 1979.

"I'm not really extreme . . ." ibid.

"I've never been into the celebrity trip . . ." Ray Davies, interviewed by Charles Catchpole. *Daily Mail*: 7 August 1980.

"Maybe that's why I was a bad husband . . ." Ray Davies/Rogan. London: 1 October 2013.

"This sounds daffy . . ." Ray Davies/Small. *People Magazine* Vol. 28, issue 1: 6 July 1987.

"He wanted to make the ultimate heavy metal album . . ." Trevisick/Rogan. London: July 1982.

"It was surreal . . ." Gibbons/Rogan. London: 4 July 1994.

"I think it's a good record . . ." Ray Davies, relating the story of the French journalist to Ken Sharp. *Goldmine*: March 1996.

"I felt cheated . . ." Ray Davies. 'The Inspiration'. *Independent*: 7 December 2010.

"I lit a candle . . ." Ray Davies/Sharp. *Goldmine*: March 1996.

"They seemed paranoid . . ." Donnie Burke, interviewed by the author. London: 4 November 1982. Burke's spiky account was partly supported by a contemporaneous review of the show at the Apollo Theatre, Victoria, 14 December 1980. *Melody Maker*'s Karl Dallas dared compare the Gas with the old Kinks noting, "It was rather like comparing the High Numbers with the parody on their lifestyle that was the *Quadrophenia* movie. One is more polished, but there's no doubt which is the original article. I mean Ray Davies must be all of thirty-six, if he's a day, and here he is carrying on like a nineteen-year-old . . . Ray seemed to be enjoying himself, but there were some strange vibes going down between Dave and he – but then, aren't there always?"

"They should have stopped . . ." ibid.

"I was visualizing all the people . . ." John Lennon. RKO Radio: 8 December 1980.

Chapter Thirty-Three: *State Of Confusion*

"I think people should . . ." Ray Davies, interviewed by Anne Nightingale. *Daily Express*: 5 November 1981.

"That's just like putting on make-up . . ." Barrie Keeffe, interviewed by Sandy Craig. *Time Out*: 3 April 1978.

"Davies . . . managed to complete 12 songs . . ." See 'Unreleased Compositions at the end of the Discography for the full listing.

"I saw his parents . . ." Ray Davies/Tamarkin. *The Aquarian/Manhattan*: 7–14 October 1981.

". . . did not appear in Britain until the following January . . ." Bizarrely, review copies had been sent out to the British press in September 1981 and there was no indication of any likely delay. It was reviewed in the *Guardian* in the autumn, for instance. Subsequently, there were suggestions that extra tracks were to be added, but the later version was identical. The *Guardian* reviewed the album again on New Year's Day 1982 with the amusing caveat, "apologies to those who tried to buy the album last time I reviewed it."

"I used to live . . ." Ray Davies/Tamarkin. *The Aquarian/Manhattan*: 7–14 October 1981.

"I run in Regent's Park . . ." ibid.

"The children *were* able to see Ray . . ." Rasa Didzpetris, email to author: 16 June 2013.

"I feel that . . ." Ray Davies/Small. *People Magazine* Vol. 28, issue 1: 6 July 1987.

"You must never . . ." Ray Davies in Jon Savage, *The Kinks: The Official Biography* (London: Faber & Faber, 1984), p. 159.

"Obviously, I'm besotted . . ." Chrissie Hynde, quoted in *Evening Standard*: 14 December 1981.

"Ray and Chrissie bought a house . . ." Dave Davies/Rogan. London: 1 March 1996.

"I went upstairs into the attic . . ." press cutting on Davies/Hynde relationship: undated.

"I got a phone call from Peggy . . ." Dave Davies/Rogan. London/Cornwall: 3 October 2012.

"They got on well . . ." ibid.

". . . brought me and Ray . . ." ibid.

"We asked him to come . . ." Ray Davies, interviewed by George Kalogerakis. *Musician*: March 1990.

"He was a bit of a storyteller . . ." Gibbons/Rogan. London: 4 July 1994.

"I sat opposite this man . . ." Reviewer Ken Gurguson, 'Box View' article: undated.

". . . visited by five 'intelligences' . . ." A full account of Dave Davies' 'visitation' and its significance on his life and belief systems is featured in his autobiography *Kink* (London: Boxtree, 1996), page 209 ff.

". . . we talked some more . . ." Ray Davies, quoted in the *Sun*: 12 August 1983.

"The registrar wouldn't marry us . . ." ibid.

"Now we've decided . . ." ibid.

"It wasn't through . . ." Ray Davies/George. *Independent*: 27 August 1994.

"If you care . . ." Ray Davies/Schruers. *Rolling Stone*: 4 February 1982.

"There was conflict . . ." Gibbons/Rogan. London: 4 July 1994.

"Dave wanted to be as far away . . ." ibid.

"I don't like working with him . . ." Ray Davies, *The Story Of The Kinks*. Original unedited film footage, dated 7 November 1984. Courtesy of Cyriel Van den Hemel.

"A winsome evocation . . ." Davies later explained to Alan de Perna (*Guitar World*: January 1997): "I just wanted the record to be a little tribute to my sisters, who were big fans of the dance halls. It was inspired by a photograph that my sister showed me of her dancing at the local hop on Saturday night. It's just about her and her husband." In a later interview with the BBC's Johnnie Walker, Davies added: "I got the characterization right. It wasn't like 'You Really Got Me', it was an energy that was based on being young and wanting to punch your way out into the world . . . an arrival song. I remember typing out the lyrics, first draft, I didn't really do any rewrites."

"What chance has he got . . ." Ray Davies, interviewed by Moira Petty. *Daily Mail*: 7 September 1983.

"I don't think I'm very good . . ." ibid.

"I wrote about it . . ." ibid.

". . . deliberately excising the information . . ." Dave cited four songs: 'Don't Forget To Dance', 'Property', 'Cliches Of The World (B Movie)' and 'Bernadette'.

"Dave Davies has checked into . . ." *Good Times*: October 1983.

". . . fatigue . . ." Ken Jones, interviewed by the author. London: 23 August 1983.

Chapter Thirty-Four: Nineteen Eighty-Four

". . . that far-off year . . ." While recognizing that Orwell's *Nineteen Eighty-Four* was, in many respects, a satirical comment on the author's present, its 'futuristic' aspects and unrelenting negativity – and most obviously its title – affected later generations.

"In 1984 . . ." Illustrated magazine clipping titled 'Kinks 1984 And All That'. Likely interviewer, Keith Altham: *c.* September 1964.

"That was when it really started . . ." Gibbons/Rogan. London: 4 July 1994.

"His attitude was changing . . ." Dave Davies/Rogan. London: 1 March 1996.

"The situation between Dave and Mick . . ." Ray Davies, interviewed by Elliot Stephen Cohen. *Record Collector* 345: January 2008.

"Even the group's staunchest fans . . ." *Kinky Mirror* editor Peter Seeger summed up the indignation of many a supporter: "You go to see a show and you know you can expect the same set, no matter if it's 1982 or 1984. Three or four songs from the current album are really no compensation . . . I can understand Dave feeling to get out of the whole thing. When will Mr Know-it-all-everything-under-control Ray Davies understand that people's patience isn't endless?"

"Ray Davies has had a brilliant, if uneven, career . . ." Reviewer Robin Denselow. *Guardian:* 4 April 1984.

"Self-destruction is quite dominant . . ." Gibbons/Rogan. London: 4 July 1994.

"Other people have said . . ." Chrissie Hynde, interviewed by Jan Moir. *Daily Telegraph*: 21 September 1999. There was no indication from Hynde who these "other people" might have been. This author has never heard of any such suggestions from anyone in the Kinks, or elsewhere. Nor are there rumours of anything said 'off the record' to my knowledge.

"There were terrible . . ." Ray Davies/Small. *People Magazine* Vol. 28, issue 1: 6 July 1987.

"It was a sunny day . . ." Ray Davies, interviewed by Jim Sullivan. *Boston Globe*: 13 December 1984.

"Ray's all right . . ." Tom Robinson, quoted in *Out Of The Wardrobe*: undated, issue 5, p. 4.

"It's a human thing . . ." Ray Davies, interviewed by Chrissie Iley. *The Times*: 6 June 2009.

"I'd like to do something . . ." Ray Davies/Small. *People Magazine* Vol. 28, issue 1: 6 July 1987.

"There were terrible fights . . ." Ray Davies/Murray. *Q* 36: September 1989.

"Dave said he wanted . . ." ibid.

"There was something . . ." Avory/Rosser. Unedited interview despatched to author: 30 November 2005.

"His scores were brilliant . . ." Rasa Didzpetris/Rogan. London: 4 March 2013.

"He was very pleased . . ." ibid.

"It's Ray . . ." Larry Page, interviewed by the author. London: 6 April 1996.

"Ray, who? . . ." ibid.

"I didn't even know . . ." Page/Rogan London: 12 July 1994.

"Most days I'd get up . . ." Ray Davies, interviewed by Jim Sullivan. *The Record*: April 1985.

"Er, could you bring a bottle of milk . . ." Page/Rogan. London: 6 April 1996.

"Well, it'll save him nineteen pence . . ." ibid.

"It was completely different . . ." Page/Rogan London: 12 July 1994.

"Ken had been a loyal roadie . . ." ibid.

"It's like being back in 1965 . . ." Larry Page, interviewed by the author. London: 14 September 1994.

"When you're involved with Ray . . ." Page/Rogan. London: 12 July 1994.

"Where is he? . . ." . . . "In the hotel room, next door . . ." . . . "Well, why don't you . . ." ibid.

"I used to have Dave . . ." ibid.

"It seemed to help . . ." Avory/Rogan. Broxbourne, Hertfordshire: 9 October 1994.

"I took Mick . . ." Ray Davies/Murray. *Q* 36: September 1989.

"Mick had had enough . . ." Page/Rogan. London: 12 July 1994.

"They were saying . . ." ibid.

"I think everybody . . ." ibid.

"It was just a completely different style . . ." Gibbons/Rogan. London: 4 July 1994.

". . . an updated version . . ." *New Statesman*: *c.* November 1984.

"It worried me . . ." Page/Rogan. London: 12 July 1994.

"There was very little dialogue . . ." Reviewer: Miles Kington. *Listener*: 8 November 1984.

"I can't remember the exact details . . ." Dave Davies/Rogan. London: 1 March 1996. Dave claimed he learned these details during a conversation with manager Elliot Abbott. The affair soured their relationship, even though it had previously been close. "Elliot was good," Dave admits. "He was a warm guy, but we had a bit of a falling-out because a lot of DJs in America thought 'Living On A Thin Line' should have been the single from the album. I had terrible arguments with Elliot. Once you lose that trust it does eat away at the relationship."

"What does Dave think? . . ." Page/Rogan. London: 12 July 1994.

"Dave? . . ." ibid.

"Oh, we'll *definitely* . . ." ibid.

"When we got to Germany . . ." ibid.

"I can't sleep . . ." ibid.

"Don't let us down . . ." ibid.

"He didn't let us down . . ." ibid.

"The Kinks acted . . ." Review of the Kinks' performance at the Festhalle, Frankfurt: 23 November 1984.

"It was an excellent gig . . ." Page/Rogan. London: 12 July 1994.

"It's wonderful . . ." Ray Davies/Sullivan. *The Record*: April 1985.

"I wish I could . . ." Ray Davies, interviewed by Divino Infusino. *San Diego Union*: 28 August 1988.

Chapter Thirty-Five: The Third Marriage

"When I mentioned . . ." Page/Rogan. London: 12 July 1994.

"Even if the UK . . ." ibid.

". . . provide for me financially . . ." Papers submitted to Manhattan Supreme Court. February: 1985.

". . . harassed and abused . . ." ibid.

"I have paid defendant thousands of dollars . . ." ibid.

"I was a very small part . . ." Yvonne Gunner, email to author: 9 December 2013.

"We all give out a persona . . ." Yvonne Gunner. *Chronogram*: February 2008.

"I really loved Pat . . ." Dave Davies/Rogan. London/Cornwall: 3 October 2012.

"I guess the Kinks . . ." Ray Davies/Ward & Hammer. *RockBill*: May 1988.

"If he had worked . . ." Ray Davies/Murray. *Q* 36: September 1989.

"We're not interested . . ." Page/Rogan. London: 12 July 1994.

"Ray, like all artistes . . ." ibid.

"Couldn't you get someone . . ." ibid.

"The girl who said it . . ." ibid.

"Elliot subsequently . . ." ibid.

"We were trying to avoid . . ." ibid.

"We've done the deal . . ." ibid.

"It was pass . . ." ibid.

"He was enthusiastic . . ." ibid.

"I hate contracts . . ." Ray Davies, interviewed by Merle Ginsberg. *LA Weekly*: 16–22 January 1987.

"He went to see a doctor . . ." Page/Rogan. London: 12 July 1994.

"That boy . . ." ibid.

"But Ray doesn't do parties . . ." Page/Rogan. Avoca Beach, New South Wales, Australia: 18 May 2011.

"Well, don't buy a bloody wedding gift . . ." ibid.

"We've just got married . . ." ibid.

"They'd cut the dad's part . . ." Ray Davies, interviewed by Peter Doggett. *Record Collector* 169: September 1993.

"You went down . . ." Page/Rogan. London: 12 July 1994.

"There was a punch-up . . ." ibid.

"The funny thing . . ." ibid.

"The silliest thing . . ." ibid.

"It's trendy to be bitter . . ." Page/Rogan. London: 12 July 1994.

"My philosophy for this record . . ." Ray Davies interviewed by J. Hutchinson. *Musician*: January 1986. "I had to make a new Kinks record, whatever that is," Ray added, "and although I wasn't really working to a market strategy, I knew it had to have driving music on it." Davies found the perfect "driving music" courtesy of his brother, whose run-of-the-mill travelogue 'Rock 'n' Roll Cities' took the tired clichés of the 'road song' into new realms of banality. "When I first heard that song, it made me sick", Ray confessed, "but then the next day I saw the humour in it. I thought, 'Well, possibly, it's a good way of breaking through to an audience that hasn't heard us for two years.'"

Despite a US singles release and promotional video, 'Rock 'n' Roll Cities' failed to make any commercial impact. Whatever the Kinks represented to the masses could no longer be translated into healthy record sales.

While Dave's lyric presented a litany of US cities, Ray offered a corrosive commentary on Cleveland in 'Welcome To Sleazy Town'. "I wanted the song to be about the American Midwest, that's why I adopted the accent. I did the opposite in 'Come Dancing' where I went to great lengths to convey a sense of Englishness." The inspiration for 'Killing Time' came from a personal observation. "It's about a couple I know who haven't worked since they left school. They got up in the morning, turned on the television and just kept watching." It was a measure of Davies' desperation that he considered the thumbnail sketch 'The Video Shop' as a possible musical. This was a potentially strong song with a weak plot.

"I don't think . . ." ibid.

"Ray could be a right arsehole . . ." Page/Rogan. London: March 1996.

Chapter Thirty-Six: *80 Days*

"He ended up . . ." Page/Rogan. Avoca Beach, New South Wales, Australia: 18 May 2011.

"If you were with him . . ." ibid.

"I was at an Indian restaurant . . ." Ray Davies, interviewed by Bryan Miller. *New York Times*: 13 November 1996.

"When we were on tour . . ." Page/Rogan. London: 12 July 1994.

"In the Fifties . . ." Ray Davies/Infusino. *San Diego Union*: 28 August 1988.

"From what I can gather . . ." Page/Rogan. London: 12 July 1994.

"It worried me . . ." ibid.

"Everyone was a bit unsure . . ." Gibbons/Rogan. London: 4 July 1994.

"It's true . . ." Dave Davies/Rogan. London/Cornwall: 3 October 2012.

"Pat's a nice girl . . ." Page/Rogan. London: 3 July 1987. Reiterated, London: 12 July 1994.

"There was talk of him . . ." Gibbons/Rogan. London: 4 July 1994.

"Pete was working . . ." David Quaife/Rogan. London: 27 February 2013.

"One reason Ray . . ." Des McAnuff, interviewed by Richard Stayton. *LA Herald Examiner*: 21 August 1988.

"Our musical . . ." ibid.

"I wanted my score . . ." Ray Davies/Infusino. *San Diego Union*: 28 August 1988.

"I should have listened . . ." Dave Davies/Hardy. *Daily Mail*: 30 October 2010. It was once suggested to me that Ray's absence around this time may have been due to his tax position, but this was a misconception. "That could be the case but it seems funny that he was able to come over a week later for the funeral," Dave told me. "I know he's taken tax years out – but I don't think that was the case at the time. It's a valid thing to think, but I don't believe that was the case then."

"There was a kids' disco . . ." Gibbons/Rogan. London: 4 July 1994.

"It was so over the top . . ." quoted in *Sunday Mirror*: 17 January 1988.

"When Terry got on the plane . . ." Page/Rogan. London: 12 July 1994.

"It was serious enough . . ." Joan Crosbie, interviewed by Gordon Blair. *Sunday Mirror*: 17 January 1988.

"I thought it was amazingly sexy . . ." Ray Davies, interviewed by Pamela Des Barres. *Detail*: 1990.

"He wrote his own . . ." Page/Rogan. London: 12 July 1994.

"I didn't think . . ." Ray Davies, interviewed by Jay Lustig. *East Coast Rocker*: 13 September 1989.

"We were always available . . ." Gibbons/Rogan. London: 4 July 1994.

"*80 Days* is a dizzy . . ." Reviewer: Welton Jones. *San Diego Union*: 30 August 1988. A similar point was made by a rival critic who praised the musical for its populist appeal ("they pleased the indulgent La Jolla audience") but felt that it lacked the quality to make that all-important transition to Broadway and the world stage.

"Davies is . . ." Reviewer: Gregory Sandow. *Herald Examiner*: August 1988.

"The music does have one great virtue . . ." ibid.

Chapter Thirty-Seven: The Whip Hand

"That's how Dave heard it . . ." Gibbons/Rogan. London: 4 July 1994.

"It meant a lot . . ." Dave Davies/Hardy. *Daily Mail*: 30 October 2010.

"How am I supposed . . ." ibid.

"He said, 'I can do what I want . . .'" ibid.

"I've never seen . . ." ibid.

"It was getting too much . . ." Gibbons/Rogan. London: 4 July 1994.

"I couldn't do anything . . ." Page/Rogan. London: 12 July 1994.

"He's right . . ." ibid.

"I think that would be good . . ." Page/Rogan. Avoca Beach, New South Wales, Australia: 18 May 2011.

"What are we going to do? . . ." Larry Page, interviewed by the author. London: July 1989.

"We'll do what we always do . . ." ibid.

"Mingus was an insomniac . . ." Ray Davies, interviewed by Robert Yates. *Observer*: June 1993.

"With this new tour . . ." Ray Davies/Lustig. *East Coast Rocker*: 13 September 1989.

"I'd like to do an album . . ." ibid.

"Putting out a record . . ." Ray Davies, interviewed by Dave Hinkley. *New York Daily News*: 13 September 1989.

"Maybe we should . . ." Ray Davies, interviewed by Chris Twomey. *Strangled*: December 1990.

"That's how much belief . . ." ibid.

"He plays the same tricks . . ." Ray Davies, interviewed by George Kalogerakis. *Musician*: March 1990.

"Aggravation" . . . Inspired by his experiences as a newly qualified driver, this song was far removed from the idyllic, relaxed tone of 'Drivin''. As Ray told Al Pereira (*Music Paper*: December 1990): "On 'Aggravation' the first thing that happens is the guy gets stuck in a traffic jam. Things just seem to go downhill from there. I delved into his personality and in the song I became him . . . A lot of people believe it's me."

"I don't think *UK Jive* . . ." Ray Davies/Twomey. *Strangled*: December 1990.

"I was never even daddy . . ." Ray Davies interviewed by Sharon Feinstein. *News Of The World*: 17 December 1989.

"I'd like to have a boy . . ." ibid.

"Drink a lot . . ." Ray Davies/George Kalogerakis. *Musician*: March 1990.

"We've never won anything . . ." ibid.

"I would like to have . . ." Ray Davies, extract from undated, handwritten letter to Ken Jones.

"They were from the street . . ." Graham Nash, Rock 'n' Roll Hall of Fame. New York: 17 January 1990.

"I don't want to see the brothers fighting . . ." ibid.

"Thanks for the award . . ." Dave Davies, Rock 'n' Roll Hall of Fame. New York: 17 January 1990.

"My name's Ray Davies . . ." Ray Davies, speaking at the Kinks' induction to the Rock 'n' Roll Hall of Fame. New York: 17 January 1990.

"This is the third release . . ." ibid.

"This is a very posh event . . ." ibid.

"I just wrote lyrics . . ." ibid.

"I was very intimidated . . ." ibid.

"And if they need any help . . ." ibid.

". . . the craziest drummer . . ." ibid.

"I just have one question . . ." Pete Quaife, Rock 'n' Roll Hall of Fame. New York: 17 January 1990.

"Why don't you give that . . ." Pete Quaife/Kirby. *Now And Then* 7: 1994.

"That really pissed him off . . ." ibid.

"It was funny . . ." Dave Davies/Rogan. London: 1 March 1996.

"I've always said . . ." Ray Davies, interviewed by Mark Holan. *The Scene, Cleveland*: 12–18 August 1990.

"We got drenched . . ." Ray Davies/Twomey. *Strangled*: December 1990.

"It's infested with attorneys . . ." ibid.

"I have nothing against feminists . . ." Ray Davies/Des Barres. *Details*: 1990.

"I liked Nigel . . ." Dave Davies/Rogan. London: 1 March 1996.

"It's about me . . ." Ray Davies/Doggett. *Record Collector* 169: September 1993. That 'Did Ya' sounded so convincing as a novelty pastiche was a backhanded compliment to the Kinks. While it emphasized the enduring quality of their music, its charm also underlined how chained the group had become to their key era. The five-track CD was not released in the UK and was commercially unsuccessful in America, where its irony was not appreciated. The package included a live version of 'Gotta Move' and a remake of 'Days', which was clearly inspired by Kirsty MacColl's recent re-reading of the song. The otherwise unavailable 'New World' and obligatory Dave workout 'Look Through Any Doorway' completed the set.

"Ken was a good worker . . ." Page/Rogan London: 12 July 1994.

"Ken Jones was with them . . ." Page/Rogan London: March 1996.

"There was this genuine undercurrent . . ." Dave Davies, interviewed by Harold de Muir. *Pulse*: May 1993.

"I like to think . . ." ibid.

"rat-arsed drunk" . . . "still shaking . . ." Ray Davies, interviewed by Harold de Muir. *Pulse!*: May 1993.

"I set out to write . . ." Ray Davies/Doggett. *Record Collector* 169: September 1993.

"That is the *real* Ray Davies . . ." Peter 'Jonah' Jones/Rogan. London/Montreal, Canada: 8 May 2013.

"The experimental workshop . . ." Ray was not the only Kink undertaking new activities. Former Kinks' drummer Mick Avory had teamed up with several musician friends to form Shut Up Frank. The line-up featured Noel Redding, Dave Clark (formerly of the Noel Redding Band), Jimmy Leverton (ex-Fat Mattress/Steve Marriott) and Dave Rowberry (the Animals/Mike Cotton Sound). A veritable mini-supergroup, they played pubs and small clubs, spicing their set with oldies such as the Move's 'I Can Hear The Grass Grow', the Animals' 'We Gotta Get Out Of This Place' and the Kinks' 'All Day And All of The Night', 'Sunny Afternoon' and 'Lola'.

Chapter Thirty-Eight: Beyond Britpop

"It was awful . . ." Ray Davies/Rogan. London: 1 October 2013.

"I have considered . . ." Ray Davies, interviewed by David Wild. *Rolling Stone*: 13 May 1993.

"That's what Ray will do . . ." Page/Rogan. London: 26 November 1996.

"Committed to promotion . . ." During the spring of 1993, the Kinks undertook an extensive tour of small theatres across America. The final date at the River Jam Festival in Kaukauna, Wisconsin, on 5 June, coincided with the death of Conway Twitty. Ray paid the singer an unexpected tribute by singing one of his best remembered songs, 'It's Only Make Believe'.

"He's got the right . . ." Ray Davies/Doggett. *Record Collector* 169: September 1993.

"'Scattered' (. . . partly inspired by Annie Davies' death . . .)" Ray remembers a secondary inspiration for the song: "I couldn't crack the lyric. I tried it again in 1989 but it didn't work. It was about a man being left by a woman. Then I lost a really close friend; she died of cancer. She was quite young. She was there one day but not the next. And that made me crack the song, gave it another element other than 'I've been left by my girlfriend and I'm emotionally scattered.' But it's still not a downer song, it's a laugh."

"It has IRA connotations . . ." Ray Davies, interviewed by Michael Amicone. *Music Connection*: 24 May 1993.

"If there are any journalists here . . ." Ray Davies, quoted words onstage at Royal Albert Hall. London: 11 July 1993.

"When British pop is great . . ." John Harris, *The Last Party* (London: Fourth Estate, 2003), p. 87. Jarvis Cocker quote originally published in *Select* magazine.

"Fifty years from now . . ." John Major speech to the Conservative Group For Europe: 22 April 1993.

"We were superimposed . . ." Brett Anderson, interviewed by the author. London: 27 August 1996.

". . . silly Little Englanders . . ." ibid.

"Ray Davies . . . embraced Albarn like a canny patriarch . . ." They shared an art school background and, coincidentally, Albarn's mother Hazel had worked as a stage designer at the Theatre Royal, Stratford East, the setting of *Chorus Girls* and the later musical, *Come Dancing*.

"I'm very interested . . ." Ray Davies/DeMuir. *Pulse!*: May 1993.

"It's kind of my lost lifelong project . . ." ibid.

"I didn't assume . . ." Gibbons/Rogan. London: 4 July 1994.

"Ray did one of his instant composing tricks . . ." ibid.

"That was a farce . . ." ibid.

"Everybody went crazy! . . ." ibid.

"Ray sent a beautiful bouquet . . ." Rasa Didzpetris, email to author: 5 March 2013.

"You go through a lot . . ." Ray Davies/George. *Independent*: 27 August 1994.

"They have a love/hate relationship . . ." Page/Rogan London: 12 July 1994.

"The great bands . . ." Prime Minister Tony Blair, speech at Park Lane Hotel, Piccadilly, London: 9 November 1994.

"It's my brain . . ." Ray Davies/Rogan. London: 1 October 2013.

"He shortened it . . ." ibid.

"Ray's way" . . . "quite funny . . ." Avory/Rogan. Broxbourne, Hertfordshire: 9 October 1994.

"When she first came to me . . ." Ray Davies, interviewed by Stephen Pitalo. *Flatiron*: summer 1996.

"Obviously I do love Ray . . ." Dave Davies/Rogan. London: 1 March 1996.

"Truly wonderful – Oasis . . ." Ray Davies, speaking at the Brit Awards. London: 20 February 1995.

"I was in love . . ." Damon Albarn, oft-repeated quote on admiration for Ray Davies.

"My Generation . . ." The series also featured filmed contributions from this author, along with Ray and Dave, Mick Avory and Larry Page.

"Fashions come in and out . . ." Ray Davies/Pitalo. *Flatiron*: summer 1996.

"I listen to the current [Oasis] album . . ." ibid.

"Ray's asking for silly money . . ." Page/Rogan. London: 26 November 1996.

Chapter Thirty-Nine: End Of The Century

"Deke Arlon . . ." Christened Anthony Howard Wilson, Arlon changed his name before entering the pop game. He fronted a couple of groups, the Tremors and the Offbeats, and recorded several singles before moving into acting.

"I think if they meet . . ." Larry Page, interviewed by the author. London: 28 February 1996.

"Of course . . ." Dave Davies/Rogan. London: 1 March 1996.

"The fact is . . ." Ray Davies/Doggett. *Record Collector* 200: April 1996.

"There is that parallel . . ." Ray Davies/Pitalo. *Flatiron*: summer 1996.

"The sensitive Britpop . . ." ibid.

"They were a good band . . ." Ray Davies/Rogan. London: 1 October 2013.

"After a couple of Scandinavian shows . . ." As Doug Hinman records, the final show took place on 15 June 1996 at the Frognerbadet in Oslo, Norway, for the 'Norwegian Wood Music Festival'.

"I didn't see a wreath . . ." Page/Rogan. London: 26 November 1996.

"Ray had the money . . ." Dave Davies/Hardy. *Daily Mail*: 30 October 2010.

"It was like . . ." Ray Davies, interviewed by Buddy Seigel. *Los Angeles Times*: April 1997.

"As I was about to cut the cake . . ." Dave Davies/Hardy. *Daily Mail*: 30 October 2010.

". . . different spirit . . ." Michael Horovitz, quoted in Diary section. *Evening Standard*: 10 June 1996.

". . . with a nine-song set . . ." Ray Davies' show at the Royal Albert Hall (7 July 1996) included 'Dedicated Follower Of Fashion', 'Session Man', 'Days', 'London Song', 'Really Animal', 'A Well Respected Man', 'Waterloo Sunset', 'Parklife' and 'Lola'.

"London reigns . . ." *Newsweek*: November 1996.

"The fun won't last . . ." *Newsweek*: November 1996.

"As it was in the mid-Sixties . . ." *Vanity Fair*: March 1997.

". . . the internationally acclaimed film actress . . ." ibid.

"a wonderful, big busty, black woman . . ." Sherrin/Rosser. Unedited interview despatched to author: 30 November 2005.

"People were only starting . . ." ibid.

". . . another explosion . . ." ibid.

"That will never happen . . ." Pete Quaife/Smith & Orton. *The Official Kinks Fan Club Magazine*: 25 June 1999.

"It was lovely . . ." Ray Davies, interviewed by Kate Bohdanowicz. *Times Educational Supplement*: 18 October 2013.

". . . a tantalizing hint . . ." Donnachadh McCarthy article. *Dance Europe Magazine*: undated.

"You can't whip the road . . ." Ray Davies/Rogan. London: 1 October 2013.

". . . messed things up . . ." Dave Davies/Rogan. London/Cornwall: 3 October 2012.

"I haven't had that many . . ." Ray Davies, interviewed by Neil McCormick. *Daily Telegraph*: 26 January 2006.

"Women like you to be . . ." Ray Davies/Cavanagh. *Uncut* 163: December 2010.

"They say, 'You wrote about this . . .'" Ray Davies/McCormick. *Daily Telegraph*: 26 January 2006.

"He was eccentric . . ." Patricia Crosbie, interviewed by Helen O'Callaghan. *Feelgood Magazine. Irish Examiner*: 19 November 2010.

"I started writing . . ." Ray Davies, interviewed by Chris Willman. *Entertainment Weekly*: 2006.

"It was a decision . . ." Ray Davies, interviewed by Nick Hasted. *Uncut* 189: February 2013.

Chapter Forty: The Shooting Of Ray Davies

"Not many people know . . ." Ray Davies/Pat Gilbert. *Mojo* 226: September 2012.

"I totally lost my confidence . . ." Ray Davies/Cohen. *Record Collector* 345: January 2008.

"When you go in . . ." Ray Davies/McCormick. *Daily Telegraph*: 26 January 2006.

"I didn't trust them . . ." Ray Davies/Doggett. *Mojo* 111: February 2003.

"People have come . . ." Liner notes to *Other People's Lives*, CD. Italics mine.

"If you listen . . ." Ray Davies/McCormick. *Daily Telegraph*: 26 January 2006.

". . . *BBC Sessions 1964–1977* . . ." The album was originally titled *The Songs We Sang For Auntie* and CD artwork was produced with that title but changed at the last minute following objections from the BBC. *Mojo* magazine actually reviewed the album under the censored 'Auntie' title.

"I saw bits . . ." Ray Davies, interviewed by David Dye. *World Café From WXPN*: 24 February 2006.

"The next album . . ." Ray Davies/Sciaky for *The Low Budget Interview* disc: July 1979.

"I found the place . . ." Liner notes to *Other People's Lives*, CD.

"Another reason . . ." Ray Davies, interviewed by Charles M. Young. *Rolling Stone*: 6 March 2008.

"Even in New Orleans . . ." Al Nodal article. *Los Angeles Times*: 21 February 1993.

"He was delightfully intelligent . . ." Jeanne Nathan, interviewed by the author. New Orleans: 28 January 2014.

"Thinking back . . ." Robert 'Bob' Tannen, interviewed by the author. New Orleans: 28 January 2014.

"It's a wonderful thing . . ." Nathan/Rogan. New Orleans: 28 January 2014.

"I used to go to school . . ." Ray Davies, speaking at the Ivor Novello Awards. London: 25 May 2006.

"in a fake world" . . . "a lost, clumsy imitation . . ." Ray Davies, cited in *Americana* (London: Virgin Books, 2013).

"It wasn't real . . ." cited in Ray Davies, *X-Ray* (London: Viking, 1994). The same words were repeated to the author by Davies. London: 1 October 1996.

"Yes . . ." Ray Davies/Rogan. London: 1 October 2013.

"He put himself . . ." Press statement by Police Chief Superintendent Eddie Compass: January 2004.

"It was a ridiculous thing . . ." Ray Davies/Cohen. *Record Collector* 345: January 2008.

"I saw a lot . . ." ibid.

"It's not really serious . . ." BBC News online: January 2004.

"It's not like in the westerns . . ." Ray Davies, brief, uncredited interview at *Q* Awards: 2005.

"That was a scary time . . ." Ray Davies/Rogan. London: 1 October 2013.

"He wanted as much privacy . . ." Tannen/Rogan. New Orleans: 28 January 2014.

". . . seven-year-old daughter, Eva . . ." In at least one tabloid newspaper Eva was wrongly identified as Natalie, Ray's daughter with Chrissie Hynde who was 21 years old at the time.

"We do need victims . . ." District Attorney Eddie Jordan, commenting on Davies' non-appearance in court: April 2005.

"I was supposed to be in court . . ." Ray Davies, interviewed by Paul Du Noyer. *The Word*: December 2007.

"What I'm trying to get to . . ." Ray Davies/Cavanagh. *Uncut* 163: December 2010.

"No . . ." ibid.

"There was a lot of eerie significance . . ." Ray Davies/Rogan. London: 1 October 2013.

The extent to which Davies may have been 'reading into things' was evident from an earlier extraordinary outburst to David Cavanagh. The interview's conspiratorial content was worthy of his brother at his most fantastical. "Our rights will be gradually eroded," Ray insisted with crystal ball conviction. "There'll be no freedom of movement. They'll use terrorism as an excuse. I sound crazy, but so be it. They're eroding our right to travel. Ryanair is making life more complicated. What was sixty quid a pop is now two hundred-plus a pop . . . I'm talking about reality."

"**I was nostalgic . . .**" Ray Davies/Rogan. London: 1 October 2013.

Chapter Forty-One: Dave's Stroke

"**I could tell . . .**" Ray Davies/Cavanagh. *Uncut* 163: December 2010.

"**I knew I was going to have . . .**" Dave Davies, quoted in *Daily Mail*: 10 October 2006.

"**Now, I appreciate . . .**" ibid.

"**I'm undecided . . .**" Dave Davies/Hardy. *Daily Mail*: 30 October 2010.

"**I wouldn't know . . .**" Dave Davies/Rosser. Unedited interview despatched to author: 30 November 2005.

"**She only sang . . .**" Ray Davies/McCormick. *Daily Telegraph*: 26 January 2006.

"**What a load of bollocks . . .**" Dave Davies, quoted in *Daily Express*: 4 December 2005.

"**Max is always there . . .**" Ray Davies/Rogan. London: 1 October 2013.

"**It's difficult . . .**" Ray Davies, interviewed by Alan Franks. *The Times*: 11 December 2009.

"**I'm a lonely adult . . .**" ibid.

"**This is a first . . .**" Katie Vanneck, interviewed by Mark Sweney. *Guardian*: 12 October 2007.

"**. . . truly excited . . .**" Ray Davies, interviewed by BBC Television: 12 October 2007.

"**I've had calls . . .**" Ray Davies/Cohen. *Record Collector* 345: January 2008.

"**I thought they were only going . . .**" Ray Davies/Cavanagh. *Uncut* 163: December 2010.

"**Ray has been doing Karaoke Kinks . . .**" Dave Davies, posting on his messageboard: 17 November 2007.

"**I really would like . . .**" Ray Davies/Du Noyer. *The Word*: December 2007.

"**I would like to work . . .**" Ray Davies, interviewed by Dan Cairns. *Sunday Times*: 21 October 2007.

"**Inside I'm just this . . .**" Ray Davies, interviewed by Lois Wilson. *Mojo* 169: December 2007.

"**I quite like . . .**" Dave Davies, interviewed by Charles M. Young. *Rolling Stone*: 6 March 2008.

Chapter Forty-Two: The Custodian

"**. . . the Kinks' box set *Picture Book* . . .**" Frustratingly, the original Shel Talmy version of 'You Really Got Me' remained undiscovered, as did the instrumental prototype which had been given to Rose when she moved to Adelaide. A sense of anti-climax when discussing the last three discs popped up in several reviews. "Thank heavens it's sequenced in chronological order," quipped critic David Cavanagh, who found it difficult to stomach the entire package: "*Picture Book*, in the end, is simply too honest for its own good." (*Uncut* 140, January 2009). The same point had been made in the *Guardian* (12 December 2008) by Alex Petridis ("Still it's hard to stifle an apprehensive gulp when their last great album, 1971's *Muswell Hillbillies*, hoves into view and you realize that there was still three CDs to go."). Both critics awarded the album three stars out of five.

"*Come Dancing* needed somebody . . ." Roden/Rogan. London: 16 January 2014. Roden's comments were based on experience and insider knowledge. After touring with the Kinks for three years, she later worked with Bill Kenwright on various musicals, as did her former partner John Miller who was also employed at Konk as a producer for Café Society.

"**I never wanted to ask . . .**" Alice Kingston, interviewed by Olivia Kelleher. *Irish Independent*: 20 June 2009.

"**She's done some dancing . . .**" Patricia Crosbie/O'Callaghan. *Feelgood Magazine*. *Irish Examiner*: 19 November 2010.

"**It was interesting . . .**" Eva Davies, recollected quote by Ray Davies, interviewed by Cole Morton. *Independent*: 22 July 2012.

"**He likes Galaxy bars . . .**" Eva Davies, quoted in interview with Olivia Kelleher. *Irish Independent*: 20 June 2009.

"**We would very much like . . .**" Ray Davies/Tatham. *Valentine*: 21 October 1967.

"**Chrissie came into the studio . . .**" Ray Davies, quoted in the *Independent*: 11 December 2009.

"**That was difficult . . .**" Ray Davies/Cavanagh. *Uncut* 163: December 2010.

"**Pete wouldn't have been able . . .**" David Quaife/Rogan. London: 27 February 2013.

"**There wasn't a single wreath . . .**" ibid.

"**Because so many people . . .**" Ray Davies, posting on his Facebook page: July 2010.

"**Hopefully . . .**" ibid.

"**I'm going to do a memorial concert . . .**" Ray Davies/Cavanagh. *Uncut* 163: December 2010.

"**After Pete died . . .**" Dave Davies/Hardy. *Daily Mail*: 30 October 2010.

"**You've heard of vampires? . . .**" ibid.

"**Ray's a narcissist . . .**" ibid.

"**Emotional vampire? . . .**" Ray Davies/Iley. *The Times*: 6 June 2009.

"**First off I would like to state . . .**" Ray Davies, posting on his Facebook page: July 2010.

"**I wanted Ray . . .**" David Quaife/Rogan. London: 27 February 2013.

"**Compared to the way . . .**" *Imaginary Man* documentary. Broadcast BBC 1: 21 December 2010.

"**Why did they put me there? . . .**" Ray Davies, interviewed by Jim Sullivan. *Boston Phoenix*: 1 April 2008.

"**I'd like to highlight . . .**" Ray Davies, interviewed by Elizabeth Gehrman. *Buffalo Spree*: November 2011.

"**. . . the real glories . . .**" Reviewer David Cavanagh. *Uncut*: December 2011.

"**They said, 'We always felt . . .'**" Ray Davies/Rogan. London: 1 October 2013.

"**I love him to death . . .**" Ray Davies, interviewed by Rachel Cooke. *Observer*, 10–19 June 2011; first published in *Observer News Review*: 1 May 2011.

"I'm in between girlfriends . . ." ibid.

"That's the one thing . . ." ibid.

"It took me . . ." Ray Davies/Gehrman. *Buffalo Spree*: November 2011.

"I've always had a thing . . ." Dave Davies/Rogan. London/Cornwall: 3 October 2012.

"Dave, the mad one . . ." Ray Davies, speaking at the Pete Quaife blue plaque unveiling at Fortismere School, London: 16 October 2011.

". . . the most friendly one . . ." Mick Avory, speaking at the Pete Quaife blue plaque unveiling at Fortismere School, London: 16 October 2011.

"If he saw that . . ." ibid.

"Yeah, it was your eyebrow! . . ." Ray Davies, speaking at the Pete Quaife blue plaque unveiling at Fortismere School, London: 16 October 2011.

"Pete made everyone mix together . . ." Ray Davies, speaking at the Pete Quaife memorial dinner. London: 16 October 2011.

"Don't mix with him! . . ." ibid.

"The drummer [Mick Avory] . . ." ibid.

"I don't know what . . ." Ray Davies, interviewed by Joe Bream. *Star Tribune*: 5 November 2011.

"About an hour . . ." Dave Davies, interviewed by Neil McCormick. *Daily Telegraph*: 13 October 2011.

"He's a great eccentric English genius . . ." Townshend/Rosser. Unedited interview despatched to author: 30 November 2005.

"They're more than they were . . ." ibid.

"I've always respected . . ." ibid.

"I feel sorry for the trees . . ." Natalie Hynde. *IB Times*: 2013.

"Ms Hynde 28, . . ." Article by David Jones. *Mail Online*: 26 July 2013.

"Ms Hynde describes herself . . ." ibid.

"His current intimate was Alma Karen Eyo . . ." She also receives 'special thanks' on the dedication page of Davies' memoir, *Americana*. One source fancifully suggested that they had first met on a park bench near a gym, a story far too apocryphal to be included in the main text, but wonderfully endearing in its imagery.

"I wrote until I thought . . ." Ray Davies/Rogan. London: 1 October 2013.

"Travis is three people . . ." ibid.

". . . the names . . ." Ray Davies, *Americana: The Kinks, The Road And The Perfect Riff* (London: Virgin Books, 2013), imprint page. The book is free from the various misspellings of names that blighted *X-Ray*. That said, Davies refers to Andy Pyle as 'Pile' whenever his name is mentioned. Nicolas Cage becomes Nicholas Cage, although there's probably no deep significance in that.

"There's a story . . ." Ray Davies/Rogan. London: 1 October 2013.

"The Kinks music is going to last . . ." Dave Davies/Rogan. London/Cornwall: 3 October 2012.

"A little footnote at the end . . ." ibid. Ray had been encouraging Mick Avory to reconnect with Dave via email, but his efforts proved counter productive, at best.

Epilogue

"I am such a secretive person . . ." Ray Davies, quoted in *Daily Mail*: 24 October 2014.

"The songs lend themselves . . ." Ray Davies, interviewed by Richard Godwin. *Evening Standard*: 11 June 2015.

"Certainly, things like Soap Opera . . ." Beecham/Rogan. London/Weston-super-Mare, north Somerset: 2 June 2014.

"It wasn't an easy process . . ." Julien Temple, interviewed by the author. London: 3 November 2015.

"They're different genres . . ." ibid.

" . . . with a lot of humour . . ." ibid. Temple adds that the film's writers, Ian La Frenais and Dick Clement, knew the Davies brothers back in the Sixties when "they played celebrity football".

"It's a natural place . . ." ibid.

"There is no Kinks . . ." ibid. Temple famously cast Avory in the video shoot for 'Do It Again', even though the drummer did not play on the recording and was no longer a member of the band. "I was shocked. I didn't know he'd left. I said, 'Let's have Mick, and Ray thought it was a good idea. It's amazing that we did that video in a day. It was shot in Aldwych, then we went to Brighton."

"We used to bunk off . . ." ibid.

"I had this amazing day . . ." ibid. Temple never did find out what had reduced Davies to tears, but one person had a mischievous, if cynical, theory. "Larry Page told me he must have lost a fiver. That was Larry's take, but I'm sure it was more than that. I doubt it was losing a fiver! In *Imaginary Man* we did have Ray pick up a 50-pence piece in the gutter."

". . . about understanding the world . . ." ibid.

"I asked them if they'd do the music . . ." ibid.

"Nothing's easy with Ray . . ." ibid.

"I was telling him . . ." ibid. Temple had mixed feelings about *Imaginary Man*. "The drag was that I had to do it through that album [*See My Friends*] which was a bit of an albatross around my neck because I wasn't really interested in that. I was interested in making a film about Ray. I think they wanted me to make it about that album, Bruce Springsteen and the collection of singers. That was the trigger. We had to have Springsteen in it, basically. I liked Metallica, though. That was funny. Ray grins as he watches them doing it. They massacre his song!"

"Alan found me the money . . ." ibid.

"I really love both of them . . ." email to author, dated 3 November 2015. Asked what he hoped the film might achieve, Temple quipped: "Hopefully peace. Peace on Earth. That would be good. I'd love to get Ray and Dave on two stages at once at Glastonbury playing the same song. That's my version of any reunion. On the stage is Dave Davies. And on the Pyramid Stage is Ray Davies. And they play 'You Really Got Me'. The whole site would be irradiated with the nuclear power of music. They'd only need to play the one song."

"You have to remember . . ." Temple/Rogan. London: 3 November 2015.

"He's legendarily mean . . ." ibid.

"When I met Ray Davies . . ." Reviewer Will Hodgkinson. *The Times*: 28 February 2015.

". . . was rather nondescript . . ." Colin Huggett, letter to the author: 24 June 2015.

"Dave said he would not go onstage with Mick . . ." Letter from Paul Ainsley Morgan, dated March 2015. Courtesy of Larry Page, who confirms that the story is correct.

"My life is defined . . ." Ray Davies, interviewed by Russell Davies. BBC Radio 2: 8 June 2015.

"Most people spend a third of their life . . ." Temple/Rogan. London: 3 November 2015.

"I think creativity happens . . ." ibid.

"I think the songs will be remembered . . ." Davies/Godwin. *Evening Standard*: 11 June 2015.

SELECT DISCOGRAPHY

This select discography covers UK and US releases and is divided into three main sections – Singles, EPs and Albums (incorporating CDs). All record numbers are UK/US originals unless stated otherwise. Significant changes of release date or serial number between the two territories are also noted. Releases outside the UK/US, straight reissues, promotional releases, singles exclusively distributed to radio stations, sampler albums, various artistes collections, interview discs and specific guest appearances are not included.

SINGLES

KINKS

'Long Tall Sally'/'I Took My Baby Home' Pye 7N 15611(UK)/Cameo 308 (US)
Reissued in US in December, Cameo 345.
Released: February 1964 (UK)/March 1964 (US).

'You Still Want Me'/'You Do Something To Me' Pye 7N 15636 (UK)
Released: April 1964 (UK). Not issued in US.

'You Really Got Me'/'It's Alright' Pye 7N 15673 (UK)/Reprise 0306 (US)
Released: August 1964 (UK)/September 1964 (US).

'All Day And All Of The Night'/'I Gotta Move' Pye 7N 15714/Reprise 0334 (US)
Released: October 1964 (UK)/December 1964 (US).

'Tired Of Waiting For You'/'Come On Now' Pye 7N 15759 (UK)/Reprise 0347 (US)
Released: January 1965 (UK)/February 1965 (US).

'Ev'rybody's Gonna Be Happy'/'Who'll Be The Next In Line' Pye 7N 15813 (UK)
Released: March 1965 (UK).

'Who'll Be The Next In Line'/'Ev'rybody's Gonna Be Happy' Reprise 0366 (US)
Released: July 1965 (US).

'Set Me Free'/'I Need You' Pye 7N 15854 (UK)/Reprise 0379 (US)
Released: May 1965 (UK/US).

'See My Friend'/'Never Met A Girl Like You Before' Pye 7N 15919 (UK)/Reprise 0409 (US)
Released: July 1965 (UK)/September 1965 (US).

'A Well Respected Man'/'Such A Shame' Reprise 0420 (US)
Released: November 1965 (US).

'Till The End Of The Day'/'Where Have All The Good Times Gone' Pye 7N 15981 (UK)/Reprise 0454 (US)
Released: November 1965 (UK)/March 1966 (US).

'Dedicated Follower Of Fashion'/'Sittin' On My Sofa' Pye 7N 17064 (UK)/Reprise 0471 (US)
Released: February 1966 (UK)/April 1966 (US).

'Sunny Afternoon'/'I'm Not Like Everybody Else' Pye 7N 17125 (UK)/Reprise 0497 (US)
Released: June 1966 (UK)/July 1966 (US).

'Dead End Street'/'Big Black Smoke' Pye 7N 17222 (UK)/Reprise 0540 (US)
Released: November 1966 (UK/US).

'Mister Pleasant'/'This Is Where I Belong' Pye 7N 17314 (Holland)/Reprise 0587 (US).
The US version features 'Harry Rag' on the B-side.
Released: April 1967 (Holland)/May 1967 (US). Not issued in UK.

'Waterloo Sunset'/'Act Nice And Gentle' Pye 7N 17321 (UK)/Reprise 0612 (US)
Released: May 1967 (UK)/July 1967 (US).

'Autumn Almanac'/'Mister Pleasant' Pye 7N 17400 (UK)/Reprise 0647 (US). The US version features 'David Watts' on the B-side.
Released October 1967 (UK)/November 1967 (US).

'Wonderboy'/'Polly' Pye 7N 17468 (UK)/Reprise 0691 (US)
Released: April 1968 (UK)/May 1968 (US).

'Days'/'She's Got Everything' Pye 7N 17573 (UK)/Reprise 0762 (US)
Released: June 1968 (UK)/July 1968 (US).

'Starstruck'/'Picture Book' Reprise 0806 (US)
Released: January 1969 (US). Not issued in UK.

'Plastic Man'/'King Kong' Pye 7N 17724 (UK)
Released: March 1969 (UK). Not issued in US.

'Drivin''/'Mindless Child Of Motherhood' Pye 7N 17776 (UK)
Released: June 1969 (UK). Not issued in US.

'Shangrila'/'This Man He Weeps Tonight' Pye 7N 17812 (UK)
Released: September 1969 (UK). Not issued in US.

'The Village Green Preservation Society'/'Do You Remember Walter' Reprise 0847 (US)
Released: August 1969 (US). Not issued in UK.

'Victoria'/'Mr Churchill Says' Pye 7N 17865 (UK)/Reprise 0863 (US). The US version features 'Brainwashed' on the B-side.
Released: December 1969 (UK)/October 1969 (US).

'Lola'/'Berkeley Mews' Pye 7N 17961 (UK)/Reprise 0930 (US). The US version features 'Mindless Child Of Motherhood' on the B-side.
Released: June 1970 (UK)/July 1970 (US).

'Apeman'/'Rats' Pye 7N 45016 (UK)/Reprise 0979 (US)
Released: November 1970 (UK)/December 1970 (US).

'God's Children'/'The Way Love Used To Be' Reprise 1017 (US). See EP section for corresponding UK release.
Released: July 1971 (US).

'20th Century Man'/'Skin And Bone' RCA 74-0620 (US)
Released: December 1971. Not issued in UK.

'Supersonic Rocket Ship'/'You Don't Know My Name' RCA 2211 (UK)/RCA 74-0807 (US)
Released: May 1972 (UK)/September 1972 (US).

'Celluloid Heroes'/'Hot Potatoes' RCA 2299 (UK)/RCA 74-0852 (US). The US A-side is edited.
Released: November 1972 (UK/US).

'One Of The Survivors'/'Scrapheap City' RCA 74-0940 (US)
Released: April 1973 (US). Not issued in UK. B-side is a different take from the version on *Preservation Act 2*.

'Sitting In The Midday Sun'/'One Of The Survivors' RCA 2387 (UK)/RCA LPBO 5001 (US). The US version features 'Sweet Lady Genevieve' on the B-side.
Released: June 1973 (UK)/August 1973 (US).

'Sweet Lady Genevieve'/'Sitting In My Hotel' RCA 2418
Released: September 1973 (UK). Not issued in US.

'Mirror Of Love'/'Cricket' RCA 5015 (UK)
Released: April 1974 (UK). Not issued in the US.

'Money Talks'/'Here Comes Flash' RCA APBO 0275 (US)
Released: April 1974 (US). Not issued in UK.

'Mirror Of Love'/'He's Evil' RCA 5042 (UK)/RCA PB 10019 (US). The A-side is a different recording to the April 1974 single version.
Released: July 1974 (UK/US).

'Holiday Romance'/'Shepherds Of The Nation' RCA 2478 (UK)
Released: October 1974 (UK). Not issued in US.

'Preservation'/'Salvation Road' RCA PB 10121 (US)
Released: November 1974 (US). Not issued in UK.

'Starmaker'/'Ordinary People' RCA PB 10251 (US)
Released: April 1975 (US). Not issued in UK.

'Ducks On The Wall'/'Rush Hour Blues' RCA 2546 (UK)
Released: April 1975. Not issued in US.

'You Can't Stop The Music'/'Have Another Drink' RCA 2567 (UK)
Released: May 1975. Not issued in US.

'I'm In Disgrace'/'The Hard Way' RCA PB 10551 (US)
Released: January 1976 (US). Not issued in UK.

'No More Looking Back'/'Jack The Idiot Dunce'/'The Hard Way' RCA RCM 1 (UK)
Released: January 1976 (UK). Not issued in US.

'Sleepwalker'/'Full Moon' Arista ARISTA 97 (UK)/Arista AS 0240 (US)
Released: March 1977 (UK/US).

'Juke Box Music'/'Sleepless Nights' Arista ARISTA 114/Arista AS 0249 (US). The US
version features 'Life Goes On' on the B-side.
Released: June 1977 (UK)/May 1977 (US).

'Father Christmas'/'Prince Of The Punks' Arista ARISTA 153 (UK)/Arista AS
0296 (US)
Released: November 1977 (UK)/December 1977 (US).

'A Rock 'n' Roll Fantasy'/'Artificial Light' Arista ARIST 189 (UK)/Arista AS 0342 (US).
The US version features an edited 'Live Life' on the B-side.
Released: May 1978 (UK)/June 1978 (US).

'Live Life'/'In A Foreign Land' Arista ARIST 199 (UK)/Arista AS 0372 (US). The US
version features 'Black Messiah' on the B-side. The UK A-side is edited.
Released: July 1978 (UK)/October 1978 (US).

'Black Messiah'/'Misfits' Arista ARIST 210 (UK)
Released: September 1978 (UK). Not issued in US.

'(Wish I Could Fly Like) Superman'/'Low Budget' Arista ARIST 240 (UK)/Arista AS
0409 (US). Also issued as an extended 12-inch single.
Released: January 1979 (UK)/March 1979 (US).

'A Gallon Of Gas'/'Low Budget' Arista AS 0448 (US)
Released: April 1979 (US). Not issued in UK.

'Catch Me Now I'm Falling'/'Low Budget' Arista 0458 (US)
Released: September 1979 (US). Not issued in UK.

'Lola'/'Celluloid Heroes' Arista AS 0541 (US). Both sides are live performances taken from the album *One For The Road*.
Released: July 1980 (US). Not issued in UK.

'You Really Got Me'/'Attitude' Arista AS 0577 (US). A-side is a live version taken from the album *One For The Road*.
Released: October 1980 (US). Not issued in UK.

'Better Things'/'Massive Reductions' Arista ARIST 415 (UK). A bonus single (Kinks 1) was included in this package featuring live versions of 'Lola' and 'David Watts'.
Released: June 1981 (UK). Not issued in US.

'Destroyer'/'Back To Front' Arista AS 0619 (US)
Released: September 1981. Not issued in UK.

'Predictable'/'Back To Front' Arista ARIST 426 (UK)
Released: October 1981. Not issued in US.

'Better Things'/'Yo-Yo' Arista AS 0649 (US)
Released: November 1981. Not issued in UK.

'Come Dancing'/'Noise' Arista ARIST 502 (UK)/Arista AS 1054 (US). Also issued in UK as an extended 12-inch single.
Released: November 1982 (UK)/April 1983 (US).

'Don't Forget To Dance'/'Bernadette' Arista ARIST 524 (UK)/Arista AS1-9075 (US). Also issued in UK as an extended 12-inch single. 'Bernadette' is an alternate take. The US version features 'Young Conservatives' on the B-side.
Released: September 1983 (UK)/August 1983 (US).

'Good Day'/'Too Hot' Arista ARIST 577 (UK). Also issued as a 12-inch single with the extra track 'Don't Forget To Dance'.
Released: August 1984 (UK). Not issued in US.

'Do It Again'/'Guilty' Arista ARIST 617 (UK)/Arista AS1-9309 (US). Also issued as a 12-inch in the UK with the extra track 'Summer's Gone'.
Released: April 1985 (UK)/December 1984 (US).

'Summer's Gone'/'Going Solo' Arista AS1-9334 (US)
Released: March 1985 (US). Not issued in UK.

'Rock 'n' Roll Cities'/'Welcome To Sleazy Town' MCA 52960 (US)
Released: November 1986 (US). Not issued in UK.

'How Are You'/'Killing Time' London LON 119 (UK). Also issued as a 12-inch single with the extra track 'Welcome To Sleazy Town'.
Released: December 1986.

'Lost And Found'/'Killing Time' London LON 132 (UK)/MCA 53015 (US). Also issued as a 12-inch single in the UK with 'The Ray Davies Interview'. A-side edited in US.
Released: April 1987 (UK)/February 1987 (UK).

'How Are You'/'Working At The Factory' MCA 53093 (US)
Released: June 1987 (US).

'The Road'/'Art Lover' London LON 165 (UK). Also issued as a 12-inch single with the
extra track 'Come Dancing'.
Released: February 1988 (UK). Not issued in US.

'Down All The Days (Till 1992)'/'You Really Got Me' (live) London LON 239 (UK).
Also issued as a 12-inch single and CD in the UK with the extra track 'Entertainment'.
The single was issued in the US as a cassette single with no B-side.
Released: September 1989 (UK)/May 1990 (US).

'How Do I Get Close'/'Down All The Days (Till 1992)', London LON 250 (UK)
Released: February 1990 (UK). Not issued in US.

'Scattered'/'Hatred (A Duet)'/'Days' Columbia 658992 2 (UK). CD single
Released: March 1993 (UK). Not issued in US.

'Only A Dream'/'Somebody Stole My Car' Columbia 6599922 7 (UK). The CD single
version features an extra track, 'Babies'.
Released: November 1993 (UK). Not issued in US.

EPs

KINKS

Kinksize Session Pye NEP 24200 (UK)
'Louie Louie'; 'I Gotta Go Now'; 'Things Are Getting Better'; 'I've Got That Feeling'.
Released: November 1964 (UK). Not issued in US.

Kinksize Hits Pye NEP 24203 (UK)
'You Really Got Me'; 'It's Alright'; 'All Day And All Of The Night'; 'I Gotta Move'.
Released: January 1965 (UK). Not issued in US.

Kwyet Kinks Pye NEP 24221 (UK)
'Wait Till The Summer Comes Along'; 'Such A Shame'; 'A Well Respected Man'; 'Don't
You Fret'.
Released: September 1965 (UK). Not issued in US.

Dedicated Kinks Pye NEP 24258 (UK)
'Dedicated Follower Of Fashion'; 'Till The End Of The Day'; 'See My Friend'; 'Set Me
Free'.
Released: July 1966 (UK). Not issued in US.

The Kinks Pye NEP 24296 (UK)
'David Watts'; 'Two Sisters'; 'Lazy Old Sun'; 'Situation Vacant'.
Released: April 1968 (UK). Not issued in US.

The Kinks (Percy) Pye 7NX 8001 (UK). Issued on 33rpm,
'God's Children'; 'The Way Love Used To Be'; 'Moments'; 'Dreams'.
Released: April 1971 (UK). Issued in US as single only.

The Kinks – Mini Monsters Pye PMM 100 (UK)
'You Really Got Me'; 'Set Me Free'; 'Wonderboy'; 'Long Tall Shorty'.
Released: August 1971 (UK). Not issued in US.

Big Deal Pye BP 105 (UK)
'Lola'; 'Sunny Afternoon'; 'Waterloo Sunset'; 'Dedicated Follower Of Fashion'.
Released: May 1977 (UK). Not issued in US.

Yesteryear Pye AMEP 1001 (UK)
'Long Tall Sally'; 'I Took My Baby Home'; 'You Still Want Me'; 'You Do Something
To Me'.
Released: November 1978. Not issued in US.

Flashbacks Pye FBEP 104 (UK)
'Waterloo Sunset'; 'David Watts'; 'Well Respected Man'; 'Stop Your Sobbing'.
Released: June 1980 (UK). Not issued in UK.

The Kinks Live EP Arista ARIST 360 (UK)
'David Watts'; 'Where Have All The Good Times Gone'; 'Attitude'; 'Victoria'.
Released: July 1980 (UK). Not issued in US.

Better Things Arista ARIST 415/KINKS 1 (UK)
'Better Things'; 'Massive Reduction(s)'; 'Lola'; 'David Watts'.
Released: June 1981 (UK). Not issued in US.

You Really Got Me PRT KD 1 (UK)
'You Really Got Me'; 'All Day And All Of The Night'; 'Misty Water'; 'Medley: All Day
And All Of The Night/You Really Got Me'.
Released: October 1983 (UK). Not issued in US.

State Of Confusion Arista ARIST 560 (UK)
'State Of Confusion'; 'Heart Of Gold'; 'Lola'; '20th Century Man'.
Released: March 1984 (UK). Not issued in US.

Did Ya Columbia 44 K 74050 (US). CD release.
'Did Ya'; 'I Gotta Move'; 'Days'; 'New World'; 'Look Through Any Doorway'.
Released: October 1991 (US). Not issued in UK.

Waterloo Sunset '94 Konk/Grapevine KNKCD 2 (UK)
'Waterloo Sunset'; 'You Really Got Me'; 'Elevator Man'; 'On The Outside'.
Released: October 1994 (UK). Not issued in US.

The Days EP When! WEN X 1016 (UK).
'Days'; 'You Really Got Me'; 'Dead End Street'; 'Lola'.
Released: January 1997 (UK). Subtitled *30 Years Of Yellow Pages 1966–1996*, this CD
EP was inspired by the *Yellow Pages* television advertisement featuring 'Days'. Not issued
in US.

The EP Collection Castle ESFCD 667 (UK)

Ten-EP reproduction box set.

Kinksize Session; *Kinksize Hits*; *Kwyet Kinks*; *Dedicated Kinks*; *The Kinks*; *Dave Davies Hits*; *Kinks In Sweden* (Swedish release); *Waterloo Sunset* (French release); *Dead End Street* (French release); *The Village Green Preservation Society* (Portuguese release).

Released: November 1998 (UK). Not issued in US.

The EP Collection 2 Castle/Sanctuary ESFCD 904 (UK)

Ten-EP reproduction box set.

Dandy (French release); *The Kinks* (Swedish release); *The Kinks At Drop In* (Swedish release); *En Una Tarde De Sol* (Spanish release); *Dedicated Follower Of Fashion* (French release); *Till The End Of The Day* (French release); *Mister Pleasant* (French release); *Los Kinks Vol 9* (Mexican release); *Los Kinks Vol 10* (Mexican release); *Callejon Sin Salda* (Spanish release).

Released: August 2000 (UK). Not issued in US.

ALBUMS (ORIGINAL ISSUES)

KINKS

Kinks Pye NPL 18096 (mono); NSPL 83021 (stereo) (UK)/ Reprise R 6143 (US)

'Beautiful Delilah'; 'So Mystifying'; 'Just Can't Go To Sleep'; 'Long Tall Shorty'; 'I Took My Baby Home'; 'I'm A Lover Not A Fighter'; 'You Really Got Me'; 'Cadillac'; 'Bald Headed Woman'; 'Revenge'; 'Too Much Monkey Business'; 'I've Been Driving On Bald Mountain'; 'Stop Your Sobbing'; 'Got Love If You Want It'.

The 11-song US issue was titled *You Really Got Me* and omitted three tracks: 'I Took My Baby Home', 'I'm A Lover Not A Fighter' and 'Revenge'.

Released: October 1964 (UK)/November 1964 (US).

Kinda Kinks Pye NPL 18112 (UK)/Reprise R 6173 (US)

'Look For Me Baby'; 'Got My Feet On The Ground'; 'Nothin' In This World (Can Stop Me Worryin' 'Bout That Girl)'; 'Naggin' Woman'; 'Wonder Where My Baby Is Tonight'; 'Tired Of Waiting For You'; 'Dancing In The Street'; 'Don't Ever Change'; 'Come On Now'; 'So Long'; 'You Shouldn't Be Sad'; 'Something Better Beginning'. The 12-song US issue omits 'Naggin' Woman' and 'Come On Now', but adds 'Set Me Free' and 'Ev'rybody's Gonna Be Happy'.

Released: March 1965 (UK)/August 1965 (US).

Kinks-Size Reprise R 6158 (US)

'Tired Of Waiting For You'; 'Louie Louie'; 'I've Got That Feeling'; 'Revenge'; 'I Gotta Move'; 'I'm A Lover Not A Fighter'; 'Come On Now'; 'All Day And All Of The Night'.

Released: March 1965 (US). Not issued in UK.

Kinks Kinkdom Reprise R 6184 (US)

'A Well Respected Man'; 'Such A Shame'; 'Wait Till The Summer Comes Along'; 'Naggin' Woman'; 'Never Met A Girl Like You Before'; 'See My Friend'; 'Who'll Be The Next In Line'; 'Don't You Fret'; 'I Need You'; 'It's Alright'; 'Louie Louie'.

Released: November 1965 (US). Not issued in UK.

The Kinks Kontroversy Pye NPL: 18131 (mono); SSPL 18131 (stereo)
(UK); Reprise R (S) 6197 (US)
'Milk Cow Blues'; 'Ring The Bells'; 'Gotta Get The First Plane Home'; 'When I See That
Girl Of Mine'; 'I Am Free'; 'Till The End Of The Day'; 'The World Keeps Going Round';
'I'm On An Island'; 'Where Have All The Good Times Gone'; 'It's Too Late'; 'What's In
Store For Me'; 'You Can't Win'. The UK cover artwork mistitles the album 'The Kink
Kontroversy' but it is titled *The Kinks Kontroversy* on the record label and spine. Different
sleeve in US.
Released: November 1965 (UK)/March 1966 (US).

Face To Face Pye NPL 18149 (mono)/NPSL 18149 (stereo) (UK)/Reprise R (S) 6226 (US)
'Party Line'; 'Rosy, Won't You Please Come Home'; 'Dandy'; 'Too Much On My Mind';
'Session Man'; 'Rainy Day In June'; 'House In The Country'; 'Holiday In Waikiki'; 'Most
Exclusive Residence For Sale'; 'Fancy'; 'Little Miss Queen Of Darkness'; 'You're Looking
Fine'; 'Sunny Afternoon'; 'I Remember'.
Released: October 1966 (UK)/December 1966 (US).

Something Else By The Kinks Pye NPL 18193 (mono)/NSPL 18193 (stereo) (UK)/Reprise
RS 6279 (US)
'David Watts'; 'Death Of A Clown'; 'Two Sisters'; 'No Return'; 'Harry Rag'; 'Tin Soldier
Man'; 'Situation Vacant'; 'Love Me Till The Sun Shines'; 'Lazy Old Sun'; 'Afternoon Tea';
'Funny Face'; 'End Of The Season'; 'Waterloo Sunset'.
Released: September 1967 (UK)/January 1968 (US).

The Kinks Live At Kelvin Hall Pye NPL 18191 (mono)/NSPL 18191 (stereo) (UK)/
Reprise 6260 (US)
'Till The End Of The Day'; 'A Well Respected Man'; 'You're Looking Fine'; 'Sunny
Afternoon'; 'Dandy'; 'I'm On An Island'; 'Come On Now'; 'You Really Got Me'; 'Medley:
Milk Cow Blues, Batman Theme, Tired Of Waiting For You'. First issued in the US under
the title *The Live Kinks*.
Released: January 1968 (UK)/August 1967 (US).

The Kinks Are The Village Green Preservation Society Pye NPL 18233 (mono)/NSPL
18233 (stereo) (UK)/Reprise 6327 (US)
'The Village Green Preservation Society'; 'Do You Remember Walter'; 'Picture Book';
'Johnny Thunder'; 'Last Of The Steam-Powered Trains'; 'Big Sky'; 'Sitting By The
Riverside'; 'Animal Farm'; 'Village Green'; 'Starstruck'; 'Phenomenal Cat'; 'All Of My
Friends Were There'; 'Wicked Annabella'; 'Monica'; 'People Take Pictures Of Each Other'.
See Notes (p. 677) for discussion on artwork and album title.
Released: November 1968 (UK)/February 1969 (US).

Arthur Or The Decline And Fall Of The British Empire Pye NPL 18317 (mono)/NSPL
18317 (stereo) (UK)/Reprise RS 6366 (US)
'Victoria'; 'Yes Sir, No Sir'; 'Some Mother's Son'; 'Drivin''; 'Brainwashed'; 'Australia';
'Shangri-la'; 'Mr Churchill Says'; 'She Bought A Hat Like Princess Marina'; 'Young And
Innocent Days'; 'Nothing To Say'; 'Arthur'.
Released: October 1969 (UK/US).

Kinks Part One – Lola Versus Powerman And The Moneygoround Pye NSPL 18359 (UK)/Reprise RS 6423 (US)
'The Contenders'; 'Strangers'; 'Denmark Street'; 'Get Back In Line'; 'Lola'; 'Top Of The Pops'; 'The Moneygoround'; 'This Time Tomorrow'; 'A Long Way From Home'; 'Rats'; 'Apeman'; 'Powerman'; 'Got To Be Free'.
Released: November 1970 (UK)/December 1970 (US).

Percy Pye NSPL 18365 (UK)
'God's Children'; 'Lola (Instrumental)'; 'The Way Love Used To Be'; 'Completely'; 'Run Round Town'; 'Moments'; 'Animals In The Zoo'; 'Just Friends'; 'Whip Lady'; 'Dreams'; 'Helga'; 'Willesden Green'; 'God's Children – End'.
Released: March 1971. Not issued in US.

Muswell Hillbillies RCA Victor LSP 4644 (UK); RCA Victor SF 8243 (US)
'20th Century Man'; 'Acute Schizophrenia Paranoia Blues'; 'Holiday'; 'Skin And Bone'; 'Alcohol'; 'Complicated Life'; 'Here Come The People In Grey'; 'Have A Cuppa Tea'; 'Holloway Jail'; 'Oklahoma USA'; 'Uncle Son'; 'Muswell Hillbilly'.
Released: November 1971 (UK/US).

Everybody's In Show-biz, Everybody's A Star RCA Victor DPS 2035 (UK)/RCA Victor VPS 6065 (US)
'Here Comes Yet Another Day'; 'Maximum Consumption'; 'Unreal Reality'; 'Hot Potatoes'; 'Sitting In My Hotel'; 'Motorway'; 'You Don't Know My Name'; 'Supersonic Rocketship'; 'Look A Little On The Sunny Side'; 'Celluloid Heroes'; 'Top Of The Pops'; 'Brainwashed'; 'Mr Wonderful'; 'Acute Schizophrenia Paranoia Blues'; 'Holiday'; 'Muswell Hillbilly'; 'Alcohol'; 'Banana Boat Song'; 'Skin And Bone'; 'Baby Face'; 'Lola'.
Released: September 1972 (UK); August 1972 (US).

Preservation Act 1 RCA Victor SF 8392 (UK)/RCA Victor LPL1-5002 (US)
'Morning Song'; 'Daylight'; 'Sweet Lady Genevieve'; 'There's A Change In The Weather'; 'Where Are They Now?'; 'One Of The Survivors'; 'Cricket'; 'Money & Corruption/I Am Your Man'; 'Here Comes Flash'; 'Sitting In The Midday Sun'; 'Demolition'.
Released: November 1973 (UK/US).

Preservation Act 2 RCA Victor LPL2 5040 (UK)/RCA Victor CPL 2-5040 (US)
'Announcement'; 'Introduction To Solution'; 'When A Solution Comes'; 'Money Talks'; 'Announcement'; 'Shepherds Of The Nation'; 'Scum Of The Earth'; 'Second Hand Card Spiv'; 'He's Evil'; 'Mirror Of Love'; 'Announcement'; 'Nobody Gives'; 'Oh Where Oh Where Is Love?'; 'Flash's Dream (The Final Elbow)'; 'Flash's Confession'; 'Nothing Lasts Forever'; 'Announcement'; 'Artificial Man'; Scrapheap City'; 'Announcement'; 'Salvation Road'.
Released: July 1974 (UK)/May 1974 (US).

The Kinks Present A Soap Opera RCA Victor SF 8411 (UK)/RCA Victor LPL1-5081 (US)
'Everybody's A Star (Starmaker)'; 'Ordinary People'; 'Rush Hour Blues'; 'Nine To Five'; 'When Work Is Over'; 'Have Another Drink'; 'Underneath The Neon Sign'; 'Holiday Romance'; 'You Make It All Worthwhile'; 'Ducks On The Wall'; '(A) Face In The Crowd'; 'You Can't Stop The Music'.
Released: May 1975 (UK)/April 1975 (US).

The Kinks Present Schoolboys In Disgrace RCA Victor RS 1028 (UK)/RCA Victor LPL1-5102 (US)
'Schooldays'; 'Jack The Idiot Dunce'; 'Education'; 'The First Time We Fall In Love'; 'I'm In Disgrace'; 'Headmaster'; 'The Hard Way'; 'The Last Assembly'; 'No More Looking Back'; 'Finale'.
Released: January 1976 (UK)/November 1975 (US).

Sleepwalker Arista SPARTY 1002 (UK)/Arista AL 4106 (US)
'Life On The Road'; 'Mr Big Man'; 'Sleepwalker'; 'Brother'; 'Juke Box Music'; 'Sleepless Night'; 'Stormy Sky'; 'Full Moon'; 'Life Goes On'.
Released February 1977 (UK/US).

Misfits Arista AL 4167 (UK)/Arista AB 4167 (US)
'Misfits'; 'Hay Fever'; 'Live Life'; 'A Rock 'n' Roll Fantasy'; 'In A Foreign Land'; 'Permanent Waves'; 'Black Messiah'; 'Out Of The Wardrobe'; 'Trust Your Heart'; 'Get Up'.
Released: May 1978 (UK)/(US).

Low Budget Arista SPART 1099 (UK)/Arista AB 4240 (US)
'Attitude'; 'Catch Me Now I'm Falling'; 'Pressure'; 'National Health'; '(Wish I Could Fly Like) Superman'; 'Low Budget'; 'In A Space'; 'Little Bit Of Emotion'; 'A Gallon Of Gas'; 'Misery'; 'Moving Pictures'.
Released: September 1979 (UK)/July 1979 (US).

One For The Road Arista DARTY 6 (UK)/Arista A2L 8401 (US)
'Opening'; 'The Hard Way'; 'Catch Me Now I'm Falling'; 'Where Have All The Good Times Gone'; 'Introduction To Lola'; 'Lola'; 'Pressure'; 'All Day And All Of The Night'; '20th Century Man'; 'Misfits'; 'Prince Of The Punks'; 'Stop Your Sobbing'; 'Low Budget'; 'Attitude'; '(Wish I Could Fly Like) Superman'; 'National Health'; 'Till The End Of The Day'; 'Celluloid Heroes'; 'You Really Got Me'; 'Victoria'; 'David Watts'.
Released: August 1980 (UK)/June 1980 (US).

Give The People What They Want Arista SPART 1171 (UK)/Arista AL 9567 (US)
'Around The Dial'; 'Give The People What They Want'; 'Killer's Eyes'; 'Predictable'; 'Add It Up'; 'Destroyer'; 'Yo-Yo'; 'Back To Front'; 'Art Lover'; 'A Little Bit Of Abuse'; 'Better Things'.
Released: January 1982 (UK)/ August 1981 (US).

State Of Confusion Arista 205 275 (UK)/Arista AL8-8018 (US)
'State Of Confusion'; 'Definite Maybe'; 'Labour Of Love'; 'Come Dancing'; 'Property'; 'Don't Forget To Dance'; 'Young Conservatives'; 'Heart Of Gold'; 'Cliches Of The World (B Movie)'; 'Bernadette'. The cassette version features two additional tracks, 'Noise' and 'Long Distance'.
Released: June 1983 (UK)/May 1983 (US).

Word Of Mouth Arista 206 685 (UK)/Arista AL8-8264 (US)
'Do It Again'; 'Word Of Mouth'; 'Good Day'; 'Living On A Thin Line'; 'Sold Me Out'; 'Massive Reductions'; 'Guilty'; 'Too Hot'; 'Missing Persons'; 'Summer's Gone'; 'Going Solo'.
Released: November 1984 (UK/US).

Think Visual London LONLP 27 (UK)/MCA MCA-5822 (US)
'Working At The Factory'; 'Lost And Found'; 'Repetition'; 'Welcome To Sleazy Town'; 'The Video Shop'; 'Rock 'n' Roll Cities'; 'How Are You'; 'Think Visual'; 'Natural Gift'; 'Killing Time'; 'When You Were A Child'.
Released: November 1986 (UK/US).

The Road – The Kinks Live London LONLP 49 (UK)/MCA MCA-42107 (US)
'The Road'; 'Destroyer'; 'Apeman'; 'Come Dancing'; 'Art Lover'; 'Clichés Of The World (B Movie)'; 'Think Visual'; 'Living On A Thin Line'; 'Lost And Found'; 'It (I Want It)'; 'Around The Dial'; 'Give The People What They Want'.
Released: May 1988 (UK)/January 1988 (US).

UK Jive London 828 165-2 (UK)/MCA MCA-6337 (US)
'Aggravation'; 'How Do I Get Close'; 'UK Jive'; 'Now And Then'; 'What Are We Doing'; 'Entertainment'; 'War Is Over'; 'Down All The Days (Till 1992)'; 'Loony Balloon'; 'Dear Margaret'; 'Bright Lights'; 'Perfect Strangers'. The last two tracks appeared on the CD version of the album.
Released: October 1989 (UK/US).

Phobia Columbia 4872489 2 (UK)/Columbia CK 48724 (US)
'Opening'; 'Wall Of Fire'; 'Drift Away'; 'Still Searching'; 'Phobia'; 'Only A Dream'; 'Don't'; 'Babies'; 'Over The Edge'; 'Surviving'; 'It's Alright (Don't Think About It)'; 'The Informer'; 'Hatred (A Duet)'; 'Somebody Stole My Car'; 'Close To The Wire'; 'Scattered'; 'Did Ya'. The final track does not appear on the US issue.
Released: March 1993 (UK/US).

To The Bone Konk/Grapevine KNKLP 1 (UK)
'All Day And All Of The Night'; 'Apeman'; 'Tired Of Waiting [For You]'; 'See My Friends'; 'Death Of A Clown'; 'Waterloo Sunset'; 'Muswell Hillbilly'; 'Better Things'; 'Don't Forget To Dance'; 'Autumn Almanac'; 'Sunny Afternoon'; 'Dedicated Follower Of Fashion'; 'You Really Got Me'. The last three songs feature Ray Davies as soloist.
Released: October 1994 (UK). Not issued in US.

To The Bone Guardian 7243 837303 21 (UK)/ Guardian 7243 837303 22 (US)
'All Day And All Of The Night'; 'Apeman'; 'Tired Of Waiting [For You]'; 'See My Friends'; 'Death Of A Clown'; 'Muswell Hillbilly'; 'Better Things'; 'Don't Forget To Dance'; 'Sunny Afternoon'; 'Dedicated Follower Of Fashion'; 'Do It Again (acoustic)'; 'Do It Again'; 'Celluloid Heroes'; 'Picture Book'; 'Village Green Preservation Society'; 'Do You Remember Walter'; 'Set Me Free'; 'Lola'; 'Come Dancing'; 'I'm Not Like Everybody Else'; 'Till The End Of The Day'; 'Give The People What They Want'; 'State Of Confusion'; 'Dead End Street'; 'A Gallon Of Gas'; 'Days'; 'You Really Got Me'; 'Animal'; 'To The Bone'. Tracks 9–11 feature Ray Davies as soloist.
Released: March 1997 (UK)/November 1996 (US).

COMPILATIONS/ARCHIVE ALBUMS

The Kinks catalogue has been recycled on countless compilation albums. Although this has been criticized by many commentators, including this author, it is worth noting that the early UK issues on Pye's Marble Arch label (priced at 14s 6d) introduced the group's music to a much larger audience than might otherwise have been the case. The Golden Hour series – although well selected – suffered from poor sound quality as a result of cramming too many songs on to each side. The vinyl quality in later years exacerbated the disappointing sonic fidelity. By the late Nineties, the group's catalogue was presented with greater care, ushering in the era of Expanded Editions.

Back in the early Eighties, I produced a more ambitious, expansive Kinks' discography embracing Continental Releases, which appeared in *The Sound And The Fury*. This was subsequently eclipsed by Doug Hinman's voluminous, privately published *You Really Got Me: An Illustrated World Discography Of The Kinks, 1964–1993*, now rightly considered the standard work. Alas, space restrictions herein preclude continental issues or a complete track listing of *every* UK/US anthology. Instead, I offer a best of the 'best ofs', a personal selection featuring key archival releases, kitsch budget items, memorable hits collections and sumptuous box sets. The others are listed by title, label and release date.

Interestingly, the first hits compilation appeared in America: *The Kinks Greatest Hits* Reprise R6217 (August 1966). Thereafter, the flood gates opened in the UK, as demonstrated below.

Well Respected Kinks Marble Arch MAL 612 (UK)
'A Well Respected Man'; 'Where Have All The Good Times Gone'; 'Till The End Of The Day'; 'Set Me Free'; 'Tired Of Waiting For You'; 'All Day And All Of The Night'; 'I Gotta Move'; 'Don't You Fret'; 'Wait Till The Summer Comes Along'; 'You Really Got Me'.
Released: September 1966 (UK). Not issued in US.

Sunny Afternoon Marble Arch MAL 716 (UK)
'Sunny Afternoon'; 'I Need You'; 'See My Friend'; 'Big Black Smoke'; 'Louie Louie'; 'Dedicated Follower Of Fashion'; 'Sitting On My Sofa'; 'Such A Shame'; 'I'm Not Like Everybody Else'; 'Dead End Street'.
Released: November 1967 (UK). Not issued in US.

The Kinks Pye NPL 18326 (UK)
'You Really Got Me'; 'Long Tall Shorty'; 'All Day And All Of The Night'; 'Beautiful Delilah'; 'Tired Of Waiting For You'; 'I'm A Lover Not A Fighter'; 'A Well Respected Man'; 'Till The End Of The Day'; 'See My Friend'; 'Don't You Fret'; 'Dedicated Follower Of Fashion'; 'Sunny Afternoon'; 'Dead End Street'; 'Death Of A Clown'; 'Two Sisters'; 'Big Black Smoke'; 'Susannah's Still Alive'; 'Waterloo Sunset'; 'Last Of The Steam-Powered Trains'; 'Wonderboy'; 'Do You Remember Walter'; 'Dandy'; 'Animal Farm'; 'Days'.
Released: February 1970 (UK). Not issued in US.

Lola Marble Arch HMA 201 (UK)
'Lola'; 'Dedicated Follower Of Fashion'; 'Dancing In The Street'; 'Where Have All The Good Times Gone'; 'You Really Got Me'; 'A Well Respected Man'; 'Dead End Street'; 'Got My Feet On The Ground'; 'Don't Ever Change'; 'All Day And All Of The Night'.
Released: October 1971 (UK). Not issued in US.

Golden Hour Of The Kinks Pye Golden Hour GH 501 (UK)
'Days'; 'Wonderboy'; 'Autumn Almanac'; 'Waterloo Sunset'; 'Dedicated Follower Of Fashion'; 'Dead End Street'; 'Set Me Free'; 'Sunny Afternoon'; 'Till The End Of The Day'; 'Sitting On My Sofa'; 'Victoria'; 'A Well Respected Man'; 'You Really Got Me'; 'All Day And All Of The Night'; 'Tired Of Waiting For You'; 'See My Friend'; 'Louie Louie'; 'Animal Farm'; 'Shangri-la'; 'Where Have All The Good Times Gone'.
Released: October 1971 (UK). Not issued in US.

The Kink Kronikles Reprise 2XS 6454 (US)
'Victoria'; 'The Village Green Preservation Society'; 'Berkeley Mews'; 'Holiday In Waikiki'; 'Willesden Green'; 'This Is Where I Belong'; 'Waterloo Sunset'; 'David Watts'; 'Dead End Street'; 'Shangri-la'; 'Autumn Almanac'; 'Sunny Afternoon'; 'Get Back In Line'; 'Did You See His Name'; 'Fancy'; 'Wonderboy'; 'Apeman'; 'King Kong'; 'Mister Pleasant'; 'God's Children'; 'Death Of A Clown'; 'Lola'; 'Mindless Child Of Motherhood'; 'Polly'; 'Big Black Smoke'; 'Susannah's Still Alive'; 'She's Got Everything'; 'Days'.
Released March 1972 (US). Not issued in UK.

The Great Lost Kinks Album Reprise MS 2127 (US)
'Till Death Us Do Part'; 'There Is No Life Without Love'; 'Lavender Hill'; 'Groovy Movies'; 'Rosemary Rose'; 'Misty Water'; 'Mr Songbird'; 'When I Turn Out [sic] The Living Room Light'; 'The Way Love Used To Be'; 'I'm Not Like Everybody Else'; 'Plastic Man'; 'This Man He Weeps Tonight'; 'Pictures In The Sand'; 'Where Did My Spring Go'.
Released: January 1973 (US). Not issued in UK.

The Kinks Hallmark HMA 244 (UK)
'Beautiful Delilah'; 'So Mystifying'; 'Just Can't Go To Sleep; 'Long Tall Shorty'; 'I Took My Baby Home'; 'I'm A Lover Not A Fighter'; 'Cadillac'; 'Bald Headed Woman'; 'Revenge'; 'Too Much Monkey Business'; 'I've Been Driving On Bald Mountain'; 'Stop Your Sobbing'.
Released: April 1973 (UK). Not issued in US.

Golden Hour Of The Kinks Volume Two Pye Golden Hour GH 558 (UK)
'Wonder Where My Baby Is Tonight'; 'Don't Ever Change'; 'Got Love If You Want It'; 'Come On Now'; 'I'm Not Like Everybody Else'; 'Something Better Beginning'; 'Dancing In The Street'; 'Just Can't Go To Sleep'; 'Long Tall Shorty'; 'Got My Feet On The Ground'; 'It's Alright'; 'Don't You Fret'; 'I Need You'; 'Such A Shame'; 'Look For Me Baby'; 'Ev'rybody's Gonna Be Happy'; 'Wait Till The Summer Comes Along'; 'Beautiful Delilah'; 'I Gotta Move'; 'So Long'; 'Nothing In The World'; 'You Shouldn't Be Sad'; 'Stop Your Sobbing'.
Released: October 1973 (UK). Not issued in US.

Lola Percy And The Apeman Face To Face With The Village Green Preservation Society . . . Something Else Pye Golden House GHD 50 (UK)
Released: November 1974 (UK). Not issued in US.

Celluloid Heroes – The Kinks Greatest RCA Victor RS 1059/Reprise APL1-1743 (US)
'Everybody's A Star (Starmaker)'; 'Sitting In My Hotel'; 'Here Comes Yet Another Day' (live); 'Holiday'; 'Muswell Hillbilly'; 'Celluloid Heroes'; '20th Century Man'; 'Sitting In The Midday Sun'; One Of The Survivors'; 'Alcohol'; 'Skin And Bone'; '(A) Face In The Crowd'.
Released: June 1976 (UK)/May 1976 (US).

The Kinks File Pye FILD001/1/2 (UK)
Released: October 1977 (UK). Not issued in US.

20 Golden Greats Ronco RPL 2031 (UK)
Released: September 1978 (UK). Not issued in US.

You Really Got Me Pye NSPL 18615 (UK)
Released: April 1980 (UK). Not issued in US.

Second Time Around RCA Victor AFL 1-3520 (US)
Released: August 1980 (US). Not issued in UK.

The Kinks Collection Pickwick PDA 072 (UK)
Released: September 1980 (UK). Not issued in US.

Spotlight On The Kinks Pye SPOT 1009 (UK)
Released: March 1981 (UK). Not issued in US.

Spotlight On The Kinks Vol. 2 Pye SPOT 1029 (UK)
Released: September 1982 (UK).

Shape Of Things To Come PRT DOW 4 (UK)
10-inch LP record. 'You Really Got Me'; 'All Day And All Of The Night'; 'Till The End Of The Day'; 'Set Me Free'; 'Lola'; 'Tired Of Waiting For You'; 'Sunny Afternoon'; 'Waterloo Sunset'.
Released: April 1983 (UK). Not issued in US.

Candy From Mister Dandy PRT DOW 12 (UK)
10-inch LP record. 'Dedicated Follower Of Fashion'; 'Dead End Street'; 'Death Of A Clown'; 'Ev'rybody's Gonna Be Happy'; 'A Well Respected Man'; 'See My Friend'; 'Days'; 'Autumn Almanac'.
Released: July 1983 (UK). Not issued in US.

Dead End Street – The Kinks Greatest PRT KINK 1 (UK)
'You Really Got Me'; 'All Day And All Of The Night'; 'Ev'rybody's Gonna Be Happy'; 'Till The End Of The Day'; 'Dead End Street'; 'Sunny Afternoon'; 'Dedicated Follower Of Fashion'; 'Victoria'; 'Set Me Free'; 'Apeman'; 'Tired Of Waiting For You'; 'See My Friend'; 'Death Of A Clown'; 'Days'; 'Lola'; 'Waterloo Sunset'; 'Wonderboy'; 'Plastic Man'; 'Autumn Almanac'; 'Susannah's Still Alive'. This compilation included a bonus

10-inch LP record featuring six tracks previously unissued in the UK: 'Misty Water'; 'Pictures In The Sand'; 'Spotty Grotty Anna'; 'Groovy Movies'; 'Time Will Tell'; 'Rosemary Rose'. However, these tracks were soon deleted from the PRT catalogue and replaced with *Six Mod Anthems*: 'David Watts'; 'Stop Your Sobbing'; 'Dancing In The Street'; 'Louie Louie'; 'Beautiful Delilah'; 'Long Tall Shorty'. Released: October 1983 (UK). Not issued in US.

A Complete Collection Complete CPL 2-2001 (US)
Released: February 1984 (US). Not issued in UK.

20th Anniversary Edition Complete CDL2-2003 (US)
Released: August 1984 (US). Not issued in UK.

The Kinks Kollectibles PRT KINK 7252 (UK)
'I'm Not Like Everybody Else'; 'This Is Where I Belong'; 'Rats'; 'Act Nice And Gentle'; 'You Still Want Me'; 'You Do Something To Me'; 'I Took My Baby Home'; 'Creeping Jean'; 'Hold My Hand'; 'Lincoln County'; 'Susannah's Still Alive'; 'Polly'; 'Sitting On My Sofa'; 'Mindless Child Of Motherhood'.
Released: November 1984 (UK). Not issued in US.

The Kinks Kovers PRT KINK 7253 (UK)
'Cadillac'; 'Dancing In The Street'; 'Louie Louie'; 'Long Tall Sally'; 'Naggin' Woman'; 'Too Much Monkey Business'; 'Milk Cow Blues'; 'Beautiful Delilah'; 'Bald Headed Woman'; 'I've Been Driving On Bald Mountain'; 'I'm A Lover Not A Fighter'; 'Long Tall Shorty'; 'Got Love If You Want It'.
Released: November 1984 (UK). Not issued in US.

The Kinks – 20th Anniversary Box Set PRT KINKX 7254 (UK)
'You Really Got Me'; 'All Day And All Of The Night'; 'Tired Of Waiting For You'; 'Ev'rybody's Gonna Be Happy'; 'Set Me Free'; 'See My Friends'; 'Till The End Of The Day'; 'Dedicated Follower Of Fashion'; 'Sunny Afternoon'; 'Dead End Street'; 'Waterloo Sunset'; 'Autumn Almanac'; 'Wonderboy'; 'Days'; 'Plastic Man'; 'Victoria'; 'Lola'; 'Apeman'; 'I'm Not Like Everybody Else'; 'This Is Where I Belong'; 'Rats'; 'Act Nice And Gentle'; 'You Still Want Me'; 'You Do Something To Me'; 'I Took My Baby Home'; 'Creeping Jean'; 'Hold My Hand'; 'Lincoln County'; 'Susannah's Still Alive'; 'Polly'; 'Sitting On My Sofa'; 'Mindless Child Of Motherhood'; 'Cadillac'; 'Dancing In The Street'; 'Louie Louie'; 'Long Tall Sally'; 'Naggin' Woman'; 'Too Much Monkey Business'; 'Milk Cow Blues'; 'Beautiful Delilah'; 'Bald Headed Woman'; 'I've Been Driving On Bald Mountain'; 'I'm A Lover Not A Fighter'; 'Long Tall Shorty'; 'Got Love If You Want It'.
Released: December 1984 (UK). Not released in US.

The Kinks Collection Castle Communications CCSLP 113 (UK)
Released: September 1985 (UK). Not issued in US.

Backtrackin' Starblend Track 1 (UK)
Released: December 1985 (UK). Not issued in US.

Come Dancing With The Kinks – The Best Of The Kinks 1977–1986 Arista 302 778 (UK)/Arista A2CD-8428 (US)

'You Really Got Me' (live); 'Destroyer'; '(Wish I Could Fly Like) Superman'; 'Juke Box Music'; 'A Rock 'n' Roll Fantasy'; 'Come Dancing'; 'Sleepwalker'; 'Catch Me Now I'm Falling'; 'Do It Again'; 'Better Things'; 'Lola' (live); 'Low Budget'; 'Long Distance'; 'Heart Of Gold'; 'Don't Forget To Dance'; 'Misfits'; 'Living On A Thin Line'; 'Father Christmas'; 'Celluloid Heroes' (live).
Released: October 1986 (UK)/June 1986 (US).

Hit Singles PRT PYL 4001 (UK)
'You Really Got Me'; 'All Day And All Of The Night'; 'Tired Of Waiting For You'; 'Ev'rybody's Gonna Be Happy'; 'Set Me Free'; 'See My Friend'; 'Till The End Of The Day'; 'Dedicated Follower Of Fashion'; 'Sunny Afternoon'; 'Dead End Street'; 'Waterloo Sunset'; 'Death Of A Clown'; 'Autumn Almanac'; 'Susannah's Still Alive'; 'Wonderboy'; 'Days'; 'Plastic Man'; 'Victoria'; 'Lola'; 'Apeman'.
Released: September 1987 (UK). Not issued in US.

The Kinks Are Well Respected Men PRT PYL 7001 (UK)
Released: September 1987 (UK). Not issued in US.

Greatest Hits Rhino R2 70086 (US)
'You Really Got Me'; 'All Day And All Of The Night'; 'Set Me Free'; 'Who'll Be The Next In Line'; 'Come On Now'; 'Ev'rybody's Gonna Be Happy'; 'I Need You'; 'Till The End Of The Day'; 'Tired Of Waiting For You'; 'A Well Respected Man'; 'You Do Something To Me'; 'You Still Want Me'; 'Stop Your Sobbing'; 'Something Better Beginning'; 'Dedicated Follower Of Fashion'; 'I'm Not Like Everybody Else'; 'Where Have All The Good Times Gone'; 'Sunny Afternoon'.
Released: March 1989 (US). Not issued in UK.

The Best Of The Kinks 1964–65 Pickwick SHM 3265 (UK)
Released: May 1989 (UK). Not issued in US.

The Ultimate Collection Castle Communications CTVLP 001/CTV CD 001 (UK)
Two-LP set. 'You Really Got Me'; 'All Day And All Of The Night'; 'Tired Of Waiting For You'; 'Ev'rybody's Gonna Be Happy'; 'Set Me Free'; 'See My Friend'; 'Till The End Of The Day'; 'Dedicated Follower Of Fashion'; 'Sunny Afternoon'; 'Dead End Street'; 'Waterloo Sunset'; 'Autumn Almanac'; 'Wonderboy'; 'Days'; 'Plastic Man'; 'Victoria'; 'Lola'; 'Apeman'; 'David Watts'; 'Where Have All The Good Times Gone'; 'A Well Respected Man'; 'I'm Not Like Everybody Else'; 'End Of The Season'; 'Death Of A Clown'; 'Susannah's Still Alive'.
Released: September 1989 (UK). Not issued in US.

The EP Collection See For Miles SEE 295 (UK)
'See My Friend'; 'All Day And All Of The Night'; 'I Gotta Move'; 'Louie Louie'; 'I've Got That Feeling'; 'A Well Respected Man'; 'Don't You Fret'; 'It's Alright'; 'Things Are Getting Better'; 'I Gotta Go Now'; 'Set Me Free'; 'You Really Got Me'; 'Wait Till The Summer Comes Along'; 'Till The End Of The Day'; 'Such A Shame'; 'Dedicated Follower Of Fashion'; 'David Watts'; 'Two Sisters'; 'Lazy Old Sun'; 'Situation Vacant'; 'Death Of A Clown'; 'Love Me Till The Sun Shines'; 'Funny Face'; 'Susannah's Still Alive'.
Released: June 1990 (UK). Not issued in US.

Lost And Found 1986–89 MCA MCAD-10338 (US)
Released: August 1991 (US). Not issued in UK.

The EP Collection Volume Two See For Miles SEE 329 (UK)
'Long Tall Shorty'; 'I Took My Baby Home'; 'Got Love If You Want It'; 'Tired Of Waiting For You'; 'Come On Now'; 'You Can't Win'; 'Where Have All The Good Times Gone'; 'Never Met A Girl Like You Before'; 'Party Line'; 'Dandy'; 'Sunny Afternoon'; 'Dead End Street'; 'I'm Not Like Everybody Else'; 'Big Black Smoke'; 'Session Man'; 'Fancy'; 'This Is Where I Belong'; 'Sitting On My Sofa'; 'Mister Pleasant'; 'Waterloo Sunset'; 'Act Nice And Gentle'; 'Village Green'.
Released: November 1991 (UK). Not issued in US.

The Definitive Collection Polygram TV 516 465-2 (UK)
Released: September 1993 (UK). Not issued in US.

Tired Of Waiting For You Rhino R2 71489 (US)
Released: January 1995 (US). Not issued in UK.

The Kinks Remastered Castle Communications ESB CD 268 (UK)
Three-CD set.
'You Do Something To Me'; 'So Mystifying'; 'Stop Your Sobbing'; 'You Still Want Me'; 'Got Love If You Want It'; 'I Gotta Go Now'; 'Things Are Getting Better'; 'Too Much Monkey Business'; 'Revenge'; 'Long Tall Sally'; 'Long Tall Shorty'; 'Louie Louie'; 'I Gotta Move'; 'I Took My Baby Home'; 'I'm A Lover Not A Fighter'; 'I've Been Driving On Bald Mountain'; 'I've Got That Feeling'; 'Just Can't Go To Sleep'; 'It's Alright'; 'You Really Got Me'; 'All Day And All Of The Night'; 'Gotta Get The First Plane Home'; 'Bald Headed Woman'; 'Beautiful Delilah'; 'Cadillac'; 'Come On Now'; 'Dancing In The Street'; 'Don't Ever Change'; 'Don't You Fret'; 'A Well Respected Man'; 'I Need You'; 'Set Me Free'; 'It's Too Late'; 'Look For Me Baby'; 'Milk Cow Blues'; 'Naggin' Woman'; 'Never Met A Girl Like You Before'; 'See My Friend'; 'Till The End Of The Day'; 'The World Keeps Going Round'; 'Tired Of Waiting For You'; 'Ev'rybody's Gonna Be Happy'; 'I Am Free'; 'You Shouldn't Be So Sad'; 'Who'll Be The Next In Line'; 'Wonder Where My Baby Is Tonight'; 'I'm Not Like Everybody Else'; 'I'm On An Island'; 'Where Have All The Good Times Gone'; 'Dedicated Follower Of Fashion'; 'Dandy'; 'Sunny Afternoon'; 'Waterloo Sunset'; 'Dead End Street'; 'Autumn Almanac'; 'Death Of A Clown'; 'Till The End Of The Day'; 'You Really Got Me'; 'Lola'; 'Apeman'.
Released: March 1995 (UK). Not issued in US.

The Very Best Of The Kinks Polygram TV 537 554-2 (UK)
'You Really Got Me'; 'All Day And All Of The Night'; 'Stop Your Sobbing'; 'Tired Of Waiting For You'; 'Ev'rybody's Gonna Be Happy'; 'Set Me Free'; 'See My Friends'; 'Till The End Of The Day'; 'Where Have All The Good Times Gone'; 'A Well Respected Man'; 'Dedicated Follower Of Fashion'; 'Sunny Afternoon'; 'Dead End Street'; 'Waterloo Sunset'; 'Death Of A Clown'; 'Autumn Almanac'; 'Susannah's Still Alive'; 'David Watts'; 'Wonderboy'; 'Days'; 'Plastic Man'; 'Victoria'; 'Lola'; 'Apeman'; 'Louie Louie'.
Released: May 1997 (UK). Not issued in US.

The Singles Collection Essential ESS CD 592 (UK)
'Long Tall Sally'; 'You Still Want Me'; 'You Really Got Me'; 'All Day And All Of The Night'; 'Tired Of Waiting For You'; 'Ev'rybody's Gonna Be Happy'; 'Set Me Free'; 'See My Friend'; 'Till The End Of The Day'; 'Where Have All The Good Times Gone'; 'Dedicated Follower Of Fashion'; 'A Well Respected Man'; 'Sunny Afternoon'; 'Dead End Street'; 'Waterloo Sunset'; 'Death Of A Clown'; 'Autumn Almanac'; 'David Watts'; 'Susannah's Still Alive'; 'Wonderboy'; 'Days'; 'Plastic Man'; 'Victoria'; 'Lola'; 'Apeman'. (For contents of Disc Two see *The Songs Of Ray Davies Waterloo Sunset*). Released: September 1997 (UK).

Come Dancing With The Kinks – The Best Of The Kinks 1977–1986 Konk/Velvel/Koch VEL-79733 (US)
'Come Dancing'; 'Low Budget'; 'Catch Me Now I'm Falling'; 'A Gallon Of Gas'; '(Wish I Could Fly Like) Superman'; 'Sleepwalker'; 'Full Moon'; 'Misfits'; 'A Rock 'n' Roll Fantasy'; 'Do It Again'; 'Better Things'; 'Lola'; 'You Really Got Me'; 'Good Day'; 'Living On A Thin Line'; 'Destroyer'; 'Don't Forget To Dance'; 'Father Christmas'. Released: October 2000 (US). Not issued in UK.

The Marble Arch Years Essential/Castle/Sanctuary CMGBX318 (UK)
Three-CD box set, combining *Well Respected Kinks*, *Sunny Afternoon* and *Kinda Kinks*. Released: July 2001 (UK). Not issued in US.

BBC Session 1964–1977 BBC/Sanctuary SANDD010 (UK)/Sanctuary 06076 84504-2 (US)
Interview; 'You Really Got Me'; Interview; 'Cadillac'; 'All Day And All Of The Night'; 'Tired Of Waiting For You'; 'Ev'rybody's Gonna Be Happy'; 'See My Friend'; 'This Strange Effect'; 'Milk Cow Blues'; 'Wonder Where My Baby Is Tonight'; 'Till The End Of The Day'; 'Where Have All The Good Times Gone'; 'Death Of A Clown'; 'Love Me Till The Sun Shines'; 'Harry Rag'; 'Good Luck Charm'; 'Waterloo Sunset'; 'Monica'; 'Days'; 'The Village Green Preservation Society'; 'Mindless Child Of Motherhood'; 'Holiday'; 'Demolition'; 'Victoria'; 'Here Comes Yet Another Day'; 'Money Talks'; 'Mirror Of Love'; 'Skin And Bone'/'Dry Bones'; 'Get Back In Line'; 'Did You See His Name'; 'When I Turn Off The Living Room Light'; 'Skin And Bone'; 'Money Talks'. Released: March 2001 (UK/US).

The Ultimate Collection Sanctuary RTV0023 (UK)
'You Really Got Me'; 'All Day And All Of The Night'; 'Tired Of Waiting For You'; 'Ev'rybody's Gonna Be Happy'; 'Set Me Free'; 'See My Friend'; 'Till The End Of The Day'; 'Dedicated Follower Of Fashion'; 'Sunny Afternoon'; 'Dead End Street'; 'Waterloo Sunset'; 'Death Of A Clown'; 'Autumn Almanac'; 'Susannah's Still Alive'; 'Wonderboy'; 'Days'; 'Plastic Man'; 'Victoria'; 'Lola'; 'Apeman'; 'Supersonic Rocket Ship'; 'Better Things'; 'Come Dancing'; 'Don't Forget To Dance'; 'David Watts'; 'Stop Your Sobbing'; 'Dandy'; 'Mister Pleasant'; 'I Gotta Move'; 'Who'll Be The Next In Line'; 'I Need You'; 'Where Have All The Good Times Gone'; 'Sitting On My Sofa'; 'A Well Respected Man'; 'I'm Not Like Everybody Else'; 'Love Me Till The Sun Shines'; 'She's Got Everything'; 'Starstruck'; 'Shangri-la'; 'God's Children'; 'Celluloid Heroes'; '(Wish I Could Fly Like) Superman'; 'Do It Again'; 'Living On A Thin Line'. Released: May 2002 (UK).

The Kinks' Greatest – Celluloid Heroes Konk/Velvel/Koch VEL-CD-79734 (US)
'20th Century Man'; 'Complicated Life'; 'Muswell Hillbilly'; 'Alcohol'; 'Celluloid Heroes'; 'Here Comes Yet Another Day'; 'Sweet Lady Genevieve'; One Of The Survivors'; 'Sitting In The Midday Sun'; 'He's Evil'; 'Mirror Of Love'; 'Artificial Man'; 'Everybody's A Star (Starmaker)'; '(A) Face In A Crowd'; 'You Can't Stop The Music'; 'I'm In Disgrace'; 'The Hard Way'; 'No More Looking Back'.
Released: September 2001 (US). Not issued in UK.

Greatest Hits 1970–1986 Konk/Velvel/Koch VEL-79822 (US)
Three-CD set. Disc 1 features *The Kinks' Greatest – Celluloid Heroes*. Disc 2 assembles the US version of *Come Dancing With The Kinks – The Best Of The Kinks 1977–1986*. Disc 3 adds the DVD *One For The Road*.
Released: October 2007 (US).

Picture Book Sanctuary/Universal KINKSSPBCD1-6 (UK)/Universal/Sanctuary 531304 9 (US)
Six-CD box set, includes previously unreleased material.
Volume One: 'Brian Matthew Introduces The Kinks'; 'You Really Got Me'; 'I'm A Hog For You, Baby'; 'I Believed You'; 'Long Tall Sally'; 'I Don't Need You Anymore'; 'Stop Your Sobbing'; 'I Gotta Move'; 'Don't Ever Let Me Go'; 'All Day And All Of The Night'; 'Tired Of Waiting For You'; 'Come On Now'; 'There's A New World Just Opening For Me'; 'Ev'rybody's Gonna Be Happy'; 'Who'll Be The Next In Line'; 'Time Will Tell'; 'Set Me Free'; 'I Need You'; 'See My Friend'; 'Wait Till The Summer Comes Along'; 'I Go To Sleep'; 'A Little Bit Of Sunlight'; 'This I Know'; 'A Well Respected Man'; 'This Strange Effect'; 'Milk Cow Blues'; 'Ring The Bells'; 'I'm On An Island'; 'Till The End Of The Day'; 'Where Have All The Good Times Gone'; 'All Night Stand'; 'And I Will Love You'; 'Sittin' On My Sofa'.
Volume Two: 'Dedicated Follower Of Fashion'; 'She's Got Everything'; 'Mr Reporter'; 'Sunny Afternoon'; 'I'm Not Like Everybody Else'; 'This Is Where I Belong'; 'Rosy Won't You Please Come Home'; 'Too Much On My Mind'; 'Session Man'; 'End Of The Season'; 'Dead End Street'; 'Village Green'; 'Two Sisters'; 'David Watts'; 'Mister Pleasant'; 'Waterloo Sunset'; 'Death Of A Clown'; 'Lavender Hill'; 'Good Luck Charm'; 'Autumn Almanac'; 'Susannah's Still Alive'; 'Animal Farm'; 'Rosemary Rose'; 'Berkeley Mews'; 'Lincoln County'; 'Picture Book'; 'Days'; 'Misty Water'.
Volume Three: 'Love Me Till The Sun Shines'; 'The Village Green Preservation Society'; 'Big Sky'; 'King Kong'; 'Drivin''; 'Some Mother's Son'; 'Victoria'; 'Shangri-la'; 'Arthur'; 'Got To Be Free'; 'Lola'; 'Get Back In Line'; 'The Moneygoround'; 'Strangers'; 'Apeman'; 'God's Children'; 'The Way Love Used To Be'; 'Moments'; 'Muswell Hillbilly'; 'Oklahoma USA'; '20th Century Man'; 'Here Come The People In Grey'.
Volume Four: 'Skin And Bone'; 'Alcohol' (live); 'Celluloid Heroes'; 'Sitting In My Hotel'; 'Supersonic Rocketship'; 'You Don't Know My Name'; 'One Of The Survivors'; 'Sitting In The Midday Sun'; 'Sweet Lady Genevieve'; 'Daylight'; 'Mirror Of Love'; 'Artificial Man'; 'Preservation'; 'Slum Kids' (live); 'Holiday Romance'; '(A) Face In The Crowd'; 'No More Looking Back'; 'Sleepwalker'; 'The Poseur' (aka 'The Poser').
Volume Five: 'Sleepless Nights'; 'Father Christmas'; 'Misfits'; 'A Rock 'n' Roll Fantasy'; 'A Little Bit Of Emotion'; 'Attitude'; 'Hidden Quality'; 'Gallon Of Gas'; 'Catch Me Now

I'm Falling'; 'Nuclear Love'; 'Duke'; 'Maybe I Love You'; 'Stolen Away Your Heart'; 'Low Budget' (live); 'Better Things'; 'Destroyer'; 'Yo-Yo'; 'Art Lover'; 'Long Distance'. Volume Six: 'Heart Of Gold'; 'Come Dancing'; 'State Of Confusion'; 'Do It Again'; 'Living On A Thin Line'; 'Summer's Gone'; 'How Are You?'; 'The Road' (live); 'Million-Pound-Semi-Detached'; 'Down All The Days (Till 1992)'; 'The Informer'; 'Phobia'; 'Only A Dream'; 'Drift Away'; 'Scattered'; 'Do You Remember Walter?' (live). Released: December 2008 (UK/US).

The Kinks In Mono Sanctuary/Universal Music 602527769448 (UK)
Ten-CD set featuring mono versions of *Kinks, Kinda Kinks, The Kinks Kontroversy, Face To Face, Something Else, The Village Green Preservation Society* and *Arthur*. Disc 8 includes the group's EP tracks from the Sixties and Discs 9–10 feature previously issued collectible tracks.
Released: November 2011 (UK).

The Kinks At The BBC – Radio & TV Sessions And Concerts: 1964–1994 Sanctuary/Universal 279 721-8 (UK)
Six-CD box set.
Disc 1: Meet The Kinks (BBC interview); 'Cadillac'; 'You Really Got Me'; 'Little Queenie'; 'I'm A Lover Not A Fighter'; The Shaggy Set (BBC interview); 'You Really Got Me'; 'All Day And All Of The Night'; Ray Talks About the USA (BBC interview); 'I've Got A Feeling'; 'All Day And All Of The Night'; 'You Shouldn't Be Sad'; Ray Talks About Records (BBC interview); 'Tired Of Waiting For You'; 'Ev'rybody's Gonna Be Happy'; 'This Strange Effect'; Ray Talks About 'See My Friends' (BBC interview); 'See My Friends'; 'Hide And Seek'; 'Milk Cow Blues'; Ray Talks About Songwriting (BBC interview); 'Never Met A Girl Like You Before'; 'Wonder Where My Baby Is Tonight'; 'Till The End Of The Day'; 'A Well Respected Man'; 'Where Have All The Good Times Gone'; 'Love Me Till The Sun Shines'; Meet Dave Davies (BBC interview); 'Death Of A Clown'; 'Good Luck Charm'; 'Sunny Afternoon'; 'Autumn Almanac'; 'Harry Rag'; 'Mister Pleasant'. Disc 2: 'Susannah's Still Alive'; 'David Watts'; 'Waterloo Sunset'; Ray Talks About Working (BBC interview); 'Days'; Ray Talks About Solo Records (BBC interview); 'Love Me Till The Sun Shines'; 'Monica'; Ray Talks About 'Village Green' (BBC interview); 'The Village Green Preservation Society'; 'Animal Farm'; 'Where Did My Spring Go?'; 'When I Turn Off The Living Room Light'; 'Plastic Man'; 'King Kong'; 'Do You Remember Walter'; Ray Talks About Rumours (BBC interview); 'Victoria'; 'Mr Churchill Says'; 'Arthur'; Ray Talks With Keith Altham (BBC interview); 'Lola'; 'Mindless Child Of Motherhood'; 'Days'; 'Apeman'; 'Acute Schizophrenia Paranoia Blues'; 'Holiday'; 'Skin And Bone'. Disc 3: 'Supersonic Rocket Ship'; 'Here Comes Yet Another Day'; 'Demolition'; 'Mirror Of Love'; 'Money Talks'; DJ Alan Black introduces *In Concert*; 'Victoria'; 'Here Comes Yet Another Day'; 'Mr Wonderful'; 'Money Talks'; 'Dedicated Follower Of Fashion'; 'Mirror Of Love'; 'Celluloid Heroes'; 'Medley: You Really Got Me/All Day And All Of The Night'; DJ Alan Black talks about *Preservation Act* 2; 'Daylight'; 'Here Comes Flash'; 'Demolition'; 'He's Evil'; 'Lola'; Outro; 'Skin And Bone'. Disc 4: Alan Freeman introduction; 'Juke Box Music'; Bob Harris introduction; 'Sleepwalker'; 'Life On The Road'; 'A Well Respected Man'; Death Of A Clown'; 'Sunny Afternoon'; 'Waterloo Sunset'; 'All Day And All Of The Night'; 'Slum Kids'; 'Celluloid

Heroes'; 'Get Back In Line'; 'The Hard Way'; 'Lola'; 'Alcohol'; 'Skin And Bone'; 'Father Christmas'; 'You Really Got Me'; Ray Talks To Johnnie Walker (BBC interview); 'Phobia'; Ray Introduces 'Over The Edge' (BBC interview); 'Over The Edge'; 'Wall Of Fire'; 'Till The End Of The Day'.

Disc 5: 'All Day And All Of The Night'; 'Waterloo Sunset'; 'I'm Not Like Everybody Else'; 'Till The End Of The Day'; 'You Really Got Me'; 'Louie Louie'; 'Stop Your Sobbing'; 'Milk Cow Blues'; 'I Am Free'; 'Susannah's Still Alive'; 'Days'; 'Medley: Dedicated Follower Of Fashion/A Well Respected Man/Death Of A Clown'; 'Sunny Afternoon'; 'Two Sisters'; 'Sitting By The Riverside'; 'Lincoln County'; 'Picture Book'; 'Days'.

Disc 6: bonus DVD.

Released: August 2012 (UK).

Best Of The Kinks 1964–1971 Sanctuary Legacy Camden BMG Sony 8887500299 (UK)/ BMG 14018 (US)

'You Really Got Me'; 'I Need You'; 'Tired Of Waiting For You'; 'See My Friends'; 'Till The End Of The Day'; 'Dedicated Follower Of Fashion'; 'Where Have All The Good Times Gone'; 'Sunny Afternoon'; 'David Watts'; 'Wonderboy'; 'Death Of A Clown'; 'Days'; 'Picture Book'; 'Victoria'; 'Lola'; 'Strangers'; 'God's Children'.

Released: August 2014 (UK)/September 2014 (US).

The Essential Kinks Legacy/Sony Music RCA/Arista/Legacy 88843066622 (US)

'You Really Got Me'; 'Stop Your Sobbing'; 'All Day And All Of The Night'; 'Tired Of Waiting For You'; 'Nothin' In This World (Can Stop Me Worryin' 'Bout That Girl)'; 'Ev'rybody's Gonna Be Happy'; 'A Well Respected Man'; 'Dedicated Follower Of Fashion'; 'Who'll Be The Next In Line'; 'Set Me Free; 'See My Friends'; 'Sunny Afternoon'; 'Dead End Street'; 'Death Of A Clown'; 'Autumn Almanac'; 'David Watts'; 'Waterloo Sunset'; 'Days'; 'The Village Green Preservation Society'; 'Do You Remember Walter'; 'Picture Book'; 'Victoria'; 'Apeman'; 'Strangers'; '20th Century Man'; 'Supersonic Rocket Ship'; 'Celluloid Heroes' (US single version); 'Here Comes Yet Another Day'; 'You Don't Know My Name'; 'Till The End Of The Day'(live); 'One Of The Survivors'; 'Sweet Lady Genevieve'; 'Everybody's A Star (Starmaker)'; 'Life On The Road'; 'A Rock 'n' Roll Fantasy'; 'Father Christmas'; '(Wish I Could Fly Like) Superman'; 'Lola' (live); 'Where Have All The Good Times Gone' (live); 'Better Things' (single version); 'Destroyer'; 'Come Dancing'; 'Don't Forget To Dance'; 'Do It Again'; 'Living On A Thin Line'; 'Scattered'.

Released: October 2014 (UK/US).

The Kinks Anthology 1964–1971 Sanctuary BMG/Sony/Legacy 88875021542 (UK)/(US)

Five-CD box set.

Disc 1: 'I'm A Hog For You, Baby' (Bo-Weevils); 'I Don't Need You Anymore' (demo); 'Ev'rybody's Gonna Be Happy' (demo); 'Long Tall Sally'; 'I Took My Baby Home'; 'You Still Want Me'; 'You Do Something To Me'; 'You Really Got Me'; 'It's All Right'; 'Beautiful Delilah' (mono mix); 'Just Can't Go To Sleep'; 'I'm A Lover, Not A Fighter' (mono mix); 'Little Queenie' (live); 'Too Much Monkey Business' (alternate take); 'Stop Your Sobbing' (mono); 'All Day And All Of The Night'; 'I Gotta Move'; 'I Gotta Go Now'; 'I've Got That Feeling' (live); 'Tired Of Waiting For You'; 'Come On Now' (alternate mix); 'Look For Me Baby'; 'Nothin' In The World Can Stop Me Worryin'

'Bout That Girl'; 'Wonder Where My Baby Is Tonight'; 'Don't Ever Change'; 'You Shouldn't Be Sad'; 'Something Better Beginning'; 'Ev'rybody's Gonna Be Happy'; 'Who'll Be The Next In Line' (session excerpt – backing track, take one; previously unreleased); 'Who'll Be The Next In Line' (alternate mix; previously unreleased); 'Set Me Free'; 'I Need You'; Interview: 'Clay Cole Meets The Kinks' (previously unreleased).

Disc 2: 'See My Friend'; 'Never Met A Girl Like You Before'; 'I Go To Sleep' (demo); 'A Little Bit Of Sunlight' (demo); 'Tell Me Now So I'll Know' (alternate demo; previously unreleased); 'When I See That Girl Of Mine' (demo); 'There's A New World Just Opening For Me' (demo); 'This Strange Effect' (live); 'Hide And Seek' (live); 'A Well Respected Man'; 'Such A Shame'; 'Don't You Fret'; 'Till The End Of The Day'; 'Where Have All The Good Times Gone'; 'Milk Cow Blues'; 'I Am Free'; 'The World Keeps Going Round'; 'I'm On An Island'; 'You Can't Win'; 'Time Will Tell'; 'Dedicated Follower Of Fashion' (session excerpt – takes 1–3; previously unreleased); 'Dedicated Follower Of Fashion'; 'Sittin' On My Sofa'; 'She's Got Everything' (backing track, take two; previously unreleased); 'She's Got Everything' (alternate mono mix; previously unreleased); 'Mr Reporter' (version one); 'All Night Stand' (demo).

Disc 3: 'Sunny Afternoon'; 'I'm Not Like Everybody Else'; 'Dandy'; 'Party Line'; 'Rosy Won't You Please Come Home'; 'Too Much On My Mind'; 'Session Man'; 'Most Exclusive Residence For Sale'; 'Fancy'; 'Dead End Street'; 'Big Black Smoke' (alternate stereo mix; previously unreleased); 'Mister Pleasant' (previously unreleased mix); 'This Is Where I Belong' (previously unreleased mix); 'Village Green' (previously unreleased mix); 'Two Sisters' (previously unreleased mix); 'Waterloo Sunset' (session excerpt – backing track, take two; previously unreleased); 'Waterloo Sunset'; 'Act Nice And Gentle' (previously unreleased mix); 'Harry Rag' (session excerpt; previously unreleased); 'Harry Rag'; 'Death Of A Clown'; 'Love Me Till The Sun Shines'; 'David Watts'; 'Tin Soldier Man'; 'Afternoon Tea' (alternate stereo mix; previously unreleased); 'Funny Face'; 'Lazy Old Sun' (alternate stereo mix; previously unreleased); 'Suzanah's Still Alive'; 'Good Luck Charm' (previously unreleased mix).

Disc 4: 'Autumn Almanac'; 'Lavender Hill'; 'Rosemary Rose'; 'Wonderboy'; 'Polly'; 'Lincoln County' (Dave Davies: previously unreleased mix); 'Did You See His Name?' (previously unreleased alternate ending); 'Days' (session excerpt: previously unreleased); 'Days'; 'Misty Water' (alternate previously unreleased mix); 'Do You Remember Walter' (mono); 'Picture Book' (mono); 'Johnny Thunder' (stereo mix); 'Big Sky' (mono); 'Animal Farm' (mono); 'Starstruck'; 'Pictures In The Sand' (mono); 'People Take Pictures Of Each Other' (European stereo mix); BBC Ray Davies Interview; 'The Village Green Preservation Society' (live); 'Hold My Hand' (Dave Davies); 'Creeping Jean' (Dave Davies); 'Berkeley Mews' (stereo); 'Till Death Us Do Part'; 'When I Turn Off The Living Room Light'; 'Where Did My Spring Go?'; 'Plastic Man' (stereo); 'King Kong'; 'This Man He Weeps Tonight' (Dave Davies); Reprise US Tour Spot.

Disc 5: 'Victoria'; 'Some Mother's Son'; 'Drivin''; 'Shangri-La'; 'She Bought A Hat Like Princess Marina'; 'Young And Innocent Days'; 'Mindless Child Of Motherhood' (Dave Davies); 'Lola' (mono); 'Apeman'; 'Strangers'; 'Get Back In (The) Line'; 'Anytime'; 'This Time Tomorrow'; 'A Long Way From Home'; 'Powerman'; 'Got To Be Free'; 'Dreams'; 'Moments'; 'The Way Love Used To Be'; 'God's Children'.

Released: November 2014 (UK)/December 2014 (US).

EXPANDED EDITIONS

The Kinks' catalogue has been enhanced by a series of CD expanded editions of the original albums. This is an ongoing process. Below is a list of these releases up until late 2014 (excluding any reissues on which *no* bonus tracks or new material appear).

Kinks Essential ESS 482 (UK)
Original album, followed by bonus tracks: 'Long Tall Sally'; 'You Still Want Me'; 'You Do Something To Me'; 'It's Alright'; 'All Day And All Of The Night'; 'I Gotta Move'; 'Louie, Louie'; 'I Gotta Go Now'; 'Things Are Getting Better'; 'I've Got That Feeling'; 'Too Much Monkey Business' (unreleased alternate take); 'I Don't Need You Anymore' (previously unreleased).
Released: April 1998 (UK)

Kinks Sanctuary/Universal UMC 275 627-4 (UK)
Deluxe Edition, double CD. Disc 1 features original stereo version of the album, plus: 'I Believed You' (mono demo); 'I'm A Hog For You Baby' (mono demo); 'I Don't Need You Anymore'; 'Ev'rybody's Gonna Be Happy' (alternate take); 'Long Tall Sally'; 'You Still Want Me'; 'You Do Something To Me'; 'It's Alright'; 'All Day And All Of The Night'; I Gotta Move'; 'Louie Louie'; 'I've Got That Feeling'; 'I Gotta Go Now'; 'Things Are Getting Better'.
Disc 2 features the original mono album, plus: 'Don't Ever Let Me Go' (mono); 'I Don't Need You Anymore' (mono); 'Bald Headed Woman' (mono, US album mix); 'Too Much Monkey Business' (alternate take); 'Got Love If You Want It' (alternate take); Meet The Kinks (BBC interview); 'Cadillac' (BBC live); Ray Talks About 'You Really Got Me' (BBC interview); 'You Really Got Me' (BBC live); 'Little Queenie' (BBC live); 'I'm A Lover Not A Fighter' (BBC live); 'All Day And All Of The Night' (BBC live); Ray Talks About The USA (BBC interview); 'I've Got That Feeling' (BBC live).
Released: March 2011 (UK).

Kinda Kinks Essential ESS CD 483 (UK)
Original album, followed by bonus tracks: 'Ev'rybody's Gonna Be Happy'; 'Who'll Be The Next In Line'; 'Set Me Free'; 'I Need You'; 'See My Friend'; 'Never Met A Girl Like You Before'; 'Wait Till The Summer Comes Along'; 'Such A Shame'; 'A Well Respected Man'; 'Don't You Fret'; 'I Go To Sleep' (unreleased demo recording).
Released: April 1998 (UK).

Kinda Kinks Sanctuary/Universal UMC 275 632-6 (UK)
Deluxe Edition, double CD. Disc 1 features original mono version of the album in full. Disc 2 includes the bonus tracks from the April 1998 edition, plus 'A Well Respected Man', with the following additions: 'When I See That Girl Of Mine' (demo); 'Tell Me Now So I'll Know' (demo); 'A Little Bit Of Sunlight' (demo); 'There's A New World Just Opening For Me' (demo); 'This I Know' (demo); 'See My Friends' (alternate version); 'Come On Now' (alternate vocals); 'You Shouldn't Be Sad' (BBC live); 'Tired Of Waiting For You' (BBC live); 'Ev'rybody's Gonna Be Happy' (BBC live); 'This Strange Effect' (BBC live); 'Hide And Seek' (BBC live).
Released: March 2011 (UK).

The Kinks Kontroversy Essential ESS CD 507 (UK)
Original album, followed by bonus tracks: 'Dedicated Follower Of Fashion'; 'Sittin' On My Sofa'; 'When I See That Girl Of Mine' (unreleased demo recording); 'Dedicated Follower Of Fashion' (unreleased alternate stereo take).
Released: April 1998 (UK).

The Kinks Kontroversy Sanctuary/Universal UMC 275 628-5 (UK)
Deluxe Edition, double CD. Disc 1 features original mono version of the album in full.
Disc 2: 'Dedicated Follower Of Fashion' (mono); 'Sittin' On My Sofa' (mono); 'Mr Reporter' (outtake); 'Dedicated Follower Of Fashion' (alternate take); 'Time Will Tell' (outtake); 'And I Will Love You'; 'I'm Not Like Everybody Else' (alternate vocal); 'All Night Stand' (demo); 'Milk Cow Blues' (BBC live); Ray Talks About Songwriting; 'Never Met A Girl Like You Before' (BBC live); 'Wonder Where My Baby Is Tonight' (BBC live); Pete Talks About Records; 'Till The End Of The Day' (BBC live); 'A Well Respected Man' (BBC live); 'Where Have All The Good Times Gone' (BBC live).
Released March 2011 (UK).

Face To Face Essential ESS CD 479 (UK)
Original album, followed by bonus tracks: 'I'm Not Like Everybody Else'; 'Dead End Street'; 'Big Black Smoke'; 'Mister Pleasant'; 'This Is Where I Belong'; 'Mr Reporter' (previously unreleased); 'Little Women' (previously unreleased backing track).
Released: April 1998 (UK).

Face To Face Sanctuary/Universal UMC 277 262-0 (UK)
Deluxe Edition, double CD. Disc 1 features original mono version of the album in full, plus bonus tracks: 'Dead End Street' (mono); 'Big Black Smoke' (mono); 'This Is Where I Belong' (mono); 'She's Got Everything' (mono); 'Little Miss Queen Of Darkness' (alternate take); 'Dead End Street' (alternate take).
Disc 2 features original album in stereo, and bonus tracks: 'This Is Where I Belong'; 'Big Black Smoke'; 'She's Got Everything'; 'You're Looking Fine' (alternate stereo mix); 'Sunny Afternoon' (alternate stereo mix); 'Fancy' (alternate stereo mix); 'Little Miss Queen Of Darkness' (alternate stereo mix); 'Dandy' (alternate stereo mix).
Released: June 2011 (UK).

Something Else By The Kinks Essential ESS CD 480 (UK)
Original album, followed by bonus tracks: 'Act Nice And Gentle'; 'Autumn Almanac'; 'Susannah's Still Alive'; 'Wonderboy'; 'Polly'; 'Lincoln County'; 'There's No Life Without Love'; 'Lazy Old Sun' (unreleased alternate stereo take).
Released: April 1998 (UK).

Something Else By The Kinks Sanctuary/Universal UMC 273 214-1 (UK)
Deluxe Edition, double CD. Disc 1 features original mono version of the album in full, plus bonus tracks: 'Act Nice And Gentle'; 'Mister Pleasant'; 'Susannah's Still Alive'; 'Harry Rag' (alternate take, mono mix); 'David Watts' (alternate take, mono mix); 'Afternoon Tea' (alternate take, mono mix); 'Sunny Afternoon' (BBC live); 'Autumn Almanac' (BBC live); 'Mister Pleasant' (BBC live); 'Susannah's Still Alive' (BBC live); 'David Watts' (BBC live); 'Love Me Till The Sun Shines' (BBC live); 'Death Of A Clown' (BBC live); 'Good

Luck Charm' (BBC live); 'Harry Rag' (BBC live); 'Little Women' (backing track).
Disc 2 features original album in stereo, and bonus tracks: 'Susannah's Still Alive'; 'Autumn Almanac'; 'Sand On My Shoes'; 'Afternoon Tea' (alternate version); 'Mister Pleasant' (alternate version); 'Lazy Old Sun' (alternate vocals); 'Funny Face' (alternate version); 'Afternoon Tea' (alternate mix); 'Tin Soldier Man' (alternate backing track). Released: June 2011 (UK).

Live At Kelvin Hall Essential ESM CD 508 (UK)
Original album in mono, followed by original album in stereo. No bonus tracks. Released: June 1998 (UK).

The Kinks Are The Village Green Preservation Society Essential ESM CD 481 (UK)
Original album in mono, plus the 12-track stereo Continental issue which featured the stereo 'Days' and a bonus track of 'Days' (mono single version). Released: June 1998 (UK).

The Kinks Are The Village Green Preservation Society Sanctuary SMETD 102 (UK)
Three-CD set.
Disc 1 features original version of the 15-song album in stereo, with bonus tracks: 'Mr Songbird'; 'Days'; 'Do You Remember Walter' (12-track album version); 'People Take Pictures Of Each Other' (12-track album version).
Disc 2 features original version of the 15-song album in mono, with bonus tracks in mono: 'Days'; 'Do You Remember Walter'; 'People Take Pictures Of Each Other'; 'Days'; 'Mr Songbird'; 'Polly'; 'Wonderboy'; 'Berkeley Mews'; 'Village Green' (without strings).
Disc 3: 'Village Green' (backing track with strings); 'Misty Water'; 'Berkeley Mews'; 'Easy Come, There You Went'; 'Polly'; 'Animal Farm' (alternate mix); 'Phenomenal Cat' (backing track); 'Johnny Thunder' (alternate mix); 'Did You See His Name' (alternate ending); 'Mick Avory's Underpants'; 'Lavender Hill'; 'Rosemary Rose'; 'Wonderboy'; 'Spotty Grotty Anna'; 'Where Did My Spring Go'; 'Groovy Movies'; 'Creeping Jean'; 'King Kong'; 'Misty Water'; 'Do You Remember Walter' (BBC mix, new vocals); 'Animal Farm' (BBC mix, new vocals); 'Days' (BBC mix, new vocals). Released: June 2004 (UK).

Arthur Or The Decline And Fall Of The British Empire Essential ESM CD 511 (UK)
Original album, plus bonus tracks: 'Plastic Man' (mono); 'King Kong' (mono); 'Drivin'' (mono); 'Mindless Child Of Motherhood' (mono); 'This Man He Weeps Tonight' (mono); 'Plastic Man' (stereo); 'Mindless Child Of Motherhood' (stereo); 'This Man He Weeps Tonight' (stereo); 'She Bought A Hat Like Princess Marina' (mono); 'Mr Shoemaker's Daughter' (previously unreleased). Released: June 1998 (UK).

Arthur Or The Decline And Fall Of The British Empire Sanctuary/Universal UMC 273 227-4 (UK)
Deluxe Edition, double CD. Disc 1 features original mono version of the album in full, plus bonus tracks: 'Plastic Man'; 'This Man He Weeps Tonight'; 'Mindless Child Of Motherhood'; 'Creeping Jean'; 'Lincoln County'; 'Hold My Hand'; 'Victoria' (BBC live); 'Mr Churchill Says' (BBC live); 'Arthur' (BBC live).

Side 2 features original album in stereo, and bonus tracks: 'Plastic Man'; 'This Man He Weeps Tonight'; 'Drivin" (alternate stereo mix); 'Mindless Child Of Motherhood'; 'Hold My Hand'; 'Lincoln County'; 'Mr Shoemaker's Daughter'; 'Shangri-la' (backing track). Released: June 2011 (UK).

The Kinks Part One – Lola Versus Powerman And The Moneygoround Essential ESM CD 509 (UK)
Original album, plus bonus tracks: 'Lola' (single version); 'Apeman' (demo); 'Powerman' (demo).
Released: June 1998 (UK).

Percy Essential ESM CD 510 (UK)
Original album, plus bonus tracks: 'Dreams' (shorter version, minus the group's backing); 'Moments' (42-second instrumental fragment); 'The Way Love Used To Be' (orchestral; vocal, and instrumental takes).
Released: June 1998 (UK).

The Kinks – Lola Versus Powerman And The Moneygoround & Percy Legacy/Sony Music. BMG 88843089592 (UK)/BMG 14040 (US)
Deluxe Edition, double CD. Disc 1 features the original album, plus bonus tracks: 'Anytime'; 'The Contenders' (instrumental demo); 'The Good Life'; 'Lola' (alternate version); 'This Time Tomorrow' (instrumental); 'Apeman' (alternate stereo version); 'Got To Be Free' (alternate version).
Side 2 features the original *Percy*, plus bonus tracks: 'Dreams' (remixed); 'Apeman' (remastered); 'Rats' (single version); 'Powerman' (mono); 'The Moneygoround' (mono, alternate version); 'Apeman' (mono, alternate version); 'God's Children' (mono film mix); 'The Way Love Used To Be' (mono film mix); 'God's Children (End)' (mono film mix).
Released: August 2014 (UK/US).

Muswell Hillbillies Kink/Koch/Universal UMC 2738367 (UK) Konk/Velvel 63467-79719-2 (US)
Original album, plus bonus tracks: 'Mountain Woman'; Kentucky Moon'.
Released: June 2010 (UK)/July 1998 (US).

Muswell Hillbillies Sanctuary/Universal UMC 273 227-4 (UK)
Deluxe Edition, double CD. Disc 1 features original version of the album in full.
Side 2: 'Lavender Lane'; 'Mountain Woman'; 'Have A Cuppa Tea' (alternate version); 'Muswell Hillbilly' (edited); 'Uncle Son' (alternate version); 'Kentucky Moon'; 'Nobody's Fool' (demo, mono mix); '20th Century Man' (alternate instrumental take); '20th Century Man' (edited); 'Queenie' (instrumental backing track); 'Acute Schizophrenia Paranoia Blues' (BBC live); 'Holiday' (BBC live); 'Skin And Bone' (BBC live).
Released: October 2013 (UK).

Everybody's In Show-biz, Everybody's A Star Konk/Koch/Universal UMC 2738353 (UK)/Konk/Velvel 63467-79720-2 (US)
Original album, plus bonus tracks: 'Till The End Of The Day'; 'She Bought A Hat Like Princess Marina'.
Released: June 2010 (UK)/July 1998 (US).

Preservation (A Play In Two Acts) Rhino R2 70523 (US)
Two-CD set. Combination of *Preservation Act 1* and *Preservation Act 2*, with additional track, 'Preservation'.
Released: July 1991 (US). Not issued in UK.

Preservation Act 1 Konk/Koch/Universal Music 2738375 (UK)/ Konk/Velvel 63467-79721-2 (US)
Original album, bookended by bonus tracks 'Preservation' and 'One Of The Survivors'.
Released: June 2010 (UK)/July 1998 (US).

The Kinks Present A Soap Opera Konk/Velvel/BMG 63467-79723-2 (US)
Original album, plus bonus tracks: 'Everybody's A Star (Starmaker)' (mono mix); 'Ordinary People' (live); 'You Make It All Worthwhile' (live); 'Underneath The Neon Sign' (live).
Released: November 1998 (US).

Sleepwalker Konk/Velvel/BMG 63467-75725-2 (US)
Original album, plus bonus tracks: 'Artificial Light'; 'Prince Of The Punks'; 'The Poseur'; 'On The Outside'; 'On The Outside' (1994 mix).
Released: November 1998 (US).

Misfits Konk/Velvel/BMG 63467-79726-2 (US)
Original album, plus bonus tracks: 'Black Messiah' (single mix); 'Father Christmas'; 'A Rock 'n' Roll Fantasy' (edited); 'Live Life' (single mix).
Released: November 1998 (US).

Low Budget Konk/Velvel/BMG 63467-79727-2 (US)
Original album, plus bonus tracks: 'A Gallon Of Gas' (extended version); 'Catch Me Now I'm Falling' (backing track); '(Wish I Could Fly Like) Superman' (stereo mix, extended version).
Released: April 1999 (US).

One For The Road Konk/Velvel/BMG 63467-79728-2 (US)
Original album, plus CD Rom with videos.
Released: April 1999 (US).

State Of Confusion Konk/Velvel/BMG 63467-79731-2 (US)
Original album, plus bonus tracks: 'Don't Forget To Dance'; 'Once A Thief'; 'Long Distance'; 'Noise'.
Released: April 1999 (US).

Word Of Mouth Konk/Velvel/BMG 63467-79732-2 (US)
Original album, plus bonus tracks: 'Good Day' (extended version); 'Summer's Gone' (extended version).
Released: April 1999 (US).

BOOTLEGS/CONCERT TAPES

During the early Eighties, I produced a detailed list of Kinks bootlegs, cover versions and taped concerts (complete with song listings and gradings) which, even then, could only be partly accommodated in book form. Space restrictions preclude any attempt to include that information here. Interested parties should consult the extensive bootleg releases and related sections featured in the author's *A Mental Institution* and *The Sound And The Fury*.

DAVE DAVIES SINGLES

During the Sixties, Dave Davies released several tracks under his own name, but some of these also appeared on records by the Kinks. Although his full discography is outside the scope of this book, it would be misleading not to mention these singles which were generally considered as a crucial addendum to the Kinks' discography.

'Death Of A Clown'/'Love Me Till The Sun Shines' Pye 7N 17356 (UK)/Reprise 0614 (US)
Released: July 1967 (UK)/August 1967 (US).

'Suzanah's Still Alive'/'Funny Face' Pye 7N 17429 (UK)/Reprise 0660 (US)
Released: November 1967 (UK)/January 1968 (US).

'Lincoln County'/'There Is No Life Without Love' Pye 7N 17514
Released: August 1968 (UK). Not issued in US.

'Hold My Hand'/'Creeping Jean' Pye 7N 17678
Released: January 1969 (UK). Not issued in US.

In addition to the above, Pye Records released an EP *Dave Davies Hits* (Pye NEP 24289) in April 1968 featuring 'Love Me Till The Sun Shines', 'Death Of A Clown', 'Susannah's Still Alive' and 'Funny Face'. The archival *The Album That Never Was* (PRT PYL 6012), released in October 1987 (UK), and the 2011 CD *Hidden Treasures* (Sanctuary/Universal 277765-3) collect solo recordings and Kinks' contributions from the Sixties.

RAY DAVIES

SINGLES
'Quiet Life'/'Voices In The Dark' Virgin VS 865 (UK)
Released: May 1986 (UK). Not issued in US.

'London Song'/'London Song'/'Storyteller' EMI STORY 1 (UK)
Released March 1998 (UK). Not issued in US.

'Postcard From London' Universal single track download
Released: December 2009 (UK/US).

EPs

The Tourist V2 VVR 5036183P (UK)
'The Tourist'; 'Yours Truly, Confused N10'; 'London Song'; 'Storyteller'. Includes bonus
CD-Rom: 'The Making Of *Other People's Lives*'.
Released: September 2005 (UK). Not issued in US.

Thanksgiving Day V2 63881-27286-2 (US)
'Thanksgiving Day'; 'Yours Truly, Confused N10'; 'London Song'; 'Storyteller';
'Thanksgiving Day' (alternate mix).
Released November 2005 (US). Not issued in UK.

ALBUMS

The Songs Of Ray Davies Waterloo Sunset Essential ESS CD 592 (UK)
The publication of Ray Davies' short story collection *Waterloo Sunset* inspired this
intriguing compilation of demos and original tracks. Includes remixes of 'Voices In The
Dark' and 'Art Lover', plus three unreleased tracks: 'The Shirt', 'The-Million-Pound-
Semi-Detached' and 'My Diary'. The 15-track selection was included as a bonus disc
with *The Kinks: The Singles Collection*, complete with liner notes from Ray Davies.
'The Shirt': 'Rock 'n' Roll Fantasy'; 'Mister Pleasant'; 'Celluloid Heroes'; 'Voices In The
Dark'; 'Holiday Romance'; 'Art Lover'; 'Still Searching'; 'Return To Waterloo'; 'Afternoon
Tea'; 'The Million-Pound-Semi-Detached'; 'My Diary'; 'Drivin''; 'Waterloo Sunset'; 'Scattered'.
Released: September 1997 (UK). Not issued in US.

The Storyteller EMI 494 1682 (UK)/Konk/EMI-Capitol 7243 4 94168 2 6 (US)
'Storyteller'; Introduction; 'Victoria'; My Name (dialogue); '20th Century Man'; 'London
Song'; My Big Sister (dialogue)'; 'That Old Black Magic'; 'Tired Of Waiting'; 'Set Me
Free' (instrumental); Dad And The Green Amp (dialogue); 'Set Me Free'; The Front
Room (dialogue); 'See My Friends'; 'Autumn Almanac'; Hunchback (dialogue); 'X-Ray';
Art School (dialogue); 'Art School Babe'; 'Back In The Front Room'; Writing The Song
(dialogue); When Big Bill Speaks/The Man Who Knew A Man (Mick Avory's Audition
– dialogue); 'It's Alright' (Managers – dialogue)'; 'It's Alright' (Havana version, the Kinks'
name – dialogue); 'It's Alright (uptempo, on the road – dialogue); Julie Finkle (dialogue);
'The Ballad Of Julie Finkle'; The Third Single (dialogue); 'You Really Got Me'; 'London
Song' (studio version).
Released: March 1998 (UK)/April 1998 (US).

Other People's Lives V2 VVR 1035352 (UK)/V2 ADV-27285-2 (US)
'Things Are Gonna Change (The Morning After)'; 'After The Fall'; 'Next Door Neighbour';
'All She Wrote'; 'Creatures Of Little Faith'; 'Run Away From Time'; 'The Tourist'; 'Is
There Life After Breakfast?'; 'The Getaway (Lonesome Train)'; 'Other People's Lives';
'Stand Up Comic'; 'Over My Head'. Bonus track 'Thanksgiving Day' is not listed on the
album artwork.
Released: February 2006 (UK/US).

Working Man's Café V2 VVR 1048572; New West NW 5010 (vinyl) (UK)/New West NW 5010; New West NW 6136 (vinyl)/NW 6137 (CD limited edition) (US)
'Vietnam Cowboys'; 'You're Asking Me'; 'Working Man's Café'; 'Morphine Song'; 'In A Moment'; 'Peace In Our Time'; 'No One Listen'; 'Imaginary Man'; 'One More Time'; 'The Voodoo Walk'; 'Hymns For A New Age'; 'The Real World'. The edition given away free with the *Sunday Times* omitted the last two tracks. The vinyl versions feature further additional tracks: 'Angola (Wrong Side Of The Law)', 'Vietnam Cowboys' (demo) and 'The Voodoo Walk' (demo). The limited edition includes the bonus tracks: 'Angola (Wrong Side Of The Law)'; 'I, The Victim' (rough mix); 'Vietnam Cowboys' (demo); 'The Voodoo Walk' (demo), plus a DVD: *Americana A Work In Progress*.
Released: October 2007 (UK)/February 2008 (US).

The Kinks Choral Collection Universal Music TV 2724050 (UK)/Decca/Universal 2703909 (US)
Credited to Ray Davies & the Crouch End Festival Chorus.
'Days'; 'Waterloo Sunset'; 'You Really Got Me'; 'Victoria'; 'See My Friends'; 'Celluloid Heroes'; 'Shangri-la'; 'Working Man's Café'; 'Village Green'; 'Picture Book'; 'Big Sky'; 'Do You Remember Walter'; 'Johnny Thunder'; 'The Village Green Preservation Society'; 'All Day And All Of The Night'. 'Postcard From London' appears on the 'Special Edition', issued December 2009.
Released: June 2009 (UK/US).

See My Friends Universal 2752942 (UK)/Decca B0015310-02 (US)
'Better Things' [with Bruce Springsteen]; 'Celluloid Heroes' [with Jon Bon Jovi and Richie Sambora]; 'Days'/'This Time Tomorrow (Medley)' [with Mumford & Sons]; 'A Long Way From Home' [with Lucinda Williams and the 88]; 'You Really Got Me' [with Metallica]; 'Lola' [with Paloma Faith]; 'Waterloo Sunset' [with Jackson Browne]; 'Till The End Of The Day' [with Alex Chilton and the 88]; 'Dead End Street' [with Amy MacDonald]; 'See My Friends' [with Spoon]; 'This Is Where I Belong' [with Black Francis]; 'David Watts' [with the 88]; 'Tired Of Waiting For You' [with Gary Lightbody]; 'All Day And All Of The Night'/'Destroyer' [with Billy Corgan]. Two additional tracks sold as digital downloads: 'Victoria' [with Mando Diao] and 'Moments' [with Arno Hintjens].
Released: November 2010 (UK/US).

SOUNDTRACKS

Return To Waterloo Arista AL6 8386 (US)
Three songs from the film are also on the Kinks' *Word Of Mouth*, while two compositions remain unissued: 'Good Times Are Gone' and 'Ladder Of Success'.
'Intro'; 'Return To Waterloo'; 'Going Solo'; 'Missing Persons'; 'Sold Me Out'; 'Lonely Hearts'; 'Not Far Away'; 'Expectations'; 'Voices In The Dark (End Title)'.
Released: July 1985 (US). Not issued in UK.

Absolute Beginners Virgin V 2386 (UK)/EMI America SV 17182 (US)
Includes the Ray Davies cameo 'Quiet Life'.
Released: March 1986 (UK/US).

COMPILATIONS

Collected Universal 2721099 (UK)
'After The Fall'; 'Vietnam Cowboys'; 'Next Door Neighbour'; 'Working Man's Café';
'You're Asking Me'; 'The Tourist'; 'Things Are Gonna Change (The Morning After)';
'One More Time'; 'No One Listen'; 'Thanksgiving Day'; 'In A Moment'; 'Imaginary
Man'; 'Morphine Song'; 'London Song'; 'The Getaway (Lonesome Train)'; 'Storyteller';
'Yours Truly, Confused N10'.
Released: October 2009 (UK).

Waterloo Sunset: The Very Best Of The Kinks & Ray Davies Sanctuary/Universal 371
248-9 (UK)
Disc 1: Kinks Classics. 'Waterloo Sunset'; 'You Really Got Me'; 'Tired Of Waiting For
You'; 'Sunny Afternoon'; 'All Day And All Of The Night'; 'Till The End Of The Day';
'Autumn Almanac'; 'Days'; 'Lola'; 'Set Me Free'; 'See My Friends'; 'Death Of A Clown';
'Apeman'; 'Dead End Street'; 'This Time Tomorrow'; 'Strangers'; 'You Don't Know My
Name'; 'Wonderboy'; 'Plastic Man'; 'Supersonic Rocket Ship'; 'Better Things'; 'Don't
Forget To Dance'; 'David Watts'.
Disc 2: London Songs. 'Dedicated Follower Of Fashion'; 'Come Dancing'; 'Where Have
All The Good Times Gone'; 'Victoria'; 'Big Black Smoke'; 'Yours Truly, Confused N10';
'Working Man's Café'; 'London Song'; 'Fortis Green'; 'Postcard From London'; 'Muswell
Hillbilly'; 'Denmark Street'; 'Berkeley Mews'; 'Holloway Jail'; 'Lavender Hill'; 'Willesden
Green'; 'Life On The Road'; 'End Of The Season'; 'Next Door Neighbour'; 'Did Ya';
'Most Exclusive Residence For Sale'; 'Waterloo Sunset'.
Released: August 2012 (UK). Not issued in US.

UNRELEASED COMPOSITIONS

Ray Davies is a prolific songwriter whose archive includes countless unreleased compositions and recordings. Over recent decades, many of Davies' demos and working tapes
have appeared as bonus tracks on reissues and Kinks' archival albums. Among these are
such former rarities as 'Till Death Us Do Part', 'There Is No Life Without Love', 'Lavender
Hill', 'Groovy Movies', 'Rosemary Rose', 'Misty Water', 'Mr Songbird', 'When I Turn
Off The Living Room Light', 'The Way Love Used To Be', 'Pictures In The Sand', 'Where
Did My Spring Go', 'Time Will Tell', 'Spotty Grotty Anna', 'This Strange Effect', 'I Go
To Sleep', 'Did You See His Name', 'I Don't Need You Anymore', 'When I See That Girl
Of Mine', 'Mr Reporter', 'Little Women', 'I Believed You', 'Don't Ever Let Me Go',
'There's A New World (Just) Opening For Me', 'A Little Bit Of Sunlight', 'Entertainment',
'This I Know', 'All Night Stand', 'And I Will Love You', 'Slum Kids', 'The Poseur', 'Hidden
Quality (aka Hidden Qualities)', 'Nuclear Love', 'Duke', 'Stolen Away Your Heart', 'Tell
Me Now So I'll Know', 'Hide And Seek', 'Sand On My Shoes', 'Mick Avory's Underpants',
'Mountain Woman', 'Kentucky Moon', 'Easy Come, There You Went' and 'Once A Thief'.

There are still several Ray Davies compositions released by other artists that have
never appeared on any of his solo or Kinks recordings.

'I Bet You Won't Stay' Cascades (Liberty 55822) October 1965 (UK)
'Emptiness' Honeycombs (album *All Systems Go* Pye 18132) December 1965 (UK)

'King Of The Whole Wide World' Leapy Lee (Decca F 12369) March 1966 (UK)
'Little Man In A Little Box' Barry Fantoni (Fontana 707) May 1966 (UK)
'Oh What A Day It's Gonna Be' Mo And Steve (Pye 7N 17175) September 1966 (UK)
'Virgin Soldier March' John Schroeder (Pye 7N 17861) November 1969 (UK)
'Ballad Of The Virgin Soldiers' Leon Bibb (RCA 74-0332) 1970 (US)
'Nobody's Fool' Cold Turkey (Pye 7N 45142) March 1972 (UK)

Kinks Era Compositions Unreleased

'Au Nom De La Loi'
'Back To 64/Decade'
'Beginning'
'Blasé Blasé'
'Child Bride'
'Could Be Right, Could Be Wrong'
'Don't Lie To Me'
'Drop Out'
'East West'
'Easy Action'
'Everybody Wants To Be A Personality'
'Everything Is Alright'
'Fallen Idol'
'Fancy Kitchen Gadgetry'
'For You'
'Give My Fondest Regards To Her'
'Having A Good Time'
'History'
'Hong Kong Moon'
'I Can't Wait To See You Smile'
'I Just Wanna Walk With You'
'I Just Want To Be With You'
'I'm Going Home'
'In A Space'
'It's You'
'La La La La'
'Laugh At The World'
'Lazy Day'
'Lilacs And Daffodils (aka Sir Jasper)'
'Listen To Me'

'Louise'
'Marathon'
'My Moment Of Decision'
'Never Say Yes'
'One Woman Man'
'Oobadiaboo'
'Power Of Gold'
'Radio'
'Regret It'
'Restless'
'Rocky Mountain'
'Rosie Rooke'
'She's My Girl'
'Shoe Without A Lace' (co-written with John Dalton)
'Sing Sing Sing'
'Stagefright'
'Student In The Game'
'Television'
'Tender Loving Care'
'That Will Make My Dreams Come True'
'That's All I Want'
'The Cake'
'The Optimist'
'Time Song'
'Tokyo'
'Using Me'
'We All Understand'
'When I'm Walking'
'You Ain't What You Used To Be"

At The Eleventh Hour Contributions Unreleased

'You Can't Give More Than What You Have'
'If Christmas Day Could Last Forever'
'We're Backing Britain'
'Poor Old Intellectual Sadie'

'Could Be You're Getting Old'
'Just A Poor Country Girl'
'The Man Who Conned Dinner From The Ritz'
'This Is What The World Is All About'

Ray Davies wrote nine songs for the BBC 1's *At The Eleventh Hour*, broadcast between December 1967 and February 1968, but only one of these, 'Did You See His Name?', has ever been released.

Where Was Spring? Contributions Unreleased

'Darling I Respect You'   'We Are Two of A Kind'
'Let's Take Off Our Clothes'

Ray Davies wrote five songs that were broadcast during February 1969 on BBC 2's *Where Was Spring?,* two of which have since been released: 'Where Did My Spring Go', 'When I Turn Off The Living Room Light'

Chorus Girls Contributions Unreleased

'A Woman In Love Will Do Anything'   'Newham At Work'
'Everybody's Got A Body'   'Payback'
'Everybody's Slagging Off England'   'Privilege'
'Glorious Sight'   'Reputation'
'Let's Have A Dance'   'The Man Of Destiny'
'Men Are Fools'   'Up On A High Rise Block'

80 Days Musical Unreleased Songs

'A Place In Your Heart'   'Members Of The Club'
'Against The Tide'   'Mongolia Song'
'Be Rational'   'No Surprises'
'80 Days'   'On The Map'
'Here!'   'Tell Him Tell Her'
'It Could Have Been Him'   'The Empire Song'
'Just Passing Through'   'Welcome To India'
'Ladies Of The Night'   'Well Bred Englishman'
'Let It Be Written'   'Who Is This Man?'

Ray Davies Solo Era Unreleased Songs

'A Long Drive To Tarzana'   'Otis Riffs'
'A Street Called Hope'   'Poetry'
'Back In The Day'   'Rock 'n' Roll Cowboys'
'Bringing Up Baby'   'Security'
'Brothers And Sisters'   'She's So Contrary'
'Cover Band'   'The Art Of Moving On'
'Depressed I Am Not'   'The Big Guy'
'Empty Room'   'The Big Weird'
'Green Carnation'   'The Deal'
'Honest'   'The Fields Are On Fire'
'I've Heard That Beat Before'   'The Great Highway'
'Olympicland'   'The Invaders'
'Major Barmy From The Army   'Wings Of Fantasy'
    Loved The Miller's Daughter'

INDEX

Singles releases are in roman type and albums are in italics.